AN INTRODUCTION TO THE AMERICAN LEGAL SYSTEM

ASPEN COLLEGE SERIES

AN INTRODUCTION TO THE AMERICAN LEGAL SYSTEM

Fourth Edition

John M. Scheb II

Professor of Political Science University of Tennessee, Knoxville

Hemant Sharma

Lecturer in Political Science University of Tennessee, Knoxville

Published by Wolters Kluwer in New York.

Wolters Kluwer serves customers worldwide with CCH, Aspen Publishers, and Kluwer Law International products. (www.wolterskluwerlb.com)

To contact Customer Service, e-mail customer.service@wolterskluwer.com, call 1-800-234-1660, fax 1-800-901-9075, or mail correspondence to:

Wolters Kluwer
Attn: Order Department
PO Box 990
Frederick, MD 21705

Printed in the United States of America.

3 4 5 6 7 8 9 0

ISBN 978-1-4548-5120-2

Library of Congress Cataloging-in-Publication Data

Scheb, John M., II, 1955- author.
   An introduction to the American legal system / John M. Scheb II, Professor of Political Science, University of Tennessee, Knoxville, Hemant Sharma, Lecturer in Political Science, University of Tennessee, Knoxville. —Fourth edition.
      pages cm
   Includes index.
   ISBN 978-1-4548-5120-2
   1. Law—United States. I. Sharma, Hemant, 1974- author. II. Title.
   KF385.S34 2015
   349.73—dc23

                                        2014041689

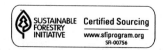

About Wolters Kluwer Law & Business

Wolters Kluwer Law & Business is a leading global provider of intelligent information and digital solutions for legal and business professionals in key specialty areas, and respected educational resources for professors and law students. Wolters Kluwer Law & Business connects legal and business professionals as well as those in the education market with timely, specialized authoritative content and information-enabled solutions to support success through productivity, accuracy and mobility.

Serving customers worldwide, Wolters Kluwer Law & Business products include those under the Aspen Publishers, CCH, Kluwer Law International, Loislaw, ftwilliam.com and MediRegs family of products.

CCH products have been a trusted resource since 1913, and are highly regarded resources for legal, securities, antitrust and trade regulation, government contracting, banking, pension, payroll, employment and labor, and healthcare reimbursement and compliance professionals.

Aspen Publishers products provide essential information to attorneys, business professionals and law students. Written by preeminent authorities, the product line offers analytical and practical information in a range of specialty practice areas from securities law and intellectual property to mergers and acquisitions and pension/benefits. Aspen's trusted legal education resources provide professors and students with high-quality, up-to-date and effective resources for successful instruction and study in all areas of the law.

Kluwer Law International products provide the global business community with reliable international legal information in English. Legal practitioners, corporate counsel and business executives around the world rely on Kluwer Law journals, looseleafs, books, and electronic products for comprehensive information in many areas of international legal practice.

Loislaw is a comprehensive online legal research product providing legal content to law firm practitioners of various specializations. Loislaw provides attorneys with the ability to quickly and efficiently find the necessary legal information they need, when and where they need it, by facilitating access to primary law as well as state-specific law, records, forms and treatises.

ftwilliam.com offers employee benefits professionals the highest quality plan documents (retirement, welfare and non-qualified) and government forms (5500/PBGC, 1099 and IRS) software at highly competitive prices.

MediRegs products provide integrated health care compliance content and software solutions for professionals in healthcare, higher education and life sciences, including professionals in accounting, law and consulting.

Wolters Kluwer Law & Business, a division of Wolters Kluwer, is headquartered in New York. Wolters Kluwer is a market-leading global information services company focused on professionals.

This book is dedicated to
Judge John M. Scheb, who passed away on November 17, 2010.
He is sorely missed by his family, his many friends, and by the entire judiciary
and legal profession in the state of Florida.

BRIEF CONTENTS

CONTENTS

PREFACE

This book is designed as an introductory text on American law and the legal system. It is meant for undergraduate students in political science, sociology, criminal justice, and legal studies, as well as students in paralegal programs. Our goal is to introduce students to basic legal concepts, principles, and procedures. Of necessity, we have painted with a broad brush, as American law and legal procedures are extremely complex and highly dynamic, and vary considerably across jurisdictions.

The first two editions of this book were coauthored by Judge John M. Scheb, a distinguished member of the legal profession and judiciary in the state of Florida. During his long career, Judge Scheb served as an attorney, a municipal judge, an appellate judge, a city attorney, a mediator, a law professor, and a reserve officer in the Judge Advocate General's Department of the United States Air Force. Judge Scheb was a living encyclopedia of the law, and he loved sharing his knowledge with students and colleagues. He enjoyed working on this book precisely because it introduces the American legal system and the broad scope of the law. Judge Scheb believed that all citizens should have at least a rudimentary understanding of the law.

Judge Scheb passed away in November 2010 and is sorely missed by his family and his many friends, former students and colleagues. We were pleased to carry on Judge Scheb's legacy with the third edition of *An Introduction to the American Legal System*, which was published in 2013. We are now pleased to offer the fourth edition of this textbook, which we dedicate to Judge Scheb's memory.

Organization

We have maintained the structure of the book from its previous editions and have concentrated our efforts on updating and clarifying the material. Part I sets forth the fundamental concepts and concerns of the law, examines the historical development of the American legal system from its English common law roots, and surveys the structures of the American legal system as well as the legal profession. Part II provides an overview of the substantive law, including constitutional law, criminal law, torts, property law, contracts and business law, and family law. Part III surveys the procedural law, covering civil and criminal procedure, the rules of evidence, and the appellate process. Finally, Part IV looks at two very important areas of modern law: legislation and administrative law and procedure. Because this book will be many students' first encounter with legal studies, we have included an extensive glossary of legal terms (see Appendix B).

Special Features

To the beginning student, an introduction to the law can be somewhat overwhelming. To make the book more accessible and useful to the student, every chapter contains a list of learning objectives, a chapter outline, a chapter summary, and a set of boldfaced key terms, all of which are defined in the glossary. To make the book more provocative, each chapter also contains a set of questions for thought and discussion. For the student who wishes to learn more about the topics addressed in the book, each chapter also contains a list of additional reference materials.

Because judicial decisions are central to the development of the law, we have incorporated two features into the text designed to alert students to especially important cases. One of these features, entitled "Case in Point," is a short summary of a significant court decision. There are multiple Case in Point features in each chapter. A related feature, "Opinion of the Court," appears in each chapter and provides substantial excerpts from landmark opinions of the U.S. Supreme Court.

Another special feature, entitled "The Law in Action," focuses on practical applications of the law and real-world controversies involving legal issues. Topics addressed in this feature range from "Civil Disobedience and the Struggle for Civil Rights" (Chapter 1) to "Purchasing a House" (Chapter 6). Students will also find a set of "Sidebar" features throughout the book. These features provide miscellaneous information relevant to chapter topics. For example, see the Sidebar in Chapter 5, "The Infamous McDonald's Coffee Case," which is of interest to every student of tort law. Other Sidebar features focus on such topics as canons of judicial conduct (Chapter 2), warranty deeds (Chapter 6), and the law regarding employment discrimination (Chapter 11). We hope that all these features will make the text more informative and more interesting.

Acknowledgments

Previous editions of this book relied on the excellent assistance of a number of able persons, whose efforts we gratefully acknowledge once again:

- Richard R. Garland, Esq., an attorney in Sarasota, Florida, who is certified in appellate practice.
- Robert P. Scheb, Esq., an attorney in Sarasota, Florida, who practices in the field of estates and trusts.
- Rebecca A. Rider, Esq., an attorney in Sarasota, Florida, who practices in the field of domestic relations.
- William T. Brown, an attorney and lecturer in the Political Science Department and College of Law at the University of Tennessee, Knoxville.
- Dr. Mark D. Welton, Professor in the Department of Law at the United States Military Academy, West Point.

Finally, we extend our appreciation to the editorial staff at Wolters Kluwer Law & Business for their encouragement and support throughout this project.

Of course, we assume full responsibility for any errors of commission or omission contained in these pages.

John M. Scheb II

Hemant Sharma

January 2015

ABOUT THE AUTHORS

John M. Scheb II is Professor of Political Science at the University of Tennessee, Knoxville, where he specializes in public law and the judicial process. He attended the University of Florida from 1974 to 1982, receiving the B.A., M.A., and Ph.D. in political science. Professor Scheb has authored numerous articles in professional journals, including *Social Science Quarterly, Justice System Journal, Political Behavior, American Politics Quarterly, Judicature, Journal of Politics, Law and Policy*, and *Tennessee Law Review*. He is the coauthor of several other textbooks, including: *American Constitutional Law*, 6th ed. (Cengage Learning 2015); *Criminal Law & Procedure*, 8th edition (Cengage Learning 2014), and *Law and the Administrative Process* (Thomson/ Wadsworth 2005).

Hemant Sharma is a lecturer in the Department of Political Science at the University of Tennessee, Knoxville, where he teaches courses on law, courts, and judicial processes. Sharma received his B.A. in English in 1997 from Cornell University, where he was a member of the Dean's List, winner of the prestigious James E. Rice Writing Prize, and the goalkeeper for Cornell's men's soccer team, which reached the NCAA Tournament in 1995 and 1996. He subsequently earned an M.A. and a Ph.D. in Political Science from the University of Tennessee, Knoxville. His published research has appeared in *Politics and Policy, Judicature*, the *National Soccer Coaches Association of America Journal*, and the *Tennessee Journal of Law and Policy*.

FOUNDATIONS OF THE LEGAL SYSTEM

PART I

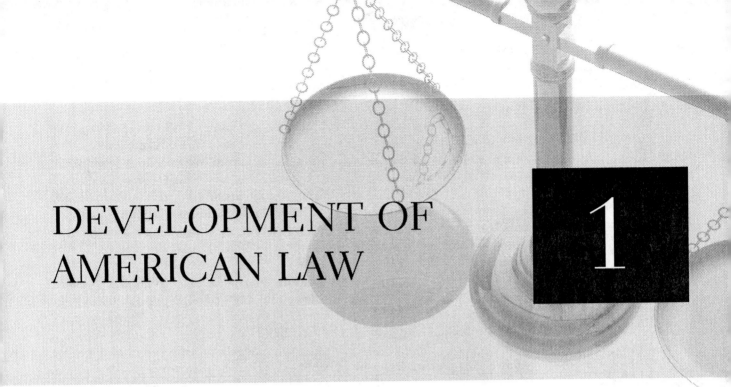

DEVELOPMENT OF AMERICAN LAW

1

LEARNING OBJECTIVES

This chapter should enable the student to understand:

- the functions of law in society
- the forms and sources of law
- the influence of the English common law on the American legal system
- the ideas and experiences that led to formation of the U.S. Constitution
- the supremacy of the U.S. Constitution and the Bill of Rights
- the role of statutory law and judicial decision making
- the functions of courts, legislatures and administrative agencies with respect to the development of the law

CHAPTER OUTLINE

INTRODUCTION

From our nation's earliest moments through the present-day, law has held an important place in American society. Our Founders devoted great care to crafting a system of government in which the rule of law was a crucial feature. We have since developed an elaborate system to make and enforce the law. A large professional class is now engaged in the practice of law. Numerous academic institutions are devoted to teaching the law. There are thousands of publications dedicated to legal education, research, and advocacy. Our mass media and popular culture reflect the social preoccupation with law, in that we are exposed to a steady barrage of books, films, newspaper articles, television shows, and web sites dealing with the law.

Despite this cultural preoccupation with the law, an essential question remains: What precisely is "law"? Numerous definitions have been proposed, reflecting the variety of philosophical and theoretical orientations to the concept. Bearing in mind that any definition is imperfect, we begin with the following simple formulation: *law is a set of rules promulgated and enforced by government.*[1] This formulation is often referred to as **positive law**, which the nineteenth century English legal theorist John Austin defined simply as "the command of the sovereign." Positive law is indeed the command of the sovereign, in that it is enunciated by government and backed by the coercive power of the state. But there is more to law than this. To be law, the command of the sovereign must take the form of a rule, a principle, or a directive that applies with equal force to everyone.[2] Moreover, to be accepted as legitimate, the law must be perceived as rational, fair, and just. Some would argue that for positive law to be legitimate, it must conform to a higher law.

Higher Law

Natural law is law that is presumed to flow from man's "natural" condition, that is, the social condition existing prior to the emergence of government. Natural law is sometimes used to refer to universal principles of morality and justice; however, precisely what those principles are is subject to conflicting interpretations. In *De Republica*, the ancient Roman orator Cicero (106–43 B.C.) defined natural law as "right reason in agreement with nature." In *Summa Theologica*, the medieval philosopher Thomas Aquinas (1225–1274) viewed natural law as the "participation in the Eternal Law by rational creatures." In a less theological approach, the seventeenth century Dutch jurist Hugo Grotius defined natural law as rules of human conduct that can be discovered solely by the use of reason. Elsewhere, in his influential *Commentaries on the Laws of England* (1769), William Blackstone asserted the primacy of natural law. Blackstone's *Commentaries* would become something of a legal bible in America, and helped to perpetuate natural law theory in this country.

To understand this concept, we can turn to a seminal document associated with our nation's founding. Our Declaration of Independence (1776) asserts that "all men are created equal, that they are endowed by their Creator with certain unalienable rights, that among these are Life, Liberty, and the pursuit of Happiness." Those who

CIVIL DISOBEDIENCE AND THE STRUGGLE FOR CIVIL RIGHTS

THE LAW IN ACTION

In 1963, Dr. Martin Luther King Jr. was arrested in Birmingham, Alabama, after leading a civil rights demonstration in the city. The specific charge against him was "parading without a permit." Dr. King had led the demonstration to protest segregation and had applied for a permit but had been denied. In his famous "Letter from the Birmingham Jail," King defended his disobedience of an "unjust" law. Echoing St. Thomas Aquinas, Dr. King wrote, "An unjust law is a human law that is not rooted in eternal and natural law." In a more modern vein, he also argued that an unjust law is one "that a majority inflicts on a minority that is not binding on itself." King was referring to the entire regime of laws that maintained racial segregation. King argued that "an individual who breaks a law that conscience tells him is unjust, and willingly accepts the penalty...is in reality expressing the very highest respect for the law." Not everyone at the time agreed with Dr. King's goals or tactics. But today, he is widely hailed as an American hero.

created the basic framework of our legal system and system of government believed that rights ultimately are not of secular origin. Rather, they flow from natural law as ordained by God. Even today, legal theorists, lawyers, lawmakers, and judges sometimes invoke natural law. But natural law as such is not an enforceable body of rules. It is more of a philosophical concept—the idea that there is a set of principles of morality and justice that transcends the positive law. In this regard, natural law provides a basis for the criticism, and sometimes the disobedience, of the positive law.

Natural law and religious precepts continue to be important because they provide a basis upon which to evaluate and contextualize the positive law. For example, quite often opponents of the death penalty will cite the Biblical injunction "Thou shalt not kill." Similar arguments are often made regarding abortion and euthanasia. Obviously, people can and will disagree on the requirements of natural law, Scripture, and divine ordinance. Because we have a secular government committed to the ideas of separation of church and state and religious tolerance, religious precepts are not enforceable through our legal institutions. But religious precepts, like natural law, can provide citizens with a philosophical anchor—a sense that there is a higher law by which positive law can be judged.[3]

The Problem of Civil Disobedience

If we assume that there is no higher law than the law promulgated by the state, how do we ever justify disobedience to the positive law? By the same token, how do we punish those who have perpetrated wrongs but have done so within the confines of the law? This problem confronted the prosecutors at the Nuremberg war crimes trials after World War II. What the Nazis did was atrocious, yet much of it was authorized by

German law at the time. A somewhat similar problem accompanied the civil rights movement in the United States during the 1950s and 1960s. Much of the segregation and discrimination faced by African-Americans at that time was authorized by law. What gave protesters the right to break these laws, to engage in **civil disobedience**? Some would argue that without a belief in some form of higher law, there is no way to justify a breach of the positive law. Belief in a higher law or some higher standard of justice permits us to evaluate the operations and policies of our legal system, to object when a particular legal rule is established or a particular legal decision is rendered, and to argue for the need for legal change. In extreme circumstances, belief in a higher law may provide a justification for violating the positive law, as long as the violator is willing to accept the consequences of disobedience.

The nineteenth century American writer Henry David Thoreau is best known for his advocacy of civil disobedience when the demands of conscience conflict with the dictates of law. Thoreau argued that the conscience of the individual is superior to the law of the state and that individuals have the right, indeed the duty, to violate the law when the law contravenes conscience.

Like all philosophical positions, Thoreau's views on civil disobedience are not universally accepted. There have been two principal criticisms of his views. One is that citizens have an obligation to obey laws that are adopted by legitimate democratic procedures. Another objection is that an individual conscience provides insufficient basis for disobedience—that an individual cannot be permitted to become a law unto himself or herself. Despite these objections, Thoreau's view of civil disobedience has been extremely influential in the United States and throughout the world.

A great deal of discussion continues, however, about exactly what types of behavior fall under the heading of "civil disobedience." The case of Edward Snowden, who revealed information about the scope of the National Security Agency's surveillance programs, provides an interesting example to consider. Snowden collected thousands of classified documents while working as an NSA contractor and then leaked that information to members of the media. His actions provided individuals around the world with an awareness of the breadth of NSA activities—including surveillance that was described as targeting the cell phone and Internet activities of millions of Americans, citizens of other countries, and even some prominent international leaders. According to Snowden, the information collected by the NSA included "metadata," which encompassed the phone numbers that a person might have called from a cell phone, as well as "content analysis," which might involve the actual words uttered in a conversation.

The U.S. government ultimately brought criminal charges against Snowden for alleged violations of the Espionage Act, but he had fled the country by that point and was granted temporary asylum in Russia. Debate remains about whether his actions should be viewed through the lens of civil disobedience—perhaps to laud Snowden for revealing a government intrusion upon the privacy interests of millions of people—or whether he has simply committed acts of treason that will weaken the United States's ability to defend itself against acts of terror; such dualities often provide the parameters for dialogue about civil disobedience.

Legitimacy of Law in a Democratic Society

The legitimacy of law does not depend solely on its content or its perceived relationship to some higher authority. In a democratic society, the legitimacy of law depends greatly on how the law is made. In a representative democracy, law is made by elected representatives serving in a **legislature**. All members of the legislature have the right to introduce legislation; a majority is required to enact a law. Furthermore, legislators are elected through free and fair elections in which all adult citizens have the right to participate.

The United States relies on representative democracy, but our system of government is much more complex than that. We are not a simple representative democracy but rather a constitutional republic in which majority rule is tempered by protections afforded to minority rights by law. Moreover, lawmaking power is vested not only in legislators but also in executive officials, in regulatory agencies, and in courts of law. However, the way in which these bodies make law remains very important and is key to whether their legal pronouncements are regarded as legitimate. Thus, in thinking about the legitimacy of law, we need to think about both **substantive legitimacy** and **procedural legitimacy**. Substantive legitimacy refers to the content of law; procedural legitimacy refers to how the law is enacted and applied.[4] The law is substantively legitimate if people believe that it is based on fair, just, and reasonable principles. It is procedurally legitimate if it is enacted, applied, and enforced according to procedures that people regard as fair, just, and reasonable.

Forms and Sources of Positive Law

As we have suggested, law emanates from several sources. It also takes on different forms. In the American legal system, the major forms of law are the following:

- **constitution** The fundamental law. It sets forth the structure and powers of government as well as the rights of citizens vis-à-vis that government.
- **statute** A law enacted by a legislature that is generally applicable within the jurisdiction of that legislature.
- **ordinance** A law enacted by a local governing body such as a city council or a county commission. Ordinances deal principally with matters of local concern.
- **executive order** An order issued by a president, governor, county executive, or mayor relating to matters over which the executive official has authority.
- **treaty** A legally binding agreement between countries.
- **regulation** A rule promulgated by a regulatory agency.
- **judicial decision** A decision by a court of law enunciating a principle of law.

When we speak of the "law," we are really talking about the sum total of all of these elements as they coexist at any point in time. As such, the law is extremely complex, somewhat uncertain, always dynamic, and sometimes self-contradictory.

THE FUNCTIONS OF LAW IN SOCIETY

Law performs many different functions in society. Law promotes social order and stability, but it can also be a force for change.[5] Law seeks to establish justice, but law is no guarantee thereof. Law determines to a great extent how government operates, although law cannot ensure good government.

Fundamentally, law protects people and their property. To the social contract thinkers of the seventeenth and eighteenth centuries, this was the primary purpose of law. Without law backed by the coercive power of the state, people would have no choice but to protect themselves, their families, their land, and their possessions by force. Law, at least ideally, protects the rights of the weak as well as the strong.

Law, Liberty, and Morality

Classical liberals like Thomas Jefferson viewed law as a means of protecting not only life and property but also liberty. To the classical liberals, freedom of speech and freedom of religion were as important as the right to own property and to engage in private enterprise. In the classical liberal view, the purpose of law was to safeguard these basic human rights. In the nineteenth century, the English philosopher and economist John Stuart Mill argued that the law should be limited to protecting the security of the individual and should not enforce traditional notions of morality. Today, this **libertarian view of law** commands considerable support in the United States and other advanced democratic countries.

Conservatives, on the other hand, see law and morality as inextricably intertwined. They believe that the maintenance of societal morality is one of the essential functions of law. One of the best statements of this perspective can be found in Lord Devlin's *The Enforcement of Morals*, published in 1959.[6] Devlin argued that law must preserve traditional morality to prevent disintegration of the society. In a response to Devlin, H.L.A. Hart suggested that a society willing to sacrifice freedom by imposing morality through law may not be a society worthy of maintaining.[7] Although the "debate" between Devlin and Hart took place in Great Britain in the late 1950s and early 1960s, the debate over law and morality continues today. Ultimately, that debate must take place within the context of any legal system that values individual freedom along with social cohesion.

Law and Economic Life

A society's economic system affects its law, and vice versa. As the great social theorist Max Weber recognized, a capitalist economy requires a highly developed legal system.[8] The legal system must be capable of enforcing contracts and property claims and must generally provide a predictable climate in which business can take place. Uncertainty in the law regarding property, contracts, and commercial transactions impedes voluntary economic activity. Therefore, it is not surprising that one tends to find the most highly developed legal systems in the most advanced capitalist countries of Europe and North America. It should be pointed out, however, that while law facilitates economic development by regulating transactions and rationalizing risk, it can also serve as an impediment to economic innovation. When too many conflicting demands are placed on the law, it becomes excessively complex, redundant, and inscrutable, a condition which may stifle economic activity. Some commentators believe that we have such a situation in the contemporary United States!

Of course, not everyone takes a benign view of the relationship between law and capitalism. Marxists, anarchists, and radicals of various persuasions generally see law, at least in capitalist society, as a tool of oppression and an agent of inequality. From the Marxist perspective, law in a capitalist society is little more than a cloak for the power of the ruling class. Today, the **critical legal studies** movement carries on this radical tradition in legal thought.

The Marxist view of law is based on the assumption that all conflict derives from material inequality. In contrast, most social theorists today regard economic inequality as only one of many sources of human conflict. And most also regard law as an essential element of modern society—both as an expression of societal consensus and as a means of conflict resolution.

Social Control

Law is a means of social control, but it is certainly not the only one. Informal, unwritten rules are transmitted and enforced by social groups, including families, peers, and colleagues. Moral principles are developed and enforced by the individual conscience. Religious precepts are developed, transmitted, and reinforced by religious institutions. Social norms, moral principles, and religious precepts constrain the behavior of most people, at least most of the time. Yet, they are inadequate in some instances. Social norms can be vague or weak, religious precepts vary somewhat across faiths and denominations, and moral principles can be totally lacking in some individuals. Law is necessary to pick up where informal means of social control leave off.

Resolution of Conflict

Law is a means of conflict resolution, but, again, there are numerous methods of conflict resolution at work in our society every day. Individuals, groups, families, corporations, and governments usually can work out their differences informally through discussion, negotiation, and compromise. The law serves as a framework for such interactions. When informal means of conflict resolution are not fruitful, parties often seek recourse through formal legal means. Law provides a mechanism for the peaceful resolution of conflict, but it is by no means always successful at preventing violence.

Most theorists believe that modern society, which is increasingly conflictual, requires a formal system of law. As society becomes more diverse, impersonal, complex, and specialized, this requirement grows ever stronger. At the same time, however, the strains on the legal system become increasingly powerful. Law is the command of the sovereign, and therefore reflects the existing structure of power in society. But in a democratic society such as ours, law also depends on a reasonable degree of social consensus. With increasing social, economic, and political diversity, such a consensus can be difficult to achieve.

Law and Societal Values

Law is an expression of a society's values. In our complex and diverse society, the law expresses many competing values which often come into conflict. A few prominent examples of such conflict are

- private enterprise versus the public good
- freedom versus equality
- privacy versus crime control
- private property versus environmental protection
- national security versus freedom of the press
- public order versus the right of public assembly
- freedom of expression versus decency and civility
- majority rule versus minority rights.

Although law expresses many competing values, it also provides mechanisms to resolve conflicts between competing values.

THE DEVELOPMENT OF LAW

Primitive, tribal societies had no formal systems of law. These societies were governed by rulers who relied on sheer power and charisma buttressed by claims of supernatural authority. Individual behavior and social and economic relationships were governed by custom—and often reinforced by religion, magic, and superstition. Offenses against the tribe, such as sacrilege or consorting with an enemy, were dealt with by sanctions such as shunning, banishment, or even death. Wrongs against individuals, like murder, rape, and theft, were avenged by the victim's family, often through actions against the family of the wrongdoer that were grossly disproportionate to the offense that gave rise to the vengeance.

With the emergence of agriculture, isolated tribal societies evolved into territorial confederations. Systems of government emerged, and with them came the beginnings of law, as leaders (usually monarchs) began formalizing and enforcing customs that had evolved among their peoples. Eventually, informal norms and customs came to be formalized as written codes of law.

Ancient Legal Codes

The oldest known written legal code is the Code of Hammurabi, which was produced in Babylonia some two thousand years before Christ. Although the Emperor Hammurabi promulgated the Code that bears his name, popular acceptance of the idea that law was of divine origin helped buttress its legitimacy. The Code of Hammurabi dealt with property rights, family relationships, personal injuries, and the collection of debts. It also covered legal procedure and imposed penalties for unjust accusations and false testimony. In terms of crimes and punishments, the Code adopted the *lex talionis*, or law of retaliation, which is similar to the Hebrew law calling for "an eye for an eye." Perhaps the most striking feature of the Code of Hammurabi, however, is that it purported to protect people of both genders and all social classes, including slaves. Thus, in this most ancient legal code, we find the seeds of a concept that is so fundamental to our system of law today—the ideal of equal protection of the law.

The ancient Greeks also contributed to the development of law. In the seventh century B.C., Draco, an Athenian legislator, developed a very strict legal code for the Athenian city-state. Even today, one hears strict rules or penalties characterized as "Draconian." A century later, the Code of Draco would be replaced by the Code of Solon. Beyond its more liberal character, the distinctive feature of this Code was that it permitted litigants to appeal the decisions of magistrates to public assemblies of Athenians, an innovation that foreshadowed the right to trial by a jury of one's peers.

Roman Law

By far the most significant of the ancient legal codes was the **Roman Law**, which formally began with the introduction of the Twelve Tables in the mid-fifth century B.C. Prior to the Twelve Tables, disputes between Roman citizens were decided on the basis of unwritten customary rules. When these rules were in doubt, the College of Pontiffs, made up of patrician aristocrats, rendered authoritative interpretations. Plebeians (common citizens) often objected to the interpretations rendered by the Pontiffs, and eventually demanded that the Roman Law be codified. The resulting Twelve Tables would serve as the basis of Roman Law for one thousand years. Over the centuries, however, Roman Law was modified, expanded, and extended through a series of imperial edicts. In the early sixth century A.D., the Byzantine Emperor Justinian commissioned the legal scholar Tribonian to produce a systematic codification of the Roman Law. The result was the *Corpus Juris Civilis*, or Body of Civil Law, also known as the **Code of Justinian**. When completed, it was supplemented by the *Novellae* (new laws), placing long-established Roman customs in statutory form. After the decline of the Roman Empire, the feudal system relied largely on customs and later on royal decrees. A remnant of the Roman Law remained, and during the twelfth century the study of the Roman Law was revived in Italy and, later, in France. Throughout the Middle Ages, the **canon law** of the Roman Catholic Church exercised great control in personal relations such as marriage and inheritance. The Roman Law eventually became the basis of law throughout the entire continent of Europe.

The Napoleonic Code

The **Napoleonic Code**, promulgated under Napoleon Bonaparte in 1804 as a codification of all the civil and criminal laws of France, was based in large part on the Code of

Justinian. The Code was decidedly modern in that it was secular, rational, comprehensive, and written in the common language of the people. The Napoleonic Code became a model for a uniform system of law for the nations of Western Europe. This is why the legal systems of Western Europe are often said to be "Roman law" systems.[9] Roman law systems are based on the primacy of statutes enacted by the legislature. These statutes are integrated into a comprehensive code designed to be applied by the courts with a minimum of judicial interpretation.

THE COMMON LAW TRADITION

American law is derived largely from the **English common law**, which dates from the eleventh century. At the time of the Norman Conquest of 1066, English law was a patchwork of local laws and customs, often applied by feudal courts, and church law enforced by ecclesiastical courts. William the Conqueror, the first Norman king of England, strengthened the royal courts established by his Anglo-Saxon predecessors. His son, King Henry I, dispatched royal judges to preside in county courts. His successor, Henry II, greatly expanded the role of the royal judges by instructing them to travel throughout the kingdom, taking jurisdiction in cases formerly under the province of feudal and local courts.

The King's judges settled disputes based on the customs of the Anglo-Saxon people and the well-established principles of feudal society. These royal courts grew increasingly popular due to their reliance on trial by jury, which of course would become a bedrock principle of Anglo-American justice. The judges of these courts began to look to the decisions of their colleagues in similar cases to guide their judgments. Out of the decisions of these courts grew a law common to the entire kingdom, hence the term "common law."

Magna Carta

One of the most important moments in the development of Anglo-American law occurred in 1215, when a reluctant King John placed his seal on **Magna Carta**. Essentially, Magna Carta was a series of promises that the King would follow the dictates of the law in dealing with his subjects and vassals. This document established the principle that government is subject to the rule of law, which is the essential idea upon which the United States Constitution is based. Magna Carta is also the source of another bedrock principle in our legal system today—the idea of **due process of law**. Magna Carta stipulated that "[n]o free man shall be taken or imprisoned or disseised or outlawed or exiled or in any way destroyed, nor will we go or send against him, except by the lawful judgment of his peers or by the law of the land." Later statutes and court decisions would use the term "due process of law" as synonymous with "the law of the land." The American Bill of Rights even uses the term "due process of law" in protecting citizens' rights to life, liberty, and property. But the essential idea was expressed nearly six hundred years earlier in Magna Carta.

The Common Law Courts

By the time Magna Carta was signed, there were three common law courts: the King's Bench, the Court of Common Pleas, and the Court of Exchequer. The Court of King's Bench dealt primarily with "pleas of the Crown," which later came to be known as criminal cases. The Court of Common Pleas had jurisdiction over "common pleas," disputes between individuals that would later come to be termed "civil" cases. The Court of Exchequer originally dealt with matters involving the King's property and revenue. Later, through a procedural device called the writ of Quominus, the Court of Exchequer extended its jurisdiction to private controversies.[10]

The Doctrine of *Stare Decisis*

In 1292, court clerks began recording the rulings of the common law courts, and by the fourteenth century these decisions were serving as **precedents** to guide judges who addressed similar cases. As the centuries passed, coherent principles of law emerged from the decisions of the judges. Thus, in contrast to Roman law systems, which are based on **legal codes**, the common law developed primarily through judicial decisions. The common law doctrine of following precedent became known as *stare decisis*, which means "to stand by that which is decided." This idea took hold with the development of the printing press in the fifteenth century. Today, it remains an important component of both the English and American legal systems. The doctrine holds that a court should follow the principle of law enunciated in previous decisions by the highest court within its jurisdiction, assuming that the principle is relevant to the decision at hand and that it makes sense in the context of contemporary circumstances.

Civil and Criminal Law

Early on, the common law developed a distinction between **civil law** and **criminal law**. The criminal law sought to punish people for offenses against the Crown; the civil law provided remedies for essentially private wrongs. As defined by the common law, a **crime** was an intentional evil act that produced harm to the society. Thus, **criminal prosecutions** were brought by the Crown in cases styled, for example, *Rex v. Jones* or *Regina v. Smith* (in Latin, "Rex" means king; "Regina" means queen). In criminal cases, the sovereign was always the **plaintiff**, that is, the party initiating the legal action. The accused offender was always the **defendant**, the party against whom legal action was brought.

By 1600, the common law classified criminal offenses as **felonies**, which were punishable by death, and **misdemeanors**, which were punishable by less severe sanctions. Felonies included the crimes of murder, manslaughter, mayhem, robbery, burglary, arson, larceny, rape, suicide, and sodomy. Misdemeanors included various offenses against public order and the administration of justice.

Civil wrongs were not seen as offenses against the entire society but only against private parties. In a **civil suit**, the plaintiff was the aggrieved party; the defendant was the party accused of the wrongful act. Much of the early common law litigation involved disputes over land, giving rise to a complex body of property law. Other civil offenses came to be classified as breaches of contract or torts. A **breach of contract** occurred when a party to a contract violated the terms of the agreement. A **tort**, on the other hand, was a wrongful act that did not violate any enforceable agreement but nevertheless violated a legal right of the injured party.

The Writ System

The common law developed a complex series of writs. A **writ** is simply another term for a court order. In order to obtain justice at common law, a plaintiff had to petition a court for the appropriate writ. For example, a plaintiff who had been wrongfully dispossessed of personal property sought a writ of replevin. One seeking to collect money owed brought an action in debt. However, if the debt was based on a sealed contract, one brought an action of covenant. An action of trespass was filed to recover damages in cases of torts. Failure to seek the proper writ was fatal to a plaintiff's case. To the average plaintiff, the writ system was bewildering. This meant that plaintiffs had to rely on experts in litigation, which gave rise to the legal profession.

Without question, the most celebrated common law writ was **habeas corpus**. Literally meaning "you have the body," habeas corpus was a device by which a court of law would require a person to show just cause for holding another person in custody. The primary purpose of the writ was to protect people from unlawful confinement. The Framers of the U.S. Constitution believed the writ of habeas corpus to be so important that they provided that "the Privilege of the Writ of Habeas Corpus shall not be suspended unless when in Cases of Rebellion or Invasion the public Safety may require it."[11]

Juries

One of the keys to the success of the common law was the emergence of the institution of the jury trial. Prior to the advent of the common law, trials in England took the form of combat, ordeal, or compurgation. In trial by combat, opposing parties would engage in combat or hire champions to do battle on their behalf. In the most ritualistic form of trial by combat, knights acting as champions would do battle by joust, charging one another on horseback and wielding lances. The assumption was that God would intervene on the side of justice and truth. Thus, the litigant whose champion prevailed in the joust prevailed in the legal dispute.

In a trial by ordeal, the defendant was tortured by fire or water. If a defendant survived the ordeal, it was said that God had intervened to prove the defendant's innocence before the law. In a trial by compurgation, a person accused of wrongdoing would recruit a body of men to attest to his honor. Custom required that any oath be repeated according to an exact form; any deviation undermined the value of the oath.

In the place of these irrational modes of trial, the common law courts substituted a more rational process of fact-finding. Early on, common law judges heard testimony from witnesses. Eventually, neighbors of the accused or of the litigants served as fact-finders, basing their conclusions only on evidence introduced in court. By the fourteenth century, the jury system was well established. Indeed, by that time, the law recognized two types of juries: the grand jury, which would decide whether an individual should be indicted for a crime; and the petit jury, which would serve as fact-finder in both civil and criminal cases.

The jury system developed at common law became an integral part of the American legal system. In many civil cases in American society today, the defendant has the right to a jury trial. Further, all individuals accused of serious crimes have a right to a trial by jury. Finally, grand juries continue to be widely used to review whether criminal charges should result in a defendant being bound over for trial.[12]

The Adversarial System

As noted above, early on, the English common law developed the concept of trial by jury as a means of resolving both civil and criminal cases. The jury would hear the evidence and decide the factual issues in the case; the judge would preside over the trial and decide questions of law.

Arguing the case would be "barristers," lawyers permitted to cross the "bar" in the courtroom that separated the judge's bench from the spectators. Thus, in England, a barrister is a trial lawyer. The barristers received their training in the Inns of Court, institutions in London located close to Westminster Hall, where the higher courts sat. Experienced barristers, called benchers, gave lectures and presided over moot courts (practice courts). After several years of training, students became eligible to serve as barristers. Although we do not use the term barrister in the United States, we do refer to licensed attorneys as having been "admitted to the bar."

In contrast to the more "inquisitorial" style of trial developed under the Roman Law tradition, the English common law developed an **adversarial system of justice**. This refers to a system of administering justice in which opposing parties contend with one another to achieve a favorable outcome. In this system, the role of the judge is one of neutral referee. In what is derisively called the "sporting theory of justice," barristers would do battle in the courtroom, much like knights on horseback charging one another with lances. Indeed, the adversarial legal system has its roots in the medieval joust. If the barristers can be seen as knights, their lances were their legal acumen and their rhetorical skills.

Today, we carry on the common law adversarial tradition, although there is much in the everyday working of the law that is more cooperative than combative. Many cases today end with plea bargains (criminal cases) or settlements (civil cases). However, when a legal "dream team" defending a celebrity accused of a crime does battle against the prosecution in a highly publicized trial, we see the adversarial system in its starkest form. Indeed, in such instances people often question whether the adversarial system obfuscates the search for truth. The assumption behind the medieval joust was that God was on the side of the victor. Similarly, the adversarial system of justice assumes that truth and justice are most likely to emerge from the clash of opposing factual and legal claims. In general, this may be true—but there is no assurance that competition in the courtroom will always produce truth or justice.

Equity

In its formative period, the common law was characterized by considerable flexibility. By the fourteenth century, the common law had become highly technical and rigid. Moreover, litigation was expensive. Aggrieved parties who were unable to secure a remedy at common law would appeal directly to the King for justice. The King often delegated such matters to his Chancellor, who was a cleric and a member of the King's court, often referred to as the "keeper of the King's conscience." Eventually, this practice of referring disputes to the Chancellor evolved into a secular tribunal called the Court of Chancery, which developed its own jurisprudence called **equity**.

The term "equity" comes from the Latin *aequitas*, which means justice or equality. The idea of equity as a supplement to law can be traced to the Roman Law, and ultimately, to the ancient Greek philosopher Aristotle (384–322 B.C.). The idea is that when existing legal rules and procedures are insufficient to remedy injustice, a court should rely on general principles of fairness in granting relief. The Court of Chancery did not follow the writ system, nor did it utilize juries; chancellors made factual determinations in addition to fashioning equitable remedies. Although the Court of Chancery did not follow the common law or the doctrine of *stare decisis*, chancellors eventually came to rely on "maxims" derived from previous equitable decisions. A maxim is a statement of a generally accepted principle, for example: "He who seeks equity must have clean hands"; "Equity aids the vigilant, not those who sleep on their rights."

Perhaps the chief distinction between the common law and equity was that common law courts were limited to awarding damages to plaintiffs who prevailed in civil actions, while the Court of Chancery could issue an **injunction** to prevent or terminate injurious conduct and could also order **specific performance** in cases of breach of contract. Development of the law of trusts represented one of the principal achievements of the Chancery Courts. Eventually, common law and equity would be merged, both in England and in the United States—at least in the sense that law and equity jurisdiction would be vested in the same courts.

The Emergence of Parliament

The English Parliament stems from a thirteenth century dispute between King Henry III and the feudal lords and originally was convened without royal authority. The Parliament convened by King Edward I in 1295 became the model for future Parliaments. By the fourteenth century, Parliament was a well institutionalized feature of the English political system. It heard petitions from aggrieved subjects and presided over abdications of kings.[13] Later in the century, Parliament was divided into two chambers: the House of Lords and the House of Commons. Parliament came to play a significant role in the formation of the law by adopting statutes that revised and supplemented the common law. For example, in 1540 Parliament enacted the Statute of Wills, which allowed people to will real estate to their heirs. Prior to that enactment, the common law recognized only the right to will personal property. Numerous other enactments followed, and they modified, extended, or superseded the common law in many ways.

The most significant moment in the history of the English Parliament was the Glorious Revolution of 1688, which established the supremacy of Parliament over the Crown. Events that occurred in England from 1688–1689 resulted in the ousting of King James II and the installation of William III and Mary II as king and queen. They accepted the Declaration of Rights, which were formalized by Parliament through enactment of the English Bill of Rights. These events collectively brought about the supremacy of Parliament over the Crown and ushered in major advances for individual rights. In fact, many of the ideals expressed in the American Bill of Rights, which the states ratified in 1791, are direct descendants of this era in English history, an era often referred to as the Glorious Revolution.

With the popularization of democratic political ideas, the role of the English monarchy became an increasingly symbolic one. Today, executive power resides in the British prime minister and the cabinet ministers, all of whom are members of Parliament. Thus, **sovereignty** (the right to rule), which once resided solely in the Crown, is now vested in Parliament.

Reception of the Common Law in America

As England became a colonial power, the common law tradition was exported throughout its Empire. Thus, the common law was extended not only throughout the United Kingdom but also to Australia, New Zealand, Canada (with the exception of Quebec), and to some extent India. The American colonies for the most part followed the common law, but there were significant variations. New York, Maryland, Virginia, Georgia, and the Carolinas followed the common law closely, while New Jersey and the New England colonies did not.

After independence was declared, some of the new American states adopted "reception statutes" or constitutional provisions adopting the English common law to the extent that it did not conflict with the new state and federal constitutions.[14] Other states adopted the common law, in whole or in part, through judicial decision making. Of the fifty states in the Union, Louisiana is currently the only one whose legal system is not based essentially on the common law. Rather, due to its settlement by the French, it is based primarily on the Napoleonic Code.

In the decades prior to the American Revolution, American lawyers often traveled to London to receive formal legal education in the **Inns of Court**. After independence, the new American judges and lawyers were greatly aided by ***Blackstone's Commentaries***, published in 1769. Therein, Sir William Blackstone, a professor at Oxford, codified the principles of the common law. Blackstone's seminal effort was a noble undertaking, but it also had the effect of demystifying English law. Consequently, Blackstone's encyclopedic treatment of the law was less than popular among English barristers, who by this time had developed a close fraternity and took great pride in offering their services to "discover the law." In America, however, *Blackstone's Commentaries* became something of a "legal bible."

THE AMERICAN CONSTITUTION

By the spring of 1776, it was apparent to most Americans that independence from England was both necessary and desirable. On July 4, the Continental Congress adopted the **Declaration of Independence**. Authored by Thomas Jefferson, the Declaration outlined the colonies' grievances against the King and asserted the right of revolution. The ideas expressed in the Declaration were by no means original to Jefferson or to the American colonies. Many were articulated a century earlier in John Locke's *Two Treatises of Government*. For example, when the Declaration of Independence refers to "life, liberty and the pursuit of happiness" as being the "unalienable rights" of individuals, it echoes John Locke's formulation of the natural rights of "life, liberty and property." Although the Declaration asserted American independence from the Mother Country, it did so by drawing on ideas that had already taken hold in England. Thus, in a sense, the Declaration of Independence was an affirmation of the linkage between English and American political cultures. Despite considerable cultural differences that led to the Revolution, then, the essential ideas of the Declaration of Independence actually came from England.

The Articles of Confederation

After the American Revolution, the United States was a confederation of sovereign states barely held together by an agreement called the **Articles of Confederation.** Congress had no power to tax and no power to regulate interstate commerce. There was no presidency to provide leadership or to speak for the new nation with a unified voice. Nor was there a national court system to settle disputes between states or parties residing in different states. Finally, the Articles of Confederation could not be amended except by unanimous consent of the states. Any state could veto a proposed change in the confederation. This system was not working. Consequently, in early 1787 Congress issued the call for a federal convention to meet in Philadelphia "for the sole and express purpose of revising the Articles of Confederation."

Adoption of the Constitution

The delegates to the Philadelphia Convention decided to scrap the Articles of Confederation and draft a new constitution. The Framers accepted the existence of the states as sovereign political entities. Indeed, they drew inspiration from the recent experience of the states in adopting their own constitutions after independence from England was declared in 1776. Yet most of the delegates knew that without a strong national government, economic growth and political stability would be seriously undermined by interstate rivalries. Hence, their central objective was to create a viable political system based on the principle of **federalism**, one in which sovereignty is exercised by the national government and the states, although it is vested ultimately in the people.

To create a viable federal system, the delegates had to confront a number of contentious issues. The two greatest sources of contention were (1) a disagreement between the small and large states over representation in Congress and (2) the conflict between northern and southern states over slavery. For a time it appeared that the Convention might fail altogether. Ultimately, through persuasion and compromise, the Convention reached agreement. On September 17, 1787, thirty-nine delegates representing twelve states placed their signatures on what would become the nation's new fundamental law. Although ratification of the Constitution was a close question in some states, by the end of 1790 all thirteen of the original states had ratified the document.

The Constitution succeeded in correcting the major deficiencies of the Articles of Confederation. It strengthened the national government, gave Congress ample legislative powers, established an executive branch, and provided for a national court system. Above all, it provided a blueprint for a workable government, one that could adapt to dramatic social, economic, and technological change.

The Rule of Law and Constitutional Supremacy

The **United States Constitution** stands in sharp contrast to the English model. The English constitution is not a written document but rather a collection of documents, statutes, judicial decisions, and customs dating back to Magna Carta. The English constitution can be altered at any time by an act of Parliament. The U.S. Constitution stands above ordinary legislation and is extremely difficult to amend, requiring a two-thirds vote of each house of Congress and ratification by at least three-fourths of the states.

The United States Constitution is the embodiment of the Founders' belief in the **rule of law**. The idea is that government and society can be regulated by law, as opposed to being subjected to the whims of powerful, but potentially capricious, rulers. The Constitution rests on the belief that no one in power should be above the law. Even the legislature, the people's elected representatives, should be bound to respect the principles and limitations contained in the "supreme law of the land." The subordination of government to law was seen by the Framers as a means of protecting individual rights to life, liberty, and property.

Separation of Powers

The Framers of the Constitution had no interest in creating a **parliamentary system,** because they believed that parliaments could be manipulated by monarchs or captured by impassioned but short-lived majorities. Accordingly, parliaments provided insufficient security for liberty and property. The delegates believed that only by distributing the three basic functions of government (legislative, executive, and judicial) among three separate, coordinate branches of government could power be appropriately dispersed. Thus, the first three articles of the Constitution, known as the **distributive articles**, define the structure and powers of Congress (Article I), the executive (Article II), and the judiciary (Article III).

The Framers of the Constitution believed that a system of checks and balances would be necessary if separate, coordinate branches of government were to be maintained. As a result, the Constitution contains a number of "auxiliary precautions." The President is authorized to veto bills passed by Congress, but Congress can override the President's veto by a two-thirds majority in both houses. The President is given the power to appoint judges, ambassadors, and other high government officials, but the Senate must consent to these appointments. The President is commander-in-chief, but Congress has the authority to declare war, raise and support an army and a navy, and make rules governing the armed forces. The President is empowered to call Congress into special session but is duty-bound to appear "from time to time" to inform Congress as to the "state of the Union." These provisions were designed to create a perpetual competition between Congress and the Executive for control of the government, with the expectation that neither institution would permanently dominate the other. And, ultimately, that is in fact how things have worked out.

The Framers said much less about the judiciary, which Alexander Hamilton described as the "least dangerous branch" of the new national government.[15] The President and the Senate are given the shared power to appoint federal judges, but these appointments are for life. Congress is authorized to establish lower federal courts and determine their jurisdiction; it may even regulate the appellate jurisdiction of the Supreme Court. But Congress is prohibited from reducing the salaries of sitting judges. The only means of removing members of the judiciary is through a cumbersome impeachment process, but this requires proof that the judge has committed "high crimes or misdemeanors." Clearly, the Framers wanted to create an independent federal judiciary that would be insulated from partisan political pressures.

Judicial Review

The text of the Constitution is silent on the means by which the judiciary can check and balance the other branches. In *Marbury v. Madison* (1803),[16] the single most important case in American constitutional history, the Supreme Court asserted the power to review acts of Congress and declare them null and void if they are found to be contrary to the Constitution. Later, the Court extended this power to encompass the validity of state laws under the Federal Constitution. Commonly referred to as **judicial review**, the power of the federal courts to rule on the constitutionality of legislation is nowhere explicitly provided for in the Constitution. However, many of the Framers of the Constitution supported the concept of judicial review, and most probably expected the courts to exercise this power. In any event, the power of judicial review is now well-established. By assuming this power, the federal judiciary greatly enhanced its role in the system of checks and balances. Moreover, the courts took on primary responsibility for interpreting and enforcing the Constitution. Today, both state and federal courts exercise this authority.

The Bill of Rights

There is no question that the protection of the liberty and property of the individual was one of the Framers' highest goals. Yet the original Constitution had little to say about individual rights. This is because the Framers assumed that the limited national

CASE IN POINT

ESTABLISHMENT OF THE POWER OF JUDICIAL REVIEW
Marbury v. Madison
United States Supreme Court
5 U.S. (1 Cranch) 137, 2 L. Ed. 60 (1803)

William Marbury's commission as justice of the peace for the District of Columbia had been signed by President John Adams following Senate confirmation on March 3, 1801, President Adams's last day in office. Everything was in order, but Marbury never received the commission.

Thomas Jefferson was sworn in as the Nation's third President on March 4, 1801. His Secretary of State, James Madison, declined to deliver the commission to Marbury. Marbury filed suit in the Supreme Court, invoking the Court's original jurisdiction. Marbury asked the Court to issue a writ of mandamus, an order directing Madison to deliver the disputed judicial commission to him.

The Supreme Court held that Marbury was entitled to the commission but declined to issue the writ of mandamus. The Court held that the Act of Congress giving the Supreme Court the power to issue the writ of mandamus in cases brought under its original (as opposed to appellate)

jurisdiction was unconstitutional. Although the Court denied to itself the power to issue writs of mandamus in cases of original jurisdiction, it claimed the much more important power to declare acts of Congress null and void. In support of this assumption of power, Chief Justice John Marshall reasoned that, since the Constitution is the "supreme law of the land," and it is the duty of the judiciary to interpret the law, judicial review is both necessary and inevitable. It was in this context that Marshall made his frequently quoted assertion that "[i]t is emphatically the province and duty of the judicial department, to say what the law is." In reaching this conclusion, Marshall stressed the fact that judges take an oath to support and defend the Constitution. Marshall ended his landmark opinion with the question: "Why does a judge swear to discharge the duties agreeable to the Constitution of the United States, if that constitution forms no rule for his government?"

---

government they were creating would not be a threat to individual liberty and property. Moreover, citizens were already protected against their respective state governments by provisions in their own state constitutions. Still, the Framers found it desirable to enumerate certain particular protections for individual liberty. Article I, Section 9 recognized the writ of habeas corpus. And Section 10 prohibited state legislatures from interfering with rights and obligations under contracts. Indeed, the desire to protect private contracts from governmental interference was one of the principal motivations of the delegates to the Constitutional Convention.

However, not everyone thought that the Constitution went far enough in protecting individual rights. Thomas Jefferson, who did not attend the Constitutional Convention because he was Minister to France, was disappointed that the Framers failed to include a more complete enumeration of rights in the document. Jefferson's concern was widely shared in his native state of Virginia, where ratification of the Constitution was a close question. Fortunately, a "gentlemen's agreement" was worked out whereby ratification was obtained in Virginia and other key states on the condition that Congress would immediately take up the matter of creating a bill of rights. The first ten amendments to the Constitution, known collectively as the **Bill of Rights**, were adopted by the First Congress in 1789 and ratified by the requisite nine states by the end of 1791. All of the provisions of the Bill of Rights were responses to abuses of official power and the perceived inadequacies of the common law in curtailing such abuses.

The First Amendment Freedoms

The First Amendment to the United States Constitution, which is the first article of the Bill of Rights, recognizes the fundamental freedoms of religion, speech, press, and assembly, as well as the right to petition government for a redress of grievances.

The desire for religious freedom was one of the principal motivations for people to come to the New World. English history was to a great extent the history of religious warfare. Prior to the Protestant Reformation, the Roman Catholic Church was the established religious authority in England. After the Reformation, the Church of England assumed that role. Prior to the modern era, both the Catholic Church and the Church of England were intolerant of dissent and persecuted those who differed on matters of faith. The common law permitted the state establishment of religion and offered no protection for dissenters. One of the principal motivations in the settlement of the American colonies, then, had been the desire to escape religious persecution. The Framers of the Bill of Rights decided that there would be no official religion in the United States, at least none established by the national government. Beyond that, the national government would not attempt to interfere with the practices of different religions. So, it is no accident that the Framers of the Bill of Rights placed freedom of religion first in the First Amendment: "Congress shall make no law respecting an establishment of religion or prohibiting the free exercise thereof. . . ." Freedom of religion as a constitutional principle has two distinct components: the prohibition against official establishment and the guarantee of free exercise. Together, these clauses demonstrate the fundamental character of the Founders' devotion to freedom of religion.

Freedom of speech has been called "the matrix, the indispensable condition, of nearly every other form of freedom."[17] Certainly, freedom of speech and freedom of the press are essential to the functioning of a democratic society. Although the English common law recognized the right of the press to be free from "prior restraints," the common law did not go very far in protecting freedom of speech or freedom of the press. Indeed, the common law offense of seditious libel permitted the Crown to prosecute its critics, even if their statements were true. For example, in 1735 John Peter Zenger was tried for seditious libel by the colonial government of New York after Zenger published newspaper articles criticizing the governor. Although truth was not a defense to a charge of seditious libel under common law, the jury nevertheless acquitted Zenger. The celebrated case helped build support in the American colonies for freedom of the press, a value enshrined in the First Amendment to the Constitution. Historically, and especially in the modern era, the First Amendment protections of speech, press, assembly, and petition have been extremely important in facilitating free political activity and a "free marketplace of ideas" in American society. See Chapter 3 for more discussion of these vital First Amendment freedoms.

Rights of Persons Accused of Crimes

The Framers of the Bill of Rights were acutely aware of the abuses of the criminal law that had characterized England, and all of Europe, for many centuries. They wanted to abolish barbaric methods of obtaining confessions and inflicting punishments. They also believed that the English common law provided inadequate protection of individual rights in this area. The authors of the Bill of Rights wanted to ensure that persons charged with crimes would be treated fairly—that they would have ample opportunity to defend themselves. In turn, the Fourth, Fifth, Sixth, and Eighth Amendments contain provisions protecting the right to be free from unreasonable search and seizure, the right to a speedy and public trial by an impartial jury, the right to counsel, the right to confront prosecution witnesses, and the right to compel the testimony of witnesses for the defense. They also contain protections against compulsory self-incrimination, double jeopardy, excessive bail, excessive fines, and cruel and unusual punishments. All of these provisions remain extremely important in the day-to-day administration of justice in this country. In the 1960s, under the leadership of the United States Supreme Court, courts in this country greatly expanded the rights of the accused by broadly interpreting many of the provisions of the Bill of Rights. Many commentators praised the courts for reforming criminal justice; others believed that the courts were coddling criminals. That debate remains alive today.

Other Notable Constitutional Amendments

The Constitution has been amended seventeen times since the ratification of the Bill of Rights. Arguably, the most important of these amendments are the Thirteenth, Fourteenth, and Fifteenth, ratified in 1865, 1868, and 1870, respectively. The Thirteenth Amendment abolished slavery, or "involuntary servitude." The Fourteenth Amendment was designed primarily to prohibit states from denying equal protection and due process of law to the newly freed former slaves. The Fifteenth Amendment forbade the denial of voting rights on the basis of race. These so-called Civil War Amendments attempted to eradicate the institution of slavery and the inferior legal status of black Americans. Although the abstract promises of the Civil War Amendments went unfulfilled for many years, they represented the beginning of a process of democratization that has fundamentally altered the character of the American political system. It is important to recognize that the Fourteenth Amendment in particular, with its broad requirements of equal protection and due process, has become a major source of legal protection for civil rights and liberties, extending far beyond issues of racial discrimination.

Beyond the Bill of Rights, the **Fourteenth Amendment** (1868) is the most important constitutional amendment in the field of civil rights and liberties. This amendment places broad restrictions on the power of states to infringe upon the rights and liberties of citizens. The Equal Protection Clause of Section 1 of the Fourteenth Amendment serves as the primary basis for protecting the civil rights of minority groups against discriminatory state action. In addition, the Due Process Clause of Section 1 of the Fourteenth Amendment prohibits states from depriving persons of life, liberty, or property without due process of law. In its most generic sense, due process refers to the exercise of governmental power under the rule of law with due regard for the rights and interests of individuals. Due process has both procedural and substantive aspects. The concept of **procedural due process** embraces government's obligation to provide **fair**

Earl Warren—Champion of Justice

Earl Warren, a former governor of California, was appointed Chief Justice of the United States Supreme Court by President Dwight Eisenhower in 1953. He served until his retirement in 1969. The Warren Court greatly expanded individual rights by reinterpreting provisions of the Bill of Rights and the Fourteenth Amendment. But the Warren Court's most memorable achievement was the 1954 decision in *Brown v. Board of Education*, which declared unconstitutional state laws that required racially segregated public schools. Chief Justice Warren was known not for his technical command of the law but rather for his abiding sense of fairness. His favorite question in reference to a law or ruling was "Is it fair?" Warren believed that a court decision or law should be "evaluated in terms of practical application. Everything we do must include the human equation, for what we do with our legal system will determine what American life will be. . . ."

notice and a **fair hearing** to individuals before depriving them of "life, liberty or property." Under **substantive due process**, government is barred from enforcing policies that are irrational, unfair, unreasonable, or unjust, even if such policies do not run counter to other specific constitutional prohibitions.

Incorporation of the Bill of Rights

The Bill of Rights was created as a set of limitations on the power of the national government.[18] However, citizens of the states originally had to look to the rights enshrined in their state constitutions for legal protection against the actions of their state or local governments. One of the most significant effects of the Fourteenth Amendment has been to make the provisions of the Bill of Rights enforceable against state and local governments as well as the national government. Under the **doctrine of incorporation**, the Supreme Court has held that most of the provisions of the Bill of Rights are embraced within the terms "liberty" or "due process" and are thus applicable to the states.[19] This is significant because it means that there are now national standards of liberty and due process by which governments at all levels must abide.

MODERN STATUTES AND CODIFICATION

Although the American legal system is based on English common law, Congress and the fifty state legislatures have become extremely active in crafting statutes to meet modern conditions. Once adopted, a statute supersedes the common law within that jurisdiction. Many modern statutes deal with subjects unknown to the common law, such as civil rights, public health, antitrust law, environmental protection, and social welfare (see Chapter 11). While Congress was not vested with a general **police power** under the Constitution, it has relied upon its broad authority under the Commerce Clause (Article I, Section 8) to legislate in many areas that are only indirectly related to commerce.

Historically, many of the landmark statutes passed by Congress have resulted from great political struggles. For example, the Civil Rights Act of 1964 is one of the most significant pieces of federal legislation in the civil rights area. It was passed only after the civil rights movement of the late 1950s and early 1960s overcame staunch public resistance and after President Lyndon Johnson used all of his political skills to shepherd the legislation through Congress.

Statutory Construction

Although the adversarial system of justice and the basic common law concepts are defined today essentially as they were by the common law judges centuries ago, the law has now been codified by legislatures to a great extent. Accordingly, when attempting to answer questions of law, lawyers and judges now look first to the relevant statutes. Of course, statutory provisions do not always have plain or obvious meanings. One of the principal functions of contemporary courts, therefore, is **statutory construction**, which is the task of assigning concrete meaning to statutory provisions that may allow for different interpretations. For example, the Civil Rights Act of 1964 contained provisions barring racial discrimination in employment. Even so, it remained for the courts to decide what constituted discrimination in particular instances and what policies could be utilized to combat discrimination in the workplace. In particular, courts have had to decide whether and under what circumstances employers could utilize affirmative action programs to remedy discrimination and to promote diversity in the workplace.

Codification

One of the most important developments in the American legal system has been the codification of the common law. Through codification, a legislature transforms the common law in a given area into a clear, systematic code of laws. The first area of law in which this took place was civil procedure.

Civil procedure under English common law was extremely complex, technical, and esoteric. In the mid-nineteenth century, a movement began to codify the rules of civil procedure. The leader of this movement was David Dudley Field, whose 1846 monograph entitled *The Reorganization of the Judiciary* was instrumental in persuading the state of New York to codify its laws. In 1848, the state legislature adopted a code of civil procedure drafted by Field. Subsequently, the code was adopted, at least in part, by more than half of the states. Even the British Parliament adopted the code in 1873. A code of criminal procedure drafted by Field also diffused widely among the states. In 1857, Field chaired a commission to codify the entire body of substantive law in New York. Other states followed suit, so that today every state has its laws codified. Thus, for example, one wishing to research a point of criminal law in Indiana would begin with Title 35 of the Indiana Code, which is entitled "Criminal Law and Procedure." Similarly, the laws of the United States are codified in the United States Code. One interested in researching a question of federal criminal law would begin with Title 18, "Crimes and Criminal Procedure." Of course, statutory provisions often require interpretation, which is the function of the courts. Therefore, one must also examine any court decisions interpreting the code provision in question.

The Diffusion of Uniform Codes

One way that the law has been standardized is through the diffusion of **uniform codes**. Consider the case of commercial law, which covers sales, leases, negotiable instruments, insurance, brokerage, shipping, and other matters pertaining to business. The common law, which had developed in a rural, agrarian, pre-industrialized setting, was not very relevant to modern commercial practices. States had enacted statutes in this area, but prior to the 1950s there was little uniformity among states' commercial laws. In 1952, the Uniform Commercial Code (UCC) was developed by legal scholars and business practitioners. It spread rapidly among the states, as state legislators saw the wisdom of adopting uniform business laws. All fifty states have now adopted the UCC, in whole or in part, which has greatly facilitated interstate commerce.

Another area in which we have seen the influence of a uniform code is the criminal law. The American Law Institute, an organization of prominent lawyers, judges, and academics, drafted the Model Penal Code (MPC) in 1962. Although the MPC is not itself law, many of its provisions defining crimes have either been adopted by, or led to reform of, the criminal statutes in the majority of states.

ADMINISTRATIVE REGULATION

The role of government has changed dramatically in the two centuries since the American nation was founded. In the early days of the republic, government essentially followed the dictum that "that government is best which governs least." For the most part, the national government left such functions as social welfare and education to state and local governments, and instead concerned itself primarily with the regulation of foreign trade, the facilitation of internal improvements such as canals and post roads, and the protection of the national security. State and local governments, in turn, tended to leave matters of social welfare and education to neighborhoods, churches, and families. Perhaps most fundamentally, individuals were regarded as responsible for their own problems in addition to their own good fortune.

In the wake of post-Civil War industrialization and the emergence of an economy dominated by giant corporations, the limited role of government began to change. A new ethos emerged, one in which government assumed primary responsibility for solving social problems. With the passage of the Interstate Commerce Act in 1887 and the concomitant establishment of the Interstate Commerce Commission, the relatively unobtrusive government envisaged by the Founders began to move in the direction of increasingly complex and intrusive regulation. The era of Progressive reform in the early twentieth century and the subsequent New Deal fostered by President Franklin D. Roosevelt in the 1930s contributed mightily to the growth of such regulation, as did the New Frontier and Great Society of the 1960s.

The expansive role now played by the national government renders the legislative task of Congress considerably more difficult. Consequently, Congress has come to rely more and more on "experts" for the development and the implementation of regulations. These experts are found in a host of government departments, commissions, agencies, boards, and bureaus that make up the modern administrative state. Through a series of broad delegations of legislative power, Congress has transferred to the **federal bureaucracy** much of the responsibility for making and enforcing the rules and regulations deemed necessary for a technological society. The Food and Drug Administration (FDA), the Nuclear Regulatory Commission (NRC), the Federal Aviation Administration (FAA), the Occupational Safety and Health Administration (OSHA), the Environmental Protection Agency (EPA), and the Securities and Exchange Commission (SEC) are just a few of the myriad government agencies to which Congress has delegated broad authority to make public policy.

Frequently, the enabling legislation creating these agencies provides little more than vague generalities to guide agency **rulemaking**. For example, in 1970, Congress gave OSHA the power to make rules that are "reasonably necessary or appropriate to provide safe and healthful employment and places of employment." The rules that OSHA promulgates as "necessary" or "appropriate" take on the force of law.

A good example of legislative delegation is seen in the Americans with Disabilities Act (ADA) of 1990. The ADA, which built upon the existing body of federal civil rights law, mandates the elimination of discrimination against individuals with disabilities. A number of federal agencies, including the Department of Justice, the Department of Transportation, the Equal Employment Opportunity Commission (EEOC), and the Federal Communications Commission (FCC), are given extensive regulatory and enforcement powers under the ADA.

Most observers agree that broad delegations of legislative power are necessary to enable agencies to develop the programs required to deal with targeted problems. These delegations of power may be to a great extent desirable or even inevitable, but they do raise serious questions of constitutional theory. As we shall see in Chapter 12, one of these questions stems from the fact that, in many instances, agencies exercise lawmaking, law enforcement, and quasi-judicial functions, which flies in the face of the constitutional principle of separation of powers.

THE DECISIONAL LAW

Although substantive law and procedural law are often modified by the adoption of federal and state statutes, courts play an equally important role in the development of law. **Trial courts** exist primarily to make factual determinations, apply settled law to established facts, and impose sanctions. In reviewing the decisions of trial courts, **appellate courts** must interpret the federal and state constitutions and statutes. The federal and state constitutions are replete with majestic phrases, such as "equal protection of the laws" and "privileges and immunities," which require interpretation. That is, courts must define exactly what these grand phrases mean within the context of particular legal disputes. Likewise, federal and state statutes often use vague language like "affecting commerce" or "reasonable likelihood." Courts must assign meaning to these and a multitude of other terms. Although the majority of states have abolished all, or nearly all, common law crimes and replaced them with statutorily defined offenses, the common law remains a valuable source of statutory interpretation. This is because legislatures frequently use terms known to the common law without defining such terms. For example, in proscribing burglary, the legislature may use the term "curtilage" without defining it. In such an instance, a court would look to the common law, which defined the term to mean "an enclosed space surrounding a dwelling."

In rendering interpretations of the law, appellate courts generally follow precedent, in keeping with the common law doctrine of *stare decisis.* However, in our rapidly changing society, courts often encounter situations to which precedent arguably does not or should not apply. In these situations, courts will sometimes deviate from or even overturn precedent. Moreover, there are situations in which there is no applicable precedent. When this occurs, the appellate courts will have the opportunity to make new law. Therefore, appellate courts perform an important **lawmaking function** as well as an **error correction function**. Today, any serious student of law must follow developments in the **decisional law**, that is, law as developed by courts in deciding cases.

Constitutional Law

The U.S. Constitution and the constitutions of the fifty states are more than mere suggestions or exhortations. This is due primarily to the institution of judicial review, through which federal and state courts can evaluate government action and ordinary law against constitutional principles. Consequently, we have an elaborate body of constitutional law, which consists of the decisions of federal and state courts interpreting constitutional provisions (see Chapter 3).

CONCLUSION

As we have seen, the foundations of American law have a rich cultural and political history. The English common law, with its emphasis on precedent, its requirement that the sovereign be subject to the law, and with its eventual incorporation of the concept of equity, laid the foundation for law and political institutions in America. The laws established by sovereign authority, referred to as the positive law, would become the essence of American law—yet the natural law and its concept of right and wrong have also played an important role in affecting the application of those laws.

Ultimately, the law has many dimensions. Today, American law is based on the supremacy of written federal and state constitutions and laws enacted pursuant to those constitutions by elected representatives. Yet in allocating power among the branches of the government, the Framers of the United States Constitution and the Bill of Rights painted with a broad brush, allowing an independent judiciary the prerogative of interpreting and applying the Constitution and laws enacted pursuant to it. Wisely, the states have followed the same pattern. Thus, in America we have created a government that is ruled by the majority but which remains protective of the rights of the minority.

The framework of our national and state constitutions is sufficiently flexible to allow the creation and implementation of laws, as well as the delegation of power to administrative agencies that can enact regulations made necessary as the United States has advanced from an agrarian economy to an industrial and, more recently, a technological society. But laws and regulations are words spread upon documents, and, no matter how positive the law, it is the application of the law that affects society. Congress and the state legislatures have the primary role in enacting laws. No one, however, has succeeded in drafting a law that provides for every contingency. Consequently, it becomes the function of independent federal and state courts to interpret those laws with wisdom and, often, with compassion. There will always be "gaps" in the law, and today, every serious student of law and government must realize that the courts must at times "make law" to fill in those gaps.

In studying the remaining chapters, it is important to observe how the dynamic nature of our society is reflected in the laws that govern us. It is also essential to remember that the United States Constitution, as interpreted by the Supreme Court, is the law of the land. The Court holds the power of judicial review over acts of Congress, acts of administrative agencies, and certain decisions of the highest tribunals of the states, all of which may, at times, contravene the Constitution. In the succeeding chapters, we will examine how the Supreme Court's actions have effectively set national standards for administration of the criminal law, and to a lesser extent, have affected the ongoing development of the civil law.

SUMMARY OF KEY CONCEPTS

In describing the foundations of American law, we have identified the forms and sources of law, explained how law functions in the economic and social life of our nation, and described how law plays an increasingly significant role in conflict resolution in our public and private lives.

As we move through the remaining chapters, it will be important to recognize how law developed and to understand how the American legal system was influenced by earlier forms of law. The primary influence was the English common law, and we will see frequent references to common law principles in many of the remaining chapters.

To fully comprehend the American legal system, though, one must also be aware of the concepts and experiences that led to its adoption. It is essential to understand the pivotal role of the U.S. Constitution and the Bill of Rights as well as succeeding constitutional amendments. The most significant of these later amendments has been the Fourteenth Amendment, which has become the bedrock of "due process of law" and "equal protection of the laws." Yet, the framework of our national and state constitutions is sufficiently flexible to allow Congress and state legislatures to enact statutory laws and to permit federal, state, and local executive agencies to promulgate administrative regulations. Finally, at this point the student should begin to understand how courts, legislatures, and administrative agencies function, as well as the crucial role played by the judicial branch, particularly through the concept of judicial review.

FOR FURTHER READING

Adams, David M., *Philosophical Problems in the Law* (4th ed., Wadsworth 2004).

Amar, Akhil Reed, *The Bill of Rights: Creation and Reconstruction* (Yale University Press 1998).

Barone, Michael, *Our First Revolution* (Crown Publishers 2007).

Devlin, Lord, *The Enforcement of Morals* (Oxford University Press 1959).

Friedman, Lawrence M., *A History of American Law* (3d ed., Touchstone 2005).

Hall, Kermit L., *The Magic Mirror: Law in American History* (Oxford University Press 1989).

Hart, H.L.A., *Law, Liberty and Morality* (Stanford University Press 1963).

Horowitz, Morton, *The Transformation of American Law, 1780–1860* (Harvard University Press 1977).

Horowitz, Morton, *The Transformation of American Law, 1870–1960* (Oxford University Press 1994).

Musson, Anthony, and W.M. Ormrod, *The Evolution of English Justice: Law, Politics and Society in the Fourteenth Century* (St. Martin's Press 1999).

QUESTIONS FOR THOUGHT AND DISCUSSION

1. What would society be like in the absence of positive law? Under what conditions could society function without law?
2. Under what conditions, if any, is civil disobedience justified?
3. Why has the English common law been important in the development of the American legal system?
4. What is the difference between the substantive and the procedural law?
5. Why did the Framers of the United States Constitution not include the Bill of Rights in the original document?

KEY TERMS

adversarial system of justice
appellate courts
Articles of Confederation
Bill of Rights
Blackstone's Commentaries
breach of contract
canon law
civil disobedience
civil law
civil suit
Code of Justinian
codification
constitution
crime
criminal law
criminal prosecutions
critical legal studies

decisional law
Declaration of Independence
defendant
distributive articles
doctrine of incorporation
due process of law
English common law
equity
error correction function
executive order
fair hearing
fair notice
federal bureaucracy
federalism
felonies
Fourteenth Amendment
habeas corpus

injunction
Inns of Court
judicial decision
judicial review
lawmaking function
legal codes
legislature
lex talionis
libertarian view of law
Magna Carta
misdemeanors
Napoleonic Code
natural law
ordinance
parliamentary system
plaintiff
police power

positive law
precedents
procedural due process
procedural legitimacy
regulation
Roman Law
rule of law

rulemaking
sovereignty
specific performance
stare decisis
statute
statutory construction
substantive due process

substantive legitimacy
tort
treaty
trial courts
uniform codes
United States Constitution
writ

ENDNOTES

1. By "rules," we mean authoritative directions as to what should be done or how it should be done. By "promulgated," we mean made known officially, publicly, and formally. By "enforced," we mean imposed by force or the threat of force. Finally, by "government," we mean the set of officials and institutions exercising a monopoly on the legitimate use of force in society.

2. Of course, the law does not always achieve this rule-like quality, but most commentators believe that this remains an ideal to which the law must strive and by which it must be judged.

3. Some would argue that utilitarianism, the doctrine that the goal of any policy should be to promote the greatest happiness of the greatest number of people, is an adequate basis upon which to evaluate law. Others would argue that utilitarianism fails to provide adequate protection for the rights of individuals and minority groups. If, in a hypothetical population of 100, 99 people are extremely happy that one troublesome individual has been put to death, is the sum total of their happiness enough to offset the "unhappiness" of the one who is killed? Of course, this assumes that one can quantify happiness in a way that would permit such a calculation. Assuming this could be done, can the morality of the execution be judged merely on the basis of comparative happiness?

4. *See* Lon L. Fuller, *The Morality of Law* (Yale University Press 1964).

5. *See,* for example, *Brown v. Board of Education,* 347 U.S. 483, 74 S. Ct. 786. 98 L. Ed. 873 (1954), in which the U.S. Supreme Court interpreted the Equal Protection Clause of the Fourteenth Amendment to the U.S. Constitution to prohibit compulsory racial segregation in the public schools.

6. *See* Lord Devlin, *The Enforcement of Morals* (Oxford University Press 1959).

7. *See* H.L.A. Hart, *Law, Liberty and Morality* (Stanford University Press 1963).

8. *See* Max Weber, *The Protestant Ethic and the Spirit of Capitalism* (Scribner's 1958).

9. The term "civil law" is often used to denote the Roman Law tradition. We prefer to use "civil law" in reference to the law governing disputes between private parties, as distinguished from criminal matters.

10. A private party wishing to collect an unpaid debt from another private party could claim that he was indebted to the King and was less able (quo minus) to pay the King due to the unpaid debt. Even though the claim of indebtedness to the King was often fictitious, the Court of Exchequer would routinely issue the writ of Quominus to take jurisdiction of the case. By this ingenious legal device, the Court was able to expand its jurisdiction to a category of private suits.

11. U.S. Const. art.I, §9.

12. In the United States, grand juries are used in criminal prosecutions in the federal courts and in many states. Great Britain abolished the institution of the grand jury in 1933. In Britain today, criminal indictments are prepared by clerks of the criminal courts.

13. Parliament presided over the abdications of King Edward II in 1327 and King Richard II in 1399.

14. For example, Article 25 of the Delaware Constitution of 1776 provided: "The common law of England, as well as so much of the statute law as has been heretofore adopted in practice in this state, shall remain in force unless they shall be altered by a future law of the Legislature, such parts only excepted as are repugnant to the rights and privileges contained in this Constitution and the declaration of rights, & agreed by this convention."

15. Alexander Hamilton, *The Federalist* No. 78.

16. *Marbury v. Madison,* 5 U.S. 137, 2 L. Ed. 60 (1803).

17. *Palko v. Connecticut,* 302 U.S. 319, 327 (1937).

18. *See Barron v. Baltimore,* 32 U.S. 243, 8 L. Ed. 672 (1833).

19. *See, e.g., Duncan v. Louisiana,* 391 U.S. 145, 88 S. Ct. 1444, 20 L. Ed. 2d 491 (1968).

STRUCTURES OF AMERICAN LAW

2

LEARNING OBJECTIVES

This chapter should enable the student to understand:

- the role of the U.S. Congress and state legislatures and the processes they follow in exercise of their powers
- the organization, jurisdiction, and functions of federal and state trial and appellate courts
- the role of the federal and state executive officers and regulatory and administrative agencies
- the operation of law enforcement and prosecutorial agencies
- the legal profession and the adversary and alternative dispute resolution processes

CHAPTER OUTLINE

INTRODUCTION

Any explanation of the American legal system necessarily involves the principle of **federalism**. As is clear from the discussion in Chapter 1, federalism is one of the hallmarks of the American constitutional system: the fundamental division of authority between the national government in Washington, D.C., and the fifty state governments. Each of the states has its own machinery of government as well as its own constitution that empowers and limits that government. Of course, the provisions of the state constitutions, as well as the statutes adopted by the state legislatures, are subordinate to the provisions of the U.S. Constitution and the laws adopted by Congress.

There are significant legal differences between the national government and that of the states. The authority of the federal government extends throughout the United States and its territories, whereas state authority is confined within state borders. The national government has sole authority to make treaties with other nations, enact laws governing the high seas, coin money, regulate standards of weights and measures, regulate international trade, regulate immigration and naturalization, and provide for the national defense. The national government also has primary, although not exclusive, authority to regulate interstate commerce, which is a major source of federal legislative power.

The states, on the other hand, have exclusive authority over their own machinery of government. They have exclusive power to establish and control local governments (cities, counties, and townships). States have sole responsibility for conducting elections and apportioning electoral districts, although in exercising these functions they must comply with federal constitutional standards. States are the primary locus of the **police power**—the power to make laws in furtherance of the public health, safety, welfare, and morality. States also have primary (though no longer exclusive) authority over commerce within their borders.

The federal government and the states also possess a number of **concurrent powers**, that is, powers vested in both levels of government. These powers include the power to tax, to spend and borrow money, to enact legislation, to charter and regulate banks, and to establish courts of law and administrative and regulatory agencies. The national government and the states also both possess the power of eminent domain, which is the power to take private property for public use, as long as property owners are compensated for the taking.

Fifty-One Legal Systems

Although this book is entitled *An Introduction to the American Legal System*, the national government and each of the states have their own legal systems. While there is significant variance among these systems, there are certain common features. Each system is based on a constitution, which represents the fundamental and supreme law within the system. Like the United States Constitution, each of the fifty state constitutions is based on the principle of separation of powers, which means that governmental power is distributed among coordinate legislative, executive, and judicial branches. Each system has a **legislature** empowered to enact statutes—laws that apply generally within the system. Each has a chief executive responsible for administering the government, and each has its own bureaucracy located within its executive branch. Each jurisdiction has its own set of **law enforcement agencies**, which are also located within the executive branch.

In addition, each of the fifty-one legal systems in the United States has its own "governmental law office" in the form of a department of justice or attorney general's office. These government lawyers represent the interests of the people within their jurisdictions in both civil and criminal matters. That is to say that they prosecute crimes, defend against lawsuits, file suits on the public's behalf, and present legal arguments in court. Many state attorneys general also render opinions for public officials and agencies on questions of law.

Finally, each of the fifty-one legal systems has its own system of courts, the structures of which we examine in some detail in the next chapter. Courts of law play the pivotal role in the legal system. They preside over the resolution of civil and criminal cases by conducting trials and hearing appeals. In so doing, courts interpret the constitutional provisions, statutes, ordinances, regulations, executive orders, treaties, and principles of common law that bear on the outcome of these cases. They also exercise the power of **judicial review**—the power to determine the constitutionality of all governmental enactments and actions.

LEGISLATURES

All governments make laws, or legislation. In a democracy, the governmental institution with primary responsibility for enacting legislation is the legislature. Legislatures in the United States and other democratic countries are composed of the people's elected representatives chosen through free and fair elections. The members of these assemblies are known as **legislators**. In the lawmaking process, legislators follow either the preferences of their constituents or their own best judgment, depending on whether they consider themselves to be **delegates** or **trustees**. The delegate tries to discern what his or her constituents prefer the laws to be and votes accordingly. The trustee relies on a sense of what is best, irrespective of what his or her constituents prefer. In reality, legislators often alternate between these approaches, depending on the issue involved. And, of course, because nearly all legislators are elected as Democrats or Republicans, and because legislatures are organized along party lines, the positions taken by their respective parties are usually quite important in determining how legislators will vote. Ultimately, what legislators do *en masse* is a function of constituent preferences, individual policy judgments, and partisan politics.

The U.S. Congress

In the United States, the national legislature is called the **Congress**. The Framers of the Constitution wanted a strong legislature to be the central feature of the new national government. Thus, the Constitution gave Congress much broader powers than the legislature that existed under the Articles of Confederation. Congress's legislative authority may be divided into two broad categories: **enumerated powers** and **implied powers**. The former category includes those powers that are mentioned specifically in the Constitution, such as the power to tax and the power to regulate interstate commerce. The latter category includes those powers that are deemed to be "necessary and proper for carrying into Execution the foregoing Powers, and all other Powers vested . . . in the Government of the United States, or in any Department or Officer thereof."[1] Under the doctrine of implied powers, scarcely any area exists over which Congress is absolutely barred from legislating, because most social and economic problems have a conceivable relationship to the broad powers and objectives contained in the Constitution. Of course, Congress may not enact laws that violate constitutional limitations such as those found in the Bill of Rights.

In addition to adopting laws governing the Nation, Congress has the responsibility to see that the laws it passes are administered by the Executive Branch in the ways that Congress intended when it passed them. This function, known as **oversight**, has become extremely important in the modern era as Congress has found it necessary to delegate a considerable degree of lawmaking power to agencies within the Executive Branch (see Chapter 12).

Congress is also occasionally required to act in a judicial fashion, such as when considering whether to impeach and remove the President, the Vice President, or a federal judge. After President Clinton was impeached by a majority vote of the House of Representatives in late 1998, the case went to the Senate for trial, as required by Article I, Section 3 of the U.S. Constitution. But the Senate failed to muster the necessary two-thirds majority to remove the President, so Bill Clinton completed his second term in the White House.

How a Bill Becomes Law

Congress is made up of two chambers, the House of Representatives and the Senate. Laws enacted by Congress begin as bills introduced by members of either chamber. (The only exception is that bills to raise revenue must originate in the House of Representatives.) Once introduced, a bill is assigned to a committee for discussion and possible approval. Most bills never make it out of committee. Those that do are sent to the floor for a vote. For ordinary legislation, a simple majority is needed to pass a bill. To become law, both houses of Congress must pass a bill in the identical form. Once this happens, the bill is sent to the President, who has several options: (1) sign the bill into law, which is what usually occurs; (2) **veto** the bill, which can be overridden by a two-thirds majority of both houses of Congress; or (3) neither sign nor veto the bill, thus allowing it to become law automatically after ten days.[2]

Publication of Federal Statutes

Once a bill has become law, it is published in *United States Statutes at Large*, an annual publication dating from 1789 in which federal statutes are arranged in order of their adoption. Statutes are not arranged by subject matter nor is there any indication of how they affect existing laws. Because the body of federal statutes is quite voluminous, and because new statutes often repeal or amend their predecessors, it is essential that

Title 1	General Provisions	Title 28	Judiciary and Judicial Procedure
Title 2	The Congress	Title 29	Labor
Title 3	The President	Title 30	Mineral Lands and Mining
Title 4	Flag and Seal, Seat of Government, and the States	Title 31	Money and Finance
		Title 32	National Guard
Title 5	Government Organization and Employees	Title 33	Navigation and Navigable Waters
Title 6	Surety Bonds (repealed)	Title 34	Navy (repealed)
Title 7	Agriculture	Title 35	Patents
Title 8	Aliens and Nationality	Title 36	Patriotic Societies and Observances
Title 9	Arbitration	Title 37	Pay and Allowances of the Uniformed Services
Title 10	Armed Forces		
Title 11	Bankruptcy	Title 38	Veterans' Benefits
Title 12	Banks and Banking	Title 39	Postal Service
Title 13	Census	Title 40	Public Buildings, Property, and Works
Title 14	Coast Guard		
Title 15	Commerce and Trade	Title 41	Public Contracts
Title 16	Conservation	Title 42	The Public Health and Welfare
Title 17	Copyrights		
Title 18	Crimes and Criminal Procedure	Title 43	Public Lands
		Title 44	Public Printing and Documents
Title 19	Customs Duties		
Title 20	Education	Title 45	Railroads
Title 21	Food and Drugs	Title 46	Shipping
Title 22	Foreign Relations and Intercourse	Title 47	Telegraphs, Telephones, and Radiotelegraphs
Title 23	Highways	Title 48	Territories and Insular Possessions
Title 24	Hospitals and Asylums		
Title 25	Indians	Title 49	Transportation
Title 26	Internal Revenue Code	Title 50	War and National Defense
Title 27	Intoxicating Liquors		

FIGURE 2.1 Overview of the U.S. Code

new statutes be merged into legal codes that systematically arrange the statutes by subject. To find federal law as it currently stands, arranged by subject matter, one must consult the latest edition of the Official Code of the Laws of the United States, generally known as the **U.S. Code**. The U.S. Code is broken down into fifty subjects, called "titles" (see Figure 2.1 above). It is indexed by subject matter and by statutes' popular names, making it relatively easy to find what the U.S. Code currently has to say on a given matter.[3] One popular compilation of the federal law widely used by lawyers, judges, and criminal justice professionals is the *United States Code Annotated*

(U.S.C.A.). Published by West Group, the U.S.C.A. contains the entire current U.S. Code, but each section of statutory law in U.S.C.A. is followed by a series of annotations consisting of court decisions interpreting the particular statute along with historical notes, cross-references, and other editorial features.

State Legislatures

Under the U.S. Constitution, each state must have a democratically elected legislature because that is the most fundamental element of a "republican form of government." State legislatures generally resemble the U.S. Congress. Each is composed of representatives chosen by the citizens of their respective states. All of them, except that of Nebraska, are bicameral (i.e., two-house) institutions. In adopting statutes, they all follow the same basic procedures. When state legislatures adopt statutes, the statutes are published in volumes known as **session laws**. Then statutes are integrated into state codes. Annotated versions of all fifty state codes are available to anyone who wishes to see how state statutes have been interpreted and applied by the state courts.

As we noted in Chapter 1, after the American Revolution, states adopted the English common law as their own state law. (Congress, on the other hand, never did.) Eventually, however, state legislatures codified much of the common law by enacting statutes, which in turn have been developed into comprehensive state codes. Periodically, states revise portions of their codes to make sure they retain relevancy to a constantly changing society. For example, in 1989 the Tennessee General Assembly undertook a modernization of its criminal code. Old offenses that were no longer being enforced were repealed, other offenses were redefined, and sentencing laws were completely overhauled.

JUDICIAL SYSTEMS

Law evolves not only through the legislative process but also through a process of judicial interpretation in the context of particular cases. These cases may arise in either federal or state courts. The federal government and each of the fifty state governments maintain their own systems of courts. These systems include both **trial courts** and **appellate courts**. Trial courts conduct civil and criminal trials and various types of hearings. Trial courts make factual determinations and are the primary settlers of legal disputes. Appellate courts hear appeals from the trial courts. The appellate courts are not fact-finding bodies. Rather, their role is to review the proceedings of lower courts, correct errors, and settle unresolved legal issues.

The Federal Court System

Article III of the United States Constitution provides that "[t]he judicial Power of the United States, shall be vested in one supreme Court, and in such inferior Courts as the Congress may from time to time ordain and establish." Beginning with the landmark Judiciary Act of 1789,[4] Congress has used this authority to create, empower, and regulate the federal court system. Congress determines the structure of the federal judiciary (see Figure 2.2), sets the number of federal judges, determines the jurisdiction of the lower federal courts, and provides for the funding of the federal judiciary.

Federal Court Jurisdiction

Jurisdiction refers to a court's ability to hear and decide a case. Courts have jurisdiction with respect to certain categories of persons, specific geographical areas, and particular types of issues. The jurisdiction of the United States Supreme Court is provided for in Article III of the Constitution, although Congress may regulate to some extent the Supreme Court's authority to hear appeals.[5] The jurisdiction of the lower federal courts is determined solely by Congress. The jurisdiction of the federal courts, while broad, is not unlimited. There are two basic categories of federal jurisdiction. First, and most important for students of constitutional law, is **federal question jurisdiction.**[6] The essential requirement here is that a case must present a federal question, that is, a question arising under the United States Constitution, a federal statute, regulation, executive order, or treaty. Of course, given its expansive modern role, the federal government has produced a myriad of statutes, regulations, and executive orders. Consequently, most important questions of public policy can be framed as issues of federal law, thus permitting the federal courts to play a tremendous role in the policymaking process.

The second broad category, **diversity of citizenship jurisdiction,** applies only to civil suits and is unrelated to the presence of a question of federal law. To qualify under federal diversity jurisdiction, a case must involve parties from different states and an amount in controversy that exceeds $75,000.[7]

Federal courts also have sole jurisdiction over bankruptcies, actions by which individuals and corporations seek protection from their creditors.

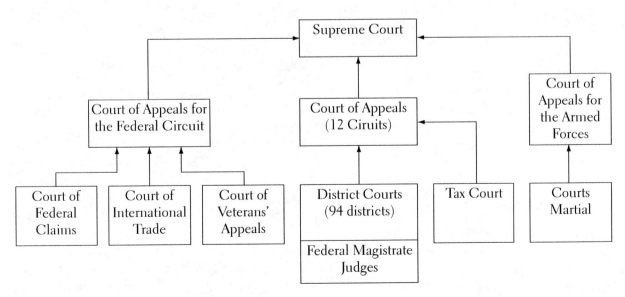

FIGURE 2.2 The Federal Court System

United States District Courts

The **United States District Courts** are the major trial courts in the federal system.[8] These courts are granted authority to conduct trials and hearings in civil and criminal cases meeting the previously discussed jurisdictional requirements. Each of the federal district courts also has its own bankruptcy court. Because the Constitution gives the federal government exclusive power over bankruptcies, all bankruptcy cases are filed in federal bankruptcy courts.[9]

There are currently ninety-four federal judicial districts, with each state being allocated at least one.[10] Some states have more districts, depending on population and geographical size. Tennessee, for example, has three federal judicial districts corresponding to the traditional eastern, middle, and western "grand divisions" of the state.[11] California, New York, and Texas are the only states with four federal judicial districts.[12]

As of 2014, there were 677 judgeships in the federal district courts.[13] The number of judges assigned to a specific district depends primarily on caseload, which is in turn largely a function of population within the district. There are currently fourteen judges assigned to the Northern District of Texas, which is based in Dallas;[14] twenty-four judges assigned to the Southern District, based in Houston;[15] sixteen judges assigned to the Western District, based in San Antonio;[16] and seven judges assigned to the Eastern District, based in Tyler.[17] Although there are multiple judges assigned to each federal judicial district, and although federal law permits certain exceptional cases to be decided by panels of three judges, normally only one judge presides at hearings and trials.

For the twelve-month period ending in September of 2013, there were 284,604 civil cases and 91,266 criminal cases filed in the federal district courts; approximately 1.1 million cases were filed in the bankruptcy courts.[18] In 1982, 206,193 civil cases, 31,623 criminal cases, and 412,852 bankruptcy cases were filed.[19] Thus, over a thirty-year period, civil filings rose slightly while criminal cases nearly tripled. To a great extent, the dramatic increase in criminal caseload can be attributed to the "war on drugs" that was launched during the 1980s, as well as the expansion of other federal law enforcement activities over the last several decades.

The United States Courts of Appeals

The intermediate appellate courts in the federal system are the **United States Courts of Appeals**.[20] These courts did not exist until passage of the Judiciary Act of 1891.[21] Prior to that time, appeals from the decisions of the District Courts were heard by the Supreme Court or by the Circuit Courts, which no longer exist. Today, the Courts of Appeals are commonly referred to as "circuit courts," because each one of them presides over a geographical area known as a circuit. The Nation is divided geographically into twelve circuits, with each circuit containing one or more federal judicial districts (see Figure 2.3). The circuit courts hear appeals from the federal districts within their circuits. For example, the United States Court of Appeals for the Eleventh Circuit, based in Atlanta, hears appeals from the District Courts located in Alabama, Georgia, and Florida. The Court of Appeals for the District of Columbia Circuit, based in Washington, D.C., has the very important additional function of hearing appeals from numerous "quasi-judicial" tribunals in the federal bureaucracy (see Chapter 12). In addition, there is a "thirteenth

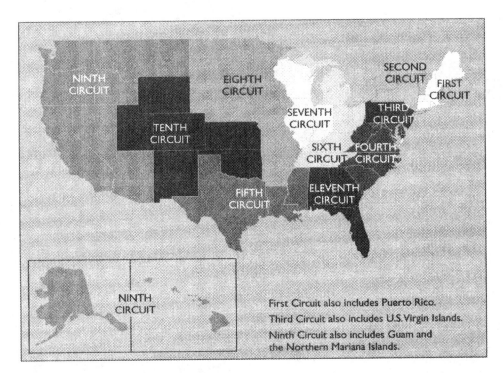

FIGURE 2.3 The Federal Judicial Circuits

circuit"—called the United States Court of Appeals for the Federal Circuit. It has nationwide jurisdiction over a number of different subjects, including international trade, intellectual property, patents, and veterans' benefit claims.[22]

Appeals in the circuit courts are normally decided by rotating panels of three judges, although under exceptional circumstances these courts will decide cases *en banc*, meaning that all of the judges assigned to the court will participate in the decision. On average, fourteen judges are assigned to each circuit, but the number varies from six judges in the First Circuit (Maine, Massachusetts, New Hampshire, Rhode Island, and Puerto Rico) to twenty-nine judges in the Ninth Circuit (Alaska, Arizona, California, Hawaii, Idaho, Montana, Nevada, Oregon, Washington, Guam, and the Northern Mariana Islands).[23] As of 2014, there are 179 judgeships across the U.S. circuit courts.[24]

In 1982, the caseload of the U.S. Courts of Appeals was 27,946 filings.[25] However, for the twelve-month period ending September 30, 2013, that figure had evolved to 56,475 cases.[26] Approximately 54 percent of the cases filed in the circuit courts were civil appeals, and about 21 percent were criminal appeals; the remainder consisted of appeals from administrative agency actions, bankruptcy courts, and other miscellaneous proceedings.[27]

The United States Supreme Court
Although the **United States Supreme Court** is explicitly recognized in Article III of the Constitution, it was not formally established until passage of the Judiciary Act of 1789.[28] The Judiciary Act provided for a Court composed of a Chief Justice and five Associate Justices. In 1807, the Court was expanded to include seven justices, and in 1837

Name	Born	State Appointed from	Year Appointed	Appointed by President	Political Party Affiliation
John G. Roberts (Chief Justice)	1955	Maryland	2005	Bush, G.W.	Republican
Samuel Alito	1950	New Jersey	2006	Bush, G.W.	Republican
Antonin Scalia	1936	New Jersey	1985	Reagan	Republican
Anthony M. Kennedy	1936	California	1987	Reagan	Republican
Clarence Thomas	1948	Virginia	1991	Bush	Republican
Ruth Bader Ginsburg	1933	Washington, D.C.	1993	Clinton	Democrat
Stephen G. Breyer	1938	Massachusetts	1994	Clinton	Democrat
Sonia Sotomayor	1954	New York	2009	Obama	Democrat
Elena Kagan	1960	New York	2010	Obama	Democrat

FIGURE 2.4 The Justices of the Supreme Court, 2014

Congress increased the number to nine. During the Civil War, the number of justices was briefly increased to ten. In 1869, Congress reestablished the number at nine, where it has remained to this day (see Figure 2.4). Although Congress theoretically could expand or contract the membership of the Court, powerful tradition militates against doing so.

The Supreme Court's first session was held in February of 1790. It had no cases on the docket and adjourned after ten days. During its first decade, 1790–1801, the Court met twice a year for brief terms beginning in February and August. Over the years, the Court's annual sessions have expanded along with its workload and its role in the political and legal system. As the Nation has become more populous, more complex, and more litigious, the Supreme Court's agenda has swelled. In the 2009–10 term, there were 6,576 filings by parties seeking review from the Supreme Court, 82 cases were argued, 77 decisions were reached and 73 written opinions[29] were produced.

Since 1917, the Court's annual term has begun on the "first Monday of October." Until 1979, the Court adjourned its sessions for the summer, necessitating special sessions to handle urgent cases arising in July, August, or September. Since 1979, however, the Court has stayed in continuous session throughout the year, merely declaring a recess (typically near the end of June) for a summer vacation.

Article III of the Constitution declares that the Supreme Court shall have **original jurisdiction** "[i]n all Cases affecting Ambassadors, other public Ministers and Consuls, and those in which a state shall be a party..." (although this was modified by the Eleventh Amendment). Congress has enacted legislation giving the District Courts **concurrent jurisdiction** in cases dealing with "Ambassadors, other public Ministers and Consuls," as well as in cases between the United States government and one or more state governments. As a result, the Supreme Court exercises exclusive original jurisdiction only in suits between state governments, which often involve boundary disputes or disputes over water rights. These cases, while important in themselves, represent a minute proportion of the Court's caseload.

The Supreme Court's **appellate jurisdiction** extends to all federal cases "with such Exceptions, and under such Regulations as the Congress shall make."[30] Appellate cases coming to the Supreme Court from the lower federal courts usually come from the thirteen Courts of Appeals, although they may come from the United States Court of Appeals for the Armed Forces, or, under special circumstances, directly from the District Courts. Appellate cases may also come from the state courts of last resort, which are usually, but not always, designated as state supreme courts.[31]

In recent years, Congress made the appellate jurisdiction of the Supreme Court almost entirely discretionary by greatly limiting the so-called **appeals of right**. Today, the Court's appellate jurisdiction is exercised almost exclusively through the **writ of certiorari**, which is issued at the Court's discretion. Federal law authorizes the Court to grant certiorari to review all cases, state or federal, which raise substantial federal questions. This broad discretion permits the Court to set its own agenda, facilitating its role as a policymaker, but allowing the Court to avoid certain issues that may carry

HOW THE SUPREME COURT GRANTS CERTIORARI

In most instances, a litigant who has exhausted all available remedies in the lower federal courts may file a petition for certiorari in the Supreme Court. As long as a substantial federal question is involved, a party who has exhausted appellate remedies in the state courts may also seek certiorari in the Nation's highest court. The chances of the Supreme Court's granting review in a given case are very slim. Of the approximately seven thousand petitions for certiorari ("cert") coming to it each year, the Court will normally grant review in only about a hundred. The Court tends to favor those cases in which the federal government is a party, cases where lower courts are in conflict, and cases involving issues of great public importance. The process of case selection actually begins with the Justices' **law clerks** (staff attorneys) reading the numerous petitions for certiorari and preparing summary memoranda. With the assistance of law clerks, the Chief Justice, who bears

THE LAW IN ACTION

primary responsibility for Court administration, prepares a list of cases to be considered. The associate justices may add cases to the list. Unless at least one justice indicates that a petition should be discussed, review is automatically denied, which disposes of more than 70 percent of the petitions. The Court considers petitions on the discuss list in private conferences. Regular conferences are held throughout the term, both for the purpose of reviewing cert petitions and for discussing and deciding the cases in which the Court has granted review. At least four justices must vote to grant certiorari in order for the Court to accept a case for review. The denial of cert carries no weight as precedent. The fact that the Court has decided not to review a lower court decision does not mean that the Court necessarily approves of the way it was decided. Should the same issue be presented to the Court in a later case, the previous denial of certiorari would have no bearing on the Court's decision.

undesirable institutional consequences. The Court may deflect, or at least postpone dealing with, issues that it considers "too hot to handle." This flexible jurisdiction, then, can be used as a means to expand or limit the Court's policymaking role, depending on the issue at hand.

Although Congress is authorized to regulate the appellate jurisdiction of the Supreme Court, it rarely has used this power to curtail the Court's authority. Rather, Congress has facilitated the institutional development of the Court by minimizing its mandatory appellate jurisdiction and thus giving the Court control over its own agenda. Likewise, Congress has delegated to the Court the authority to promulgate **rules of procedure** for itself and the lower federal courts.[32] Consequently, the Supreme Court is nearly autonomous with respect to the determination of its decision-making process.

Specialized Federal Tribunals

All of the federal tribunals we have discussed thus far are considered "Article III courts," which means that they are part of the judicial branch. Congress has also created a set of specialized tribunals under its authority under Article I of the Constitution. The principal difference between Article III courts and Article I courts is that the judges of the former are appointed for life whereas the judges of the latter serve for set terms of office (in most instances, fifteen years). Otherwise, the distinction between these two types of tribunals is rather blurred. The Article I courts include

- the **Tax Court**, established in 1924 to resolve disputes between taxpayers and the Internal Revenue Service
- the **Court of Veterans' Appeals**, created in 1988 to review decisions of the Board of Veterans' Appeals regarding veterans' claims to benefits
- the **Court of Federal Claims** (first established in 1855 as the Court of Claims), which is responsible for adjudicating **tort claims** (civil suits for damages) against the federal government.

The **Court of International Trade** (first established in 1926 as the Customs Court) adjudicates controversies between the federal government and importers of foreign goods. This specialized tribunal located in New York City has been declared by Congress to be an Article III court; therefore, its nine judges are appointed for life.[33]

Decisions of the Tax Court are appealable to the U.S. Court of Appeals for the District of Columbia Circuit. Appeals from the Court of Veterans' Appeals, the Court of Federal Claims, and the Court of International Trade are directed to the Court of Appeals for the Federal Circuit.[34]

Selection, Tenure, and Removal of Federal Judges

As provided by the Constitution, the President, subject to the consent of the Senate, appoints all federal judges. With the exception of those serving on the Article I courts, the appointments are for life.[35] Normally, the Senate consents to presidential judicial appointments with a minimum of controversy. However, Senatorial approval is by no means pro forma, especially when it involves appointments to the Supreme Court. Historically, of the 151 nominations to the Supreme Court as of 2014, 12 were formally rejected by the Senate, and seven were withdrawn by the President before a Senate vote. The most recent Senate rejection was that of Robert Bork in 1987, while the most recent withdrawal came in 2005, when President George W. Bush withdrew Harriet Miers' name from consideration.

On November 21, 2013, the Democrat-controlled Senate voted to alter long-standing rules regarding the confirmation of district and circuit court judges.[36] This change has been described as the invocation of a "nuclear option," ostensibly because it is considered a "last-resort" tactic for securing the confirmation of judges with minimal resistance from the minority party. Specifically, by a vote of 52-48—with 52 Democrats in favor and all 45 Republicans (plus three Democrats) opposing—Senate rules were changed so that filibusters of district and circuit court confirmation hearings would no longer be permitted. As many students of American politics know, a filibuster is a delay tactic that requires a "super-majority" of 60 senators to invoke "cloture" in order to end the delay and proceed to a vote. In practical terms, then, this shift in rules allowed for the confirmation of judges with a simple majority vote—as opposed to requiring the support of 60 senators. The change does not apply to confirmation hearings of Supreme Court justices—but only to District and Circuit court nominees.

Ultimately, in the aftermath of this shift, three Obama nominees to the D.C. Circuit that had previously been stymied by Republicans were confirmed by majority vote.[37] The President attempted to justify the rule change by stating that the Republican Party was engaging in a "pattern of obstruction"; however, Senate minority leader Mitch McConnell lamented this limitation on a minority's right to object by declaring, "It's a sad day in the history of the Senate"—with Alabama Senator Richard Shelby adding, "Democrats won't be in power in perpetuity . . . This is a mistake—a big one for the long run."[38] Along these lines, it is worth noting that in 2006, Obama—then a Senator from Illinois—spoke out against utilization of the "nuclear option" when a Republican majority had suggested its usage, even suggesting that the elimination of judicial filibusters would "change the character of the Senate forever."[39]

The importance of confirmation battles over judicial positions is connected largely to the idea that federal judges can hold their positions for life. Article III, Section 1 of the Constitution specifically states that "judges, both of the supreme and inferior Courts, shall hold their Offices during good Behaviour. . . ." This grant of life tenure to federal judges was intended to make the federal courts independent of partisan forces and transitory public passions so that they could dispense justice impartially, according to the law. But not everyone accepts the need for a life-tenured, appointed federal judiciary. In a democratic nation that extols the will of the people, such sentiments are apt to be viewed as elitist, even aristocratic. From time to time, proposals have surfaced to impose limitations on the terms of federal judges, but no such effort has ever gained serious political momentum. Life tenure for federal judges, like most of the elements of our eighteenth century Constitution, remains a firmly established principle of the political order.

The only means of removing a federal judge is through the **impeachment** process provided in the Constitution. First, the House of Representatives must approve one or more articles of impeachment by at least a majority vote.[40] Then, a trial is held in the Senate presided over by the Chief Justice of the Supreme Court. To be removed from office, a judge must be convicted by a vote of at least two-thirds of the Senate.[41]

Since 1789, the House of Representatives has initiated impeachment proceedings against thirteen federal judges, and only seven of these have been convicted in the Senate. The first federal judge to be impeached was John Pickering, a district judge from New Hampshire, who was impeached and removed from office in 1803 for reasons of mental instability and intoxication. The most recent impeachment was that of Judge Walter L. Nixon from the Southern District of Mississippi, who was impeached and removed from office in 1989 for committing perjury before a federal grand jury.

Only once has a Supreme Court Justice been impeached by the House. In 1804, Justice Samuel Chase fell victim to President Jefferson's attempt to control a federal judiciary largely composed of Washington and Adams appointees. Justice Chase had irritated the Jeffersonians by his haughty and arrogant personality and his extreme partisanship. Nevertheless, there was no evidence that he was guilty of any crime. Consequently, Chase narrowly escaped conviction in the Senate. The Chase affair set an important precedent—a federal judge may not be removed simply for reasons of partisanship, ideology, or personality. Thus, despite strong support in conservative quarters for the impeachment of Chief Justice Earl Warren during the 1960s, there was never any real prospect of Warren's removal. Barring criminal conduct or serious breaches of judicial ethics, federal judges do not have to worry that their decisions might cost them their jobs.

Federal Magistrate Judges

Federal magistrate judges (formerly called "federal magistrates") are appointed by the judges of the federal district courts for a period of eight years. Magistrate judges preside over pretrial proceedings in civil and criminal cases. They try misdemeanors and can preside over civil trials with the consent of both parties. The position of federal magistrate was created by Congress in 1968 to replace the ancient system of federal judicial commissioners. In 1990, Congress changed their title to "federal magistrate judge." Today, they tend to be experienced lawyers who are appointed based on the

---

SIDEBAR

Canons of Conduct for Federal Judges

1. A judge should uphold the integrity and independence of the judiciary.
2. A judge should avoid impropriety and the appearance of impropriety in all activities.
3. A judge should perform the duties of the office impartially and diligently.
4. A judge may engage in extra-judicial activities to improve the law, the legal system and the administration of justice.
5. A judge should regulate extra-judicial activities to minimize the risk of conflict with judicial duties.
6. A judge should regularly file reports of compensation received for law-related and extra-judicial activities.

Source: Judicial Conference of the United States

recommendations of merit selection committees. There are currently more than 500 federal magistrate judges.

The Military Justice System

Pursuant to Article I, Section 8 of the U.S. Constitution, Congress enacted the **Uniform Code of Military Justice** (UCMJ),[42] which gives **courts-martial** jurisdiction to try all offenses against the Code committed by military personnel. This includes those members on active duty, students at military academies, prisoners of war, and, in some instances, retired or reserve personnel.[43]

Offenses proscribed by the UCMJ embrace not only those commonly defined by civilian criminal laws but also certain offenses peculiar to military and naval service, for example, being absent without leave (AWOL) or desertion. (These military offenses are described in more detail in Chapter 4.) Historically, military jurisdiction was dependent on one's military status, but in 1969 the U.S. Supreme Court held that military jurisdiction was limited to "service-connected" offenses.[44] In 1987, the Court changed its view and said that courts-martial jurisdiction depends solely on whether an accused is a military member.[45]

Court-martial proceedings are initiated by commanders of military units, referred to as convening authorities, who appoint court members who sit in a way that is similar to a civilian jury. Military lawyers, called judge advocates, serve as judge and trial (prosecutor) counsel and defense counsel. Although accused military members are furnished counsel, they may, at their own expense, retain civilian counsel. The President, by executive order, prescribes rules of evidence and procedures to implement the provisions of the UCMJ. These are incorporated into the **Manual for Courts-Martial** (MCM) and are similar to the rules applied in federal district courts.

Decisions of courts-martial are reviewed by military courts of review in each branch of the armed forces. In specified instances, appeals are heard by the **United States Court of Appeals for the Armed Forces** (USCAAF). This court is staffed by civilian judges who are appointed to fifteen-year terms by the President with the consent of the U.S. Senate. It hears appeals when the death penalty is imposed, when cases are forwarded by the judge advocate general for a specific service (after the reviewing court of that service has acted), and when certain discretionary appeals are appropriate. Its decisions are subsequently appealable to the U.S. Supreme Court.

Historically, the Supreme Court has permitted "enemy aliens" captured during wartime to be tried by military tribunals.[46] In 2001, President George W. Bush issued an executive order authorizing military commissions to try foreign nationals accused of acts of terrorism against the United States. The Supreme Court, however, ruled that these commissions were neither authorized by federal law nor required by military necessity and that they ran afoul of the Geneva Conventions.[47] Congress responded by passing the Military Commissions Act of 2006,[48] which provided for "the use of military commissions to try alien unlawful enemy combatants engaged in hostilities against the United States for violations of the law of war and other offenses triable by military commission." Although the commissions are still in use, a 2008 Supreme Court decision declared that enemy combatants are entitled to basic habeas corpus protections.[49]

State Court Systems

Each of the fifty states has its own court system, responsible for cases arising under the laws of that state, which include the state constitution, statutes enacted by the state legislature, orders issued by the governor, regulations promulgated by various state agencies, and ordinances (local laws) adopted by cities and counties. State courts have jurisdiction over most criminal cases, because most crimes are offenses against state laws (see Chapter 4). State courts address most questions of property law, including real estate, probate, and inheritance questions (see Chapter 6). State courts handle most torts (see Chapter 5) and most contract disputes (see Chapter 7). Finally, state courts resolve almost all family law cases, including issues of divorce, child custody, guardianship, and juvenile delinquency (see Chapter 8). Indeed, the great majority of cases are decided not by the federal courts but by state courts.

Although no two state court systems are identical, all of them contain trial and appellate courts. Trial courts go by many names: county court, superior court, district court, circuit court, court of common pleas, and so forth. The New York Supreme Court has both trial and appellate divisions, which sometimes is a source of confusion. Many states have trial courts of limited jurisdiction to handle minor or specialized matters. They, too, have many names: probate court, juvenile court, municipal court, sessions court, mayor's court, and so forth. Some states, such as Idaho, Illinois, Iowa, and South Dakota, have one consolidated trial court that handles all civil and criminal cases. Other states have multiple trial courts, each with specialized jurisdiction.

Each state has a **court of last resort**, usually called the **state supreme court**, which speaks with finality on matters of state law. Most states now have **intermediate appellate courts** to handle routine appeals, which allows the state supreme court to focus on the most important cases. However, the jurisdictional characteristics of appellate courts vary considerably. In Florida, for example, the district courts of appeal are ostensibly the intermediate appellate courts. But under Florida law they are final in most matters. The Florida Supreme Court only reviews district court decisions on constitutional issues or where the district courts are in conflict or certify a question as one of great public importance.

Figure 2.5 displays a "model" state court system. Some state court structures are fairly close to this model, but there is enormous variation across the states with respect to judicial structure.

Selection and Retention of State Judges

State judges are selected in a variety of ways. Most are elected, though some run on partisan ballots and others run in non-partisan races. Many state judges are appointed by governors, either directly or through a nominating process known as merit selection. Even appointed judges typically must face the voters eventually in a contested election, or a merit-retention election, in which voters are asked whether a judge should be given another term. There is considerable controversy over judicial selection and retention. Advocates of **judicial accountability** to the people usually support some sort of elective system. Proponents of **judicial independence** generally argue for an appointive process with life tenure (the federal model) or at least long terms of office. A compromise

FIGURE 2.5 A Model State Court System

approach that has been steadily gaining acceptance since it was first adopted in 1940 is known as the **Missouri Plan**. It consists of three elements:

1. When a vacancy occurs, qualified persons submit applications to a non-partisan judicial nominating commission. The commission reviews the applications, conducts interviews, and submits a "short list" to the governor.
2. The governor appoints an individual from the list submitted by the nominating commission.
3. When the judge's term of office expires, the judge faces the voters in a retention election. The voters are asked simply, "Should Judge X be retained in office for another term?"

By combining merit-based, appointive, and elective elements, the Missouri Plan attempts to balance the values of judicial competency, independence, and account-ability. It is no guarantee of excellence, but at least incompetent or unsuitable prospects are screened out. Governors can often still use judicial appointments as patronage, which is something they have done historically. Finally, the voters can oust those judges whom they believe have abused their authority or acted unwisely. It is important to realize that the overwhelming majority of judges who stand for retention are retained. But sometimes the electorate can become aroused over an issue like capital punishment and vote out of office judges they believe to be acting contrary to public preferences. Such was the case in 1986 when Chief Justice Rose Bird and two of her colleagues on the California Supreme Court were removed by the voters. In her decade-long tenure as chief justice, Bird voted to reverse the death sentence in all of the sixty-four death penalty cases that came before the court. Her ouster by the voters probably had an effect on the California judiciary, making judges more cautious in dealing with controversial issues. Critics of judicial elections saw the defeat of Chief Justice Bird as a real threat to judicial independence. But those of a more populist bent celebrated what they regarded as a victory for judicial accountability.

Judicial Discipline and Removal

Every state has some mechanism (other than the ballot box) by which judges who commit serious legal or ethical violations can be removed from office. Generally speaking, this process is impeachment and basically follows the federal model discussed above. In recent years, state legislatures have created **judicial disciplinary commissions** to reprimand, censure, and even suspend judges whose violations do not rise to the level where impeachment is warranted. In Tennessee, for example, this body is known as the Court of the Judiciary. Composed of judges, attorneys, and laypersons, the Court of the Judiciary reviews complaints about judicial conduct, often from disgruntled litigants or attorneys. Where these complaints are determined to have merit, the Court of the Judiciary may issue a reprimand, issue a cease and desist order, suspend the offending judge for a period of thirty days, or recommend the judge's removal altogether. If the Court of the Judiciary recommends removal, the matter is referred to the General Assembly for impeachment.

Judicial Administration, Rulemaking, and Supervision of the State Judiciary

Most state courts have substantial, if not total, control over the process of making procedural rules for the courts. In most states, the state supreme court is the rulemaking body for the state judiciary. Local courts usually have some authority to establish their own **rules of practice**, but these must not conflict with the rules of procedure that apply statewide. Typically, the state supreme court has administrative responsibility for the entire state court system, although in some states administration is still fairly decentralized. The state supreme court generally has supervisory power over the practice of law, which includes responsibility for disciplining attorneys who violate the code of professional responsibility.

How Cases Begin

All court cases can be divided into two basic categories: **criminal prosecutions** and **civil suits**. Criminal cases begin when a federal or state prosecutor files criminal charges against a defendant. The defendant is brought before the appropriate court of law to answer the charges. Most criminal cases are resolved by guilty pleas, which are often obtained through **plea bargaining**. When the defendant pleads "not guilty," a **trial** is conducted to determine guilt or innocence. (For a detailed examination of criminal procedure, see Chapter 10.)

All non-criminal cases are by definition civil cases. A civil case typically begins when one party files suit against another, alleging some wrong and seeking some remedy. Many civil suits are settled through negotiation. Those that are not settled or dismissed result in a civil trial. (For a detailed examination of civil procedure, see Chapter 9.)

Powers of Courts

Courts have the power to issue binding judgments in the civil and criminal cases. They can sentence persons convicted of crimes to a variety of punishments as allowed by law. They can award **damages** to persons who are the victims of civil wrongs. They can issue **injunctions** and **restraining orders** to prevent an injury from taking place or continuing. Courts also have power to issue a number of orders, writs, and decrees to effectuate their judgments. Common writs include

- the **writ of mandamus**, requiring a judge or other public official to perform a legal duty
- the **writ of habeas corpus**, ordering a party to show cause for holding a person in custody
- the **writ of prohibition**, ordering a lower court not to take jurisdiction in a particular case
- the **writ of certiorari**, calling up the record of a lower court proceeding so that it can be reviewed for error.

The Power of Contempt

Courts can hold in **contempt** parties who disrupt court proceedings or refuse to comply with court orders. **Criminal contempt** is the offense of engaging in contemptuous behavior in the presence of the court or so close to the court as to interrupt or hinder the judicial proceedings. In 1968, the Supreme Court held that criminal contempt is a crime in the ordinary sense and may be punished by fine, imprisonment, or both.[50] Perhaps the most sensational use of the contempt power in recent memory occurred in 1999 when U.S. District Judge Susan Webber Wright cited President Clinton for contempt and fined him $100,000. Clinton was cited for giving false, evasive, and misleading testimony to a federal grand jury investigating allegations of misconduct by the President.

Civil contempt is a sanction imposed to coerce a recalcitrant person—for example, a "deadbeat dad" who refuses to pay court-ordered support for his dependents—to obey a court order. A judge may order this individual to be confined in jail until he agrees to comply. How long may the individual be held in custody? There is no set limit—the standard is one of "reasonableness" in the context of the situation.

An interesting example of the use of civil contempt took place in Knoxville, Tennessee, in the early 1990s. An anti-abortion protester was arrested for criminal trespass after he refused to remain outside the property of a clinic that performed abortions. At the police station, and again when he was brought into court, the defendant refused to reveal his true identity, giving his name only as "Baby John Doe." A judge held him in contempt and ordered him jailed until he would cooperate. After several months the judge relented, noting that he had already served more time than he could serve if convicted of the trespass.

The Judicial Role

In their high school civics classes, students are taught that "legislatures make the law and judges interpret the law." Although this civics lesson is basically true, it represents an oversimplification of the role of the judge. Trial judges attempt to apply settled and clear principles of law to particular disputes. Unfortunately, the law is not always settled or clear and often trial judges must choose between conflicting interpretations of the law. When they make such choices, extra-legal factors may come into play. Of course, trial judges do not have the final say. Appellate courts review the interpretations of law rendered by trial courts. Appellate judges attempt to clarify and settle the law, drawing on legislative intent, precedent, and tradition. Appellate judges, especially in the courts of last resort, are inevitably engaged in the process of "saying what the law is," to paraphrase Chief Justice John Marshall's opinion in *Marbury v. Madison*.[51] Because the process of legal interpretation is far from an exact science, the values, preferences, and biases of individual judges may enter into the interpretive process. Yet it is important to remember that appellate courts are all **collegial courts**, in that decisions are made by panels of judges and not individuals. Moreover, appellate courts justify their interpretation of the law by producing written **opinions**. The process is designed to maximize rationality and minimize subjectivity. Appellate judges strive for objectivity, even if it is never perfectly achieved.

THE ROLE OF THE CHIEF EXECUTIVE

Chief executives at all levels of government, that is, mayors, governors, and presidents, play an important role in the American legal system. Chief executives can issue executive orders based on statutory provisions and, in some instances, direct constitutional authority. Executive orders have the force of law—they must be obeyed in the same way that statutes and court decisions command obedience.

Presidents and governors can also **veto** bills enacted by their respective legislatures. For the U.S. Congress and most state legislatures to override a veto, more than a simple majority vote is required. This ensures that controversial legislation will not be enacted without a sufficiently strong consensus in the government.

Presidents and governors play more than a negative role in the legislative process. They also propose legislation. At the federal level, the President outlines a legislative agenda in the annual state of the union speech. Much of the effort expended by the White House on a day-to-day basis involves trying to persuade Congress to enact this agenda. Much the same thing happens at the state level.

CASE IN POINT

PRESIDENTIAL ENFORCEMENT OF JUDICIAL DECISIONS
Cooper v. Aaron
United States Supreme Court
358 U.S. 1, 78 S. Ct. 1401, 3 L. Ed. 2d 5 (1958)

Undoubtedly one of the most important decisions of the Supreme Court in the modern era was *Brown v. Board of Education* (1954), where the Court said that states could no longer maintain racially segregated public schools. That decision touched off a firestorm of controversy in the South. In Arkansas, the governor called out the National Guard to block the court-ordered desegregation of Central High School in Little Rock in 1957. After meeting with President Eisenhower, Governor Orval Faubus withdrew the Guard, but an angry mob of white citizens attempted to prevent the African-American students from entering the school. President Eisenhower then ordered federal troops into Little Rock to enforce the court's desegregation order. The extreme situation led the local school board to petition the federal district court for a delay in the implementation of its desegregation order.

In reviewing the case, the Supreme Court refused to allow the delay. In an unusual step, the Court produced an opinion co-authored by all nine justices. The Court reaffirmed its decision in *Brown* and rebuked Governor Faubus, reminding him of his duty to uphold the Constitution. Would the Court have been able to take this position if President Eisenhower, who had reservations about court-ordered desegregation, had decided not to send the troops to Little Rock? In using military force to implement a judicial decision, Eisenhower was recognizing the authority of the Supreme Court to speak with finality on matters of constitutional interpretation. However, the ultimate decision to enforce the Court's authority belonged to the President. Accordingly, *Cooper v. Aaron* is more a testament to the importance of the executive than a bold assertion of judicial power.

Executives also perform a critical function in the enforcement of the law. Legislation and judicial decisions are not self-enforcing. Oftentimes, the chief executive or other officials within the executive branch are called upon to carry out the will of courts and legislatures. Of course, in deciding how to implement statutes and court decisions, executive officials shape the law as it is applied in concrete circumstances.

REGULATORY AND ADMINISTRATIVE AGENCIES

The modern chief executive sits atop a massive bureaucracy—a panoply of departments, boards, commissions, and other agencies. These agencies have various functions. Some are law enforcement agencies that serve to investigate crimes, apprehend offenders, and assist in their prosecution. Others are purely **administrative agencies**—their job is to carry out government programs like social security, Medicaid, or public housing programs. Still others are **regulatory agencies**, whose role is to create and enforce regulations in specific policy areas. They do this by invoking authority granted to them by the legislature, which has delegated power to agencies to act as, in effect, miniature legislatures. For example, Congress has created the Environmental Protection Agency and vested it with the authority to make and enforce regulations to give

COOPER v. AARON
358 U.S. 1, 78 S. Ct. 1401, 3 L. Ed. 2d 5 (1958)

Opinion of the Court by **The Chief Justice, Mr. Justice Black, Mr. Justice Frankfurter, Mr. Justice Douglas, Mr. Justice Burton, Mr. Justice Clark, Mr. Justice Harlan, Mr. Justice Brennan,** and **Mr. Justice Whittaker.**

. . . Article 6 of the Constitution makes the Constitution the "supreme Law of the Land." . . . Chief Justice Marshall . . . declared in *Marbury v. Madison:* . . . "It is emphatically the province and duty of the judicial department to say what the law is." This decision declared the basic principle that the federal judiciary is supreme in the exposition of the law of the Constitution, and that principle has ever since been respected by this Court and the Country as a permanent and indispensable feature of our constitutional system. . . . Every state legislator and executive and judicial officer is solemnly committed by oath taken pursuant to Article 6, clause 3, "to support this Constitution." . . .

No state legislator or executive or judicial officer can war against the Constitution without violating his undertaking to support it. Chief Justice Marshall spoke for a unanimous Court in saying that: "If the legislatures of the several states may, at will, annul the judgments of the courts of the United States, and destroy the rights acquired under those judgments, the Constitution itself becomes a solemn mockery. . . ." . . .

specific content to the Nation's environmental laws. In making these regulations, EPA and other regulatory agencies follow a rulemaking procedure outlined by Congress.

Agencies vary not only in their functions but also in their relationship to the chief executive. Most agencies are located within the major departments of the executive branch, which means that the President or governor has a good deal of control over them. Others, called **independent agencies**, are freestanding entities over which presidents and governors have less control. These agencies are typically directed by boards whose members are appointed for set terms of office and can only be removed for good cause. Of course, there are mechanisms by which legislative bodies and chief executives can control the decisions of independent agencies, for example, through the budgetary process. All of the legal issues pertaining to the functions and processes of administrative and regulatory agencies are the subject of **administrative law**, which is dealt with in some detail in Chapter 12.

LAW ENFORCEMENT AGENCIES

In the United States today, there are nearly 40,000 law enforcement agencies. Located within the executive branches of local, state, and federal governments, these agencies have the power to investigate criminal activity, to arrest suspects, and to detain arrested persons until their cases come before the appropriate courts of law. These agencies also play an important role in gathering evidence that prosecutors use in obtaining convictions. In addition to officers' testimony, these agencies provide arrest reports, statements made by persons who file complaints, witnesses' identification of perpetrators from lineups or mug shots, and many different types of **forensic evidence** obtained from victims or from crime scenes.

The role of law enforcement agencies goes well beyond investigating crime, arresting suspects, and assisting prosecutors. Society expects these agencies to prevent crimes from occurring, which is a much more demanding assignment. It also expects these agencies, especially those at the local level, to maintain public peace and order, a function that requires discretion and diplomacy and, when required, force and coercion. And, increasingly, under the rubric of **community-oriented policing**, law enforcement agencies are being viewed as social services agencies that must provide assistance to people in need and assist in resolving conflicts.

In carrying out their assigned functions, law enforcement agencies are subject to the limitations of the federal and state constitutions, in particular those clauses that protect citizens against unreasonable searches and seizures, arbitrary arrests, prolonged detentions, coerced confessions, and police brutality (see Chapter 10). In some instances, police misconduct may constitute a tort (see Chapter 5); in other instances it may even be criminal (see Chapter 4). In this country we expect law enforcement to abide by the rule of law even as it enforces the law. Of course, this does not always happen in practice, but when police violate the law, they, too, are subject to sanctions. They can be disciplined by internal affairs authorities within their agencies; they can be subject to civil suit and even prosecuted for crimes. Such was the case with four Los Angeles police officers who participated in the beating of Rodney King during an arrest in 1991. Although the officers were acquitted of criminal charges in state court, a federal grand jury indicted them under the federal civil rights laws. In 1993, a trial jury returned verdicts of guilty against two of the officers; the other two were acquitted. The two convicted officers were sentenced to thirty months in federal prison.[52]

Federal Agencies

There are more than sixty federal agencies that have law enforcement authority, including the Environmental Protection Agency, the Internal Revenue Service, the Bureau of Indian Affairs, the Federal Bureau of Prisons, the Bureau of Postal Inspection, the Tennessee Valley Authority, the National Park Service, the U.S. Forest Service, the U.S. Capitol Police, the U.S. Fish and Wildlife Service, and the U.S. Mint. As of 2008, there were approximately 12,000 federal law enforcement personnel empowered to carry firearms and make arrests.[53]

The U.S. Marshals Service

The oldest federal law enforcement agency is the U.S. Marshals Service, which was established by Congress in 1789. For most of the nineteenth century, federal marshals were the only law enforcement authorities on the western frontier. Today, federal marshals are responsible for executing warrants issued by federal courts, pursuing and arresting federal fugitives, transporting federal prisoners, and protecting federal judges and witnesses.

The FBI

The **Federal Bureau of Investigation** is the primary agency empowered to investigate violations of federal criminal laws. Located in the **Department of Justice**, the FBI is by far the most powerful of the federal law enforcement agencies, with broad powers to enforce the many criminal laws adopted by Congress. The FBI is perhaps best known for its Ten Most Wanted Fugitives program, which was inaugurated by the FBI's longtime Director, J. Edgar Hoover, in 1950. In the 1950s, the Ten Most Wanted list mainly included bank robbers and car thieves. Today, it features alleged terrorists, serial killers, international drug dealers, and organized crime kingpins.

Under J. Edgar Hoover, who served as Director from 1924 until his death in 1972, the FBI was often excessive in its zeal to enforce federal law and protect national security. In the 1950s, the FBI concentrated on the "Communist menace." In the 1960s, it turned its attention to the more radical elements of the antiwar movement. On numerous occasions, the FBI was accused of exceeding the limits of the law and infringing the rights of citizens. Today, the FBI operates under tighter legal constraints, the result of congressional action, judicial decisions, and cultural changes within the agency itself.

Although its history is somewhat checkered, the FBI generally is regarded today as embodying the highest standards of professionalism in the law enforcement community. The FBI currently employs nearly 25,000 people, including more than ten thousand Special Agents spread out over fifty-six field offices in the United States and twenty-one foreign offices. The FBI also uses the most sophisticated methods in crime prevention and investigation. Its crime laboratory even assists state and federal law enforcement agencies; thus, it figures prominently in the prosecution of numerous crimes.

The Secret Service

Most students know that the **Secret Service** protects the President and Vice President of the United States, their families, presidential candidates, and visiting heads of state. Many are not aware that the Secret Service also has an important law enforcement function. Currently located within the Department of Homeland Security, the Secret Service was created by Congress in 1865 for the purpose of preventing counterfeiting of paper money, which had been introduced in this country during the Civil War. It was not until after the assassination of President William McKinley in 1901 that the Secret Service was assigned the function of protecting the President. Today, the Secret Service enforces federal laws against forgery of federal government checks and bonds. It also investigates credit and debit card fraud, computer fraud, and electronic fund transfer fraud.[54]

ATF and Federal Gun Control Laws

Another well-known but more controversial federal law enforcement agency is the **Bureau of Alcohol, Tobacco, Firearms, and Explosives** (commonly known as the

ATF). Located within the Department of Treasury, the ATF enforces federal laws pertaining to alcohol, tobacco, guns, and explosives. With respect to alcoholic beverages, the ATF regulates distilleries, wineries, and breweries as well as importers and wholesalers. Regarding tobacco, the ATF collects federal excise taxes on cigarettes and other tobacco products. It also licenses the manufacture and importation of such products. With regard to firearms, the ATF enforces the regime of federal gun control laws. It was the exercise of this function that ultimately led to the catastrophic encounter between the ATF and the Branch Davidians in Waco, Texas, in April 1993. It was then that many Americans first became aware of the ATF and its law enforcement activities. The allegation that tear gas canisters fired by federal agents started the fire that destroyed the Branch Davidians' compound and killed eighty members of their group led to congressional investigations that basically exonerated federal agents. But the public's perception of the ATF was nevertheless marred.

Today, a debate rages in Congress and in the media over the adequacy of current federal gun control legislation. Advocates of gun control support tougher and more extensive federal gun laws. Others argue that existing laws need to be more vigorously enforced. The ATF contends that it needs more resources to enforce existing laws, but if new laws are passed, the responsibility for enforcing them will fall on the ATF, regardless of whether it gets more resources.

Federal Agencies at the Front Line of the War on Drugs

In the 1980s, the federal government declared "war on drugs." Congress toughened the criminal laws prohibiting drug offenses; various federal agencies instituted drug-testing programs for their employees; efforts at interdiction were stepped up; more money was appropriated to fund agencies to enforce the drug laws; and a Drug Czar was appointed to coordinate federal policy and programs. Of course, despite some success in stemming the tide of illegal drugs flowing into this country and curtailing the consumption of illicit drugs by the American public, the drug problem remains an epidemic. Today, many people question the efficacy of the war on drugs; others lament the increased intrusiveness of law enforcement as it tries to ferret out drug smugglers, dealers, and users. Still others question the wisdom of incarcerating drug users along with violent criminals.

At the front lines of the war on drugs is the Drug Enforcement Administration (DEA), which was established in 1973. Located within the Department of Justice, the DEA has more than 11,000 special agents and investigators. Its mission is to enforce federal drug laws and provide assistance to other federal agencies, such as the Immigration and Customs Enforcement (ICE), as well as state and local authorities involved in the war on drugs. The DEA's total budget for the 2014 fiscal year was $2.87 billion.[55] In 2012, the DEA made 30,476 domestic arrests.[56]

ICE and the Battle Against Illegal Immigration

Immigration and Customs Enforcement (ICE), located within the Department of Homeland Security, is responsible for maintaining control of America's 8,000-mile-long border, which means apprehending and deporting those who enter the country illegally. Today, the focus of ICE attention is the prevention of illegal immigration from

Mexico, as Mexicans looking to improve their economic condition have streamed across the porous southern border in search of employment. ICE is also a key component of the federal government's Joint Terrorism Task Force.

State and Local Agencies

All fifty states have their own law enforcement agencies, although the agencies vary quite a bit in how they are organized. Some states have their own counterpart to the FBI. For example, the Oklahoma Bureau of Investigation works with local law enforcement agencies to investigate crimes. Its criminalistics division provides forensic analysis, including drug and alcohol testing, toxicology, fingerprints, DNA sampling, and ballistics. It also serves as the central repository for crime data and criminal history information. The principal statewide law enforcement agency in Oklahoma is the Highway Patrol, which is responsible for policing all state highways as well as lake and river shorelines. By way of contrast, Illinois has combined the investigative, enforcement, and forensic functions into one comprehensive agency: the Illinois State Police. In most states there are multiple agencies charged with law enforcement in specific areas such as traffic safety, agricultural importation, casino gambling, alcoholic beverages, and hunting and fishing.

County Sheriffs

At the local level, we find both county and municipal law enforcement agencies. Nearly every county in America has a **sheriff**. The institution of sheriff dates from the Reign of Alfred the Great in ninth century England. The kingdom was divided into "shires," which eventually became counties. The "shire reeve" was appointed by the King to represent the King in local affairs. As the English legal system evolved, sheriffs came to be responsible for arresting and detaining persons accused of crimes, serving summonses and subpoenas, and maintaining jails and workhouses. The institution of county sheriff was brought to America by the colonists. Early on, sheriffs were appointed by governors. In the early nineteenth century, states made this position elective, as it remains today. In some areas, particularly the urban Northeast, many of the powers traditionally exercised by sheriffs have been assumed by state or metropolitan police forces. However, in the rest of the country, especially in the rural areas, sheriffs (and their deputies) are the principal law enforcement agents at the county level.

Municipal Law Enforcement Agencies

The idea that a city should have its own professional police force is generally credited to Sir Robert Peel, who in 1829 persuaded Parliament to establish a metropolitan police force for the city of London.[57] Soon cities throughout the world emulated London's example. Today, more than 20,000 cities and towns in the United States have their own police departments. Local police are charged with enforcing the criminal laws of their states as well as the ordinances enacted by their municipalities. Although the county sheriff usually has jurisdiction within the municipalities of the county, generally the sheriff concentrates enforcement efforts on those areas outside municipal boundaries.

Traditionally, police officers in America were provided little in the way of formal job training. In the latter half of the twentieth century, law enforcement became much more professional. Most states now have standards for certification of officers based on their completion of training programs and meeting certain standards. Often, attainment of these standards is the key to promotion. Increasingly, modern police agencies are seeking candidates who have completed college-level courses in criminal justice and other social sciences. Some police agencies even subsidize community-college-level courses for in-service officers.

PROSECUTORIAL AGENCIES

While law enforcement agencies are the "gatekeepers" of the criminal justice system, **prosecutors** are central to the administration of criminal justice. They determine whether to bring charges against suspected criminals. They have enormous **prosecutorial discretion**, not only in determining whether to prosecute but also in determining what charges to file. Moreover, prosecutors frequently set the tone for plea bargaining and have a powerful voice in determining the severity of sanctions imposed on persons convicted of crimes. Accordingly, prosecutors play a crucial role in the criminal justice system.

The chief prosecutor at the federal level is the **Attorney General**, who is the head of the Department of Justice. Below the Attorney General are a number of **United States Attorneys**, each responsible for prosecuting crimes within a particular federal district. The United States Attorneys in turn have a number of assistants who handle most of the day-to-day criminal cases brought by the federal government. The Attorney General and the United States Attorneys are appointed by the President, subject to the consent of the Senate. The assistant U.S. Attorneys are federal civil service employees who acquire their positions through a rigorous application process.

In addition to the regular federal prosecutors, Congress has provided for the appointment of **independent counsel** (special prosecutors) in cases involving alleged misconduct by high government officials. By far the most infamous such case was the Watergate scandal of 1972-1974, which resulted in the convictions of several high-ranking officials and the resignation of a president. But there have been numerous cases where, under congressional direction, a special prosecutor has been appointed. One of the best-known recent examples of this was the appointment of former federal judge Kenneth Starr to investigate the Whitewater scandal that involved close associates of President Bill Clinton and First Lady Hillary Rodham Clinton. In 1998, Starr alleged, among other things, that President Clinton had given false and misleading statements to a federal grand jury. This led to President Clinton's impeachment by the House of Representatives, although he was acquitted after trial in the Senate. In the wake of the Starr investigation, Congress voted not to extend the law under which Starr was appointed, but Congress could provide for a new independent counsel at any time.

Each state likewise has its own attorney general and a number of assistant attorneys general, plus a number of district or **state's attorneys** at the local level. Generally speaking, local prosecutors are elected for set terms of office. In most states, local prosecutors act autonomously and possess broad discretionary powers.

Cities and counties also have their own attorneys. These attorneys sometimes prosecute violations of city and county ordinances, but increasingly their function is limited to representing their cities or counties in civil suits and giving legal advice to local councils and officials. These city and county attorneys generally are appointed by the governing bodies they represent.

THE LEGAL PROFESSION

As we noted in Chapter 1, the American legal profession has its roots in English common law practice. In England, trial lawyers were (and are) called "barristers," while attorneys who provided other legal services were (and are) known as "solicitors." In the United States, we do not use that nomenclature, although the distinction between "trial lawyer" and "office lawyer" remains relevant. Indeed, lawyers in the United States have become extremely specialized. As in medicine, the general practitioner is becoming increasingly rare. Lawyers today specialize in torts, estate planning, taxation, civil rights, contracts, real estate, criminal defense work, and every other conceivable area of the law.

Legal Education and Admission to the Bar

About half the Framers of the U.S. Constitution were lawyers who "read law" and served apprenticeships with those who practiced law. A few states still allow some alternatives to formal study at a law school, but even where permitted, this option is infrequently exercised. Most commonly, the path to becoming a lawyer today is to successfully complete a three-year course from one of the 184 law schools accredited by the American Bar Association.[58] Indeed, all but a few states now require that to take a bar examination for admission to the practice of law an applicant must possess a Juris Doctor (J.D.) degree. Prior to the 1960s, law schools awarded graduates a Bachelor of Laws (LL.B.) degree.

The number of applicants who annually seek admission to law schools has leveled off somewhat from the vast increase that occurred from the late 1960s to the 1970s, a time of social upheaval when many students were inspired to channel social and economic changes through law. A prospective law student must have a four-year college degree and generally score well on a Law School Aptitude Test (LSAT) and have a credible grade point average (GPA). Law schools are selective but do not demand that pre-legal education be in a particular field. Business, history, political science, and economics have been popular undergraduate majors. Admission committees often employ various criteria beyond LSAT and GPA scores to enroll a diverse group. Prior to 1960, women and minority students represented a very small percentage of law students. Today, they represent a substantial percentage of the enrollment in most law schools.

Law schools usually require completion of basic courses in contracts, property, torts, criminal law, civil procedure, constitutional law, legal research and writing, evidence, and professional responsibility. Electives are available in fields such as estates and trusts, taxation, administrative law, and commercial law and often include skills courses in trial and appellate advocacy and clinical training in client counseling. Some newer electives are in the fields of environmental, employment discrimination, eminent domain, and intellectual property law. Classes in alternative dispute resolution also are becoming increasingly popular.

Since first introduced at the Harvard Law School in the 1870s, the "case method" has become the principal method of instruction in law schools. Casebooks today contain not only reported appellate court cases but also related materials. Professors frequently employ the "Socratic method," with students reciting cases and responding to in-depth questions concerning analysis of a case and its implications in the law. Use of the Socratic method has declined somewhat in recent years, particularly in classes beyond basic required courses. In elective courses, many professors now follow traditional college lecturing and discussion. Most basic law courses culminate in a written examination requiring a detailed analysis of hypothetical factual situations with discussion of applicable rules of law. Many law schools now place an increased emphasis on clinical and skills training where students learn "to perform like lawyers" and are graded on their performance rather than on written examination.

The Organized Bar

Although we do not use the term "barrister" in the United States, we do refer to licensed attorneys as having been "admitted to the bar." State laws govern the admission requirements and require passage of a written bar examination before an applicant can be admitted to practice in a particular state. Usually, the highest court in the state has oversight of the bar admission policies and requires a thorough check of the applicant's background. Successful applicants take an oath to support the federal and state constitution and adhere to the ethical requirements of being a lawyer.

Some states have a **unified bar** that has been delegated authority to regulate the profession, usually under the oversight of the state's highest court. One who practices law in the state must be a dues-paying member of the state bar association. Dues furnish the administrative support for activities relating to disciplinary measures and continuing legal education. In some instances, however, a unified bar has used its funds to pay for lobbying to secure legislation favorable to causes advocated by bar leadership. Some members have disagreed with positions taken by unified bar associations, and in 1990 their disagreement came into sharp focus when the U.S. Supreme Court ruled that a bar member cannot be forced to pay dues to support political and ideological activities with which a lawyer-member disagrees.[59] In other states, bar association membership is optional. In either instance, lawyers usually form voluntary bar associations at the local level to further their social and professional contacts, to foster continuing legal education, and to provide legal assistance to the poor.

Being admitted to the bar in one state does not permit a lawyer to practice in another state. Nevertheless, a lawyer usually can be admitted to practice in another state on a limited basis when accompanied by a lawyer admitted in that state. Admission to the practice of law in a state does not carry with it admission to practice in a federal court. Instead each federal trial and appellate court has its own requirements. These requirements are largely administrative, but in some instances an oral examination is given.

Prior to 1975, bar associations often adopted minimum fee schedules designed to limit "cost-cutting practitioners" that established lawyers deemed to be unethical. In 1975, the Supreme Court turned a deaf ear to such contentions and held that enforcement of a mandatory minimum fee schedule violated antitrust laws.[60]

Specialization and Certification

The law has grown exceedingly complex, and the practice of law has become quite competitive. These factors have led to extensive advertising—especially when coupled with the Supreme Court's 1977 ruling that the First Amendment protects a lawyer's right to engage in commercial speech.[61] Furthermore, advertising fosters specialization, and this in turn has led to the certification of lawyers who practice in particular areas. Certification is generally conferred by a state bar organization under the oversight of the state's highest court. It is achieved by having practiced in a given area for a stated period of time and by having successfully completed a written examination of the law and procedures applicable to that area of the law. Board-certified attorneys are deemed to have special knowledge and skill in their area of certification. Certification enables a lawyer to publicly announce his or her competency in a given field. Usually, one who is certified must fulfill certain practice requirements and complete a number of continuing legal education courses in order to be periodically recertified.

Paralegals

Lawyers have long placed great responsibilities on their legal secretaries, who often acquire considerable experience in assisting with the drafting of legal documents and with the preparation of cases for settlement or trial. With the increased specialization of the legal profession, in recent years the **paralegal** (sometimes referred to as a legal assistant) has come on the legal scene to work in conjunction with the attorney and the legal secretary. A paralegal is one who has been educated in basic legal studies and trained to assist attorneys in drafting legal documents and in preparing cases. The duties and responsibilities of a paralegal depend on the practice of the lawyer being assisted. For example, lawyers who specialize in handling personal injury cases often rely on paralegals to prepare suggested drafts of interrogatories to opposing parties, to assemble medical reports, and to keep track of a client's expenses that may be eligible for reimbursement. In real estate practice, a paralegal may obtain appraisals and title insurance commitments, handle property insurance transfers, draft routine legal documents for review by the lawyer, and prepare closing statements for transactions. Paralegal institutes now train individuals to become professionals and, in some instances, use this text for instruction in basic principles of law. In addition to the examples given, in probate, employment discrimination, criminal law, and other specialized areas, the paralegal has become an established professional in the delivery of legal services.

Finding a Lawyer

Although more than two-thirds of lawyers engage in private practice, a prospective client often finds it difficult to select a lawyer to serve the client's needs. Telephone books and local bar directories carry names and increasingly indicate a lawyer's area of practice. Yet, as is the case in selecting a physician, one often must depend on a referral. Historically, advertising by lawyers was prohibited, and many members of the legal profession are disdainful of advertising, believing it to be unprofessional. Nonetheless, truthful advertising is permitted and can enable a prospective client to become informed about the qualifications and areas of practice of lawyers without the necessity of making repetitive calls to law offices. In some instances, membership organizations, prepaid legal insurance, and group legal plans assist in making referrals.

Legal Assistance for Indigent Persons

In most areas, bar associations have established legal aid offices to assist persons of limited means in obtaining legal advice. Congress has also provided limited federal funds for such assistance, and state and local agencies, including bar associations, often assist in funding these offices. These offices often employ staff lawyers, and in many areas law students assist as interns. In many instances, a legal aid office will refer a case to a practicing attorney who agrees to handle a case on a *pro bono* (for benefit of the

CASE IN POINT

LIMITATIONS ON ATTORNEY SOLICITATION
Florida Bar v. Went For It, Inc.
United States Supreme Court
515 U.S. 618, 115 S. Ct. 2371, 132 L. Ed. 2d 541 (1995)

To practice law in Florida, an attorney must be a member of the Florida Bar and must abide by its rules of professional responsibility. One of these rules forbids personal injury lawyers from mailing solicitations to victims and their relatives for one month after an accident or disaster. G. Stewart McHenry, who operated an attorney referral service called Went For It, Inc., filed suit in federal district court challenging the Bar's prohibition as a violation of the First Amendment. Reviewing the case on certiorari, the Supreme Court rejected the challenge. Writing for a sharply divided Court, Justice Sandra Day O'Connor recognized that the Florida Bar had "substantial interest both in protecting injured Floridians from invasive conduct by lawyers and in preventing the erosion of confidence in the profession that such repeated invasions have engendered." Writing for the four dissenters, Justice Anthony Kennedy observed that lawyers "who communicate their willingness to assist potential clients are engaged in speech protected by the First and Fourteenth Amendments." In his view, the Court's decision "undercuts this guarantee in an important class of cases and unsettles leading First Amendment precedents, at the expense of those victims most in need of legal assistance."

Some states have lawyer referral services whereby lawyers agree to hold a brief initial conference with a client for a modest fee. During the conference, the client can arrange either to go forward with that lawyer or to receive a referral to one who practices in a specialized field. Still, the most common method of selection of a lawyer is probably based on a recommendation by a friend, business associate, fellow employee, or organization.

public) basis without charge to the client. Of course, indigent criminal defendants are furnished legal counsel, a topic we examine in Chapter 10.

Professional Responsibility

Professional responsibility of lawyers has become a major issue. Lawyers are regulated by codes of professional conduct often patterned after the Model Code of Professional Conduct promulgated by the American Bar Association (ABA), a voluntary association of lawyers. The Model Code has no legal effect because the ABA is a private organization, but many state legislatures and the highest court of the states have adopted the ABA Model Code with some variations. Because lawyers are deemed to be "officers of the court," judges exercise inherent power to discipline them and even hold them in contempt of court for violations of ethical standards in the conduct of litigation.

Among the ethical concerns these codes of professional responsibility address are standards to be abided by lawyers concerning their duties to

- charge reasonable fees (often with limitations on contingency fees)
- provide a client competent representation
- act with reasonable diligence in handling a client's interests
- be loyal to the client
- keep the client advised of the progress of legal matters undertaken
- avoid conflicts of interest
- exercise candor in dealings with courts and agencies.

Bar associations customarily provide a mechanism for clients to file a grievance against an attorney whom the client believes to have violated the standards of professional responsibility. Grievances that have merit result in disciplinary action that ranges from a reprimand to suspension or disbarment. Moreover, a client may institute a malpractice suit against an attorney for misconduct or negligence in handling legal matters. If successful, the client may recover damages. Many attorneys carry liability insurance to protect both the client and lawyer. Finally, some bar associations have established client security funds to reimburse a client who suffers a financial loss due to a lawyer's misconduct.

The Changing Profession

In the latter half of the twentieth century, the legal profession in the United States experienced rapid growth. Indeed, the prevailing attitude among the mass public today is that there are too many lawyers. In 1951, there were about 220,000 lawyers in the United States, but by 2012 that number had increased to more than 1.2 million.[62] To put this in perspective, in 1951 there was one lawyer per 700 people; more recently, the ratio approximates one per 300.[63] With one lawyer for every twenty-four persons, Washington, D.C., has the highest density of lawyers in the country.[64] In contrast, Arkansas has the lowest density of lawyers with one for every 556 persons.[65]

The demographics of the legal profession also have changed, especially with regard to gender. In 1951, there were about 5,500 female lawyers in the United States—less than 3 percent of the profession. By 1980, females constituted 8 percent of the profession, but by 2005 their representation had grown to 30 percent.[66] In the 1950s, it was common for law school classes to be all-male. However, by the 2011-2012 academic year, 47 percent of law students were female.[67] And, it is not uncommon today for women to outnumber men in law school classes.[68] The legal "fraternity" is rapidly vanishing and is being replaced by a more diverse profession—one that is more representative of the population it serves.

THE ADVERSARIAL SYSTEM OF JUSTICE

The American court system follows the historic **adversarial system** this nation inherited from the English common law. Unlike the system that prevails in civil law countries (see Chapter 1), the adversarial system separates the function of gathering evidence from the judge's role in pretrial and trial processes. The theory of the common law approach is that a judge's not having participated in the investigative process assures the parties that their case will be heard before a neutral decision-maker.

In the adversary process, the competing parties develop the evidence through investigation. Parties, usually through their lawyers, present their evidence and arguments in support of their positions and seek to demonstrate the weakness of the other side of the case. This affords each party an opportunity to have a lawyer-conducted examination and cross-examination of witnesses, as well as challenges to the evidence and arguments presented by the opposing side. An important aspect of the adversarial system is the development of detailed procedural rules that a judge must apply impartially irrespective of the merits of a party's case.

Juries

Juries are not a necessary part of the legal system in civil law countries (see Chapter 1); however, in some civil law countries lay judges assist the professional judge in the decision-making processes. And although a jury is not essential to the functioning of the adversarial system, in America it is a vital component of the system. Juries are deeply rooted in Anglo-American tradition. In the late eighteenth century, William Blackstone called the jury a "strong barrier between the liberties of the people and the prerogative of the crown."[69] Today, Americans continue to regard the jury as an important check on government. Even so, some Americans find frustration in the inconvenience of jury duty, and others are occasionally outraged by jury verdicts that seem unjust or even inexplicable. Famous examples of such instances include O.J. Simpson's 1995 acquittal on double murder charges, and Casey Anthony's 2011 acquittal on charges related to the death of her daughter. Nevertheless, support for the institution of the jury remains strong.

In America, juries are selected from a cross-section of the adult community without regard to educational attainments. Thus, a college professor may be seated next to an elementary school dropout. To ensure an impartial jury, parties have the right to challenge jurors as to their basic qualifications to render a fair and impartial verdict. Although a prospective juror is not usually disqualified for having heard or read about a case, a juror who has formed an opinion about a pending case or who may have an interest in the litigation will be disqualified from serving. Juries decide the facts in a case and must apply the law as instructed by the presiding judge. Historically, a juror was not permitted to ask questions, only to hear the evidence presented. The trend is to allow jurors to ask the presiding judge to have lawyers pose their questions to a witness. Where this is permitted, the judge has broad discretion in such matters. We explain the juror selection process and jurors' functions in the decision-making process in later chapters.

Trial Procedures

We also explain the procedures in civil and criminal trials in later chapters. Many of these adversary processes, such as depositions and other discovery matters, occur during pretrial phases of litigation, but for now it is helpful to become acquainted with the basic steps at trial.

1. Opening Statements: The plaintiff's attorney or the prosecutor and the defendant's attorney outline their theories of the case and the evidence to be presented.
2. Direct Examination by Plaintiff or Prosecutor: The plaintiff's attorney or prosecutor questions witnesses and presents documentary and physical evidence.
3. Cross-Examination by Defense: The defendant's attorney may cross-examine the plaintiff's or prosecutor's witnesses in an attempt to discredit their testimony.
4. Motions by Defense: The judge rules on any defense motions to dismiss the plaintiff's case or to grant acquittal and discharge the defendant.
5. Direct Examination by Defense: The defendant's attorney proceeds along the lines outlined in 2 above.
6. Cross-Examination by the Plaintiff or Prosecutor: The plaintiff or prosecutor proceeds as outlined in 3 above.
7. Closing Arguments: The plaintiff or prosecutor and the defense attorney present their closing arguments summarizing the evidence and seeking to persuade the jury (or the court in a non-jury trial) of their respective positions.
8. Jury Instructions: In a jury trial, the court instructs the jury as to the law applicable to the case and their responsibilities in arriving at a verdict.
9. Verdict and Judgment: The jury, returns its verdict and the court subsequently enters a judgment in favor of the prevailing party in a civil case or enters a judgment of conviction and proceeds to sentence the defendant or to discharge the defendant if acquitted. In a non-jury case, the court makes a disposition of the case and enters judgment accordingly.

ALTERNATIVE DISPUTE RESOLUTION

Courts and regulatory agencies represent traditional means of formal conflict resolution. They focus on adjudicatory forms of dispute resolution. With the increased involvement of government in the lives of individuals and businesses and the diminished role of informal dispute resolution in the family and religious institutions, many have seen a need for fair, efficient, economical, yet informal means of dispute resolution. These alternative methods of dispute resolution take several forms, some voluntary and some involuntary.

Private arbitration is a voluntary method of dispute resolution. It has historic roots. In an effort to ward off any possible litigation, President George Washington included an arbitration clause in his will to the effect that any disputes be decided "by three intelligent and impartial men known for their probity and good understanding."[70] Today, many construction, employment, and brokerage agreements include provisions requiring arbitration of any dispute arising out of the contract. Parties select an arbitrator or a panel of three arbitrators, usually persons who have experience in the area of the dispute. Each party has an opportunity to present various forms of proof, including live witnesses. The proceedings are usually private and the procedure is informal, with participants agreeing to be bound by the decision of the arbitrators. Judicial review is generally limited to issues of misconduct of the arbitrators.

To speed the resolution of court cases, a number of jurisdictions have recently adopted court-ordered **arbitration**. Usually, neither party is bound to accept the results; however, the court may impose sanctions on a party who has rejected the results of arbitration and then fails to obtain a more satisfactory result in court.

Negotiation remains the primary tool of **alternative dispute resolution** not involving adjudicatory procedures. Negotiation frequently takes place without court supervision. In other instances, it may be a means of settling pending litigation before trial. Much civil litigation is resolved through some form of negotiation undertaken by lawyers who are trained in evaluating the merits of positions taken by parties.

Mediation has become the most popular form of alternative dispute resolution. It is a process whereby a neutral third party acts as a facilitator in an informal and non-adversarial process to assist the disputants in reaching a mutually agreeable settlement. Some jurisdictions have mediation training programs and prescribe competency and ethical standards for mediators. Mediation may take place irrespective of pending litigation, but most mediation occurs while litigation is pending. The mediator encourages parties to communicate freely with the understanding that communications are confidential and statements made cannot be used in court proceedings. The mediator will point out problems incident to each party's position, often in private conference with a party and that party's counsel. Voluntary mediators often serve in small claims courts to assist litigants, most of whom are not represented by counsel.

In family law disputes, personal injury cases, and other major legal controversies parties often agree to mediation. The parties select and pay the fees of a mediator, which may be based on the mediator's expertise in a given field. Experienced lawyers are frequently called upon to serve as mediators. Legal counsel often represents parties, but the procedure remains informal. In some situations, a court will order the parties to mediate a pending case and will appoint the mediator.

The ability of legal counsel to successfully negotiate becomes a key factor in mediation. Much of mediation proceeds on a "give and take" basis. It has the advantage of allowing parties to fashion an agreement with more flexibility than can often be obtained in court. Where agreement is reached, it is reduced to writing and signed by the parties and mediator. In cases where litigation is pending, the agreement generally is filed with the court and enforced as a resolution of the dispute. In family law matters, the court usually determines if the agreement is in the best interests of the parties where minor children are involved.

Although arbitration and mediation are more popular, other forms of alternative dispute resolution include a mini-trial or summary jury trial. In a mini-trial, the parties present their proofs in a summary manner in a private proceeding with the expectation that they can agree on a decision proposed by the advisor. In a summary jury trial, each side in a litigated case presents a summary of that party's case to a mock jury under relaxed rules of evidence and procedure; the jury then renders an advisory verdict that is nonbinding but often accepted by the parties.

CONCLUSION

The American legal system is extremely complicated, due in large part to federalism: the division of political and legal authority among one national government and fifty state governments. No two sets of state laws are identical. Even where states have emulated laws of other states, there are likely to be nuances. Further, no two state court systems are exactly alike. Even those that are superficially similar are likely to have significant jurisdictional, procedural, and administrative differences. And, of course, the federal system is quite unique in many respects.

The American legal system depends on the contributions of many different actors, most notably the legislators who write statutes, the chief executives and other executive officials who enforce them, and the judges who apply them to specific cases. The system also depends on litigants, people who are willing to subject their disputes to courts of law for orderly and peaceful resolution, as well as the lawyers who help litigants navigate a legal maze that can be, at times, maddening. But there are many other actors who are essential to the functioning of the legal system, including legislative staffers, law clerks, research aides, bailiffs, sheriffs, jurors, stenographers, police officers, customs agents, postal inspectors, marshals, constables, corrections officers, secretaries, paralegals, and many more. Ultimately, though, the American legal system depends on the faith and support of average Americans who are asked to believe that our legal system represents a sincere effort to achieve the rule of law in this country.

SUMMARY OF KEY CONCEPTS

American government is complicated because it is a federal system with powers shared between national and state office holders. At the federal level, lawmaking is primarily a legislative function performed by elected members of the U.S. Senate and House of Representatives. At the state level, elected legislatures perform this function.

Federal and state judicial systems interpret the laws and sometimes fill in gaps by "making law." Federal District Courts are trial courts; the U.S. Courts of Appeals perform appellate review. State courts are structured similarly, with trial and appellate courts. The U.S. Supreme Court sits at the apex of the judicial system. Its jurisdiction is almost entirely discretionary, but its judgments, particularly those determining the constitutionality of federal and state laws, vitally affect the entire legal system. The President, with consent of the U.S. Senate, appoints judges of most federal courts for life; state court judges come into office by election or by various means of appointment.

Each level of government has an executive department. At the national level, the President performs this function; at the state level, the governor does. At local levels, a mayor or commission chair serves as executive. The executive branch of each level of government functions largely through various regulatory and administrative agencies. Law enforcement agencies operate at the federal, state, and local levels, as do prosecutorial offices.

Lawyers serve as advocates in criminal and civil court proceedings in our adversary system of justice, which in many instances relies on juries to determine guilt and innocence in criminal cases and awards in civil cases. In addition, lawyers serve as counselors on the law, advising clients on a variety of legal matters. They operate within an American legal system that is based on adversary practice. Despite this contextual framework, today many citizens rely on negotiation, arbitration, and mediation as alternative dispute resolution processes.

FOR FURTHER READING

Abraham, Henry J., *The Judiciary: The Supreme Court in the Governmental Process* (10th ed., Allyn and Bacon 1996).

Baum, Lawrence, *American Courts: Process and Policy* (6th ed., Houghton Mifflin 2007).

Carp, Robert A., and Ronald Stidham, *The Federal Courts* (3d ed., CQ Press 1998).

Kalven, Harry, and Hans Zeisel, *The American Jury* (University of Chicago Press 1966).

Lazarus, Edward, *Closed Chambers: The First Eyewitness Account of the Epic Struggles Inside the Supreme Court* (Times Books 1998).

Neely, Richard, *How Courts Govern America* (Yale University Press 1981).

Schwartz, Bernard, with Stephen Lesher, *Inside the Warren Court* (Doubleday 1983).

Toobin, Jeffrey, *The Nine: Inside the Secret World of the Supreme Court* (Anchor Books 2007).

Wasby, Stephen, *The Supreme Court in the Federal Judicial System* (4th ed., Nelson-Hall 1993).

Woodward, Bob, and Scott Armstrong, *The Brethren: Inside the Supreme Court* (Simon and Schuster 1979).

QUESTIONS FOR THOUGHT AND DISCUSSION

1. When seeking to determine the status of a federal or state law, what advantage is gained by consulting a set of annotated statutes?
2. What is meant by the term "police power" as it relates to state legislatures?
3. Why did the United States Congress never adopt the English common law?
4. What is the difference between the "delegate" and "trustee" models of representation? If you were elected to your state legislature, which of these models would you espouse? Why?
5. Why do we have separate state and federal court systems?

6. Which mode of selecting appellate judges makes more sense, gubernatorial appointment or popular election? How does the Missouri Plan combine elements of both?

7. Is the President required to enforce a decision of the U.S. Supreme Court that the President believes to be contrary to the U.S. Constitution?

8. When is mediation a more desirable method of dispute resolution in a civil case than to seek recourse through a jury in a trial court?

9. What are the basic procedural steps in a civil or criminal trial?

10. Explain the concept of a "unified bar." What advantages or disadvantages do you find in the unified bar concept?

11. The Supreme Court has interpreted the First Amendment to the U.S. Constitution to permit attorneys to advertise their services in the print, radio, and television media and on the Internet. What, if any, restrictions should be placed on the content of such advertising?

KEY TERMS

administrative agencies
administrative law
adversarial system
alternative dispute resolution
appeals of right
appellate courts
appellate jurisdiction
arbitration
Attorney General
Bureau of Alcohol, Tobacco and Firearms
civil contempt
civil suits
collegial courts
community-oriented policing
concurrent jurisdiction
concurrent powers
Congress
contempt
Court of Federal Claims
Court of International Trade
court of last resort
Court of Veterans' Appeals
court-martial proceedings
courts-martial
criminal contempt
criminal prosecutions
damages
delegates
Department of Justice
diversity of citizenship jurisdiction

enumerated powers
Federal Bureau of Investigation
federal magistrate judges
federal question jurisdiction
federalism
forensic evidence
impeachment
implied powers
independent agencies
independent counsel
injunctions
intermediate appellate courts
judicial accountability
judicial disciplinary commissions
judicial independence
judicial review
law clerks
law enforcement agencies
legislators
legislature
Manual for Courts-Martial
mediation
Missouri Plan
negotiation
opinions
original jurisdiction
oversight
paralegal
plea bargaining
police power
professional responsibility

prosecutorial discretion
prosecutors
regulatory agencies
restraining orders
rules of practice
rules of procedure
Secret Service
session laws
sheriff
state supreme court
state's attorneys
Tax Court
tort claims
trial
trial courts
trustees
unified bar
Uniform Code of Military Justice
United States Attorneys
United States Court of Appeals for the Armed Forces
United States Courts of Appeals
United States District Courts
United States Supreme Court
U.S. Code
veto
writ of certiorari
writ of habeas corpus
writ of mandamus
writ of prohibition

ENDNOTES

1. U.S. Const. art.I, §8.

2. A major exception applies, however, to the third option: if Congress adjourns before the ten days have expired and the President has still not signed the bill, it is said to have been subjected to a "pocket veto."

3. Students can access the U.S. Code online at *http://www4.law .cornell.edu/uscode/*.

4. 1 Stat. 73.

5. U.S. Const. art.III, §2.

6. 28 U.S.C. §1331.

7. 28 U.S.C. §1332.

8. For provisions of the U.S. Code dealing with the district courts, *see* 28 U.S.C. §§81-132.

9. *See* 28 U.S.C. §§151-158.

10. There are also federal district courts in Guam, Puerto Rico, the Northern Mariana Islands, the Virgin Islands, and the District of Columbia.

11. The United States District Court for the Eastern District of Tennessee is based in Knoxville. The Middle District is based in Nashville. The Western District is based in Jackson.

12. California's four federal judicial districts are based in San Francisco (Northern), Sacramento (Eastern), Los Angeles (Central), and San Diego (Southern). New York's four districts are based in Syracuse (Northern), Buffalo (Western), Brooklyn (Eastern), and Manhattan (Southern).

13. Administrative Office of the United States Courts http:// www.uscourts.gov/JudgesAndJudgeships/FederalJudgeships .aspx.

14. http://www.txnd.uscourts.gov/judges/index.html.

15. http://www.txs.uscourts.gov/district/judges/.

16. http://www.txwd.uscourts.gov/General/Judges/biographylist .asp.

17. http://www.txed.uscourts.gov/page1.shtml?location=info.

18. http://www.uscourts.gov/Statistics/JudicialBusiness/2013/ judicial-caseload-indicators.aspx.

19. Administrative Office of the United States Courts, *Annual Report of the Director, 1982* (Administrative Office of the United States Courts 1982).

20. For provisions of the U.S. Code dealing with the United States Courts of Appeals, *see* 28 U.S.C. §§41-49.

21. 26 Stat. 828.

22. http://www.cafc.uscourts.gov/the-court/court-jurisdiction .html.

23. http://www.uscourts.gov/JudgesAndJudgeships/Viewer.aspx? doc=/uscourts/JudgesJudgeships/docs/appeals-judgeships.pdf.

24. http://www.ca9.uscourts.gov/content/view_seniority_list.php? pk_id=0000000035.

25. Administrative Office of the United States Courts, *Annual Report of the Director, 1999* (Administrative Office of the United States Courts 1999).

26. http://www.uscourts.gov/Statistics/JudicialBusiness/2013/ judicial-caseload-indicators.aspx.

27. http://www.uscourts.gov/Statistics/JudicialBusiness/2013/ us-courts-of-appeals.aspx.

28. For provisions of the U.S. Code dealing with the Supreme Court, *see* 28 U.S.C. §§1-6.

29. http://www.uscourts.gov/news/TheThirdBranch/11-01-01/ The_Supreme_Court_of_the_United_States.aspx.

30. U.S. Const. art.III, §2.

31. The Supreme Court's jurisdiction is set forth in 28 U.S.C. §§1251-1259.

32. *See* 28 U.S.C. §2071.

33. *See* 28 U.S.C. §§251-258, 1581-1585, 2631-2647.

34. *See* 28 U.S.C. §1295.

35. U.S. Const. art.II, §2.

36. The rule shift also applies to many appointments to executive branch positions.

37. Patricia Millett was confirmed on December 10, 2013 by a vote of 56-38; Nina Pillard was confirmed on December 12, 2013 by a vote of 51-44; Robert Wilkins was confirmed on January 13, 2014 by a vote of 55-43.

38. "Reid, Democrats, Trigger 'Nuclear' Option; Eliminate Most Filibusters on Nominees," http://www.washingtonpost.com/ politics/senate-poised-to-limit-filibusters-in-party-line-vote-that- would-alter-centuries-of-precedent/2013/11/21/d065cfe8-52b6- 11e3-9fe0-fd2ca728e67c_story.html.

39. "Obama Quotes on Senate Rules in 2005 Given New Scrutiny," http://abcnews.go.com/blogs/politics/2010/02/obama- quotes-on-nuclear-option-in-2005-given-new-scrutiny/.

40. U.S. Const. art.I, §2.

41. U.S. Const. art.II, §3.

42. 10 U.S.C. §801 et seq.

43. Prior to Congress's enactment of the UCMJ in 1950, each military service had its own system of military justice, known as the Articles of War in the Army and the Articles for the Government of the Navy. The UCMJ is designed to provide uniformity and ensure all members of the armed forces the same substantive charges and procedural rules.

44. *O'Callahan v. Parker*, 395 U.S. 258, 89 S. Ct. 1683, 23 L. Ed. 2d 291 (1969).

45. *Solorio v. United States*, 483 U.S. 435, 107 S. Ct. 2924, 97 L. Ed. 2d 364 (1987).

46. *Ex parte Quirin*, 317 U.S. 1, 63 S. Ct. 2, 87 L. Ed. 3 (1942).

47. *Hamdan v. Rumsfeld*, 548 U.S. 547, 126 S. Ct. 2749, 165 L. Ed. 2d 723 (2006).

48. Pub. L. No. 109-366, 120 Stat. 2600 (Oct. 17, 2006).

49. *Boumediene v. Bush*, 553 U.S. 723, 128 S. Ct. 2229, 171 L. Ed.2d 41 (2008).

50. *Bloom v. Illinois*, 391 U.S. 194, 88 S. Ct. 1477, 20 L. Ed. 2d 522 (1968).

51. 5 U.S. 137, 2 L. Ed. 60 (1803).

52. *See Koon v. United States*, 518 U.S. 81, 116 S. Ct. 2035, 135 L. Ed. 2d 392 (1996).

53. U.S. Department of Justice, Office of Justice Programs, *Bureau of Justice Statistics*, "Federal Law Enforcement Officers, 2008" (NCJ 238250). http://www.bjs.gov/index.cfm?ty=pbdetail&iid=4372.

54. The law enforcement authority of the Secret Service is provided by 18 U.S.C. §3056.

55. http://www.justice.gov/dea/about/history/staffing.shtml.

56. http://www.justice.gov/dea/resource-center/statistics.shtml.

57. This why London police officers are still referred to as "Bobbies."

58. The *U.S. News and World Report* annually presents a magazine feature listing what it considers the Top 100 Law Schools. Additionally, it identifies law schools ranked by faculty who teach in different fields of legal education and a Law School Diversity Index.

59. *Keller v. State Bar of Cal.*, 496 U.S. 1, 110 S. Ct. 2228, 110 L. Ed. 2d 1 (1990).

60. *Goldfarb v. Virginia State Bar*, 421 U.S. 773, 95 S. Ct. 2004, 44 L. Ed. 2d 572 (1975).

61. *Bates v. State Bar of Ariz.*, 433 U.S. 350, 97 S. Ct. 2691, 53 L. Ed. 2d 810 (1977).

62. http://www.americanbar.org/content/dam/aba/administrative/market_research/lawyer_demographics_2013.authcheckdam.pdf.

63. *See* Carson, *The Lawyer Statistical Report, The U.S. Legal Profession in 1995*, at 1 (1999).

64. *Id.* at 61.

65. *Id.* at 41.

66. http://www.americanbar.org/content/dam/aba/administrative/market_research/lawyer_demographics_2013.authcheckdam.pdf.

67. http://www.americanbar.org/content/dam/aba/administrative/market_research/lawyer_demographics_2013.authcheckdam.pdf.

68. Carson, at 4.

69. W. Blackstone, *Commentaries on the Laws of England* 349-350 (T. Cooley 4th ed. 1896).

70. http://gwpapers.virginia.edu/documents/will/index.html.

THE SUBSTANCE
OF THE LAW

PART II

CONSTITUTIONAL LAW 3

LEARNING OBJECTIVES

This chapter should enable the student to understand:

- the concept of judicial review and interpretive powers of courts
- legislative functions based on constitutionally enumerated and implied powers
- the means by which executive powers have been expanded
- the principle of separation of powers and the related system of checks and balances and the principle of federalism
- the ways in which the U.S. Constitution protects civil rights and liberties
- the significance of the Fourteenth Amendment provisions and the judicial interpretations of "due process of law" and "equal protection of the laws"

CHAPTER OUTLINE

INTRODUCTION

The federal government and each of the fifty state governments are based on written constitutions. Each of these constitutions sets forth the structure and powers of government as well as the rights of citizens. The term "constitutional law" refers to the judicial interpretation of these constitutions in the context of legal disputes. These disputes arise in both state and federal courts. Each of the fifty states has its own court system, which is responsible for interpreting its own state constitution and, in some instances, the federal constitution. Because of the variations in state constitutional law, this chapter focuses on federal constitutional law. It is important to understand, however, that because the federal constitution is the "supreme law of the land," state constitutions (as well as statutes and local ordinances) must conform to the principles of the U.S. Constitution. All federal courts interpret the U.S. Constitution, but because the U.S. Supreme Court sits at the apex of the federal judicial hierarchy, the Supreme Court is the most important developer of constitutional law.

Constitutional law has two basic components: the institutional component and the civil rights/civil liberties component. The former component embraces issues of congressional, presidential, and judicial power as well as questions of state versus national authority and problems of interstate relations. The latter component involves claims of personal freedom and legal and political equality, usually asserted in opposition to exercises of governmental power.

JUDICIAL REVIEW

In its most general sense, **judicial review** refers to the authority of a court of law to review a particular legal issue. In constitutional law, the term has more specific meaning. It refers to the power of courts to declare government actions invalid if the actions are determined to be contrary to constitutional principles. The U.S. Constitution does not explicitly grant the power of judicial review. However, in *Marbury v. Madison* (1803),[1] the Supreme Court assumed the power to strike down unconstitutional federal statutes. Later, the Court extended the scope of judicial review to encompass executive actions[2] as well as state statutes.[3] Today, all actions of government, from the conduct of police officers on the street to orders issued by the President, are subject to judicial review. Judicial review has become a bedrock principle of the American legal and political systems. It is generally regarded as essential to preserve the ideal of constitutional supremacy.

Constitutional Interpretation

The exercise of judicial review requires courts to interpret the Constitution. Whenever possible, courts rely on the plain meaning of the text, but the meaning of many constitutional provisions is not self-evident. Accordingly, courts often seek to discern the **intentions of the Framers** of the Constitution. In determining original intent, courts often rely on the debate that took place during the Constitutional Convention

MARBURY v. MADISON

1 Cranch (5 U.S.) 137, 2 L. Ed. 60 (1803)

OPINION OF COURT

Mr. Chief Justice Marshall delivered the opinion of the Court.

. . . The Constitution is either a superior paramount law, unchangeable by ordinary means, or it is on a level with ordinary legislative acts, and, like other acts, is alterable when the legislature shall please to alter it. If the former part of the alternative be true, then a legislative act, contrary to the Constitution, is not law; if the latter part be true, then written constitutions are absurd attempts, on the part of the people, to limit a power, in its own nature, illimitable.

Certainly, all those who have framed written constitutions contemplate them as forming the fundamental and paramount law of the nation, and consequently, the theory of every such government must be, that an act of the legislature, repugnant to the Constitution, is void. . . .

If an act of the legislature, repugnant to the Constitution, is void, does it notwithstanding its invalidity, bind the courts, and oblige them to give it effect? Or, in other words, though it be not law, does it constitute a rule as operative as if it was a law? This would be to overthrow, in fact, what was established in theory; and would seem, at first view, an absurdity too gross to be insisted on. . . .

It is, emphatically, the province and duty of the judicial department, to say what the law is. Those who apply the rule to particular cases, must of necessity expound and interpret that rule. If two laws conflict with each other, the courts must decide on the operation of each.

So, if a law be in opposition to the Constitution; if both the law and the Constitution apply to a particular case, so that the court must either decide that case, conformable to the law, disregarding the Constitution; or conformable to the Constitution, disregarding the law; the court must determine which of these conflicting rules governs the case: this is of the very essence of judicial duty. . . .

in 1787. They also look to essays by James Madison, Alexander Hamilton, and John Jay written during the debate over ratification of the Constitution and later published as *The Federalist Papers.*

However, the **doctrine of original intent** is not universally accepted. Many judges and commentators believe that the intentions of the Framers are impossible to discern on a number of issues. Others argue that original intent, even if knowable, should not control contemporary constitutional decision making. These commentators extol the virtues of **the living Constitution**, whose meaning evolves according to what Justice Oliver Wendell Holmes called the "felt necessities" of the times. The Supreme Court has never resolved the issue of constitutional interpretation. Rather, the Court's numerous decisions reflect an ongoing debate over how the eighteenth century Constitution should be applied to contemporary circumstances.

Precedent

In the common law tradition, courts rely on **precedent**, which means that they generally follow what courts have said and done in the past. This doctrine of *stare decisis*, which literally means "to stand by things decided," applies to constitutional law as well. Courts tend to interpret provisions of the Constitution in the same fashion that they have been interpreted by courts in previous cases. But the doctrine of precedent is by no means absolute, and courts will at times overturn or abandon precedent in constitutional cases. As the Supreme Court has observed,

> Adhering to precedent "is usually the wise policy, because in most matters it is more important that the applicable rule of law be settled than it be settled right." . . . Nevertheless, when governing decisions are unworkable or are badly reasoned, "this Court has never felt constrained to follow precedent." . . . *Stare decisis* is not an inexorable command; rather, it "is a principle of policy and not a mechanical formula of adherence to the latest decision." . . . This is particularly true in constitutional cases, because in such cases "correction through legislative action is practically impossible."[4]

Perhaps the best-known example of a long-standing precedent that was later overturned is the Supreme Court's decision in *Plessy v. Ferguson* (1896).[5] In *Plessy*, the Court upheld a Louisiana law that required racial segregation on passenger trains. The statute was merely one of many such "Jim Crow laws" that were common in the American South well into the twentieth century. The law was challenged as a violation of the Fourteenth Amendment, which forbids states from denying equal protection of the laws to persons within their jurisdiction. Under the pretense that segregation was not inherently unequal, the Supreme Court found no violation of equal protection and upheld the statute. Thus, the "separate but equal" doctrine became the law of the land. Fifty-eight years later, in the landmark case of *Brown v. Board of Education* (1954),[6] the Supreme Court repudiated the "separate but equal" doctrine in the context of public education. In later decisions during the 1950s and 1960s, the Court would abolish the separate but equal doctrine altogether.

Limiting Doctrines

Because judicial review is inherently counter-majoritarian, and because the exercise of judicial review can produce intense political conflict, courts tend to be cautious in exercising this authority. This caution is often referred to as **judicial self-restraint**, whereas the absence of caution is dubbed **judicial activism**. Judicial self-restraint is manifested in a number of doctrines limiting the exercise of judicial review. Judicial activism consists largely in ignoring or circumventing these limiting doctrines.

Perhaps the most fundamental limiting doctrine is the **presumption of constitutionality**. Under this doctrine, courts will presume a challenged statute or governmental action is valid until it is demonstrated otherwise. In other words, the party bringing the constitutional challenge carries the burden of persuasion. This doctrine is based on an appreciation for the counter-majoritarian character of judicial review and a fundamental respect for the legislative bodies in a democratic system. However, the

Supreme Court has modified the doctrine of presumptive constitutionality with respect to laws discriminating against citizens on grounds of race or national origin. Such laws are now viewed as inherently suspect and are subjected to **strict judicial scrutiny**.[7] Similarly, laws abridging fundamental rights such as freedom of speech are not afforded the traditional presumption of validity either.[8]

Another fundamental limiting doctrine is that of **standing**. A party seeking judicial review of a law must have standing to challenge that law, which means that the operation of the law must produce a substantial injury to the rights of the party seeking review. For example, a federal taxpayer who believes that a particular federal program is unconstitutional does not normally have standing to challenge the law on which the program is based.[9] Yet a person who is prosecuted criminally under an arguably unconstitutional statute certainly has standing to challenge that statute.[10] In many instances, one who is likely to be prosecuted or whose activities are chilled or deterred by the existence of a statute can bring a civil suit seeking to enjoin enforcement of the law. Such was the case in *Roe v. Wade* (1973),[11] where a woman facing an unwanted pregnancy brought suit in federal court to challenge the constitutionality of a Texas law criminalizing most abortions. The Supreme Court's decision to strike down the Texas law, and thus effectively legalize abortion throughout the country, was perhaps the most controversial exercise of judicial review in the modern age.

In a concurring opinion in *Ashwander v. Tennessee Valley Authority* (1936),[12] Associate Justice Louis D. Brandeis set forth the basic limiting doctrines observed by courts in the exercise of judicial review:

1. The Court will not pass upon the constitutionality of legislation in a friendly, nonadversary, proceeding, declining because to decide such questions "is legitimate only in the last resort, and as a necessity in the determination of real, earnest, and vital controversy between individuals. It never was the thought that, by means of a friendly suit, a party beaten in the legislature could transfer to the courts an inquiry as to the constitutionality of the legislative act."

2. The Court will not "anticipate a question of constitutional law in advance of the necessity of deciding it."

3. The Court will not "formulate a rule of constitutional law broader than is required by the precise facts to which it is to be applied."

4. The Court will not pass upon a constitutional question although properly presented by the record, if there is also present some other ground upon which the case may be disposed of. . . . Thus, if a case can be decided on either of two grounds, one involving a constitutional question, the other a question of statutory construction or general law, the Court will decide only the latter.

5. The Court will not pass upon the validity of a statute upon complaint of one who fails to show that he is injured by its operation.

6. The Court will not pass upon the constitutionality of a statute at the instance of one who has availed himself of its benefits.

7. "When the validity of an act of the Congress is drawn in question, and even if a serious doubt of constitutionality is raised, it is a cardinal principle that this Court will first ascertain whether a construction of the statute is fairly possible by which the question may be avoided."

The so-called *Ashwander* **rules** obviously limit the exercise of judicial review and, accordingly, reduce the potential for political conflict flowing from an ill-advised or untimely use of judicial power. Yet it must be pointed out that the *Ashwander* rules are frequently honored in the breach. In the modern era, courts tend to be less cautious in their exercise of judicial review. Under Chief Justice Earl Warren (1954-1969), the Court was particularly active in its use of judicial review. The Warren Court rendered numerous decisions that contradicted public opinion and aroused the ire of politicians at all levels of government. Of course, because the courts function within the constitutional system of checks and balances, there are a number of external constraints on judicial power. These constraints prevent the courts from straying too far from mainstream opinion.

Restriction of the Court's Jurisdiction

The Supreme Court's original jurisdiction is fixed by Article III of the Constitution. *Marbury v. Madison* made clear that Congress may not alter the Court's original jurisdiction. Congress may, however, authorize lower federal courts to share the Court's original jurisdiction. The Supreme Court's appellate jurisdiction is another matter. Article III indicates that the Court ". . . shall have appellate Jurisdiction, both as to Law and Fact, with such Exceptions, and under such Regulations as the Congress shall make."

On only one occasion has Congress significantly limited the appellate jurisdiction of the Supreme Court. It happened during the turbulent Reconstruction period that followed the Civil War. Congress restricted the Court's appellate jurisdiction in a certain category of cases to prevent the Court from ruling on the constitutionality of the Reconstruction program. In *Ex Parte McCardle* (1869), the Court acquiesced in the curtailment of its jurisdiction, thus buttressing congressional control of the Court.[13]

Congress has, on several occasions, debated limitations on the Supreme Court's appellate jurisdiction. In the late 1950s, there was a movement in Congress to deny the Supreme Court appellate jurisdiction in cases involving national security, a reaction to Warren Court decisions protecting the rights of suspected Communists. Although the major legislative proposals were narrowly defeated, the Court retreated from some of its most controversial decisions.[14]

Does *Ex Parte McCardle* suggest that Congress could completely abolish the Court's appellate jurisdiction? Whatever the answer might have been in 1869, the answer today would certainly be "no." It is highly unlikely that Congress would ever undertake such a radical measure, but if it did, the Supreme Court would almost certainly declare the act invalid. Because the Court's major decision-making role is a function of its appellate jurisdiction, any serious curtailment of that jurisdiction would in effect deny the Court the ability to perform its essential function in the constitutional system.

In the early 1980s, a flurry of activity in Congress was aimed at restricting Supreme Court jurisdiction to hear appeals in cases dealing with abortion and school prayer. A number of proposals surfaced, but none were adopted. The constitutionality of such proposals is open to question, in that they might be construed as undermining the Court's ability to protect fundamental constitutional rights. The question remains academic, though, because Congress has not enacted such a restriction on the Court. Denial of jurisdiction as a limiting strategy depends greatly on the substantive issue-area involved, what the Court has done in the area thus far, and what it is likely to do in the future. As retaliation against the Court for one controversial decision, the curtailment of appellate jurisdiction is not likely to be an effective strategy.

Constitutional Amendment

From time to time Congress will attempt to overturn, evade, or modify a Supreme Court decision through the enactment of legislation. The Court will generally not permit this, as it reserves to itself the final word in matters of constitutional interpretation.[15] The only conclusive means of overruling a Supreme Court or any federal court decision is through adoption of a constitutional amendment. If Congress disapproves of a particular judicial decision, it may be able to override that decision through a simple statute, but only if the decision was based on statutory interpretation. It is much more difficult to override a federal court decision that is based on the United States Constitution. Congress alone cannot do so. Ever since *Marbury v. Madison,* our system of government has conceded to the courts the power to authoritatively interpret the Nation's charter. A Supreme Court decision interpreting the Constitution is therefore final unless and until one of two things occurs. First, the Court may overrule itself in a later case. This has happened numerous times historically. The only other way to overturn a constitutional decision of the Supreme Court is through constitutional amendment. This is not easily done, since Article V of the Constitution prescribes a two-thirds majority in both houses of Congress followed by ratification by three-fourths of the states. Yet on at least four occasions in our history specific Supreme Court decisions have been overturned in this manner.[16]

Over the years, numerous unsuccessful attempts have been made to overrule Supreme Court decisions through constitutional amendments. In 1983, an amendment providing that "[t]he right to an abortion is not secured by this Constitution," obviously aimed at *Roe v. Wade,* failed to pass the Senate by only one vote. The most recent example of a proposed constitutional amendment aimed at a Supreme Court decision dealt with the emotional public issue of flag burning. In 1989, the Court held that burning the American flag as part of a public protest was a form of symbolic speech protected by the First Amendment.[17] Many, including President George H. W. Bush, called on Congress to overrule the Court. Congress considered an amendment that read, "The Congress and the States shall have power to prohibit the physical desecration of the flag of the United States." Votes were taken in both houses, but neither achieved the necessary two-thirds majority. As recently as 1997, the U.S. House of Representatives passed another proposed constitutional amendment designed to overrule the Court's flag-burning decisions. But this measure was not approved by the requisite two-thirds vote in the Senate.

The Appointment Power as a Check on the Courts

As we discussed in Chapter 2, all federal judges are appointed by the President subject to the consent of the Senate. Normally, the Senate consents to presidential judicial appointments with a minimum of controversy. However, Senatorial approval is by no means automatic, especially when the opposing political party controls the Senate. The shared presidential/Senatorial power of appointing federal judges is an important means of influencing the judiciary. For example, President Richard Nixon made a significant impact on the Supreme Court and on American constitutional law through his appointment of four justices. During the 1968 presidential campaign, Nixon criticized the Warren Court's decisions, especially in the criminal law area, and promised to appoint "strict constructionists" to the bench. President Nixon's first appointment came in 1969 when Warren E. Burger was selected to succeed Earl Warren as Chief Justice. Nixon would appoint three more justices to the Court: Lewis Powell, Harry Blackmun, and William Rehnquist (who was elevated to Chief Justice by President Reagan in 1986). The four Nixon appointments had a moderating influence on the Supreme Court and set the stage for the emergence of the more conservative Rehnquist Court in the 1980s. This shows how the appointment process provides an indirect democratic control on the courts, ensuring that judicial interpretation of the Constitution will not move too far from a national consensus.

Presidents can, however, temporarily avoid the need to acquire Senatorial approval of nominations; this is accomplished through a process called "recess appointment." Article 2, Section II of the U.S. Constitution sanctions this mechanism, and specifically allows the president to "fill up all Vacancies that may arise during the Recess of the Senate." Therefore, if the Senate is in a recess—during a holiday break, for example—the president ostensibly can fill a government position through a unilateral act. Even so, recess appointments must be confirmed in the Senate by the end of the next congressional session. President Eisenhower actually used this power to appoint three justices to the Supreme Court of the United States: William Brennan, Potter Stewart, and Earl Warren—all of whom were subsequently confirmed when the Senate reconvened.

On June 26, 2014, in a case called *National Labor Relations Board v. Noel Canning*, the Court put some limitations on the president's ability to use recess appointments. In reviewing three Obama appointments to executive branch positions, the Court declared that the Senate determines when it is officially in recess—not the president. In fact, Justice Breyer's majority opinion bluntly declared: "The Senate is in session when it says it is."[18] More specifically, in the case at hand, Republican senators had claimed to keep the Senate "open" during a holiday break by having a single Senator appear at the Senate chamber to call to order a session that might have lasted for mere minutes (at most). The Supreme Court's decision indicated that such activity was enough to consider the Senate "open," and thus is tantamount to a recognition that one Senator can effectively block recess appointments. Ultimately, although this case concerned nominations to executive branch positions, the Court's ruling will have implications for a president's ability to fill subsequent judicial vacancies via the recess appointment power.

LEGISLATIVE POWER

Having discussed the power of judicial review and its exercise under the system of checks and balances, we turn now to the substance of constitutional law, beginning with the interpretation of Article I, which defines the legislative power. Article I, Section 1 of the Constitution provides that "[a]ll legislative powers herein granted shall be vested in a Congress of the United States, which shall consist of a Senate and a House of Representatives." Article I delineates the composition of both houses of Congress, indicates minimal requirements for members, specifies how members are to be chosen, grants broad authority to each house to determine its own procedures, and extends certain privileges to members of Congress. Article I also defines the legislative powers of Congress, although grants of congressional authority are even found elsewhere in the Constitution.

Enumerated Powers

Most of the **enumerated powers** of Congress are located in Article I, Section 8, which consists of seventeen brief paragraphs enumerating specific powers followed by a general clause permitting Congress to "make all laws which shall be necessary and proper for carrying into Execution the foregoing powers, and all other powers vested by this Constitution in the Government of the United States. . . ." The powers enumerated in Article I, Section 8 authorize Congress to lay and collect taxes, borrow money, regulate commerce among the states, control immigration and naturalization, regulate bankruptcy, coin money, fix standards of weights and measures, establish post offices and post roads, grant patents and copyrights, establish tribunals "inferior to the Supreme Court," declare war, raise and support an army and a navy, regulate the militia when called into service, and perform other more restricted functions.

In reading Article I, Section 8, one will note that, although Congress is empowered to "provide for the common defense and general welfare of the United States," there is no general grant of police power to Congress. Consequently, the power to make any and all laws deemed necessary for the protection of the public health, safety, welfare, and morals is reserved to the states under the Tenth Amendment. Yet Congress exercises substantial legislative power by linking laws to the specific powers contained in Section 8. For example, Congress is not empowered to prohibit prostitution per se, but it can make it a crime to transport persons across state lines for "immoral purposes" by drawing on its broad power to regulate "commerce among the states."[19] Over the years, the power to regulate interstate commerce has been invoked to justify a wide range of federal legislation, including laws relating to telecommunications, the natural environment, civil rights, and organized crime. One is tempted to argue that Congress has effectively acquired a police power through its reliance on the Commerce Clause and the courts' willingness to interpret the Clause liberally.

However, in 1995, the Supreme Court held that the Commerce Clause is not boundless and does not confer a general police power on Congress. In *United States v. Lopez*, the Court struck down a federal law making it a crime to possess a firearm in close proximity to a school.[20] Noting that most states already had similar prohibitions, the Court held that the mere act of possessing a firearm was not sufficiently related to interstate commerce to permit Congress to reach this activity. In a similar vein, the Court in *United States v. Morrison* (2000) struck down the Violence Against Women Act of 1994 on the ground that Congress had exceeded its power under the Commerce Clause.[21] And in *National Federation of Independent Business v. Sebelius* (2012), the Court said that the Commerce Clause does not empower Congress to require Americans to purchase health insurance (although the Court ultimately upheld this mandate by relying on Congress' broad taxing power).[22] Despite the Supreme Court's opinions in *Lopez, Morrison,* and *Sebelius,* Congress's powers under the Commerce Clause remain broad and formidable.

Implied Powers

It is obvious that Congress today exercises far more powers than are specifically enumerated in the Constitution. Over the years, the American people have come to expect, even demand, as much. Yet arguably, Congress has remained within the scope of powers delegated to it by the Constitution. The linchpin of this argument is the Necessary and Proper Clause (Article I, Section 8, clause 18) and the related doctrine of **implied powers**. In fact, the Necessary and Proper Clause is today, along with the Commerce, Taxing, and Spending Clauses, one of the key sources of congressional power.

The doctrine of implied powers was firmly established in the landmark case of *McCulloch v. Maryland* (1819).[23] The doctrine holds that Congress may enact laws that are reasonably related to its enumerated powers, as long as Congress does not violate a specific prohibition of the Constitution. Under the doctrine of implied powers, scarcely any area exists in which Congress is absolutely barred from acting, since most problems have a conceivable relationship to the broad powers and objectives contained in the Constitution.

Congress has many sources of constitutional authority. Some of these are quite explicit, as the list of enumerated powers in Article I, Section 8 makes clear. Others are implicit, open-ended, and subject to no complete or conclusive definition. These implied powers are fully recognized in the Necessary and Proper Clause and in the enforcement provisions of several constitutional amendments, most notably the Thirteenth, Fourteenth, and Fifteenth. Within this broad range of explicit and implicit powers, Congress has ample latitude to address the major problems, needs, and goals of the Nation, as perceived by succeeding generations of Americans during two centuries of constitutional history.

The Power to Investigate

Although legislation is Congress's principal function, **oversight** of the executive branch is also an important responsibility of Congress. To this end, congressional committees conduct investigations in which they hold hearings and call witnesses to testify. Sometimes these investigations have been great public events, such as the Watergate hearings of 1973 and 1974, which led to the demise of the Nixon presidency. Quite often, these

CASE IN POINT

THE SUPREME COURT RULES ON "OBAMACARE"
National Federation of Independent Business v. Sebelius
United States Supreme Court
567 U.S., 132 S. Ct. 2566; 183 L. Ed. 2d 450 (2012)

Although Congress' legislative powers are very broad, they are not without limits. A test of those limits came when Congress enacted the Patient Protection and Affordable Care Act of 2010. Embodying President Barack Obama's campaign promise to reform the nation's health care system, the Act sought to expand health insurance coverage to millions of uninsured Americans. The complicated bill, which spanned some 2,700 pages, expanded eligibility for Medicaid, the nation's health care system for the poor, prohibited insurance companies from rejecting applicants based on pre-existing medical conditions, and allowed children to remain on their parents' health insurance plans until age 26. Most controversially, the law mandated that all Americans obtain health insurance, either through the marketplace or a government program. Those who failed to obtain the required insurance would pay a fine. The idea was to bring all Americans, including the young and healthy ones, into the risk pool and thereby reduce costs for insurers and, ultimately, the insured.

Conservatives and Republicans railed against the new law, which they referred to caustically as "Obamacare," claiming that it represented nothing short of a government takeover of the nation's health care system. President Obama eventually embraced the term "Obamacare," and said that the law shows "the President cares." By June of 2012, Obamacare had become a major issue in the 2012 presidential election. It also had become a major constitutional question for the judiciary.

The mandate that individuals obtain health care coverage was at the heart of a case that came before the U.S. Supreme Court in the spring of 2012. The government defended the mandate as a regulation of interstate commerce under Article I, Section 8 of the Constitution. On the other side, those challenging the mandate, including the National Federation of Independent Business, argued that it was an unprecedented exercise of federal power and transcended regulation of commerce. On June 28, 2012, the U.S. Supreme Court announced its decision in *National Federation of Independent Business v. Sebelius.* To many people's surprise, the Court upheld the mandate, not as a regulation of commerce, but rather as an exercise of Congress' broad taxing power.

President Obama hailed the Court's decision, which upheld his signature legislative achievement, while Republicans vowed to seek repeal of the entire law by Congress. The deciding vote in *National Federation of Independent Business v. Sebelius* was cast by Chief Justice John Roberts, who also wrote the majority opinion. In a long opinion, Roberts rejected the idea that the mandate could be construed as a regulation of interstate commerce, but nevertheless concluded that the "requirement that certain individuals pay a financial penalty for not obtaining health insurance may reasonably be characterized as a tax." He also noted that "[b]ecause the Constitution permits such a tax, it is not our role to forbid it, or to pass upon its wisdom or fairness." Justices Antonin Scalia, Anthony Kennedy, Samuel Alito, and Clarence Thomas dissented, observed that the "holding that the Individual Mandate is a tax raises a difficult constitutional question... that the Court resolves with inadequate deliberation."

The fact that Chief Justice Roberts, a Republican appointed to the Court by President George W. Bush, cast the deciding vote upholding the Affordable Care Act helped reinforce the idea that the Supreme Court is supposed to transcend partisan politics in its interpretation of the laws and the Constitution.

McCULLOCH v. MARYLAND
4 Wheat. (17 U.S.) 316, 4 L. Ed. 579 (1819)

Mr. Chief Justice Marshall delivered the opinion of the Court.

. . . We admit, as all must admit, that the powers of the government are limited, and that its limits are not to be transcended. But we think the sound construction of the Constitution must allow to the national legislature that discretion, with respect to the means by which the powers it confers are to be carried into execution, which will enable the body to perform the high duties assigned to it, in the manner most beneficial to the people. Let the end be legitimate, let it be within the scope of the Constitution, and all means which are appropriate, which are plainly adapted to that end, which are not prohibited, but consist with the letter and spirit of the Constitution, are constitutional.

. . . Should Congress, in the execution of its powers, adopt measures which are prohibited by the Constitution; or should Congress, under the pretext of executing its powers pass laws for the accomplishment of objects not entrusted to the government, it would become the painful duty of this tribunal, should a case requiring such a decision come before it, to say that such an act was not the law of the land. But where the law is not prohibited, and is really calculated to effect any of the objects entrusted to the government, to undertake here to inquire into the degree of its necessity, would be to pass the line which circumscribes the judicial department, and to tread on legislative ground. This court disclaims all pretensions to such a power. . . .

investigations have led to significant changes in public policy. However, Article I makes no mention of Congress's having the **power to investigate**. In 1881, the Supreme Court confronted this problem.[24] It held that the power of Congress to investigate is a necessary auxiliary of the legislative function. Yet the implied power to investigate is not unlimited. It must be exercised only in relation to potential legislation. Of course, today, there are few areas in which Congress may not potentially legislate; thus, there are few areas off limits to congressional investigation. Still, an investigation purely for its own sake is subject to judicial challenge.[25]

EXECUTIVE POWER

Article II, Section 1 of the Constitution provides that the "executive power shall be vested in a President of the United States." Sections 2 and 3 enumerate specific powers granted to the President. These include authority to appoint judges and ambassadors, veto legislation, call Congress into special session, grant pardons, and serve as commander-in-chief of the armed forces. Each of these designated powers is obviously a part of **executive power**, but that general term is not defined in Article II. Thus, it is debatable whether the opening statement of Article II was intended to be merely a summary of powers later enumerated in the Article or, as Alexander Hamilton argued, an independent grant of power to the President.

For the most part, Hamilton's argument has prevailed, as the Supreme Court generally has acquiesced in the expansion of executive authority beyond the powers enumerated in Article II. It would be naive to expect the Court to stem the flow of power into the executive branch, given the fundamental economic, social, technological, and military needs that have led to concentration of power in the presidency. There are cases in which the Court has invalidated particular exercises of executive power—for example, the Steel Seizure Case in 1952[26] and the Watergate Tapes Decision of 1974,[27] but the overall trend has been to legitimize broad presidential power as the Supreme Court did in 1936 when it placed its stamp of approval on presidential primacy in the realm of foreign affairs, referring to the President as the "sole organ of the federal government in the field of international relations."[28]

War Powers

Perhaps the most contentious aspect of presidential power is the power to make war. The Constitution recognizes the President as **commander-in-chief**, but it does not define this term. The prevailing understanding of the term at the time the Constitution was ratified was that the President would be "first among generals, first among admirals" during a war that Congress had declared. Few thought that the power of commander-in-chief included the power to make war absent prior congressional authorization. But presidents going back to Thomas Jefferson have asserted the power to use limited military force abroad prior to approval from Congress. In *The Prize Cases* (1863),[29] the Supreme Court lent credence to this position when it upheld President Lincoln's order imposing a naval blockade on southern ports at the outset of the Civil War. Congress never declared war on the South, because to do so would have been a *de facto* recognition of the Confederacy as a sovereign government.

The modern tendency has been for presidents to conduct major wars based on resolutions authorizing the use of force rather than full declarations of war. In fact, the last declared war was World War II. For example, President George H.W. Bush won congressional approval before launching operation Desert Storm in 1991. Similarly, George W. Bush obtained congressional authorization before commencing operation Iraqi Freedom in 2003. As the latter operation evolved into an ongoing military occupation and counter-insurgency, public support for the enterprise declined, leading many in Congress to call for the termination of funds to support the operation. This illustrates why the **power of the purse** is Congress's most effective means of controlling a President's ability to sustain a long war effort in the face of public disapproval.

In passing the Gulf of Tonkin Resolution in 1964, Congress authorized the President to use military force to defend the government of South Vietnam from Communist North Vietnam and the Viet Cong guerillas. Of course, the Vietnam War expanded far beyond anything envisioned by Congress in 1964. Unhappy with the conduct of the Vietnam War by the Johnson and Nixon administrations, Congress in 1973 enacted the War Powers Resolution, which attempted to control presidential

CASE IN POINT

IS EXECUTIVE PRIVILEGE ABSOLUTE?
United States v. Nixon
United States Supreme Court
418 U.S. 904, 94 S. Ct. 3193, 41 L. Ed. 2d 1152 (1974)

This case stems from President Nixon's refusal to comply with a *subpoena duces tecum* (an order to produce documents or other physical evidence) obtained by Watergate Special Prosecutor Leon Jaworski. The subpoena directed President Nixon to produce the infamous Watergate Tapes on which were recorded conversations that took place in the Oval Office between President Nixon and his advisers. In refusing to honor the subpoena, President Nixon argued that the tapes were protected by executive privilege. Indeed, the President's counsel asserted that executive privilege is absolute and not subject to subpoena. The United States District Court for the District of Columbia, which had issued the subpoena, rejected the President's arguments and ordered him to produce the tapes. The President appealed to the Court of Appeals, but before the Circuit Court could act the Supreme Court granted Leon Jaworski's petition for certiorari, citing great public importance of the matter and the need for prompt resolution of the conflict. On the merits, the Supreme Court ruled in favor of the Special Prosecutor. Writing for a unanimous Court, Chief Justice Warren E. Burger (a Nixon appointee) concluded that "when the ground for asserting privilege as to subpoenaed materials sought for use in a criminal trial is based only on the generalized interest in confidentiality, it cannot prevail over the fundamental demands of due process of law in the fair administration of criminal justice." President Nixon reluctantly complied with the Supreme Court's decision, surrendered the incriminating tapes, and resigned as President. *United States v. Nixon* generally is regarded as a vindication of the rule of law over political power and a fundamental reaffirmation of our constitutional democracy.

action in this area. The Act contained a provision allowing Congress to veto presidential deployments of military forces into combat situations abroad. Although some critics, including several presidents, have questioned the constitutionality of the War Powers Resolution, the Act has never been subjected to judicial review. To some extent, this is because the Act's principal component, the veto provision, has never been acted upon. It is also true that the federal courts tend to stay away from controversies between Congress and the Executive, especially when they involve questions of war and peace.

SEPARATION OF POWERS

The Constitution allocates the legislative, executive, and judicial functions of the national government to separate branches. Moreover, each branch has the means to resist encroachments and to check excesses by the other branches. The Framers of the Constitution viewed the constitutional principle of **separation of powers** and the related system of **checks and balances** as essential to the maintenance of limited government and, ultimately, individual liberty. As James Madison observed in *The Federalist* No. 47, "The accumulation of all powers, legislative, executive, and judiciary, in the same hands . . . may justly be pronounced the very definition of tyranny."

Of course, the separation of powers is not absolute, and the courts have on many occasions recognized exceptions to the principle. But in general the following rules apply. Congress may not exercise the appointment power, for that power is reserved to the President.[30] Congress may not invest itself, its members, or its agents with executive power.[31] Nor can Congress delegate wholesale legislative power to the executive branch.[32] However, as long as Congress "shall lay down by legislative act an intelligible principle to which the person or body authorized to [exercise the delegated power] is directed to conform, such legislative action is not a forbidden delegation of legislative power."[33] In the modern era, the Supreme Court has tended to be somewhat permissive in applying this principle, which has facilitated substantial delegations of power to federal regulatory agencies. The Court has observed that "in our increasingly complex society, replete with ever changing and more technical problems, Congress simply cannot do its job absent an ability to delegate power under broad general directives."[34]

One of the more difficult separation of powers issues came to the Supreme Court in 1988. *Morrison v. Olson*[35] tested the constitutionality of the independent counsel provisions of the Ethics in Government Act of 1978.[36] A legacy of the Watergate scandal, this Act allowed for the appointment of an **independent counsel** to investigate and, if appropriate, prosecute certain high-ranking government officials for violations of federal criminal laws. The issue before the Court was whether the appointment of the independent counsel could be vested in a panel of federal judges rather than the President. The Court upheld the provision, saying that "we do not think that the Act 'impermissibly undermine[s]' the powers of the Executive Branch . . . or 'disrupts the proper balance between the coordinate branches [by] prevent[ing] the Executive Branch from accomplishing its constitutionally assigned functions'. . . ." Dissenting, Justice Scalia observed that "the President's constitutionally assigned duties include complete control over investigation and prosecution of violations of the law. . . ." In Scalia's view, vesting the appointment of the independent counsel in the courts deprived the President of such control.

The competing views expressed in *Morrison v. Olson* were especially interesting in light of the 1994 appointment of Kenneth Starr to investigate allegations of misconduct by President Clinton. This investigation led to President Clinton's **impeachment** by the House of Representatives in 1998. Like federal judges, presidents can be removed from office upon conviction of "high crimes and misdemeanors." President Clinton was charged with perjury and obstruction of justice but was acquitted by the Senate in early 1999. Later that year, Congress decided not to renew the independent counsel statute under which Starr was appointed.

FEDERALISM

Separation of powers is one of the two basic structural characteristics of the American constitutional system, the other being **federalism**. In a federal system, power is divided between a central government and a set of regional governments. A **unitary system**, by contrast, vests all authority in the central government. In the American context, federalism refers to the division of power between the national government on the one hand and the state and local governments on the other. In the American system of federalism, both the national government and the states are sovereign entities. Each of the fifty states has the right to exist; none can be done away with by the national government. Each of the fifty states has its own constitution and its own machinery of government—its own legislature, executive branch, and court system. Ultimately, each state has the authority to govern its citizenry, as long as it does so in a way that conforms to the U.S. Constitution.

Historically, the states preceded the Nation as political communities. After the Revolutionary War, citizens thought of themselves primarily as Virginians, New Yorkers, Rhode Islanders, and so forth, and only secondarily as Americans. The **Articles of Confederation**, under which this country was governed between the end of the Revolution and the time the Constitution was ratified in 1788, created a loose confederation of states held together by a weak central government. The Framers of the Constitution of 1787 sought to create an effective but limited national government. Still, during the debate over ratification, critics charged that the new national government might become too powerful and intrude on the rights of the states. Thus, the Tenth Amendment was adopted in 1789, and reserved to the states all powers not delegated to the national government.

In the early days of the Republic, the national government played a fairly limited role. As that role began to expand, conflicts emerged between the national government and the states. Under Chief Justice John Marshall (1801-1835), the Supreme Court established the doctrine that state policies may not contravene policies of the national government, assuming the latter are consistent with the Constitution.[37] This doctrine of national supremacy is based on the Supremacy Clause of Article VI, paragraph 2 of the Constitution, which states:

> "This Constitution, and the Laws of the United States which shall be made in Pursuance thereof; and all Treaties made, or which shall be made, under the Authority of the United States, shall be the supreme Law of the Land; and the Judges in every State shall be bound thereby, any Thing in the Constitution or Laws of any State to the Contrary notwithstanding."

The opposing doctrine, that states could "nullify" actions of the federal government they believed to be unconstitutional, was first proposed by Thomas Jefferson in the Kentucky Resolution of 1798. Although the doctrine of nullification failed to find support in the Supreme Court, it was extended in the mid-nineteenth century by southern states that claimed the right to secede from the Union. In *Texas v. White* (1869), handed down four years after General Robert E. Lee's surrender at Appomattox, the Supreme Court rejected the idea that states could secede from the Union.

The Civil War, the Industrial Revolution, the Great Depression, and two world wars had a profound impact on American political culture. In the twentieth century, people came to think of themselves first and foremost as Americans. Increasingly, they looked to the national government to solve problems the state and local governments could not, or would not, address. This cultural change produced a corresponding change in constitutional law. Whereas in the late nineteenth and early twentieth

---

CASE IN POINT

CAN THE FEDERAL GOVERNMENT COMMAND LOCAL OFFICIALS TO IMPLEMENT A FEDERAL GUN CONTROL PROGRAM?
Printz v. United States
United States Supreme Court
521 U.S. 898, 117 S. Ct. 2365, 138 L. Ed. 2d 914 (1997)

The Supreme Court struck a blow to congressional power by invalidating a provision of the Brady Handgun Violence Prevention Act. The offending provision required local law enforcement officials to perform background checks on prospective handgun purchasers. According to Justice Scalia's opinion for the sharply divided Court, this provision violated "the very principle of separate state sovereignty," which Scalia characterized as "one of the Constitution's structural protections of liberty." The *Printz* decision suggests that Congress cannot require state and local officials to assist in the administration of federal programs. Of course, there are many joint federal-state programs, but most of them involve voluntary cooperation by the states.

---

centuries the Supreme Court adopted a conservative model known as **dual federalism**,[38] in the wake of the Great Depression the Court embraced a more progressive model of federalism in which the national government was clearly recognized as the paramount authority.[39]

Over the two centuries since the republic was founded, the relationship between the national government and the states has changed dramatically. Today, there is no question of the dominance of the national government in most areas of policymaking. There is also considerable interaction between federal and state agencies, an arrangement often referred to as **cooperative federalism**. In the contemporary age, the federal government often uses its superior fiscal resources to prod the states into adopting policies they might not otherwise adopt. A good example of this sort of **coercive federalism** was Congress's decision in the early 1980s to force the states to raise the legal drinking age to twenty-one by threatening to cut off badly needed federal highway funds.[40] Despite clear federal dominance, states remain viable actors in the political system. And the courts continue to take the concept of federalism seriously.[41] Thus, as a constitutional principle, federalism retains considerable vitality.

CIVIL RIGHTS AND LIBERTIES

One of the principal objectives of the U.S. Constitution, as stated in its preamble, is "to secure the Blessings of Liberty to ourselves and our Posterity." The Framers of the Constitution thus recognized the protection of individual liberty as a fundamental goal of constitutional government. The Framers sought to protect liberty by creating a system of government that would be inherently restricted in power, hence limited in its ability to transgress the rights of the individual. However, the original Constitution contained few explicit protections of individual rights. This was not because the Framers did not value rights but rather because they thought it unnecessary to deal with them explicitly. Significantly, most of the state constitutions adopted during the American Revolution contained fairly detailed bills of rights placing limits on state and local governments. The Framers did not anticipate the growth of a pervasive national government and thus did not regard the extensive enumeration of individual rights in the federal Constitution as critical. They did, however, recognize a few important safeguards in the original Constitution, most notably the limitation on prosecution of **treason**, the guarantee of **habeas corpus**, and the prohibition against **bills of attainder** and **ex post facto laws**.

Circumscribing the Crime of Treason

At common law, the offense of high treason included plotting to kill or overthrow the King, making war against the King, or giving aid to the enemies of the Crown. In some instances, mere words were deemed sufficient wrongful acts to allow for conviction of high treason. Indeed, in one seventeenth century case, a writer was convicted of treason for suggesting that the King should be accountable to his subjects. Prior to the American Revolution, the Crown accused some supporters of American independence of treason. Consequently, the Framers of the Constitution believed that the crime of treason needed to be defined more narrowly. Thus, they provided in Article III, Section 3 that:

(1)   Treason against the United States, shall consist only in levying War against them, or in adhering to their Enemies, giving them Aid and Comfort. No Person shall be convicted of Treason unless on the Testimony of two Witnesses to the same overt Act, or on Confession in open Court.

(2)   The Congress shall have Power to declare the Punishment of Treason, but no Attainder of Treason shall work Corruption of Blood, or Forfeiture except during the Life of the Person attainted.

Habeas Corpus

Article I, Section 9 of the Constitution states, "[T]he privilege of the Writ of Habeas Corpus shall not be suspended, unless when in Cases of Invasion or Rebellion the public Safety may require it." Grounded in English common law, the writ of habeas corpus gives effect to the all-important right of the individual not to be held in unlawful custody. Specifically, habeas corpus enables a court to review a custodial situation and order the release of an individual who is being held in custody illegally. While the right has many applications, the most common is in the criminal context where an individual is held in custody but denied due process of law.[42] Indeed, the writ of habeas corpus is an important and controversial element of modern criminal procedure (see Chapter 10).

The scope of federal habeas corpus became a hotly contested issue under the war on terrorism launched after the horrendous attacks of 9-11-2001. Hundreds of "enemy aliens" captured in Afghanistan and elsewhere were incarcerated at the American naval base at Guantanamo Bay, Cuba. Under an executive order issued by President George W. Bush, these detainees were to be tried by military tribunals. Moreover, the government took the position that the detainees were beyond the reach of federal habeas corpus review. In a series of decisions, the Supreme Court held otherwise.[43] What some observers saw as a defeat for national security, others saw as a victory for the rule of law.

Ex Post Facto Laws and Bills of Attainder

The Constitution also prohibited both Congress and the state legislatures from adopting ex post facto laws and bills of attainder.[44] Ex post facto laws are laws passed after the occurrence of an act that alter the legal status or consequences of that act. A bill of attainder is a legislative act that imposes punishment upon a person without benefit of a trial in a court of law. The English Parliament had, often at the king's behest, passed ex post facto laws subjecting people to punishment for acts that were not illegal when performed. Parliament had also adopted bills of attainder imposing punishments on individuals without granting them the benefit of trial by jury. The common law did not prohibit ex post facto laws or bills of attainder, nor did the English Bill of Rights of 1689. The Framers of the American Constitution decided that Congress would not be permitted to foster such abuses.

Article I, Section 9 of the Constitution prohibits Congress from passing ex post facto laws. Article I, Section 10 imposes the same prohibition on state legislatures. The ex post facto clauses apply to criminal but not to civil laws.[45] For an act to be invalidated as an ex post facto law, two key elements must exist. First, the act must be retroactive—it must apply to events that occurred before its passage. Second, it must seriously disadvantage the accused, not merely by changes in procedure but also by means that render conviction more likely or punishment more severe.

Judicial decisions relying on the Ex Post Facto Clauses are uncommon today. However, in *Carmell v. Texas* (2000),[46] the Supreme Court reversed a series of sexual assault convictions on ex post facto grounds. The assaults had occurred in 1991 and 1992, when under Texas law a defendant could not be convicted merely on the testimony of the victim unless the victim was under age fourteen. At the time of Carmell's alleged assaults, the victim was fourteen or fifteen. The law was later amended to extend this "child victim exception" to victims under eighteen years old. Carmell was convicted under the amended law, which the Supreme Court held to be an impermissible ex post facto law.

Article I, Sections 9 and 10 also prohibit Congress and the states, respectively, from adopting bills of attainder. After the Civil War, the Supreme Court struck down a federal statute forbidding attorneys from practicing before federal courts unless they took an oath that they had not supported the Confederacy.[47] The Court also invalidated a provision of the Missouri Constitution that required a similar oath of all persons who wished to be employed in a variety of occupations, including the ministry.[48] The Court found that these laws violated both the bill of attainder and ex post facto provisions of Article I.

Since World War II, the Supreme Court has declared only two acts of Congress invalid as bills of attainder. The first instance was *United States v. Lovett* (1946),[49] in which the Court struck down a measure that prohibited three named federal employees from receiving compensation from the government. The three individuals had been branded by the House Committee on Un-American Activities as "subversives." The Court said that legislative acts "that apply either to named individuals or to easily ascertainable members of a group in such a way as to inflict punishment on them without a judicial trial are bills of attainder prohibited by the Constitution." In *United States v. Brown* (1965), the Court invalidated a law that prohibited members of the Communist party from serving as officers in trade unions, saying that "legislative acts, no matter what their form, that apply either to named individuals or to easily ascertainable members of a group in such a way as to inflict punishment on them without a judicial trial are bills of attainder prohibited by the Constitution."[50]

The Contract Clause

One of the principal motivations behind the Constitutional Convention of 1787 was the desire to secure overriding legal protection for contracts. Thus, Article I, Section 10 prohibits states from passing laws "impairing the obligation of contracts." The Contract Clause must be included among the provisions of the original Constitution that protect individual rights—in this case, the right of individuals to be free from governmental interference with their contractual relationships. By protecting contracts, Article I, Section 10 performed an important function in the early years of American economic development. Historically, the Contract Clause was an important source of litigation in the federal courts. In modern times, it is seldom interpreted to impose significant limits on the states in the field of economic regulation, especially when states are responding to economic emergencies. For example, during the Great Depression the Supreme Court upheld a Minnesota law that postponed foreclosures on real estate mortgages, observing that "the reservation of the reasonable exercise of the protective power of the state is read into all contracts."[51]

Adoption of the Bill of Rights

The omission of a bill of rights from the original Constitution was regarded as a major defect by numerous critics and even threatened to derail ratification in some states. Thomas Jefferson, who had not participated in the Constitutional Convention due to his diplomatic duties in France, was among the most influential critics. In a letter to his close friend James Madison, Jefferson argued, "You must specify your liberties, and put them down on paper." Madison, the acknowledged father of the Constitution, thought it unwise and unnecessary to enumerate individual rights, but Jefferson's view eventually prevailed. Honoring a "gentlemen's agreement" designed to secure ratification of the Constitution in several key states, the First Congress considered a proposed bill of rights drafted by Madison. Madison's original bill of rights called for limitations on the states as well as the federal government, but this proposal was defeated by states' rights advocates in Congress. The Bill of Rights was adopted by Congress in September 1789 and was ratified in November 1791.

The **Bill of Rights** was adopted as a set of limitations on the new federal government; it was not intended to apply to the states.[52] Accordingly, citizens had to look to their respective state constitutions and state courts for protection against actions of their state governments. That changed beginning in the late nineteenth century, as the Supreme Court held that various provisions of the Bill of Rights were applicable to the states as well. Today, virtually all of the provisions of the Bill of Rights apply with equal force to all levels of government. (To learn how this was accomplished, see the discussion of the Fourteenth Amendment below.)

The First Amendment: Freedom of Religion

The First Amendment provides a number of crucial guarantees of freedom, including protections of freedom of speech, freedom of the press, freedom of assembly, and the right to petition government for a redress of grievances. The First Amendment also prohibits Congress from making laws "respecting an establishment of religion or prohibiting the free exercise thereof"; the Establishment Clause prohibits Congress from making laws "respecting an establishment of religion," while the Free Exercise Clause enjoins the national government from "prohibiting the free exercise thereof."

Free Exercise of Religion

The Free Exercise Clause provides virtually absolute protection for the right to express one's religious beliefs and to assemble with other believers. It also protects people's right to solicit funds and proselytize on behalf of religious organizations, although these rights are subject to reasonable time, place, and manner restrictions.[53] The Free Exercise Clause prohibits government from adopting laws or regulations aimed specifically at the practices of one religious sect.[54] It does not, however, generally permit citizens to flout criminal laws that are applicable to everyone.[55] Thus, under current interpretation, one cannot be exempt from criminal laws proscribing polygamy even though one's religion might condone or even sacramentalize such conduct. Nor can parents use freedom of religion as a justification for their refusal to seek medical treatment for their seriously ill children.[56]

However, the Court has carved out an exception for the use of certain controlled substances in religious ceremonies. This occurred in large part due to the passage of the Religious Freedom Restoration Act in 1993.[57] That legislation stated that First Amendment claims of free exercise of religion should be evaluated with something called the Sherbert Test. This test mandates that a claimant demonstrate a "sincere belief" and also show that the government has placed an "undue burden" on that belief. If the claimant is successful on these two "prongs" of the test, the government must then demonstrate a "compelling interest" for imposing a burden and must also demonstrate that it is using the "least restrictive means" to further that interest. In 2006, the Supreme Court used the *Sherbert* Test in granting members of the O Centro Espirita Benficiente Uniao do Vegetal church an exception that permitted the use of a controlled substance in a religious ceremony. Specifically, at their ceremonies, the church members ingested a tea called hoasca, which contains DMT, a Schedule 1 controlled substance. Although the Court did find that the government held valid compelling interests in regard to preventing harm to the users and in preventing recreational abuse of the drug outside of the church, the Court added that these interests were not advanced in the "least restrictive means" when customs agents seized tea leaves imported by the church. Thus, the church members were successful in asserting a "free exercise" claim.[58]

CASE IN POINT

THE SUPREME COURT RULES IN FAVOR OF HOBBY LOBBY
Burwell v. Hobby Lobby
United States Supreme Court
June 30, 2014
573 U.S. _____; 134 S. Ct. 2751; 189 L. Ed. 2d 675 (2014)

On the final day of its 2013-14 term, the Supreme Court released a sharply-divided decision addressing the constitutionality of a portion of the Affordable Care Act. Executives from Hobby Lobby Stores, Inc. and a company called Conestoga Wood Specialties Corp. brought suit to challenge the Affordable Care Act's mandate that businesses provide employees with access to health care plans that covered certain types of contraceptives. The specific contraceptives at issue included intrauterine devices and so-called "morning after pills," items that the companies' lawyers said "may have the effect of preventing an already fertilized egg from developing any further by inhibiting its attachment to the uterus," thus making these contraceptives incompatible with religious beliefs that are linked to the idea that life begins at conception. Consequently, company executives claimed that the contraceptive requirement violated their First Amendment rights to "free exercise of religion."

In *Burwell v. Hobby Lobby*, a 5-4 majority ruled in favor of Hobby Lobby. Justice Alito's majority opinion began by noting that "family-owned" (or "closely-held"), for-profit companies could in fact claim the same free exercise of religion rights that individuals can assert. (From a semantic standpoint, the Internal Revenue Service defines "closely-held" companies as those where five or fewer individuals control 50% or more of the company stock.)

After asserting that a "free exercise" claim could be recognized here, the majority opinion then evaluated this matter through the lens of the Sherbert Test. Although the opinion did grant that "providing contraception to women" was in fact a compelling interest, Alito added that the government had not achieved the "least restrictive means" for furthering this compelling interest. His opinion even suggested that the government itself could pay for women to acquire contraceptive coverage, or that it could require insurance companies to do so.

Justice Ginsburg's dissent derided the majority for offering "a decision of startling breadth" that, in her opinion, would allow corporations to "opt out of any law (saving only tax laws) they judge incompatible with their sincerely held religious beliefs." She expressed particular concern about possible challenges to providing health insurance that covered blood transfusions, antidepressants, and vaccines.

Justice Alito responded to Justice Ginsburg by noting that, "Our holding is very specific. We do not hold, as the principal dissent alleges, that for-profit corporations and other commercial enterprises can 'opt out of any law,'" and he specifically stated that the decision does not sanction denial of vaccinations or transfusions, or any type of workplace discrimination.

Two primary areas for future litigation remain after this decision. First, subsequent cases will be needed to determine the application of these principles to other forms of birth control besides "emergency contraception"; second, additional cases will be required to assess whether other types of organizations besides "closely-held, for profit companies" can successfully advance similar claims. In the end, the precise scope of the exceptions to existing law that the Supreme Court is willing to grant under the auspices of "free exercise of religion" provides a matter for ongoing debate about the First Amendment.[59]

Separation of Church and State

The Supreme Court has said that the Establishment Clause was intended to erect a "wall of separation between church and state."[60] Of course, people often disagree as to how high or thick the wall of separation should be. Those of a liberal persuasion usually argue for strict **separation of church and state**, while those of a more conservative mindset generally are less troubled by governmental acknowledgments and accommodations of religious belief.

Several decades ago, the Supreme Court fashioned a three-part test to determine whether a challenged law or policy violates the Establishment Clause. It is referred to as the *Lemon* test, as it was first articulated in the Court's 1971 decision in *Lemon v. Kurtzman*.[61] To pass muster, (1) the law or policy must have a secular legislative purpose; (2) its principal or primary effect must be one that neither advances nor inhibits religion; and (3) it must not foster an excessive government entanglement with religion. Of course this test is not self-executing. Judges often disagree about what constitutes a "secular purpose," "principal or primary effect," and "excessive entanglement." A number of commentators and even some of the justices of the Supreme Court have questioned the value of the *Lemon* test, and in recent years the Court has modified the test somewhat. But the Court has yet to produce an alternative formulation.

Nowhere is the debate over separation of church and state more intense than in the context of public education, where the courts have dealt with such emotional issues as prayer and the teaching of "creation science" in the public schools.[62] With respect to both of these issues, the Supreme Court has taken the position that the Constitution requires strict separation of church and state. In the early 1960s, the Supreme Court under Chief Justice Warren invalidated the long-standing practice of prayer and Bible reading in the public schools.[63] That position has been reaffirmed by the Supreme Court many times since then and indeed has been made more stringent.[64] For example, in 1985 the Court struck down an Alabama law that required students in public schools to observe a minute of silence each day for the purpose of prayer or meditation.[65] And in 2000, the Court struck down a public high school practice in which an elected student "chaplain" delivered a prayer over the public address system before each home football game.[66]

On the other hand, the Court has permitted states and communities to provide assistance to children in religious schools as long as it is part of a general program of assistance that benefits all schoolchildren. For example, in 1997 the Court upheld a New York City program that placed public school teachers in parochial schools for the purpose of providing federally financed remedial courses to disadvantaged students. In her opinion for the Court, Justice Sandra Day O'Connor stressed the neutrality of the remedial instruction and noted that this program could not reasonably be viewed as an endorsement of religion by the City.[67] In a similar vein, the Court in 2000 upheld Chapter 2 of the Education Consolidation and Improvement Act of 1981, under which the federal government makes grants to state and local agencies that provide materials and equipment to public and private schools, including religious schools.[68] As long as government is merely aiding the education of all children in secular subjects on a nondiscriminatory basis, the Establishment Clause is not breached.

Another "accomodationist" decision, one that sanctioned prayer in a particular public setting, was released in 2014. With its 5-4 decision in *Town of Greece v. Galloway*, the Supreme Court stated that a prayer read before the start of a town council meeting in upstate New York did not violate the Establishment Clause. Although Justice Kagan's dissenting opinion decried the prayers as "government-sponsored worship," the Court's majority opinion focused on the lack of "coercion" in this situation, meaning that such prayer did not necessarily compel citizens in attendance to alter their religious beliefs.[69] Future cases likely will assess the impact of this principle for prayer in other contexts, for the *Town of Greece v. Galloway* decision was limited to prayer in legislative settings.

The First Amendment: Freedom of Expression

The First Amendment also protects freedom of speech and freedom of the press, often referred to jointly as **freedom of expression**. One can argue that freedom of expression is the most vital freedom in a democracy, in that it permits the free flow of information between the people and their government. Certainly, the Framers of the Bill of Rights were aware of its fundamental importance, which is why the freedoms of speech and press were placed in the First Amendment. Finally, the First Amendment protects the "right of the people peaceably to assemble and petition the Government for a redress of grievances." Freedom of assembly remains an important right, and one that is often controversial, as when an extremist group such as the Ku Klux Klan stages a public rally. The freedom to petition government for a redress of grievances is no less important. Today, it is referred to as "lobbying," a principal activity of interest groups.

Legitimate Restrictions on Expression

Freedom of expression is not absolute. As Justice Oliver Wendell Holmes Jr. observed in 1919, it does not give a person the right to falsely shout "Fire" in a crowded theater.[70] Thus was born the **clear and present danger doctrine**, which marked the outer limits of First Amendment protection (see Case in Point). In 1969, the Supreme Court reformulated the clear and present danger standard by stating that speech that posed a danger of **imminent lawless action**, that is, a condition in which violence or lawbreaking is about to take place, would not be protected by the First Amendment.[71]

Expression in a public forum is also subject to reasonable **time, place, and manner regulations**, although such regulations may not be employed on a discriminatory basis or invoked only to suppress particular messages that authorities deem undesirable. A valid time, place, and manner regulation must pass the test of "intermediate scrutiny," which mandates that the regulation be "narrowly tailored" to serve the State's "significant" interests—and must also leave open ample alternative channels of communication.[72]

The Supreme Court used intermediate scrutiny in *McCullen v. Coakley*, a decision released on June 26, 2014. In this case, the Court confronted a Massachusetts law that required protestors near abortion clinics to remain outside of a 35-foot "buffer zone" surrounding the clinic. In deciding this matter, the Court found that although the notion of preserving public safety and order could amount to a "significant interest," because the law "burden[ed] more speech than necessary," it failed on the component of "narrow-tailoring." In particular, the majority opinion noted that even the peaceful distribution of literature on sidewalks would be circumscribed by the statute in question; that crystallized the reasons why this law constituted an impermissible restriction on speech.[73]

Freedom of expression does not include the right to commit libel or slander, although the Supreme Court has made it very difficult for public officials and other "public figures" to sue their detractors for **defamation**, requiring a showing of "actual malice" for such individuals to prevail.[74] **Obscenity** also is not protected by the First Amendment;[75] however, most pornography falls outside the current definition of obscenity—which relies upon "contemporary community standards,"[76] and prosecutorial efforts today focus almost exclusively on child pornography. Additionally, expressions of hatred and bigotry are protected by the First Amendment except when such expression constitutes **fighting words**, that is, threats or insults that are inherently likely to incite violence.[77] Overall, the Supreme Court's First Amendment jurisprudence is based on the premise that "debate on public issues should be uninhibited, robust, and wide-open."[78] The Court has also conferred free speech rights on corporations wishing to engage in spending on certain political advertisements,[79] although purely commercial speech may not receive the same level of protection as other forms of speech.[80]

Furthermore, the Court consistently has observed that even "offensive" speech retains protection under the First Amendment, a principle articulated in *Snyder v. Phelps* (2011). In this case, the majority opinion upheld the rights of Westboro, Kansas, Baptist Church members to hold protests 1,000 feet away from funerals for American soldiers. The church has drawn widespread attention for the inflammatory messages its members convey at military funerals around the United States. Typically, church members bring signs to these funerals and stand on a public sidewalk at a distance from the actual funeral itself; the signs usually levy criticisms at the military, homosexuals, or the country as a whole. The family of one fallen solider, Matthew Snyder, brought suit against the church for civil damages.

Ultimately, although many find Westboro's content to be highly offensive, Justice Roberts' majority opinion in *Snyder v. Phelps* relied on the First Amendment in insulating church members from the civil suit. In particular, Roberts stated that, "Speech is powerful. It can stir people to action, move them to tears of both joy and sorrow and—as it did here—inflict great pain. On the facts before us, we cannot react to that pain by punishing the speaker. As a nation, we have chosen a different course—to protect even hurtful speech on public issues to ensure that we do not stifle public debate."

Justice Alito's dissent, however, responded with the assertion that, "Our profound national commitment to free and open debate is not a license for the vicious verbal assault that occurred in this case," and he further lambasted the church members' messages as "verbal attacks that make no contribution to public debate."[81]

In the end, forging a balance between the concerns articulated in these competing opinions lies at the core of First Amendment "freedom of expression" jurisprudence. Additional freedom of speech cases are discussed in Chapter 4.

CASE IN POINT

ESTABLISHMENT OF THE CLEAR AND PRESENT DANGER DOCTRINE
Schenck v. United States
United States Supreme Court
249 U.S. 47, 39 S. Ct. 247, 63 L. Ed. 470 (1919)

Charles T. Schenck, general secretary of the Socialist Party, was convicted under the Espionage Act of 1917 for interfering with military recruitment by conspiring to print and circulate leaflets "to men who had been called and accepted for military service." The leaflets urged resistance to the draft on the ground that it violated the Thirteenth Amendment of the Constitution. Although sharply critical of the war effort, the Socialists' message was confined to the advocacy of peaceful measures such as petition for repeal of the draft. No disruption or actual draft resistance occurred as a result of Schenck's efforts; however, the United States Supreme

Court unanimously upheld his conviction on the ground that speech intended to obstruct the war effort was not entitled to constitutional protection. Writing for the Court, Justice Oliver Wendell Holmes Jr. reasoned that "the character of every act depends upon the circumstances in which it is done. The most stringent protection of free speech would not protect a man in falsely shouting fire in a theater, and causing a panic. . . . The question in every case is whether the words used are used in such circumstances and are of such a nature as to create a clear and present danger that they will bring about the substantive evils that Congress has a right to prevent."

The Supreme Court also has established a body of precedent related to school speech. In a 1969 case, the Court overturned the suspensions of three students who were punished for wearing black armbands to an Iowa school in protest of the Vietnam War. The majority opinion noted that students do not "shed their constitutional rights at the schoolhouse gates."[82] However, other cases have upheld the power of school principals who wish to suppress certain forms of student speech. For example, in a 1988 decision, the Court upheld a principal's decision to censor a story about divorce and teen pregnancy written for a school newspaper.[83] In 2007, the Court afforded leeway to a school principal to suspend a student for displaying a sign that read "BONG HITS 4 JESUS" at an off-campus, school-sponsored function.[84] In that case, the Court noted that schools could exercise control over speech in keeping with the furtherance of an "important—indeed, perhaps compelling interest"—provided the censorship was "narrowly-tailored" to furthering this interest.

The Prior Restraint Doctrine
One of the reasons that the Framers of the Bill of Rights saw the need for the First Amendment was that the English common law provided little protection to personal expression. However, one common law doctrine has been grafted onto the First Amendment through judicial interpretation: the rule against **prior restraint**. The concept was first discussed by the Supreme Court in 1931 in a case involving a dispute over

publication of a newspaper.[85] The case involved a state law that permitted public officials to seek an injunction to stop publication of any "malicious, scandalous and defamatory newspaper, magazine or other periodical." Writing for the Court, Chief Justice Charles Evans Hughes characterized this law as "the essence of censorship" and declared it unconstitutional. Chief Justice Hughes acknowledged that the rule against prior restraint would not, for example, prevent government in time of war from pro-hibiting publication of "the sailing dates of transports or the number and location of troops." In these and related situations, national security interests are almost certain to prevail over freedom of the press. But where is the line to be drawn? How far can the "national security" justification be extended in suppressing publication?

The Court revisited the question of prior restraint on the press in the much-her-alded Pentagon Papers case of 1971.[86] Here, the federal government attempted to prevent the *New York Times* and the *Washington Post* from publishing excerpts from a classified study entitled "History of U.S. Decision-Making Process on Vietnam Policy," better known as the Pentagon Papers. By a 6-3 vote, the Supreme Court held that the government's effort to block publication of this material amounted to an unconstitutional prior restraint. The majority was simply not convinced that such publication—several years after the events and decisions discussed in the Pentagon papers—constituted a significant threat to national security.

Freedom of Association

The First Amendment makes no mention of the right to associate freely with people of one's own choosing, but the courts have recognized that this right is implicit in the First Amendment. In recent years, this implicit **freedom of association** has come into con-flict with government efforts to eliminate various forms of social discrimination. In one case, a unanimous Supreme Court found that Minnesota's interest in eradicating sex discrimination was sufficiently compelling to justify a decision of its human rights commission requiring local chapters of the Jaycees to admit women. The Court rejected the Jaycees' argument that their First Amendment rights were being violated.[87] However, in June 2000, the Court ruled that the Boy Scouts of America had a constitutional right to prohibit openly gay men from serving as scout leaders. This controversial ruling came in a case where the New Jersey courts had prohibited the Scouts from engaging in such discrimination under that state's civil rights laws.[88] The 5-4 decision by the Supreme Court was denounced by leaders of the gay rights move-ment but hailed by those who wish to see private organizations protected from govern-mental intrusion.

The Second Amendment: The Right to Keep and Bear Arms

The Framers of the Bill of Rights did not see the need for the United States to maintain a standing army. Rather, they believed that all adult male citizens should be prepared to serve in the militia when the need arose. Therefore, they provided in the Second Amendment that "[a] well-regulated Militia, being necessary to the security of a free state, the right of the people to keep and bear arms shall not be infringed." Most Americans believe that the Constitution protects their **right to keep and bear arms**.

Yet the Second Amendment refers not only to the keeping and bearing of arms but also to the need for a "well-regulated militia." In 1875, the Supreme Court held that the Second Amendment guaranteed states the right to maintain militias but did not guarantee to individuals the right to possess guns.[89] Accordingly, in the modern era the Court uniformly upheld federal **gun control legislation**.[90] However, in a landmark ruling in June 2008, the Court reversed course and declared that the Second Amendment does protect a personal right to possess a firearm for "traditionally lawful purposes" irrespective of one's service in any militia.[91] In the same case, the Court declared unconstitutional a District of Columbia ordinance effectively prohibiting the possession of handguns, even in the home. Writing for a sharply divided Court, Justice Antonin Scalia observed:

> "Undoubtedly some think that the Second Amendment is outmoded in a society where our standing army is the pride of our Nation, where well-trained police forces provide personal security, and where gun violence is a serious problem. That is perhaps debatable, but what is not debatable is that it is not the role of this Court to pronounce the Second Amendment extinct."[92]

Even so, Justice Scalia was also quick to note that the Court's decision did not render invalid most of the nation's gun control laws, saying that "nothing in our opinion should be taken to cast doubt on longstanding prohibitions on the possession of firearms by felons and the mentally ill, or laws forbidding the carrying of firearms in sensitive places such as schools and government buildings, or laws imposing conditions and qualifications on the commercial sale of arms."[93] The Court would reinforce these ideas in a 2010 case, *McDonald v. Chicago*, that made Second Amendment rights applicable in the states.[94] Although the *Heller* and *McDonald* cases spoke directly to a right to possess handguns in the home, matters such as the possession of other types of weapons and the carrying of weapons outside the home remain for future cases.

The Third Amendment: Subordination of the Military

The Third Amendment prohibits military authorities from quartering troops in citizens' homes without their consent. This was a matter of serious concern to the Founders, because English troops had been forcibly billeted in colonists' homes during the Revolutionary War. Today, the Third Amendment is little more than a historical curiosity, since it has not been the subject of any significant discussion. The Third Amendment, however, reflects an important principle of American government: the military is subordinate to civilian authority.

The Fourth Amendment: Prohibition against Unreasonable Searches and Seizures

One of the colonists' principal grievances against the Crown was that the King's agents had unbridled powers of search and seizure. The Fourth Amendment addressed this concern by stating that "[t]he right of the people to be secure in their persons, houses, papers, and effects, against unreasonable searches and seizures, shall not be violated, and no Warrants shall issue, but upon probable cause, supported by Oath or affirmation, and particularly describing the place to be searched, and the persons or things to be seized." The Fourth Amendment thus protects citizens from **unreasonable searches and seizures** conducted by police and other government agents. The Fourth Amendment remains extremely important today, especially in light of the pervasiveness of crime and the national war on drugs. In the late twentieth century, the Fourth Amendment was the source of numerous important Supreme Court decisions that generated a tremendous and complex body of legal doctrine. Under Chief Justice Earl Warren, the thrust of the Court's Fourth Amendment jurisprudence was to protect the rights of suspects and defendants. For example, in *Mapp v. Ohio* (1961), the Court held that evidence obtained in violation of the Fourth Amendment could not be used in state criminal prosecutions. And in *Katz v. United States* (1967), the Court expanded the scope of Fourth Amendment protection to include wiretapping.[95] The succeeding Burger and Rehnquist Courts were decidedly more conservative in this area, facilitating police efforts to ferret out crime. (For additional discussion, see Chapter 10.)

The Fifth Amendment: Rights of the Accused

The Fifth Amendment contains a number of important provisions involving the rights of persons accused of crime. It requires the federal government to obtain an **indictment** from a **grand jury** before trying someone for a major crime. It also prohibits **double jeopardy**, that is, being tried twice for the same offense. Additionally, the Fifth Amendment protects persons against **compulsory self-incrimination**, which is what is commonly meant by the phrase "taking the Fifth." (For additional discussion, see Chapter 10.)

The Fifth Amendment: Property Rights and Due Process

The Fifth Amendment also protects people against arbitrary use of **eminent domain**, the power of government to take private property for public use. In 2005, the Supreme Court sanctioned the taking of private property even by private developers, as long as such development served a "public purpose." However, the Just Compensation Clause[96] forbids government from taking private property without paying **just compensation** to the owner. Finally, the Fifth Amendment prohibits the federal government from depriving persons of life, liberty, or property without **due process of law**. A virtually identical clause is found in the Fourteenth Amendment, which applies specifically to the states. The Due Process Clauses have implications both for civil and criminal cases, as well as for a variety of relationships between citizen and government. Due process is the broadest and most basic protection afforded by the Constitution.

Protection against Arbitrary Use of Eminent Domain
As noted above, the power of government to take private property for public use is known as eminent domain. The Takings Clause of the Fifth Amendment specifically protects citizens against whom this power is used by requiring that property owners be justly compensated for such takings. Moreover, the Due Process Clause of the Fifth

Amendment permits owners to challenge in court takings of their property. Protection of private property was a major goal of the Framers of the Constitution. The Bill of Rights added additional protections in this area. Today, questions of governmental authority to take or even regulate private property continue to be important issues of law.

The Sixth Amendment: Rights of the Accused

The Sixth Amendment is concerned exclusively with the **rights of the accused**. It requires, among other things, that people accused of crimes be provided a "speedy and public trial, by an impartial jury. . . ." The right of **trial by jury** is one of the most cherished rights in the Anglo-American tradition, predating Magna Carta of 1215. The Sixth Amendment also grants defendants the right to confront, or cross-examine, witnesses for the prosecution and the right to have **compulsory process** (the power of subpoena) to require favorable witnesses to appear in court. Significantly, considering the incredible complexity of the criminal law, the Sixth Amendment guarantees that accused persons have the "Assistance of Counsel" for their defense. The Supreme Court has regarded the **right to counsel** as crucial to a fair trial and since 1963 has held that defendants charged with a crime who face jail or imprisonment and who are unable to afford private counsel must be afforded counsel at public expense.[97]

Protecting citizens against crime is one of the fundamental obligations of government. In the United States, however, government must perform this function while respecting the constitutional rights of individuals. Courts of law are constantly trying to balance the interest of society in crime control with the rights of individuals accused or convicted of crimes. Given the prevalent fear of crime in contemporary America, the balance can be difficult to maintain. For an extensive discussion of the rights of persons accused or convicted of crimes, see Chapter 10.

The Seventh Amendment: The Right to a Jury Trial in Civil Suits

The Seventh Amendment guarantees the right to a jury trial in federal civil suits "at common law" where the amount at issue exceeds twenty dollars. Originally, it was widely assumed that the Seventh Amendment required jury trials only in traditional common law cases, for example, actions for libel, wrongful death, and trespass. But over the years, the Supreme Court expanded the scope of the Seventh Amendment to encompass civil suits seeking enforcement of statutory rights.[98] However, the Seventh Amendment does not apply to the adjudication of certain issues by administrative or regulatory agencies.[99] Although at common law a jury in a civil trial consisted of twelve jurors, the Supreme Court has approved the use of six-person juries in civil cases.[100]

The Eighth Amendment: Prohibitions against Excessive Bail, Excessive Fines, and Cruel and Unusual Punishments

The Eighth Amendment protects persons accused of federal crimes from being required to post **excessive bail** to secure **pretrial release**. The Supreme Court held that bail is excessive if it is higher than is reasonably necessary to ensure a defendant's appearance for trial.[101] But it has also said that the Eighth Amendment does not require that defendants be released on bail, only that, if the court grants bail, it must not be "excessive."[102]

The Eighth Amendment also forbids the imposition of **excessive fines**. Recently, the Supreme Court held that this prohibition also applies to forfeitures of property used in illicit activities. Federal law allows the government to sue to recover property used to facilitate criminal offenses. The Court ruled that **forfeitures**, although they are not technically criminal proceedings, are subject to the Excessive Fines Clause of the Eighth Amendment.[103]

Finally, the Eighth Amendment prohibits the infliction of **cruel and unusual punishments** on persons convicted of crimes. Originally designed to proscribe torture, the Cruel and Unusual Punishments Clause now figures prominently in the ongoing national debate over the **death penalty**.[104] The Supreme Court has said that the Cruel and Unusual Punishments Clause "must draw its meaning from the evolving standards of decency that mark the progress of a maturing society."[105] (For additional discussion, see Chapter 10.)

The Ninth Amendment: Rights Reserved to the People

The Ninth Amendment was included in the Bill of Rights as a solution to a problem raised by James Madison; namely, that the specification of particular liberties might suggest that individuals possessed only those specified. The Ninth Amendment makes it clear that individuals retain a reservoir of rights and liberties beyond those listed in the Constitution by stating that "[t]he enumeration in the Constitution, of certain rights, shall not be construed to deny or disparage others retained by the people." This amendment reflects the dominant thinking of late eighteenth-century America: individual rights precede and transcend the power of government; individuals possess all rights except those that have been surrendered to government for the protection of the public good.

Although they have seldom relied explicitly on the Ninth Amendment, federal and state courts have over the years recognized a number of rights that Americans take for granted but that are not specifically enumerated in the Constitution. The right to marry, to determine how one's children are to be reared and educated, to choose one's occupation, to start a business, to travel freely across state lines, to sue in the courts, and to be presumed innocent of a crime until proven guilty are all examples of individual rights that have been recognized as "constitutional," despite their absence from the text of the Constitution. Quite often these rights have been recognized under the broad Due Process Clauses of the Fifth and Fourteenth Amendments.

The Fourteenth Amendment

Arguably, the most important amendment to the Constitution outside the Bill of Rights is the Fourteenth Amendment. Ratified in 1868, the principal objective of the Fourteenth Amendment was to protect the civil rights and liberties of African-Americans. Although slavery had been formally abolished by the Thirteenth Amendment, ratified in 1865, questions remained about the legal status of the former slaves. In *Dred Scott v.*

Sandford (1857),[106] the Supreme Court had not only defended the institution of slavery but also indicated that blacks were not citizens of the United States and possessed "no rights or privileges but such as those who held the power and the Government might choose to grant them." Section 1 of the Fourteenth Amendment made clear that *Dred Scott* was no longer the law of the land:

> All persons born or naturalized in the United States, and subject to the jurisdiction thereof, are citizens of the United States and of the State wherein they reside. No state shall make or enforce any law which shall abridge the privileges or immunities of citizens of the United States; nor shall any State deprive any person of life, liberty, or property, without due process of law; nor deny to any person within its jurisdiction the equal protection of the laws.

Due Process of Law

The Fourteenth Amendment prohibits states from depriving persons within their jurisdiction of life, liberty, or property without due process of law. In its most generic sense, due process refers to the exercise of governmental power under the rule of law with due regard for the rights and interests of individuals. The concept of procedural due process embraces government's obligation to provide **fair notice** and a **fair hearing** to individuals before depriving them of "life, liberty or property." Thus, for example, in 1967 the Supreme Court relied on the Due Process Clause of the Fourteenth Amendment in a landmark decision revolutionizing the juvenile justice system, holding that juveniles must be afforded certain procedural protections before they can be judged "delinquent" and sent to a reformatory.[107] Similarly, the Supreme Court has invoked due process to say that police may not use methods that "shock the conscience" in attempting to gather evidence of criminal wrongdoing.[108]

Historically, the concept of due process was extremely important in defending private property rights from government regulation. More recently, the courts have recognized government employment and government benefits as "property interests" subject to the requirements of due process. Thus, while there is no constitutional right to receive welfare assistance, government may not terminate a person's welfare benefits without observing certain procedural safeguards.[109]

Incorporation of the Bill of Rights

One of the most important consequences of the Fourteenth Amendment has been to make the Bill of Rights applicable to the states. Although it is unclear whether the Framers of the Fourteenth Amendment intended this result, the Supreme Court has interpreted the Due Process Clause to this effect. In 1897, the Supreme Court held that the Fifth Amendment's Just Compensation Clause is incorporated within the concept of due process and thereby enforceable against the states.[110] In 1937, the Court said that those protections of the Bill of Rights that are essential to "a scheme of ordered liberty" are enforceable against the states via the Fourteenth Amendment.[111] Over the years, the Court used this **doctrine of incorporation** to apply most of the other provisions of the Bill of Rights to the states.[112] This is one of the principal reasons that the federal courts have assumed something of a supervisory role with regard to the state and local governments.

The most recent instance of incorporation came in 2010, when the Supreme Court took the step of incorporating the Second Amendment.[113] The Court centered its decision around the notion of keeping a handgun in the home for the purpose of self-defense. In effect, the incorporation of the Second Amendment confers "fundamental right" status on the Second Amendment, and essentially forces states to justify restrictions on the right to bear arms with a "compelling interest" that is "narrowly-tailored."

Levels of Judicial Scrutiny

The Supreme Court has recognized certain rights as "fundamental." Courts typically afford fundamental rights the protection of a legal test called "strict scrutiny." Strict scrutiny requires that a government restriction on individual liberties be justified by a compelling interest, and that it also be narrowly tailored. Narrow tailoring can best be

SIDEBAR

Cases Incorporating Provisions of the Bill of Rights into the Fourteenth Amendment

Amendment	Clause	Case	Year
1st	Establishment of Religion	*Everson v. Bd of Education*	1947
1st	Free Exercise of Religion	*Cantwell v. Connecticut*	1940
1st	Freedom of Speech	*Gitlow v. New York*	1925
1st	Freedom of the Press	*Near v. Minnesota*	1931
1st	Freedom of Assembly	*DeJonge v. Oregon*	1937
1st	Petition for Redress of Grievances	*Edwards v. South Carolina*	1963
2nd	Right to Bear Arms	*McDonald v. Chicago*	2010
4th	Unreasonable Search and Seizure	*Wolf v. Colorado*	1949

Amendment	Clause	Case	Year
5th	Double Jeopardy	*Benton v. Maryland*	1969
5th	Self-Incrimination	*Malloy v. Hogan*	1964
5th	Just Compensation	*Chicago, B & Q RR v. Chicago*	1897
6th	Right to Speedy Trial	*Klopfer v. North Carolina*	1967
6th	Right to Public Trial	*In re Oliver*	1948
6th	Right to Trial by Impartial Jury	*Duncan v. Louisiana*	1968
6th	Right to Confront Witnesses	*Pointer v. Texas*	1965
6th	Right to Compulsory Process	*Washington v. Texas*	1967
6th	Right to Counsel	*Gideon v. Wainwright*	1963
8th	Cruel and Unusual Punishment	*Robinson v. California*	1962

described as a close fit between the government action and the purported compelling interest. Rights that are not considered "fundamental" are typically protected less vigorously using something called the "rational basis test," which merely requires the government to show a "legitimate" interest that is rationally related to the action taken. In short, the rational basis test tilts in favor of the government, while strict scrutiny tilts in favor of the individual. (A third, "middle ground" test, called "intermediate scrutiny," applies to the "Time-Place-Manner" restrictions discussed earlier.)

Substantive Due Process

In addition to providing procedural protections against arbitrary and capricious government action, due process has been held to impose substantive limits on government policies as well. Under the concept of **substantive due process**, government is barred from enforcing policies that are irrational, unfair, unreasonable, or unjust, even if such policies do not run counter to other specific constitutional prohibitions. For almost fifty years (roughly 1890 to 1937), the Supreme Court relied on substantive due process to invalidate a variety of state and federal laws regulating aspects of economic life. For example, in the leading case of the era, *Lochner v. New York* (1905),[114] the Court struck down a state law setting maximum working hours in bakeries. The Court held that the restriction violated both the employer's and the employee's liberty of contract, a right not specifically enumerated in the Constitution but held to be embraced within the substantive prohibitions of the Due Process Clause of the Fourteenth Amendment. While the liberty of contract aspect of substantive due process has been repudiated by the modern Supreme Court, substantive due process lives on under the rubric of the constitutional **right of privacy**.

The Right of Privacy

First recognized in *Griswold v. Connecticut* (1965),[115] the right of privacy is not found in any specific provision of the Bill of Rights. Nevertheless, the Supreme Court has held that privacy is an un-enumerated "fundamental right" enforceable against the state

SIDEBAR

Levels Of Judicial Scrutiny

Test	Required State Interest	Degree of Fit
Strict Scrutiny	Compelling Interest	Narrow Tailoring
Intermediate Scrutiny	Significant Interest	Narrow Tailoring + Ample Alternatives
Rational Basis Test	Legitimate Interest	Rational Relationship

governments via the Due Process Clause of the Fourteenth Amendment. In *Griswold*, the right of privacy was invoked to invalidate a state law prohibiting the use of birth control devices. Eight years later, in *Roe v. Wade* (1973),[116] the right of privacy was held to be broad enough to include a woman's decision to have an abortion, touching off a constitutional debate that continues to rage. The *Roe* decision remains one of the most hotly debated decisions of the modern Supreme Court. Although the Court has reaffirmed its *Roe* decision on several occasions,[117] it has relaxed somewhat the standard by which it judges whether particular regulations of abortion violate a woman's constitutional rights.[118] And in 2007, the Court upheld a federal statute banning a controversial procedure known colloquially as "partial-birth abortion."[119] (Abortion and other reproductive issues are discussed more fully in Chapter 8.)

The right of privacy has been applied to a number of other controversial questions of social policy. For example, the Supreme Court has struck down state laws prohibiting private homosexual activity between consenting adults.[120] The Court also has recognized that terminally ill patients have a **right to die**, that is, to refuse artificial means of prolonging life.[121] But it has refused to extend the right to encompass physician-assisted suicide.[122] (Legal issues involving refusal of medical treatment are discussed more fully in Chapter 8.)

Earl Warren believed that the most important decisions rendered by the Supreme Court during his tenure as Chief Justice were those in which the Court used the Equal

CASE IN POINT

ABORTION AS A CONSTITUTIONAL RIGHT
Roe v. Wade
United States Supreme Court
410 U.S. 113, 93 S. Ct. 705, 35 L. Ed. 2d 147 (1973)

Norma McCorvey, a.k.a. Jane Roe, was a 25-year-old unmarried Texas woman who was faced with an unwanted pregnancy. Because abortion was illegal in Texas, Roe brought suit in federal court against district attorney Henry Wade to challenge the constitutionality of the state's anti-abortion statute. The District Court declared the Texas law unconstitutional but refused to issue an injunction barring its enforcement. On appeal, the Supreme Court handed down a 7-2 decision striking down the Texas law. Justice Harry Blackmun wrote the majority opinion, concluding that the right of privacy was broad enough to encompass a woman's decision to terminate her pregnancy. However, Blackmun noted, "the right [to abortion] is not unqualified and must be considered against important state interests...." Although a fetus was not, in the Court's view, a "person" within the language of the Constitution, states would be permitted (except in cases where the mother's life was endangered by carrying the fetus to term) to ban abortion after "viability" (that point in gestation where the fetus is capable of surviving outside the mother's womb). Dissenting, Justice Rehnquist wrote that "the fact that a majority of the States ... have had restrictions on abortion for at least a century is a strong indication ... that the right to an abortion is not so rooted in the traditions and conscience of our people to be ranked as fundamental." Although the Supreme Court has reaffirmed *Roe v. Wade* several times, most recently in 2000,[123] the abortion issue remains the most divisive constitutional question of our age.

Protection Clause to require **reapportionment** of state legislatures. For many years, there had been wide population disparities among legislative districts, which meant that rural districts had disproportionate influence over state legislatures. In 1964, the Supreme Court held that these districts had to be reapportioned on the principle of "one person, one vote."[124] American politics changed dramatically as a result.

The Fourteenth Amendment prohibits **state-sponsored discrimination**. Discrimination by private actors is beyond the reach of the Equal Protection Clause.[125] Of course, private discrimination can be addressed by federal, state, and local civil rights legislation. The best known example of this is Title II of the Civil Rights Act of 1964, which prohibits racial discrimination by privately owned places of public accommodation (businesses that open their doors to the general public) (see Chapter 11).

Equal Protection of the Laws

One of the philosophical foundations of American democracy is the idea that all individuals are equal before the law. This ideal is expressed both in the Declaration of Independence and in the Equal Protection Clause of the Fourteenth Amendment, which provides that no state shall "deny to any person within its jurisdiction the **equal protection of the laws**." The Equal Protection Clause prohibits states from denying any person or class of persons the same protection and rights that the law extends to other similarly situated persons or classes of persons.

In the late nineteenth century, the Supreme Court declared that the word "person" in the Equal Protection Clause included corporations.[126] Occasionally, the Clause was employed as a basis for invalidating discriminatory business regulation.[127] In the modern era, the federal courts have relied heavily on the Equal Protection Clause of Section 1 in advancing the civil rights of African-Americans and other minority groups. The "case of the century," *Brown v. Board of Education* (1954),[128] in which the Supreme Court abolished racial segregation in the public schools, was based squarely on the Equal Protection Clause.

Like other rights guaranteed by the post–Civil War Amendments, the Equal Protection Clause was motivated in large part by a desire to protect the civil rights of African-Americans recently freed from slavery. However, the text of the Clause makes no mention of race; rather, it refers to any person within the jurisdiction of a state. Although in 1873 the Supreme Court attempted to limit the scope of the Equal Protection Clause to discrimination claims brought by African-Americans,[129] the Clause has been developed into a broad prohibition against unreasonable governmental discrimination directed at any identifiable group. In the 1970s, 1980s, and 1990s, advocates for women's rights successfully used the Equal Protection Clause to combat sex discrimination.[130] More recently, gay rights activists have employed the Equal Protection Clause to attack discrimination based on sexual orientation.[131]

Today, one of the most difficult equal protection problems involves the controversial policy of **affirmative action**, a broad term referring to a variety of efforts designed to assist women and minority groups in employment, government contracting, and higher education. Affirmative action has been a major source of litigation, as it is often

CASE IN POINT

IS AN ALL-MALE STATE MILITARY ACADEMY CONSTITUTIONAL?
United States v. Virginia
United States Supreme Court
518 U.S. 515, 116 S. Ct. 2264, 135 L. Ed. 2d 735 (1996)

In this widely publicized decision, the U.S. Supreme Court struck down the male-only admissions policy of the Virginia Military Institute (VMI), a public educational institution. The lawsuit had been brought by the Justice Department, after a complaint was filed by a female high school student who wanted to go to VMI but was barred from doing so by the Institute's absolute prohibition against admitting women. In a 7-1 decision, the Supreme Court, speaking through Justice Ginsburg, ruled that the state of Virginia had "fallen far short of establishing the 'exceedingly persuasive justification,' that must be the solid base for any gender-defined classification...." In a scathing dissent, Justice Scalia questioned the majority's "amorphous 'exceedingly persuasive justification' phrase" and lamented the fact that the Court had, in his view, "shut down an institution that has served the people of the commonwealth of Virginia with pride and distinction for over a century and a half." He ended by observing that "I do not think any of us, women included, will be better off for its destruction."

characterized by its critics as "reverse discrimination." In the 1970s, the Supreme Court sought middle ground in the affirmative action area, approving the basic concept but rejecting the policy of using numerical quotas.[132] In the 1990s, the Court took a more negative view of affirmative action but stopped short of repudiating the concept altogether.[133] In recent years, the Court has maintained support for the concept but has continued to strictly scrutinize its application. For example, in 2003 the Court upheld the use of race as one of many criteria to be used to determine who gets into law schools but on the same day struck down an affirmative action policy that the Court believed gave too much weight to race in the undergraduate admissions process.[134]

Voting Rights

While the Fourteenth Amendment is the broadest, and most important, source of protection for civil rights and liberties outside the Bill of Rights, a number of other constitutional amendments address specific civil rights issues. These Amendments (Fifteenth, Nineteenth, Twenty-Fourth, and Twenty-Sixth) focus on the **right to vote**, which is arguably the most essential right in a democracy. The original Constitution left the matter of voting rights to the states. In 1787, voting in the United States was confined for the most part to "freeholders," that is, white male landowners above the age of twenty-one. As our society has become progressively more democratic, the Constitution has been amended to make the franchise more inclusive. Moreover, Congress has enacted legislation to protect access to registration and voting, most significantly the Voting Rights Act of 1965 (see Chapter 11).

CONCLUSION

After the new Americans won their freedom, the Articles of Confederation that attempted to tie together the citizens of the new American states proved unworkable. The Articles were thus replaced by the United States Constitution, which created a workable framework that enabled a loosely knit group of states to become a nation. The Framers incorporated into the Constitution a process for orderly, albeit difficult, amendment. In allocating powers, the Framers painted with a broad brush. Congress and the President have the ability to make and execute laws. The Supreme Court exercises the power to interpret the constitutional aspects of government in light of the vast social, economic, and political differences that have evolved in our society since ratification of the Constitution in 1789. Thus, the Constitution has provided an enduring foundation for the American political system for more than two centuries.

Rather than becoming a mere document to be outdated by generations that followed its ratification, the new Constitution was promptly followed by a Bill of Rights. The concepts of separation of powers, judicial independence, and federalism have bolstered the enduring quality of the Constitution. But the Constitution became the bulwark of civil liberties through adoption of the Bill of Rights. While designed to protect the rights and liberties of citizens from actions of the federal government, over time these guarantees largely have been applied against the states as well.

Today, the constitutional makeup embraces not only the original constitution and the Bill of Rights, but significantly, the Fourteenth Amendment, which prohibits states from depriving any citizen of life, liberty, or property without due process of law or from denying any citizen the equal protection of the laws. Through the Constitution, as amended, and as interpreted, Americans have become national citizens in a sovereign nation with fifty sovereign states that has expanded from a framework for government to include a charter for a democracy to protect the rights and liberties of the citizens of the new republic.

SUMMARY OF KEY CONCEPTS

In this chapter, we have endeavored to portray the significance of the U.S. Constitution, the Bill of Rights, and later amendments. Central to comprehending constitutional law is an understanding of how the Supreme Court developed the doctrine of judicial review and how the exercise of interpretive powers by the courts has given continued viability to the Constitution. In interpreting the Constitution, the Supreme Court has generally followed the doctrine of precedent, at times demonstrating judicial restraint while at other times displaying judicial activism.

The Constitution stands as the bedrock for operation of the government. Its meaning has been expanded not only through the processes of amendment and judicial interpretation but also through Congress's exercise of its enumerated and implied powers. Through judicial deference to the exercise of implied powers, the legislative branch is enabled to enact laws providing for the economic and social development of the Nation.

Two characteristics define the basic structure of American constitutional government. First, the principle of separation of powers and related checks and balances are essential to the maintenance of limited government and ultimately to individual liberty. Second, the concept of federalism allows the power to govern to be shared between the national and the state and local governments.

A variety of constitutional provisions protect civil rights and liberties in the United States. Basic are constitutional guarantees of the writ of habeas corpus, the prohibitions against ex post facto laws and bills of attainder, and the clause that prevents impairment of contracts. But to most Americans, the guarantees of the Bill of Rights characterize freedom in everyday life in America. These include the freedom of expression and religion, protections against unreasonable searches and seizures, the many rights afforded an accused, the right to trial by jury, and the right to just compensation when private property is taken for public use.

In contemporary America, the Supreme Court has amplified these specifically defined rights by developing a right of privacy and by broadly interpreting provisions of the Fourteenth Amendment that guarantee all citizens "due process of law" and "equal protection of the laws." We will discuss these protections further, but the student who grasps these basic concepts of constitutional law at this point will better understand the American legal system as developed in later chapters.

FOR FURTHER READING

Abraham, Henry J., and Barbara A. Perry, *Freedom and the Court: Civil Rights and Liberties in the United States* (8th ed., University Press of Kansas 2003).

Amar, Akhil Reed, *The Bill of Rights: Creation and Reconstruction* (Yale University Press 1998).

Berger, Raoul, *Government by Judiciary: The Transformation of the Fourteenth Amendment* (Harvard University Press 1977).

Carter, Lief H., *Contemporary Constitutional Lawmaking: The Supreme Court and the Art of Politics* (Pergamon Press 1985).

Ely, John Hart, *War and Responsibility: Constitutional Lessons of Vietnam and Its Aftermath* (Harvard University Press 1993).

Fisher, Louis, *The Politics of Shared Power: Congress and the Executive* (Congressional Quarterly Press 1987).

Irons, Peter, *May It Please the Court: The First Amendment* (The New Press 1997).

Kelly, Alfred H., Winfred A. Harbison, and Herman Belz, *The American Constitution: Its Origins and Development* (7th ed., 2 vols., Norton 1991).

McDonald, Forrest, *Novus Ordo Seclorum: The Intellectual Origins of the Constitution* (University of Kansas Press 1985).

Swisher, Carl Brent, *American Constitutional Development* (2d ed., Houghton-Mifflin 1954).

QUESTIONS FOR THOUGHT AND DISCUSSION

1. What is judicial review and how did it become a part of our constitutional fabric?

2. To what extent, if at all, can Congress restrict the jurisdiction of the U.S. Supreme Court?

3. What process must be followed before an amendment to the U.S. Constitution can become effective?

4. How has the Supreme Court's 1819 decision in *McCulloch v. Maryland* affected the lawmaking role of Congress?

5. Explain the constitutional principle of federalism. How has this principle affected governmental policymaking over the last two centuries?

6. What are the two prongs of the First Amendment in relation to freedom of religion? Give an example of state action that would likely violate each of these proscriptions.

7. Do you think the Eighth Amendment to the U.S. Constitution provides a basis for the Supreme Court to conclude that in our contemporary society death by electrocution constitutes a "cruel and unusual punishment"? Why or why not?

8. What is the basis of the authors' statement that "the most important amendment to the Constitution outside the Bill of Rights is the Fourteenth Amendment"? How has the Supreme Court expanded the role of the Fourteenth Amendment?

9. What are the two basic requirements of procedural due process of law?

10. What is meant by "substantive due process of law?" Give an example.

KEY TERMS

affirmative action	excessive fines	power of the purse
Articles of Confederation	executive power	power to investigate
Ashwander rules	fair hearing	precedent
Bill of Rights	fair notice	presumption of constitutionality
bills of attainder	federalism	pretrial release
checks and balances	fighting words	prior restraint
clear and present danger doctrine	forfeitures	reapportionment
coercive federalism	freedom of association	right of privacy
commander-in-chief	freedom of expression	right to counsel
compulsory process	grand jury	right to die
compulsory self-incrimination	gun control legislation	right to keep and bear arms
cooperative federalism	habeas corpus	right to vote
cruel and unusual punishments	imminent lawless action	rights of the accused
death penalty	impeachment	separation of church and state
defamation	implied powers	separation of powers
doctrine of incorporation	independent counsel	standing
doctrine of original intent	indictment	*stare decisis*
double jeopardy	intentions of the Framers	state-sponsored discrimination
dual federalism	judicial activism	strict judicial scrutiny
due process of law	judicial review	substantive due process
eminent domain	judicial self-restraint	time, place, and manner regulations
enumerated powers	just compensation	treason
equal protection of the laws	the living Constitution	trial by jury
ex post facto laws	obscenity	unitary system
excessive bail	oversight	unreasonable searches and seizures

ENDNOTES

1. *Marbury v. Madison*, 5 U.S. 137, 2 L. Ed. 60 (1803).
2. *The Prize Cases*, 67 U.S. 635, 17 L. Ed. 459 (1863).
3. *Fletcher v. Peck*, 10 U.S. 87, 3 L. Ed. 162 (1810).
4. *Payne v. Tennessee*, 501 U.S. 808, 827-828, 111 S. Ct. 2597, 2609-2610, 115 L. Ed. 2d 720, 737 (1991).
5. *Plessy v. Ferguson*, 163 U.S. 537, 16 S. Ct. 1138, 41 L. Ed. 256 (1896).
6. *Brown v. Board of Educ.*, 347 U.S. 483, 74 S. Ct. 686, 98 L. Ed. 873 (1954).
7. *Korematsu v. United States*, 323 U.S. 214, 65 S. Ct. 193, 89 L. Ed. 194 (1944).
8. *Shapiro v. Thompson*, 394 U.S. 618, 89 S. Ct. 1322, 22 L. Ed. 2d 600 (1969).
9. *Frothingham v. Mellon*, 262 U.S. 447, 43 S. Ct. 597, 67 L. Ed. 1098 (1923).
10. *See, e.g., Texas v. Johnson*, 491 U.S. 397, 109 S. Ct. 2533, 105 L. Ed. 2d 342 (1989).
11. *Roe v. Wade*, 410 U.S. 113, 93 S. Ct. 705, 35 L. Ed. 2d 147 (1973).
12. *Ashwander v. Tennessee Valley Auth.*, 297 U.S. 288, 56 S. Ct. 466, 80 L. Ed. 688 (1936).
13. 74 U.S. 506, 19 L. Ed. 264 (1869).
14. In this regard, it is instructive to compare *Pennsylvania v. Nelson*, 350 U.S. 497, 76 S. Ct. 477, 100 L. Ed. 640 (1956), and *Watkins v. United States*, 354 U.S. 178, 77 S. Ct. 1173, 1 L. Ed. 2d 1273 (1957), with *Uphaus v. Wyman*,

360 U.S. 72, 79 S. Ct. 1040, 3 L. Ed. 2d 1090 (1959), and *Barenblatt v. United States*, 360 U.S. 109, 79 S. Ct. 1081, 3 L. Ed. 2d 1115 (1959).

15. *See, e.g., United States v. Eichman*, 496 U.S. 310, 110 S. Ct. 2404, 110 L. Ed. 2d 287 (1990); *City of Boerne v. Flores*, 521 U.S. 507, 117 S. Ct. 2157, 138 L. Ed. 2d 624 (1997).

16. The Eleventh Amendment was adopted to overturn the Supreme Court's decision in *Chisholm v. Georgia*, 2 U.S. 419, 1 L. Ed. 440 (1793). The infamous *Dred Scott* decision of 1857 was effectively overruled by adoption of the Thirteenth Amendment, abolishing slavery, and the Fourteenth Amendment, granting citizenship to all persons born or naturalized in the United States. The Sixteenth Amendment, granting Congress the power to "lay and collect" income taxes, overruled *Pollock v. Farmer's Loan & Trust*, 157 U.S. 429, 15 S. Ct. 673, 39 L. Ed. 759 (1895), in which the Court had declared a federal income tax law unconstitutional. Finally, in *Oregon v. Mitchell*, 400 U.S. 112, 91 S. Ct. 260, 27 L. Ed. 2d 272 (1970), the Supreme Court ruled that Congress had no power to regulate the voting age in state elections. The Twenty-Sixth Amendment, ratified in 1971, accomplished what Congress was not permitted to do through statute. The Amendment provides: "The right of citizens of the United States, who are eighteen years of age or older, to vote shall not be denied or abridged by the United States or by any State on account of age."

17. *Texas v. Johnson*, 491 U.S. 397, 109 S. Ct. 2533, 105 L. Ed. 2d 342 (1989).

18. *NLRB v. Noel Canning*, 573 U.S. _____ (2014).

19. *See Hoke v. United States*, 227 U.S. 308, 33 S. Ct. 281, 57 L. Ed. 523 (1913).

20. *United States v. Lopez*, 514 U.S. 549, 115 S. Ct. 1624, 131 L. Ed. 2d 626 (1995).

21. 529 U.S. 598; 120 S. Ct. 1740; 146 L. Ed. 2d 658 (2000).

22. 567 U.S. _____; 132 S. Ct. 2566; 183 L. Ed. 2d 450 (2012).

23. *McCulloch v. Maryland*, 17 U.S. (4 Wheat.) 316, 4 L. Ed. 579 (1819).

24. *Kilbourn v. Thompson*, 103 U.S. 168, 26 L. Ed. 377 (1881).

25. *See, e.g., Watkins v. United States*, 354 U.S. 178, 77 S. Ct. 1173, 1 L. Ed. 2d 1273 (1957).

26. *Youngstown Sheet & Tube Co. v. Sawyer*, 343 U.S. 579, 72 S. Ct. 863, 96 L. Ed. 1153 (1952).

27. *United States v. Nixon*, 418 U.S. 904, 94 S. Ct. 3193, 41 L. Ed. 2d 1152 (1974).

28. *United States v. Curtiss-Wright Export Corp.*, 299 U.S. 304, 320, 57 S. Ct. 216, 221, 81 L. Ed. 255, 262 (1936).

29. 67 U.S. 635, 17 L. Ed. 459 (1863).

30. *Buckley v. Valeo*, 424 U.S. 1, 96 S. Ct. 612, 46 L. Ed. 2d 659 (1976).

31. *Bowsher v. Synar*, 478 U.S. 714, 106 S. Ct. 3181, 92 L. Ed. 2d 583 (1986).

32. *A.L.A. Schechter Poultry Corp. v. United States*, 295 U.S. 495, 55 S. Ct. 837, 79 L. Ed. 1570 (1935).

33. *J.W. Hampton, Jr., & Co. v. United States*, 276 U.S. 394, 409, 48 S. Ct. 348, 352, 72 L. Ed. 624, 630 (1928).

34. *Mistretta v. United States*, 488 U.S. 361, 372, 109 S. Ct. 647, 655, 102 L. Ed. 2d 714, 731 (1989).

35. *Morrison v. Olson*, 487 U.S. 654, 108 S. Ct. 2597, 101 L. Ed. 2d 569 (1988).

36. The Act was codified at 28 U.S.C.A. §§591-599.

37. *McCulloch v. Maryland*, 17 U.S. 316, 4 L. Ed. 579 (1819); *Gibbons v. Ogden*, 22 U.S. 1, 6 L. Ed. 23 (1824).

38. See, for example, *Hammer v. Dagenhart*, 247 U.S. 251, 38 S. Ct. 529, 62 L. Ed. 1101 (1918), in which the Court struck down federal child labor legislation on the ground that it intruded on an area reserved to the states.

39. For example, in *United States v. Darby Lumber Co.*, 312 U.S. 100, 61 S. Ct. 451, 85 L. Ed. 609 (1941), the Supreme Court relegated the status of the Tenth Amendment to that of a mere "truism" rather than a meaningful limitation on the power of the national government. Although the Court has on occasion resurrected the Tenth Amendment, *see, e.g., National League of Cities v. Usery*, 426 U.S. 833, 96 S. Ct. 2465, 49 L. Ed. 2d 245 (1976), the classical model of federalism belongs to a bygone era.

40. *See South Dakota v. Dole*, 483 U.S. 203, 107 S. Ct. 2793, 97 L. Ed. 2d 171 (1987).

41. *See, e.g., Printz v. United States*, 521 U.S. 898, 117 S. Ct. 2365, 138 L. Ed. 2d 914 (1997).

42. *See, e.g., Felker v. Turpin*, 518 U.S. 651, 116 S. Ct. 2333, 135 L. Ed. 2d 827 (1996).

43. *See, e.g., Rasul v. Bush*, 542 U.S. 466, 124 S. Ct. 2686, 159 L. Ed. 2d 548 (2004); *Boumediene v. Bush*, 553 U.S. 723, 128 S. Ct. 2229, 171 L. Ed. 2d 41 (2008).

44. U.S. Const. art. I, §§9-10.

45. *Calder v. Bull*, 3 U.S. 386, 1 L. Ed. 648 (1798).

46. 529 U.S. 513, 120 S. Ct. 1620, 146 L. Ed. 2d 577 (2000).

47. *Ex parte Garland*, 71 U.S. 333, 18 L. Ed. 366 (1867).

48. *Cummings v. Missouri*, 71 U.S. 277, 18 L. Ed. 356 (1867).

49. 328 U.S. 303, 66 S. Ct. 1073, 90 L. Ed. 1252 (1946).

50. 381 U.S. 437, 449, 85 S. Ct. 1707, 1715, 14 L. Ed. 2d 484, 492 (1965).

51. *Home Bldg. & Loan Assn. v. Blaisdell*, 290 U.S. 398, 54 S. Ct. 231, 78 L. Ed. 413 (1934).

52. *Barron v. Baltimore*, 32 U.S. 243, 8 L. Ed. 672 (1833).

53. *Heffron v. International Socy. for Krishna Consciousness*, 452 U.S. 640, 101 S. Ct. 2559, 69 L. Ed. 2d 298 (1981).

54. *Church of the Lukumi Babalu Aye v. City of Hialeah*, 508 U.S. 520, 113 S. Ct. 2217, 124 L. Ed. 2d 472 (1993).

55. *Employment Div., Dept. of Human Res. v. Smith*, 494 U.S. 872, 110 S. Ct. 1595, 108 L. Ed. 2d 876 (1990).

56. *See, e.g., Walker v. Superior Court*, 763 P.2d 852 (Cal. 1988).

57. The RFRA itself was passed in the wake of the Court's decision in *Employment Division v. Smith* (494 U.S. 872, 110 S. Ct. 1595, 108 L. Ed. 2d. 876), which effectively prohibited an exception for those who use the drug peyote in religious contexts.

58. *Gonzales v. O Centro Espirita Beneficiente Uniao do Vegetal*, 546 U.S. 418, 126 S. Ct. 1211, 163 L. Ed. 2d 1017 (2006).

59. A case involving Wheaton College, a private, religiously-based school in Ohio has already entered the lower courts, with the Supreme Court issuing a July 3, 2014 order for the government to cease application of the Affordable Care Act to the school until the case is resolved. The government had previously granted an exception from the Affordable Care Act's "contraception mandate" for religiously-based non-profit organizations like Wheaton; such organizations were simply required to submit a form that permitted them to "opt-out" of the mandate to provide health plans that include contraception coverage. If such an organization "opts out," then the insurance provider is to offset the cost of the service, and the individual would still acquire contraception coverage. However, Wheaton is asserting a right to refuse to complete the "opt out" form in the first place. Lower courts—and perhaps ultimately the Supreme Court—are left to untangle the appropriate course of action in applying the Affordable Care Act to this conduct, in light of the high Court's opinion in *Burwell v. Hobby Lobby*.

60. *Everson v. Board of Educ.*, 330 U.S. 1, 67 S. Ct. 504, 91 L. Ed. 711 (1947).

61. *Lemon v. Kurtzman*, 403 U.S. 602, 91 S. Ct. 2105, 29 L. Ed. 2d 745 (1971).

62. *See Edwards v. Aguillard*, 482 U.S. 578, 107 S. Ct. 2573, 96 L. Ed. 2d 510 (1983).

63. *See, e.g., School Dist. of Abington Twp. v. Schempp*, 374 U.S. 203, 83 S. Ct. 1560, 10 L. Ed. 2d 844 (1963).

64. *See, e.g., Lee v. Weisman*, 505 U.S. 577, 112 S. Ct. 2649, 120 L. Ed. 2d 467 (1992).

65. *Wallace v. Jaffree*, 472 U.S. 38, 105 S. Ct. 2479, 86 L. Ed. 2d 29 (1985).

66. *Santa Fe Indep. Sch. Dist. v. Doe*, 530 U.S. 290, 120 S. Ct. 2266, 147 L. Ed. 2d 295 (2000).

67. *Agostini v. Felton*, 521 U.S. 203, 117 S. Ct. 1997, 138 L. Ed. 2d 391 (1997).

68. *Mitchell v. Helms*, 530 U.S. 793, 120 S. Ct. 2530, 147 L. Ed. 2d 660 (2000).

69. *Town of Greece, v. Galloway*, 572 U.S. _____ (2014).

70. *Schenck v. United States*, 249 U.S. 47, 39 S. Ct. 247, 63 L. Ed. 470 (1919).

71. *Brandenburg v. Ohio*, 395 U.S. 444, 89 S. Ct. 1827, 23 L. Ed. 2d 430 (1969).

72. *See, e.g., Ward v. Rock Against Racism*, 491 U.S. 781, 109 S. Ct. 2746, 105 L. Ed. 2d 661 (1989).

73. *McCullen v. Coakley*, 573 U.S. _____ (2014).

74. *New York Times v. Sullivan*, 376 U.S. 254, 84 S. Ct. 710, 11 L. Ed. 2d 686 (1964); *Curtis Publg. Co. v. Butts*, 388 U.S. 130, 87 S. Ct. 1975, 18 L. Ed. 2d 1094 (1967).

75. *Miller v. California*, 413 U.S. 15, 93 S. Ct. 2607, 37 L. Ed. 2d 419 (1973).

76. *Miller v. California*, 413 U.S. 15, 93 S. Ct. 2607, 37 L. Ed. 2d 419 (1973).

77. *Cohen v. California*, 403 U.S. 15, 91 S. Ct. 1780, 29 L. Ed. 2d 284 (1971).

78. *New York Times v. Sullivan*, 376 U.S. at 270, 84 S. Ct. at 721, 11 L. Ed. 2d at 701.

79. *Citizens United v. FEC*, 558 U.S. 50, 130 S. Ct. 876, 175 L. Ed. 2d. 753 (2010).

80. *Ohralik v. Ohio State Bar*, 436 U.S. 447, 98 S. Ct. 1912, 56 L. Ed. 2d. 2 (1978).

81. *Snyder v. Phelps*, 562 U.S. _____, 131 S. Ct. 1207, 179 L. Ed. 2d. 172 (2011).

82. *Tinker v. Des Moines*, 393 U.S. 503, 89 S. Ct. 733, 21 L. Ed. 2d. 731 (1969).

83. *Hazelwood v. Kuhlmeier*, 484 U.S. 260, 108 S. Ct. 562, 98 L. Ed. 2d. 592 (1988).

84. *Morse v. Frederick*, 551 U.S. 393, 127 S. Ct. 2618, 168 L. Ed. 2d. 290 (2007).

85. *Near v. Minnesota*, 283 U.S. 697, 51 S. Ct. 625, 75 L. Ed. 1357 (1931).

86. *New York Times Co. v. United States*, 403 U.S. 713, 91 S. Ct. 2140, 29 L. Ed. 2d 822 (1971).

87. *Roberts v. United States Jaycees*, 468 U.S. 609, 104 S. Ct. 3244, 82 L. Ed. 2d 462 (1984).

88. *Boy Scouts of Am. v. Dale*, 530 U.S. 290, 120 S. Ct. 2266, 147 L. Ed. 2d 295 (2000).

89. *United States v. Cruikshank*, 92 U.S. 542, 23 L. Ed. 588 (1875).

90. *See, e.g., United States v. Miller*, 307 U.S. 174, 59 S. Ct. 816, 83 L. Ed. 1206 (1939); *Lewis v. United States*, 445 U.S. 55, 100 S. Ct. 915, 63 L. Ed. 2d 198 (1980).

91. *District of Columbia v. Heller*, 554 U.S. 570, 128 S. Ct. 2783, 171 L. Ed. 2d 637 (2008).

92. 554 U.S. at 636, 128 S. Ct. at 2822, 171 L. Ed. 2d at 684.

93. 554 U.S. at 626, 128 S. Ct. at 2816, 171 L. Ed. 2d at 678.

94. *McDonald v. Chicago*, 561 U.S. 3025; 130 S. Ct. 3020; 177 L. Ed. 2d. 894 (2010).

95. 389 U.S. 347, 88 S. Ct. 507, 19 L. Ed. 2d 576 (1967).

96. *Kelo v. City of New London*, 545 U.S. 469, 125 S. Ct. 2655, 162 L. Ed. 2d 439 (2005).

97. *Gideon v. Wainwright*, 372 U.S. 335, 83 S. Ct. 792, 9 L. Ed. 2d 799 (1963). See also: *Argersinger v. Hamlin*, 407 U.S. 25, 92 S. Ct. 2006, 32 L. Ed. 2d. 530 (1972).

98. *Curtis v. Loether*, 415 U.S. 189, 94 S. Ct. 1005, 39 L. Ed. 2d 260 (1974).

99. *Thomas v. Union Carbide*, 473 U.S. 568, 105 S. Ct. 3325, 87 L. Ed. 2d 409 (1985).

100. *Colgrove v. Battin*, 413 U.S. 149, 93 S. Ct. 2448, 37 L. Ed. 2d 522 (1973).

101. *Stack v. Boyle*, 342 U.S. 1, 72 S. Ct. 1, 96 L. Ed. 3 (1951).

102. *United States v. Salerno*, 481 U.S. 739, 107 S. Ct. 2095, 95 L. Ed. 2d 697 (1987).

103. *Austin v. United States*, 509 U.S. 602, 113 S. Ct. 2801, 125 L. Ed. 2d 488 (1993).

104. *See, e.g., Furman v. Georgia*, 408 U.S. 238, 92 S. Ct. 2726, 33 L. Ed. 2d 346 (1972); *Gregg v. Georgia*, 428 U.S. 153, 96 S. Ct. 2909, 49 L. Ed. 2d 859 (1976).

105. *Trop v. Dulles*, 356 U.S. 86, 78 S. Ct. 590, 2 L. Ed. 2d 630 (1958).

106. *Scott v. Sandford*, 60 U.S. 393, 15 L. Ed. 691 (1857).

107. *In re Gault*, 387 U.S. 1, 87 S. Ct. 1428, 18 L. Ed. 2d 527 (1967).

108. *Rochin v. California*, 342 U.S. 165, 72 S. Ct. 205, 96 L. Ed. 2d 183 (1952).

109. *Goldberg v. Kelly*, 397 U.S. 254, 90 S. Ct. 1011, 25 L. Ed. 2d 287 (1970).

110. *Chicago, Burlington & Quincy R.R. v. City of Chicago*, 166 U.S. 226, 17 S. Ct. 581, 41 L. Ed. 979 (1897).

111. *Palko v. Connecticut*, 302 U.S. 319, 58 S. Ct. 149, 82 L. Ed. 288 (1937).

112. The only provisions of the Bill of Rights that have not been made applicable to the states are the Third Amendment, the Grand Jury Clause of the Fifth Amendment, the Seventh Amendment, and the Excessive Bail and Excessive Fines Clauses of the Eighth Amendment.

113. *McDonald v. Chicago*, 561 U.S. 3025, 130 S. Ct. 3020, 177 L. Ed. 2d. 894 (2010).

114. *Lochner v. New York*, 198 U.S. 45, 25 S. Ct. 539, 49 L. Ed. 937 (1905).

115. *Griswold v. Connecticut*, 381 U.S. 479, 85 S. Ct. 1678, 14 L. Ed. 2d 510 (1965).

116. *Roe v. Wade*, 410 U.S. 113, 93 S. Ct. 705, 35 L. Ed. 2d 147 (1973).

117. *See, e.g., Stenberg v. Carhart*, 530 U.S. 914, 120 S. Ct. 2597, 147 L. Ed. 2d 743 (2000).

118. *Planned Parenthood v. Casey*, 505 U.S. 833, 112 S. Ct. 2791, 120 L. Ed. 2d 674 (1992).

119. *Gonzales v. Carhart*, 550 U.S. 124, 127 S. Ct. 1610, 167 L. Ed. 2d 480 (2007).

120. *Lawrence v. Texas*, 539 U.S. 558, 123 S. Ct. 2472, 156 L. Ed. 2d 508 (2003).

121. *Cruzan v. Director, Mo. Dept. of Health*, 497 U.S. 261, 116 S. Ct. 2841, 111 L. Ed. 2d 224 (1990).

122. *Washington v. Glucksberg*, 521 U.S. 702, 117 S. Ct. 2258, 138 L. Ed. 772 (1997).

123. *Stenberg v. Carhart*, 530 U.S. 914, 120 S. Ct. 2597, 147 L. Ed. 2d. 743 (2000).

124. *Reynolds v. Sims*, 377 U.S. 533, 84 S. Ct. 1362, 12 L. Ed. 2d 506 (1964).

125. *The Civil Rights Cases*, 109 U.S. 3, 3 S. Ct. 18, 27 L. Ed. 835 (1883).

126. *Santa Clara County v. Southern Pac. R.R. Co.*, 118 U.S. 394, 6 S. Ct. 1132, 30 L. Ed. 118 (1886).

127. *See, e.g., Yick Wo v. Hopkins*, 118 U.S. 356, 6 S. Ct. 1064, 30 L. Ed. 220 (1886).

128. *Brown v. Board of Educ.*, 347 U.S. 483, 74 S. Ct. 686, 98 L. Ed. 873 (1954).

129. *The Slaughterhouse Cases*, 83 U.S. 36, 21 L. Ed. 394 (1873); *Strauder v. West Virginia*, 100 U.S. 303, 25 L. Ed. 664 (1880).

130. *See, e.g., Craig v. Boren*, 429 U.S. 190, 97 S. Ct. 451, 50 L. Ed. 2d 397 (1976); *Mississippi Univ. for Women v. Hogan*, 458 U.S. 718, 102 S. Ct. 3331, 73 L. Ed. 2d 1090 (1982); *United States v. Virginia*, 518 U.S. 515, 116 S. Ct. 2264, 135 L. Ed. 2d 735 (1996).

131. In *Romer v. Evans*, 517 U.S. 620, 116 S. Ct. 1620, 134 L. Ed. 2d 855 (1996), the Court struck down an amendment to the Colorado Constitution that precluded "all legislative, executive, or judicial action at any level of state or local government designed to protect the status of persons based on their 'homosexual, lesbian or bisexual orientation, conduct, practices or relationships.'" Writing for the Court, Justice Kennedy observed: "It is not within our constitutional tradition to enact laws of this sort. Central both to the idea of the rule of law and to our own Constitution's guarantee of equal protection is the principle that government and each of its parts remain open on impartial terms to all who seek its assistance." 517 U.S. at 634, 116 S. Ct. at 1628, 134 L. Ed. 2d at 866.

132. *See, e.g., Regents of the Univ. of Cal. v. Bakke*, 438 U.S. 265, 98 S. Ct. 2733, 57 L. Ed. 2d 750 (1978).

133. *See Adarand Constructors v. Peña*, 515 U.S. 200, 115 S. Ct. 2097, 132 L. Ed. 2d 158 (1995).

134. *See Grutter v. Bollinger*, 539 U.S. 306, 123 S. Ct. 2325, 156 L. Ed. 2d 304 (2003); *Gratz v. Bollinger*, 539 U.S. 244, 123 S. Ct. 2411, 156 L. Ed. 2d 257 (2003).

CRIMINAL LAW

4

LEARNING OBJECTIVES

This chapter should enable the student to understand:

▦ the role of federal, state, and local legislative bodies in defining criminal laws

▦ constitutionally imposed limitations on defining criminal conduct

▦ the essential elements of crimes and classification of parties to crimes

▦ the rationale for and definition of inchoate offenses

▦ the way in which common law crimes evolved into statutory offenses against persons, property, public order, justice, and the environment

▦ the American statutory assault on white-collar and organized crime and vice

▦ the basic substantive military offenses

▦ defenses based on lack of capacity, excuse and justification, use of force, constitutional and statutory rights, and wrongful governmental conduct

▦ theories and practices involving punishment of offenders

▦ the rights of prisoners and corrective measures alternative to incarceration

CHAPTER OUTLINE

INTRODUCTION

Criminal law is that branch of the law that deals with crimes and punishments. **Substantive criminal law** defines crimes and establishes penalties. **Procedural criminal law** regulates the enforcement of the substantive law, the determination of guilt, and the punishment of those found guilty of crimes. In this chapter, we examine the substantive criminal law. We examine criminal procedure in Chapter 10.

Crime and the Evolving Social Consensus

The law distinguishes between serious crimes, known as **felonies**, and less serious offenses, called **misdemeanors**. The distinction between felonies and misdemeanors is that the former carry terms of incarceration for one year or more, whereas the latter usually are punishable by shorter terms of confinement. Most felonies are considered *mala in se*, or evils in themselves. These crimes, which include such offenses as murder, rape, robbery, theft, kidnapping, and arson, are universally condemned by civilized societies. Misdemeanors, on the other hand, are generally considered *mala prohibita*—they are wrong because the law has declared them to be incompatible with the public good. Many so-called "victimless crimes," such as gambling, prostitution, and possession of marijuana, are considered *mala prohibita* and are punished as misdemeanors. However, possession of even a small quantity of cocaine is a felony in most American jurisdictions, even though this behavior is *malum prohibitum*. And petit theft is a misdemeanor, even though larceny or grand theft is *malum in se*.

Cocaine possession is a crime because our society has made a collective judgment that cocaine use is inimical to the public welfare. Obviously, this is not a unanimous judgment. Many people believe that criminalizing cocaine and other "recreational" drugs is unwise public policy. But our federal and state legislative bodies have come to the opposite conclusion. Of course, our system is a constitutional democracy, which means that legislation must conform to the requirements of the federal and state constitutions. Some would argue that laws prohibiting the private recreational use of cocaine and other drugs infringe the constitutionally protected liberty of the individual, but this argument has not prevailed in the courts.[1]

As society has evolved and its standards have changed, behaviors that were once *mala prohibita* are no longer subject to criminal sanction. Sexual offenses are a good example. Not long ago the law criminalized sexual relations outside of marriage. Today, adultery and fornication are not even crimes in most jurisdictions, and in states where such prohibitions remain on the books they are no longer enforced. In 2003, the Supreme Court also struck down a Texas law that banned sodomy.[2] That decision overruled a 1986 Supreme Court decision that upheld a similar law in Georgia.[3] Between 1986 and 2003, many state legislatures actually had taken the step of repealing laws that proscribed certain types of sexual conduct. Generally, once a particular criminal prohibition no longer is supported by societal consensus, it is apt to go unenforced or be stricken from the laws.

By the same token, new prohibitions are enacted as society comes to recognize certain behaviors as harmful. Recent years have seen the establishment of many new criminal prohibitions, including offenses against the environment, smoking in public buildings, transmission of HIV, failure to wear seat belts, texting while driving, and improper disposal of sewage, to name but a few.

Crime: An Offense against Society

Our legal system regards crimes not merely as wrongs against particular victims but as offenses against the entire society. Indeed, there does not have to be an individual victim for there to be a crime. For example, it is a felony to possess cocaine, even though it is unlikely that a particular individual will claim to have been victimized by another person's use of the drug.

Because crime is an injury against society, it is government, as society's legal representative, that brings charges against persons accused of committing crimes. In the United States, we have a federal system, that is, a division of power and responsibility between the national and state governments. Both the national government and the states enact their own criminal laws—although the national government is limited to passing laws that correspond to appropriate enumerated powers in Article 1, Section 8 of the Constitution. Thus, both the national and state governments may prosecute persons accused of crimes. The national government initiates a prosecution when a federal law has been violated; a state brings charges against someone who is believed to have violated one of its laws.

The Role of the Crime Victim

The principal parties in a criminal case are the prosecution (i.e., the government) and the defendant (i.e., the accused person). Crime victims play a very limited role. Even where a crime victim files a complaint with a law enforcement agency that leads to prosecution, once the prosecution begins, the victim's participation is primarily that of being a witness. Victims often complain that the system is insensitive to their interests, and states have begun to address their concerns in several ways. Some states now provide for notice to enable a victim to observe how a case is handled at the trial and sentencing stages. In addition, many prosecutors will ask victims to complete a "Victim Impact Statement" which may play a role in guiding a prosecutor's sentencing request. Increasingly, courts also order convicted defendants who are placed on probation to make restitution to their victims. Several states have even enacted statutes providing compensation to victims who suffer direct financial losses as a result of crime. Finally, a civil suit to recover damages for losses or injuries is also an option for the victim of a crime, but all too often the defendant is financially unable to respond to an award of damages.

Criminal Responsibility

The criminal law, indeed our entire legal system, rests on the idea that individuals are responsible for their actions and must be accountable for them. This is the essential justification and rationale for imposing punishments on persons convicted of crimes.

On the other hand, society recognizes that certain individuals (for example, young children) lack the capacity to appreciate the wrongfulness of their conduct. Similarly, factors beyond individuals' control may lead them to commit criminal acts. In such instances, the law exempts individuals from responsibility. Moreover, there are situations in which acts that would otherwise be crimes may be justified. The best example of this is committing a homicide in self-defense. Ultimately, there are a host of defenses that individuals may invoke beyond a simple denial of guilt. We discuss the topic of criminal responsibility and defenses later in this chapter.

THE ORIGIN AND SOURCES OF THE CRIMINAL LAW

American criminal laws basically came from the **English common law** as it existed at the time that America proclaimed its independence in 1776. After independence, the new American states, through the legislative enactment of "reception statutes," adopted the English common law—to the extent that it did not conflict with the new state and federal constitutions. Though Louisiana is the only state in the Union whose legal system is not based on the common law, instead being based on the Napoleonic Code of France, in Louisiana as in the other states, crimes are largely defined by statutes. However, the federal government did not adopt the common law of crimes. From the outset, statutes passed by Congress defined federal crimes.

The new American judges and lawyers were greatly aided by *Blackstone's Commentaries*, published in 1769, in which Sir William Blackstone, a professor at Oxford, codified the principles of the common law. Blackstone's seminal effort was a noble undertaking, but it had the effect of demystifying English law. Consequently, Blackstone's encyclopedic treatment of the law was less than popular among English barristers, who by this time had developed a close fraternity and took great pride in offering their services to "discover the law." In America, however, *Blackstone's Commentaries* became something of a "legal bible."

State and Local Authority to Enact Criminal Prohibitions

At the time of the American Revolution, the English common law constituted the criminal law of the new United States. Eventually, most common law definitions of crimes were superseded by statutes adopted by the state legislatures. Today, the state legislatures are the principal actors in defining crimes and punishments. For the most part, modern criminal statutes retain the *mala in se* offenses defined by the common law, but many of the old common law crime definitions have been modified to take into account social and economic changes. As we shall see, modern criminal statutes often go far beyond the common law in prohibiting offenses that are *mala prohibita*.

When authorized by state constitutions or acts of state legislatures, cities and counties may adopt ordinances that define certain criminal violations. Local ordinances typically deal with traffic offenses, animal control, land use, building codes, licensing of businesses, and so forth. Usually, these offenses are prosecuted in courts of limited jurisdiction such as municipal or county courts.

Federal Authority to Define Crimes

The national government's responsibility in the criminal justice area has always been more limited than that of the states. Yet, Congress has adopted statutes defining criminal offenses that relate to Congress's legislative powers and responsibilities. Thus, there are federal criminal laws that relate to military service, immigration and naturalization, use of the mail, interstate commerce, civil rights violations, and so forth. Criminal offenses may also be defined by federal regulatory agencies where Congress has specifically delegated such authority and provided sufficient guidelines. Persons who commit federal crimes are subject to prosecution in the federal courts.

The Model Penal Code (MPC)

The American Law Institute (ALI) is an organization of distinguished judges, lawyers, and academics that have a strong professional interest in drafting model codes of laws. In 1962, after a decade of work that produced several tentative drafts, the ALI published its Proposed Official Draft of the **Model Penal Code** (MPC). The MPC consists of general provisions concerning criminal liability, sentences, defenses, and definitions of specific crimes. The MPC is not law; rather, it is designed to serve as a model code of criminal law for all states. It has had a significant impact on legislative drafting of criminal statutes, particularly during the 1970s when the majority of the states accomplished substantial reforms in their criminal codes. Additionally, the MPC has been influential in judicial interpretation of criminal statutes and doctrines, thereby making a contribution to the continuing development of the decisional law.

The Role of Courts in Developing the Criminal Law

Although substantive criminal law and procedural criminal law are often modified by the adoption of federal and state statutes, courts play an equally important role in the development of law. Trial courts make factual determinations, apply settled law to established facts, and impose sanctions. In reviewing the decisions of trial courts, appellate courts must interpret the federal and state constitutions and statutes, which are replete with majestic phrases such as "equal protection of the laws" and "privileges and immunities" that require interpretation. Courts must define exactly what these grand phrases mean within the context of particular legal disputes. Likewise, federal and state statutes often use vague language like "affecting commerce" or "reasonable likelihood." Courts must assign meaning to these and a multitude of other terms. Although the majority of states have abolished all, or nearly all, common law crimes, and replaced them by statutorily defined offenses, the common law remains a valuable source of statutory interpretation. This is because legislatures frequently use terms known to the common law without defining such terms. For example, in proscribing burglary, the legislature may use the term "curtilage" without defining it. In such an instance, a court would look to the common law, which defined the term to mean "an enclosed space surrounding a dwelling."

In rendering interpretations of the law, appellate courts generally follow precedent, in keeping with the common law doctrine of *stare decisis*, which means "to stand by that which is decided." However, in our rapidly changing society, courts often encounter situations, to which precedent arguably does not, or should not, apply. In such situations courts will sometimes deviate from or even overturn precedent. Moreover, where there is no applicable precedent, appellate courts often perform an important lawmaking function, as well as an error correction function.

CONSTITUTIONAL LIMITATIONS ON CRIMINAL LAW

Because it is the "supreme law of the land," the United States Constitution limits the power of Congress and the state legislatures to enact criminal statutes. For example, Article III, Section 3 provides that the crime of **treason** against the United States "shall consist only in levying War against them, or in adhering to their Enemies, giving them Aid and Comfort." Incidentally, treason is the only crime actually defined in the Constitution; all other crimes are defined by the common law, state and federal statutes, or both. Other constitutional limitations on the criminal law include the prohibitions against bills of attainder and ex post facto laws contained in Article I, Sections 9 and 10,[4] and many of the provisions of the Bill of Rights (see Chapter 3).

First Amendment Limitations

Among the most significant protections of the Bill of Rights in the criminal law context are the First Amendment freedoms of religion, speech, and assembly. The following cases represent several well-known instances in which the United States Supreme Court struck down or limited the enforcement of criminal statutes on First Amendment grounds:

- *Brandenburg v. Ohio* (1969).[5] Here, the Court struck down an Ohio statute prohibiting "criminal syndicalism." The law made it a criminal act to advocate violence as a means of political change. The Court held that it is unconstitutional to punish someone merely for advocating violence unless the speech is "directed at inciting or producing imminent lawless action" and is "likely to produce or incite such action."
- *Wisconsin v. Yoder* (1972).[6] In this case, members of the Old Order Amish religion were convicted of violating a state law requiring school attendance through age sixteen. The Amish argued that sending their children to school beyond the eighth grade would be psychologically and spiritually damaging to them and would ultimately have a destructive effect on their tight-knit community. The Supreme Court held that the compulsory school attendance law as applied to the Amish was a violation of the Free Exercise Clause.
- *Texas v. Johnson* (1989).[7] After burning an American flag as part of a public protest at the Republican National Convention in 1984, Gregory Lee Johnson was convicted of desecrating a flag in violation of Texas law. The Texas Court of Criminal Appeals reversed the conviction, holding that the statute under which Johnson was convicted was unconstitutional as applied to his particular conduct. The State of Texas

petitioned the United States Supreme Court for certiorari. The Supreme Court, in a very controversial 5-4 decision, upheld the Texas Court of Criminal Appeals. Writing for the Court, Justice Brennan observed that punishing desecration of the flag would dilute the freedom that it represents.

▪ *Reno v. American Civil Liberties Union* (1997).[8] In 1996, Congress adopted the Communications Decency Act, which made it a crime to display "indecent" material on the Internet in a manner that might make it available to minors. In *Reno v. ACLU* the Court declared this statute unconstitutional as an abridgment of freedom of speech. Speaking for the Court, Justice Stevens concluded that the interest in freedom of expression in a democratic society outweighs any benefits achieved by trying to censor the Internet.

▪ *Ashcroft v. American Civil Liberties Union* (2004).[9] The Supreme Court upheld a lower court injunction against the enforcement of the Child Online Protection Act, a federal statute making it a crime to knowingly post on the Internet content that is harmful to minors. In upholding the injunction, the Court noted, "Content-based prohibitions, enforced by severe criminal penalties, have the constant potential to be a repressive force in the lives and thoughts of a free people."[10] While trumpeted by many as a victory for free speech, the decision seriously undermined efforts to curb online child pornography.

Of course, as we noted in Chapter 3, the protections of the First Amendment are not absolute, and there are numerous cases where the Court has rejected First Amendment claims and allowed criminal statutes to be enforced. For example, in *Virginia v. Black* (2003),[11] the Supreme Court upheld a state statute making it crime to burn a cross with the intent to intimidate a person or group. Writing for the Court, Justice Sandra Day O'Connor concluded that the "First Amendment permits Virginia to outlaw cross burnings done with the intent to intimidate because burning a cross is a particularly virulent form of intimidation."[12]

Due Process and Equal Protection of the Laws

The Due Process Clauses of the Fifth and Fourteenth Amendments also provide important constraints on the criminal law, as does the Equal Protection Clause of the Fourteenth Amendment. Due process requires, among other things, that criminal statutes be written in such a way that a person of ordinary intelligence has a reasonable opportunity to know what is prohibited. As the Supreme Court observed in 1948, "Legislation may run afoul of the Due Process Clause because it fails to give adequate guidance to those who would be law-abiding, to advise defendants of the nature of the offense with which they are charged, or to guide courts in trying those who are accused."[13] When legislatures fail to meet this obligation, they have succumbed to the **vice of vagueness**.

Due process has a *substantive* component as well. Courts have long recognized that the term "liberty" contained in the Due Process Clauses of the Fifth and

Fourteenth Amendments embraces freedoms beyond those specifically enumerated in the Constitution. For instance, in *Lawrence v. Texas* (2003),[14] the U.S. Supreme Court struck down a Texas law making it a crime to engage in "deviant sexual intercourse with another individual of the same sex." Speaking for the Court, Justice Anthony Kennedy concluded that, "The Texas statute furthers no legitimate state interest which can justify its intrusion into the personal and private life of the individual."[15] The decision effectively terminated the ability of government to criminalize private, consensual sexual activity by adults.

Equal protection prohibits legislatures from criminalizing conduct only for certain groups of people, at least not without a very strong justification. For example, in 1976 the Supreme Court declared unconstitutional as a violation of equal protection an Oklahoma law that prohibited eighteen to twenty-year-old men from consuming beer with 3.2 percent or greater alcohol content but did not apply the same prohibition to women of the same age.[16] The Court concluded that the state lacked a sufficient justification for discriminating between the sexes in the availability of the contested beverage.

Ultimately, while courts cannot prevent legislatures from enacting unconstitutional criminal laws, they can enjoin enforcement of those laws. They can also reverse convictions of persons who are prosecuted under such laws. Of course, the burden is on the defendant to raise a constitutional objection to the enforcement of a criminal statute.

OPINION
OF
COURT

GRAYNED v. CITY OF ROCKFORD
408 U.S. 104, 92 S. Ct. 2294, 33 L. Ed. 2d 222 (1972)

Mr. Justice Marshall delivered the Opinion of the Court.

. . . It is a basic principle of due process that an enactment is void for vagueness if its prohibitions are not clearly defined. Vague laws offend several important values. First, because we assume that man is free to steer between lawful and unlawful conduct, we insist that laws give the person of ordinary intelligence a reasonable opportunity to know what is prohibited, so that he may act accordingly. Vague laws may trap the innocent by not providing fair warning. Second, if arbitrary and discriminatory enforcement is to be prevented, laws must provide explicit standards for those who apply them. A vague law impermissibly delegates basic policy matters to policemen, judges, and juries for resolution on an ad hoc and subjective basis, with the attendant dangers of arbitrary and discriminatory application. Third, but related, where a vague statute "abut[s] upon sensitive areas of basic First Amendment freedoms," it "operates to inhibit the exercise of [those] freedoms." Uncertain meanings inevitably lead citizens to "'steer far wider of the unlawful zone' . . . than if the boundaries of the forbidden areas were clearly marked." . . .

ELEMENTS OF CRIMES

To constitute a crime there must be a **wrongful act or omission (*actus reus*)** accompanied by **criminal intent (*mens rea*)**. The criminal law requires a wrongful act because it is concerned with infliction of harm and not simply with someone's evil thoughts. Thinking about killing someone may be sinful, but the evil thought is not in and of itself a crime. But an actual homicide is an evil act unless it is justifiable or excusable.

Even an omission may constitute the required "act," but only where there is a duty to act. For example, a physician who undertakes surgery has a duty to complete the necessary operation. And while there is ordinarily no duty to come to the aid of a stranger who is drowning, parents have a duty to take care of their children, and their failure to perform that duty, for example, their failure to furnish their children nourishment, can suffice as a criminal act.

The second element of a crime is the mental state, or criminal intent. The common law described this as either **general intent** or **specific intent**. A person who performs an act without the intent to do a particular type of injury is said to act with a general intent, while one who acts to accomplish some specific harmful result is said to act with a specific intent. For example, a person who voluntarily sets fire to a building commits an act with an awareness of the general consequences and has acted with a general intent. One who then files a false claim to require an insurance company to pay damages for the loss of the building commits an act with a specific intent; that is, the intent to defraud the insurer.

The Model Penal Code classifies culpability for crimes by using a different terminology. Under the MPC, there is a hierarchy of culpable mental states. In descending order of culpability, they are "purposely," "knowingly," "recklessly," and "negligently." A person who acts "purposely" would generally fall within the common law designation of specific intent, while the other MPC culpable states seem to fall within the general-intent category. Students should become familiar with these newer classifications, as they are widely used in contemporary criminal law; however, in this text, we generally refer to crimes as involving general or specific intent.

In certain instances, one may be held criminally responsible irrespective of intent. Crimes of this nature are classified as **strict-liability offenses**. The classic example of a strict-liability offense is statutory rape, where a person who has sexual intercourse with a minor is guilty irrespective of intent. Recently, though, some jurisdictions have begun to allow a "mistake of age" defense in such situations. Another example of a strict-liability offense is selling liquor to a minor. Most minor traffic offenses also fall into this category of offenses.

In addition to the essential elements of *actus reus* and *mens rea*, the concept of **causation** becomes important when an offense is defined in a manner that a specific result must occur. For example, the various degrees of homicide require that to be guilty of murder or manslaughter, the defendant's conduct must have resulted in the death of a human being. Sometimes causation is referred to as **proximate cause**, a requirement satisfied if the result that occurs was foreseeable.

PARTIES TO CRIMES

Historically, the common law classified parties to crimes as either **principals** or **accessories**. A person directly involved in committing a felony was classified as a principal; a person whose conduct did not involve direct participation was classified as an accessory. Principals were further classified by the degree of their participation. A person who directly or through the acts of an innocent agent actually committed the crime was a principal in the first degree. A principal in the second degree was a person not directly involved but actually or constructively present at the commission of the crime who aided and abetted the perpetrator. The concept of actual presence is self-explanatory; however, the concept of constructive presence requires further explanation. To be constructively present, one had to be sufficiently close to render assistance to the perpetrator. For example, suppose a man led a woman's escort away from her so that another man could sexually attack the woman. The man who led the escort away would be constructively present at the crime and would be classified as a principal in the second degree because he was **aiding and abetting** a crime. Aiding and abetting another in the commission of a crime means assenting to an act or lending countenance or approval, either by active participation in it or by encouraging it in some other manner.

An accessory at common law was classified as either an accessory before the fact or an accessory after the fact. An accessory before the fact procured or counseled another to commit a felony but was not actually or constructively present at commission of the offense. An accessory after the fact knowingly assisted or gave aid or comfort to a person who had committed a felony.

Because misdemeanors were far less serious than felonies, the common law found no necessity to distinguish between participants. As in the case of treason, all participants in misdemeanor offenses were regarded as principals. Accessories to felonies were not regarded as being as culpable as the principals, so they were punished less severely at common law.

The trend in American criminal law has been to abolish the distinction between principals and accessories before the fact. Federal law stipulates that "[w]hoever commits an offense against the United States or aids, abets, counsels, commands, induces, or procures its commission, is punishable as a principal. . . ."[17] The federal statute reflects the law of most of the states insofar as it abolishes the distinction between principals and accessories before the fact.

Even though the common law distinction between principals and accessories before the fact has been largely abolished, the concept of accessory after the fact as a separate offense has been retained by many jurisdictions. Modern statutes view an accessory after the fact as less culpable than someone who plans, assists, or commits a crime. Thus, statutes generally define accessory after the fact as a separate offense and provide for a less severe punishment.[18] In most states, a lawful conviction as an accessory after the fact requires proof that the defendant knew that the person aided or assisted had committed a felony. The gist of being an accessory after the fact lies essentially in obstructing justice, and a person is guilty who knows that an offense has been committed and receives, relieves, comforts, or assists the offender in order to hinder the offender's apprehension, trial, or punishment.[19] Federal law, however, does not distinguish between whether the person assisted has committed a felony or has committed a misdemeanor.[20]

Because of a wife's duty at common law to obey her husband, a woman who gave aid and comfort to her husband was exempt from the law governing accessories after the fact. While this exemption no longer prevails, some state statutes exempt spouses and other classes of relatives from penalty for being accessories after the fact. For example, Florida law prevents the prosecution as an accessory after the fact of any person standing in the relation of husband or wife, parent or grandparent, child or grandchild, brother or sister, either by blood or marriage—except for child abuse and homicide offenses.[21]

INCHOATE OFFENSES

The word "inchoate" means underdeveloped or unripened. Thus, an **inchoate offense** is one involving activity or steps directed toward the completion of a crime. There are three such offenses: **attempt**, **solicitation**, and **conspiracy**. Although preparatory to commission of other offenses, they are separate and distinct crimes. During the 1800s, each was recognized as a misdemeanor at common law, too late to become a part of the common law under the reception statutes adopted by most new American states. Most American jurisdictions now define these offenses by statute, frequently classifying them as felonies.

Inchoate offenses were originally created by the courts in response to the need to prevent commission of serious crimes. The development of the law in this area has been primarily through the courts. Frequently, the courts have found difficulty in determining when mere noncriminal activity has reached the stage of criminal conduct. Yet, by making certain inchoate conduct illegal, the law affords law enforcement officers an opportunity to terminate such conduct at an early stage.

Attempt

Attempt is the most frequently charged of the inchoate crimes. A criminal attempt consists of an intent to commit a specific offense coupled with an act that goes beyond mere preparation toward the commission of that offense. No particular federal statute proscribes the offense of attempt. In general, federal courts have recognized the requisite elements of attempt as (1) an intent to engage in criminal conduct, and (2) the performance of an act that constitutes a substantial step toward the completion of the substantive offense.[22] State penal codes often specifically provide for attempts to commit the most serious crimes such as murder. A general attempt statute then covers the remaining offenses. A typical statute that covers all attempts provides, "Whoever attempts to commit an offense prohibited by law and in such attempt does any act toward the commission of such an offense, but fails in the perpetration or is intercepted or prevented in the execution of the same, commits the offense of criminal attempt."[23]

The "act" requirement contemplates an overt act that constitutes a substantial step toward commission of an offense. While the quoted statute makes no distinction between felony or misdemeanor offenses, statutes in some states limit the crime of attempt to attempts to commit felonies or certain specified crimes. The criminal law proscribes not simply an attempt but an attempt to commit a specific crime, for example, attempted murder or attempted sexual assault.

The Model Penal Code distinguishes preparatory conduct from an attempt. It allows conviction for the crime of attempt where the actor engages in "an act or omission constituting a substantial step in a course of conduct planned to culminate in the commission of the crime." Federal courts apply this test.[24] It is possible that where there are multiple intentions underlying an act, one act may establish several different criminal attempts.

To find a defendant guilty of the crime of attempt, most courts require the prosecution to prove that the defendant had a specific intent to commit the intended offense, frequently referred to as the **target crime**. Most courts reason that one cannot attempt to do something without first forming the specific intent to accomplish that particular act. The rationale for this majority view seems to be that an attempt involves the concept of intended consequences by the actor. In any event, courts require at least the level of intent that must be established in proof of the target crime.

When a criminal attempt completes a substantive crime, the attempt usually merges into the target offense. The actor is then guilty of the substantive crime rather than merely an attempt to commit it. Thus, a person who is successful in an attempt to commit murder is guilty of murder. However, there can be no attempt to commit certain crimes because some substantive offenses by definition embrace an attempt. To illustrate, the statutory crime of uttering a forged instrument is usually defined as including an attempt to pass a forged instrument to someone to obtain something of value. Therefore, one who makes such an attempt would be guilty of uttering a forged instrument, not merely an attempt to do so. In effect, the attempt is subsumed by the very definition of the substantive crime. Needless to say, it would be redundant to charge someone with attempting to attempt to commit a given crime.

Some jurisdictions have laws providing that it is a defense to the crime of attempt if the defendant abandons an attempt to commit an offense or otherwise prevents its consummation.[25] If recognized as a defense, abandonment must be wholly voluntary. It cannot be the result of any outside cause like the appearance of the police on the scene.

Solicitation

By the 1800s, the English common law specified that a person who counseled, incited, or solicited another to commit either a felony or a misdemeanor involving breach of the peace committed the offense of solicitation. A person who solicited another to commit a crime was guilty of solicitation even if the crime counseled, incited, or solicited was not committed. The offense of solicitation is now defined by statute in most American jurisdictions. The statutory definition of solicitation in Illinois is typical: "A person commits solicitation when, with intent that an offense be committed, other than first-degree murder, he commands, encourages, or requests another to commit the offense."[26] The essence of the offense remains the solicitation, so the offender may be found guilty irrespective of whether the solicited crime is ever committed. Conviction under federal law requires the solicitation to be of a federal offense.[27]

The offenses of solicitation and attempt are different crimes, analytically distinct in their elements. Although each is an inchoate offense, solicitation is complete when the request or enticement to complete the intended offense is made, and it is immaterial whether the solicitee agrees, if the offense is carried out, or if no steps were taken toward consummation of the offense. Mere solicitation is generally not sufficient to constitute an attempt, because attempt requires proof of an overt act to commit the intended criminal act.

Usually, the fact that the solicitor countermands the solicitation is not a defense to the crime of solicitation. Nor is it a defense that it was impossible for the person solicited to commit the crime. The Model Penal Code provides that a timely, complete, and voluntary renunciation of the accused's criminal purpose is a defense to a charge of solicitation.[28] Some states have adopted this position. For such a defense to prevail, though, a defendant would have to affirmatively establish that after soliciting another person to commit an offense, the defendant prevented commission of the crime under circumstances manifesting a complete and voluntary renunciation of any criminal purpose.

Conspiracy

At common law, conspiracy consisted of an agreement by two or more persons to accomplish a criminal act or to use unlawful means to accomplish a noncriminal objective. The gist of the offense was the unlawful agreement between the parties, and no overt act was required. The common law regarded a husband and wife as one person for most purposes; therefore, a husband and wife could not be guilty of conspiring with one another. Since the trend of the law in recent years has been to recognize the separate identities of the spouses, there appears to be no valid reason to continue the common law approach.

Today, the offense of conspiracy is defined by statute in all jurisdictions. Most state laws define the elements of the offense along the lines of the common law. Thus, under Florida law, both an agreement and an intention to commit an offense are necessary elements to support a conviction for conspiracy.[29] On the other hand, federal law (with some exceptions) requires an overt act in a conspiracy to commit an offense or defraud the United States.[30] A number of states also require proof of an overt act in order to convict someone for conspiracy. Texas law, for example, provides: "A person commits criminal conspiracy if, with intent that a felony be committed, (1) he agrees with one or more persons that they or one or more of them engage in conduct that would constitute the offense, and (2) he or one or more of them performs an overt act in pursuance of the agreement."[31] Note that the Texas statute also requires an intent that a felony be committed, whereas in many states it is only necessary to prove an intent to commit a criminal offense.

The range of conspiracies cuts across socioeconomic classes in society. Traditionally, state prosecutions for conspiracy have been directed at criminal offenses such as homicide, arson, perjury, kidnapping, and various offenses against property. In recent years, an increasing number of both state and federal conspiracy prosecutions have been related to illicit drug trafficking. In addition to the large number of narcotics violations, federal prosecutions include a variety of conspiracies not found under state laws. Among these are customs violations, counterfeiting of currency, copyright violations, mail fraud, lotteries, and violations of antitrust laws and laws governing interstate commerce and other areas of federal regulation.

Conspiracy is regarded as a separate and distinct crime; therefore, it usually does not merge into the target offense. Wharton's Rule, named after Francis Wharton, a well-known commentator on criminal law, provides an exception to this principle. Wharton's Rule holds that two people cannot conspire to commit a crime such as incest or bigamy because these offenses require only two participants. The rationale is that, unlike the usual conspiracy (often viewed as a wheel with many spokes or as a chain of circumstances), the offenses named do not endanger the public generally. Wharton's Rule has been applied in many state and federal courts, but it has its limitations. In holding the rule inapplicable to various federal gambling offenses under the Organized Crime Control Act of 1970, the Supreme Court pointed out that the rule itself is simply an aid to determination of legislative intent and must defer to a discernible legislative judgment.[32]

There has been an increased tendency in recent years to prosecute defendants for conspiracies as well as target crimes. The offense of conspiracy is a potent weapon in the hands of the prosecutors, particularly in coping with the problem of organized crime. But since the intent requirement and the form of agreement required are somewhat imprecise, a conspiracy is easier to prove than specific substantive crimes. On this basis, some critics argue that prosecutors, judges, and juries are given too wide latitude in finding a defendant guilty. Other critics point to the fact that conspiracy prosecutions may chill or effectively abolish First Amendment rights of free expression.

In some states, statutes specifically provide for a defense of withdrawal from and renunciation of a conspiracy. As an illustration, Missouri law specifies: "No one shall be convicted of conspiracy if, after conspiring to commit the offense, he prevented the accomplishment of the objectives of the conspiracy under circumstances manifesting a renunciation of his criminal purpose."[33]

In the absence of statutory authority, courts have been reluctant to approve a person's withdrawal as a defense. One of the difficulties in approving withdrawal as a defense is that even though a conspirator withdraws, the criminal objective of the conspiracy may proceed. Therefore, it seems reasonable to require that a person who would rely on such defense not only renounce any criminal purpose but also take the necessary steps to thwart the objective of the conspiracy. To accomplish this result, the conspirator probably would have to notify law enforcement authorities of the pertinent details of the conspiracy. If the accused is allowed to offer such a defense, then he or she has the burden of establishing a withdrawal from the conspiracy.

OFFENSES AGAINST PERSONS

The protection of people from others who would do them harm is the fundamental mission of the criminal law. Offenses against persons can be divided into five basic categories:

1. Assaultive offenses
2. Homicide
3. Rape and sexual battery
4. False imprisonment and kidnapping
5. Abusive offenses.

Assaultive Offenses

Assault and battery, terms which are familiar to everyone, derive from the common law. An **assault** is an attempt or threat to inflict bodily injury upon another person. An **aggravated assault** is an assault involving a weapon capable of inflicting death or serious bodily injury. Simple assault is a misdemeanor; aggravated assault is a felony. **Battery** is the unlawful use of force against another person that entails some injury or offensive touching. Common examples would include striking someone or even kissing someone against his or her will. **Aggravated battery** entails the infliction of serious bodily injury or use of a deadly weapon. In some jurisdictions, assault and battery is one offense, which is to say that battery is subsumed under assault. Additionally, the common law developed an offense called **mayhem**, which involve the severing of a limb or the putting out of an eye, such that the victim was rendered less able to fight. Today, some jurisdictions retain mayhem as an offense, while others consider mayhem to be aggravated battery.

Another assaultive offense is **stalking**. A relatively new development, stalking is typically defined as willfully, maliciously, and repeatedly following or harassing another and making a credible threat against that person. Usually, a stalking statute defines a general-intent crime that involves more than one incident—hence the appearance of the word "repeatedly" in the previous sentence. Most complaints are filed by women who are targeted by men. Some commentators have criticized stalking laws as being excessively vague, but courts have rejected most constitutional challenges to these laws.

Homicide

The common law recognized **murder** and **manslaughter** as criminal homicide. Murder was the "unlawful killing of another with malice aforethought." Manslaughter was an unlawful killing that did not involve malice. There were two categories of manslaughter: involuntary (unintentional) and voluntary (intentional). The common law also recognized **justifiable homicide** and **excusable homicide**. Homicide was justifiable if a killing resulted from self-defense or by a command or permission of the law. It was excusable where committed through accident or misfortune.

Criminal homicide involves actions that result in the death of a human being and is classified according to degrees. **First-degree murder** is usually defined as requiring proof of malice aforethought or premeditation; accordingly, it is a specific-intent crime. Other homicidal offenses are usually general-intent crimes. **Second-degree murder** commonly requires proof of a defendant's depraved indifference to human life or imminently dangerous or outrageous conduct. A few statutes proscribe an offense requiring a lesser level of culpability known as third-degree murder.

At common law, manslaughter was classified as voluntary or involuntary. Modern penal codes preserve manslaughter as criminal homicide; however, some jurisdictions combine voluntary and involuntary manslaughter into one offense. Manslaughter today frequently embraces responsibility for omissions as well as commissions where there is a legal duty to act. Depending on the specific jurisdiction, manslaughter usually requires proof of either reckless conduct or "gross negligence" that results in another's death. Provocation that would cause a reasonable person to lose control also may be sufficient to convert an otherwise intentional killing of another to manslaughter. Mere words, however, even if extremely insulting, are not sufficient to constitute provocation. It must generally be shown that the provocation was sufficient to excite in the defendant's mind such anger, rage, or terror as to obscure an ordinary person's reasoning and render that person incapable of cool reflection. Often, there is a fine line between a conviction for second-degree murder and manslaughter. In some instances, a verdict finding a defendant guilty of manslaughter results from a jury's desire to mitigate the seriousness of a defendant's offense.

Vehicular homicide usually involves death resulting from the negligent operation of a vehicle or driving while in the commission of an unlawful act not amounting to a felony. The offense usually carries a lesser penalty than the crime of manslaughter. Prosecutors often charge a defendant with vehicular manslaughter rather than vehicular homicide where the evidence shows the defendant was negligent but not necessarily grossly negligent or reckless.

Felony murder consists of an unintentional killing that occurs during the commission or attempted commission of another serious felony. Developed at common law when felonies were punishable by death, the doctrine has been incorporated into most criminal codes in the United States. Today, many jurisdictions outline a specific list of felonies that can lead to a charge of felony murder when a death occurs during their commission. Examples of such felonies include burglary, robbery, rape, arson, and kidnapping.

Homicide can be considered excusable when committed by accident or misfortune or in doing any other lawful act by lawful means, with usual and ordinary caution, and without any unlawful intent. Homicide also may be excusable when committed in the heat of passion, or on sudden and sufficient provocation, or on sudden combat where no dangerous weapon is used and the killing is not done in a cruel or unusual manner. A death that results from a vehicular accident where the driver is not negligent is also an example of excusable homicide.

In justifiable homicide, the intent to cause death is often present. When death is inflicted by public officers in obedience to a court judgment or in discharge of certain other legal duties, or when necessarily committed in apprehending felons, it is considered justifiable homicide.

In order to earn a conviction for a homicide offense, the prosecution must prove that the victim was alive before the homicidal act, that the victim was killed by a criminal act or agency of another (***corpus delicti***), and that the victim's death was proximately caused by the defendant. At common law, the victim's death had to occur within a year and a day of the defendant's act. Modern technology has caused courts and legislatures to recede from this inflexible requirement and the Supreme Court of the United States effectively sanctioned this retreat from the "year and a day rule" with its opinion in *Rogers v. Tennessee*.[34] Further, while cessation of heartbeat was the classic definition of death, many jurisdictions have legislatively or judicially supplemented the classic requirement of when death occurs by a new definition of "brain death."

Defenses to homicidal crimes often involve pleas of self-defense and, sometimes, insanity, as well as claims that the victim's death resulted from an accident or through actions taken in the heat of passion.

Suicide

Early English common law defined the offense of suicide as "the intentional taking of one's life by self-destruction." Suicide was not only regarded as being contrary to nature, but also was looked upon as an offense against the Biblical commandment: "Thou shalt not kill." Suicide was punishable by forfeiture of the decedent's goods and chattels because it deprived the King of one of his subjects.

The thrust of statutory criminal law has been to make it an offense for anyone to cause or aid another person to commit suicide. After several unsuccessful attempts to convict Dr. Jack Kevorkian for assisting terminally ill individuals to commit suicide, in 1999 the state of Michigan successfully prosecuted Kevorkian for second-degree murder in the death of a man suffering from Lou Gehrig's disease. After serving eight years in prison, Dr. Kevorkian was released in June 2007.

In 1997, in *Washington v. Glucksberg*, the U.S. Supreme Court upheld a Washington statute making it a crime to assist another in committing suicide.[35] Writing for a unanimous Court, Chief Justice Rehnquist discussed the historical and cultural background of laws prohibiting **assisted suicide**. He pointed out that in almost every state it is a crime to assist in a suicide and that the statutes banning assisted suicide are long-standing expressions of the states' commitment to the protection and preservation of all human life. The Court's opinion analyzed the interests that come into play in determining whether a statute banning assisted suicide passes constitutional muster. The Court rejected any parallel between a person's right to terminate medical treatment and the "right" to have assistance in committing suicide.

Laws against assisted suicide bring into play significant policy issues and require legislatures to carefully balance competing claims of individual liberty, ethics, and the interest of society. Some proponents of allowing assisted suicide argue that it simply enables a person who has a rational capacity to make a fundamental life choice that should be within their domain of decision making. Those who reject this view urge that the state has an interest in the preservation of life and that some individuals may die needlessly as a result of misdiagnosis. Moreover, they argue that allowing assisted suicide leads to an indifference to the value of life.

The Supreme Court's decision in *Washington v. Glucksberg* essentially leaves the question of doctor-assisted suicide in the hands of state legislators and voters. In 1994, Oregon voters narrowly approved a law allowing a doctor to assist terminally ill persons in committing suicide under specified circumstances.[36] Subsequently, in 2006 the Supreme Court effectively sanctioned Oregon's assisted suicide law with its decision in *Gonzales v. Oregon*,[37] which prevented the United States' Attorney General from unilaterally prohibiting the prescription of certain drugs used in the act of assisting a suicide.

Rape and Sexual Battery

At common law, **rape** was defined as "the unlawful carnal knowledge of a female by force and against her will." Later, it became a statutory offense for a male to have carnal knowledge of (sexual intercourse with) a female child under age ten irrespective of her consent. There was also a presumption at common law that a male under age fourteen could not commit rape. Further, because common law rape required that the carnal knowledge be unlawful, under "Hale's Rule" a husband could not be found guilty of raping his wife.

Early on, American courts generally followed the common law definition of rape but rejected the presumption that a male under age fourteen could not commit the offense. Beyond that, most legislatures classified intercourse with females under age sixteen or eighteen, irrespective of consent, as statutory rape. All courts recognized that to constitute common law rape, sexual intercourse had to be without the female's consent. But many American courts struggled with the requirements of force and in determining how to define what constituted consent. Some judges actually instructed juries that "in order for the defendant to be found guilty of rape, you must find that the woman resisted to her utmost." Some courts even commonly admitted evidence of a female victim's reputation and allowed inquiry concerning her prior sexual experiences. Later cases recognized that it was not necessary for a female victim to resist to the utmost; rather, the degree of resistance came to be regarded as a relative matter dependent on all the circumstances surrounding the incident. Courts have divided on the issue of whether sexual battery laws require proof of a general or specific intent, with the wording of the statute proscribing the offense generally determining the intent requirement.

Since the late 1970s, the offense of rape has evolved as a gender-neutral offense proscribing not only rape as defined by the common law but also all types of sexual impositions. Additionally, modern sexual battery laws often classify sexual battery by degree according to the conduct involved, the character and extent of force, and the age and vulnerability of the victim.

By the mid-1990s, all states had either abrogated or modified the common law marital exemption known as "Hale's Rule," which specified that a husband could not be guilty of raping his wife. Some states, however, created a new offense of spousal rape, which could carry lesser penalties or require different standards of proof than other rape statutes. As of 2014, different criteria applied to spousal rape in 13 states. South Carolina, for example, requires that the threat or use of force be of a higher nature; a few states even mandate consideration of whether the couple is living apart.

One of the most significant legal reforms concerning rape has been the enactment of **rape shield laws** by a majority of the states. In a prosecution for rape (or sexual battery), these laws preclude presentation of evidence of a victim's prior sexual activity with anyone other than the defendant on the theory that a victim's prior sexual activity is not probative of whether the victim has been violated. Even where the defendant seeks to introduce evidence of prior relations with a victim, some statutes require such evidence to be first presented to the court *in camera* to determine whether evidence of the defendant's prior relationship with the victim is relevant to the victim's consent.

The term **rape trauma syndrome** was coined in the early 1970s to describe a recurring pattern of physical and emotional symptoms experienced by rape victims. Since then, prosecutors have sought to introduce expert testimony at rape trials to establish that a victim's symptoms are consistent with the syndrome. This type of evidence has particular relevance to a prosecution where the defendant claims consent of the victim as a defense. On review of convictions, appellate courts have disagreed on whether such evidence is admissible.

Megan's Law refers to a new type of statute that requires convicted sex offenders who are released from prison to register with local law enforcement agencies. This information is then made available to the public. Failure to comply with the registration requirement is a criminal offense. The initial law was enacted in New Jersey, but now federal legislation has been enacted encouraging states to adopt similar laws.

Beyond a general denial, the most common defense in sexual battery cases is that the victim consented to have sex with the defendant. However, in some jurisdictions, the offense of statutory rape is held to be a strict-liability offense to which the defense of consent is unavailable.

False Imprisonment and Kidnapping

At common law, **false imprisonment** consisted of confining someone against that person's will; **kidnapping** involved forcibly abducting and taking a person to a foreign country. The modern statutory definition of false imprisonment is similar to the common law definition. Most statutes require proof of a general intent. To prove the offense, the prosecution must show the confinement or movement was not merely incidental to another crime.

False imprisonment is no longer a frequently charged offense. Serious cases of false imprisonment commonly result in kidnapping prosecutions, while others result in civil suits. In contrast to false imprisonment, kidnapping has become a far more serious offense and is universally proscribed by state and federal statutes. Unlike the common law, statutes now usually define kidnapping as the unlawful taking and carrying away (asportation) of a victim without that person's consent. Most require proof of a general intent. Many states distinguish between simple kidnapping and kidnapping for ransom, while others classify kidnapping by degree according to the seriousness of the acts attendant to the crime.

Federal law plays a prominent role in the prosecution of kidnapping. Federal statutes presume that a kidnapping victim who has not been returned within twenty-four hours has been taken across state lines, thus providing a basis for federal jurisdiction. The intent requirement in kidnapping is dependent upon the language of the particular statute. Recent federal statutes also criminalize hostage taking.

The term "child snatching" is now commonly applied to situations where one parent seizes his or her child from the custody of the other. The Uniform Child Custody Jurisdiction Act (UCCJA) or its revised version, the Uniform Child-Custody Jurisdiction and Enforcement Act (UCCJEA), now in force in the majority of states, and the Parental Kidnapping Prevention Act (PKPA), enacted by Congress in 1980, address the problem of interstate child abduction.

An officer, or even a private citizen, who makes a lawful arrest, or a jailer who detains a prisoner lawfully committed to custody, or a parent or a teacher who reasonably restrains a child would not be guilty of false imprisonment. Consent can be a defense to false imprisonment or kidnapping, but it must have been given by a competent person and must not have been induced by threat, coercion, or misrepresentation. A person who relies on consent as a defense has the burden of establishing its validity. Defendants frequently challenge whether there was sufficient movement of the victim to constitute the asportation element of kidnapping.

Abusive Offenses

Many cases of abusive conduct involve commission of assault or battery (or aggravated categories thereof), or some category of sexual battery. Nevertheless, with the rise of neglect, abuse, and violence against children, many states have enacted specific child abuse laws to cover a broader range of abusive behavior. Statutes now commonly require medical professionals and social workers to report instances of suspected child abuse to enforcement authorities. Child abuse cases often involve issues as to whether parents, social workers, and others who discuss these matters with an abused child are to be permitted to testify in court concerning communications with the child. Further, expert testimony by physicians, psychologists, and social workers is often relied upon to explain a child's behavior that may grow out of certain types of abuse.

Many instances of abuse of spouses and the elderly constitute criminal violations of traditional statutes previously discussed; beyond that, laws have been enacted in many states to provide for issuance of court injunctions to protect spouses from domestic violence and provide for arrest of those who violate these orders. Additionally, legislatures frequently have provided for enhanced penalties for those who commit crimes of violence against elderly persons.

PROPERTY CRIMES

If the most important goal of the criminal law is to protect persons, the next most important goal is the protection of property. The Anglo-American legal tradition places a premium on private property rights, and this emphasis can be seen in the many criminal prohibitions relative to economic and property crimes.

Theft

The basic common law offense against someone's taking another's personal property was **larceny**. The crime consisted of (1) the wrongful taking and carrying away of (2) the personal property of another (3) with the intent to permanently deprive the other person of the property. The taking was called the "caption"; the carrying away, the "asportation." The wrongful act was a "trespass" and to convict a defendant of larceny required proof of the defendant's specific intent to permanently deprive the victim of possession of the property.

Because of the many technical distinctions in larceny, the English Parliament developed two statutory offenses, **false pretenses** and **embezzlement**. False pretenses made it a misdemeanor for a seller to obtain someone else's property by false pretenses. This statute was adopted in 1757 and became a part of the common law of most new American states. Embezzlement occurred when a person who had lawful possession of another's property wrongfully appropriated that property. This statute was aimed at brokers, bankers, lawyers, trustees, and others who abused their positions of trust. Parliament enacted the offense of embezzlement in 1799, too late to be received by the new American states as part of the common law.

Most states originally followed the common law of larceny, receiving stolen property, and false pretenses, and enacted statutes making embezzlement of intangible and tangible items a crime. During the ensuing years, states passed a variety of statutes that proscribed stealing in its various forms. Since the 1970s, the trend has been for the states to replace their disparate statutes defining various aspects of stealing with an omnibus statute proscribing theft in comprehensive terms. These newer statutes replace the narrow common law concept of what constitutes a taking, carrying away, and trespass. Most retain the specific-intent requirement but generally define it as the "intent to steal" rather than the intent to permanently deprive another of his or her property.

The newer state statutes defining theft make it unlawful for a person to commit any of the common law offenses as well as various other crimes, including theft of intellectual property such as trade secrets. Theft statutes usually classify the seriousness of the offense based on the value of the goods or services stolen, an element the prosecution can establish by proving the market value of the goods or services taken. Frequently, theft of certain articles, for example, firearms, fire extinguishers, or a person's last will and testament, are classified as more serious offenses, irrespective of their market value. Likewise, some states classify the degree of theft on the basis of local economic interests, as would be the case with theft of livestock, citrus fruit, or building materials.

Most **computer crimes** violate one or more laws defining theft, fraud, embezzlement, and similar offenses at the state level, and often, mail fraud at the federal level. Nevertheless, nearly every state has adopted some laws defining such offenses as computer fraud, computer trespass, and theft of computer services. These new laws define such terms as "access," "computer program," "software," "database," "hacking," and other computer parlance, and address computer manipulation, theft of intellectual property, telecommunications crimes, and software piracy. Depending on the value of property or services actually obtained, these offenses are graded as felonies or serious misdemeanors.

Robbery

At common law, **robbery** was a felony consisting of (1) a taking of personal property (2) from another person's possession (3) by force or by placing a person in fear (4) with the intent to permanently deprive the victim of the property. Thus, in reality robbery is both a property crime and a crime against a person. Robbery became a statutory offense in all American jurisdictions. Federal statutes apply to post offices, military installations, and banks where deposits are insured by the federal government. Federal law varies from the common law requirements by not requiring the prosecution to establish the defendant's specific intent.

Most states define robbery much as did the common law; however, many now classify the offense by degrees depending on whether the accused is armed, the extent of force used or injury inflicted, and, in some instances, the vulnerability of the victim based on the victim's age or disabilities. A contemporary issue in robbery is whether the element of force or placing the victim in fear must occur prior to or contemporaneous with the taking of the victim's property.

Recognizing the serious threat that forcible auto theft poses to persons and their motor vehicles, and after a nationwide spree of "carjacking," Congress in 1994 enacted a law providing that:

> [w]hoever, with the intent to cause death or serious bodily harm takes a motor vehicle that has been transported, shipped, or received in interstate or foreign commerce from the person or presence of another by force and violence or by intimidation or attempts to do so shall be [fined or imprisoned].[38]

In 1999, the Supreme Court rejected the appeal of a defendant who claimed that he did not have the "intent to cause death or serious bodily injury" even though he pointed a gun at a person while stealing their car. The defendant claimed that any intent to harm would have been "conditional" on the car owner failing to comply with a demand to relinquish the vehicle. The Supreme Court rejected the notion that "conditional intent" could absolve the defendant of responsibility.[39]

In the years following Congress' enactment, many states have also adopted **carjacking** statutes. For example, a Tennessee law enacted in 1995 follows the federal law by defining carjacking as "the intentional or knowing taking of a motor vehicle from the possession of another by use of: (1) a deadly weapon; or (2) force or intimidation."[40]

Forgery and Uttering a Forged Instrument

At common law, **forgery** was a misdemeanor that consisted of "the fraudulent making or alteration of a writing to the prejudice of another man's rights." To convict, the prosecution had to establish the defendant's specific intent to defraud the victim. A separate and distinct misdemeanor, **uttering a forged instrument**, involved the publishing or passing of a forged instrument. The status of forgery offenses as misdemeanors attests to the lesser importance of commercial matters at common law.

The chief difference between common law and statutory forgery lies not in the definition of the offense but in the broader scope of the latter and the more serious punishments now imposed by statutes. Federal and state statutes classify forgery as a felony. Federal law provides that "[w]hoever, with intent to defraud, falsely makes, forges, counterfeits, or alters any obligation or other security of the United States" commits forgery, thus retaining the specific-intent requirement. Numerous federal statutes describe instruments subject to forgery.

Most states have substantially adopted the common law definition of forgery, requiring either the intent to defraud or to injure, and have enacted statutes proscribing the uttering of forged instruments.

Worthless Checks and Credit Card Fraud

As commercial banking developed, the passing of bad checks became a serious problem. In early cases, the issuance of a check without funds in the bank was prosecuted as the use of a "false token" under statutes proscribing the use of false pretenses to obtain property. Now, a variety of statutes make it unlawful to issue checks with insufficient funds to cover payment. Earlier statutes often provided that to be guilty a person had to fraudulently obtain goods. With the widespread use of commercial and personal banking, legislatures enacted worthless-check statutes usually classifying such an offense as a misdemeanor. Often, these statutes allow an offender to avoid prosecution by making prompt restitution.

One who makes a purchase through use of a stolen or otherwise fraudulently obtained credit card is guilty of **credit card fraud** and may be prosecuted under most modern larceny and theft statutes. Credit cards, however, are now in such widespread use that many states have enacted laws creating specific offenses for their improper use.

Identity Theft

A recent development in criminal law is the prohibition of "identity theft." Identity theft involves one person pretending to be another person, often with the objective of using a Social Security number or other identifying information to acquire credit lines or to make purchases of items like automobiles or even property. This type of activity can have a deleterious impact on the lives of the persons whose identities are stolen, as they may find themselves held responsible for purchases or loans that they did not authorize. To address this problem, Congress passed the Identity Theft and Assumption Deterrence Act in 1998. Many states have since adopted similar statutes. The magnitude of the problem is highlighted by the fact that several companies now mass-market identity theft protection programs.

In 2009, the Supreme Court rejected the application of an identity theft law to illegal immigrants who had used randomly selected, fake Social Security numbers to secure employment. The Court ruled that a federal identity theft prosecution required that the individual using a false Social Security number have knowledge that the Social Security number in question belonged to an actual person.[41]

Habitation Offenses

The common law offenses of **burglary** and **arson** protected not only the dwelling house but also the buildings within the "curtilage," that is, the enclosure that typically included the cookhouse and other outbuildings. At common law, burglary consisted of (1) breaking and entering of (2) a dwelling of another (3) during the nighttime (4) with the intent to commit a felony therein.

In the United States, all jurisdictions enacted statutes to eliminate the common law requirement that the offense take place in the nighttime. Most statutes retain the requirement for a specific intent, usually providing that the entry be made "with the intent to commit a felony"; however, some have added "or theft" to broaden the scope of burglary. Today, burglary statutes usually proscribe the breaking and entering of all types of private and commercial structures as well as vehicles, aircraft, and vessels of all types. Retaining the common law tradition of the sanctity of the home, contemporary statutes commonly impose enhanced punishment for burglary of a dwelling. Most statutes use the term "curtilage," but courts construe it in a modern way to protect reasonable enclosures surrounding a dwelling, and in some instances, even commercial structures.

Many states have also enacted statutes making the possession of burglar's tools a crime. Because burglar's tools may consist of common household items, to obtain a conviction the prosecution is usually required to prove that the defendant knew the tools could be used for a criminal purpose and intended to use them for such purpose.

Arson at common law consisted of (1) the willful and malicious burning (2) of a dwelling (3) of another. There was no requirement that the dwelling be destroyed, and charring was sufficient. The requirement of "malice" was fulfilled by proof that the burning was deliberate; hence, the offense only required proof of the defendant's general intent to commit the crime.

As with burglary, modern statutes extend the offense of arson to include the intentional burning of buildings, structures, and vehicles of all types. Many statutes now provide that use of explosives to damage a structure constitutes arson. Therefore, arson can no longer be considered strictly a habitation offense. In contrast to the common law, many modern statutes provide that damage by smoke or scorching is sufficient to constitute arson. The modern approach is to classify arson by categories and provide penalties accordingly, with the most serious offense being arson of a dwelling.

Statutes also make it an offense to burn (and sometimes to otherwise destroy or injure) structures or personal property with the intent to defraud an insurer of the property. By definition, this offense requires proof of the defendant's specific intent to defraud.

Malicious Mischief

Malicious mischief was the common law misdemeanor of intentionally and maliciously causing damage to another's real or personal property. Modern statutes define the offense much as did the common law, often identifying it as **vandalism**. The punishment under contemporary statutes is often based on the value of property injured or destroyed.

Extortion

At common law, **extortion** involved the "taking by color of an office of money or other thing of value, that is not due, before it is due, or more than is due." Some modern statutes rather closely parallel the common law, while others equate with the concept of "blackmail." The essence of the modern offense is obtaining something of value from someone by inducing the victim's fear that he or she will be accused or exposed to some form of injury, embarrassment, or disgrace.

WHITE-COLLAR CRIME

White-collar crimes are offenses committed in the course of a person's occupation or profession and frequently include tax evasion, embezzlement, and various forms of fraud. Environmental crimes and violations of the federal food and drug acts are often included in the white-collar crime category, as are **obstruction of justice** and other offenses against the administration of justice. Sometimes **violations of civil rights** also are categorized as white-collar crimes. In addition, a number of federal statutes (and to a lesser extent various state statutes) proscribe acts uniquely referred to as white-collar crimes. These include **antitrust violations, bid rigging, price fixing, money laundering, insider trading, tax fraud**, and various other offenses. Essentially, these offenses involve the use of deceit and concealment (as opposed to force or violence) to obtain economic benefits or advantages. Many crimes, for example, assaultive and homicidal offenses, are not usually considered white-collar crimes although committed by "white-collar persons."

ORGANIZED CRIME

Organized crime involves offenses committed by persons or groups who conduct their business through illegal enterprises. Organized crime figures often attempt to gain political influence through graft and corruption, and they frequently resort to threats and acts of violence in commission of white-collar offenses. Organized crime gained its greatest foothold during the period when the Eighteenth Amendment to the United States Constitution, prohibiting the sale and distribution of alcoholic beverages, was extant. By the time Prohibition was repealed in 1933, organized crime had become involved in many phases of our economy, pursuing its interests through such illegal activities as loan sharking, gambling, prostitution, and drug trafficking. Protection rackets (in which proprietors are coerced into making payments to protect their businesses from theft and vandalism) and other forms of racketeering have become the methodology of organized crime as it has infiltrated many legitimate business operations. There is often an overlap between white-collar crime and organized crime.

Under its power to regulate foreign and interstate commerce, Congress enacted the Organized Crime Control Act of 1970. Title IX of the Act is entitled "Racketeer Influenced and Corrupt Organizations" and is commonly referred to by the acronym **RICO**. The law prohibits infiltration of legitimate organizations by racketeers where foreign or interstate commerce is affected. In addition to increased criminal penalties, the RICO statute provides for forfeiture of property used in criminal enterprises and also permits the government to bring civil actions against such enterprises.

RICO makes it a crime for any person "who has received any income derived, directly or indirectly, from a pattern of racketeering activity or through collection of an unlawful debt... to use or invest [in] any enterprise which is engaged in interstate or foreign commerce."[42] Second, it makes it unlawful for any such person to participate, directly or indirectly, in the conduct of the enterprise's affairs through a "pattern of racketeering."[43] Third, it makes it a crime for any person "employed by or associated with any enterprise engaged in, or the activities of which affect, interstate or foreign commerce, to conduct or participate, directly or indirectly, in the conduct of such enterprise's affairs through a pattern of racketeering activity or collection of unlawful debt."[44] This latter subsection of the Act making it unlawful to conduct the affairs of an enterprise through a pattern of racketeering has become the provision most frequently relied upon by prosecutors. Finally, the Act prohibits conspiracies to violate any of its regulations.[45] In January 2011, federal law enforcement officials made use of the RICO statute when they arrested over 110 organized crime figures in New York and New Jersey in what the FBI dubbed one of its biggest single-day operations ever.

VICE CRIMES

The common law of crimes developed based on the shared experiences of the English people. Customs were greatly influenced by the Bible and church doctrine. These concepts, in turn, became the foundation of pre-Revolutionary criminal law in America. Later, as legislative bodies began defining crimes, they took a more secular approach in the exercise of their police power, which is their authority to proscribe conduct that threatens the public health, safety, and morals. Today, there is considerable debate about whether the government should criminalize vices such as prostitution, obscenity, gambling, and illicit drugs. Certainly, these prohibitions are among the most widely violated.

Prostitution

A prostitute is one who engages in indiscriminate sexual activity for hire. Although it was not a crime at common law, historically, **prostitution** has been prohibited by most American penal codes. The Mann Act, passed in 1910, was an early federal law aimed at preventing the transportation of females across state lines for "immoral purposes." Traditionally directed at females, many state laws proscribing prostitution are now directed at both females and males. Increasingly, the police will arrest customers who solicit prostitutes. Nevada is currently the only state that permits some legalized prostitution, but it remains illegal in Nevada's most populated counties.

Obscenity

At common law, the use of vulgar and obscene language or indecent public exhibitions was considered a private nuisance and punishable as a misdemeanor. Historically, both the federal and state governments proscribed **obscenity**. With the development of mass communications in the 1950s, a flood of erotic material inundated the market.

Statutes and ordinances proscribing obscenity seldom defined it. Typically, laws simply criminalized the "buying, selling, giving or showing any obscene, indecent or impure book, paper or picture" without any definition of "obscene." Courts usually defined obscenity as being "repulsive" to the senses. Consequently, producers of sexually oriented materials and law enforcement officers lacked a guide to determine whether particular materials were in fact obscene.

In 1957, the U.S. Supreme Court in *Roth v. United States*, after first ruling that obscene materials had no First Amendment protection, declared that the test of obscenity was "whether to the average person applying contemporary community standards, the dominant theme of the material taken as a whole, appeals to the prurient interest."[46] In the ensuing years, the Court reviewed a number of lower court decisions, culminating in 1973 in its review of the seminal case, *Miller v. California*. In *Miller*, the Court clarified its *Roth* test by defining "community" so as to permit local juries to base their judgments on local, and not national, standards. Then, the Court further redefined the standards for determining obscenity by saying that the basic guidelines for the trier of fact must be (1) whether "the average person, applying contemporary community standards" would find that the work, taken as a whole, appeals to the prurient interest; (2) whether the work depicts or describes, in a patently offensive way, sexual conduct specifically defined by the applicable state law; and (3) whether the work, taken as a whole, lacks serious literary, artistic, political, or scientific value. The Court expressly rejected any requirement that the challenged materials must be found to be "utterly without redeeming social importance," and gave examples of the type of materials that would be considered "patently offensive."[47]

In 1982, in *New York v. Ferber*, the Supreme Court unanimously held that child pornography, like obscenity, is unprotected by the First Amendment.[48] Then, in 1987 the Court said that while the application of "contemporary community standards" is appropriate in evaluating the first two prongs of the *Miller* test, the third prong concerning the work's value must be gauged by the "reasonable person" test.[49]

Although most states proscribe obscenity along the lines of the federal constitutional definitions, states are free to grant greater freedom of expression than allowed under the current federal constitutional interpretations. Indeed, some have chosen to do so. In Oregon, for example, the state supreme court has interpreted the state constitution to hold that "any person can write, print, read, say, show or sell anything to a consenting adult even though that expression may be generally or universally condemned as 'obscene.'"[50]

Police and prosecutors experience difficulties chiefly in determining what is obscene based on "contemporary community standards" and in coping with Fourth Amendment problems relative to search for and seizure of allegedly obscene materials. Thus, obscenity prosecutions frequently fail. Today, much that was once considered to be obscene is readily available to anyone on the Internet and pay-per-view television. In recent years, law enforcement has shifted its attention away from traditional obscenity and toward child pornography, which the courts have said is not entitled to any constitutional protection.[51]

Gambling

To gamble means to risk money on an event, chance, or contingency in the expectation of realizing a gain. The common law did not regard **gambling** as an offense; however, the new American states made all or certain forms of gambling illegal. Today, federal laws and a variety of state statutes and local ordinances prohibit various forms of gambling. Bingo, craps, baccarat, poker, raffles, bookmaking, and slot machines are examples of common forms of gambling. However, the trend in America is toward legalization of gambling, and there now exist numerous opportunities for legal gambling.

Courts generally agree that to convict a defendant for a violation of a gambling law the prosecution must establish three elements: (1) a consideration, (2) a prize, and (3) a chance. Where gambling is prohibited, laws customarily make it unlawful to possess gambling devices and provide for their confiscation.

An analysis of the gambling laws extant in the United States is difficult because laws often authorize certain forms of gambling by certain organizations (usually church, fraternal, or other nonprofit activities) while forbidding others to do the same acts. State statutes often create exceptions for retail merchandising promotions and permit charitable, nonprofit, and veterans' organizations to conduct bingo games. Indeed, many states now promote lotteries to supplement tax revenues. Further, a number of Native American reservations have established casinos on sovereign tribal land. Internet gambling sites also have become more prevalent, but Congress's enactment of The Unlawful Internet Gambling Act, which was originally passed in 2006 but did not take effect until 2010, has curtailed the proliferation of online poker sites.

Betting on sports events is also widespread in this country, but because of the private consensual nature of such activity, any attempt to enforce laws against participants is usually futile. Gambling laws present a paradox, and enforcement must be directed primarily toward organized gambling under control of crime syndicates. Legalized sports gambling is currently permitted in Nevada, although some state legislators in New Jersey are leading a movement to legalize sports gambling there.

If a statute prohibiting gambling makes intent an element of the offense, the prosecution must prove the defendant's intent; otherwise, it is sufficient merely to prove the act of gambling. In some jurisdictions, statutes provide that it is a defense if the actor reasonably believed that the gambling conduct was permitted under bingo or charitable raffle laws. Defendants frequently raise constitutional issues relating to search and seizure problems and in some instances a defendant charged with gambling might succeed in establishing entrapment, a defense discussed later in this chapter.

Drug and Alcohol Offenses

The misuse of drugs and alcohol is among the oldest vices in society. The common law had little to say about the abuse of alcohol and did not address illicit drugs. Consequently, these offenses are based on statutory enactments reflecting the adverse social consequences of alcohol and drug abuse.

The Federal Controlled Substances Act[52] establishes schedules classifying controlled substances according to their potential for abuse and provides penalties for offenses involving the manufacture, sale, distribution, and possession of controlled substances. Specifically, there are five schedules, with Schedule I representing the most regulated class of substances and Schedule V representing the least regulated class of substances (such as cough suppressants). Schedule I drugs are said to have "high potential for abuse" and "no accepted medical usage," and include heroin and marijuana—with the latter's placement as a Schedule I substance serving as a source of controversy for many, especially in light of cocaine's placement as a Schedule II drug.

All states provide similar versions of the Federal Controlled Substances Act, usually setting mandatory penalties for those who sell large quantities of contraband or controlled substances that have a high potential for abuse. Although most narcotics offenses are felonies, it has become common for states to provide that where possession of a very small quantity of marijuana is involved, the offense is reduced to a misdemeanor. Despite numerous challenges, drug laws generally have been upheld, as courts are reluctant to reassess legislative judgments in this area. Furthermore, legislatures themselves have been reluctant to embrace any efforts to legalize certain types of controlled substances. Typically, efforts to legalize the use of illegal substances for medicinal purposes have taken the form of "ballot initiatives," whereby citizen petitions result in the passage of legislation by the people. Currently, over twenty states permit the usage of limited quantities of marijuana for medical purposes.

Additionally, in November 2012, voters in Colorado and Washington passed ballot initiatives that legalized possession of up to one ounce of marijuana. Colorado's initiative took effect on January 1, 2014, and Washington's was implemented on July 8, 2014; in both states, possession is limited to those 21 years or older. Other states have taken the step of "decriminalizing" marijuana by shifting penalties for possession from criminal offenses to civil offenses; in practical terms, such a shift means that those caught in possession would face no more than a fine. In March of 2014, legislators in Maryland and in the District of Columbia took the step of decriminalizing marijuana, joining sixteen other states that had done so previously.

Beyond regulations on the possession and distribution of illegal drug use, all states prohibit operating a vehicle in public while intoxicated (D.W.I.) or while under the influence of intoxicating liquors or drugs (D.U.I.). Some states prohibit driving with an unlawful blood alcohol level (D.U.B.A.L.). By 2000, eighteen states and the District of Columbia had decreased the level of blood alcohol required to establish legal intoxication to .08 percent or above. This nationwide trend was promoted by an act of Congress passed in the summer of 1998 under which states receive lucrative federal grants for lowering the prohibited blood-alcohol level to .08. As of 2012, all fifty states and the District of Columbia now have laws making it an offense to drive with a blood-alcohol concentration at or above 0.08 percent. Further, even in states that have legalized marijuana possession, driving under the influence of the drug remains a criminal offense.

OFFENSES AGAINST PUBLIC ORDER AND SAFETY

Government has an obligation to protect the public order and safety. Virtually all governments seek to achieve this goal by criminalizing acts that threaten society's interests in order and safety. The contemporary American offenses against public order have their roots in the English common law and include several misdemeanor offenses. Specifically, **unlawful assembly, riot**, and **disorderly conduct** were designed to preserve order, while **vagrancy** (going about without visible means of support) was designed to punish idleness and to control suspicious persons. Traffic violations and weapons offenses, while unknown to the common law, exist by virtue of modern legislation aimed at protecting the public safety.

Following the common law, most states have enacted statutes proscribing unlawful assembly, riot, and disorderly conduct. Cities frequently supplement these prohibitions by enacting ordinances against disturbing the peace and excessive noise. Arrests for crimes against public order are sometimes attacked as being violations of First Amendment freedoms of expression and assembly. In reviewing such arrests, courts must determine whether they were prompted by the need to preserve public order and safety and not a desire to suppress controversial messages or unpopular groups. In a well-known 1963 decision, the Supreme Court reversed convictions for breach of the peace where civil rights protesters conducted a peaceful, albeit vocal, demonstration on the grounds of the South Carolina state capitol.[53] The Court characterized the protestors' conduct as "an exercise of . . . basic constitutional rights in their most pristine and classic form."

Vagrancy, Loitering, and Panhandling

The common law offense of vagrancy has been replaced in most states and communities by laws that prohibit loitering. Vagrancy and loitering have been assailed as inherently vague offenses, and courts have struck down vagrancy laws and some loitering laws as violations of due process.[54] Historically, many vagrancy laws included prohibitions against public begging or panhandling. These prohibitions have been struck down by some courts as violations of First Amendment rights as well as due process. More recently, communities have enacted more narrowly tailored restrictions on "aggressive panhandling," and these prohibitions have fared better in the courts.

CASE IN POINT

THE SUPREME COURT INVALIDATES A CHICAGO LOITERING ORDINANCE AIMED AT STREET GANGS
Chicago v. Morales
United States Supreme Court
527 U.S. 41, 119 S. Ct. 1849, 144 L. Ed. 2d 67 (1999)

In 1992, the Chicago City Council enacted an ordinance prohibiting criminal street gang members from loitering in any public place. Over the next three years, the police issued more than 89,000 dispersal orders and arrested more than 42,000 people for violating the new law. In 1999, the United States Supreme Court declared the ordinance unconstitutional. Writing for the Court, Justice John P.

Stevens concluded that the ordinance did not provide "sufficiently specific limits on the enforcement discretion of the police" and failed to meet "constitutional standards for definiteness and clarity." The Court found that the ordinance succumbed to the vice of vagueness—that the city council had failed to meet its obligation to specify the criminal law with reasonable precision.

Curfews

In recent years, many cities and counties across the United States have enacted ordinances imposing curfews on juveniles. Most of these laws prohibit juveniles from being on public streets or in other public places from midnight to 6:00 a.m. unless accompanied by a parent or guardian or another adult approved by the juvenile's parent or guardian. Curfew laws that provide exceptions concerning work, school and civic events, travel, and emergencies generally have been upheld by the courts against constitutional challenges based on due process and equal protection arguments.

Motor Vehicle Violations

States, and often municipalities, have adopted laws defining a wide range of motor vehicle violations. These are typically strict-liability offenses; therefore, there is generally no requirement to prove criminal intent to find a defendant guilty of a traffic violation. Among other offenses, these laws proscribe speeding; failing to yield the right-of-way; failing to observe traffic officers, signs, and signals; and driving without required equipment. During the 1970s and 1980s, states adopted a number of model laws, so that traffic offenses are highly uniform across the states. This uniformity is both necessary and desirable given the mobility of today's populace and the volume of traffic on the Nation's highways.

Weapons Offenses

The Second Amendment to the United States Constitution provides that "a well regulated Militia, being necessary to the security of a free state, the right of the people to keep and bear Arms, shall not be infringed." Nevertheless, there are numerous statutory prohibitions against the manufacture, sale, possession, and use of firearms and other weapons. For example, states commonly enact statutes making it unlawful to carry a concealed weapon without a permit. The federal Gun Control Act of 1968 established a fairly comprehensive regime governing the distribution of firearms.[55] For example, federal law prohibits the sale, possession, and use of machine guns and other automatic weapons. The Supreme Court has upheld these prohibitions against challenges based on the Second Amendment.[56] State courts have generally been unsympathetic to challenges to state gun control laws based on state constitutional provisions.

The most notable judicial decision on gun control occurred in 2008, when the Supreme Court struck down a District of Columbia ordinance effectively prohibiting the possession of all handguns within the District.[57] The Court said that the Second Amendment confers a personal right to gun possession for personal protection, but the Court noted that there is ample room for reasonable regulation of firearms. The Court's decision prompted a new wave of constitutional challenges to local gun control laws around the country. In 2010, the Court reaffirmed the notion that gun possession in the home is protected by the Second Amendment when it struck down a city of Chicago ban.[58] That case, *McDonald v. City of Chicago*, incorporated the Second Amendment. Nevertheless, because senseless gun violence continues to plague America's cities, and even its schools and universities, a debate rages in the land over the need for tougher gun control legislation and/or increased enforcement of existing prohibitions.

OFFENSES AGAINST THE ADMINISTRATION OF JUSTICE

The common law recognized the need to deter and, if necessary, to punish those who corrupt the orderly processes of government and the administration of justice. In the United States, federal and state statutes proscribe such offenses as **bribery, perjury, subornation of perjury**, obstruction of justice, **resisting arrest, compounding a crime**, and **escape**. Bribery consists of offering, giving, requesting, soliciting, or receiving something of value to influence a public officer's decision. Perjury involves making a false statement under oath, while procuring someone to lie under oath is subornation of perjury. Resisting arrest involves behavior that keeps an officer from making an arrest. Accepting something of value in exchange for an agreement not to prosecute a crime is called compounding a crime. Finally, the crime of escape consists of a person's unlawfully leaving lawful custody. Statutory offenses defining these crimes expand the common law and generally increase the severity of these offenses from misdemeanors to felonies.

Courts have the power to hold a person in either civil or criminal **contempt**. **Civil contempt** is a sanction imposed to coerce a recalcitrant person to obey a court order, for example, for failing to pay court-ordered support for dependents. A court imposes **criminal contempt** to punish an offender whose deliberate conduct is calculated to obstruct or embarrass the court or to degrade a judicial officer in the role of administering justice.

ENVIRONMENTAL CRIME

Unlike common law crimes, offenses against the public health and the environment are defined by statutes enacted by the federal and state legislatures. While not faced with the severe environmental problems of our age, the common law did regard wildlife, game, and fish as resources to be preserved. In the United States, the state and federal governments have for many years enacted regulations and imposed criminal sanctions on poachers to protect these resources for the benefit of the public. Many offenses relating to public health developed during the industrial revolution as a result of the widespread distribution of food, drugs, and cosmetics and the need to control communicable diseases. By the early 1900s, municipalities perceived the need for zoning to control nuisances and to regulate land use. Since the middle of this century, pollution of the ground, water, and air has been recognized as a major threat to the health and welfare of the people and, indeed, to the ecological balance of the earth.

Enforcement of regulations in these fields is accomplished largely by regulatory agencies and through measures imposing civil liability. Nevertheless, legislatures have found it necessary to impose criminal sanctions to effectively enforce standards and to deter violators. In contrast to the typical common law crimes, **environmental crimes** usually involve an offender's neglect to comply with required standards or failure to take action required by law. These are *mala prohibita* offenses, and statutes criminalizing conduct in these areas generally contemplate a lower level of intent, frequently imposing a standard of strict liability.

MILITARY OFFENSES

In 1950, Congress enacted the **Uniform Code of Military Justice** (UCMJ), which has been amended several times. The UCMJ defines those persons subject to the jurisdiction of military courts. These include active military personnel, military prisoners, prisoners of war, and, under certain circumstances, reserve and retired members of the military.

Members of the armed forces enjoy constitutional rights and protections as do civilians, but some of these rights are restricted because of the military environment. The UCMJ's Article 15, which references non-judicial punishment, enables a commander to impose disciplinary measures for commission of minor offenses. However, a service member may reject such punishment and demand to be tried by a court-martial.

Articles 77-134, referred to as the punitive articles of the UCMJ, include most major crimes common to the civilian justice system. In addition, the UCMJ defines a number of offenses unique to the armed forces, such as desertion, absence without leave (AWOL), insubordination, disrespect toward a superior officer, aiding the enemy, and mutiny. Article 133 proscribes "conduct unbecoming an officer," while Article 134 includes "disorders and neglects to the prejudice of good order and discipline" and "conduct of a nature to bring discredit upon the armed forces." These latter articles appear vague by civilian standards; nevertheless, in *Parker v. Levy* (1974),[59] the Supreme Court, recognizing the different character of the military community, upheld them as not violating due process of law.

DEFENSES

Defenses are arguments that defendants use to deny criminal responsibility. Like crimes, most defenses have their roots in the English common law, though they have been modified over the years by constitutional provisions and statutes and judicial interpretations thereof.

The most common defense asserted by defendants is a general denial, often accompanied by an **alibi**. Defendants may simply deny the factual allegations of the prosecutor. A defendant who pleads alibi simply says, "I was elsewhere when the offense was committed." The Supreme Court has ruled that when the state law requires that a defendant who pleads an alibi must notify the prosecution in advance of trial and furnish the names of witnesses the defendant intends to use to support the alibi, the prosecution must make similar disclosures to the defendant concerning refutation of the evidence the defendant presents.[60]

Denial and alibi are examples of **negative defenses** in that they seek to negate the charge that the defendant committed a wrongful act. **Affirmative defenses**, on the other hand, do not dispute that the act took place, but instead deny the defendant's criminal responsibility for the act or assert other limitations on the authority of government to prosecute the defendant. Affirmative defenses to crimes may be divided into the following five categories:

1. those asserting lack of capacity;
2. those asserting excuse or justification;
3. those justifying the use of force;
4. those relying on constitutional or statutory rights; and
5. those assailing governmental conduct.

Defenses Asserting Lack of Capacity to Commit a Crime

Except in cases of strict liability, it is necessary to prove the defendant's criminal intent as well as the commission of an unlawful act. This first set of affirmative defenses involves the claim that the defendant lacks the capacity to form criminal intent due to **infancy, intoxication, insanity**, or **automatism**.

Infancy

The common law protected very young children from the harshness of the law by presuming a child under age seven to be incapable of forming criminal intent. This presumption of incapacity was rebuttable for a child over seven but under fourteen, with the prosecution having to demonstrate that a child under fourteen was capable of comprehending the wrongdoing involved in commission of an offense. Children over age fourteen were treated as adults. In many American jurisdictions, these presumptions are no longer viable because legislatures have provided that children under certain ages are subject to the jurisdiction of juvenile courts, where procedures are tailored toward less mature offenders. Although different states define "juveniles" with different age standards, under federal law, a juvenile is a person who has not attained age eighteen at the time of the commission of an offense.[61] Some jurisdictions also allow for juveniles to be tried as adults for certain offenses.

Intoxication

English common law did not excuse a person who voluntarily became intoxicated from responsibility for criminal conduct. American courts distinguish voluntary intoxication from involuntary intoxication. In most jurisdictions, voluntary intoxication may be considered in determining whether a defendant can formulate the specific intent required in such crimes as larceny, burglary, and premeditated murder. A few courts will not even permit a jury to consider voluntary intoxication on the issue of specific intent. Courts typically reject the defense of voluntary intoxication in respect to general-intent crimes such as voluntary manslaughter and most sexual offenses. Involuntary intoxication rarely occurs, but when it does, it can relieve the criminality of an act committed under its influence if, as a result of intoxication, the defendant no longer knows right from wrong.

Insanity

All persons are presumed sane unless previously adjudicated insane. The concept of mental responsibility has historic roots in Anglo-American law because common law crimes included a *mens rea*, the mental element. The **M'Naghten Rule** developed at common law provides, "it must be clearly proved that, at the time of committing the act, the party accused was labouring under such a defect of reason, from disease of the mind, as not to know the nature and quality of the act he was doing; or, if he did know it, that he did not know what he was doing was wrong."[62] By the mid-1800s, the *M'Naghten* Rule had become the test for insanity used in both federal and state courts in the United States.

In 1962, the American Law Institute (ALI) proposed a new standard sometimes referred to as the **substantial capacity test**. It provides that "a person is not responsible for criminal conduct if at the time of such conduct, as a result of mental disease or defect, a person lacks substantial capacity either to appreciate the wrongfulness of his conduct or to conform his conduct to the requirements of the law." Most federal courts have adopted the ALI standard.

The defense of insanity has never been popular with the public, sometimes being called "a rich person's defense," because defendants who invoke it frequently expend considerable financial resources to present psychiatric testimony. Few cases have caused as great a concern over the functioning of the criminal justice system in the United States as the verdict of "not guilty by reason of insanity" in the federal court trial of John Hinckley for the 1981 shooting of then President Ronald Reagan, his press secretary, and two law enforcement officers. The Hinckley verdict motivated Congress and several state legislatures to review the status of insanity defenses. Dissatisfied with the ALI test, which was applied in the Hinckley trial, Congress decided to eliminate the volitional prong in the federal test for insanity and to revert substantially to the *M'Naghten* Rule when it enacted the Insanity Defense Reform Act of 1984. This Act provides that in federal courts:

> [i]t is an affirmative defense to a prosecution under any Federal statute that, at the time of the commission of the acts constituting the offense, the defendant, as a result of a severe mental disease or defect, was unable to appreciate the nature and quality or the wrongfulness of his acts. Mental disease or defect does not otherwise constitute a defense.[63]

Additionally, the Act stipulates, "The defendant has the burden of proving the defense of insanity by clear and convincing evidence."[64] The clear and convincing evidence standard is higher than the usual civil evidentiary standard of preponderance of the evidence but somewhat lower than the standard of beyond a reasonable doubt, the evidentiary standard required for criminal convictions.

Under the Insanity Defense Reform Act, psychiatric evidence of impaired volitional control is not admissible to support an insanity defense; however in 1990, the

United States Court of Appeals for the Eleventh Circuit ruled that the language of the new federal Act does not bar the use of psychiatric evidence to negate specific intent where that level of intent is an element of the offense charged by the government.[65]

Although Congress has placed the burden on defendants who plead insanity in federal courts to prove their defense, state courts are divided on the issue. In some states where insanity is classified as an affirmative defense, the defendant bears the burden of proof of insanity, usually by a preponderance of the evidence. In other states, when a defendant pleads insanity and introduces some evidence of insanity, the state must then establish the defendant's sanity, usually by proof beyond a reasonable doubt, the standard required for establishing a defendant's guilt. Most courts permit laypersons as well as expert witnesses to testify on the issue of a defendant's insanity.

Unlike a defendant who is simply found not guilty, a defendant found not guilty by reason of insanity may, in some circumstances, be committed to a mental institution if the trial judge determines that protection of the public requires that the defendant be confined.

Some states have recently resorted to verdicts of "guilty but mentally ill" in cases where the defendant's insanity has been established, and several states have abolished the defense of insanity. While the Supreme Court has not settled the issue, its refusal to hear appeals of criminals who seek to bring an insanity defense in states that do not permit one suggests that the federal constitution does not require that states allow a defendant the opportunity to plead insanity.

Automatism

Older cases treat defendants who claim that their unlawful acts were committed because of an involuntary condition such as somnambulism (i.e., sleepwalking) within the context of the insanity defense. Newer cases tend to classify such involuntary actions as automatism and view them as a basis for an affirmative defense independent from insanity. The defense is usually limited to a situation where criminal conduct is beyond a person's knowledge and control. Where a defendant is acquitted of an offense because of automatism, generally there are no follow-up consequences such as institutionalization, which often occurs when a defendant is acquitted by reason of insanity.

Defenses Asserting Excuse or Justification

A defendant who asserts an excuse admits the offense but claims that under the circumstances such conduct should not result in punishment. A defendant who asserts a justification for conduct says, in effect, that it was justified under the circumstances. There are five principal defenses based on a defendant's asserting an excuse or justification: **duress, necessity, consent, mistake of law**, and **mistake of fact**.

Duress

The common law recognized that duress can be a defense to criminal charges if the coercion exerted involved the use of threats of harm that were present, imminent, and pending and of such nature as to include well-grounded apprehensions of death or serious bodily harm if the act was not done. Not even the threat of imminent death was sufficient to excuse the intentional killing of an innocent human being. The defense of duress, sometimes referred to as "coercion, compulsion, or duress," is recognized today either by statute or decisional law. American courts have generally ruled that a threat of future harm is not sufficient to constitute duress. Duress has been asserted most frequently by defendants who have committed robberies and thefts and by prisoners who have escaped from custody.

Necessity

Early common law cases recognized the defense of necessity. Suppose several people are shipwrecked on a cold night. One person swims to shore, breaks into an unoccupied beach cottage, and takes food and blankets to assist the injured until help can be secured. Prosecution in such an event would be unlikely, but if prosecuted, the defendant would properly plead the defense of necessity. American courts hold that if there is a reasonable legal alternative to violating the law, the defense of necessity fails.

Recently, defendants have attempted to justify actions involving "civil disobedience" on the ground of necessity in instances where they have forcefully asserted their personal or political beliefs. In most—but not all—cases, the necessity defense has been unavailing to defendants espousing social and political causes. For example, several defendants were charged with criminal trespass when they refused to leave an abortion clinic in Anchorage, Alaska. They claimed their actions were necessary to avert the imminent peril to human life that would result from performance of abortions. In rejecting their contention, the Alaska Supreme Court outlined three requirements that must be met by a person who pleads the defense of necessity: (1) the act charged must have been done to prevent a significant evil; (2) there must have been no adequate alternative; and (3) the harm caused must not have been disproportionate to the harm avoided.[66]

Consent

Because a victim may not excuse a criminal act, historically, courts have said that consent is not a defense to a criminal prosecution. But there are exceptions to this general statement. For example, where lack of consent is an element of the offense, as in larceny, consent is a defense. This may be true in a prosecution for rape, but only where competent adults freely consent before having sexual relations. Consent also is commonly given to physicians who perform surgery. In contact sports, such as football and boxing, consent is implied and may be a defense to reasonable instances of physical contact that may otherwise be regarded as batteries. Of course, a valid consent presupposes that it is voluntarily given by a person legally competent to do so.

Mistake of Law

One of the oft-quoted maxims of the law is that "ignorance of the law is no excuse." But in some instances, a defendant's honest, but mistaken, view of the law may be accepted as a defense. One example is where such a mistake negates the specific-intent element of a crime. Thus, a mistake of law may be asserted as a defense in a larceny case where there is a technical question of who has legal title to an asset. Likewise, a defendant's good-faith, but mistaken, trust in the validity of a divorce has been held to be a defense to a charge of bigamy. However, a court will never recognize a dishonest pretense of ignorance of the law as a defense.

Mistake of Fact

In contrast to the ancient common law maxim that "ignorance of the law is no excuse," at common law, ignorance or mistake of fact, guarded by an honest purpose, afforded a defendant a sufficient excuse for a supposed criminal act. American courts have agreed, but normally a mistake of fact will not be recognized as a defense to a general-intent crime unless the mistake is a reasonable one for a person to make under the circumstances. However, even an unreasonable mistake may be asserted as a defense to a crime that requires a specific intent. An example of a mistake of fact might be a person at an airport accidentally taking a piece of luggage that looked similar to their own. Because most theft statutes require a showing of specific intent, the individual's mistake in taking in the wrong piece of luggage might preclude criminal prosecution for theft.

In strict-liability offenses, though, the defense of mistake of fact is unavailing since these offenses are not based on intent. Having consensual sexual relations with a minor is considered a strict-liability offense in some jurisdictions, and a mistake of fact as to a minor's age is generally not a defense. Even if a court finds that a statutory rape statute requires proof of a general criminal intent to convict, a defendant's reasonable mistake of fact concerning a female's age is usually not available as a defense. In the past decade, trial courts have also rejected the contention that because a minor female can consent to an abortion, she should be able to consent to sexual intercourse. Yet, some judges and legislators have questioned the need to employ a strict-liability standard in consensual sexual relationships where a minor represents herself as an adult.

Defenses Justifying the Use of Force

The use of force may be a defense to a criminal charge that the defendant caused injury or death to another. Therefore, the defense of **justifiable use of force** is applicable to the assaultive and homicidal offenses where the defendant claims that the use of force was justified under the circumstances.

In general, the use of **deadly force** in self-defense typically requires that the person using such force (1) be in a place where the person has a right to be; (2) act without fault; and (3) act in reasonable fear or apprehension of imminent death or serious bodily injury.[67] In evaluating whether the use of deadly force is reasonable, courts consider numerous factors. Among these are the sizes, ages, and physical abilities of the parties, whether the attacker was armed, and perhaps even the attacker's reputation for violence. Ordinarily, a person being attacked may use whatever degree of nondeadly force appears reasonably necessary under the circumstances—although self-defense statutes can vary greatly across jurisdictions.

Self-Defense

Today, each state has laws that specifically define the circumstances under which the use of lethal force is considered justified. As a starting point, all states—with the exception of Ohio (and some Louisiana courts)—require that the prosecutor prove, beyond a reasonable doubt, that self-defense is not applicable. Thus, the burden of proof remains on the state even when this defense is invoked. Past this point of commonality, though, subtle variations in statutes from different states can dramatically impact the implementation of self-defense principles.

One common variation across state laws is the matter of a "duty to retreat," which can be contrasted with a statutory grant to "stand-your-ground." At common law, a person attacked had a duty "to retreat to the wall" before using deadly force in **self-defense**. A majority of modern courts, however, have rejected the common law doctrine of requiring a person to retreat to the greatest extent possible before "meeting force with force."[68] Rather, most state laws today suggest that a person attacked or threatened is under no obligation to flee from the situation, and may stand one's ground and use any force reasonably necessary to prevent serious bodily harm. Nevertheless, a minority of jurisdictions has adopted the principle that a person who can safely retreat must do so before using deadly force.[69] Even states that follow the 'retreat rule', though, generally have adhered to the notion that a person does not have to retreat while inside that person's own dwelling; and, this concept actually was articulated by the Supreme Court of the United States in an 1895 case called *Beard v. United States*—where a homeowner's conviction for killing an armed cow thief that had entered his property was overturned.

A widely-publicized self-defense case involving a "stand-your-ground" provision emanated from an incident that took place on the night of February 26, 2012 in Sanford, Florida. There, George Zimmerman, a neighborhood watch coordinator, fatally shot an unarmed 17-year-old named Trayvon Martin. Zimmerman claimed that he acted in self-defense after Martin repeatedly punched him, and Zimmerman exhibited wounds to his face and head. Florida self-defense laws state that one may use lethal force when that person "reasonably believes that such force is necessary to prevent imminent death or great bodily harm to himself or herself or another or to prevent the commission of a forcible felony."[70] Furthermore, Florida law also includes a "stand-your-ground" provision that absolved Zimmerman of any duty to retreat from an attack.[71] In light of these mandates, local authorities declined to press charges against Zimmerman. Subsequently, however, a special prosecutor charged him with second-degree murder. Ultimately, on July 13, 2013, following a trial that lasted approximately three weeks, a jury found that Zimmerman was not guilty of any homicide offense.

Another self-defense case from Florida, dubbed the so-called "Loud Music Shooting" by some members of the media, also has garnered national attention. On November 23, 2012, at a gas station in Jacksonville, a man named Michael Dunn was involved in a verbal dispute with four teenagers concerning loud music that was emanating from their car. As the situation escalated, Dunn fired 10 shots at the teenagers' vehicle, killing an 18-year-old named Jordan Davis. Dunn fled the scene immediately after the shooting, and later claimed that he was threatened and thought that he saw a gun pointed at him. A jury later convicted Dunn on three counts of attempted second-degree murder. However, the jury was deadlocked on the charge of murder in the matter of Davis' death, resulting in a mistrial on that count; in a re-trial, Dunn was convicted of murder and sentenced to life in prison.

Battered Woman Syndrome

In recent years, the concept of self-defense by women also has been expanded to include a situation in which a woman claims to have been continually battered by a man. **Battered woman syndrome** (BWS) refers to a pattern of psychological and behavioral symptoms of a woman living with a male in a battering relationship. Some courts now permit a female in that situation who is charged with assaulting or killing a man to show that even though she did not face immediate harm, her plea of self-defense should be recognized because her actions were a response to constant battering by the man with whom she lived. Relatively little decisional law from the higher courts has developed in this area. The trend seems to be to allow such evidence, either by judicial decision or by statute.

Following the same rationale, if there is evidence that a child has been abused continually over an extended period, there is now a movement to assert the **battered child syndrome** (BCS) in defense of a child accused of assaulting or killing a parent. In a much-discussed opinion, a Washington appellate court held: "Neither law nor logic suggest [*sic*] any reason to limit to women recognition of the impact a battering relationship may have on the victim's actions or perceptions. . . . [T]he rationale underlying the admissibility of testimony regarding the battered women syndrome is at least as compelling, if not more so, when applied to children."[72]

Defense of Others

At common law, a defender had the right to use reasonable force to prevent commission of a felony or to protect members of the household who were endangered. The trend in American jurisdictions is to allow a person "to stand in the shoes of the victim" and to use such reasonable force as is necessary to defend anyone from harm, irrespective of relationship. Courts in many states limit a person's right to defend another individual from harm to those persons who "reasonably believe" that force is necessary to protect another. Some courts take a more restrictive view and hold that an intervener is justified in using force to defend another only if the party being defended would have been justified in using the same force in self-defense. Of course, under either standard, the right to go to the defense of another does not authorize a person to resort to retaliatory force.

Defense of Habitation

The common law held that "a man's home is his castle" and placed great emphasis on the security of a person's dwelling by permitting the use of deadly force against an intruder. This is sometimes referred to as the **castle doctrine**. Courts generally have said that the use of deadly force is justified to prevent a forcible entry into a habitation in circumstances such as where threats have been made against the occupant or other occupants, or where the occupant reasonably apprehends death or great bodily harm to self or other occupants, or where the occupant reasonably believes that the assailant intends to commit a felony. Even so, variation exists across states in regard to justifying the use of lethal self-defense inside the home. Tennessee, for example, allows the use of deadly force in all situations where an intruder "forcibly enters" the home,[73] while Minnesota permits the use of deadly force in the home only when necessary to prevent another from committing a felony.[74] In 2014, a 65-year-old Minnesota man named Byron Smith actually was found guilty of murder for shooting two teenage burglars multiple times; prosecutors were able to convince a jury that Smith's multiple shots exceeded the scope of what was necessary to prevent commission of a felony.

Application of the castle doctrine also can vary in other situations. For example, while a householder may, under some circumstances, be justified in using deadly force, the householder normally would not be justified in taking a life to repel a mere trespass onto surrounding property—although states vary in regard to how they treat the "curtilage," a term that refers to areas immediately surrounding the home (such as a porch). Jurisdictions also have been divided as to whether the castle doctrine applies to incidents involving co-occupants or other people who are legally on the premises. As with other self-defense provisions, then, different states evince subtle variations in their applications of the castle doctrine.

Defense of Property

The right to defend your property is more limited than the right to defend your home or yourself. The common law allowed a person in lawful possession of property to use reasonable, but not deadly, force to protect it. Today, the use of force to protect a person's property is often defined by statute. Typically, these laws are similar to an Iowa law that provides: "[A] person is justified in the use of reasonable force to prevent or terminate criminal interference with his or her possession or other right to property."[75] Most states generally follow this standard, but recently some have adopted "stand-your-ground" laws that allow the use of deadly force to protect property.

Defenses Based on Constitutional and Statutory Authority

Everyone is familiar with the scenario of the witness who invokes the constitutional privilege against self-incrimination based on the Fifth Amendment to the Constitution, which provides that "no person . . . shall be compelled in any criminal case to be a witness against himself." The privilege against self-incrimination is applicable to the states through the Fourteenth Amendment. The privilege against self-incrimination guaranteed by the federal Constitution is a personal one that applies only to natural persons and not to corporations. A strict reading of the clause would limit the privilege to testimony given in a criminal trial. The Supreme Court, however, has held that an individual may refuse to answer official questions posed in any proceeding, civil or criminal, formal or informal, where the answers might be incriminating.[76] A classic example is the privilege of suspects in police custody to invoke their *Miranda* rights, a subject we discuss in Chapter 10.

Immunity

A witness compelled to give incriminating testimony receives **use immunity** (i.e., the testimony given cannot be used against the witness). This form of immunity meets the demands of the Constitution.[77] In some states, a witness who testifies under a grant of immunity is given **transactional immunity**, a broader protection than required under the federal Constitution. Transactional immunity protects a witness from prosecution for any activity mentioned in the witness's testimony. Despite a grant of immunity, a witness may be prosecuted for making material false statements under oath.

Sometimes a prosecutor, with approval of the court, grants a witness **contractual immunity** to induce a suspect to testify against someone and thereby enable the prosecution to obtain a conviction not otherwise obtainable because of the constitutional protection against self-incrimination. This type of immunity is rarely granted if other available evidence will lead to a conviction. The authority to grant immunity in federal courts is vested in the United States Attorney with approval of the Attorney General or certain authorized assistants.[78] At the state level, such authority typically is vested in the chief prosecuting officer (i.e., the district or state attorney).

Under international law, a person who has diplomatic status and serves as a part of a diplomatic mission, as well as members of the diplomat's staff and household, is immune from arrest and prosecution, thus enjoying **diplomatic immunity**.

Double Jeopardy

The concept of forbidding retrial of a defendant who has been found not guilty developed under English common law. The Fifth Amendment to the United States Constitution embodies the principle by stating, "[N]or shall any person be subject for the same offence to be twice put in jeopardy of life or limb." The Double Jeopardy Clause forbids a second prosecution for the same offense after a defendant has been acquitted or even after a conviction.[79] But, if a defendant appeals from a conviction and prevails, it is not **double jeopardy** for the prosecution to retry the defendant, unless the appellate court rules that there was insufficient evidence to sustain the defendant's conviction.[80] Nor is it double jeopardy to retry a defendant if the trial court, at the defendant's request, has declared a mistrial.[81] If, however, the government moves for a mistrial, the defendant objects, and the court grants the mistrial, the prosecution must establish a manifest necessity for the mistrial in order for a retrial to be permitted.

Some offenses are crimes against both the federal and state governments. The standard policy, and in some instances state law, forbids a second prosecution once an offender has been prosecuted in a different jurisdiction. Nevertheless, under our federal system, the Double Jeopardy Clause does not preclude a prosecution by both the federal and state governments, since separate sovereigns are involved.[82] Yet this principle does not allow two courts within a state to try an accused for the same offense.[83] In addition to protecting against a second prosecution for the same offense after conviction or acquittal, the Double Jeopardy Clause protects against multiple punishments for the same offense.[84] The Constitution, however, does not define "same offense." In *Blockburger v. United States* (1932) the Supreme Court said that "[t]he applicable rule is that, where the same act or transaction constitutes a violation of two distinct statutory provisions, the test to be applied to determine whether there are two offenses or only one is whether each provision requires proof of an additional fact which the other does not."[85]

Thus, the *Blockburger* test focuses primarily on the elements of the crimes in question, and less so on the facts. However, not all courts have regarded *Blockburger* as the exclusive method of determining whether successive prosecutions violate the principle of double jeopardy. Indeed, some courts look also to the evidence to be presented to prove those crimes.

Statutes of Limitation

A **statute of limitations** is a legislative enactment that places a time limit on the prosecution of a crime. Common law placed no time limits on prosecution. There is no federal constitutional basis to limit the time in which a prosecution can be initiated. Nonetheless, the federal government and almost all states have laws that prescribe certain time limits for prosecution of most offenses, except murder. There are two primary public policy reasons for enacting statutes of limitations on the prosecution of crimes. First, it is widely accepted that a person should not be under threat of prosecution for too long a period. Second, after a prolonged period, proof is either unavailable or, if available, perhaps not credible.

Statutes of limitations seldom place time limits on prosecutions for murder and other very serious offenses. This fact was dramatized in 1994 when Byron De La Beckwith was convicted for the June 1963 murder of Medgar Evers. Evers was an official of the National Association for the Advancement of Colored People, and his death galvanized support for the enactment of civil rights laws in the 1960s. Two trials in 1964 ended in deadlocked juries. But after extended litigation, and a lapse of more than thirty years since the victim's death, a Mississippi jury found De La Beckwith guilty of killing Evers.

Under most statutes of limitations, the period for prosecution begins when a crime is committed, and not when it is discovered. The period ends when an arrest warrant is issued, an indictment is returned, or an information is filed. The period of limitations is interrupted while a perpetrator is a fugitive or conceals him or herself from authorities. This cessation of the statute of limitations is often referred to as the "tolling" of the statutory period.

Federal statutes of limitations provide a five-year limitations period on prosecution of noncapital crimes.[86] While limitations periods vary among the states, most provide five- to seven-year limitations on the prosecution of felonies other than murder, one to two years on major misdemeanors, and a year or less on minor misdemeanors.

Defenses Based on Improper Government Conduct

Law enforcement officers may provide an opportunity for a predisposed person to commit a crime, but they are not permitted to "manufacture" crime by implanting criminal ideas into innocent minds. Therefore, a person who has been induced to commit an offense under these latter circumstances may plead the defense of **entrapment**. A defendant who claims to have committed an offense as a result of inducement by an undercover police officer or a confidential police informant often asserts the defense of entrapment. However, it is not available to a defendant who has been entrapped by a person not associated with the government or police.

Entrapment was not a defense under the common law, and strictly speaking, it is not based on the Constitution. Nevertheless, it has long been recognized in federal and state courts in the United States. In a landmark case arising during prohibition days, the Supreme Court held that a federal officer had entrapped a defendant by using improper inducements to cause him to buy illegal liquor for the officer. The Court observed that the evidence revealed that the defendant, Sorrells, had not been predisposed to commit a crime but had been induced by the government agent to do so. The Court opined that entrapment occurs when criminal conduct involved is "the product of the creative activity of [law enforcement officers]."[87] In *Sorrells*, the majority of the justices viewed the test for entrapment as whether the defendant's criminal intent originated in the mind of the officer or whether the defendant was predisposed to commit the offense. This focus on the predisposition of the defendant has come to be known as the subjective test of entrapment. A minority of justices in *Sorrells* would have applied what is now known as the objective test of entrapment. Under this view, the court would simply determine whether the police methods were so improper as to be likely to induce or ensnare a person into committing a crime.

Most courts today follow the subjective view. Thus, a person who pleads entrapment is held to have admitted commission of the offense. A jury then determines whether the defendant committed the crime because of predisposition, or if the defendant was improperly induced to do so by the police. Where courts follow the objective view, the judge, not the jury, determines whether the police methods were so improper as to constitute entrapment. Some federal courts have simply said that where police conduct is outrageous, it becomes a question of law for the judge to determine if governmental misconduct is so shocking as to be a violation of due process of law. In courts that strictly follow the objective view, the defendant's predisposition to commit an offense is irrelevant.

Two principal reasons account for the increased assertion of the defense of entrapment in recent years. First, a large number of violations of narcotics laws have been prosecuted on the basis of undercover police activity and evidence given by confidential police informants. Second, there has been increased attention to prosecuting corruption involving government officials.

Selective Prosecution

Selective enforcement of the criminal law is not itself a constitutional violation, and therefore, without more, it does not constitute a defense.[88] To prevail on the defense of **selective prosecution**, a defendant must demonstrate that other similarly situated persons have not been prosecuted for similar conduct, and that prosecution was based on some impermissible ground such as race, religion, or exercise of the First Amendment rights of free speech.

Nontraditional Defenses

Although they are rarely successful, defendants sometimes employ novel and innovative defenses. Where a novel defense leads to an acquittal, appellate courts do not have an opportunity to evaluate the legal basis of the defense, so precedent is slow to develop. Such defenses have alleged a victim's negligence, premenstrual syndrome (PMS), compulsive gambling, post-traumatic stress syndrome (PTSS) (which often refers to the psychological reaction to the unique stresses suffered during combat), the junk food defense, and pornographic or television intoxication. Other unusual defenses include urban survival syndrome, XYY chromosome abnormality, black rage, multiple personalities, and even the notion of an affluent upbringing ("affluenza").

CASE IN POINT

ENTRAPMENT IN A CHILD PORNOGRAPHY CASE
Jacobson v. United States
United States Supreme Court
503 U.S. 540, 112 S. Ct. 1535, 118 L. Ed. 2d 174 (1992)

In 1987, Keith Jacobson was indicted for violating the Child Protection Act of 1984, which criminalizes the knowing receipt through the mails of a "visual depiction [that] involves the use of a minor engaging in sexually explicit conduct." At trial, Jacobson contended the government entrapped him into committing the crime. A jury found him guilty, and his conviction was affirmed by the Court of Appeals. The United States Supreme Court granted review. In evaluating the evidence at Jacobson's trial, the Supreme Court found that while it was still legal to do so, Jacobson ordered some magazines containing photos of nude boys. After Congress enacted the Child Protection Act making this illegal, two government agencies learned that Jacobson had ordered the magazines. The agencies sent mail to Jacobson through fictitious organizations to explore his willingness to break the law. He was bombarded with solicitations, which included

communications decrying censorship and questioning the legitimacy and constitutionality of the government's efforts to restrict availability of sexually explicit materials. Jacobson finally responded to an undercover solicitation to order child pornography and was arrested after a controlled delivery of the explicit sexual materials. After pointing out that for twenty-six months the government agents had made Jacobson the target of repeated mailings, the Court held that the prosecution failed to produce evidence that Jacobson was predisposed to break the law before the government directed its efforts toward him. Adding that government agents may not implant a criminal design in an innocent person's mind and then induce commission of a crime, the Court reversed Jacobson's conviction, observing that Congress had not intended for government officials to instigate crime by luring otherwise innocent persons to commit offenses.

PUNISHMENT OF OFFENDERS

Law and society both demand that criminals be punished for their offenses. Defendants who are convicted face a variety of punishments, depending on the nature and severity of their crimes. These punishments are designed to meet one or more of the basic goals of the criminal justice system: retribution, deterrence, rehabilitation, and incapacitation.

▧ **Retribution.**   Literally, this term refers to something demanded as payment. In criminal justice, retribution is the idea that the criminal must pay for wrongs perpetrated against society. The biblical phrase "an eye for an eye" can be invoked in this regard.[89] Another oft-used phrase is that criminals must be given their "just deserts." Some people question whether retribution, or legalized vengeance, is a legitimate goal of criminal justice. One response is that the desire for revenge is deep-seated in the human psyche and that if the state does not exact vengeance, individuals will resort to vigilantism. Another defense of retribution focuses on the need for expiation of guilt—criminals must suffer in order to atone for their wrongs. Finally, defenders of retribution note that it involves **proportionality**—offenders are punished, but punishment must fit the crime.

▓ **Deterrence.** This is the idea that punishing persons who commit crimes will prevent other similarly disposed individuals from committing like offenses. Criminals must be punished to the degree necessary to impress those who would emulate them of the undesirable consequences of crime. This assumes, of course, that potential criminals are rational calculators of costs and benefits associated with particular courses of action. In many cases, this may be basically true, but it certainly does not apply to crimes of passion. Another problem with the deterrence theory is that some people discount the negative consequences of crime by the improbability of being caught. To be an effective deterrent, punishment would have to be so severe that even those who did not believe that they were going to be caught would not take the risk. We could, for example, increase compliance with speed limits by executing those who are caught speeding, but such a punishment would be unthinkable. In practice, the criminal justice system strives to achieve deterrence, but not at the expense of proportionality in punishment.

▓ **Rehabilitation.** Perhaps the loftiest goal of the criminal justice system, rehabilitation means changing the offender to function in civil society without resorting to criminal behavior. On its face, this is the most appealing theory of criminal punishment. We would like to believe that by punishing people we can improve them. Of course, rehabilitation involves more than punishment. It entails various sorts of programs and therapies, each of which is based on its own theory of what causes criminal behavior. Today, high **recidivism** (repeat offending) rates among those convicted of felonies have made society much less sanguine about its ability to rehabilitate "hardened criminals."

▓ **Incapacitation.** The idea here is that that punishment should prevent criminals from committing additional crimes. Contemporary American society resorts to imprisonment or, in extreme cases, execution to rid itself of seriously threatening behavior. While nearly everyone favors incapacitation of violent offenders, in practice, incapacitation extends beyond the execution or incarceration of violent criminals. For instance, when the state revokes the driver's license of someone convicted of driving while intoxicated, the purpose is primarily incapacitation. Similarly, some states have laws offering convicted sex offenders the option of taking a drug that may eliminate sexual impulses.

Each of these justifications for punishment is somewhat controversial, and there is not a consensus as to which of these goals should be paramount. As we examine particular punishments, the student should reflect on which of these objectives is being served.

Historical Background

Under English common law, persons convicted of misdemeanors were generally subjected to **corporal punishment** like flogging. The misdemeanant was taken into the public square, bound to the whipping post, and administered as many lashes as were prescribed by law for the offense. At common law, felonies were punishable by death. In the early days of the common law, nobles who committed **capital crimes** were shown mercy by simply being beheaded. Commoners who were sentenced to death were often subjected to more grisly forms of punishment—they were broken on the wheel, burned at the stake, or drawn and quartered. Eventually, the comparatively humane method of hanging was adopted as the principal means of execution in England.

In colonial America, criminal punishment followed common law practice, although the Massachusetts Code of 1648 mandated the **death penalty** in cases of witchcraft, blasphemy, sodomy, adultery, and "man stealing," as well as the common law capital crimes. During the colonial period of American history, and indeed well into the nineteenth century, the death penalty was often inflicted for a variety of felonies, including rape, arson, and horse theft. And corporal punishment, primarily flogging, was widely used for a variety of crimes, including many misdemeanors.

The American Bill of Rights, ratified in 1791, prohibited the imposition of "cruel and unusual punishments" through the Eighth Amendment. The Framers of the Bill of Rights sought to prevent the use of torture, which had been common in Europe as late as the eighteenth century. They did not intend, however, to outlaw the death penalty or abolish all forms of corporal punishment. The meaning of cruel and unusual punishment has changed markedly since 1791. As the Supreme Court noted in 1958, the Cruel and Unusual Punishments Clause "must draw its meaning from the evolving standards of decency that mark the progress of a maturing society."[90]

In the early nineteenth century, reformers introduced the concept of the **penitentiary**, literally, "a place to do penance." The idea was that criminals could be reformed through isolation, Bible study, and hard labor. These gave rise to the notion of rehabilitation, the belief that the criminal justice system could reform criminals and reintegrate them into society. Many of the educational, occupational training, and psychological programs found in modern prisons are based on this theory.

By the twentieth century, **incarceration** replaced corporal punishment as the mainstay of criminal punishment. All states, as well as the federal government, constructed prisons to house persons convicted of felonies. Even cities and counties constructed jails for the confinement of persons convicted of misdemeanors. The death penalty remained in wide use, however, for the most serious violent felonies. But, the gallows were replaced by the firing squad, the gas chamber, the electric chair, and, eventually, lethal injection.

The Death Penalty

By the 1960s, it appeared that the death penalty was on the way out. Public opinion no longer favored it, and a number of states had abolished it. In those that had not, the courts began to impose restrictions on its use. When the Supreme Court declared Georgia's death penalty law unconstitutional in *Furman v. Georgia* (1972),[91] many observers thought it signaled the demise of the death penalty nationwide. That decision striking the Georgia death penalty focused on the virtually unlimited discretion the state placed in trial juries empowered to impose death sentences for a number of felonies. According to Justice Stewart's concurring opinion in *Furman*, Georgia's administration of the death penalty was unpredictable to the point of being "freakishly imposed." In the wake of the *Furman* decision, Georgia, and most other states, revised their death penalty laws to address the concerns raised by the Court. In *Gregg v. Georgia* (1976),[92] the Supreme Court upheld Georgia's revised death penalty statute, thus ending a four-year moratorium on capital punishment (for further discussion, see Chapter 10).

Capital punishment officially returned to America in 1977 when the state of Utah placed convicted murderer Gary Gilmore in front of a firing squad. Since then, the administration of the death penalty has become more common. Currently, thirty-two states have statutes providing for capital punishment.[93] Congress has provided for capital punishment in certain federal crimes, including treason, murder of a federal law enforcement official, as well as kidnapping, carjacking, child abuse, and bank robbery that result in death.[94] Approximately 1,100 defendants have been executed in the United States since the death penalty was reinstated in 1976.[95]

Even though the death penalty is supported by public opinion, it remains the object of intense debate. Objections to the death penalty include moral, constitutional, and practical arguments. Some believe that state-sponsored execution is nothing more than legalized murder, although the traditional legal justification for capital punishment is that it, like war and self-defense, involves justifiable homicide. Others argue that the death penalty today is "cruel and unusual punishment" in that it is relatively infrequently applied and the United States is one of the few countries that have not abolished it. Some also have argued that the administration of capital punishment is racially discriminatory.[96]

Opponents of the death penalty might see it as barbaric and believe it is inconsistent with the aims of a civilized society. Others claim that the death penalty has no appreciable deterrent value, a claim buttressed by the fact that states that have abolished the death penalty do not have higher murder rates. Whatever the theoretical deterrence value of the death penalty, its actual deterrent effect is no doubt attenuated by the years of delay between sentencing and execution. Obviously, the death penalty has no value as a means of rehabilitation, unless it helps to rehabilitate other convicted murderers who have not been sentenced to death. Therefore, if the death penalty is to be justified, it must be primarily on grounds of retribution and incapacitation.

Since the reinstatement of capital punishment in 1976, the courts have continued to wrestle with the death penalty issue. While generally upholding state death penalty statutes and only infrequently reversing death sentences, the Supreme Court has imposed a number of additional limitations on the ultimate punishment. For example, the Court has disallowed the death penalty in cases of rape, even the rape of a child.[97] It has held that persons cannot be sentenced to death if they were under the age of legal majority (18) at the time they committed their capital crimes.[98] It also has said that the death penalty is impermissible where defendants suffer from mental retardation.[99] And, it has held that prisoners who become insane while on death row cannot be put to death until their sanity is restored.[100] The Court opined that executing a prisoner who is unable to comprehend what is taking place, and why it is taking place, is nothing more than mindless vengeance, which the Eighth Amendment prohibits.

In the nineteenth century, hanging was the most common means of capital punishment. The electric chair was introduced in the 1890s as a "humanitarian" alternative to the gallows. Until recently, electrocution was the predominant means of execution. In 1977, Oklahoma became the first state to give condemned prisoners the option of choosing death by lethal injection. Today, all states with the death penalty (as well as the federal government) allow for execution by lethal injection; in most of these states it is the only lawful means of execution. In 2008, the U.S. Supreme Court upheld the practice of execution by lethal injection against the claim that it constitutes cruel and unusual punishment.[101] Had the Court ruled otherwise, it would have effectively abolished capital punishment in America.

Incarceration

Today, incarceration is the conventional mode of punishment prescribed for persons convicted of felonies. Under federal and state law, felonies are classified by their seriousness, and convicted felons may be imprisoned for periods ranging from one year to life. Incarceration usually is available as a punishment for those convicted of the more serious misdemeanors, but only for up to one year in most jurisdictions. While it was originally thought to be an effective means of rehabilitation, most criminologists now view incarceration simply as a means of isolating those persons who pose a serious threat to society.

In 2008, the U.S. Department of Justice reported that by mid-2007, 1,595,037 inmates were incarcerated in federal and state prisons. Of these inmates, 87.5 percent of these inmates were in state prisons; the remaining 12.5 percent were under federal jurisdiction. When local jail populations were added in, the number of inmates reached nearly 2.3 million.[102] Indeed, the total number of prison and jail inmates has more than quadrupled in the last three decades. This tremendous increase reflects the fact that during the 1980s and 1990s, federal and state sentencing laws were amended to increase the length of prison terms given to convicted felons. Unfortunately, many prisons are now seriously overcrowded to the point that courts must limit the number of inmates who can be confined.

Prisoners' Rights

The federal courts have made it clear that the Eighth Amendment's prohibition against "cruel and unusual punishments" imposes obligations on prison administrators to maintain certain standards of confinement. Traditionally, courts adopted a "hands-off" policy, allowing prison officials free rein. In the late 1960s, that began to change, as federal and state tribunals came to examine prison conditions and policies. As the courts signaled their willingness to scrutinize the prisons, litigation mushroomed. In the past two decades, litigation in the federal courts by prisoners has increased dramatically, often challenging conditions of prison overcrowding. In 2011, the Supreme Court ruled that severe overcrowding in California state prisons mandated a 137.5 percent decrease in the state's prison population. The Court's rationale was connected to the adverse impact that overcrowding has on the medical care provided to inmates.[103]

A sizable number of other state prison systems have been or are currently under court orders to improve conditions of confinement or reduce overcrowding. In recent years, some state courts have begun to focus their attention on the deplorable conditions existing in many city and county jails. As currently interpreted, the Eighth Amendment requires that prisoners must be provided with reasonably adequate food, clothing, shelter, medical care, and sanitation and that there must be a reasonable assurance of their personal safety. In 1992, the Supreme Court held that a prisoner who is beaten maliciously by guards may bring a civil action for damages based on a claim of cruel and unusual punishment, even if the prisoner does not suffer "significant injuries."[104]

The courts also have held that a prison inmate retains those First Amendment rights "that are not inconsistent with his status as a prisoner or with the legitimate penological objectives of the corrections system."[105] For example, under the Free Exercise Clause of the First Amendment, courts have been generally receptive to prisoners' rights to possess bibles, prayer books, and other religious materials, as well as inmates' rights to be visited by the clergy. On the other hand, courts have upheld restrictions on religious exercises if they disrupt prison order or routine.[106]

One of the most firmly established **rights of prisoners** is the right of access to the courts. The Supreme Court made it clear decades ago that prison officials may not deny inmates access to the courts, nor penalize them for utilizing that access.[107] Similarly, the Court has held that indigent inmates must be furnished writing materials and notarial services to assist them in filing petitions and seeking writs from courts, and has upheld the right of prisoners to meet with counsel in privacy and, in the absence of other forms of legal assistance, to have access to law libraries.[108]

The courts also have recognized that prisoners retain a limited right to communicate with the outside world via the mails, although prison officials may limit and censor the mail prisoners send and receive, provided there is no interference with attorney-client relationships. Prison officials also have broad latitude to restrict visitation privileges if there is reason to believe that an inmate is receiving contraband being smuggled into the prison by visitors.[109] Likewise, prison regulations impinging on inmates' interests in free assembly and association have been consistently upheld. The federal courts have imposed limits on prison disciplinary measures such as corporal punishment and the extended use of punitive isolation. Today, prison discipline is largely accomplished by the granting and removal of **good-time credit**, that is, early release for good behavior.

Parole

Traditionally, most states have provided for early release from prison on **parole** for those inmates who can demonstrate to the satisfaction of a **parole board** their willingness to conform their conduct to the requirements of the law.[110] Of course, persons released on parole must submit to a number of conditions. If these conditions are violated, parole can be revoked and the offender returned to prison to serve the remainder of the original sentence. The Federal Sentencing Reform Act of 1984 abolished parole for federal offenders who commit offenses on or after November 1, 1987. Many states have followed the lead of the federal government and have abolished or restricted parole.

However, in jurisdictions where overcrowding is an issue, parole may be granted after as little as 30 percent of a sentence is served.

Alternatives to Incarceration

Although society must be protected from violent offenders who have shown no inclination toward reform, today we recognize that imprisonment is not the appropriate punishment for all convicted felons. Moreover, the overcrowding of penal institutions mandates the consideration of alternatives. Of course, there are other means of punishing nonviolent offenders, first-time offenders, and those who have potential for rehabilitation. One of the most common of these is **probation**, where the convicted person is not incarcerated in a penal institution but remains under the close supervision of authorities. About three million adults are on probation in the United States. Probation is usually conditioned on restrictions on the probationer's everyday conduct. The most extreme limitations on conduct and movement take the form of **house arrest**. Unfortunately, the success of probation can be hindered by inadequate staffing, resulting in inadequate supervision of probationers. Increasingly, probationers are being monitored through the use of electronic ankle bracelets that allow officials to track their whereabouts.

Boot Camps

In recent years, state legislatures have experimented with military-style **boot camps** as an alternative to prison. Boot camps are designed to instill discipline in young offenders who have committed nonviolent offenses, perhaps brought about by their drug abuse. In lieu of a prison sentence, these offenders elect to undergo three to six months of training that may include drug rehabilitation and work on public projects. Although boot camps have produced some notable success stories, there is little evidence that they are superior to conventional incarceration in terms of reducing the rates of recidivism.

Community Service

The requirement that an offender perform community service is becoming more attractive as a punishment for less serious crimes, especially for juveniles and first-time offenders. **Community service** is regarded as a more meaningful sanction than the imposition of a fine. It is also viewed as less likely than incarceration to promote future criminal behavior. The theory underlying community service is that an offender will become aware of obligations to the community and how criminal conduct violates those obligations. Community service is often imposed as a condition of probation or as part of a pretrial diversion program in which first-time nonviolent offenders are offered the opportunity to avoid prosecution by completing a program of counseling or service.

Restitution

As society becomes more cognizant of the rights of crime victims, courts are increasingly likely to require that persons convicted of crimes pay sums of money to their victims by way of **restitution**. Typically, requirements to make restitution are imposed in property crimes cases where victims have suffered some sort of economic loss. On some occasions, the requirement to pay restitution is one of several conditions that must be met in order for the offender to gain release via probation. The term "restitution" should not be confused with the term "retribution," which, as we noted above, is one of the classic justifications for imposing criminal punishments.

Fines and Forfeitures

Monetary **fines** are by far the most common punishment for those convicted of misdemeanors. Felons are likewise subject to fines in addition to, or instead of, incarceration. Usually, the law allows the sentencing judge to impose a fine, a jail term, or some combination of the two. A number of felonies, especially serious economic crimes, now carry very heavy fines. For example, violations of federal banking and securities laws are punishable by fines running into the millions of dollars. The Eighth Amendment to the United States Constitution prohibits "excessive fines," and many state constitutions contain similar protections. But appellate courts rarely overturn criminal fines on this basis.

Federal law provides for **forfeiture** of the proceeds of a variety of criminal activities. Under federal law, a "conveyance," which includes aircraft, motor vehicles, and vessels, is subject to forfeiture if it is used to transport controlled substances.[111] Real estate may also be forfeited if it is used to commit or facilitate commission of a drug-related felony.[112] Many states have similar statutes. Though technically this kind of forfeiture is a civil, and not a criminal, sanction, the U.S. Supreme Court has recognized that forfeiture constitutes significant punishment and is thus subject to constitutional limitations under the Eighth Amendment.[113] The Court, however, left it to state and lower federal courts to determine the tests of "excessiveness" in the context of forfeiture.

CONCLUSION

The criminal law expresses society's collective judgment that certain forms of conduct are inimical to social welfare and must not be permitted. Many of these proscriptions are ancient and universal. From the beginning of civilization, people everywhere have condemned murder, rape, arson, perjury, burglary, and theft. Of course, our modern criminal law applies to many activities that are not *mala in se*, such as motor vehicle infractions, drug and alcohol offenses, white-collar crimes, and offenses against public health and the natural environment. The changing prohibitions of the criminal law reflect the appearance of new social problems, as well as the evolving values of a maturing society. Behaviors that were permissible on the American frontier of the nineteenth century are no longer considered appropriate in a post-industrial, urbanized culture.

Crimes are deemed to be offenses against the entire society, which is why they are prosecuted in the name of the state or the people. The criminal law is most successful when its prohibitions are supported by a strong social consensus. This social consensus does as much to deter crime as do the penalties associated with criminal prosecution.

When the criminal law deviates from social consensus, lawbreaking inevitably increases and respect for the criminal justice system is diminished.

The criminal law assumes that people are responsible for their actions, yet advances in medicine, psychology, and the social sciences have made us aware that human behavior is influenced by a variety of internal and external factors. One of the greatest challenges to criminal law today is how to maintain the norm of criminal responsibility in the face of novel defenses that seek to deflect blame away from the defendant.

Ultimately, there is a consensus that criminals should be punished, although there is considerable disagreement as to the nature and degree of punishment that particular crimes warrant. Courts of law inevitably face the philosophical questions associated with criminal punishment as they interpret the sentencing laws enacted by legislatures and the limitations that the federal and state constitutions impose on the criminal justice system. In so doing, they tend to reflect the dominant values of the society. Thus, courts have not hesitated to invalidate torture and flogging as cruel and unusual punishments forbidden by the Eighth Amendment, yet they have been extremely reluctant to reach similar conclusions regarding the death penalty. In the end, as social norms change, judicial decisions interpreting and applying the criminal law also will evolve.

SUMMARY OF KEY CONCEPTS

To understand the criminal law, one must understand its social and political aspects and its historical development. It was against this historic common law background that the federal government and the states have enacted statutes that refine the common law crimes and define new offenses as the social, economic, and political development of this Nation has evolved.

Federal, state, and local legislative bodies define crimes, and courts interpret these legislatively enacted laws. But in each instance, the U.S. Constitution requires crimes to be defined precisely. A crime ordinarily involves two essential elements: an act and an intent; however, increasingly governments have enacted strict-liability offenses where a violator's intent is irrelevant. A violator's culpability may depend upon that person's role in the offense; under federal and state laws, one who aids and abets the commission of a crime is regarded as a principal of that offense. In some instances, an accessory after the fact is treated differently today.

In reviewing this chapter, the student should grasp a basic understanding of the inchoate crimes, crimes against persons and property, and offenses against public order, justice, and the environment. Moreover, it is important to have a basic knowledge of offenses unique to our military forces. These are the basic building blocks of

the criminal law. But, the criminal law in America has expanded to proscribe white-collar offenses and is making a concerted effort to combat organized crime. Responses to governmental assault on vice have been mixed, yet there is support for legalized protection of the most core moral values.

Historic defenses of alibi, use of force, and excuses and justifications for commission of criminal acts remain. In recent decades, the approaches to infancy and intoxication have often been modified to allow special treatment for juveniles and intoxicated persons. Yet, there has been a trend to take a firmer approach to pleas of insanity. The American penchant for timely action against a wrongdoer also has brought about the statute of limitations defense, and the U.S. Constitution has brought about defenses against double jeopardy and wrongful conduct by government.

Finally, at this stage, it is relevant to recognize the roles that retribution, deterrence, and rehabilitation have played in inflicting punishment on wrongdoers through the death penalty, incarceration, and the growing reliance on community-based alternatives. The U.S. Constitution again appears in the punishment phase of the criminal justice system in its evolving prohibition against cruel and unusual punishments and the requirement that prisoners not be deprived of the most fundamental constitutional rights.

FOR FURTHER READING

Banner, Stuart, *The Death Penalty: An American History* (Harvard University Press 2003).

Gardner, Thomas J., and Terry M. Anderson, *Criminal Law* (10th ed., Wadsworth 2008).

Samaha, Joel, *Criminal Law* (9th ed., Wadsworth 2007).

Scheb, John M., and John M. Scheb II, *American Criminal Law* (5th ed., Wadsworth 2008).

Singer, Richard G., and John Q. La Fond, *Criminal Law Examples & Explanations* (4th ed., Aspen Publishers 2007).

QUESTIONS FOR THOUGHT AND DISCUSSION

1. Why was the English common law important in the development of the American criminal law?
2. What purpose is served by criminalizing inchoate conduct? Which offenses address such conduct?
3. Is it good public policy to criminalize vices such as gambling, prostitution, and drug abuse? Why or why not?
4. What are the arguments for and against making assisted suicide a crime?
5. Give an example of a scenario when a defendant might assert the defenses of (a) duress and (b) necessity.
6. Under what circumstances does the law generally allow a person to use deadly force in defense of an attack?
7. Why has the defense of entrapment been asserted more frequently in recent years?
8. Under what circumstances should a court impose a fine in lieu of imprisonment on a defendant convicted of a felony?
9. Do you think that a judge who places a convicted defendant on probation should impose a community service obligation as a condition of probation? Support your view.
10. What is the rationale for enactment of a statute of limitations on the prosecution of crime?
11. To what extent do prisoners retain basic constitutional rights while incarcerated?
12. What rationale supports the unique character of offenses peculiar to the armed forces?

KEY TERMS

accessories
actus reus
affirmative defenses
aggravated assault
aggravated battery
aiding and abetting
alibi
antitrust violations
arson
assault
assisted suicide
attempt
automatism

battered child syndrome
battered woman syndrome
battery
bid rigging
boot camps
bribery
burglary
capital crimes
carjacking
castle doctrine
causation
civil contempt
community service

compounding a crime
computer crimes
consent
conspiracy
contempt
contractual immunity
corporal punishment
corpus delicti
credit card fraud
criminal contempt
criminal intent
deadly force
death penalty

deterrence
diplomatic immunity
disorderly conduct
double jeopardy
duress
embezzlement
English common law
entrapment
environmental crimes
escape
excusable homicide
extortion
false imprisonment
false pretenses
felonies
felony murder
fines
first-degree murder
forfeiture
forgery
gambling
general intent
good-time credit
house arrest
in camera
incapacitation
incarceration
inchoate offense
infancy
insanity
insider trading
intoxication
justifiable homicide
justifiable use of force
kidnapping

larceny
mala in se
mala prohibita
malicious mischief
manslaughter
mayhem
Megan's Law
mens rea
misdemeanors
mistake of fact
mistake of law
M'Naghten Rule
Model Penal Code
money laundering
murder
necessity
negative defenses
obscenity
obstruction of justice
organized crime
parole
parole board
penitentiary
perjury
price fixing
principals
probation
procedural criminal law
proportionality
prostitution
proximate cause
rape
rape shield laws
rape trauma syndrome
recidivism

rehabilitation
resisting arrest
restitution
retribution
RICO
rights of prisoners
riot
robbery
second-degree murder
selective prosecution
self-defense
solicitation
specific intent
stalking
stare decisis
statute of limitations
strict-liability offenses
subornation of perjury
substantial capacity test
substantive criminal law
target crime
tax fraud
transactional immunity
treason
Uniform Code of Military Justice
unlawful assembly
use immunity
uttering a forged instrument
vagrancy
vandalism
vehicular homicide
vice of vagueness
violations of civil rights
white-collar crimes
wrongful act or omission

ENDNOTES

1. Two interesting exceptions are *People v. Woody*, 394 P.2d 813 (Cal. 1964), and *Ravin v. State*, 537 P.2d 494 (Alaska 1975).
2. *Lawrence v. Texas*, 539 U.S. 558, 123 S. Ct. 2472, 156 L. Ed. 2d 508 (2003).
3. *Bowers v. Hardwick*, 478 U.S. 186, 107 S. Ct. 29, 92 L. Ed. 2d. 779 (1986).
4. Section 9 applies to the national Congress and Section 10 applies to the state legislatures.
5. 395 U.S. 444, 89 S. Ct. 1827, 23 L. Ed. 2d 430 (1969).
6. 406 U.S. 205, 92 S. Ct. 1526, 32 L. Ed. 2d 15 (1972).
7. 491 U.S. 397, 109 S. Ct. 2533, 105 L. Ed. 2d 342 (1989).
8. 521 U.S. 844, 117 S. Ct. 2329, 138 L. Ed. 2d 874 (1997).
9. 542 U.S. 656, 124 S. Ct. 2783, 159 L. Ed. 2d 690 (2004).

10. 542 U.S. at 660, 124 S. Ct. at 2788, 159 L. Ed. 2d at 698.
11. 535 U.S. 343, 123 S. Ct. 1536, 155 L. Ed. 2d 535 (2003).
12. 535 U.S. at 363, 123 S. Ct. at 1549, 155 L. Ed. 2d at 554.
13. *Musser v. Utah*, 333 U.S. 95, 97, 68 S. Ct. 397, 398, 92 L. Ed. 562, 565 (1948).
14. 539 U.S. 558, 123 S. Ct. 2472, 156 L. Ed. 2d 508 (2003).
15. 539 U.S. at 578, 123 S. Ct. at 2484, 156 L. Ed. 2d at 526.
16. *Craig v. Boren*, 429 U.S. 190, 97 S. Ct. 451, 50 L. Ed. 2d 397 (1976).
17. 18 U.S.C. §2(a).
18. *See, e.g.*, Cal. Penal Code §33.
19. *United States v. Barlow*, 470 F.2d 1245 (D.C. Cir. 1972).
20. 18 U.S.C. §3.
21. Fla. Stat. §777.03.
22. *See United States v. Manley*, 632 F.2d 978 (2d Cir. 1980), *cert. denied*, 449 U.S. 1112, 101 S. Ct. 922, 66 L. Ed. 2d 841 (1981).
23. Fla. Stat. §777.04(1).
24. *United States v. Mandujano*, 499 F.2d 370, 376 (5th Cir. 1974).
25. *See, e.g.*, Tex. Penal Code Ann. §15.04(a).
26. 720 ILCS 5/8-1.
27. *United States v. Korab*, 893 F.2d 2122 (9th Cir. 1989).
28. M.P.C. §5.02(3).
29. *Webster v. State*, 646 So. 2d 752 (Fla. App. 1994).
30. 18 U.S.C. §371.
31. Tex. Penal Code Ann. §15.02(a).
32. *Iannelli v. United States*, 420 U.S. 770, 786, 95 S. Ct. 1284, 1294, 43 L. Ed. 2d 616, 628 (1975).
33. Mo. Ann. Stat. §564.016(5)(1).
34. 532 U.S. 451, 121 S. Ct. 1693, 149 L. Ed. 2d 697 (2001).
35. 521 U.S. 702, 117 S. Ct. 2258, 138 L. Ed. 2d 772 (1997).
36. 3 Or. Rev. Stat. §127.800 (1994).
37. 546 U.S. 243, 126 S. Ct. 904, 163 L. Ed. 2d 748.
38. 18 U.S.C. §2119.
39. *Holloway v. United States*, 526 U.S. 1, 119 S. Ct. 966, 143 L. Ed. 2d. 1.
40. Tenn. Code Ann. §39-13-404.
41. *Flores-Figueroa v. United States*, 556 U.S. 646, 129 S. Ct. 1886, 173 L. Ed. 2d. 853
42. 18 U.S.C. §1962(a).
43. 18 U.S.C. §1962(b).
44. 18 U.S.C. §1962(c).
45. 18 U.S.C. §1962(d).
46. 354 U.S. 476, 489, 77 S. Ct. 1304, 1311, 1 L. Ed. 2d 1498, 1509 (1957).
47. 413 U.S. 15, 24, 93 S. Ct. 2607, 2613, 37 L. Ed. 2d 419, 423 (1973).
48. 458 U.S. 747, 102 S. Ct. 3348 73 L. Ed. 2d 1113 (1982).
49. *Pope v. Illinois*, 481 U.S. 497, 107 S. Ct. 1918, 95 L. Ed. 2d 439 (1987).
50. *State v. Henry*, 732 P.2d 9, 18 (Or. 1987).
51. *New York v. Ferber*, 458 U.S. 747, 102 S. Ct. 3348, 73 L. Ed. 2d 1113 (1982).
52. 21 U.S.C. §801 et seq.
53. *Edwards v. South Carolina*, 372 U.S. 229, 83 S. Ct. 680, 9 L. Ed. 2d 697 (1963).
54. *See, e.g., Papachristou v. City of Jacksonville*, 405 U.S. 156, 92 S. Ct. 839, 31 L. Ed. 2d 110 (1972).
55. 18 U.S.C. §921 et seq. *See also:* National Firearms Act of 1934.
56. *See United States v. Miller*, 307 U.S. 174, 59 S. Ct. 816, 83 L. Ed. 1206 (1939); *Lewis v. United States*, 445 U.S. 55, 100 S. Ct. 915, 63 L. Ed. 2d 198 (1980).
57. *District of Columbia v. Heller*, 554 U.S. 570, 128 S. Ct. 2783, 171 L. Ed. 2d 637 (2008).
58. *McDonald v. City of Chicago*, 561 U.S. 3025, 130 S. Ct. 3020, 177 L. Ed. 2d. 894.
59. 417 U.S. 733, 94 S. Ct. 2547, 41 L. Ed. 2d 439 (1974).
60. *Wardius v. Oregon*, 412 U.S. 470, 93 S. Ct. 2208, 37 L. Ed. 2d 82 (1973).
61. 18 U.S.C. §5031.
62. *M'Naghten's Case*, 8 Eng. Rep. 718 (1843).
63. 18 U.S.C. §17(a).
64. 18 U.S.C. §17(b).
65. *United States v. Cameron*, 907 F.2d 1051, 1063 (11th Cir. 1990).
66. *Cleveland v. Municipality of Anchorage*, 631 P.2d 1073, 1078 (Alaska 1981).
67. For a typical example of a state self-defense law, see the Tennessee statute at: http://law.justia.com/codes/tennessee/2010/title-39/chapter-11/part-6/39-11-611.
68. See, for example, Florida's self-defense statute: http://www.leg.state.fl.us/statutes/index.cfm?App_mode=Display_Statute&URL=0700-0799/0776/Sections/0776.013.html.
69. For a breakdown of statutes by state, see: http://criminal.findlaw.com/criminal-law-basics/stand-your-ground-laws.html.
70. http://www.leg.state.fl.us/statutes/index.cfm?App_-mode=Display_Statute&Search_String=&URL=0700-0799/0776/Sections/0776.012.html.
71. http://www.leg.state.fl.us/statutes/index.cfm?App_-mode=Display_Statute&Search_String=&URL=0700-0799/0776/Sections/0776.013.html.
72. *State v. Janes*, 822 P.2d 1238, 1243 (Wash. App. 1992).
73. http://law.justia.com/codes/tennessee/2010/title-39/chapter-11/part-6/39-11-611.
74. https://www.revisor.mn.gov/statutes/?id=609.065.
75. Iowa Code Ann. §704.4.
76. *Murphy v. Waterfront Commn.*, 378 U.S. 52, 77-78, 84 S. Ct. 1594, 12 L. Ed. 2d 678 (1964).
77. *Kastigar v. United States*, 406 U.S. 441, 92 S. Ct. 1653, 32 L. Ed. 2d 212 (1972).

78. 18 U.S.C. §6003.

79. *United States v. Wilson*, 420 U.S. 332, 95 S. Ct. 1013, 43 L. Ed. 2d 232 (1975).

80. *Burks v. United States*, 437 U.S. 1, 98 S. Ct. 2141, 57 L. Ed. 2d 1 (1978).

81. *Oregon v. Kennedy*, 456 U.S. 667, 102 S. Ct. 2083, 72 L. Ed. 2d 416 (1982).

82. *Bartkus v. Illinois*, 359 U.S. 121, 79 S. Ct. 676, 3 L. Ed. 2d 684 (1959).

83. *Waller v. Florida*, 397 U.S. 387, 90 S. Ct. 1184, 25 L. Ed. 2d 435 (1970).

84. *North Carolina v. Pearce*, 395 U.S. 711, 89 S. Ct. 2072, 23 L. Ed. 2d 656 (1969).

85. 284 U.S. 299, 304, 52 S. Ct. 180, 182, 76 L. Ed. 306, 309 (1932).

86. 18 U.S.C. §3282 et seq.

87. *Sorrells v. United States*, 287 U.S. 435, 451, 53 S. Ct. 210, 216, 77 L. Ed. 413, 422 (1932).

88. *Oyler v. Boles*, 368 U.S. 448, 82 S. Ct. 501, 7 L. Ed. 2d 446 (1962).

89. Leviticus 24:17-20.

90. *Trop v. Dulles*, 356 U.S. 86, 101, 78 S. Ct. 590, 598, 2 L. Ed. 2d 630, 642 (1958).

91. 408 U.S. 238, 92 S. Ct. 2726, 33 L. Ed. 2d 346 (1972).

92. 428 U.S. 153, 96 S. Ct. 2909, 49 L. Ed. 2d 859 (1976).

93. In 2014, the eighteen states without the death penalty were Alaska, Connecticut, Hawaii, Illinois, Iowa, Maine, Maryland, Massachusetts, Michigan, Minnesota, New Jersey, New Mexico, New York, North Dakota, Rhode Island, Vermont, West Virginia, and Wisconsin.

94. The Anti-Drug Abuse Act of 1988, 21 U.S.C. §848(e), allows the death penalty for so-called "drug kingpins" who control "continuing criminal enterprises" whose members intentionally kill or procure others to kill in furtherance of the enterprise.

95. Death Penalty Information Center, http://www .deathpenaltyinfo.org.88.

96. *See McCleskey v. Kemp*, 481 U.S. 279, 107 S. Ct. 1756, 95 L. Ed. 2d 262 (1987).

97. *Coker v. Georgia*, 433 U.S. 584, 97 S. Ct. 2861, 53 L. Ed. 2d 982 (1977); *Kennedy v. Louisiana*, 554 U.S. 407, 128 S. Ct. 2641, 171 L. Ed. 2d 525 (2008).

98. *Roper v. Simmons*, 543 U.S. 551, 125 S. Ct. 1183, 161 L. Ed. 2d 1 (2005).

99. *Atkins v. Virginia*, 536 U.S. 304, 122 S. Ct. 2242, 153 L. Ed. 2d 335 (2002).

100. *Ford v. Wainwright*, 477 U.S. 399, 106 S. Ct. 2595, 91 L. Ed. 2d 335 (1986).

101. *Baze v. Rees*, 553 U.S. 35, 128 S. Ct. 1520, 170 L. Ed. 2d 420 (2008).

102. U.S. Dept. of Justice, Bureau of Justice Statistics, *Prison Inmates at Midyear 2007*, Washington, D.C., U.S. Dept. of Justice, June 2008. See, in particular, Tables 1 and 8.

103. *Brown v. Plata*, 563 U.S. _____, 131 S. Ct. 2895, 179 L. Ed. 2d. 1185.

104. *Hudson v. McMillian*, 503 U.S. 1, 112 S. Ct. 995, 117 L. Ed. 2d 156 (1992).

105. *Pell v. Procunier*, 417 U.S. 817, 822, 94 S. Ct. 2800, 2804, 41 L. Ed. 2d 495, 501 (1974).

106. *O'Lone v. Estate of Shabazz*, 482 U.S. 342, 107 S. Ct. 2400, 96 L. Ed. 2d 282 (1987).

107. *Ex parte Hull*, 312 U.S. 546, 61 S. Ct. 640, 85 L. Ed. 1034 (1941).

108. *Bounds v. Smith*, 430 U.S. 817, 97 S. Ct. 1491, 52 L. Ed. 2d 72 (1977).

109. *Kentucky Dept. of Corr. v. Thompson*, 490 U.S. 454, 109 S. Ct. 1904, 104 L. Ed. 2d 506 (1989).

110. The Sentencing Reform Act of 1984 abolished parole eligibility for federal offenders other than military offenders who commit offenses on or after November 1, 1987. It also provided for the abolition of the U.S. Parole Commission on November 1, 1992. However, Congress subsequently extended the life of the Commission through November of 2018.

111. 21 U.S.C. §881(a)(4).

112. 21 U.S.C. §881(a)(7).

113. *Austin v. United States*, 509 U.S. 602, 113 S. Ct. 2801, 125 L. Ed. 2d 488 (1993).

TORTS

5

LEARNING OBJECTIVES

This chapter should enable the student to understand:

- the definition of a tort, its historical development, and the purpose of tort law
- the basic elements of negligence: duty, breach, causation
- defenses to actions based on negligence
- categories of intentional torts
- defenses to torts against persons and property
- the doctrine of strict liability applicable to products and to dangerous activities
- the applicability of vicarious liability in tort law
- torts involving professional malpractice, owners of land, emotional distress, survival and wrongful death actions, alcoholic beverages, and employment relationships; preconception torts; toxic torts; and quasi-torts involving deprivation of constitutional rights
- historic immunities from tort liability and trends eliminating such immunities
- new developments in tort law and areas of tort reform

CHAPTER OUTLINE

INTRODUCTION

The word **tort** comes from the Latin "tortus," which means twisted or wrong. Thus, a tort is a wrongful act committed by a person or an entity known as the **tortfeasor** resulting in injury or loss to the victim. But a tort is not always a wrongful act, because in certain instances the law imposes liability for activities that are not necessarily wrongful yet result in injury or damage.

The law of torts emanates from the English common law. In the United States, tort law has developed over the years largely by judicial decisions but also through legislative action restricting or expanding tort liability. The American Law Institute (ALI), an organization of scholarly lawyers and judges, has published the *Restatement of Torts,* First, Second, and Third Editions. The *Restatement* is not law; however, it purports to restate principles of contemporary American law and is often relied on by courts in interpreting the law. In this chapter, we refer to certain sections of the *Restatement.* We refer to a person who allegedly suffers as a result of someone's negligence or intentional act as the "plaintiff" and to the alleged tortfeasor as the "defendant."

Tort law is designed to protect persons from injury to their person, property, and reputation. One who suffers a tort may bring a civil action for damages to obtain redress of the injury or loss caused by the tortfeasor's actions. There are three basic types of torts:

1. **Negligent acts or omissions.**   Negligence is the failure to exercise reasonable care. A tortfeasor's negligent driving that causes injuries to a person or damage to someone's vehicle, or the performance of a physician or lawyer that falls below the required standard of care, are common examples of the tort of negligence. In some instances failure to perform an act—that is, an omission— may be a tort.
2. **Intentional acts.**   These are torts committed by someone who intends to do something that the law has declared wrongful, such as assault, battery, defamation, false imprisonment, trespass, or fraud. Striking someone with a stick is a battery and is a classic example of an intentional tort, unless one happens to be participating in a karate tournament.
3. Acts for which the law imposes **strict liability**.   This means that one is held liable for an injury regardless of one's intent or negligence. Historically, one who keeps wild animals or who stores or uses explosives has been held strictly liable even where damage occurs through no fault of the tortfeasor. Today, strict liability is imposed on those who engage in abnormally dangerous activities and can be imposed on designers and manufacturers of products.

Under certain circumstances, a person or an entity can be held responsible for the tortious acts of another. This is called **vicarious liability**. The most common example of vicarious liability is where an employer is held liable for acts of an employee committed within the scope of employment.

Tort law is a very dynamic area, and its development has closely paralleled the social and economic changes in society. In recent years, legislative bodies and courts began to recognize a tort action to protect a person's privacy. Thus, the tort of **invasion of privacy** came into being. By the 1970s, as society began to seriously address environmental concerns, courts recognized **toxic torts**. Courts are now being asked to impose tort liability on tobacco companies whose products allegedly have caused serious injuries to smokers and on gun manufacturers whose products have been used to kill or injure people.

NEGLIGENCE

Most contemporary law actions involving torts are based on the tort of **negligence.** Negligence is the failure of a person or entity to use reasonable care, which failure results in injury to persons or damage to property. The concept of reasonable care is often expressed in terms of what an ordinary, prudent person would do in similar circumstances. Of course, people frequently commit negligent acts or negligently omit to perform certain acts. But before a defendant can be held liable for commission of a negligent act or omission, the plaintiff must prove by the preponderance (greater weight) of the evidence the following four basic elements:

- First, there must be a **duty** to act in such a manner as not to expose the plaintiff to an unreasonable risk.
- Second, there must be a **breach of duty** on the part of the defendant.
- Third, there must be a causal connection (called **proximate cause**) between the defendant's failure to abide by the duty to act in a reasonable and prudent manner and the plaintiff's loss and the result must have been reasonably **foreseeable** by the defendant.
- Fourth, the defendant's negligent act or omission must result in injury or loss to the plaintiff.

Duty and the Required Standard of Care

A plaintiff who initiates a tort action must initially show that the defendant owed the plaintiff a duty. People must conduct their activities in ways that do not create unreasonable risks of harm to others. The standard of care that a defendant must observe is based on an objective standard of what a **reasonable person** would observe under the circumstances. The hypothetical reasonable person is not held to a perfect standard in making judgments but is held to exercise the ordinary care that a reasonable person would have exercised under the circumstances. Consequently, one who drives a vehicle is held to the standard of care of a reasonable driver.

To establish a defendant's standard of care, plaintiffs often submit evidence of the standard of performance or the safety practices customarily followed in a particular industry or business. A defendant who engages in a profession that requires special education or training is held to the standard of a reasonably competent person who performs in that area. Thus, a physician, lawyer, engineer, or accountant is held to the standard of a reasonably skilled practitioner in that profession. An aspect of a professional's duty of care is the responsibility to effectively inform clients of potential risks. Consequently, before performing non-emergency surgery, a physician generally explains the risks involved and asks the patient to sign a consent form. **Informed consent** is given by a patient after receiving an explanation of the risks and possible outcomes of the treatment or surgery.

Courts continue to review the required duty and standard of care of professionals. In 1976, in *Tarasoff v. Regents of University of California*, the Supreme Court of California ruled that when a psychotherapist determines, or pursuant to the standards of his or her profession should determine, that a patient presents a serious danger of violence to another, the therapist must use reasonable care to protect the intended victim against such danger.[1] The court held that discharge of such duty may require the therapist to warn the intended victim or others of the danger, notify the police, or take whatever steps are reasonably necessary under the circumstances. *Tarasoff* was considered a far-reaching development in tort law, yet some twenty years later the Supreme Court of Ohio observed that the majority of courts now follow the ruling and have extended it to psychiatrists, mental health clinics, and even social workers.[2]

Emergency Situations

In emergency situations, courts view the defendant's conformity to the required standard of care based on the circumstances that exist at the time of an event. Of course, a defendant must observe ordinary care in anticipating certain emergencies; for example, a theater owner must provide sufficient exits for use in the event of an emergency.

Children

Historically, children have been held liable for their own torts; however, some courts hold that a child under age seven is incapable of committing a tort.[3] The law recognizes that children are generally incapable of meeting the standard of care for adults. Thus, it tends to judge what is reasonable conduct for a child based on the child's age, intelligence, and experience and to look subjectively at the level of care observed by a minor plaintiff or defendant.[4] Nevertheless, when a child engages in an adult activity such as driving an automobile, courts generally hold the child to an adult standard.

Persons Suffering Physical and Mental Infirmities

The law recognizes that a person who suffers from physical infirmities may not meet the objective requirement of acting as a reasonably prudent person, yet such a person must act in accordance with the standard of a reasonable person with such a disability and must not take unreasonable risks. In contrast, those suffering from mental and emotional deficiencies or from voluntary intoxication may not be able to act as the hypothetical reasonable person, yet they are held to the standard of the reasonably prudent individual. Here, the law must strike a balance between the rights of a plaintiff who has suffered a loss and a defendant whose disability may have been a contributing factor in causing the plaintiff's loss.

Breach of Duty

After a plaintiff establishes that the defendant owes a duty to the plaintiff, in order to present a prima facie case, the plaintiff must then establish a breach of that duty by the defendant. The plaintiff can do this by showing the defendant's act, or failure to act, violated the standard of care that a reasonable person should observe under the circumstances.

Violation of duties imposed by statutory laws, ordinances, and governmental regulations may indicate negligence. This is a very technical area. If the particular statute or regulation is designed to specifically protect the plaintiff against the harm caused by the defendant's violation, such violation may constitute **negligence per se**, that is, the defendant's conduct may be treated as negligence without regard to any surrounding circumstances. In other instances, though, such violation may simply be evidence of negligence to be considered along with all other circumstances.[5]

In rare instances, a plaintiff may be aided in proving breach of the defendant's duty by a legal doctrine called *res ipsa loquitur* ("the thing speaks for itself"). In such cases, negligence is inferred from the simple fact that the injury occurred. For example, an Ohio court upheld use of the doctrine in a case where personal injuries resulted from explosion of a bottle of beer.[6] The bottle of beer would not have exploded had it not been defective. Another example would be an operation in which a surgeon erroneously removes a patient's gallbladder instead of her appendix. The thing speaks for itself. That can be especially useful if the only witnesses are those whose conduct led to an injury, as when a patient is unconscious during surgery. If the doctrine is properly invoked, a court may instruct the jury that it can infer the defendant's negligence. This doctrine is typically applied to situations where a defendant has exclusive control over a situation in which something goes wrong.

Causation—The Proximate or Legal Cause

To establish the defendant's liability, the plaintiff must prove that the defendant's act or omission (breach of duty) caused the plaintiff's injury. The actual cause of the plaintiff's injury is often determined by the **"but for" test**, where the court asks whether the plaintiff would have been injured *but for* the defendant's act or omission. In other instances, the court may seek to determine if the defendant's act or omission was a substantial factor in causing the plaintiff's injury. But simply proving factual cause is not sufficient. Courts not only look to the actual cause of the plaintiff's injury but also determine if the cause was the *proximate* or *legal* cause of that injury. The element of proximate cause involves proof that the natural or reasonably foreseeable consequence of the defendant's act or omission was the plaintiff's injury.

A classic case that nearly every law student studies is *Palsgraf v. Long Island Railroad*.[7] In *Palsgraf*, two railroad employees assisted a passenger in boarding a train. In assisting the passenger, the employees dislodged a package containing fireworks the passenger was carrying. The fireworks exploded and caused a scale some distance away to fall and injure Mrs. Palsgraf, a bystander. The New York Court of Appeals reversed a judgment for damages against the railroad in favor of Mrs. Palsgraf. The majority opinion of the court held that the injury to Mrs. Palsgraf was not a foreseeable result of the actions by the railroad's employees. This classic decision has been argued in hundreds of cases with lawyers parsing its language that requires that a defendant be held liable only where the injury is foreseeable. Moreover, if there is an **intervening act** by someone after a defendant's negligent act and that act causes the plaintiff's injury, courts generally hold the intervening party responsible, unless the intervening act itself was foreseeable.

Damages

Finally, to establish a prima facie case in a negligence action the plaintiff must prove an entitlement to damages. Most negligence actions are based on what the law terms as "ordinary" negligence, and a successful plaintiff may recover **compensatory damages**. In most negligence cases, a jury determines the amount of damages to be awarded. Compensatory damages are designed to attempt to "make whole" the plaintiff who has suffered economic and non-economic losses. Loss of wages, medical bills, and damage to property are examples of economic damages. Non-economic damages may consist of pain and suffering resulting from an accident and the inability to continue one's usual lifestyle. While economic damages can be measured in dollars, it is often difficult to place a dollar value on such items as the loss of one's ability to pursue sports or hobbies. A plaintiff's spouse may be awarded compensatory damages for the loss of **consortium**, that is, the loss of the injured spouse's services and companionship.

In addition to awarding compensatory damages to a plaintiff, some courts allow **punitive damages** to punish a defendant whose conduct evidences **gross negligence**. Gross negligence is generally defined as the intentional failure to perform an act required by law or the outrageous disregard of the rights of others. To illustrate, an intoxicated driver who drives in the lane of oncoming traffic and causes a vehicular accident would be considered grossly negligent. In some jurisdictions, this type of behavior may be referred to as a "reckless" tort, with §500 of the *Restatement (Second) of Torts* defining reckless torts as applying where there is a "conscious disregard of a substantial risk of serious harm." A finding of recklessness on the part of a defendant may impact an award of punitive damages. (See Chapter 9 for a further discussion of compensatory and punitive damages.)

Defenses to Negligence Actions

The most common defense in negligence cases is the defendant's denial of negligence. Beyond this, defendants commonly assert an affirmative defense, that is, a defense that the defendant is required to prove. Affirmative defenses commonly include **assumption of risk, contributory negligence**, and **comparative negligence**.

Assumption of Risk
Historically, courts have held that a plaintiff who voluntarily consents to a known risk assumes the consequences of such risk. Thus, courts have allowed a defendant to assert assumption of risk as a defense against actions brought on the theory that the defendant is negligent. Consequently, one who expressly agrees to assume a known risk is generally barred from recovery of damages for the tort of negligence.

Often, consent to a defendant's conduct is manifested by a document the plaintiff has signed agreeing to relieve the defendant from the consequences of negligence. The permission slip signed by parents allowing their child to go on a school field trip is one example. A more formal consent may take the form of an exculpatory agreement whereby a person expressly agrees not to hold another party liable for any injury or damage from a given activity. Courts view such documents cautiously, and before a party can be relieved of negligent acts the exculpatory language of the document must be very clear and explicit. Even if valid, such a document would not ordinarily relieve a person from liability for commission of an intentional tort or for conduct amounting to gross negligence.

Another type of assumption of risk is called an **implied consent**. A person's conduct may imply an assumption of risk. For example, a person who attends an athletic event and sits in a place where spectators are prohibited and is injured may be said to have assumed the risk of injury.[8] A player who willingly participates in a football game impliedly consents to being tackled and possibly being injured under the rules of the game. In one well-known, case a woman who willingly raised her arm for a nurse to administer an immunization shot was held to have impliedly consented to receiving the immunization.

Contributory and Comparative Negligence

During the early 1800s, the courts developed a doctrine that barred a plaintiff who brought suit from recovering damages if the defendant could show the plaintiff's own actions contributed to his or her injuries or losses. Courts began to universally apply this defense, called contributory negligence. By the mid-twentieth century, courts increasingly criticized the doctrine, particularly as related to manufacturers of products and owners and drivers of vehicles. In recent years, through legislation or judicial decision,[9] many states have adopted the doctrine of comparative negligence extant in civil law countries.

Comparative negligence seeks to assess damages based on the amount of negligence of the parties. Some jurisdictions apply the doctrine in its purest form and allow a plaintiff to recover damages against a negligent defendant irrespective of the amount of the plaintiff's own negligence. Thus, a plaintiff found to be 80 percent negligent could recover damages for the 20 percent of negligence attributable to the defendant. Other jurisdictions apply a modified form of comparative negligence under which a plaintiff may not recover any damages if found to be 50 percent or more negligent. Most commentators believe the doctrine of comparative negligence is a more equitable approach to assessing liability. Nevertheless, the shift from contributory negligence has resulted in complexities, particularly where multiple parties are involved or where the law traditionally allowed a defendant to assert that a plaintiff assumed the risk of injury or loss. These changes pose problems to the insurance industry, which underwrites liability protection for defendants in the majority of major tort actions based on negligence.

INTENTIONAL TORTS

An intentional tort consists of a willful act that a tortfeasor knows or is substantially certain will cause injury to another, interferes with another's property, injures a person's reputation, or wrongfully invades someone's privacy. Intent is a state of mind and is usually proved by the circumstances surrounding a person's action. Intent is distinguished from motive in that intent is the desire to cause certain immediate consequences or knowledge that they will occur, whereas motive is the actor's conscious reason for acting. The law presumes that a person intends the natural and probable consequences of one's acts. Therefore, to establish a prima facie case, a plaintiff must prove that a defendant committed a voluntary tortious act directed against a plaintiff or the plaintiff's legally protected interest. In some instances, a defendant's intent is transferred from the intended victim to an unintentional victim. This is called the doctrine of **transferred intent**. For example, if A fires a pistol at B, but instead the bullet hits C, A's intent to kill or injure B is transferred to C, who has a tort action against A.

We discuss intentional torts in four categories:

1. Assault, battery, and false imprisonment are examples of intentional torts that involve interference with a person's body.
2. Defamation is a tort that injures another's reputation.
3. Infliction of emotional distress and invasion of privacy are newer torts against persons.
4. Trespass to land or taking, misusing, or conversion of personal property belonging to another, and misrepresentation,[10] concealment, and fraud are intentional torts that involve interference with someone's property.

Assault, Battery, and False Imprisonment

Assault and **battery** frequently coexist; however, each is a distinct tort. An assault occurs when a person with apparent ability places another person in apprehension of injury or unwanted physical contact. An assault requires an overt act but does not require physical contact, and although an assault is often accompanied by threatening words, words alone do not constitute an assault. A missed punch is a classic example of an assault.

A battery is usually the act of physically injuring someone, but even an unwanted and unreasonable touching of another without that person's consent can constitute a battery. Thus, striking someone with a baseball bat or hurling a stone and hitting someone is a battery. But, even a male's offensively touching a female's body without her consent could constitute a battery.

An assault does not necessarily culminate in a battery, but more frequently an assault and a battery will be committed simultaneously. For example, an aggressor who threatens to beat up another person and then proceeds to physically attack the victim has committed an assault and battery. Of course, a battery may exist without commission of an assault; for instance, a person who is struck from behind may never have apprehended an injury.

False imprisonment consists of intentionally restraining a person's freedom or confining a person without that person's consent or without legal authority. An amorous suitor who locks the door to prevent the object of affection from leaving the room, or the jailer who refuses to release a prisoner once the prisoner has served a prescribed term, commits false imprisonment. Security personnel in a store may commit false imprisonment by preventing a customer from leaving the store; however, statutes generally allow temporary detention of a suspected shoplifter where the security personnel have a reasonable basis to believe a customer has shoplifted merchandise. In such an instance, it would not be false imprisonment if the security personnel detained the suspected shoplifter in a reasonable manner until police arrived.[11]

As we discussed in Chapter 4, assault, battery, and false imprisonment are crimes as well as torts. Such conduct is prosecuted as a crime to vindicate the right of the state, to punish the offender, and to deter others from like conduct. Irrespective of whether the state chooses to prosecute the wrongdoer, the victim may bring a civil legal action to recover monetary damages for injuries or losses resulting from commission of a tort. Actions for intentional torts are far less frequent than lawsuits alleging negligence where the defendant likely carries liability insurance. Liability insurance does not generally cover intentional torts, except in cases of vicarious liability (discussed later in this chapter). Consequently, a plaintiff who is successful in a suit based on an intentional tort may not have any assurance of collecting damages.

Defamation

Defamation consists of publishing communications that cause another person to be held in ridicule, or that injure another's reputation or business interests. Oral defamation is called **slander;** written or printed defamation is called **libel.** Courts differ on whether defamation by radio or television is slander or libel, but the difference is primarily a matter of form as essentially the same principles of law apply to each.

In 1999, quoting from *Restatement (Second) of Torts* §559, the Indiana Supreme Court stated that a defamatory communication is one that "tends so to harm the reputation of another as to lower him in the estimation of the community or to deter third persons from dealing with him." The court explained that whether a communication is defamatory depends, among other things, upon the temper of the times and contemporary public opinion, with the result that words, harmless in one age, in one community, may be highly damaging to a person's reputation at another time or in another place.[12]

To recover damages for defamation, the plaintiff usually must prove a financial loss; however, some forms of defamation give rise to an action against the tortfeasor irrespective of loss. These include such accusations as falsely imputing perjury or treason, or that a person is guilty of a crime or has a loathsome disease, or falsely alleging that a person is having deviate sexual relations with a minor.

In 1964, the U.S. Supreme Court held that the First Amendment to the U.S. Constitution precludes **public officials** from recovering damages for defamatory falsehoods related to their official conduct unless they can prove "that the statement was made with . . . knowledge that it was false or with reckless disregard whether it was false or not."[13] The Court later expanded the principle to apply to all **public figures** that sue for libel.[14] The theory underlying this holding is that public figures (usually public officials, politicians, or celebrities) have sufficient access to the mass media to defend themselves against false accusations and thus do not normally require the assistance of libel suits.

The "public figure" doctrine has made it difficult for celebrities to prevail in libel suits against the tabloid press. A notable exception occurred in 1981 when Carol Burnett prevailed in a libel suit against *The National Enquirer*. The tabloid had run a brief item asserting that a "boisterous" Carol Burnett had a loud argument with Henry Kissinger in a Washington restaurant. According to the article, "she traipsed around the place offering everyone a bite of her dessert." The article implied that Burnett was drunk. Burnett sued for defamation. The jury awarded her $300,000 in compensatory damages and $1.3 million in punitive damages. The trial judge reduced the award to $50,000 compensatory and $750,000 punitive damages. An appeals court remanded the case, holding that the punitive damages were excessive.[15] In 1986, Burnett agreed to settle the case, reportedly for $200,000.

Intentional Infliction of Emotional Distress and Invasion of Privacy

The tort of **intentional infliction of emotional distress** consists of willfully committing outrageous acts directed against another person. Historically, infliction of emotional distress upon another person was considered an actionable tort only if accompanied by another tort such as assault, battery, or false imprisonment. The trend is for courts to allow emotional distress to stand as a separate tort where the conduct of the tortfeasor is particularly reprehensible. Virginia law illustrates the high standard of proof imposed on a plaintiff who seeks to recover damages in an action for intentional infliction of emotional distress. It requires the plaintiff to establish that the defendant's conduct is intentional or reckless; that it offends generally accepted standards of decency or morality; that it is causally connected with the plaintiff's emotional distress; and that the defendant's conduct caused the plaintiff to suffer severe emotional distress.[16]

CASE IN POINT

A CELEBRITY SUES A TELEVISION NETWORK FOR LIBEL
Newton v. National Broadcasting Co.
United States Court of Appeals for the Ninth Circuit
930 F.2d 662 (9th Cir. 1990)

In 1981, Wayne Newton, a well-known entertainer, filed a defamation suit against NBC and three of its journalists. Newton claimed that NBC broadcasts conveyed false impressions that "the Mafia and mob sources" helped Newton buy a hotel and casino in Las Vegas in exchange for a hidden share of the hotel/casino and that Newton, while under oath, deceived Nevada state gaming authorities about his relationship with the Mafia. A jury awarded Newton more than $19 million in compensatory and punitive damages. A federal appeals court reversed, holding that Newton was a public figure and that he failed to prove that NBC and its journalists made false disparaging statements about him with "actual malice."

In November 1983, *Hustler Magazine* featured a parody of an advertisement, which portrayed Rev. Jerry Falwell, a nationally known minister active in politics and public affairs, as having engaged in a drunken incestuous rendezvous with his mother in an outhouse. Rev. Falwell sued and recovered damages based on the tort of emotional distress. The victory was short lived, for in 1988 the U.S. Supreme Court reversed the judgment.[17] The Court held that, as in defamation, a public figure is precluded from recovering damages for the tort of intentional infliction of emotional distress without showing that publication of a false statement of fact was made with actual malice.[18]

As we mentioned in the introductory remarks, invasion of privacy is one of the newer torts. In 1983, in recognizing this tort, the Alabama Supreme Court explained that it consists of four distinct wrongs: (1) intrusion upon the plaintiff's physical solitude or seclusion; (2) publicity which violates ordinary decencies; (3) putting the plaintiff in a false, but not necessarily defamatory position in the public eye; and (4) appropriation of some element of the plaintiff's personality for commercial use. The court went on to

HUSTLER MAGAZINE v. FALWELL
485 U.S. 46, 108 S. Ct. 876, 99 L. Ed. 2d 41 (1988)

OPINION OF COURT

Chief Justice Rehnquist delivered the opinion of the Court.

... The sort of robust political debate encouraged by the First Amendment is bound to produce speech that is critical of those who hold public office or those public figures who are "intimately involved in the resolution of important public questions or, by reason of their fame, shape events in areas of concern to society at large." ... Such criticism, inevitably, will not always be reasoned or moderate; public figures as well as public officials will be subject to "vehement, caustic, and sometimes unpleasantly sharp attacks." ...

... [A] public figure may hold a speaker liable for the damage to reputation caused by publication of a defamatory falsehood, but only if the statement was made "with knowledge that it was false or with reckless disregard of whether it was false or not." False statements of fact are particularly valueless; they interfere with the truth-seeking function of the marketplace of ideas, and they cause damage to an individual's reputation that cannot easily be repaired by counter speech, however persuasive or effective.... But even though falsehoods have little value in and of themselves, they are "nevertheless inevitable in free debate," ... and a rule that would impose strict liability on a publisher for false factual assertions would have an undoubted "chilling" effect on speech relating to public figures that does have constitutional value. "Freedoms of expression require 'breathing space.'" This breathing space is provided by a constitutional rule that allows public figures to recover for libel or defamation only when they can prove both that the statement was false and that the statement was made with the requisite level of culpability.

hold that the defendant's intrusive demands and threats, and inquiry into the nature of sex between the plaintiff and her husband, supported a claim for invasion of privacy.[19] A public official or public figure who claims to have been placed in a false light in regard to a matter of public concern bears the burden of proof required in defamation under the previously discussed rule established in *New York Times v. Sullivan.*[20]

Interference with Property

As we discussed in Chapter 1, the English common law developed largely in an agrarian economy. Consequently, the common law placed great emphasis on a person's interest in land. Today, torts involving interference with someone's property may take several forms. Going on another's land or into another's buildings without permission are classic examples of the tort of **trespass to land**. But trespass to land also extends to the use of one's own land in such a way as to damage or to create a **nuisance** affecting another's land. The tort of nuisance developed from a landowner's use of property in such a way as to adversely affect the plaintiff's land. For example, in an early case the Georgia Supreme Court held that the unlawful diversion of water from a stream to the deprivation of the lower riparian owner constituted a trespass.[21] In recent years, plaintiffs have employed trespass and nuisance actions to recover damages where pollution has caused damages, for example, to a farmer's crops.[22]

The theft of someone's personal property, failure to return that property, or damaging or depreciating the property so as to deprive the owner or rightful possessor of the use or enjoyment of the property constitutes the tort of **conversion**.

Fraud and Misrepresentation

At common law, the torts of **fraud** and **misrepresentation** consisted of (1) a false statement of a material fact, (2) knowledge by the person making the statement that the representation is false, (3) intent by the person making the statement that the representation will induce another to act, and (4) justifiable reliance on the representation to the injury of the other party.[23] Today, many statutes define fraud and misrepresentation in the context of various areas of commerce and may include concealment as a fraudulent act. Most of these statutes include the common law elements of fraud. When considering whether an action is fraudulent, one must remember that, in business dealings, there is a significant difference between "puffing" or "sales talk" (i.e., "This is the finest used car you will find in this town!"), for which there is no liability, and fraudulent misrepresentation of material facts that meet the above requirements.

The sale of securities is a prime example where both federal and state laws protect persons from fraud and misrepresentations. But despite establishing other elements of a cause of action for fraud, often the plaintiff falls short of proving that he or she justifiably relied on the seller's representations. In 1983, the U.S. Court of Appeals for the Tenth Circuit reviewed a case where a plaintiff purchased stock, suffered a financial loss, and then sued the company that issued the securities claiming violations of federal securities laws.[24] The president and vice president of the company had described an investment in the stock as a "good opportunity" and assured investors there were no risks and that the investment would achieve the potential benefits illustrated by their oral and written projections. Nevertheless, they furnished the plaintiff a private placement memorandum, a written document that explained the details concerning the securities being offered for sale and that clearly outlined the risks involved. Moreover, before purchasing the stock the plaintiff signed a subscription agreement stating the investment was subject to the risks set forth in the memorandum. Yet the plaintiff never read the memorandum. After suffering a financial loss the plaintiff sued and recovered a judgment for damages. Observing that the plaintiff had never read the memorandum furnished him, the court reversed the plaintiff's judgment and held that "knowledge of a prospectus or an equivalent document authorized by statute or regulation should be imputed to investors who fail to read such documents."[25]

Defenses to Intentional Torts against a Person

There are three common defenses to intentional conduct that results in injury or damage to another person: **consent**, **self-defense** (including **defense of a third person**), and **authority of law**.

Consent
The most common defense to an intentional tort to a person is that the plaintiff consented to the defendant's actions. Consent may be communicated expressly by words or impliedly by actions, and in some instances by a person's silence. A person who is intoxicated or unconscious is not competent to give consent, and fraud or coercion vitiates a person's consent and can render the offending party liable for committing a battery. Moreover, where statutes are enacted to protect certain classes of persons, such as minors, consent is not valid. Statutes defining statutory rape and making it a crime to have sexual relations with a minor irrespective of the minor's consent illustrate this principle.

Self-Defense
When a person reasonably believes that it is necessary to use force to protect against a threat to one's person it is proper to defend by use of **reasonable force**. Self-defense can be a defense against such torts as assault and battery. Usually, one may not become the aggressor during self-defense. Most courts extend self-defense to allow defense of a third person; however, the Supreme Court of Ohio has pointed out that one who uses force to intervene on behalf of another person may not invoke the privilege of self-defense if the person defended was the aggressor in the conflict.[26]

Authority of Law
One who acts under authority of law also may have a defense to the tort of false imprisonment. Generally, the officer who makes a legal arrest or the schoolteacher who keeps a pupil after school for a reasonable period of time could assert such a defense.

Defenses against Defamation

Truth is a defense against slander and libel. Public policy also dictates that in certain instances a person is privileged to make statements that may be defamatory. This defense of **privilege** may apply to statements made by public officials in the course of their duties and is applicable to those testifying in judicial proceedings. In other instances, the defense of **qualified privilege** may apply. For example, an employer has a qualified privilege to inform a prospective employer of a former employee's poor performance at work as long as the report is not made with malice. Likewise, a person who has a reasonable belief that someone has stolen his or her property and makes such a report to the police is exercising a qualified privilege.

Defenses to Torts against Property

A defendant sued for committing a tort against property will first seek to defend on the basis that the allegations of conduct do not constitute a tort or by a general denial of the allegations. There are, however, two classic defenses: reasonable use of force and **necessity**.

Use of Force

A possessor of property is justified in defending that property against trespass and may use such reasonable force as is necessary to prevent trespass or to remove a trespasser. Ordinarily, a person must first request an intruder to desist. **Deadly force** cannot be used simply to protect property. There must be a threat of serious harm to the owner or possessor and even then in many jurisdictions courts require that a person threatened who can safely retreat must do so. Nevertheless, our common law heritage regarded that "a man's home is his castle," and rarely do courts require a person to retreat within one's own home. As the Minnesota Supreme Court observed in 1999, "The special status of the home has persisted over time, obviating retreat requirements for people engaging in self-defense within their homes."[27]

Courts have approved the use of guard dogs and electronically charged fences to protect property. Historically, courts also permitted the use of spring guns and other mechanical devices to protect property, but modern courts have generally disallowed such means of defense. Most courts now hold that one who sets up a spring gun or other mechanical device designed to kill or injure a trespasser will be held liable for the death or injury to the trespasser. Indeed, today, the use of a spring gun could under certain circumstances result in the user being charged with a crime.

Necessity

Necessity is a defense that can be asserted by one who commits a tort of trespass or conversion in order to prevent greater harm to a person or to the public generally. An example could be where it is necessary to destroy property to prevent the spread of fire. The defense applies only in the direst calamities. Even then, it does not shield one from a duty to compensate for harm caused where the defense of necessity is invoked to protect a person's private interest as opposed to protection of the public interest.

STRICT LIABILITY

Strict liability, sometimes referred to as liability without fault, is imposed by courts based on a defendant's activities rather than fault due to a defendant's intent or negligence. The doctrine originated in early English common law, which imposed strict liability on keepers of dangerous animals. In 1868, in a landmark decision, *Rylands v. Fletcher*, an English court applied strict liability in a case where the waters from the defendant's reservoir flooded the plaintiff's coal mine.[28] Thus, the English courts broadened the doctrine of strict liability to hold liable those engaged in a particularly dangerous activity such as storing dynamite, blasting, or handling dangerous chemicals. Over the years, a majority of American courts have accepted the principle of strict liability. In determining whether to apply strict liability, courts today consider such factors as the inappropriateness of an activity and degree of risk involved. Of course, a defendant is held strictly liable only for those activities that are abnormally dangerous, while the defendant's other activities would be subject to ordinary tort liability.

In 1975, in a significant environmental ruling a Florida appellate court held that impounding of phosphate slime in connection with phosphate-mining operations constituted a "nonnatural use of land."[29] This enabled the State of Florida to invoke the doctrine of strict liability against the operator of a phosphate mine for damages to the public waters resulting from phosphate wastes. Other examples of situations where courts also have invoked the strict-liability doctrine include cases involving the use of explosives, crop dusting, and storage of inflammable gases.

Products Liability

Products liability refers to the legal responsibility of those who supply goods whose defects cause injuries or losses to others. American courts originally accepted the English doctrine of *caveat emptor* ("let the buyer beware"), but during the twentieth century they began discussing the doctrine of strict liability mentioned above in reference to manufacturers of products. At first, a manufacturer was liable for negligence only to the immediate purchaser of a product, who was usually a dealer from whom the ultimate consumer purchased. Consequently, the ultimate purchaser or user of a product could not recover damages against the manufacturer.

But in 1916, in its seminal decision *MacPherson v. Buick Motor Car Co.*, the New York Court of Appeals held that a manufacturer of an automobile was liable to a person injured as a result of the vehicle's defective wheel.[30] The court made legal history by holding the manufacturer liable to the ultimate purchaser, and its decision was eventually adopted by all American jurisdictions. Later courts extended the doctrine to hold the seller of a product liable for damages to all persons who used the product whom the manufacturer or seller could reasonably have foreseen as users or consumers of the product. The manufacturer, seller, or supplier of the defective product became responsible to not only the purchaser but also the users, and even bystanders who suffer injuries because of a defective product.

Today, a plaintiff whose person or property suffers injury causally related to an unsafe product may opt to bring suit for negligence or breach of warranty or, in most states, may have a cause of action for "products liability" based on the doctrine of strict tort liability. The rationale for imposing such liability is that it will increase the level of safety. Further, manufacturers and distributors can cover most risks of this type by liability insurance.

To recover for damages resulting from a defective product, the plaintiff must establish that the injuries or losses that have accrued are the proximate result of the defective product. In general, the defendant can prevail by establishing that the product was used in a way not reasonably foreseeable or that it was used once the plaintiff had knowledge of the defective condition of the product.

Many product liability cases involve claims of defective design of products, and until recently the comments to §402A of the *Restatement (Second) of Torts* stated that a warning could insulate a manufacturer from liability in certain instances. As previously noted, tort law is dynamic, and the *Restatement (Third) of Torts*, adopted in 1997,[31] notes that warnings are not "a substitute for the provision of a reasonably safe design" of a product. Following this view, a federal appeals court in May 1998 upheld a verdict for $16.7 million in damages. The court ruled that an adequate warning by itself does not "immunize a manufacturer from any liability caused by its defectively designed product."[32]

In two cases in 2011, the Supreme Court placed some limits on the reach of a product liability lawsuit. The first case stemmed from a bus accident in Paris that claimed the lives of two boys from North Carolina who were in France for a soccer tournament. The accident was blamed on a defective tire produced by a foreign subsidiary of Goodyear. In *Goodyear Tire v. Brown*, the Court noted that North Carolina courts lacked the jurisdiction to hear a case involving these subsidiary companies because the accident itself had no connection to the state—even though the Goodyear "parent company" did business in the state.[33]

In a second 2011 case, a man lost four fingers while using a machine designed to cut metal. He sued the manufacturer, which was based in England. Although the manufacturer had used a U.S. based distributor, the Supreme Court ruled that New Jersey state courts lacked jurisdiction over that foreign company. In the plurality opinion, Justice Kennedy did not entirely eliminate the possibility of similarly situated individuals suing foreign companies, but noted that "a forum-by-forum, or sovereign-by-sovereign, analysis" was required to assess the extent of a company's dealings in a particular jurisdiction[34]—with a company's "purposeful availment" or "targeting" of a jurisdiction providing a litmus test of susceptibility to a lawsuit.

VICARIOUS LIABILITY

Vicarious liability means that one person is held liable for the acts of another based on a relationship between the parties. Courts justify the imposition of vicarious liability based on one party's exercising control over the other. Not surprisingly, vicarious liability most frequently applies in a relationship known at common law as a master-servant. Today, this type of relationship is more commonly characterized as an employer-employee relationship, and the employer may be held liable for torts committed by employees acting within the scope of their duties. Being vicariously liable for employees gives an employer an incentive to carefully select and train employees. Employees remain liable for their own torts; however, plaintiffs usually seek recourse against the employer, who is likely to carry liability insurance to cover such claims.

Typically, an employer-employee relationship is created where an employer furnishes necessary tools and directly supervises a person working on an hourly or a salary basis. One must distinguish the employer-employee relationship from one in which the contract is with an **independent contractor**. An independent contractor is a party hired to accomplish a certain result for a stipulated payment. For example, an independent contractor relationship generally arises when a party employs a roofing company to repair a roof and the roofer brings the equipment and workers and directs the performance of their work. Ordinarily one who employs an independent contractor is not held liable for the torts of such contractor. There are exceptions. For example, a party who contracts to have dangerous work performed can be held vicariously liable for an independent contractor's torts that are inherent and foreseeable in the work to be accomplished. A good example of this would be a contract to perform blasting with explosives. There are other technical exceptions, which include duties imposed by contract or by laws and regulations.

Employer Hiring Practices

Historically, an employer was vicariously liable for acts of an employee committed within the scope of employment, but the trend of court decisions has been to broaden that liability. In 1980, a Pennsylvania appellate court ruled that employers are liable for acts of violence committed by their employees if the employer knew, or should have known, of the employee's propensity for violence.[35] Since that time, courts have held that an employer is liable for the willful tort of an employee committed against a third person if the employer knew or should have known that the employee was a threat to others. These principles have brought about the tort known as **negligent hiring** in many jurisdictions. This doctrine is based on an employer's duty to make an investigation before hiring an employee and to exercise a reasonable degree of supervision, particularly of employees who will have personal contacts with third parties. In recent years, this theory has been employed frequently to hold religious organizations liable for offenses committed against minors by clergypersons.

In an interesting application of the doctrine of negligent hiring, an occupant of a townhouse sued the developer for injuries sustained when she was assaulted by one of the developer's employees who was permitted to enter the townhouses to perform maintenance. The plaintiff was unsuccessful in the trial court, but a Florida appellate court remanded the case for trial based on the principle that when the developer permits an employee to have access to the townhouses, the developer is charged with acquiring such information about the employee's background as it could have obtained upon reasonable inquiry.[36]

Owners and Drivers of Motor Vehicles

A driver whose negligence causes an automobile accident is liable; however, frequently the owner of the vehicle is in a better financial position (often by virtue of liability insurance) to respond in damages. Yet under traditional tort law, an owner of an automobile who permits another person to drive was not liable to a party injured as a result of the driver's negligence unless the driver was an agent of the owner or was acting within the scope of employment, or if the owner had negligently entrusted the vehicle to a person not competent to operate it. Through different legal devices, states have created doctrines of law to assess liability against the owner. Some states have enacted statutes or courts have ruled that the driver is presumed to be the owner's agent, thereby making the owner liable for the negligence of anyone operating the vehicle with the owner's consent. Others treat a family much like a business and hold that an owner is liable for negligent operation of a vehicle by members of the owner's family. Very early in the history of automobiles, the Florida Supreme Court, in a landmark decision, declared that an automobile is a **dangerous instrumentality** and that therefore the owner is liable for the negligence of a driver permitted to use the vehicle.[37]

SPECIAL TORT SITUATIONS

Tort law is a complex and highly dynamic area. There are a number of special situations that do not fit neatly into the categories we have been discussing. These include professional malpractice, the liability of owners and possessors of real estate, negligent infliction of emotional distress, survival actions, wrongful death actions, preconception torts, torts involving alcoholic beverages, toxic torts, and torts involving the deprivation of constitutional rights.

Professional Malpractice

Professional malpractice consists of the failure of a professional, for example, a physician, hospital, dentist, lawyer, or engineer, to meet the reasonable standard of care of professionals with similar training and experience. Not every error by a professional equates with malpractice. To have a cause of action, the plaintiff must suffer harm as a proximate result of the professional's alleged negligence. Unless the defendant's failure to meet the standard of care of professionals in similar disciplines can be established through common knowledge, the plaintiff must prove the defendant's negligence through the testimony of expert witnesses. Handling a plaintiff's suit for malpractice often involves considerable pretrial procedures involving lengthy discovery processes to obtain documents and depositions of experts. Trials are lengthy and can involve testimony by numerous experts.

Medical malpractice and legal malpractice are the most frequent instances of professional malpractice. Medical malpractice may take the form of a physician's or other health care provider's misdiagnosing a patient's problem, failing to properly treat the patient, or prescribing or administering the wrong medication. A physician can also be guilty of medical malpractice by failing to adequately inform the patient about the risks involved in a treatment or surgical procedure. This makes it important, especially in non-emergency surgical procedures, for a physician to obtain the patient's "informed consent" prior to procedures. The publicity that attends a suit for medical malpractice can seriously reflect on the defendant's reputation. Therefore, to avoid the prospect of a "meritless suit," some states impose pre-suit screening requirements.

A lawyer who fails to use such skill, prudence, and diligence ordinarily exercised by lawyers under similar circumstances may be guilty of legal malpractice. Areas of potential malpractice span a variety of situations, including legal advice as well as performance in civil and criminal cases. Failure to file a claim on behalf of a claimant within the period allowed by a statute of limitations is one of the more frequent grounds cited in legal malpractice suits.

Owners and Possessors of Real Estate

Tort liability of owners or possessors of land or buildings depends on the duty the law imposes on such owner or occupier. Generally, an owner who leases property to a tenant is not liable to the tenant or to third parties for injuries occurring on the leased premises unless the owner knows or has reason to know of some concealed danger of the premises.

Most courts determine the possessor's duty based on whether the plaintiff is an **invitee**, **licensee**, or **trespasser**. The duty to an invitee is to exercise reasonable care for a person's safety. Therefore, it is not uncommon for a supermarket to be held liable to a person who slips and falls on a green pea or banana peel left on the floor. This usually occurs where the evidence shows the supermarket was aware of the existence of a dangerous situation or that the condition existed a sufficient length of time for the store to be on what is called **constructive notice** of the situation. Courts hold that an owner or possessor of property has a somewhat lesser standard of care to social guests and household occupants. This class of persons has historically been treated as licensees. The trend in recent years has also been for courts to hold a landowner or possessor to a reasonable standard of care to all classes of persons.[38] Some states, though, have enacted statutes limiting the liability of an owner or possessor who makes land available to the public without charge for recreational use.

Most courts take the position that a trespasser must take the property as it is found and require only that the owner or possessor of the premises not commit an intentional tort against the trespasser. Some courts, however, have imposed special rules in respect to trespassing children who are injured by an artificial condition on the land if the owner or possessor knows, or has reason to know, that children are likely trespassers. This is especially true where the possessor has created something that particularly attracts very young children. Some courts term such a condition an **attractive nuisance**.[39] An abandoned sewer drain, a house under construction, a small pumping oil well with a jack handle moving up and down like a "seesaw," and a "mud mixer" machine that exposed the revolving blades are examples of other situations that courts have considered attractive nuisances.

Most American courts have adopted the English common law doctrine called the **firefighter's rule**, which treats a firefighter or police officer as a licensee, thereby limiting a landowner's or possessor's liability to a firefighter or police officer injured as a result of the condition of premises they enter. The rationale for the rule is that those whose occupations call for them to enter premises as part of their duties assume the risks incident thereto. Yet some courts have held that this rule should not be applied to prevent a firefighter or police officer from recovering damages against someone who intentionally injures or causes injuries to a firefighter or officer on the scene.[40]

Negligent Infliction of Emotional Distress

As we pointed out earlier, the tort of intentional infliction of emotional distress consists of willfully committing outrageous acts directed against another person. In the past four decades, most courts have extended the tort of intentional infliction of emotional distress to include **negligent infliction of emotional distress**. With some variations in the states, most courts allow a plaintiff who is a bystander to recover for negligent infliction of emotional distress if the plaintiff can demonstrate physical consequences from fright or shock resulting from exposure to physical danger. For example, in 2004, the Tennessee Supreme Court upheld a mail carrier's action for negligent infliction of emotional distress against the estate of a homeowner where on her mail delivery route the carrier was exposed to watching the homeowner shoot his wife and then commit suicide.[41]

Survival Actions

Under the English common law, the right to bring a law action for personal injuries terminated at the death of either the victim or the tortfeasor. In the United States, **survival statutes** provide that most tort actions survive both the plaintiff and the defendant; however, some jurisdictions stipulate that a cause of action for defamation does not survive a deceased plaintiff. The right to continue a deceased victim's cause of action is transferred to the personal representative of the victim's estate, or in some instances, to designated family members. Any defenses that would have been available to a defendant had the decedent lived continue to be available to the defendant's estate.[42]

Wrongful Death Acts

The English common law did not provide for a civil suit against one who caused another's death. Thus, a tortfeasor who caused someone's death was in the anomalous position of not suffering the economic consequences of one who merely injured the victim. Eventually, this restriction was eliminated in England by passage in 1846 of Lord Campbell's Act.[43] In the United States, all states now have **wrongful death acts** that allow an action for wrongful death. Because many of these state statutes are patterned after the English legislation, these acts are commonly referred to as Lord Campbell's Acts. In some states, the personal representative of the decedent's estate is the plaintiff; in other states members of the decedent's family who were dependent on the decedent can bring the action. The class of persons who may recover and the elements of damage recoverable vary among the states. Usually, a decedent's spouse and children are permitted beneficiaries, but in some instances it is the decedent's estate that is entitled to certain elements of damage. Some statutes simply specify the action is for the benefit of the decedent's heirs. But courts have denied a "live-in cohabitant" the right to recover even though such person may have been dependent on the decedent for support.[44]

Wrongful Birth; Wrongful Life; Preconception Torts

The dynamic character of tort law is illustrated by recent decisions recognizing a rather distinct species of medical malpractice. The tort of **wrongful birth** is a species of medical malpractice in which parents give birth to an impaired or deformed child where negligent treatment or advice deprived them of the opportunity to avoid or terminate the pregnancy. An example could be where a child is born with severe defects because the mother contracted a serious illness. In jurisdictions that permit an action for wrongful birth, the plaintiff can recover those extra expenses associated with the birth defect. Some courts have permitted a child's parent to sue a physician for negligence in performing sterilization procedures that resulted in the birth of a child.

The tort of **wrongful life** refers to an action brought on behalf of a child born with birth defects when the birth would not have occurred but for the negligent medical advice or treatment. Most courts today recognize the tort of wrongful birth,[45] and some recognize the tort of wrongful life.[46] This area of the law is now developing with courts in wrongful life cases generally limiting damages to medical expenses rather than extending them to the costs of raising a child.

A decision by the Indiana Supreme Court furnishes another example of law developing in this area. In 1992, the court ruled that a child has a **preconception tort** cause of action for injuries allegedly resulting from the negligence of the defendant medical laboratory's failure to diagnose that the child's mother had Rh-negative blood and the defendant physician's alleged failure to administer RhoGAM (Rh immune globulin) during the mother's pregnancy.[47]

Alcoholic Beverages

Under the English common law, a vendor of intoxicating beverages was not liable to persons injured by the intoxicated purchaser. The trend in American courts in recent years, though, has been to allow a tort action against the seller of intoxicated beverages, particularly if the seller violated a statute imposing liability on vendors who sell intoxicating beverages to a minor.

These statutes, often called **dram shop acts** (a dram shop is a place of business that dispenses alcoholic beverages), eliminate the proximate cause requirement and allow a person injured by the intoxicated individual to recover damages against the vendor. Some courts have held that an injured party has a claim against the vendor under a dram shop act even though a minor with whom the purchasing minor shared the alcoholic beverage caused the injuries. In 1998, the Washington Supreme Court ruled that a vendor who illegally sold alcoholic beverages to the minor, who in turn furnished the alcoholic beverage to another minor, could be held liable for foreseeable alcohol-related injuries that arose from the initial sale.[48]

The so-called dram shop acts generally are not applicable to a **social host** who furnishes alcoholic beverages to a guest. Legislatures and courts have begun to address the issue of whether a social host can be held responsible for furnishing alcoholic beverages to a guest who becomes intoxicated and causes injury or death to another person. Observing that courts, and not only legislatures, have a duty in this area, in 1984 the New Jersey Supreme Court addressed the issue. The court held that a social host who provides intoxicating liquor to a guest knowing that guest to be intoxicated and would soon drive a vehicle is liable for injuries to a third party caused by guest's negligent operation of a motor vehicle if the driver's negligence is caused by intoxication.[49]

In 1990, the Ohio Supreme Court ruled that parents may be held liable if they know that their children are planning a party where underage drinking is likely even if the parents are not at home at the time of the party.[50] Some states require a statutory basis for assessing liability of a social host in respect to furnishing alcohol to minors or permitting minors to consume alcoholic beverages; in other states, courts have imposed liability based on common law principles and have found that a social host has a duty to avoid serving alcoholic beverages to minors.

Toxic Torts

One of the newest tort actions is based on claims of human or property exposure to toxins through absorption, contact, ingestion, inhalation, implantation, or injection. Plaintiffs have charged that asbestos, various chemical compounds, silicone breast implants, and disposal of hazardous wastes, to name a few, have caused injuries to health or the environment. Many of the substances involved in toxic tort actions are regulated by such federal agencies as the Food and Drug Administration (FDA), the Environmental Protection Agency (EPA), and the Occupational Safety and Health Administration (OSHA). (Administrative regulation is discussed in Chapter 12.)

Among the legal problems that arise in this area is whether exposure to a toxic substance, for example, asbestos, where the symptoms remained latent until after the right to bring suit, is barred by a **statute of limitations**. Another concerns the legal theory available for recovery and what defenses may be available to a defendant. In 1973, the U.S. Court of Appeals for the Fifth Circuit applied the principle of strict product liability and held a manufacturer liable for failure to adequately warn the plaintiff of the hazards of products that contained asbestos.[51]

In 1991, the Supreme Court of California reviewed a case where a shipyard worker brought a toxic tort action based on strict liability.[52] The plaintiff alleged that, while working, he contracted lung ailments through exposure to asbestos and asbestos products. The issue before the state supreme court was whether in a strict product liability action based on an alleged failure to warn of a risk of harm a defendant could present evidence of the state-of-the-art, that is, evidence that the particular risk was neither known nor knowable by the application of scientific knowledge available. The court recounted that it had previously concluded that a manufacturer of prescription drugs is exempt from strict liability for defects in design and is not strictly liable for injuries caused by scientifically unknowable dangerous propensities in prescription drugs. This principle, the court opined, should allow a defendant to present state-of-the-art evidence at trial.

In toxic tort litigation, courts must resolve disputes involving complex problems of science and technology. These actions present a problem to the legal system when they involve an issue of when a statute of limitations begins to run, where the plaintiff alleges latent injuries. Often, thousands of plaintiffs are involved in tort claims involving toxic torts resulting from massive accidents, and not infrequently, multiple defendants are charged with the responsibility for such massive occurrences. Generally, claims in mass torts are handled through class action lawsuits (see Chapter 9).

Some of the most complex and difficult product liability cases are those that involve pharmaceutical products used by millions of Americans. For example, in 2005 there were literally thousands of suits pending against the pharmaceutical giant Merck over the arthritis drug Vioxx, which was pulled from the market in 2004 over concerns that it led to increased risks of heart attack and stroke. Several of these suits had resulted in huge judgments against Merck. After appellate courts in several states reversed or reduced these judgments, Merck agreed to establish a $4.85 billion fund to settle these cases. In 2013, Merck also agreed to a $23 million settlement in response to a series of additional lawsuits regarding Vioxx. Thus, it is important to recognize that resolutions in one set of lawsuits do not necessarily preclude additional litigation on similar matters.

Employer-Employee Relationships

Under the common law, employers rarely were found liable for injuries to their employees, because employers were allowed to assert defenses that usually insulated them from liability. For example, an employer was exonerated if the court found that the employee assumed the risk of injury incident to a particular job (assumption of risk), if another employee caused the injury (fellow servant rule), or if the worker's carelessness contributed to the injury (contributory negligence).

These common law doctrines were unsuitable to an industrial age, and in the early 1900s, Congress and many state legislatures enacted laws, which today are called **worker's compensation acts**. These acts provide that if an injury occurs "in the course of employment" and "arises out of the employment" an injured worker is compensated according to a statutory schedule that covers medical expenses, loss of wages, and temporary and permanent disabilities. Dependents can recover benefits if the employee's death arises out of the worker's employment. These acts are beneficial to both employers and employees. Employers gain the advantage of averting litigation and being able to budget to pay insurance premiums for necessary coverage. Employees obtain compensation promptly without the necessity of proving fault, yet the benefits to the employee do not include compensation for pain and suffering. The Federal Employers Liability Act provides somewhat similar benefits for railroad workers; another federal statute, the Jones Act, covers maritime employees.

TOXIC TORTS

Recent decades have seen a surge in "toxic tort" litigation involving claims arising from injuries or illnesses caused by exposure to toxic chemicals, radiation, or other hazardous materials such as asbestos. Perhaps the best-known toxic tort case was that stemming from the 1984 accident at the Union Carbide plant in Bhopal, India. More than 10,000 people died and more than 300,000 people were injured as the result of exposure to a cloud of methyl isocyanate and other toxic chemicals that were accidentally released from the plant. Union Carbide paid $470 million to settle the case out of court.

THE
LAW IN
ACTION

Other well-known examples of toxic tort litigation include the Love Canal case in Niagara Falls, New York, the Times-Beach Case in Missouri, and the W.R. Grace case in Massachusetts, which was the subject of the book and film *A Civil Action.*

Toxic tort litigation was also the subject of a popular feature film. Based on a true story, *Erin Brockovich* (2000) features Julia Roberts as a legal secretary who investigated water contamination in the small desert community of Hinckley, California. The resulting lawsuit brought by 652 Hinckley residents against Pacific Gas & Electric Company resulted in a $333 million out-of-court settlement in 1996.

Toxic tort lawsuits usually involve claims of negligence or strict liability. This type of litigation also typically incorporates analysis of complex factual issues. Thus, plaintiffs and defendants tend to rely heavily on the testimony of expert witnesses—and many claims result in settlements that avoid the expense of a lengthy trial (and any subsequent appeals). A recent example of this kind of settlement comes from Charleston, West Virginia, where a January 2014 chemical spill in the Elk River contaminated drinking water for 300,000 residents. In July 2014, the company responsible for the spill agreed to establish a $2.9 million dollar trust fund to benefit residents of the affected area.

Deprivation of Constitutional Rights—A Quasi-Tort

A federal statute passed after the Civil War, 42 U.S.C. §1983, creates a cause of action for an **intentional tort committed under color or authority of law** which deprives a person of federal constitutional rights or rights under federal laws. The basic purpose of the law is to deter state actors from using their authority to deprive individuals of their federally guaranteed rights. Section 1983 provides:

> Every person, who under color of any statute, ordinance, regulation, custom, or usage, of any State or Territory, subjects or causes to be subjected, any citizen of the United States or other person within the jurisdiction thereof to the deprivation of any rights, privileges, or immunities secured by the Constitution and laws, shall be liable to the party injured in action at law, and in equity, or other proper proceeding for redress.

The statute is the basis for actions, commonly referred to as Section 1983 suits, against state and local officials in both federal and state courts. Section 1983 does not create a basis for a tort action against a federal official; the U.S. Constitution is the basis for such actions.[53]

Tort actions based on Section 1983 span a variety of situations in employment, education, housing, and public facilities as well as prisoners' rights, voting rights, and other areas. Many Section 1983 actions focus on law enforcement activities.

CASE IN POINT

THE *EXXON VALDEZ* CASE: TWENTY YEARS OF LITIGATION RESULTS IN A DRAMATIC DECISION BY THE U.S. SUPREME COURT
Exxon Shipping Co. v. Baker
United States Supreme Court
554 U.S. 471, 128 S. Ct. 2605, 171 L. Ed. 2d 570 (2008)

When the supertanker *Exxon Valdez* ran aground on a reef along the Alaska coast in June 1989, the hull fractured and almost 11 million gallons of crude oil were spilled into Prince William Sound. Nearly 1,300 miles of Alaska coastline were fouled by the oil, and thousands of birds and other marine creatures were killed. More than 30,000 residents were economically affected by the disaster; many of them lost their livelihoods altogether. It turned out that the ship's captain had been drinking and was not on the bridge at the time of the accident. The U.S. government and the state of Alaska brought suit against Exxon, alleging negligence on the part of the company. The suit was settled when Exxon agreed to pay more than $900 million for the cost of the cleanup and the restoration of the natural environment. Exxon agreed to pay another $300 million to settle claims brought by various private parties. A number of private civil suits that were not settled were consolidated for trial in the federal district court in Alaska. The jury awarded $287 million in compensatory damages and, because it found that Exxon was reckless, imposed an additional $5 billion in punitive damages. The U.S. Court of Appeals reduced the punitive damages award to $2.5 billion, but Exxon asked the U.S. Supreme Court to review the case. In a 5-3 decision rendered in June 2008, the Supreme Court further reduced the punitive damages to $507.5 million. Writing for the majority, Justice David Souter concluded that the $2.5 billion award was excessive, and therefore a violation of due process, because in maritime cases punitive damages tend to be equivalent to actual damages where the harm was not deliberate or malicious. Limiting punitive damages is necessary, according to Souter, "given the need to protect against the possibility . . . of awards that are unpredictable and unnecessary, either for deterrence or for measured retribution. . . ." In dissent, Justice Ruth B. Ginsburg questioned "whether there is an urgent need in maritime law to break away from the 'traditional common law approach' under which punitive damages are determined by a properly instructed jury, followed by trial-court, and then appellate-court review, to ensure that [the award] is reasonable."

Because negligence does not constitute a violation of constitutional rights, a negligent shooting death of an individual by a police officer would not ordinarily constitute a violation of Section 1983. But a complaint alleging that police officers illegally arrested a black man, contrived charges to justify his arrest, falsified police reports, and initiated prosecution in bad faith, all with racial animus and pursuant to official policy, was held to state a claim for deprivation of equal protection of the law under Section 1983.[54]

Perhaps the most famous Section 1983 case was the suit brought by Rodney King, who alleged that Los Angeles police officers had used excessive force in violation of the federal Constitution when they stopped King's car after a high-speed chase in 1991. The officers were charged criminally in a California court but were acquitted, which spawned the Los Angeles riot of 1992. The officers were subsequently convicted of federal civil rights violations and went to prison. In the related civil action, King won a $3.8 million judgment from the City of Los Angeles.

Section 1983 is not itself a source of substantive rights, but rather is a method for vindicating rights recognized by the United States Constitution or conferred by federal statutes. Thus, the first issue in a Section 1983 lawsuit is to identify the substantive right allegedly infringed. An interesting case in this regard is *Board of County Commissioners, Wabaunsee County, Kansas v. Umbehr.*[55] The case began when a county commission terminated a garbage collection contract with a company whose owner had been extremely critical of the commission. The owner, Umbehr, claimed that the commission had violated his First Amendment rights by retaliating against him economically. The federal district court dismissed the suit, holding that the First Amendment does not prohibit government from considering a contractor's expression as a factor in deciding not to continue the contract. The court reasoned that, as an independent contractor, Umbehr was not entitled to the First Amendment protection that is afforded public employees.[56] The Supreme Court reinstated the complaint, recognizing "the right of independent government contractors not to be terminated for exercising their First Amendment rights."[57] Thus, the existence of an "injury" in a Section 1983 case depends on whether courts are willing to recognize a plaintiff's constitutional claims.

IMMUNITIES FROM LIABILITY

Under the English common law, no action could be brought against the Crown because "the King could do no wrong." As early as the thirteenth century, the common law held that the King could not be sued in his own courts. This doctrine of **sovereign immunity** was received by the American courts and became a part of the American common law. The doctrine holds that the United States as a sovereign nation and the states as sovereign states cannot be sued without their consent. In a democratic society based on the principle that government is subject to the rule of law, the principle of sovereign immunity is difficult to defend. Of course, Congress and the state legislatures can, and often do, waive sovereign immunity in whole or in part.

CASE IN POINT

ARE MUNICIPALITIES IMMUNE FROM FEDERAL CIVIL RIGHTS LAWSUITS?
Monell v. New York City Department of Social Services
436 U.S. 658, 98 S. Ct. 2018, 56 L. Ed. 2d 611 (1978)

Female employees of the New York City Department of Social Services brought suit under 42 U.S.C. §1983 against the Department and a number of local officials. The essence of their complaint was that the Department had compelled pregnant employees to take unpaid leaves of absence before they were medically necessary. Relying on precedent, the federal district judge held that local governments were immune from suits for damages under 42 U.S.C. §1983 and that local officials were cloaked with this immunity. The Court of Appeals affirmed. The U.S. Supreme Court reversed, holding that local governments and local government officials can be sued under Section 1983 in situations where employees' constitutional rights are deprived as a matter of policy or custom. The Court said that Congress did not intend for municipalities to be immune from lawsuits seeking to vindicate constitutional rights.

Federal Tort Liability

To prevent injustices to those who suffer injuries or losses at the hands of the federal government, Congress enacted the Federal Tort Claims Act of 1946.[58] The Act waives the federal government's sovereign immunity for "negligent or wrongful acts or omissions"; therefore, the federal government is not liable under the doctrine of strict tort liability. Claims must first be presented to the appropriate federal agency before an injured party can file suit in the U.S. Court of Federal Claims. The Act contains numerous exceptions, for example, claims in respect to postal matters, intentional torts against a person, misrepresentation, fraud and deceit, defamation, interference with contract rights, and monetary matters involving the U.S. Treasury.

State and Local Tort Liability

In 1793, in *Chisholm v. Georgia*, the U.S. Supreme Court ruled that sovereign immunity did not apply to states when sued in federal court.[59] The Eleventh Amendment to the U.S. Constitution was promptly ratified and effectively nullified the Court's decision in *Chisholm*. The Eleventh Amendment provides: "The Judicial power of the United States shall not be construed to extend to any suit in law or equity, commenced or prosecuted against one of the United States by Citizens of another State, or by Citizens or Subjects of any Foreign State." The Supreme Court has said that the Eleventh Amendment exists both to prevent federal court judgments that must be paid out of state funds and to protect states from the coercion of the federal courts.[60]

Through a variety of constitutional and statutory provisions, the states have provided various means for asserting claims and filing suits for torts. In some instances, there are limits to amounts recoverable, in others, claimants are limited to coverage provided by the state's liability insurance. Tort claims against the state and local units of government are usually limited to **proprietary or operational activities**, and the states retain their sovereign immunity for such **discretionary activities** that are incident to governance. Utilities and road maintenance often are classified as operational activities, while passage of laws and ordinances and planning activities generally fall within the area of discretionary activities.

With the availability of liability insurance, the trend is to abolish or restrict immunities of state and local governments. In some instances, state and local governments waive their immunity to the extent that they are covered by liability insurance coverage.

Interspousal and Parent-Child Immunity

The English common law identified spouses as one. Thus, one spouse could not sue the other. By the middle of the nineteenth century, statutes and court decisions in the United States began to recognize married women as having a separate legal identity; however, most jurisdictions still maintained that one spouse could not sue the other for a tort. Courts said this doctrine of **interspousal immunity** was justified by the need to preserve marital harmony and to protect defendants and their liability insurers from the prospect of collusive lawsuits. Today, many states have abolished interspousal immunity, either by statute or by court decision.

Historically, courts found that the parental immunity rule was essential to protect family relationships and not interfere with parental responsibilities with respect to the discipline and care of children. Although the issue is unsettled, the trend is toward abolition or modification of parent-child immunity. In 1994, the Tennessee Supreme Court overruled its precedents and held that **parental immunity** is limited to conduct that involves exercise of parental authority, performance of parental supervision, and provision of parental care and custody.[61] But even as recently as 2005, the Arkansas Supreme Court held that the parental immunity doctrine precluded a minor child from recovering in a negligence action against his father for injuries to the child when his father ran over him while operating a lawnmower.[62] Even where courts continue to adhere to the parental immunity doctrine, many have held that the doctrine is not applicable to actions arising from motor vehicle accidents.

Charitable Immunity

Historically, nonprofit organizations conducting charitable activities were immune from liability under the doctrine of **charitable immunity**. In 1942, the U.S. Court of Appeals for the District of Columbia Circuit, in a landmark decision, rejected the doctrine of charitable immunity.[63] Other courts also have ruled that there is no such immunity; some, though, have upheld immunity for certain types of charitable institutions by drawing distinctions between paying and non-paying parties. With the increasing availability of liability insurance, most courts now hold charitable organizations liable to the same extent as individuals and private corporations.

RECENT DEVELOPMENTS IN TORT LAW

In our litigious society, there are always new developments in tort law. Increasingly, governments and interest groups are relying on tort law as a way of addressing social problems. Some of the more important recent developments include

- suits against the tobacco industry brought by smokers who have become ill and by states seeking to recover costs associated with treating illnesses due to smoking.
- suits against manufacturers of firearms brought by governments seeking to recover costs associated with gun violence.
- suits against pharmacists for failing to warn customers about possible dangers of prescription drugs.

Tobacco Litigation: A Reversal of Judicial Attitudes

Before the 1990s, tobacco companies were generally successful in their defense of suits for damages by smokers who claimed to have developed tobacco-related illnesses, but the defense of such claims was greatly undermined by the U.S. Supreme Court's 1992 decision in *Cipollone v. Liggett Group, Inc.*[64] There, the Court held that the federal law which established cigarette warnings in advertising did not bar a claimant from seeking damages under state laws. In later litigation, tobacco companies were ordered to produce documents that revealed scientific evidence concerning the adverse health consequences to tobacco users. In a number of instances, appellate courts have reversed jury verdicts awarding damages to plaintiffs.

In 1997, the attorneys general of many states successfully negotiated settlements with tobacco companies in Medicaid reimbursement lawsuits. Nevertheless, by 1999, individual and class action suits were filed on behalf of smokers and the estates of deceased smokers seeking both compensatory and punitive damages for illnesses and death alleged to have resulted from smoking. Substantial verdicts have been rendered against major tobacco companies. For example, in March 2000, a San Francisco jury awarded $1.7 million in compensatory damages and $20 million in punitive damages to a terminally ill woman who smoked cigarettes for several decades. In April 2000, a Miami jury found a cigarette manufacturer liable in a class action suit and awarded $12.7 million in compensatory damages. And, in 2003, tobacco giant Phillip Morris was ordered to pay 10.1 billion dollars in damages in a class-action lawsuit brought in Illinois. However, the Illinois Supreme Court overturned that decision in 2005. Even so, in 2011, a lower appellate court in Illinois opened the possibility for the suit to be revived, and in April 2014, the original damages actually were reinstated—although future appeals remain a possibility.

Elsewhere, in 2011, a 1999 judgment against Philip Morris in Oregon was upheld by the state's Supreme Court, and in January 2012, the company agreed to pay the state $56 million for punitive damages for a claim brought by the family of a former school custodian who died of lung cancer.[65] The Supreme Court of the United States was twice involved with earlier appeals stemming from that Oregon case,[66] but Phillip Morris decided to settle the matter rather than pursue further appeals. In July 2014, a Florida jury awarded $23.6 billion in damages against R.J. Reynolds—although an appeal is also expected to be heard in that case. The Supreme Court of the United States, however, has recently kept itself out of such matters. For example, in June of 2014, it refused to hear appeals brought by R.J. Reynolds, Phillip Morris, and Lorillard, who were contesting $70 million in damages awarded by juries in a series of cases that were also from Florida; the high Court's denial of certiorari ostensibly leaves damage awards from lower courts intact.

Ultimately, many of the awards related to tobacco litigation—even some that are more than a decade old—are still under review by appellate courts. In the end, the rules of law that develop from such litigation will be crystallized in the appellate courts that review jury awards of damages.

Are Manufacturers of Firearms to Be Held Liable for Acts of Violence?

In the late 1990s and early 2000s, in the aftermath of the tragic deaths of the increasing number of victims of firearm violence, a number of cities and counties filed lawsuits against gun manufacturers. These plaintiffs were seeking to recover millions of dollars spent on medical care and police protection incident to violence, which the local governments attributed to use of guns. Some plaintiffs claimed the sale of guns to criminals constitutes a public nuisance, while others sought to recover on product liability theories or claims that the manufacturers had been negligent in failing to incorporate safety features into their products.

However, in 2005, Congress passed the Protection of Lawful Commerce in Arms Act, which limited lawsuits against gun manufacturers based on consumer use of their products (although no limitations on suits related to defective products were imposed). In 2009, the Supreme Court effectively sanctioned this law when it refused to review a lower court's dismissal of New York City's lawsuit against gun manufacturers.[67] Suits against ammunition dealers are still permitted, though.

Are New Duties of Pharmacists on the Horizon?

Traditionally, pharmacists were liable only if they failed to accurately fill a prescription. But a June 1999 article in the *American Bar Association Journal* states, "Most states still do not hold pharmacists liable for failure to warn of possible drug hazards, but that may be changing."[68] The author cites two cases in point. In 1992, the Arizona Court of Appeals found that a pharmacist has a duty to warn patients about the possible adverse side effects of prescription medications or the combining of different ones.[69] In 1996, the Michigan Court of Appeals ruled that a pharmacy assumed a duty of care when it advertised that its computers could detect harmful drug interactions.[70] Again, this is a developing area of tort law.

TORT REFORM

In the early twentieth century, state and federal legislative bodies enacted laws that provide a uniform schedule of compensation to employees injured in the course of their employment. This usually takes the form of worker's compensation laws previously discussed. These laws have been modified frequently, with the trend being to provide more generous benefits to injured workers. In the latter part of the twentieth century, legislative bodies began to seriously revise the laws concerning tort liability in respect to motor vehicle accidents.

No-Fault Automobile Insurance Laws

As automobile liability insurance became commonplace, litigation became increasingly costly and often subject to great delays. In the latter part of the twentieth century, reformers who pointed to uncertainties, delays, and costs to victims to obtain a fair award in automobile accident litigation persuaded a number of states to enact **no-fault automobile insurance laws**.[71] These laws provide for reimbursement to injured parties irrespective of fault. Thus, an injured party collects from his or her own insurance company instead of asserting a claim against the party alleged to be at fault. There are variations among no-fault laws, with some applying to property damage as well as personal injuries. In general, these laws allow an injured party to collect for medical expenses, loss of wages, and other economic losses. Some no-fault laws allow traditional tort actions where an injured party suffers permanent injury or disability or where medical expenses and loss of income exceed certain threshold amounts. These laws are still a "work in progress" in the halls of state legislatures and in the courts.

As we have noted, courts and legislative bodies have limited or abolished the historic immunity of governmental bodies and charitable institutions. Moreover, they have formulated new torts, particularly in the areas of products liability and environmental liability. Many reformers argue that some juries have awarded excessive amounts to injured plaintiffs.

The Focal Points of Tort Reform Today

Present advocacy for tort reform centers largely on six areas.

1. Joint and several liability. Historically, where joint tortfeasors are involved, an award of damages is issued on a **joint and several liability** basis. This means that where more than one tortfeasor is found responsible, each is liable to the plaintiff for the entire damages award. This allows a successful plaintiff to collect the entire judgment from one tortfeasor if the others are unable to pay. There is considerable criticism of the joint and several liability doctrine, and some states have adopted laws to provide that joint and several liability is either not applicable, or applicable only in respect to awards under a certain amount, say $50,000.

2. Collateral sources. Legislatures have frequently modified the **collateral source rule**, a rule that historically prohibited juries from hearing about the sources available to a plaintiff to receive reimbursement for losses, for example, personal disability insurance. Where the common law collateral source rule has been overridden by legislation, the court instructs the jury that in awarding damages it must take into consideration the amount of compensation a plaintiff receives from personal insurance or other sources.

3. Non-economic damages. Legislatures in a number of states have enacted laws (and in some instances, the voters have amended their state constitutions) to provide caps on non-economic awards, that is, amounts awarded to compensate a victim for pain and suffering. In more than half of the states, such caps have been created specifically to address medical malpractice claims.

4. Punitive damages. Legislatures in a majority of the states have placed some caps on the award of punitive damages, the so-called "smart money" (see Chapter 9) that juries have been permitted to award if they find the tortfeasor's conduct to be outrageous.

5. Statutes of limitations. Some legislatures have enacted laws shortening the time that plaintiffs are allowed to bring suit, particularly in the fields of professional malpractice, construction defects, and product liability claims.

SIDEBAR

The Infamous McDonald's Coffee Case

A popular example of an allegedly excessive jury award is the $2.7 million "scalding coffee award" against McDonald's in 1997. Stella Liebeck ordered coffee from the drive-through at a McDonald's restaurant in Albuquerque, New Mexico, in 1992. As she removed the lid, the coffee, which was more than 180 degrees Fahrenheit, spilled into her lap causing third-degree burns. Liebeck was hospitalized for eight days, during which time she received skin grafts. Evidence at trial showed that similar injuries had occurred in the past and that McDonald's was aware of the danger of maintaining its coffee at a high temperature. McDonald's argued that its customers preferred its coffee to be served hot and were aware of the risks associated with hot liquids. The jury awarded Liebeck $160,000 in compensatory damages and $2.7 million in punitive damages. The trial court subsequently reduced the punitive award to $480,000. The case was eventually settled for an undisclosed amount. Nevertheless, the fact that the jury was willing to make such an immense award of punitive damages provided impetus for the movement to reform tort laws.

6. Restrictions on legal fees. Lawyers frequently handle personal injury claims and lawsuits for plaintiffs on a **contingent fee** based on the amount of damages recovered. This arrangement enables injured plaintiffs who otherwise may not be able to afford legal counsel to effectively assert their rights. If the lawyer is unsuccessful in recovering damages, the plaintiff's obligation to the lawyer is generally limited to payment of necessary court costs. Lawyers who handle personal injury suits argue that contingent fees are essential to "level the playing field" between plaintiffs and defendants. Critics of contingent fee arrangements claim they lead to unnecessary litigation and are subject to abuse by lawyers. Some states have enacted laws to limit an attorney to a stated percentage of a plaintiff's recovery, perhaps providing for a lesser percentage for recovery through out-of-court settlements.

Congress has been unable to agree on any major tort reforms in recent years. In contrast, state legislation in the above areas has been prolific, meeting varied reactions from the courts. In a number of states, the highest courts have upheld various state laws initiating tort reforms. Many, however, have struck down, in whole or in part, laws capping tort awards and shortening statutes of limitation. Courts have often found such reforms contrary to state constitutional provisions guaranteeing the right to trial by jury in civil cases. Despite reformers having made gains in state legislatures, proponents of restrictions on tort suits now are fighting in the courts to protect their gains.

Some laws that have been invalidated have been unclear as to how they are to be applied by judges and juries. Many advocates of tort reform contend that courts are more likely to sustain reform legislation where the laws provide clear outlines for making awards of damages. One thing is certain: the concept of tort reform will remain viable, with legislative and judicial activity continuing to demonstrate the dynamic qualities of this area of the law.

CONCLUSION

The basic function of tort law is to compensate those who are injured or who suffer economic losses as a result of someone else's intentional or negligent conduct or unreasonably dangerous activity. But it also serves to deter persons from improper conduct, and, in some instances, to punish wrongdoers. Moreover, the availability of tort remedies is designed to prevent those who suffer injuries or losses from resorting to retaliation or self-help against those perceived to be at fault.

Although of common law origin, tort law and its development have paralleled the dynamics of American society, and the principle of fairness has played an increasing role in determining standards of care. Liability based on negligence (rather than strict liability), the economic distribution of risks through worker's compensation, and the availability of liability insurance allowed America to become the world's greatest industrial nation.

In recent decades, as ownership of motor vehicles became almost universal, many states replaced the doctrine of contributory negligence with a fairer doctrine of comparative negligence, and the trend has been to distribute risks among motorists under a no-fault concept. Modern technology also has enabled manufacturers to produce safer products. Courts have responded by holding manufacturers and sellers of products to strict liability for damages resulting from defective products.

Old immunities of governmental and charitable institutions have been severely limited, as insurance has provided a method of risk management compatible with modern conditions.

Legislatures and courts will continue to struggle to enact reforms to fairly compensate those who suffer injuries and losses while not unfairly penalizing those whose actions cause those injuries and losses. These are the dynamics of tort law.

SUMMARY OF KEY CONCEPTS

A tort is a wrongful act that results in injury or loss to the victim. The most common tort today is the tort of negligence based on a tortfeasor's wrongful act or omission and is illustrated by negligent operation of a motor vehicle. Another prominent example is malpractice by a professional. One simple way of remembering the required elements of the tort of negligence are four key words: duty, breach, causation, and damages. Defenses to actions based on negligence include contributory or comparative negligence of a plaintiff or a plaintiff's consent or assumption of risk.

Intentional torts against persons or property include such common examples as assault, battery, false imprisonment, trespass to land or personal property, defamation, fraud, and misrepresentations. Among the defenses commonly asserted by defendants sued for intentional torts against a person are consent, self-defense, and authority of the law. In actions based on torts against property, defendants often assert reasonable use of force and necessity as defenses. In an action for defamation, a defendant may assert the defense that the statements made were true or privileged.

A species of historic torts now broadened in the American legal system is known as strict liability. Originally applied against keepers of dangerous animals and persons conducting such inherently dangerous activities as blasting, the doctrine has been made applicable to those who supply goods whose defects cause injuries or losses to others. In another social development, worker's compensation insurance has largely replaced the uncertainties associated with suits by employees against their employers.

Tort law also provides that a party may be vicariously liable, that is, one person is held legally responsible for the actions of another person based on control over someone's activities. The most common example is an employer's being held liable for acts of an employee committed within the scope of employment. In many instances, legislatures and courts have imposed vicarious liability on owners of motor vehicles who permit others to operate their vehicles.

The student should gain an awareness of the many special tort situations such as survival actions, wrongful death, wrongful birth and life, and preconception torts as well as the growing field of toxic torts and the quasi-tort involving liability for deprivation of a person's constitutional rights. These torts and the elimination of traditional immunities based on sovereignty and the relationship of parties illustrate this very dynamic area of the law. The newest areas of developing tort law concern no-fault automobile insurance laws and attempts to establish new principles of tort law concerning tobacco and pharmaceuticals.

Finally, the student should become conversant with the legislative and judicial trends in tort reform. Attempts to limit non-economic damages and awards of punitive damages, and to shorten some statutes of limitations and limit joint and several liability, are now under way in many states.

FOR FURTHER READING

Helland, Eric, and Alexander Tabarrok, *Judge and Jury: American Tort Law on Trial* (Independent Institute 2006).

Kionka, Edward J., *Torts: Injuries to Persons and Property* (West Group 1999).

Lewis, Anthony, *Make No Law: The Sullivan Case and the First Amendment* (Vintage Books 1992).

Litan, Robert E., and Clifford Winston (eds.), *Liability: Perspectives and Policy* (Brookings Institution 1988).

O'Connell, Jeffrey, *The Injury Industry* (University of Illinois Press 1971).

Olson, Walter (ed.), *New Directions in Liability Law* (Academy of Political Science 1988).

Posner, Richard A. (ed.), *Tort Law: Cases and Economic Analysis* (Little Brown 1977).

Rabin, Robert L. (ed.), *Perspectives on Tort Law* (4th ed., Aspen Publishers 2003).

Schuck, Peter H. (ed.), *Tort Law and the Public Interest* (W.W. Norton 1991).

Shavell, Steven, *Economic Analysis of Accident Law* (Harvard University Press 1987).

QUESTIONS FOR THOUGHT AND DISCUSSION

1. Give an example of conduct that might give rise to (a) a claim for damages based on the tort of invasion of privacy; and (b) a claim based on intentional infliction of emotional distress.

2. Would a court likely hold an owner liable to a person injured by a mechanical device such as a spring gun that was actuated when a trespasser came on the owner's premises?

3. What elements must a plaintiff establish in order to recover damages for injuries or losses suffered as a result of a defendant's alleged negligence?

4. Explain the differences between the defenses of contributory negligence and comparative negligence. Which doctrine do you find to be fairer and more practical? Why?

5. A seven-year-old boy enters an unfenced lot in his neighborhood without the owner's permission. The child drowns when he falls into a small vat of water that the owner left when the house that formerly stood on the land was demolished. Under what theory might the child's parents bring an action against the landowner?

6. Name the defenses that employers were allowed to assert in an employee's common law tort action to recover damages for job-related injuries. What development in the law brought about a compensation system of employees injured in job-related activities?

7. How has the action for products liability developed from the common law concept of strict liability? To what extent has its development been influenced by the *Restatement of Torts*?

8. Give an example of an action by a state official that would likely be a violation of 42 U.S.C. §1983?

9. Why have courts tended to limit tort liability of local government entities to operational activities, thereby excluding liability for discretionary activities?

10. Evaluate the validity and fairness of tort reform legislation that would (a) shorten the statutes of limitations; (b) abolish the collateral source rule; (c) place caps on non-economic punitive damages; and (d) adopt no-fault automobile insurance.

KEY TERMS

assault
assumption of risk
attractive nuisance
authority of law
battery
breach of duty
"but for" test
caveat emptor
charitable immunity
collateral source rule
comparative negligence
compensatory damages
consent
consortium
constructive notice
contingent fee
contributory negligence
conversion
dangerous instrumentality
deadly force
defamation
defense of a third person
discretionary activities
dram shop acts
duty
false imprisonment
firefighter's rule
foreseeable
fraud

gross negligence
implied consent
independent contractor
informed consent
intentional acts
intentional infliction of emotional distress
intentional tort committed under color or authority of law
interspousal immunity
intervening act
invasion of privacy
invitee
joint and several liability
libel
licensee
misrepresentation
necessity
negligence
negligence per se
negligent acts or omissions
negligent hiring
negligent infliction of emotional distress
no-fault automobile insurance laws
nuisance
parental immunity
preconception tort
privilege

products liability
professional malpractice
proprietary or operational activities
proximate cause
public figures
public officials
punitive damages
qualified privilege
reasonable force
reasonable person
res ipsa loquitur
self-defense
slander
social host
sovereign immunity
statute of limitations
strict liability
survival statutes
tort
tortfeasor
toxic torts
transferred intent
trespass to land
trespasser
vicarious liability
worker's compensation acts
wrongful birth
wrongful death acts
wrongful life

ENDNOTES

1. 551 P.2d 334 (Cal. 1976).
2. *Estate of Morgan v. Fairfield Family Counseling Ctr.*, 673 N.E.2d 1311 (Ohio 1996).
3. *See, e.g., DeLuca v. Bowden*, 329 N.E.2d 109 (Ohio 1975).
4. *See, e.g., Dunn v. Teti*, 421 A.2d 782 (Pa. Super. 1980).
5. *See, e.g., Sanchez v. Galey*, 733 P.2d 1234 (Idaho 1986).

6. *Fick v. Pilsener Brewing Co.*, 86 N.E.2d 515 (Ohio C.P. 1949).

7. 162 N.E. 99 (N.Y. 1928).

8. *See Dusckiwicz v. Carter*, 52 A.2d 788 (Vt. 1947).

9. *See, e.g., Hoffman v. Jones*, 280 So.2d 431 (Fla. 1973).

10. There also can be instances of negligent misrepresentation.

11. *See, e.g., Vaughan v. Wal-Mart Stores, Inc.*, 734 So.2d 156 (La. App. 1999).

12. *Journal Gazette Co. v. Bandido's Inc.*, 712 N.E.2d 446 (Ind. 1999).

13. *New York Times v. Sullivan*, 376 U.S. 254, 84 S. Ct. 710, 11 L. Ed. 2d 686 (1964).

14. *Curtis Publg. Co. v. Butts*, 388 U.S. 130, 87 S. Ct. 1975, 18 L. Ed. 2d 1094 (1967) (declaring Wally Butts, a well-known football coach, to be a public figure).

15. *Burnett v. National Enquirer, Inc.*, 144 Cal. App. 3d 991 (1983).

16. *Womack v. Eldridge*, 210 S.E.2d 145 (Va. 1974).

17. *Hustler Magazine v. Falwell*, 485 U.S. 46, 108 S. Ct. 876, 99 L. Ed. 2d 41 (1987).

18. 485 U.S. at 55, 108 S. Ct. at 882, 99 L. Ed. 2d at 52.

19. *Phillips v. Smalley Maint. Servs., Inc.*, 435 So.2d 705 (Ala. 1983).

20. 376 U.S. 254, 84 S. Ct. 710, 11 L. Ed. 2d 686 (1964).

21. *McNabb v. Houser*, 156 S.E. 595 (Ga. 1931).

22. *See, e.g., Borland v. Sanders Lead Co.*, 369 So.2d 523 (Ala. 1979).

23. *See First Union Disc. Brokerage Servs., Inc. v. Milos*, 997 F.2d 835 (11th Cir. 1993).

24. *Zobrist v. Coal-X, Inc.*, 708 F.2d 1511 (10th Cir. 1983).

25. 708 F.2d at 1519.

26. *Ellis v. State*, 596 N.E.2d 428 (Ohio 1992).

27. *State v. Carothers*, 594 N.W.2d 897, 900 (Minn. 1999).

28. L.R. B.H.L. 330 (1868).

29. *Cities Serv. Co. v. State*, 312 So.2d 799 (Fla. App. 1975).

30. 111 N.E. 1050 (N.Y. 1916).

31. American Law Institute, St. Paul, Minn. (1998).

32. *Rogers v. Ingersoll-Rand Co.*, 144 F.3d 841 (D.C. Cir. 1998).

33. *Goodyear Dunlop Tires Operations, S.A. v. Brown*, 564 U.S. _____, 131 S. Ct. 2846, 180 L. Ed. 2d. 796 (2011).

34. *J. McIntyre Machinery, Ltd. v. Nicastro*, 564 U.S. _____, 131 S. Ct. 2780, 180 L. Ed. 2d. 765. *See also: Hertz v. Friend*, 559 U.S. 77, 130 S. Ct. 1181, 175 L. Ed. 2d 1029 (2010), which addressed the need to locate a business' "nerve center" when determining jurisdiction for a civil suit.

35. *Coath v. Jones*, 419 A.2d 1249 (Pa. Super. 1980).

36. *Williams v. Feather Sound, Inc.*, 386 So.2d 1238 (Fla. App. 1980).

37. *Southern Cotton Oil Co v. Anderson*, 86 So. 629 (Fla. 1920).

38. *See, e.g., Rowland v. Christian*, 443 P.2d 561 (Cal. 1968).

39. *See, e.g., Banker v. McLaughlin*, 208 S.W.2d 843 (Tex. 1948).

40. *See Lang v. Glusica*, 393 N.W.2d 181 (Minn. 1986).

41. *Lourcey v. Estate of Scarlett*, 146 S.W.3d 48 (Tenn. 2004).

42. *See, e.g., Wright v. Davis*, 53 S.E.2d 335 (W. Va. 1949).

43. 9 & 10 Vict. C. 93 (1846).

44. *See, e.g., Cassano v. Durham*, 436 A.2d 118 (N.J. Super. 1981).

45. *See, e.g., Kush v. Lloyd*, 616 So.2d 415 (Fla. 1992).

46. *See, e.g., Procanik v. Cillo*, 478 A.2d 755 (N.J. 1984).

47. *Walker v. Rinck*, 604 N.E.2d 591 (Ind. 1992).

48. *Schooley v. Pinch's Deli Mkt., Inc.*, 951 P.2d 749 (Wash. 1998).

49. *Kelly v. Gwinnell*, 476 A.2d 1219 (N.J. 1984).

50. *Huston v. Konieczny*, 556 N.E.2d 505 (Ohio 1990).

51. *Borel v. Fibreboard Paper Prods. Corp.*, 493 F.2d 1076 (5th Cir. 1973).

52. *Anderson v. Owens-Corning Fiberglass Corp.*, 810 P.2d 549 (Cal. 1991).

53. *Bivens v. Six Unknown Named Agents*, 403 U.S. 388, 91 S. Ct. 1999, 29 L. Ed. 2d 619 (1971).

54. *Usher v. Los Angeles*, 828 F.2d 556 (9th Cir. 1987).

55. 518 U.S. 668, 116 S. Ct. 2342, 135 L. Ed. 2d 843 (1996).

56. *Umbehr v. McClure*, 840 F. Supp. 837, 839 (D. Kan. 1993).

57. 518 U.S. at 686, 116 S. Ct. at 2352, 135 L. Ed. 2d at 858.

58. 28 U.S.C. §1346 et seq.

59. *Chisholm v. Georgia*, 2 U.S. 419, 1 L. Ed. 440 (1793).

60. *Seminole Tribe v. Florida*, 517 U.S. 44, 116 S. Ct. 1114, 134 L. Ed. 2d 252 (1996).

61. *Broadwell v. Holmes*, 871 S.W.2d 471 (Tenn. 1994).

62. *Verdier v. Verdier*, 219 S.W.3d 143 (Ark. 2005).

63. *President & Dirs. of Georgetown Coll. v. Hughes*, 130 F.2d 810 (D.C. Cir. 1942).

64. 505 U.S. 504, 112 S. Ct. 2509, 120 L. Ed. 2d 407 (1992).

65. In the state of Oregon, a portion of punitive damages in such cases are paid directly to the state, while the rest go to the plaintiff.

66. *Phillip Morris USA v. Williams*, 549 U.S. 346, 127 S. Ct. 1057, 166 L. Ed. 2d. 940 (2007), see also *Phillip Morris USA v. Williams*, 556 U.S. 178, 129 S. Ct. 1436, 173 L. Ed. 2d 346 (2009).

67. Dismissal was by the United States Court of Appeals for the Second Circuit, *New York City v. Beretta U.S.A. Corp.*, 524 F.3d 384 (2008). The Supreme Court's refusal to hear the appeal was issued on April 30, 2009.

68. P. Barnes, *Prescription for Liability*, 40 ABA J., June 1999, at 40.

69. *Lasley v. Shrake's Country Club Pharmacy*, 880 P.2d 1120 (Ariz. App. 1994).

70. *Baker v. Arbor Drugs, Inc.*, 544 N.W.2d 727 (Mich. App. 1996).

71. According to the Insurance Information Institute, twelve states currently invoke no-fault automobile provisions: http://www .iii.org/issue-update/no-fault-auto-insurance.

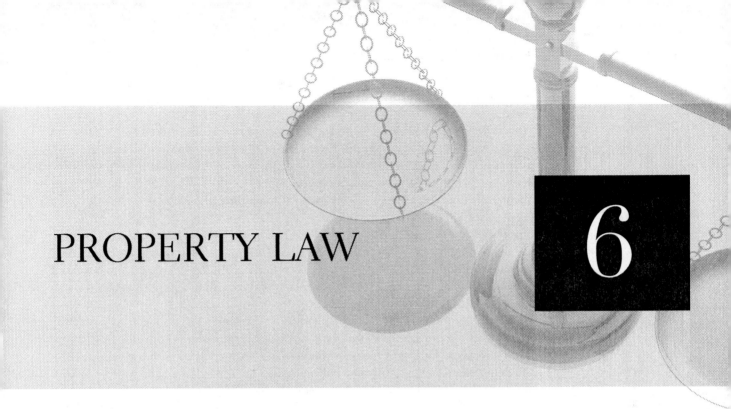

PROPERTY LAW

6

LEARNING OBJECTIVES

This chapter should enable the student to understand:

- the historical background of private property, and the distinctions between personal and real property
- the forms of property ownership; how real estate is acquired, mortgaged, and transferred; and what constitutes nonpossessory interests in land
- the historic and modern-day concepts of the lessor-lessee relationship
- the restriction of land use by deed covenants and zoning regulations
- the government's power of eminent domain and what constitutes a "taking" of property
- the creation and use of living and testamentary trusts in estate planning
- the law of wills and intestate succession
- the means by which trusts allow one party to hold title to property for the benefit of another party
- federal and state estate and inheritance taxes

CHAPTER OUTLINE

Introduction
Personal Property
Real Estate
The Lessor-Lessee Relationship
Regulation of the Use of Real Property
Eminent Domain
Trusts
Wills and Intestate Succession
Estate, Gift, and Inheritance Taxes
Conclusion
Summary of Key Concepts
For Further Reading
Questions for Thought and Discussion
Key Terms

INTRODUCTION

Although property may be classified as either private or public, this chapter focuses on private property, a cornerstone of American political philosophy. The Fifth Amendment to the U.S. Constitution concludes with the proviso: "nor shall private property be taken for public use without just compensation." In 1897, the U.S. Supreme Court incorporated this clause into the Fourteenth Amendment, making it applicable to the states as well as the federal government.[1]

Property concepts and the language of property law are based primarily on the English common law. The somewhat archaic language of property law reflects its feudal origins. Perhaps more than any other area of the law, property law bears out Justice Oliver Wendell Holmes Jr.'s oft-cited observation that "a page of history is worth more than a volume of logic."

Today, property law reflects the changes in the American economy. As protecting our natural resources and environment has become a greater priority, Congress, state legislatures, and local governmental bodies have responded by enacting various regulatory measures that limit private control of property. Indeed, the U.S. Supreme Court has held that laws may be enacted to require property owners to use their property in ways not to injure the property rights of others.[2] In recent decades, laws enacted at the national and state levels and land use zoning ordinances and building codes adopted at the local level have diminished the extent of private control over property.

Real and Personal Property

Property is basically classified as **real property** or **personal property**. Real property consists of land and the structures that are built upon or attached to the land, growing timber and crops, airspace above the land, and the minerals underneath the surface of the land. All other types of property are considered personal property. Questions may arise as to whether some types of property, for example, window blinds installed in a building, are real or personal. The determination is based on the character of the property, how it is affixed to the building, the intent of the parties and their legal relationship, that is, whether the parties are mortagor-mortagee or lessor-lessee, and so forth. Some items of property that are personal, for example, a mobile home, become real property when permanently affixed to the land. On the other hand, growing trees are considered real property, but once severed from the land they become personal property.

"Ownership" in respect to property is a generic rather than a legal term. The law attempts to define property rights with more precision. Because there are often different rights to the same property, law professors suggest students visualize ownership of property as a "bundle of sticks." A person's residence is generally classified as real property, and one who receives a deed to the property is generally regarded as the owner. But if there is a mortgage on the property, the lender (mortgagee) also has a property interest. If the home was recently remodeled and the owner did not pay the contractor or the lumber company in full, the law provides that either or both may have a **lien** against the property. This, too, is a property interest. And if the owner

CASE IN POINT

IS A MODULAR HOME REAL OR PERSONAL PROPERTY?
Far West Modular Home Sales, Inc. v. Proaps
Oregon Court of Appeals
604 P.2d 452 (Or. App. 1979)

As a result of a dispute over the price of a modular home the plaintiff sold to the defendants, the plaintiff filed a suit for replevin (an action to recover personal property) against the defendants, who purchased a modular home from the plaintiff. Upon purchasing the modular home the defendants had it bolted to a concrete foundation and connected to utility lines and it became the family residence. The trial court concluded that the modular home sold to the defendants was personal property, and allowed the plaintiff's action for replevin. The defendants appealed, contending that their home was so annexed to their real property that it lost its character as personal property, and, therefore, was not subject to the replevin action. The appellate court agreed with the defendants and reversed the trial court's judgment.

In ruling for the defendants, the appellate court observed that the paramount factor to be considered is the objective intent of the annexor to make the item a permanent accession of the freehold. The court explained that the annexor's intent can be inferred from "the nature of the article, the relation of the party annexing, the policy of law in relation thereto, the structure and mode of annexation, and the purpose and use for which the item was annexed." The court concluded, "[T]he fact that this chattel is a home, coupled with evidence that it was bolted and nailed to a foundation and connected to all utilities, established that it was annexed to defendants' real property." Thus, the modular home was no longer personal property and not subject to the plaintiff's action for replevin to regain possession of the home.

---

leases the property to others, they, too, have a property interest called a **leasehold**. These are some of the "sticks" in the bundle of property rights.

Personal property may either be tangible, that is, something that is personal and movable, or intangible, that is, something that evidences a property interest. A person's car, furniture, golf clubs, and clothing are classified as **tangible personal property**. Shares of stock in a corporation, a promissory note, and a government or corporate bond are **intangible personal property**. Another species of intangible property is the **chose in action**, which is illustrated by one's having a legal right to enforce a contract or to bring an action for a tort. (We discussed torts in Chapter 5; contracts are discussed in Chapter 7.)

Patents, Copyrights, and Trademarks
Patents, **copyrights**, and **trademarks** are also forms of intangible property rights, and are often discussed under the heading of "intellectual property." The U.S. Constitution authorizes Congress "to promote Progress of Science and useful Arts, by securing for limited times to Authors and Inventors the exclusive Right to their respective Writings and Discovery."[3] Accordingly, federal law defines the scope of patent, trademark, and copyright protections. Additionally, the United States is also a party to a treaty known as the Berne Convention for the Protection of Literary and Artistic Works—an agreement among over 160 countries that respects intellectual property across international

borders. Ultimately patents, trademarks, and copyrights each shield different kinds of items; thus, it is critical to understand the differences among the three.

A **patent** is a government grant for the exclusive right to make and sell an invention. The U.S. Patent and Trademark Office, located in the Department of Commerce, grants patents upon an applicant's proof that the machine or method is original and useful. Currently, patent protection extends for twenty years in most instances.[4] Patent disputes often are settled at the level of federal district courts, with the U.S. District Courts for the Eastern District of Texas and the District of Delaware accounting for approximately 40% of the nationwide caseload in this issue area—perhaps because of a perceived penchant for these courts to rule in favor of plaintiffs that are patent holders.[5]

A major patent case reached the Supreme Court in 2013. In *Association for Molecular Biology v. Myriad Genetics, Inc.*, the Court prohibited a pharmaceutical company from patenting a human DNA sequence for use in a breast cancer detection test; the practical result was that the cost of this test decreased dramatically as more companies were allowed to utilize it. The Supreme Court's decision did permit the possibility of patenting "synthetic DNA"[6] (or DNA that had been altered in some fashion by researchers), essentially maintaining an incentive for businesses to pursue innovation in the pharmaceutical field.

A **copyright** is an exclusive right granted to an author of an original literary, musical, photographic, video, or artistic work. A work created on or after January 1, 1978, is protected by statutory copyright for the life of the author plus fifty years after the author dies.[7] Although registration is not required, it can be accomplished by depositing copies of an original work with the U.S. Copyright Office. It is essential to register a copyright before filing suit for infringement. The Supreme Court has provided guidelines for defining the "originality" that is requisite for acquiring a copyright, noting that it is a low standard requiring only a "minimal degree" of creativity.[8]

Limited utilization of another's copyrighted material might even be allowed via the "fair use doctrine"—particularly in non-profit and educational contexts. A "balancing test" commonly used for evaluating applicability of this doctrine was derived from Judge Joseph Story's opinion in an 1841 Massachusetts case called *Folsom v Marsh*;[9] that test also was codified into American law with the passage of the Copyright Act of 1976.

An evolving modern area of copyright law addresses the proliferation of unauthorized downloads. In the early 2000s, members of the Recording Industry Association of America (RIAA) brought numerous lawsuits accusing individuals of improperly accessing copyrighted music on the Internet. The majority of those lawsuits ended in settlements for $3,500, but a Minnesota woman named Jammie Thomas-Rassett challenged the case against her and ultimately was ordered to pay $220,000 in fines. In 2013, the Supreme Court of the United States refused to hear her appeal, effectively allowing the fine to stand. In a similar ruling in 2012, the Court also refused to hear the appeal of a Boston man named Joel Tenenbaum, leaving intact a $675,000 damage award for illegal acquisition of copyrighted music.

In June 2014, a case concerning copyrighted video material reached the Supreme Court. In this matter, major television networks ABC, NBC, CBS, and FOX successfully brought suit against Aereo, Inc., which streamed broadcast television channels on its website while charging users a viewing fee. Ultimately, the Supreme Court found that Aereo was profiting from material that had been copyrighted by others, and Aereo was ordered to cease this activity.[10]

Additionally, creators of the movie *Dallas Buyers Club* brought multiple lawsuits in 2014 against people whom they accuse of illegally downloading the film, particularly through a file sharing website called "Bit Torrent." Cases such as these often ascribe responsibility for the illegal download to the end-user whose name is attached to an Internet Protocol (IP) address. However, because multiple computers can access a single wireless router, forging such a link may be a tenuous proposition. In fact, early in 2014, a federal judge on the U.S. District Court for the Western District of Washington dismissed an illegal download case brought by the studio that produced the movie *Elf-Man*. The judge declared, "Simply identifying the account holder associated with an IP address tells us very little about who actually downloaded *Elf-Man*."[11] It remains to be seen if this notion will usher in a new trend in copyright law; if it does, it seems logical to infer that lawsuits alleging online copyright infringements will become more difficult to win.

Finally, beyond the acquisition of copyrights or patents, an individual may protect their intellectual creations with a **trademark**. Like a patent, a trademark also may be registered with the U.S. Patent and Trademark Office. A trademark is a distinctive word, symbol, or emblem used to identify a particular product in the marketplace. Trademarks are valid for 10-year intervals, but indefinite renewals are possible. There is no trademark protection for the use of everyday common names or phrases. Although federal and state laws allow registration of trademarks, it is the use of the trademark that is important. Registration, however, establishes a presumption of the user's priority.

Nevertheless, simply being the first to register a trademark does not preclude the possibility of a legal challenge. Professional football quarterback Johnny Manziel, for example, became embroiled in a dispute with long-time friend Nate Fitch over who holds the stronger claim to trademarking the phrase "The House That Johnny Built." Both have filed paperwork to register it. Fitch actually was the first to register the trademark, but Manziel may have the stronger claim in court, as the phrase speaks directly to his accomplishments.

Although trademark cases seldom reach the Supreme Court, litigation over perceived trademark violations is fairly common in lower courts. For example, in 2014 a U.S. District Court in California weighed a dispute between Duke University and the family of John Wayne. Members of Wayne's family produced a whiskey called "Duke" in honor of the late movie star's nickname, but Duke University officials objected to this utilization of their trademarked name.

Elsewhere, officials in the town of Lake City, Tennessee faced a legal challenge after changing the town's name to Rocky Top. A company called House of Bryant, which had trademarked a popular song called "Rocky Top," brought a lawsuit seeking an injunction to bar the name change. However, Judge Thomas Varlan of the U.S. District Court for the District of Eastern Tennessee ruled in favor of Lake City, permitting the name change. House of Bryant then filed an appeal with the U.S. Court of Appeals for the Sixth Circuit, but the name change has been enacted—pending future litigation. In theory, the Supreme Court would have jurisdiction to hear a subsequent appeal on this matter.

PERSONAL PROPERTY

To "own" personal property one must have **dominion and control** over it. Usually, this is accomplished by possession of the tangible item that a person has either created or produced or acquired by purchase or gift. One who paints a picture or who grows crops has created or produced property. Acquisition by purchase is a simple concept, but sometimes controversies arise as to whether a **donor** has made a legal gift to a **donee**. To determine if a gift has been made, courts examine evidence of the donor's intent and whether a delivery of the gift has been made by the donor and accepted by the donee. If the size of the item permits, a gift should ordinarily be delivered manually; if too large to be manually delivered, something symbolic of the gift, for example, the keys to an automobile, should be given to the donee.

In addition to dominion and control, some items of personal property, for example, motor vehicles, airplanes, and boats, require a certificate of title in order for a person to have an ownership interest that can be transferred. Items of intangible property such as cash in a checking account, a promissory note, or shares of stock in a corporation are usually transferred by check, endorsement, or a written assignment, respectively.

Possession and Ownership of Personal Property

Personal property may be in someone's **actual possession** or **constructive possession**. A person is in actual possession of a finger ring or the clothes being worn. But a person may also "own" items not in actual possession. For example, a person who has the only key to a safe deposit box containing a gold watch or diamond ring is said to be in constructive possession of those items and thus may own those items in the box.

In addition to individual ownership, personal property may be owned as **tenants in common** by two or more persons, each owning an undivided interest. Or, individuals may own such property as **joint tenants with right of survivorship.** In this way, upon the death of one party, the surviving party or parties become the sole owner(s). A bank or securities customer may see this designated as "JTROS" on bank signature cards and stock certificates. In some states, the fact that a husband and wife own property jointly determines, as a matter of law, that upon death of one spouse the surviving spouse becomes the sole owner of the property.

Personal property may be pledged as **collateral** to secure repayment of a loan. The debtor signs a **security agreement**, and the secured party (creditor) acquires a **security interest** in the personal property. Upon default by the debtor, the secured creditor has the right to the collateral, and the debtor has the right to any surplus proceeds realized upon disposition of the collateral. The debtor may be liable for any deficiency remaining after the collateral is sold. These matters are generally governed by the Uniform Commercial Code and are discussed in more detail in Chapter 7.

Lost and Abandoned Property

Personal property is sometimes either lost or abandoned. If property is lost, the true owner continues to be the owner, but a finder of **lost property** has a right to it against everyone but the true owner. Lost property is property lost through inadvertence or neglect. **Abandoned property** is property that an owner voluntarily parts with, with no intention to reclaim it. If a person finds lost or abandoned property, the finder who first exercises control over the property with intent to claim it usually becomes the owner. We say "usually" because in certain instances someone else may have an entitlement. For example, an employer may be entitled to lost or abandoned property found by an employee within the scope of employment. An Ohio appellate court required a hospital receptionist to return to the hospital jewelry found in an eyeglass case on top of the information desk. The hospital was directed to hold the jewelry as a gratuitous bailee for the rightful owner.[12]

Bailments

Another instance where a party receives possession or custody of personal property without acquiring an ownership interest is called a **bailment.** A bailment is created where one party, the **bailor** (usually but not necessarily the owner), delivers temporary possession of personal property to another party, the **bailee**, who accepts the property. Any type of personal property may be the subject of a bailment. There are two basic types of bailments: **gratuitous bailments** and **mutual benefit bailments**. The rights and duties of parties to a bailment are often defined by contract, but in the absence of such an agreement the law provides for the rights and duties depending on the type of bailment and the relationship of the parties.

A gratuitous bailment is usually an informal arrangement whereby the transfer of possession of property is without any compensation. It can refer to a bailment that benefits only the bailor, for example, where a bailee agrees to store property for the bailor. Or it can refer to a bailment that benefits only the bailee, for example, a home-owner who lends a lawn mower to a neighbor is a bailor and the neighbor who borrows it is a bailee. If a gratuitous bailment is solely for the benefit of the bailor, the bailee's standard of care is minimal. But if a gratuitous bailment is for benefit of the bailee, the bailee must exercise reasonable care and return the property to the bailor in good condition.

A more formal example is the mutual benefit bailment that is common in commercial relationships. There, one party receives a benefit and another party receives compensation. Examples include a bailor who delivers an automobile to a mechanic for repairs or who stores goods in a commercial warehouse. In each instance, the bailor pays a fee for services. If hidden dangers exist in the bailed property, the bailor must inform the bailee. The bailee must handle the property according to the bailor's instructions and owes the bailor the duty of exercising ordinary care. Upon payment for services, the bailee must return the bailed items to the bailor. Although the bailee is not an insurer of the property bailed, if the bailee is negligent and such negligence is the proximate cause of damage to the bailor's goods, courts hold the bailee liable.

A lease of personal property that expressly or impliedly requires the lessee to return the property to the lessor at the termination of the lease is, in effect, a bailment.[13] Likewise, the usual commercial lease of an automobile is generally considered a bailment for mutual benefit.

Parking an automobile in a commercial parking facility is a common experience. If the car is delivered to the parking attendant, who retains the owner's keys and who has authority to move the owner's car, a bailment is often created. In contrast, a Missouri appellate court found that no bailment was created between the owner of a self-service parking lot and the automobile owner. The owner parked an automobile, locked it, and retained control of the ignition keys. The access card to the parking lot stated that the owner of the parking lot was not liable for personal property stolen from the automobile. The court held the automobile owner merely had a license to park.[14]

Confusion and Accession

Where personal property of different owners is commingled and cannot be separated, laws relating to **confusion** apply and courts attempt to determine the proportionate interest of those who contributed to the confusion of the property. For example, where farmers combine their grain, the product owned by each loses its identity and each then has a proportionate interest in the confused product. **Accession** occurs where an owner's personal property enjoys a natural increase. Thus, one who owns a cow becomes owner of the calf born to the cow.

Can a Thief Transfer Title?

Despite acquiring possession, a thief does not acquire title to property. In the area of property law, the general rule is that a person can transfer no better title to personal property than the transferor has. Thus, one who has acquired possession of property by theft cannot confer title by a sale, even to a **bona fide purchaser**.

REAL ESTATE

Under early English law, the King was considered as the dominant owner of the lands of the country. The King made certain grants to feudal lords who possessed various tracts of land referred to as manors. In the manorial system of land holding, the lord of the manor, in turn, would grant his tenants certain rights in the land accompanied by certain obligations of the tenant to the lord. This system was known as **land tenure**. There existed several types of tenure, but primarily there were three. One who had a **fee simple estate** could dispose of it at will. Those who had **fee tail estates** could only dispose of their estates within their family, while those who had simply **life estates** or **estates during the life of another** were further restricted in transfer of their interests. A significant development occurred in 1290 by enactment of the Statute of Quai Emptores. This English statute allowed freemen to transfer their estates in real property to another, with the new possessor to have the same obligations to the lord of the manor.

The early English system of land conveyancing became part of the common law and was adopted by the new American states. Even today, we speak of fee simple ownership to indicate the highest estate in land. Today, sales of real estate are completed by a deed, a written document by which an owner transfers title. Gifts of real estate occur by a deed, by a **will** upon an owner's demise, or by the laws of inheritance. Indeed, while most deeds or devises under a decedent's will transfer fee simple title, a deed or will may transfer a life estate, that is, ownership rights to the property during the owner's lifetime. A **life tenant** must maintain the improvements on the property and ordinarily must pay the real estate taxes assessed against the property. The life tenant of the property must protect the value of the property for benefit of the person who becomes the owner upon decease of the life tenant. At that time, another party (called a **remainderman**) designated in the deed or will, usually becomes the owner.

Acquiring and Transferring Title to Real Property

When real estate is sold, the buyer generally requires the seller, often referred to as the **grantor**, to transfer the title to the property by a **warranty deed**. A warranty deed is a document that contains certain promises called **covenants** to protect the buyer, often referred to as the **grantee**, and to require the seller, if necessary, to defend the validity of the buyer's new title. In most states, there is a form of warranty deed that by reference to the state law includes various common law covenants, including the covenant of warranty. To be effective, a deed must not only be executed but also be delivered to the grantee by or with the grantor's permission. A deed recorded in the public records is presumed to have been delivered and accepted.

Early English common law regarded the title to land as extending "from the heavens to the center of the earth." In modern times, of course, the title to land must be balanced against the rights of the population. Hence, American courts have long recognized the right of aircraft to fly over lands to the extent permitted by federal regulations of aircraft.[15] Moreover, in some areas of the United States it is not uncommon for the seller of real estate to reserve certain interests, for example, the right to gas, oil, and other minerals.

When real estate is transferred to a buyer, it is generally described in the deed of conveyance by its boundaries or by lot and block numbers with reference to a map or subdivision plat recorded in the county land records. For the protection of the new owner, a deed transferring real estate is recorded in the public records of the city or county where the property lies.

Another common form of deed is known as a **quitclaim deed**. This form of deed is used to clear the title to real estate of some possible adverse claim. In a quitclaim deed, the grantor makes no representation as to having an interest in the property but simply releases any such possible interest. Therefore, if the grantee does not acquire any interest in property as a result of the quitclaim deed, the grantor has no liability.

Mortgages

One who borrows money using real property as collateral signs a promissory note payable to the lender providing for repayment of the loan and interest according to the terms of the note. The borrower secures payment of the note by executing a contractual document known as a **mortgage** creating a lien against the borrower's

SIDEBAR

Warranty Deeds

Under the common law, a warranty deed would set out a number of covenants by the grantor. State statutes often prescribe a form of warranty deed that is deemed to include such covenants if drafted substantially as provided by the statute. For example, Section 689.02, Florida Statutes prescribes the following form:

* * * * *

This indenture, made this day of _____ A.D. _____ between _____ of the County of _____ in the State of _____, party of the first part, and _____ of the County of _____ in the State of _____, party of the second part,
   Witnesseth:
   That the said party of the first part, for and in consideration of the sum of _____ dollars, to her or him in hand paid by said party of the second part, the receipt whereof is hereby acknowledged, has granted, bargained and sold to the said party of the second part, her or his heirs and assigns forever, the following described land, to wit: _____.
   And the said party of the first part does hereby fully warrant the title to said land, and will defend the same against the lawful claims of all persons whomsoever.

* * * * *

Section 689.02, Florida Statutes provides that "[a] conveyance executed substantially in the foregoing form shall be held to be a warranty deed with full common-law covenants, and shall just as effectually bind the grantor, and the grantor's heir, as if said covenants were specifically set out therein."
   Other statutes provide for the proper signing of the deed and the requirements for witnesses to the signers' signatures and for acknowledgment of the signers before a notary public or other officer before the deed can be recorded in the public records.

real property. Some loans carry a fixed rate of interest; others provide for an adjustable rate of interest based on fluctuations in the interest rate in the credit markets. In most states, a mortgage must be executed in a manner similar to execution of a deed. In fact, the typical mortgage appears much like a conveyance of property but includes a number of stipulations designed to protect the lender. The party mortgaging property is known as the **mortgagor**, and the lender is known as the **mortgagee**. In some instances, particularly in the sale of a residence, a seller often agrees to "take back a mortgage" as part of the purchase price. This type of legal instrument is known as a **purchase money mortgage**. To prevent subsequent purchasers of the property or a later mortgagee from gaining priority, it is essential for the mortgagee to record a mortgage in the office where deeds are recorded.

Many institutional lenders require a mortgagor to purchase private mortgage insurance (PMI) to guarantee the mortgagee against loss in the event of a foreclosure of the mortgage. In home financing, often the homeowner (mortgagor) makes monthly payments of principal and interest on the mortgage loan and deposits an additional sum to pay real estate taxes, insurance, and PMI. Banks and other commercial lenders frequently sell mortgages to institutions that invest in mortgages.

A mortgage document contains a number of covenants that bind the mortgagor. Among these are covenants to promptly make all payments required by the note secured by the mortgage, pay real estate taxes and assessments against the property, and keep any improvements on the property insured against casualty losses such as fire and windstorm. If the mortgagor transfers title to the real estate, the mortgagee's interest remains intact and the new owner of the real estate takes title subject to the lien of any recorded mortgage. In some instances, a mortgage includes a **due-on-sale clause** and the mortgagor must secure approval of the new buyer by the mortgagee in order to allow the new buyer to **assume the mortgage**, otherwise the mortgagee can declare the entire loan due upon the sale.

The common law treated a mortgage much as it did a deed and provided the mortgagee had title even though the mortgage loan was not in default. Most states today treat a mortgage as a lien that does not ripen into a title until the necessary steps to foreclose the property are completed. The mortgagee can foreclose a mortgage if the mortgagor fails to make required payments under the note secured by the mortgage or fails to comply with the other covenants contained in the mortgage. If a court enters a judgment of foreclosure, the owner of the property is generally afforded the **right of redemption.** This means that the mortgagor can pay off all sums due the mortgagee and continue to own the property. One problem with exercising this right is the cost, including court costs, attorney's fees, and other expenses associated with the foreclosure. If the mortgagor does not exercise this right, the property is sold at a public sale and the proceeds of the sale are applied as determined by the court, usually giving a first mortgagee priority after payment of costs associated with the foreclosure. In some instances, where sale of the property does not provide sufficient funds to pay the costs of foreclosure and repay the mortgagee, the court will enter a **deficiency judgment** against the mortgagor for the balance due the mortgagee.

Some states follow a different procedure. They use a **deed of trust** instead of a mortgage. The borrower deeds the property that secures the loan to a trustee. The trustee, in turn, holds title to the property. If the borrower defaults, the trustee notifies all interested parties and conducts a public sale of the property in order to pay the sums due the mortgagee. Lenders consider this arrangement preferable because it allows the lender to recover the money loaned without the formalities and delays attendant with a court proceeding.

The Mortgage Meltdown of 2008

Throughout the 1990s and into the 2000s, housing prices in the United States rose dramatically—in some areas as much as 100 percent. During that time, lending standards of many financial institutions declined greatly, with lenders often requiring only minimal down payments from borrowers seeking to finance the purchase of houses. In fact, many lenders offered "no doc mortgage loans," that is, a loan supported simply by an appraisal of the property offered to secure the loan with no documentary evidence of the borrower's financial standing or ability to repay. Mortgages were approved for subprime borrowers (borrowers with a less than stellar credit rating) who had a limited ability to repay their loans. The situation was exacerbated by lenders offering borrowers adjustable rate mortgages (ARMs), with the expectation that housing prices and wages would continue to rise and enable the borrowers to make increased payments after a few years. In 2006, the "housing bubble" burst as housing prices went into steep decline and many homeowners found it impossible to meet the increased payments. As housing prices continued to drop, many homeowners found their homes worth less than the balance due on their mortgages. This resulted in a high rate of default, especially on subprime mortgages and ARMs.

This high-risk lending led to a "mortgage meltdown" in 2007 and 2008. And by 2008, unemployment was rising and defaults and foreclosures increased dramatically. For several years prior to this time, it had become common for banks and insurance companies to exchange their mortgage portfolios for "collateralized debt obligations" (CDOs), a bundle of mortgages often including subprime mortgages. When lenders sought to foreclose, borrowers began to raise issues of fraud and misrepresentations by mortgage brokers and financial institutions in the origination of the mortgages. Financial institutions experienced heavy losses, and stockholders saw their investments in these institutions dwindle. By the latter part of 2008, the U.S. government took over two giant lending institutions and attempted to provide government backing of some home mortgages. Congress appropriated billions of dollars to bail out major financial institutions in order to make credit available to creditworthy borrowers seeking to acquire homes and automobiles and to obtain credit cards. But by the end of 2008, the mortgage market in the United States was still in crisis mode. Even four years later, in February 2012, Ben Bernanke, Chairman of the Federal Reserve, referred to the housing market as a "key impediment" to the nation's economic recovery. In 2013 and 2014, positive signs came in the form of decreased foreclosures and increased home sales, but the recovery in the housing market was uneven and erratic.[16]

Adverse Possession

In what today has become rare, title to land may, in some instances, be acquired by **adverse possession**. To acquire land by adverse possession, a person must comply strictly with the statutory requirements of state law. These laws vary but usually require that the adverse possessor hold the property "openly and notoriously" and continuously for a period of time usually varying from seven to twenty years. The adverse possessor may also be required to fence, cultivate, or otherwise use the land consistent with local land use practices for the type of property involved. Many laws require the adverse possessor to file a property tax return with local taxing authorities describing the land and pay real estate taxes on the property.

Estates in Real Property

Estates in real property refer to how title to real estate is held and are derived from the English common law. In addition to individual title, these estates commonly exist in the following forms: join tenancy, tenancy in common, and tenancy by the entirety.

Joint Tenancy
In a **joint tenancy**, the owners each own an undivided (usually equal) portion of the real estate. The legal instrument (deed or will) creating the joint tenancy usually

provides that upon the death of one joint tenant the remaining joint tenant or tenants become(s) the owner or owners of the decedent's share. Sometimes joint tenants cannot agree on how to manage their property and they may choose to divide the property. If they cannot agree on how to divide the property, one party might institute a court action known as a **partition suit**. In a partition suit, the court divides the property, if feasible, and if not, it orders the property sold and the net proceeds divided according to the interests of the joint tenants.

Tenancy in Common

A **tenancy in common** is similar to a joint tenancy but does not provide for survivorship rights. A tenant in common owns an undivided interest in the real estate. Upon death of a tenant in common, who held his or her interest in his or her individual name, the decedent's heirs at law would inherit the deceased tenant's share of the property. If the decedent died with a valid will, the deceased tenant's share would be distributed according to the terms of the will. As in the case of joint tenants with right of survivorship, tenants in common can alter their interests by executing the necessary deeds or resorting to a partition suit.

Tenancy by the Entirety

A **tenancy by the entirety** is very similar to a joint tenancy, but it can only exist between a husband and wife. Upon the death of one spouse, the other spouse becomes the sole owner of the property. Married couples frequently own their home place as tenants by the entirety. Unlike a joint tenancy, neither spouse can transfer his or her interest to anyone except the other spouse. Upon dissolution of marriage, a tenancy by the entirety usually becomes a tenancy in common unless the court awards one spouse's share to the other spouse in settlement of marital assets.

Community Property

Several states, largely in the western United States, have **community property** laws. Community property laws were unknown to the English common law. They originated from the Spanish and French laws during colonization in the western United States. Community property states have statutes defining community property rights, and while they vary somewhat, they generally provide that each spouse is deemed to own one-half of property acquired during the marriage. The community property concept does not affect ownership of property acquired by either spouse prior to their marriage or to property acquired by gift or inheritance. The concept of community property is discussed more extensively in Chapter 8.

Condominium and Cooperative Ownership

Condominium ownership is an increasingly popular form of ownership. Title may be acquired in any of the forms discussed above. Condominium ownership may exist in business as well as residential properties. But the most common condominium ownership is the residential unit where amenities vary from simple walkways and parking spaces to luxurious recreational facilities and services. Unlike the usual freestanding residence, residential condominium properties are divided into units much like apartments, either freestanding or in one or several buildings. A person who acquires a condominium in a building receives a deed vesting the owner with title to a certain space in the building that includes the interior walls and space of the unit. The unit owner also acquires an interest in common with the other condominium owners in the roof and exterior walls, the common walkways, stairways, driveways, and amenities provided in the condominium complex. The condominium owner's rights and obligations are set out in a declaration of condominium (usually recorded in the office where property deeds are recorded) and in the bylaws adopted by the condominium association.

Unit owners become members of a **condominium association** whose officers and directors usually hire professional management to ensure proper exterior maintenance of the units and common facilities. In addition to real estate taxes, unit owners are required to pay fees to the condominium association to cover routine maintenance. Moreover, unit owners are subject to assessments to cover major expenses, such as re-roofing and exterior painting. Often, condominium associations impose regulations that may restrict unit owners as to whether pets or young children are permitted to occupy their units. Before purchasing a condominium unit, one is well advised to carefully examine all the various legal documents affecting the interest being acquired. It is wise for a purchaser of a condominium to have an attorney examine all relevant legal documents and explain the various obligations incident to condominium ownership.

In a **cooperative form of ownership** in real estate, the owner acquires shares of stock in a corporation that owns a building or complex of units. Thus, unlike the ownership of a condominium unit, the shareholder has an interest in the entire complex. The corporation leases the right to occupy a unit to a shareholder who usually makes stipulated payments to the corporation to cover mortgage payments and maintenance.

Real Estate Taxes

Real estate is subject to state and local taxes assessed by a local official who is usually called a tax assessor. The assessor appraises each parcel of real estate and generally declares that appraised value (or a fraction thereof) to be the taxable value of the property. Thus, real estate taxes are called *ad valorem* (at value) **taxes**, and the property owner is generally billed once a year. Some states grant certain exemptions to home-owners to allow a portion of the assessed value of the home to be exempt from real estate taxes. In most states, a property owner may challenge the assessor's determination of value by appealing to a board of review usually called a **board of equalization**. Failure to pay taxes when due can result in a requirement to pay interest and penalties. Eventually, if taxes are not paid, an owner's property can be sold to allow the taxing authorities to recoup the unpaid taxes.

The transfer of real estate may require payment of certain fees and taxes, including a fee for recording necessary legal documents. Of course, the sale of real estate may

PURCHASING A HOUSE

The purchase of a residence illustrates an everyday application of the law of property. Sales of homes (and other real properties such as farms and buildings) are common transactions in today's mobile society. To illustrate the process, we consider a young couple looking to purchase a home. After selecting the area where they intend to reside, often the next step is to scan the advertisements of homes for sale, look for signs offering a home for sale by an owner, or engage the services of a real estate broker. Real estate brokers usually (but not always) receive their compensation in the form of a sales commission paid by the seller.

THE LAW IN ACTION

Once the couple finds a house within their price range that meets their requirements, the next step is to sign a written offer to purchase that includes the offering price, legal description of the property, terms, and conditions of purchase. Often, the offer to purchase will be conditioned on the buyers' being approved to assume an existing mortgage or to obtain a mortgage loan for a certain amount. The offer to purchase normally is accompanied by a good-faith cash deposit, and the seller is then allowed a short period of time to accept or reject the offer. Where a broker is involved, it is the broker who retains the deposit in an escrow account. A standard form of offer to purchase and deposit receipt becomes a binding contract once accepted by the seller. This contract usually provides that if the buyers do not perform their part of the contract, the seller may retain the good-faith deposit as liquidated damages. Where a real estate broker is involved, the deposit money that is forfeited is generally divided between the seller and the broker.

An offer to purchase usually contains a number of other provisions. These include whether the purchase price is to be paid in cash or through financing, who is to furnish an abstract of title or title insurance policy, how real estate taxes and assessments are to be handled, an inventory of personal property, if any, to be included,

and the closing date and place. In recent years, standard contracts for purchase of homes have included provisions to assure the buyers that there are no structural defects in the house and that electrical, plumbing, air conditioning, heating, and other systems and all appliances will be in good working order at time of closing. Depending on local customs, other provisions may be included. Many of the items in offers to purchase are subject to negotiation. Real estate agents typically perform this function on behalf of the seller and buyers, but a couple buying a home may be well advised to secure advice from a real estate attorney before signing a document that commits them to purchase. The attorney will advise as to the form of the contract and concerning zoning, deed restrictions (including dues to and assessments by homeowners' associations), easements, and other factors that may be important to the buyers.

In most instances, the buyers will obtain a mortgage loan from a bank or other institutional lender. The buyers will complete an application for the loan. Before approving a loan, the lender will impose certain requirements. Initially, the lender obtains a credit report to find out if the purchasers are creditworthy. If so, the lender will usually have a qualified appraiser determine the market value of the house and hire a land surveyor to prepare a survey of the property and depict the location of the house on the land and show that there are no encroachments on the property being purchased. A real estate broker will assist the purchasers in handling many of the details of financing. The buyers' attorney will examine the title to the property or secure a commitment from a title insurance company to issue the new owners a title insurance policy upon their acquiring title to the property.

At the time of closing, the buyers (and their lender, if financing has been secured) will pay the balance of the contract price to the seller. The seller will execute a deed (usually a warranty deed) conveying the title to the purchasers, usually as husband and wife, and will deliver the deed to the buyers. The lender will examine the deed and submit the buyers a note and mortgage and certain disclosure statements concerning the financing of the property. The buyers then execute the note and mortgage. If the buyers are assuming an existing mortgage, approval of the present mortgage holder should be obtained along with evidence of the balance of the mortgage loan being assumed. The lender will see that the necessary documents are recorded in the land records of the city or county. An attorney who represents the buyers will examine all the relevant documents to ensure everything is properly completed.

have income tax consequences under the Internal Revenue Code and any applicable state tax laws and regulations.

Nonpossessory Interests in Land

Besides the estates discussed above, a person may have an interest in land or a right to use land without having a right of possession. Two such interests are known as **easements** and **licenses.** An easement is a right of use over the property of another. This term frequently refers to a right-of-way across privately owned land. A license is merely a permit that allows someone to exercise a privilege in respect to land.

An owner of land can create an easement by executing a deed or by reserving an easement when transferring property. An easement is an interest in land but not an estate in land because the holder of the easement gains only the right to use a part of the land for a specified purpose, but not the right to possess the land. For example, an owner might grant a utility easement to allow a power company to install power lines and poles on his or her property. The easement may be permanent or for a specified period. When given to a utility company, it is usually a permanent easement. If the owner who granted the easement transfers the title to the land, the easement probably would remain viable or as lawyers would say, "it runs with the land." Of course, the interested parties may agree in writing to terminate an easement.

There are some instances when a landowner acquires an **easement of necessity**. This arises where a landowner transfers title to a purchaser of a part of the owner's land without providing access to the land being transferred. To obtain an easement of necessity, the new owner must require an easement for necessary ingress and egress and not simply desire one for convenient access.

An easement also may be acquired by **prescription**, that is, where a person makes a continuous and uninterrupted use of property, for example, if a person has used a road right-of-way for an extended period of time. Generally, to acquire an easement by prescription the user must comply with statutory laws similar to those we previously discussed concerning adverse possession of real property.

A license in real property is a right permitting someone to do some specified thing on another person's land.[17] For example, one whose land has a pond may permit a friend or neighbor to fish there. Unlike an easement, a license is not an interest in land. A license may be granted orally, and in most instances it is revocable by the landowner.[18]

CASE IN POINT

DOES AN EASEMENT OF NECESSITY "RUN WITH THE LAND"?
Broadhead v. Terpening
Mississippi Supreme Court
611 So. 2d 949 (Miss. 1992)

The Ratcliffs divided a tract of land and sold parcels to the defendants Broadhead and others. The Terpenings, plaintiffs, acquired a parcel of the former Ratcliff tract from someone who had purchased it from the Ratcliffs. The only established way of ingress and egress to the Terpenings' property required traversing the property now owned by Broadhead and the other defendants. The plaintiffs claimed that an easement of necessity was created in favor of those who purchased the landlocked property now owned by the Terpenings. The Mississippi Supreme Court observed that "...the Broadheads were not the parties responsible for dividing up the Ratcliff estate in such a way that the portion now owned by the Terpenings was rendered inaccessible except by passing over other portions of the formerly unified lands." Nevertheless, the court reasoned that when the Ratcliffs parceled up their property and sold it to others, an easement of necessity was created for the person who purchased the landlocked portion of the estate now owned by the Terpenings. Such an easement of necessity, the court declared, runs with the land and passes with each conveyance to subsequent owners.

THE LESSOR-LESSEE RELATIONSHIP

Historically, the relationship between an owner of property and the owner's tenant was referred to as **landlord-tenant law**. The term "landlord" was derived from the relationship between the lord of the English manor to whom certain obligations were due and the tenant of the land who was responsible to fulfill those obligations. As previously explained, the laws concerning real property are deeply rooted in history. Even though it is not uncommon to hear the terms "landlord" and "tenant" used today, we prefer to discuss the relationship in the modern context as between a **lessor** and a **lessee**. Lessor-lessee relationships commonly occur in either residential or commercial leasing.

Historically, a lessee was required to pay rent and abide by various lease provisions but was granted only limited rights against the lessor. A lessee is often in a disadvantageous bargaining position in respect to the lessor. During the latter half of the twentieth century, courts began to look more favorably on the rights of a lessee of residential property. Legislative bodies enacted laws and ordinances to require that lessors of rental properties meet certain standards in respect to habitability, convenience, safety, and sanitation. Some laws even prescribe certain mandatory provisions that must be included in residential leases and permit a lessee to withhold rental payments when the lessor fails to comply with the requirements of the law. In some instances, where a lessee would report a lessor to local authorities as not complying with the requirements to maintain safe and sanitary premises, a lessor would resort to evicting the lessee. The common law imposed no restriction on a lessor's motives in evicting a tenant if the action had a legal basis. But since the 1970s, statutes have been enacted that restrict a lessor from evicting a lessee in retaliation for reporting violations of law concerning habitability of the leased premises. Some states have enacted statutes to enable a tenant to recover damages from a lessor if the tenant suffers a **retaliatory eviction**.[19]

Residential leases, especially where the premises are furnished, often require the lessee to make a prepayment of rent and post a security deposit. Prepayment of rent affords the lessor compensation should the lessee breach the lease, and the security deposit guarantees payment to the lessor for any damages to the leased premises beyond ordinary wear and tear. A federal appeals court has described a **security deposit** as being in the nature of a trust fund.[20] Upon termination of the lease, the security deposit (less any sums retained by the lessor for damages to the leased premises) must be refunded to the lessee at the end of the lease term. Courts have issued conflicting opinions as to whether the lessor is required to pay interest on the security deposit. Often, this depends on statutory law.

The common law did not restrict the right of a lessee to sublet the leased premises; however, written leases commonly restrict the lessee's right to assign the lease or sublet the premises without consent of the lessor. Many written leases add that the lessor will not unreasonably withhold consent for the lessee to assign the leasehold interest. Even if the lessee is permitted to assign rights, the lessee cannot assign duties. Therefore, the lessee remains liable to the lessor for performance of the lease covenants.

Today, short-term rental arrangements may be handled on an oral basis and can be terminated by either party on short notice. Many of these oral rental arrangements are on a weekly or monthly basis, and generally the parties are required to furnish a reasonable notice of termination. In many states, though, the Statute of Frauds (see Chapter 7) requires that a lease for more than a year be in writing.

The Fair Housing Act of 1968 prohibits a lessor from refusing to sell or rent a dwelling on the basis of race, color, religion, sex, national origin, familial status, or disability.[21] Some lessors have contended they have a First Amendment right based on the free exercise of religion to decline to rent to those persons whose living arrangements violate the lessor's religious convictions. In recent years, trial courts have been called upon to determine whether a lessor's refusal to rent a dwelling to unmarried cohabitants violates the federal Act or similar state statutes.

In contrast to residential leases, commercial leases are usually negotiated between more sophisticated parties and bargaining is generally on a more even basis. Professionals usually handle the negotiation and drafting of a major commercial lease, and attorneys often represent the parties. Commercial leases are frequently entered into on a long-term basis and stipulate the uses of the property and include provisions for remodeling and an option for renewal. A commercial lease may include a number of other provisions, including easements for vehicular parking, sometimes in common with other lessees. The forms of commercial leases are less standard than the terms of a residential lease. In a commercial lease, the rent is sometimes based on a percentage of the lessee's sales and may include an "inflation index" requiring the lessee to pay additional rent to cover annual increases in real estate taxes and property insurance. Shopping center leases and leases in mall complexes often mandate conformity with uniform business hours and include restrictions on the types of goods and services offered for sale in order to protect lessees from excessive competition.

REGULATION OF THE USE OF REAL PROPERTY

Some restrictions on use of real property are privately agreed upon by contract. Others are imposed by legislation or regulation. All levels of government impose restrictions on the use of real property. The federal government imposes certain **environmental regulations** to preserve endangered species of birds and animals, control the discharge of industrial wastes and sewage pollutants, and reduce air pollution. State and local governmental agencies impose most regulations on the development and uses of land. Because private control of private property is a fundamental value in American culture, such restrictions are often controversial. Sometimes compliance with these regulations imposes significant economic costs on property owners. The thrust of modern American law, however, is to allow reasonable restrictions on private property that furthers societal interests in public health, safety, welfare, and environmental integrity.

Planning and Zoning Activities

Land use planning is a modern method of achieving a balance of land uses within a state and a community. To ensure orderly land development, many states have initiated a comprehensive plan that requires local governmental agencies to adhere to certain standards in their planning and zoning activities. Two primary tools that local governmental agencies use to regulate the use of privately owned lands are **zoning** and **building codes**.

Land Use Zoning

Land use zoning is a facet of the police power, and state legislatures can grant authority to counties and municipalities to adopt comprehensive land use plans and enact zoning regulations for lands within their jurisdiction. When a county or city initially undertakes to enact zoning ordinances and regulations, it divides the community into zones and classifies those zones as permitting residential, office, business, recreational, and industrial uses. When zoning is originally imposed and thereafter when rezoning occurs, existing uses that are incompatible with the zoning are generally "**grandfathered in**" for a period of time to allow the owner of the property to recover the economic value of nonconforming improvements.

Zoning is a product of the twentieth century. It originally was undertaken on the legal premise that the police power of government is sufficient to allow it to abate nuisances and that zoning, in effect, was simply "keeping the pig out of the parlor." Disparate court decisions by state courts created considerable doubt as to the validity of zoning enactments until 1926 when the U.S. Supreme Court sustained the constitutionality of a comprehensive zoning ordinance in its seminal decision in *Village of Euclid v. Ambler Realty Co.*[22] In upholding Euclid's right to enact a comprehensive zoning ordinance, the Court rejected Ambler Realty's arguments concerning due process of law, equal protection of the laws, and contentions that the zoning resulted in unauthorized taking of property. The *Euclid* decision firmly established the right of legislatures to grant local communities the power to enact zoning controls over private lands. Courts continue to entertain constitutional challenges to zoning ordinances as they affect particular parcels of land. However, these disputes are primarily handled in state courts.

The latter half of the twentieth century witnessed considerable sophistication in the zoning process. In addition to its traditional function of establishing residential, business, and industrial districts, zoning is now used as a tool to create historical and architectural districts. It also provides for conditional uses, and to enforce certain aesthetic values such as specifying off-street parking requirements for business and apartment complexes and regulating the size of on-premises and off-premises signs.

Local governments provide for applications for rezoning of property and for **special exceptions** based on specified criteria that must be observed in certain uses of property in a given neighborhood or area. A comprehensive zoning ordinance must provide for a **board of adjustment** authorized to grant **variances** where because of the character or size of a parcel of land, enforcement of a zoning regulation would impose an undue hardship on the property owner. If zoning goes beyond its permitted scope, it may bring into question whether a landowner's property has effectively been taken by government and require the local government to pay the landowner just compensation.

Restrictive Covenants

A land developer who subdivides land often files a written declaration of **restrictive covenants** to bind those who purchase vacant lots or houses in the subdivision. This is to provide a certain level of quality and may limit the use of the land solely to residential purposes and prescribe that houses built are to be of a certain size within specified distances from one another. These are very common where there are no local zoning controls or in instances where the developer deems the zoning inadequate to maintain the desired quality of the neighborhood. The restrictive covenants may provide for enforcement by the subdivider of the land or by property owners within the subdivision. Historically, restrictive covenants were sometimes used to restrain homeowners from selling their homes to people of certain races. In 1948, though, the Supreme Court said that judicial enforcement of racially restrictive covenants constitutes a violation of the Equal Protection Clause of the Fourteenth Amendment to the U.S. Constitution.[23]

EMINENT DOMAIN

An inherent attribute of federal and state sovereignty is the power of **eminent domain**, that is, the ability of government to take private property for public use.[24] The federal government and the government of each state have this power, and the legislatures of the states can grant this power to certain levels of local government, usually to counties and cities. The power to condemn property for public use is most commonly exercised by government to acquire lands for such public improvements as government buildings, military bases, highways, parks, and recreation areas.

The portion of the Fifth Amendment to the U.S. Constitution that stipulates "private property [shall not] be taken for public use without just compensation" is known as the Takings Clause. In addition to establishing that property may be taken for public purposes, it requires a condemning authority to pay just compensation to the owners of the property taken. Thus, the cost of acquiring property for public purposes is borne by the taxpayers.

Public Use

Previously, the term **public use** has included improvements to infrastructure (roads, bridges, canals, etc.) as well as public amenities such as parks and schools. In the twentieth century, courts approved takings to allow construction of stadiums, railroad lines, and power plants, even though title often was transferred to private parties. Indeed, governments have used eminent domain to engage in urban renewal programs and even to redistribute land. Consequently, through government action and judicial approval, "public use" has been redefined as "public purpose" or even "public interest."

In *United States v. Gettysburg Electric Railway Co.* (1896),[25] the Supreme Court said that "when the legislature has declared the use or purpose to be a public one, its judgment will be respected by the courts, unless the use be palpably without reasonable foundation." Similarly, in *Berman v. Parker* (1954),[26] the Court stated that "when the legislature has spoken, the public interest has been declared in terms well-nigh conclusive." And in *Hawaii Housing Authority v. Midkiff* (1984),[27] the Court indicated that a taking should not be invalidated under the Public Use Clause as long as it is "rationally related to a conceivable public purpose." Clearly, such language gives elected officials broad latitude to use eminent domain as they see fit.

In *Kelo v. City of New London* (2005),[28] the U.S. Supreme Court permitted a city to use eminent domain to facilitate an ambitious waterfront development project, even though title to real property would be transferred to private developers. The city claimed that the new development would create jobs, generate substantial tax revenues, and help revitalize its downtown area. And even though a private developer would undertake the project, there would be restaurants, stores, and other amenities that members of the public could enjoy. Dividing 5-4, the Supreme Court agreed that this combination of benefits was sufficient to meet the requirements of the Public Use Clause. Writing for the majority, Justice Stevens had no difficulty concluding that New London's plan "unquestionably serves a public purpose."

Because *Kelo* can be seen as giving cities *carte blanche* in their exercise of eminent domain, it was roundly condemned by advocates of private property rights. Of course, state courts may provide greater protection to private property rights under the relevant provisions of their state constitutions.[29] It is also noteworthy that since the *Kelo* decision, thirty-four states have enacted laws restricting the exercise of eminent domain by state and local agencies. For example, in 2006 Florida voters approved an amendment to the state constitution providing, "Private property taken by eminent domain . . . may not be conveyed to a natural person or private entity except as provided by general law passed by a three-fifths vote of the membership of each house of the Legislature."[30]

In 2013, officials in the town of Richmond, California discussed a unique justification for using eminent domain. Specifically, they proposed seizing properties that were in foreclosure for the purpose of permitting the delinquent homeowners to remain in their dwellings; however, investment firms with interests in the foreclosed properties have threatened legal action if the town invokes eminent domain for this reason, and perhaps as a result, the town has not yet moved forward with its plan.

Just Compensation

When the condemning authority and the property owner cannot agree on what constitutes **just compensation**, the amount of compensation is determined by a court. The condemning authority introduces evidence that the property being taken is required for public purposes and presents real estate appraisers who offer expert opinions on the value of the property being condemned. The property owner, in turn, has the right to testify concerning the value and use of the property being taken and to present appraisers as expert witnesses to testify as to the market value of the property. In most cases, a jury determines the amount of compensation due the property owner. Judges usually instruct juries that "just compensation" equates to fair market value. Courts generally determine fair market value as the price at which the property being condemned would change hands between a willing buyer and a willing seller, neither being under any compulsion to buy or sell and both being knowledgeable of relevant facts.

OPINION
OF
COURT

MISSISSIPPI & RUM RIVER BOOM CO. v. PATTERSON
98 U.S. 403, 25 L. Ed. 206 (1878)

Mr. Justice Field delivered the Opinion of the Court.

. . . The right of eminent domain, that is, the right to take private property for public uses, appertains to every independent government. It requires no constitutional recognition; it is an attribute of sovereignty. The clause found in the Constitutions of the several States providing for just compensation for property taken is a mere limitation upon the exercise of the right. When the use is public, the necessity or expediency of appropriating any particular property is not a subject of judicial cognizance. The property may be appropriated by an act of the legislature, or the power of appropriating it may be delegated to private corporations, to be exercised by them in the execution of works in which the public is interested. But notwithstanding the right is one that appertains to sovereignty, when the sovereign power attaches conditions to its exercise, the inquiry whether the conditions have been observed is a proper matter for judicial cognizance. If that inquiry take the form of a proceeding before the courts between parties,—the owners of the land on the one side, and the company seeking the appropriation on the other,— there is a controversy which is subject to the ordinary incidents of a civil suit, and its determination derogates in no respect from the sovereignty of the State. . . .

The testimony as to the amount of compensation to be awarded can become very technical when the condemning authority takes real estate that effectively abolishes or diminishes the owner's ongoing business. In such instances, accountants and economists often appear as expert witnesses on behalf of the owner. In some states, courts can award a condemnee attorney's fees in addition to damages to compensate for a taking.

Regulatory Takings

The drafters of the Fifth Amendment Takings Clause undoubtedly had in mind physical takings by government; however, courts have long recognized applicability of the Clause to governmental regulatory actions as well as physical takings. In some instances, government regulations have greatly affected the economic value of an owner's property. For example, in 1987 the U.S. Supreme Court ruled that a land use regulation can effectively become a taking where the regulation does not substantially advance legitimate interests of the government or where such regulations deny the owners use of their land.[31] The Court has noted the Takings Clause "is designed not to limit the governmental interference with property rights per se, but rather to secure compensation in the event of otherwise proper interference amounting to a taking."[32]

The need to protect the environment has caused governmental agencies to take steps, for example, denying a permit to fill wetlands, which have greatly burdened an owner's use of private property. Some instances where courts have required the

CASE IN POINT

CAN LOCAL GOVERNMENT CONDITION THE GRANTING OF A BUILDING PERMIT ON THE PROPERTY OWNER'S GRANTING AN EASEMENT?
Nollan v. California Coastal Commission
United States Supreme Court
483 U.S. 825, 107 S. Ct. 3141, 97 L. Ed. 2d 677 (1987)

James and Marilyn Nollan owned a beachfront lot in Ventura County, California. They wanted to tear down the small house on the lot and build a larger one. To do this they had to obtain a permit from the California Coastal Commission. The Commission granted the permit on the condition that the Nollans allow the public to pass across their beach, which was situated between two public beaches. The required condition was "part of a comprehensive program to provide continuous public access along Faria Beach as the lots undergo development or redevelopment." The Nollans unsuccessfully challenged this requirement in the California courts, arguing that their property

was effectively being taken for public use without just compensation.

The United States Supreme Court agreed with the Nollans. Writing for the Court, Justice Antonin Scalia said, "California is free to advance its 'comprehensive program,' if it wishes, by using its power of eminent domain for this 'public purpose' . . . but if it wants an easement across the Nollans' property, it must pay for it." In dissent, Justice William Brennan castigated the Court's "narrow view" of the case, saying that its "reasoning is hardly suited to the complex reality of natural resource protection in the 20th century."

government to pay just compensation include governmental efforts to protect coastal areas from erosion.[33] In a case where the government sought to protect water quality from strip-mining activities, a federal court even held that the Surface Mining Control and Reclamation Act, which permitted such governmental action, effected a compensable taking.[34]

Further, it is not uncommon for a local government to require certain concessions from a property owner before approval of rezoning or issuance of a building permit. For example, a city may require an owner to grant an easement or dedicate land for public use. In such instances, an issue of **regulatory taking** may come into play. In *Dolan v. City of Tigard* (1994), the U.S. Supreme Court held that requiring the owner to deed a portion of the property to the city for use as a public greenway before allowing the owner to expand her plumbing and electrical supply store went too far and was inconsistent with the Takings Clause of the Fifth Amendment.[35]

TRUSTS

A **trust** is an arrangement whereby one party (the **trustee**) holds title to property for the benefit of another (the **beneficiary**). It is created by a **grantor** (or **settlor**) executing a legal instrument known as a **trust agreement**. In some instances, the grantor, trustee, and beneficiary during the grantor's lifetime may be the same person. Trusts that are created during the grantor's lifetime are referred to by lawyers as **inter vivos trusts**, but more commonly, laypersons refer to such trusts as **living trusts**. In most states, any competent adult may create a trust or act as a trustee.

The transfer of assets into the trust is essential. This is usually accomplished by retitling assets into the name of the trustee. The grantor of an inter vivos or living trust can, and typically does, retain the right to revoke the trust. This is called a **revocable trust**. If a grantor does not reserve the right to revoke the trust, it is known as an **irrevocable trust**. Inter vivos trusts are often created to coordinate the management of assets with the objective of providing for the needs of beneficiaries and conserving income, gift, and estate taxes. Additionally, a grantor of an inter vivos trust may desire to avoid the publicity and costs that may be attendant to the grantor's property being administered under supervision of a probate court.

A trust created by a will is known as a **testamentary trust** and does not become effective until death of the **testator** or **testatrix** (the legal designations for a man or woman who signs a will). In most instances, one who creates a testamentary trust may revoke it simply by revoking the will or executing a new will.

Whether inter vivos or testamentary, trusts are often established by those seeking competent, professional management, and a trust company is selected to serve as trustee. There are significant advantages in having professional management and corporate trustees fulfill this role because they customarily have a staff of officers who are trained in administration and investments. Trustees are entitled to receive a fee for services, and such fees typically are negotiated between the grantor and trustee. A corporate trustee who assumes its duties upon the grantor's death may ask those who bear the impact of the fee (beneficiaries) to consent to the fee.

WILLS AND INTESTATE SUCCESSION

A will is a legal instrument by which a person disposes of property at death. Traditionally referred to as a **last will and testament**, during the early stages of our law, the will provided for the disposition of real property and the testament covered personal property. A man who made a valid will was called a **testator**, while a woman who did so was referred to as a **testatrix**, but the law now commonly uses the term **testator** irrespective of gender.

A testator must have **testamentary capacity**. This means the testator (testatrix) must be of sound mind and must understand the nature and extent of his or her property, the natural objects of his or her bounty, and the disposition being accomplished by the will being executed. To be valid, a will must be executed by a competent adult and must comply with certain formal requirements set forth in the statutes of the state of the testator's **domicile** at the time the will was signed. Generally, a will must be signed by a competent person in the presence of two witnesses and declared by the signer to be his or her will. The witnesses must sign the will in the presence of the testator and each other. During lifetime, a competent testator may either revoke a will or may revise a will by signing an amendment called a **codicil**. A codicil must be executed with the same formalities as a will. A testator who dies without a valid will is said to have died **intestate**.

Traditional legal terminology designated beneficiaries of a will who receive real estate as **devisees** and beneficiaries of personal property as **legatees**. Now, both devisees and legatees are commonly referred to as devisees or beneficiaries. A testator has considerable freedom in determining who are to be the beneficiaries under the will. Nevertheless, most state laws provide that if a surviving spouse is dissatisfied with the share provided under the deceased spouse's will, he or she may choose to receive an **elective share** of the decedent's property. Originally, this was a device to protect widows and was known as a right to elect a dower interest. In the past several decades, most states have broadened the concept to equally protect widows and widowers. Usually, the elective share entitlement is about 30 percent of the decedent's estate. A spouse married to a testator after the will was signed is commonly entitled to the share he or she would have received if the testator died without a valid will. Pre-nuptial or post-nuptial agreements (agreements made between spouses prior to or after marriage) may waive the rights of spouses to elective or intestate shares. These agreements are strictly regulated because they can have significant effects on the rights of spouses for whom the laws were designed to protect. In some states, a child born after a will is executed is entitled to a share of the estate unless the testator's will expressly excludes **after-born children**.

A will is an important legal document, but it does not control the disposition of all property owned by a decedent. If a person has created an inter vivos trust, the property held by the trustee passes pursuant to the terms of the trust. Also, in many instances property is owned jointly with the **right of survivorship**, whereby the survivor becomes the owner, or certain accounts may be designated as pay or transfer on death, whereby the named beneficiary on the account receives the asset automatically at the death of the owner. Additionally, life insurance, annuities, and retirement death benefits typically pass by contract to the named beneficiary rather than by the decedent's will or by the laws of intestate succession.

A testator's will generally appoints a **personal representative** (traditionally called an **executor** [male] or **executrix** [female]) to handle the administration of the estate. This may be any competent adult or a corporate trust company that is qualified to act under state law. Some states require the personal representative to be a resident of the state where the administration takes place. Upon a testator's death, the personal representative named in the decedent's will petitions the court to admit the will to probate and officially appoint the named personal representative, who then administers the estate under oversight of the **probate court**. This is known as the **probate** process, which was established to protect two classes: beneficiaries and creditors. The probate court's function is to ensure that the personal representative properly inventories and protects the decedent's assets; has the assets appraised; publishes notice to creditors; sells assets where necessary; files necessary tax returns; pays all taxes, administrative fees, and expenses; addresses any valid claims filed against the estate; and distributes the remaining assets according to the provisions of the decedent's will. The personal representative must collect all sums due the decedent, keep detailed records of receipts and expenditures, file such accountings as required, and apprise the beneficiaries of these activities. At the conclusion of administration, the court determines whether the personal representative has properly completed his or her duties and, if so, discharges the personal representative from any further responsibility or liability with regard to the estate. The formalities and time requirements of the probate process often depend on the value and character of the decedent's assets and liabilities.

Property owned by a person who dies without a will passes to the decedent's **heirs** by intestate succession. The law of the state of the decedent's domicile determines the decedent's heirs. Usually, state intestate succession laws provide for inheritance by the decedent's spouse and children or descendants of deceased children. The probate court appoints someone to serve as a personal representative (traditionally called an **administrator** or **administratrix**) to handle the administration of the decedent's estate. An individual who is appointed personal representative of an intestate estate generally must post a surety bond in an amount set by the court to guarantee faithful performance of duties. (With a will, the testator may waive the requirement of a bond; however, it is still up to the court as to whether a bond will be required. Generally, where a will waives the bond requirement and the personal representative is a resident of the state where the administration is occurring or is a corporation, no bond will be required.) That appointed person or corporate entity must notify the decedent's heirs and in general carry out the duties as outlined for testate estates, making any distribution according to law. Again, the formalities and time requirements often depend on the value and character of the decedent's assets and liabilities.

Every state has a probate court or a division of the civil court that supervises the administration of estates and the distribution of the decedent's property to the decedent's beneficiaries or heirs at law. The personal representative of an estate and the attorney who advises the personal representative are each entitled to a fee for services. In some instances, the fee is based on a percentage allowed by state law. In other instances, interested parties agree upon the fee; however, where there is a disagreement the probate court is available to determine the reasonableness of fees. On occasion, approval of fees by the probate court is required. Where the decedent owned real estate in a state other than where the decedent was domiciled, it may even become necessary to have an **ancillary administration** of a decedent's estate in the state where the real property is located.

The Contest of a Will

To contest a will, the contestant must have standing. An heir who has been **disinherited** or a person who was named as a beneficiary in a prior will generally has standing. Will contests usually take one of two forms. The contestant claims either that the testator did not have testamentary capacity when the will was executed, or that the will was the result of fraud, duress, or **undue influence** of the testator.

Of the grounds named, undue influence is the most common. To prove undue influence, the contestant generally must show the testator's mind was unduly influenced in executing the will. Disinheriting a relative does not create a presumption of undue influence. But when a testator names as a beneficiary a person who was in a close relationship with the testator (for example, the testator's doctor, nurse, business

CASE IN POINT

A WILL EXECUTED UNDER UNDUE INFLUENCE
Boehm & Allen v. Allen
Iowa Court of Appeals
506 N.W.2d 781 (Iowa App. 1993)

For twenty-eight years Duane Allen was married to Belva Allen. The couple had two children, Fred and Louise. Belva died in 1970, and in 1972 Duane married Mary. He executed wills in 1975 and 1976 that included his children, Fred and Louise. Then in 1980, Duane and Mary executed new wills leaving their estates to each other. Duane died on October 20, 1989, and Fred and Louise received nothing under their father's new will. They filed an action to set aside the decedent's will, contending that Mary unduly influenced her husband to execute his 1980 will. A jury returned a verdict in their favor. Mary, as estate representative, filed an appeal contending the evidence at trial was insufficient to show that she had exercised undue influence on Duane in executing his will.

"Undue influence," the appellate court observed, "must be such as to substitute the will of the person exercising the influence for that of the testator" and "is usually established by circumstantial evidence and may be and often is based upon an accumulation of many factors."

The evidence at trial revealed that Fred and Louise had a close relationship with their father and were beneficiaries under a former will. The record further disclosed that Duane suffered from a painful arthritic condition, was debilitated, and had an alcohol abuse problem and was therefore more susceptible to influence. The lawyer who prepared Duane's 1980 will testified that Mary had come to his office alone to request that he draft simple wills for her and Duane, leaving their estates to each other, and that he had no private conversations with Duane regarding the changes Duane's will was making. Finally, there was evidence that before Duane executed the 1980 will, he had prepared but never executed a will devising his estate to his children, with a life estate to his wife, whereas the contested will left his entire estate to Mary.

The court found the evidence sufficient and affirmed the trial court's judgment invalidating the decedent's 1980 will.

adviser, or housekeeper) to the exclusion of close family members, a question of undue influence may arise. If such a person possessed a confidential relationship with the testator, assisted the testator in procuring the will, and is to receive a substantial benefit under the will, many courts raise a presumption of undue influence. Such a presumption requires the proponent of the challenged will to offer a reasonable explanation for having actively procured the testator to sign the will. The court then determines whether the explanation is reasonable and whether the will should be upheld.

ESTATE, GIFT, AND INHERITANCE TAXES

Since the early decades of the twentieth century, the United States government has imposed a tax on estates and gifts. Since 1977, taxes on gifts and estates have been combined. A decedent's gross estate for **estate tax** purposes consists not only of property in the decedent's sole name that is subject to probate but also life insurance and annuities on the decedent's life where the decedent owned the policies, property in certain types of trusts the decedent established, business interests, the decedent's interest in jointly owned property, "pay or transfer on death" accounts, as well as certain pension and profit-sharing interests. A person may make annual exclusion gifts of certain amounts without tax consequences (currently $13,000 to each donee); however, beyond these exempt amounts the gifts made during a person's lifetime are added to the value of the decedent's estate to determine the value of the estate for federal estate tax purposes.

The decedent's adjusted gross estate, that is, the value of the decedent's estate less debts of the decedent and costs of administration, is entitled to an applicable credit amount (**unified credit**). However, as the estate tax continues to be a divisive political issue, the exact amount of this credit continuance is often changed by acts of Congress. For example, in the year 2009, the exemption was set at $3.5 million. In 2010, there was no estate tax at all, and in 2011, the exemption returned at a level of $5 million for individual persons and $10 million for a couple that receives an inheritance. In 2013, President Obama signed legislation called the American Taxpayer Relief Act, which set the 2014 exemption at $5.34 million for individuals and $10.68 million for married couples, with future exemptions slated to increase these amounts based on inflation rates. In practical terms, in 2014, this information means that an estate valued at $5.34 million or less will not incur any federal taxes upon transfer of assets (although state taxes could apply). An estate that exceeds the specified exemption in a given year, though, will be taxed at a rate of 40%. Ultimately, the specific details of estate tax exemptions are regular topics of debate in Congress, with many Republicans not only calling for lower estate tax rates and higher exemptions, but even for the abolition of estate taxes altogether.

In determining the decedent's taxable estate, the adjusted gross estate is reduced by deductions for charitable gifts, debts, and funeral expenses. In addition, the estate of a married person is entitled to a **marital deduction** of the value of the property transferred outright or in certain other ways to a surviving spouse. Under current federal law, there is no limit on the amount of the marital deduction; thus, assets of any value can be transferred to a surviving spouse without a tax being levied. There are, however, limitations on the marital deduction where the surviving spouse is not a U.S. citizen. Of course, when the surviving spouse subsequently dies, that spouse's estate—having been increased by property received as part of a marital deduction—may be quite large and thus subject to considerable estate taxes for those who inherit it.

Another interesting aspect of this discussion lies in how the Internal Revenue Service (IRS) treats same-sex marriages. In 2013, in *United States v. Windsor*, the Supreme Court struck down a federal law called the Defense of Marriage Act, which had defined marriage as a union between a man and a woman. This ruling, in turn, potentially allows a married same-sex couple to derive the benefits of federal marital deductions related to estate taxes. The caveat, though, is that the couple must have a marriage that is recognized as valid by one of the fifty states—and the Supreme Court's decision did not mandate that any state must permit same-sex marriages. For more on this case and the matter of same-sex marriage in general, see Chapter 8.[36]

As a result of the complex issues that can arise with an inheritance—and the significant sums of money that are often at stake—for many individuals, **estate planning** has become a very important activity in present-day America. Estate planning takes into consideration a person's assets, family situation, and desires. It is designed to provide an effective method of accomplishing one's objective of distribution of assets while minimizing taxes and costs of administration. In order to maximize the estate that will be available to beneficiaries, a person who has an estate that may be subject to federal estate taxes should seek the advice of an attorney who practices in this field of law and other experts in the field of taxes and financial management. In this way, one can be guided in making lifetime and testamentary gifts and structuring an estate plan to take advantage of available deductions.

State Estate and Inheritance Taxes

Some states impose a similar additional estate tax and some impose a tax that is due only if there is a federal estate tax, and the laws are frequently written in such a way that the decedent's estate pays a portion of the total estate taxes to the state rather than the federal government. Other states impose an **inheritance tax** on the value of the assets received from a decedent's estate; in these states, there are usually certain levels of exemptions for assets received by close family members.

CONCLUSION

One concept unmistakably emerges from this chapter: Property law, long regarded as stable and unchanging, has become dynamic. History has provided a needed stability in the law of property, yet as our nation's economy has changed from agricultural to industrial, and as it now advances into the information age, new approaches to property rights have evolved. In the early history of the United States, ownership of real property represented by far the predominant wealth of individuals and businesses. By the twentieth century, however, intangible assets represented the greatest source of wealth in the nation.

Beyond that, the notion of an individual's absolute right over the use of private property is no longer feasible. Zoning laws and building standards that were originally designed to control nuisances have become very sophisticated in their restrictions on the use of real property. Additionally, in response to environmental concerns, regulations necessarily have altered the concept of free and unrestricted use of land. Even so, where such regulations constitute a "taking" of an owner's property, the owner is entitled to receive just compensation from the government just as surely as if the government effected a physical taking of the owner's property.

Modern forms of financing also have enabled home ownership to become widespread, and laws have been enacted to protect the interests of those whose materials and labor have created or enhanced real property. Further, condominium and cooperative ownership of real property is popular and growing.

Ultimately, the transfer of wealth from one generation to another is no longer accomplished by a simple will. During the past few decades, many persons have accumulated large estates. Thus, estate planning to avoid guardianships and excessive taxes has become commonplace, as have the uses of trusts in the transmission of property to new generations.

SUMMARY OF KEY CONCEPTS

In this chapter, we have endeavored to present the historical background of the law of private property, which has its roots in the English common law, and to explain how these historic concepts pervade the present law, particularly the laws relating to ownership and transfer of real estate.

It is important to comprehend the different forms of personal property (tangible and intangible) and the ownership and possessory rights that arise under the doctrines of bailments, confusion, and accession.

It is important to grasp the various forms of ownership of real property and how such property is transferred and mortgaged, as well as the nonpossessory interests in land, such as licenses and easements. Although much of the law of real estate follows the English common law, the relationship between a lessor and lessee of residential property has undergone considerable changes, mostly to the benefit of the lessee.

Owners of real estate sometimes impose restrictions on its use, for example, subdivision restrictions. And although the concept of private ownership of property is protected by the U.S. Constitution, government at all levels regulates the use of property, primarily through land use zoning, building codes, and environmental regulations. Governmental units have the power of eminent domain, that is, the power to condemn private property for public use. But the U.S. Constitution requires that the owners must be fairly compensated. In some instances, governmental regulations can become so restrictive that courts will hold such regulations constitute a compensable taking.

Creation of a trust is a legal method of providing for the management and eventual transfer of property interests. Living or inter vivos trusts are created during a person's lifetime; trusts created under a will are known as testamentary trusts. By execution of a will, a testator or testatrix can, subject to certain restrictions, provide for transfer of property at death and designate a personal representative to carry out the terms of the will. Otherwise, property is distributed to heirs according to the intestate succession laws of the state of the decedent's domicile. Of course, estates must reckon with the payment of debts and costs of administration. Larger estates are subject to federal estate taxes, and in many states, heirs who receive property are subject to payment of inheritance taxes.

FOR FURTHER READING

Ackerman, Bruce, *Private Property and the Constitution* (Yale University Press 1977).

Bernhardt, Roger, & Amy M. Burkhart, *Real Property in a Nutshell* (5th ed., West Publishing 2005).

Ely, James W. Jr. (ed.), *Property Rights in American History* (6 vols., Garland 1997).

Epstein, Richard A., *Takings: Private Property and the Power of Eminent Domain* (Harvard University Press 2005).

Nedelsky, Jennifer, *Private Property and the Limits of American Constitutionalism: The Madisonian Framework and Its Legacy* (University of Chicago Press 1990).

Seigan, Bernard H., *Economic Liberties and the Constitution* (2d ed., Transaction Publishers 2005).

QUESTIONS FOR THOUGHT AND DISCUSSION

1. The authors state that private property is essential to American political philosophy. Is this the case? Why or why not?

2. Explain the distinction between an easement and a license as related to the law of real property.

3. You are offered a three-year lease on a residence for a monthly rental agreeable to you. What provisions would you consider to be essential in the lease? What other provisions would you look for that might affect your use and enjoyment of the property?

4. Should the law impose definite requirements on a party who leases property for residential use, or should parties be free to negotiate the terms of a lease without interference from government? Justify your answer.

5. Before the city of Plainville would grant a developer a permit to construct houses in a new subdivision the city required that the developer deed to the city a large tract of land for use for the construction of a school. Do you think this would constitute a regulatory taking in violation of the Takings Clause of the Fifth Amendment? Why or why not?

6. A person who accumulates property pays various taxes such as real estate taxes, sales taxes, federal and state income taxes, and in some instances intangible taxes. In view of the taxes exacted upon the creation of wealth, is the imposition of a federal gift and estate tax a justifiable form of taxation?

7. Why is it usually more advantageous to have a will rather than to die intestate?

8. What is meant by an "elective share" in regard to a decedent's estate?

9. Outline the functions that must be performed by a personal representative in the administration of a decedent's estate.

10. Describe a family situation where it may be advisable for an individual with dependent children to place property in a trust rather than will it outright to the children under a will.

KEY TERMS

abandoned property
accession
actual possession
ad valorem taxes
administrator
administratrix
adverse possession
after-born children

ancillary administration
assume the mortgage
bailee
bailment
bailor
beneficiary
board of adjustment
board of equalization

bona fide purchaser
building codes
chose in action
codicil
collateral
community property
condominium
condominium association

confusion
constructive possession
cooperative form of ownership
copyrights
covenants
deed of trust
deficiency judgment
devisees
disinherited
domicile
dominion and control
donee
donor
due-on-sale clause
easement of necessity
easements
elective share
eminent domain
environmental regulations
estate planning
estate tax
estates during the life of another
estates in real property
executor
executrix
fee simple estate
fee tail estates
"grandfathered in"
grantee
grantor
gratuitous bailments
heirs
inheritance tax
intangible personal property

inter vivos trusts
intestate
irrevocable trust
joint tenancy
joint tenants with right of
   survivorship
just compensation
land tenure
land use planning
landlord-tenant law
last will and testament
leasehold
legatees
lessee
lessor
licenses
lien
life estates
life tenant
living trusts
lost property
marital deduction
mortgage
mortgagee
mortgagor
mutual benefit bailments
partition suit
patents
personal property
personal representative
prescription
probate
probate court
public use

purchase money mortgage
quitclaim deed
real property
regulatory taking
remainderman
restrictive covenants
retaliatory eviction
revocable trust
right of redemption
right of survivorship
security agreement
security deposit
security interest
settlor
special exceptions
tangible personal property
tenancy by the entirety
tenancy in common
tenants in common
testamentary capacity
testamentary trust
testator
testatrix
trademarks
trust
trust agreement
trustee
undue influence
unified credit
variances
warranty deed
will
zoning

ENDNOTES

1. *Chicago, Burlington, & Quincy R.R. v. Chicago*, 166 U.S. 226, 17 S. Ct. 581, 41 L. Ed. 979 (1897).
2. *See Walls v. Midland Carbon Co.*, 254 U.S. 300, 41 S. Ct. 118, 65 L. Ed. 276 (1920).
3. U.S. Const. art.I, §8, cl. 8.
4. 35 U.S.C. §154(a)(3).
5. "2012 Trends in Patent Case Filings and Venue," by James Pistorino, available at: http://www.perkinscoie.com/files/upload/LIT_13_02Pistorino_2012Article.pdf
6. *Association for Molecular Pathology v. Myriad Genetics*, 569 U.S. _____, 133 S. Ct. 2107, 186 L. Ed. 2d 124 (2013).
7. 17 U.S.C. §302 (a).

8. *See Feist Publications v. Rural Telephone*, 499 U.S. 340, 111 S. Ct. 1282; 113 L. Ed. 2d 358 (1991); in this case, the Court ruled against a phone company's attempt to copyright names in a phone book, suggesting that although the standard for defining originality was a low one requiring only a "minimal degree" of creativity, a compilation of names did not meet this baseline threshold. Furthermore, the court noted that the substantial labor and effort associated with transcribing the names was irrelevant to any assessment of originality.

9. 9 F. Cas. 342 (C.C.D. Mass. 1841).

10. *American Broadcasting Companies, Inc., et al. v. Aereo, Inc.*, 573 U.S._____, 134 S. Ct. 2498, 189 L. Ed. 2d 476 (2014).

11. *Elf-Man, LLC v. Cariveau*, W.D. Wash. (Jan 17, 2014).

12. *Ray v. Flower Hosp.*, 439 N.E.2d 942 (Ohio App. 1981).

13. *Franklin v. Jackson*, 847 S.W.2d 305 (Tex. App. 1992).

14. *Weinberg v. Wayco Petroleum Co.*, 402 S.W.2d 597 (Mo. App. 1966).

15. *See, e.g., State v. Chippewa Cable Co.*, 180 N.W.2d 714 (Wis. 1970).

16. *See* Nick Tamiraos, "The Foreclosure Fade and What it Means for the Housing Market," *Wall Street Journal Online*, available at: http://blogs.wsj.com/economics/2014/07/22/the-foreclosure-fade-and-what-it-means-for-the-housing-market/.

17. *Thornhill v. Caroline Hunt Trust Estate*, 594 So.2d 1150 (Miss. 1992).

18. *Mueller v. Keller*, 164 N.E.2d 28 (Ill. 1960).

19. *See, e.g., Morford v. Lensey Corp.*, 442 N.E.2d 933 (Ill. App. 1982).

20. *Peterson v. Oklahoma City Hous. Auth.*, 545 F.2d 1270 (10th Cir. 1976).

21. 42 U.S.C. §3604.

22. 272 U.S. 365, 47 S. Ct. 114, 71 L. Ed. 303 (1926).

23. *Shelley v. Kraemer*, 334 U.S. 1, 68 S. Ct. 836, 92 L. Ed. 1161 (1948).

24. *Kohl v. United States*, 91 U.S. 367, 23 L. Ed. 449 (1876).

25. 160 U.S. 668, 16 S. Ct. 427, 40 L. Ed. 576 (1896).

26. 348 U.S. 26, 75 S. Ct. 98, 99 L. Ed. 27 (1954).

27. 467 U.S. 229, 104 S. Ct. 2321, 81 L. Ed. 2d 186 (1984).

28. 545 U.S. 469, 125 S. Ct. 2655, 162 L. Ed. 2d 439 (2005).

29. *See, e.g.*, the Ohio Supreme Court's decision in *City of Norwood v. Horney*, 110 Ohio St. 3d 353 (2006).

30. Fla. Const. art. X, §6(c).

31. *See Keystone Bituminous Coal Assn. v. DeBenedictis*, 480 U.S. 470, 107 S. Ct. 1232, 94 L. Ed. 2d 472 (1987).

32. *First English Evangelical Lutheran Church of Glendale v. County of Los Angeles*, 482 U.S. 304, 315, 107 S. Ct. 2378, 2386, 96 L. Ed. 2d 250, 264 (1987).

33. *See Lucas v. South Carolina Coastal Council*, 505 U.S. 1003, 112 S. Ct. 2886, 120 L. Ed. 2d 798 (1992).

34. *See Whitney Benefits, Inc. v. United States*, 926 F.2d 1169 (Fed. Cir. 1991).

35. *Dolan v. City of Tigard*, 512 U.S. 374, 114 S. Ct. 2309, 129 L. Ed. 2d 304 (1994).

36. *United States v. Windsor*, 570 U.S. _____, 133 S. Ct. 2675, 186 L. Ed. 2d 808 (2013). In this case, the same-sex marriage actually occurred in Canada, but had been recognized as valid by the state of New York; therefore, the Supreme Court's decision suggests that a marriage that is recognized by a state can also be recognized by the federal government.

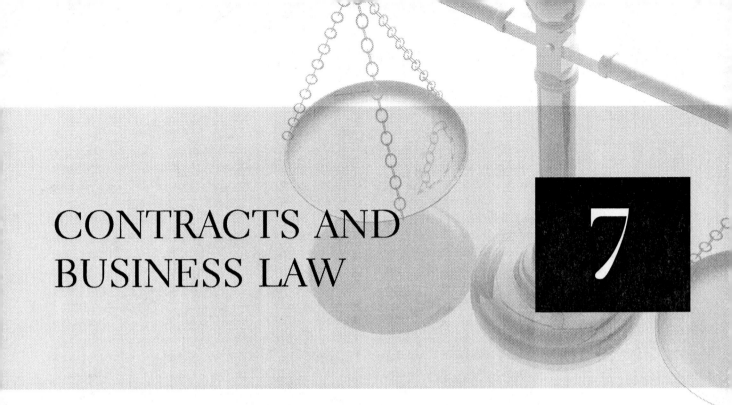

CONTRACTS AND BUSINESS LAW

7

LEARNING OBJECTIVES

This chapter should enable the student to understand:

- the constitutional and commercial significance of the right to contract
- how contracts are classified
- the elements of a contract
- the legal meaning of "offer and acceptance," "consideration," "capacity to contract," and "legality of purpose"
- the effect of the statute of frauds and the parol evidence rule
- assignment and performance of contracts; legal remedies for breach of contract
- the applicability of the Uniform Commercial Code to sales, commercial paper, secured transactions, and warranties
- the organization and regulation of sole proprietorships, partnerships, and corporations and why businesses choose a particular legal structure
- the basic principles of federal consumer protection laws, consumer credit legislation, and bankruptcy proceedings

CHAPTER OUTLINE

Introduction
Contracts
The Uniform Commercial Code (UCC)
Business Associations
Consumer Protection
Bankruptcy
Conclusion
Summary of Key Concepts
For Further Reading
Questions for Thought and Discussion
Key Terms

INTRODUCTION

In this chapter, we examine the basic principles of contract and business law. The right to contract is a core value in the United States, and the freedom of individuals, organizations, and businesses to enter into contracts is basic to the free enterprise system. Article I, Section 10 of the U.S. Constitution, which provides that "No State shall pass any . . . Law impairing the Obligation of Contracts," reveals the importance the Founders placed on contractual relations. This provision came into sharp focus in 1819 when Chief Justice John Marshall, in a landmark decision of the U.S. Supreme Court, wrote that the charter King George III granted to Dartmouth College in 1769 gave the trustees the contractual right to govern the college. Consequently, the Court ruled that the state legislature could not impair the obligation of that contract by transferring control of the College to a new board of overseers.[1]

The basic law of contracts as developed in the English common law was accepted in the United States; however, federal and state statutes have considerably modified laws concerning contracts. As a result, the freedom to contract is regulated to a considerable extent by legislative bodies and by the courts. As mentioned in Chapter 5, the American Law Institute (ALI) has developed Restatements of the Law in an attempt to bring uniformity in the application of legal principles. Because the law of contracts is so vital to commerce and the need for stability and uniformity in the law is so great, the Restatement assumes a particularly significant role in this area. The principles of contract law as restated by the ALI are frequently followed by the courts. In this chapter, we make frequent references to the *Restatement (Second) of Contracts*.

Every day, we enter into contracts when we buy a cup of coffee, fill up the car with gas, grab a bite to eat at the drive-through window, or download a new song from an online vendor. These contracts seldom result in controversies and rarely do the contracting parties resort to litigation. Contracts form the backbone of modern business, as individuals contract to purchase real estate, executives enter into employment contracts with corporations, and promoters raise capital from investors to start new businesses. The federal government procures material to equip the armed forces, and states contract with construction firms to build roads and bridges. Overall, the basic principles of law applicable to simple contracts apply to those involving millions of dollars.

The development of business entities has been an outgrowth of the right to contract. In this chapter, we also examine the basic structure and legal aspects of sole proprietorships, partnerships, and the artificial legal beings we know as corporations. In discussing business organizations, it is helpful to understand some of the basic concepts of antitrust law, labor law, and laws relating to employment contracts and employment discrimination. We discuss these topics in Chapter 11.

CONTRACTS

A contract is basically an agreement between two or more parties that is enforceable by law. Gaining familiarity with the various classifications of contracts is a good way to start. Contracts may be oral or written. An **express contract** exists where the parties explicitly state the terms of their agreement. An **implied contract**, on the other hand, exists where the conduct of the parties evidences a contract. For example, one who orders a hamburger at a fast-food restaurant implicitly agrees to pay the price posted on the menu. In other instances, the issue of whether the conduct of parties constitutes an express or implied contract (or both) can become complex, as illustrated by the Case in Point below.

Classifications of Contracts

Another method of classifying contracts is whether they are bilateral or unilateral. A **bilateral contract** is one where parties exchange promises. Most written contracts are bilateral. In contrast, a **unilateral contract** is one where one party responds to another party's offer by performing some act. To illustrate: A homeowner offers a gardener $40 if

CASE IN POINT

THE LEGAL RELATIONSHIP BETWEEN A COLLEGE AND A STUDENT IS CONTRACTUAL
Johnson v. Schmitz
United States District Court for the District of Connecticut
119 F. Supp. 2d 90 (D. Conn. 2000)

Johnson, a graduate student in the doctoral program at Yale University, sued his faculty advisors, Oswald Schmitz and David Skelly, as well as the University, charging them with breach of express and implied contract for misappropriating his doctoral theory. Johnson alleged that in 1995 he developed a theory for his dissertation and later learned that other students who had read his private notes explained his theory to Schmitz. Johnson hesitated when Schmitz requested that he explain his ideas in order to complete his qualifying exam. Nevertheless, Johnson explained his theory to Schmitz but expressed concern to another member of his dissertation committee that Schmitz would misappropriate his ideas. He was assured this would not happen when he took the written part of his doctoral exam. Later, when he appeared for his oral examination he was discouraged from pursuing his ideas and told his ideas were "ridiculous and unoriginal." Following the oral exam, Schmitz and Skelly allegedly published Johnson's theory without attribution to him, thus precluding Johnson from further research and forcing him to abandon it as his dissertation topic.

At this stage of the case, the issue was whether Johnson's factual allegations, assuming them to be true, could establish express and implied contracts. Johnson argued

that based on distributed documents, including admissions literature and matriculation representations given to all doctoral students, Yale made an express contract with him and that an implied contract resulted from Yale's implied promise of the rights, privileges, and protections to which doctoral students are entitled in exchange for his agreement to become a graduate student. Defendants countered that Johnson's allegations were simply educational malpractice claims in disguise and characterized them as not cognizable as merely alleging a failure "to provide an effective course or manner of education."

"The basic legal relation between a student and a private university or college is contractual in nature," the court observed. Further, the court explained that a student bases a decision to attend a college or university, in significant part, on the documents received concerning core matters, such as faculty, curriculum, requirements, costs, facilities, and special programs, application of contract principles based on these documents, and other express or implied promises. Accordingly, the court denied the defendants' motion to dismiss, noting that Johnson's breach of contract claims against Schmitz, Skelly, and Yale must await further factual development.

the gardener mows the homeowner's lawn, and the gardener complies. The gardener's act represents the acceptance of the homeowner's offer. This is a unilateral contract.

In contract law, an **executory contract** refers to one that has not yet been fully performed, while an **executed contract** is one where performance has been completed. A **voidable contract**, such as a minor's contract to purchase an automobile, may be legitimately cancelled. A **void contract**, though, is one the law does not recognize; an example would be a contract between parties to injure or kill someone.

Finally, some contracts are classified as **formal contracts** while others are called **informal contracts**. A **negotiable instrument** such as a **check** or **promissory note** requires the use of certain language and legal terms; hence it is called a formal contract. Other contracts are called informal contracts, for although some written contracts are very detailed and complex, the law does not specify the exact language that the contracting parties must use.

Requisites of a Contract

The three basic components of a contract are typically referred to as **offer, acceptance**, and **consideration**. More specifically, to have an enforceable contract, there must be **mutual assent** of two or more parties who have the **capacity to contract** and there must be **consideration**. The mutual assent is based on one party's offer and another party's acceptance. To have the capacity to contract, a person must have attained the age of legal majority and must be mentally competent. Consideration is often thought of as being synonymous with money, but it can involve an exchange of benefits between parties, a promise, or even forbearance.

Offer and Acceptance

In contract law, one who makes an **offer** (**offeror**) must manifest an intention to become legally bound, while the one to whom the offer is made (**offeree**) must accept the offer on the terms proposed. Those terms must be definite and properly communicated to the offeree.

Not every proposal constitutes a legal offer to enter into a contract. For example, an offer made in jest, such as "I'll give you a million dollars for that beer," would not legally bind the offeror, as a reasonable person would understand the statement to be a joke. However, in a famous case called *Lucy v. Zehmer*,[2] the Supreme Court of Virginia used a "reasonableness" standard to find that a contract to sell a 471-acre farm for $50,000 was valid even though it was written on a restaurant napkin, and despite the seller's claim that the deal was a joke.

Another illustration concerns advertisements. A circular arrives in the mail and advertises certain dresses for sale. A woman orders a particular dress, but it is not available. Has a contract been formed by the customer's acceptance of a legal offer? In most instances, the answer is no, because the law generally looks upon an advertisement as an invitation for someone to make an offer to purchase.[3] Certain advertisements, however, can be construed as offers. For example, Big Bargain Store places an advertisement in the newspaper stating, "The first ten people who come to our store on December 1 may purchase a [particularly described] pocket radio for $12." This probably would be construed as an offer rather than merely an invitation to make an offer. Why? Because it is definite as to time, place, and description of the goods, thus indicating an intention to be bound.[4]

An offer must be accepted by the means specified in the offer, but if no means are specified, then the offer may be accepted in a reasonable manner consistent with the circumstances and customs. An offer should state a time for acceptance, but in practice this frequently is not the case. If no time is stated, the offer is open for a reasonable period of time. When a court must determine what constitutes a "reasonable time" it considers the many circumstances surrounding the offer. If the offer is made during a conversation, the law may determine that acceptance must be made by the end of the conversation.

Customs of an industry also can play a part in a court's determination of the time of acceptance, but unless the offer specifies it is open for a set period of time, an offer may be revoked prior to acceptance. If the offeree accepts it subject to conditions, the law views such a conditional acceptance as a counter-offer, and in most cases it is deemed a rejection.[5] But an acceptance that requests some addition to the terms of the offer does not necessarily invalidate the acceptance as long as the acceptance is not made conditional on the request.[6]

Consideration

Historically, in England, the Church held that a person who took a false oath committed a serious sin. On this basis, the English common law developed "oath taking" as a basis to determine if the parties to an agreement were sufficiently serious for the court to find that a contract existed. Later, the common law courts developed the concept of placing a seal on a document to indicate that a party intended to be bound. During the sixteenth and seventeenth centuries, the common law courts decided that, in order to have an objective basis to determine whether parties to an agreement intended to be bound by their offer and acceptance, consideration should be an essential element of a contract. The requirement was unique to the common law and was imposed to enable judges to objectively determine the parties' intent to be bound by an agreement. Consideration came to consist of some benefit to a **promisor** or some detriment to a **promisee**. In this form, the doctrine of consideration in the law of contracts was accepted in America as part of the common law.

By requiring consideration, the law seeks to prevent attempts to enforce gratuitous promises. The most basic consideration is money; for example, a student orders a cup of coffee and pays fifty cents for it. But the concept of consideration goes beyond paying money for goods or services.

In addressing the requirement for consideration, the *Restatement (Second) of Contracts* §75 states:

(1) Consideration for a promise is
   (a) an act other than a promise, or
   (b) a forbearance, or
   (c) the creation, modification or destruction of a legal relation, or
   (d) a return promise,
   bargained for and given in exchange for the promise.
(2) Consideration may be given to the promisor or to some other person. It may be given by the promisee or by some other person.

The following examples illustrate some forms that consideration may take:

- An act other than a promise. George agrees to shovel all the snow from in front of Howard's home in return for Howard's promise to pay George $50.
- A forbearance from doing an act. Edgar, who has the legal right to build an addition to the family home, agrees to refrain from doing so in exchange for his neighbor Frank's granting Edgar the right to pipe water from Frank's well to irrigate Edgar's lawn.
- Creation or destruction of a legal relation. Agnes agrees to withdraw from a partnership in consideration of Cynthia's becoming a partner in her place.
- A promise for a promise. Susan promises to pay Donald $20,000 for Blackacre and Donald promises to convey (deed) Blackacre to Cynthia for that sum. But note that a promise cannot be **illusory**, that is, it must commit the promisor to do something. For example, a promise that "I will agree to pay you sometime when I have money" is illusory for it does not really commit the promisor to anything definite.

Adequacy of Consideration

Courts do not generally look to the **adequacy of consideration**. In America, parties have the freedom to contract and strike the bargains they desire. Therefore, if there is no fraud involved, a court will not be likely to set aside a contract on the ground that the consideration is inadequate. So if Alex agrees to buy a certain car from Acme Motors for $30,000, makes a deposit, and signs the agreement, but it later turns out that Alex could have bought the same car for $2,000 less from Big Town Motors, the contract would not be subject to cancellation on the grounds of inadequate consideration. There are exceptions. For example, Dana owes Adam $1,000, and there is no dispute that the amount of $1,000 is due. Dana sends Adam a check for $250 and notes on the check that it is "payment in full." The $250 would not be sufficient consideration to effect payment in full. On the other hand, if there is a genuine dispute between the parties over the amount due on the account and Dana offers and Adam agrees to accept a lesser amount, then Dana and Adam have reached what the law terms an **accord and satisfaction** and the debt is extinguished.

Past Consideration; Pre-existing Duties

A **past consideration** does not fulfill the requirement of consideration for formation of a contract. Therefore, the fact that a person has previously performed an act or furnished something of value does not support a contract, as a contract must be based on a present consideration. Likewise, performance of a **pre-existing duty** will not be regarded as consideration to support a contract to do some act or to refrain from doing an act. To illustrate: Suppose the owner of a store promises to pay the police to answer an emergency call in the event the owner's store is burglarized. Because the police are under a duty to respond to criminal acts, the promise is not supported by consideration.

Promissory Estoppel

In certain situations, courts determine that it is unfair not to enforce an agreement even in the absence of consideration. Under a doctrine known as **promissory estoppel**, a court may enforce an agreement where it was foreseeable that one party, in reliance on another's promise, has incurred expenses. For example, Joe relied on Kenneth's promise to buy Joe's boat if Joe placed the boat in first-class condition. With Kenneth's knowledge, Joe expended a large sum of money to meet that condition. Kenneth decides not to buy the boat, and Joe brings suit. A court might determine that under the doctrine of promissory estoppel, Kenneth should not be permitted to deny that a contract existed on the basis that there was no consideration for the promise to buy the boat.

Many courts have employed the doctrine of promissory estoppel as a substitute for the element of consideration where a pledge to provide funds to a charitable organization is involved and the charity has relied upon that pledge. Some even take the position that a charitable pledge is enforceable whether supported by consideration or not, and even in absence of any reliance by the charity.[7] The *Restatement* takes the position that a promise to make a gift to a charitable organization is enforceable per se without the need to show consideration or any substitute therefor.[8]

In addition to the basic elements of offer, acceptance, and consideration, parties to a contract must have the legal capacity to contract. Moreover, the contract must be for a purpose that is neither illegal nor contrary to public policy.

Capacity to Contract

A minor (usually defined as a person under age eighteen) does not have the legal capacity to enter into contracts and thus may **disaffirm** a contract. In practice, we know that minors enter into contracts to purchase food, clothing, other necessary items, and some things that may not be regarded as necessary. Buying lunch may be necessary, but clearly buying a new sports car is not. A minor who enters a contract for necessaries may be required to pay if those responsible for the minor's custody do not. But a minor who enters a contract to buy a car may disaffirm that contract upon attaining majority. Alternatively, if not disaffirmed, the minor may ratify the contract upon attaining legal majority. Marriage removes a minor's lack of capacity to contract. Furthermore, most state laws provide that a minor age sixteen or over may petition a court to remove the minor's disability to enter contracts.

Persons under **legal guardianship**, whether as minors or for physical or mental infirmities, are legally incapable of contracting. Nevertheless, an adult placed under guardianship cannot generally avoid a contract made prior to the guardianship.

A contract made by a person who is intoxicated to the extent of impairment of normal faculties is voidable. Upon becoming sober, the formerly intoxicated individual is permitted to affirm or disaffirm the contract made while in an intoxicated state. Courts usually require that action to disaffirm must be taken promptly.

Legality of Purpose

Obviously, the law will not enforce a contract to do an **illegal act**. For example, a contract to injure or damage someone's person or property in exchange for a payment or an agreement to pay a bribe to a witness or public official is void. Likewise, a contract that has as its purpose to inflict fraud on a third party would be void. Where a lender agrees to charge a **usurious rate of interest**, the contract may not be enforceable; however, in some instances the court will enforce the contract to the extent of the principal loaned but not the interest. State laws normally stipulate the rate of interest a creditor may charge a borrower. Typically, these laws provide higher levels of interest with respect to credit card and "payday" loans.

Mutual Mistake and Misrepresentations

Although not void, certain other contracts are voidable. A **mutual mistake** occurs when a contract achieves what neither party intended, and either party can avoid the contract.[9] For example, suppose a pet shop agrees to sell, and a woman agrees to buy, a pedigreed cat for $300. The buyer selects a Persian cat named Chelsea, but the seller thought the buyer had selected a different cat named Whitey. It turns out both parties were mistaken, so either party can usually avoid the contract on the basis of mutual mistake. On the other hand, where one party is mistaken (the law terms this a **unilateral mistake**) the law concerning mistake does not provide grounds to avoid the contract. If the buyer agreed to buy a cat believing the cat was worth $500 but it turns out the cat is an ordinary cat that has a minimal market value, this would be a unilateral mistake and no ground to avoid the contract.

A contract entered into based on fraud or a material misrepresentation of fact may be avoided. To illustrate: A seller of a pre-owned automobile represents to the prospective buyer that the car has been owned by one previous owner and has been driven only 15,000 miles, a fact disclosed by the car's odometer. It turns out that the car has had three previous owners and had been driven more than 55,000 miles but the seller tampered with the odometer to cause it to be turned back to 15,000. This is the type of misrepresentation on which a plaintiff (buyer) may sue to avoid a contract.

Likewise a contract is subject to being avoided on the ground of **unconscionability.** In 1977, the New York Court of Appeals defined an unconscionable bargain as one "such as no person in his or her senses and not under delusion would make on the one hand, and as one no honest and fair person would accept on the other, the inequality being so strong and manifest as to shock the conscience and confound the judgment of any person of common sense."[10] Courts have refused to enforce agreements between a debtor and creditor where the terms of the contract are oppressive or where a home improvement contract exacted a sum of money from a householder greatly disproportionate to the work performed. The **Uniform Commercial Code** (UCC), discussed later in this chapter, authorizes a court to refuse enforcement of a contract on a finding that the contract or any clause thereof was unconscionable at the time it was made.[11]

With the aforementioned parameters surrounding mutual mistakes notwithstanding, it is important to recognize that a party's failure to fully comprehend the scope of a key provision will not necessarily void a contract. In some instances, potentially confounding components of an agreement may even require judicial interpretation. A recent matter that is colloquially called the "Million Dollar Comma" highlights the value in understanding the implications of minute, seemingly insignificant details embedded in a contract. In this case, Rogers Communication, a cable television provider in Canada, had a contract with telephone company Bell Aliant for use of telephone poles. As the cost of using the poles went up, though, Bell Aliant attempted to terminate the contract.

The telephone company's lawyers successfully argued that the comma in a key portion of the contract allowed for the contract to be terminated. The critical provision said: "This agreement shall be effective from the date it is made and shall continue in force for a period of five (5) years from the date it is made, and thereafter for successive five (5) year terms, unless and until terminated by one year prior notice in writing by either party." Rogers Communication contended that the final clause, which spoke to termination of the agreement, only applied to the contract's renewal after five years. However, Bell Aliant successfully argued that the comma between the words "terms" and "unless" actually allowed the termination clause to apply *either* to the renewal or to the basic agreement referenced in the start of the passage. Consequently, the contract was renegotiated at a cost of one million Canadian dollars to Rogers Communication; that would not have been necessary if the comma in question was omitted from the initial agreement.[12]

Contracts Contrary to Public Policy

Courts also have reserved the right to void contracts that are contrary to broader principles related to society's general welfare. The meaning of **public policy** is somewhat vague. In 1897, the U.S. Supreme Court said that in the absence of constitutional or statutory provisions, the courts may find public policy in the decisions of courts and the practice of government officials.[13]

Frequently, a person who accepts employment agrees that upon termination the employee will not compete against the employer's business. Such contracts frequently involve employees who have been entrusted with trade secrets and customer lists. The law enforces such agreements if they are otherwise valid, if the length of the term for not competing is not too great, and if the geographical area in which competition is forbidden is reasonable. On the other hand, the law disfavors contracts that prevent a person from pursuing a gainful occupation; thus, public policy plays an important role in contracts containing a **covenant not to compete.** For example, suppose a physician signs a contract with a medical group that would prohibit the physician upon leaving employment from practicing medicine in the state for twenty-five years. The court would undoubtedly find such a contract to be against public policy and decline to enforce it.

Courts also have ruled that where a contract is made for sexual services, it will not be enforced; however, unmarried adult cohabitants are not precluded from entering into contracts regarding their earnings and property interests. This was highlighted by a famous "palimony" case decided by the California Supreme Court in 1976 (see the Case in Point that follows).

CASE IN POINT

CAN AN UNMARRIED COHABITANT SUE TO RECOVER DAMAGES BASED ON AN ORAL CONTRACT?
Marvin v. Marvin
California Supreme Court
557 P.2d 106 (Cal. 1976)

For seven years, Plaintiff Michelle Marvin, a single woman, lived with defendant Lee Marvin, a well-known movie star. After they separated, she brought suit to enforce an alleged oral agreement whereby they agreed to combine their efforts and earnings and share equally all property they accumulated. Plaintiff alleged she gave up her career as an entertainer to be the defendant's companion, housekeeper, and cook; that in return, the defendant agreed to provide for her for the rest of her life. The Los Angeles Superior Court granted judgment for the defendant, and the plaintiff appealed.

On appeal, the California Supreme Court rejected defendant Lee Marvin's contention that enforcement of the alleged contract would be contrary to public policy because it involved an immoral relationship between the parties. The court stated, "Agreements between nonmarital partners fail only to the extent that they rest upon a consideration of meretricious sexual services. . . . The fact that a man and woman live together without marriage, and engage in a sexual relationship, does not in itself invalidate agreements between them relating to their earnings, property, or expenses." The court returned the case to the trial court with directions to determine the plaintiff's property rights.

Formal Requirements of Contracts

As previously pointed out, a contract may be oral or written, informal or formal. But there are definite advantages that a contract, other than a simple agreement, be in writing. The English common law judges found it very perplexing to resolve disputes concerning major contracts based on conflicting and sometimes fraudulent oral testimony of witnesses. This led the English Parliament in 1667 to enact a law for "the prevention of frauds and perjuries," called the Statute of Frauds, that requires certain types of contracts to be in writing to be enforceable. Every state in the United States has a **statute of frauds** requiring certain contracts to be in writing; these are typically adopted from the basic English statute. These statutes generally require the following types of contracts to be in writing:

- for transfer, sale, and purchase of real estate or interests in real estate, usually including a lease for a period of more than one year;
- in consideration of marriage;
- that cannot be performed within a year;
- to pay a debt or obligation of another, for example, a contract of **suretyship** or an agreement by a personal representative of a decedent's estate to discharge a debt of the decedent from the personal representative's personal funds;
- involving sale of personal property beyond a stipulated amount, usually $500.

One can usually satisfy the requirement that a contract be in writing by producing evidence of informal written memoranda that sufficiently describe the parties, subject matter, and essential terms of a contract. Where real property is involved, courts often insist on a legal description of the property sufficient for a surveyor to locate the property. There is considerable litigation involving questions that arise as to whether such memoranda are sufficient. Moreover, courts often require a party who has received benefits under a contract to perform under the contract irrespective of whether the contract is evidenced by a writing. A classic example is where Joe Smith, a homeowner, watches workers put in a new driveway at his home. Smith neither ordered the work done nor paid any money to the party performing the work. He has no intention of paying for the new driveway, but he fails to inform the workers that they are at the wrong address. A court would likely hold Smith liable, even though he had not formally entered into a contract.

Parol Evidence Rule

The **parol evidence rule** states that a party cannot introduce parol (oral) evidence to contradict the terms of a written agreement that is complete. The term "parol" has broader meaning than simply "oral." It prohibits the introduction of any evidence extrinsic to the written agreement that existed at, or prior to, the execution of the written contract. Although termed a "rule," the parol evidence rule is more a principle of law than a rule of evidence.

Like many rules of law, the rule is subject to considerable interpretation by the courts. It does not prohibit a party from showing that a contract was entered into as a result of fraud, duress, or misrepresentation. Nor does it prohibit a showing that the contract was subsequently amended or modified by a new agreement. For example, construction contracts usually contain a clause that prohibits modification of the contract by oral agreements. Courts have held such a provision does not prohibit the parties from entering into subsequent contracts. This frequently occurs where the parties to a construction contract sign "change orders" to provide for additions or modifications to a building under construction. In such situations, courts sometimes admit parol evidence to resolve issues where there is an **ambiguity** in the legal writing and oral evidence is essential to ascertain the true intent of the parties to the contract.[14]

Assignments of Contracts

An **assignment** of a contract occurs when one party to a contract assigns rights under the contract to another who is not a party to the original contract. Contracts are generally assignable unless the contract or a statute provides to the contrary. Even then, courts may approve an assignment. Although rights under a contract may be assigned, a contracting party may not delegate the duties imposed on such person under the contract. Beyond that, the non-assigning party retains all rights and defenses under the contract.

Although duties under a contract may not be assigned, in some instances, they may be delegated. In all instances, however, the original contracting party remains liable. In general, duties may be delegated where the **delegatee** is in a position to perform as effectively as the delegator. Some contracts envision a delegation. For example, a building contractor customarily delegates to a subcontractor certain specialized phases

CASE IN POINT

ARE ALLEGED ORAL REPRESENTATIONS MADE BY A SELLER ADMISSIBLE IN EVIDENCE TO MODIFY AN EXPRESS WARRANTY?
Foundation Software Laboratories, Inc. v. Digital Equipment Corp.
United States District Court for the District of Maryland
807 F. Supp. 1195 (D. Md. 1992)

Foundation Software Laboratories (FSL) brought suit against Digital Equipment Corporation (DEC) after discovering that FSL's software would not run satisfactorily on the DEC computers it had purchased. The contract under which the purchase took place contained an express warranty that the hardware would be free from defects and that its operational software conformed to its published specifications. The contract disclaimed any implied warranties. FSL contended that representatives of DEC made oral representations about the performance of the hardware that extended the terms of the express warranty. The Court disagreed and granted summary judgment for the defendant, saying that "the parol evidence rule excludes evidence of oral assurances made before, or contemporaneous with, the execution of the [contract]."

---

of construction. Of course, a delegatee is not liable to the **delegator** unless the delegatee is furnished consideration necessary for performance. Other duties that may be delegated include an obligation to pay money or deliver standard goods. On the other hand, professional services such as those provided by a physician, lawyer, or architect are examples of **non-delegable duties**.

Who Can Enforce a Contract?

Ordinarily, it is the parties to a contract who have the right to enforce the terms of the contract. But most contracts can be assigned. For example, a buyer who agrees to purchase a certain automobile can generally assign that right to purchase to another party. The original purchaser is referred to as the **assignor** and the person to whom the right has been assigned is called the **assignee**.

The right to enforce a contract also extends to a party for whose benefit a contract is made, a party that is called a **third-party donee beneficiary**. Perhaps the most common form of a third-party beneficiary contract is a life insurance policy. A parent contracts with a life insurance company that upon the parent's death the insurer will pay the face amount of the policy to the parent's child. The parent and the company are the parties to the contract; the child is the beneficiary. A parent who reserves the right to change the beneficiary may do so. A **third-party creditor beneficiary** is a party to whom a party to a contract owes some legal obligation. One of the classic cases that nearly every first-year law student studies is the 1859 decision by the New York Court of Appeals in *Lawrence v. Fox*.[15] In this case, Holly loaned Fox $300, stating at the time that he owed that sum to the plaintiff Lawrence. Fox promised Holly that he would pay that sum to Lawrence the next day. But when the plaintiff Lawrence brought suit, the defendant

Fox contended that there was no proof that Holly was indebted to the plaintiff and that his agreement with Holly to pay the plaintiff was void for want of consideration. After a jury verdict, the court entered judgment against Fox, and he appealed. The Court of Appeals ruled in favor of the plaintiff Lawrence and held that when a promise is made to one person for the benefit of another, "he for whose benefit it is made may bring an action for its breach." This principle, the court ruled, previously applied in cases involving trusts, and should be applied in cases of third-party creditor beneficiaries. The overwhelming majority of American courts soon accepted that development in contract law.

Performance of Contracts

Fulfillment of the promises under a contract constitutes **performance**. Proper performance of all obligations under a contract discharges a contracting party. There are other means of discharge. A person may be excused from performing under a contract under the doctrine called **impossibility of performance**. For example, if Alan was hired to repair a beach cottage that was swept into the sea before his performance came due, Alan is excused from performance. If a law is enacted that makes it illegal to perform the obligations under a contract, the party obligated to perform is discharged. Written contracts frequently include provisions that the party required to perform will not be liable for delays due to strikes, adverse weather conditions, or **acts of God**. These clauses are sometimes referred to as *force majeure* **clauses**.

Remedies for Breach of Contract

Non-performance of a contractual obligation is known as a **breach of contract.** Where a party repudiates a contract before the time for performance, such repudiation constitutes an **anticipatory breach.** In such instances, the law provides the aggrieved party with a remedy. Three judicial remedies may be available where a breach has occurred. These are (1) a suit for damages; (2) a suit for **specific performance**; and (3) **rescission** of the contract.

Damages
The principal remedy the law affords for a breach of contract is a suit for **compensatory damages**. In law, "damages" means "dollars," and to recover damages the plaintiff must prove with reasonable certainty that the damages claimed as a result of a breach of contract were **reasonably foreseeable** by the parties. In some situations, a party must take steps to avoid damages to whatever extent possible. Failure of a party to mitigate damages can prevent recovery of such damages as could have been avoided by reasonable efforts.[16]

Damages in contract cases are usually assessed by a jury. Damages are designed to reimburse a person who has suffered losses because a contract has been breached. Damages for breach of contract follow certain general rules. Two illustrations:

▓ If a seller breaches a contract to sell goods or real estate to a buyer, the measure of damages would likely be the additional amount the buyer may have to pay to obtain similar goods or property.

▓ If a building contractor fails to complete the construction of a building but the contractor has substantially performed the contract, the damages would likely be the amount the owner would have to pay to another contractor to complete the job plus other expenses, such as rent or interest on a construction loan, that the owner may sustain.

One who suffers a breach but does not sustain actual damages may only recover **nominal damages**. A party who establishes a breach, but who is unable to prove having sustained any actual damages, may be awarded nominal damages of one dollar.

In some contracts, the parties include a provision for **liquidated damages**. This is a stipulation that in the event of a breach of the contract, damages shall be deemed to be in a certain amount or shall be calculated in a certain manner. Courts enforce liquidated damages provisions as long as they bear a reasonable relationship to damages that were anticipated or that occurred. But if the liquidated damages clause exacts a penalty, courts will disregard it and require actual proof of damages. Frequently, construction contracts for commercial buildings stipulate that in the event the building contractor does not complete the building by a certain date, the contractor will pay a certain sum for each day of delay beyond the agreed-upon date of completion.

A court will sometimes award **punitive damages** where the party who has breached a contract has committed a willful tort involving outrageous or malicious acts. Punitive damages are much like a fine. While punitive damages are not uncommon in tort suits (see Chapter 5), they are seldom awarded in contract cases.

Rescission

Rescission of a contract is not a common remedy, but in instances where a court determines that a party was fraudulently induced to enter a contract, it may allow that party to rescind, that is, to cancel, the contract. Courts may allow rescission of a contract and require restitution (repayment of sums advanced) either where a contract is void or where a contracting party is unable to perform.

Specific Performance

Where money damages would be inadequate to compensate an injured party, a court may award specific performance of a contract. Specific performance is an equitable remedy and one that a court dispenses on a discretionary basis and only where the terms of the contract are fair and the duties to be performed are clear.

Courts often require specific performance where a contract to sell some unique item of personal property is breached. An example would be where a contract involves an antique or an heirloom or a valuable work of art and where money damages would not compensate the person who contracted to buy the antique. Courts consider each parcel of real estate unique and will entertain suits for specific performance of a contract to purchase or sell real estate. Usually, a court will not order a person to render personal services in a specific performance suit, for example, requiring a singer to perform on stage, as to do so may constitute involuntary servitude. However, in such an instance the court may enjoin the singer from performing elsewhere.

CASE IN POINT

WHEN DOES A LIQUIDATED DAMAGES PROVISION BECOME AN UNENFORCEABLE PENALTY?
Lefemine v. Baron
Florida Supreme Court
573 So. 2d 326 (Fla. 1991)

Daniel and Catherine Lefemine contracted to purchase a residence from Judith W. Baron for $385,000. They made a good-faith deposit of $38,500. When unable to obtain financing, the Lefemines sued Baron for return of their deposit. Baron counterclaimed to retain the deposit money as liquidated damages pursuant to the contract. The default provision of the contract stipulated: "If the Buyer fails to perform the Contract...the deposit...may be retained or recovered by...the...Seller as liquidated damages, as consideration for the execution of the Contract and in full settlement of any claims;...or Seller at his option, may proceed at law or in equity to enforce his rights under the Contract."

The trial court ruled in favor of the seller on the counterclaim, allowing Baron to retain the deposit, and the appellate court affirmed. But on further review the Florida Supreme Court agreed that while the forfeiture provision was not unconscionable, it must fail because "the option granted to Baron either to choose liquidated damages or to sue for actual damages indicates an intent to penalize the defaulting buyer and negates the intent to liquidate damages in the event of a breach." The court remanded the case for a trial to determine the actual damages sustained as a result of the buyers' default.

THE UNIFORM COMMERCIAL CODE (UCC)

The Uniform Commercial Code (UCC) is a compilation of laws governing commercial transactions drafted by the National Conference of Commissioners on Uniform State Laws and submitted to the legislatures of the states. With some modifications, the UCC has been adopted in all states except Louisiana. The Louisiana legislature has enacted commercial laws that incorporate many of the provisions of the UCC. The purpose of the UCC is to make uniform laws dealing with sales of goods, commercial dealings with banks, warehouse receipts, investment securities, and secured transactions. The UCC has been a boon to interstate commerce, particularly among merchants.

The UCC is divided into articles and numbered by section. There is some variation in the statutory numbering system in different states. The model UCC consists of the following articles:

Article 1   General Provisions
Article 2   Sales
Article 2A   Leases
Article 3   Commercial Paper

Article 4	Bank Deposits and Collections
Article 4A	Fund Transfers
Article 5	Letters of Credit
Article 6	Bulk Transfers
Article 7	Warehouse Receipts, Bills of Lading, and Documents of Title
Article 8	Investment Securities
Article 9	Secured Transactions
Article 10	Effective Date

Much of the UCC deals with contractual matters that are commonly experienced in everyday life. For example, Articles 2 and 3 deal with sales and **commercial paper**, Article 4 deals with bank deposits and collections, and Article 9 concerns secured transactions. Articles 5, 6, 7, and 8 serve vital commercial interests, but for the most part cover more sophisticated business practices or subjects of concern primarily to bankers, security dealers, and merchants.

Sales of Goods

Article 2 of the UCC applies to contracts for the sale of goods. It does not cover service contracts or contracts for the sale of real estate. Article 2-204 allows a sales contract for goods to be "made in any manner sufficient to show agreement, including conduct by both parties which recognizes the existence of such a contract." Unlike the traditional common law rule, Article 2-207 allows an acceptance of an offer in dealings between merchants even if the acceptance proposes some changes. In addition to express warranties that may accompany the sale of goods, Article 2-314 provides that, unless excluded or modified, there is an **implied warranty of merchantability** that the goods are fit for ordinary use if the seller is a merchant with respect to goods of that kind. Article 2-315 provides for an **implied warranty of fitness of goods** for the buyer's particular purpose if the seller knows any particular purpose for which the goods are required and that the buyer is relying on the seller's skill or judgment to select or furnish suitable goods. Article 2-316 allows certain warranties to be modified or disclaimed in a conspicuous manner.

Commercial Paper

Ordinarily, in a contract between two persons the law dealing with negotiation of commercial paper does not come into play, but there developed a need to have negotiable documents that could be used as substitutes for money in commercial transactions where more than two persons are involved. From a legal standpoint, the essential difference between a **non-negotiable** and a **negotiable** legal instrument is that one who takes a negotiable instrument (1) for value, (2) in good faith, (3) without knowledge that it is overdue or has been dishonored, and (4) without knowledge that there is any defense against or claim to it by any person, becomes what the law terms a **holder in due course**. A holder in due course occupies a privileged position as a transferee and (with a few exceptions) takes the instrument free of all defenses to enforcing it.

CASE IN POINT

ARE THE CONTENTS OF A BOOK SUBJECT TO AN IMPLIED WARRANTY?
Cardozo v. True
Florida District Court of Appeal, Second District
342 So. 2d 1053 (Fla. 2d Dist. Ct. App. 1977)

Ingrid Cardozo purchased a book entitled *Trade Winds Cookery* from a local bookstore. While following a recipe for cooking a tropical plant commonly known as "elephant ears" she ate a small slice of the plant roots and suffered intense coughing, gasping, and stomach cramps that required medical attention. She sued the bookstore contending that the plant roots were poisonous and the recipes had been inadequately tested. Thus, she contended that the bookstore had breached its implied warranty under the UCC that the book was reasonably fit for its intended use, and argued that her illness occurred because of that breach.

The trial court certified the question to the appellate court, which held that the implied warranty in respect to

the sale of books by a merchant is limited to a warranty of the physical properties of the books and does not extend to the material communicated. While making no ruling as to the liability of an author or publisher, the court wrote, "It is unthinkable that standards imposed on the quality of goods sold by a merchant would require . . .a bookseller to evaluate the thought processes of the many authors and publishers of the. . .thousands of books which the merchant offers for sale." On that basis, the appellate court returned the case to the trial court for proceedings consistent with its answer to the certified question.

Negotiable instruments are vital to commercial transactions. Some have described a negotiable instrument as a "courier without luggage." The following contrasting scenarios illustrate this essential difference between a non-negotiable and a negotiable instrument:

1. Arthur contracts to furnish certain equipment to Bill. Bill is to pay Arthur in installments. Arthur assigns the contract to Charles. Bill is dissatisfied with Charles's performance and brings suit against Charles. Contract law concerning assignments provides that Charles, as an assignee of the contract, acquired the contract subject to any defenses that Bill has against Arthur.

2. On the other hand, had Bill given Arthur a negotiable promissory note that met the requirements of negotiability under the UCC, Arthur could have transferred that note to Charles, who would be a holder in due course and could have sold or otherwise transferred the note for value to a third party. Thus, negotiable instruments become a special class of commercial paper designed to be freely transferred in commerce.

As the above illustration reveals, it is very important to determine whether a particular legal document is negotiable. Article 3 of the UCC deals with commercial paper and focuses on negotiable instruments, a technical legal term dealing with checks, drafts, certificates of deposit, and promissory notes, and the specific requirements for an instrument to be negotiable. These requirements are technical but chiefly require the legal document to be an unconditional order or promise in writing payable to the bearer or "on order" (remember your check says "pay to the order of _____"), and payable on demand or at a fixed or determinable time.

A check is a legal instrument where a bank customer (**drawer**) orders the bank (**drawee**) to pay the **payee** of the check a certain amount. A promissory note is a legal document whereby one party (the **maker**) promises to pay another party (the payee) a sum of money either on demand or at a time certain. A **draft** is a written order drawn on one party by another requesting the payment of a certain sum to a third person. Checks and drafts involve three parties, whereas certificates of deposit and promissory notes usually involve only two. Historically, such matters were governed by principles of law called the law merchant, which later became a part of the common law. Prior to the UCC, the Uniform Negotiable Instruments Law governed these instruments in most states. The UCC reflects much of the context of that law.

The importance of bank checking accounts for handling financial transactions is reflected by the fact that the overwhelming majority of families in the United States have one or more checking accounts with a bank or other financial institution. Traditionally, these institutions furnished their customers a monthly statement accompanied by cancelled checks, which served as receipts. This model began to change after Congress in 1978 enacted the **Electronic Fund Transfer Act** (ETF Act), codified at 15 U.S.C. §1693 et seq. The ETF provides a basic framework establishing the rights, liabilities, and responsibilities of participants in electronic fund transfer systems. The most common types of transactions covered are those involving debit cards, direct deposits, Automated Teller Machine (ATM) transfers, and preauthorized debits from a customer's bank account. Today, after you have been notified, credit card companies, utilities, and some other creditors commonly use your check to make an electronic payment from your account. Your periodic bank statement must show all electronic transfers to and from your account, but you do not receive a cancelled check. If a financial institution does not follow the provisions of the EFT Act, you may sue for actual damages.

To further modernize the banking system, Congress enacted the **Check Clearing for the 21st Century Act**, also known as the "Check 21 Act," on October 28, 2003. The Act, codified at 12 U.S.C. §5001 et seq., became effective on October 28, 2004. Its stated purpose is to improve the overall efficiency of the Nation's payments system by fostering innovation in the check collection system and facilitating check truncation. Truncation refers to removing an original paper check from the check collection or return process and replacing it with a substitute check with an electronic image of the original check. Once a check is truncated, banks can work with either the digital image or a print reproduction of a check. Like checks processed under the ETF, the Check 21 procedures occur almost immediately. This places a premium on a checking account customer's having funds on deposit when issuing a check. Substituted checks are returned with a customer's bank statement and are the legal equivalent of the original checks for all purposes under federal or state law. The Act provides a one-year statute of limitations for enforcing claims under the Act.

SIDEBAR

Promissory Notes

A promissory note is a legal document whereby one party promises to pay another party (the payee) a sum of money either on demand or at a time certain. Following is the typical form of a promissory note:

_____ [City], _____ [State], _____ [Month], _____ [Day], _____ [Year] On _____, 201 _____, for value received, (I)(We) promise to pay to the order of _____ at _____ (name of place of payment; usually a bank) the sum of _____ dollars ($ _____) with interest thereon from date at the rate of _____ percent (_____%) per annum. If this note is not paid promptly at maturity, the maker and endorsers agree to pay all costs of collection, including a reasonable attorney's fee.

_____
Signature of maker of note

Security Agreements

Article 9 of the UCC deals with **security agreements**. A security agreement is a contract that grants a creditor a security interest in **collateral (security)** pledged by a debtor or borrower. If the debtor has rights in the collateral, a security interest attaches to the collateral as provided in Article 9. In some instances, the holder of the security interest takes possession of the collateral. In many instances, the debtor is allowed to retain the collateral, for example, a car, and the security interest is perfected by filing a **financing statement** with the appropriate government office. The financing statement gives public notice of the security holder's interest. If the debtor defaults, the security holder can convert the collateral into cash by conducting a sale in accordance with the provisions of Article 9.

BUSINESS ASSOCIATIONS

The common forms of business associations in the United States are the **sole proprietorship**, **partnership**, **corporation**, and **limited liability company**. The selection of the form of organization is based on the size of the business undertaking, the number of investors required to capitalize the business, the need for professional management, whether the business activities will involve a risk of personal liability to the owners, tax advantages, expenses of administration, and other factors. Throughout history, individuals have operated as sole proprietorships. Historians trace the development of partnerships and corporations to the Roman Law, but in the United States the legal principles governing these organizations are basically derived from the English common law. Of course, modern business law has developed from early precedents, particularly in the field of contract law, but federal and state statutes have played a key role in the last two centuries.

Sole Proprietorships

The most common form of a business organization is the sole proprietorship. The sole proprietorship is a solely owned form of enterprise in which the owner has the responsibility and control, enjoys the profits, and suffers any losses. Many professionals and retail stores and services operate as sole proprietorships. Because, unlike a corporation, a sole proprietorship has no legal identity apart from the owner, it is not taxed separately for federal income taxes. A sole proprietor is personally liable for performance of contracts and for any torts resulting from the operation of the business. Often, state laws or local ordinances require that sole proprietorships that operate under a name different from the owner register under **fictitious name laws.** For example, if Lilly Jones owns a women's clothing store under the name Lilly's Casuals, she may have to register the fact that she is the owner of that business. This alerts everyone to the true ownership of a business should any legal process be necessary.

Partnerships

A partnership is an association of two or more persons who combine their money, property, and skill to carry on a lawful business for profit. A partnership can be created orally—although it is preferable to have a written agreement that describes its purpose, the term for which it is to exist, the contributions and duties of the partners, the way that profits and losses shall be shared or borne, and the desired manner for dissolution and conclusion of the partnership's affairs.

The advantage of a partnership is that it allows co-owners to pool their talents and capital. The major disadvantages are that each partner is liable for the debts of the partnership and the withdrawal or death of a partner causes a termination of the partnership. Each partner is an agent for the other partners, and each is individually and jointly liable for contract and tort liabilities in the scope of partnership business. Consequently, if one partner is insolvent and another partner wealthy, a creditor who obtains a judgment against the partnership may enforce the judgment against the solvent partner. Partnerships file informational federal tax returns; however, the partners report their income or losses on their personal tax returns.

The foregoing describes a general partnership, yet there is another form of partnership authorized by law in states that have enacted the Uniform Limited Partnership Act. This Act authorizes formation of a **limited partnership** whereby one or more limited partners can limit their liability for the firm's debts to the amount of their investment. Organization must be accomplished as provided by the governing statute, which will include a requirement of obtaining a state certificate of partnership that usually includes the partners' written partnership agreement. A **limited partner** who actively participates in operation of a partnership business becomes liable on the same basis as a **general partner**.

In certain instances, persons who are not partners cause third parties to rely in good faith on representations that they are partners in a business. The usual scenario involves apparent partners misleading a creditor who extends credit on the assumption of dealing with partners. In these situations, courts may hold the apparent partners are estopped from denying that a partnership relationship exists.

Corporations

It was Chief Justice John Marshall who, in 1819, described a corporation as "an artificial being, invisible, intangible, and existing only in contemplation of the law."[17] In 1868, the Court further held that a corporation is a "person" within contemplation of the Fourteenth Amendment, thereby giving a corporation standing to sue in matters concerning due process of law.[18] Thus, as an artificial legal entity, a corporation has a legal existence independent from its stockholders who own shares of stock issued by the corporation. Corporations are chartered principally under state law. Delaware is the leading state for chartering corporations, due in part to the state's corporate-friendly tax laws and the fact that Delaware courts have developed a large body of law concerning corporations, which makes for more predictability. The **corporate charter** grants a corporation certain powers, provides for the shares of stock to be issued, and provides for the selection and duties of the officers and directors who are to govern the corporation. The shares of stock issued by a corporation represent the interests of its investors. The **common stock** carries with it the right to vote for directors and receive the net assets upon dissolution of the corporation. Holders of **preferred stock** are usually given priority to receive dividends and to receive assets upon dissolution.

Corporations may be publicly held as most large corporations are, with stockholders numbering in the thousands or millions. But corporations also may be quite small, where the stock is closely held, as is the case in most small business corporations. These latter corporations are frequently referred to as closed or **closely held corporations**.

Why a Corporation?

There are several advantages to operating a business as a corporation. They may be summarized as follows:

- **Limited liability.** Unlike one who invests in establishing a sole proprietorship or partnership, those who acquire shares of stock in a corporation are not liable for its debts and are not called upon to respond to legal actions involving the corporation. A variation of the business corporation is known as a professional association (PA) in which doctors, lawyers, and other professionals may incorporate. Rules for limiting the liability of such professionals, especially in the area of professional malpractice, differ from rules concerning the limited liability afforded stockholders in regular business corporations.
- **Aggregation of capital.** By selling shares of stock, a corporation can aggregate the capital it requires to carry on and expand its business.
- **Perpetual existence.** Because a corporation is itself a "being," it has perpetual life—at least until dissolved according to law. Thus, an incorporated business does not have to cease operations when a shareholder or director dies or becomes incompetent.
- **Transferability of ownership.** Because ownership of the corporation is represented by shares of stock, it is easy to transfer ownership. Changes in stock ownership, in general, will not affect the corporation's business.

■ **Continuity of management.**   A corporation's officers and board of directors can retain management to operate the business on a continuing basis.

Apart from the advantages, corporations (even closely held corporations) are burdened with considerably more administrative matters than a sole proprietorship or a partnership faces. These include furnishing notices to stockholders, holding meetings, recording minutes showing election of directors and officers, and filing annual reports with state agencies. Because a corporation is a separate entity it must file federal and state income tax returns. Its earnings are subject to taxes, and those earnings that are distributed to its shareholders are again subject to tax. In many cases, small corporations qualify for special treatment as "S corporations" under the Internal Revenue Code. Perhaps it is not a major problem for the large corporation, but a small business operating as a corporation often finds it a financial burden to employ accountants and lawyers to comply with laws and regulations.

The Corporate Structure

Both the federal and state governments have the power to charter corporations, but the great majority of corporations are chartered by state governments. The federal power is exercised mainly in connection with corporations that serve some national purpose. The Tennessee Valley Authority (TVA) is a familiar example. TVA was established by Congress during the Great Depression to provide electrical power to an economically deprived region that was not being served by private utilities. Another well-known example is the Federal National Mortgage Association (better known as "Fannie Mae"), which was chartered by Congress in 1938 to provide liquidity to the home mortgage market by purchasing or backing home loans that had been originated by private mortgage lenders.

In most instances, a corporation for profit is chartered by an executive department of a state acting under legislative authority. Usually, a group of incorporators submits their **articles of incorporation**, and if the articles meet the statutory requirements, they become the **certificate of incorporation** of the new corporation. The certificate of incorporation lists the names and addresses of the incorporators and original directors. It also outlines the powers of the corporation, its place of business, its capital structure, the rights of stockholders, and how directors and officers are to be selected. Upon organization, the corporation adopts bylaws for internal control of its operations. Corporations formed to operate banks, utilities, and insurance companies often require additional approval from other regulatory agencies.

A corporation that fully complies with the requirements of the law is known as a *de jure* corporation. A corporation is a **domestic corporation** in the state where incorporated. In other states, it is classed as a **foreign corporation** and may have to comply with certain legal requirements to do business in a particular state.

As previously pointed out, a corporation is a separate entity apart from its stockholders. One compelling reason for organizing a corporation is that the investors' liability is typically limited to their investment. If a corporate organization is not properly completed, or the investors are using it in some fraudulent manner, courts sometimes disregard the corporate entity. Courts may find stockholders personally liable where they create a "shell corporation" without assets or employees. However, lawyers who represent parties attempting to hold controlling stockholders liable face a formidable challenge when seeking to **pierce the corporate veil**.

Corporate Powers

A corporation's powers are derived from its certificate of incorporation subject to the constitution and statutes of the state of incorporation. Stockholders may agree to amend the articles. The powers listed in the corporation's articles of incorporation are its **express powers**. A corporation has **implied powers** to do those things reasonably necessary to carry out its express powers. State legislatures have adopted special provisions limiting the powers of particular corporations such as banks, utilities, and insurance companies. A corporation that acts beyond its powers is said to have committed **ultra vires** acts. The state attorney general can bring a court action to enjoin such *ultra vires* acts and, if necessary, to dissolve the corporation. Stockholders also have a standing to challenge *ultra vires* acts in court actions.

Stockholders' Rights

The management of a corporation is vested in its directors and officers. They have a duty to the stockholders to act honestly and in good faith and to avoid conflicts of interest. Stockholders do not participate in the corporate management, but they do have the right to inspect the corporation's books and records when they do so in good faith and for proper purposes. Most states require annual meetings of stockholders; however, this is usually required by the corporate bylaws. Stockholders receive notice of these annual meetings, and holders of the common stock are entitled to vote for directors and for such major actions as mergers and consolidations with other corporations. Those who own corporate stock will be familiar with these annual notices that usually include a proxy form with recommendations from the corporation's board of directors. Not infrequently today, groups of stockholders make some proposal for the corporation to take some particular action, for example, to report on employment of minorities. Most of these proposals fail because stockholders making them usually own a very small percentage of stock.

Publicly Traded Corporations

Corporations whose shares are widely held by the general public are known as **publicly traded corporations**. Federal laws relate to issuance and trading in securities of such corporations. In addition, each state has its own securities laws, sometimes called **blue sky laws**, which require issuers of securities to make certain disclosures. The objective of these laws is to protect investors who purchase stock by requiring corporations to ensure that stockholders have access to relevant financial information concerning the corporation. These laws also penalize officers, directors, employees, and even controlling stockholders who have access to information that is not available to other stockholders and who use such **insider information** to profit from stock transactions.

The federal government and state governments have enacted laws that impose duties on corporations to protect the public. The most prominent of these is the Securities and Exchange Act of 1934, which provides for civil and criminal penalties for conduct involving misrepresentations, omissions, insider trading, and other aspects of fraud in securities dealing.[19] The Securities and Exchange Commission (SEC) administers the Act, and the SEC's Rule 10(b) prohibits any person from using fraud or deception in the sale of securities. Famous prosecutions under the act include that of Martha Stewart in 2004, and those of executives from mortgage giants Fannie Mae and Freddie Mac in 2011–2012.

Limited Liability Companies

By the early 1980s, a new form of business entity made its appearance. The **limited liability company** (**LLC**) is a hybrid business organization composed of one or more owners (called members) and has characteristics of both a partnership and a corporation. It is controlled by an operating agreement and must be created under state law. The operating agreement establishes ownership interests and defines management responsibilities. An LLC requires minimal administrative compliance and although a member is personally liable for debts and obligations arising from the member's own activities or negligence, depending on state law, a member may be insulated from liability for acts of the other members. These minimal administrative requirements, and the fact that the Internal Revenue Code enables an LLC with more than one owner to elect to be taxed as a partnership, make it an attractive entity for professionals and smaller business entities.

Legal Regulation of Business

The American system of free enterprise underwent tremendous growth in the nineteenth century. The Nation's economic power became concentrated in the hands of a relatively small group of corporations. Many viewed this as injurious to the public because competition, the cornerstone of the free enterprise system, was becoming very restricted and monopolies flourished. Reliance on the common law and state antitrust laws proved inadequate to control the national industrial complex. In the late nineteenth century, by passing the Sherman Antitrust Act (1890), Congress placed limits on these monopolistic practices and agreements in restraint of trade that threatened the cherished American concepts of free enterprise.

With the growth of giant corporations in control of the Nation's basic industrial complex, tension arose between management and labor. Again, the common law proved unworkable because it regarded attempts by employees to band together in non-violent activities to improve working conditions and pay as criminal conspiracies. Early in the twentieth century, Congress responded by enacting legislation and by the mid-1930s the federal government had placed its stamp of approval on trade unions and their right to collectively bargain and to strike.

During and after World War II, the population became more diverse, and more women entered the workforce. Accordingly, the federal government began to take on a more active role in the Nation's economy. For example, in enacting the Civil Rights Act of 1964, Congress prohibited discrimination in employment on account of race, color, sex, national origin, or religion. Congress followed this by passing legislation to

CASE IN POINT

WAS THE OWNER OF MULTIPLE CORPORATIONS PERSONALLY LIABLE?
Walkovsky v. Carlton
New York Court of Appeals
223 N.E.2d 6 (N.Y. 1966)

The plaintiff was injured when struck by a taxicab owned by Seon Cab Corporation. The plaintiff alleged that Carlton was a stockholder in Seon and nine other corporations, each of which owned but two cabs. He claimed these corporations were operated as a single enterprise with regard to financing, supplies, repairs, employees, and garaging. The plaintiff asserted each stockholder was personally liable for the damages caused to the plaintiff because Carlton had used the multiple corporate structures to defraud those who might be injured by the cabs. A lower appellate court ruled that the grounds asserted were sufficient to allow the plaintiff to proceed against Carlton.

In reversing the lower appellate court's ruling, the Court of Appeals said: "[Carlton] is charged with having organized, managed, dominated and controlled a fragmented corporate entity but there are no allegations that he was conducting business in his individual capacity. . . . The corporate form may not be disregarded merely because the assets of the corporation, together with the mandatory insurance coverage of the vehicle which struck the plaintiff, are insufficient to assure him the recovery sought. If Carlton were to be held individually liable on those facts alone, the decision would apply equally to the thousands of cabs which are owned by their individual drivers who conduct their businesses through corporations."

---

provide for equal pay for women, prohibiting discrimination on the basis of age in most occupations, providing requirements for safe workplaces, and providing accommodations for those who suffer from disabilities. We discuss these legislative enactments in Chapter 11.

CONSUMER PROTECTION

Historically, the English common law relegated a consumer seeking relief from unfair business transactions to a law action for fraud and deceit. The common law proscribed only fraudulent statements of fact, not opinion, and allowed a merchant the privilege of **puffing**, that is, exaggerated sales talk. Soon the doctrine of *caveat emptor* (let the buyer beware) occupied a prominent place in the common law. American courts accepted the doctrine, but since the early twentieth century, the legislative and judicial trend of the law has been toward rejection of *caveat emptor* and toward protection of the consumer. Congress and state legislatures have adopted numerous laws to protect consumers. We discuss some of the principal federal laws below.

Federal Pure Food, Drug, and Cosmetic Law

One of the oldest consumer protection laws is the Pure Food and Drug Act (now popularly known as the Federal Food, Drug, and Cosmetic Act). Originally enacted in 1906—partly in response to publicity generated by Upton Sinclair's book *The Jungle*, which outlined poor conditions in the meat-packing industry—the Act was comprehensively amended in 1938 and has since been amended several times.[20] The Act makes it unlawful to prepare or handle food, drugs, and cosmetics under unsanitary circumstances or under conditions that render them injurious to health. Included in its broad sweep are prohibitions against misbranding and adulteration of food, drugs, and cosmetics as well as requirements for truthful labeling. In 1992, Congress amended a companion statute to strengthen laws regulating poultry inspection, adding criteria concerning pesticides and food additives in respect to poultry.[21]

The Federal Trade Commission

In 1914, Congress passed the Federal Trade Commission Act, which created the Federal Trade Commission (FTC) and declared unlawful "unfair methods of competition in or affecting commerce."[22] The objective of the law was to restrain trade practices that tend toward monopoly or restraint of trade.[23] In 2014, the FTC was expected to rule on a whether a proposed merger between cable companies Comcast and Time Warner would violate antitrust regulations by limiting competition in the marketplace. The evaluation process likely would involve assessing the market share of satellite companies like DirecTV and DISH Network, as well as providers like Verizon and AT&T, since the presence of these companies could also impact the notion of competition in this industry.

Beyond federal oversight, today, many states have "Little FTC Acts" that regulate sales of motor vehicles and mobile homes, home improvement contracts, and **unconscionable consumer contracts**. Beginning in 1982, some states adopted **"lemon laws."** These laws allow a buyer of a new automobile to obtain a replacement vehicle if, after repetitive trips to the auto dealer for repairs, and after the manufacturer has been given an opportunity to effect necessary repairs, the vehicle is still not functional.

Similar state and local ordinances also frequently address home solicitations and allow cancellation of subscriptions or of orders for merchandise solicited by a door-to-door salesperson. Misleading advertising is another aspect subject to state and local control. For example, laws often prohibit such misleading practices as **bait and switch advertising**. This is the practice of advertising an item in short supply for a low price and then attempting to sell the customer a similar but more expensive item.

The Truth in Lending Act

As the American public became more affluent, many federal approaches to consumer protection began to focus on finance and credit transactions. Many of these statutes were passed during the 1970s. One of the most important laws that protect consumers is the Consumer Credit Protection Act of 1968, better known as the Truth-in-Lending Act.[24] This Act is designed to promote the informed use of credit and to protect the credit consumer. It requires disclosure of finance charges in certain real estate transactions based on the effective **annual percentage rate of interest** (**APR**) and provides for a three-day "cooling off" period when a consumer negotiates a loan on the security of a second mortgage on a residence. Certain provisions of the law allow a consumer the right to rescind, that is, cancel, a contract under specified circumstances.

Garnishment is a process by which a creditor (**garnishor**) seeks to enforce payment of sums owed by a debtor by asserting a claim against a third party (**garnishee**) to obtain property of the debtor held by the garnishee. Common examples include a creditor's seeking to garnish a debtor's checking account at the bank or to garnish an employer to obtain a worker's wages.

The Act limits garnishment of a worker's wages for any workweek to a sum not exceeding 25 percent of the worker's disposable wages for the week.[25] State laws vary widely on a debtor's exemptions from the garnishment of wages.

Federal Consumer Credit Laws

During the 1970s, Congress enacted a spate of laws designed to protect consumers in common everyday business transactions. Among the more important statutory enactments are the following:

- The **1970 Amendment to the Truth in Lending Act**[26] furnishes important protection for **credit cardholders**. First, a credit card may only be issued in response to an application. This does not apply to a renewal.[27] Second, it limits the cardholder's liability for loss, theft, and unauthorized use of a credit card to $50 per card.[28] The statute only limits the cardholder's liability for "unauthorized use." Therefore, a cardholder is liable for purchases by a person to whom the cardholder gave the card or otherwise authorized to use the card.
- The **Fair Credit Reporting Act of 1970**[29] gives a consumer the right to verify the accuracy of credit information on file with credit reporting agencies.
- The **Fair Credit Billing Act of 1974**[30] provides protection to consumers who challenge irregularities in accounting, goods, or services that have not been delivered or accepted and incorrect application of payments. Creditors are required to investigate claims of errors, and pending investigation, they are not allowed to press for payment. A debtor must pay any sums not in dispute. Subject to certain limitations, a credit cardholder may assert claims and defenses arising out of any transaction in which the credit card is used if the cardholder has first made a good-faith attempt to satisfactorily resolve any disagreement or problem.[31]
- The **Fair Debt Collection Practices Act of 1977**[32] was enacted to eliminate **abusive debt collection practices**. The Act makes it illegal for debt collectors to use such tactics as falsely representing themselves as having some official status, making harassing phone calls, or making threats to notify a debtor's employer.

The Magnuson-Moss Warranty Act of 1975

The Magnuson-Moss Warranty Act was enacted in 1975 to make certain that consumers receive adequate information concerning consumer products and to encourage manufacturers to establish procedures for informal settlement of disputes.[33] The Federal

Trade Commission administers the Act, and some of the Act's provisions supersede those in Article 2 of the Uniform Commercial Code previously discussed. The Act requires a written warranty to be clearly and conspicuously designated as either a **full warranty** or a **limited warranty** and to disclose, in simple language, the terms and conditions of the warranty and the time period for enforcing the warranty. A full warranty must meet rather strict standards and must extend to any person who purchases the product or to any person to whom the product is transferred during the warranty period. Any warranty not meeting these standards is a limited warranty. A limited warranty may not disclaim an **implied warranty**. Recall the last time you bought a hair dryer or some similar item. It probably came with a printed limited warranty that read along the following lines:

> This warranty . . . excludes claims for indirect, incidental, or consequential damages. Some states do not allow the exclusion of incidental or consequential damages, so the above exclusion may not apply to you. This warranty, however, gives you specific legal rights and you may have other rights, which may vary from state to state.

The Act creates a right of action for a consumer who sustains damages from breach of a written, statutory, or implied warranty—but first a consumer must resort to an informal settlement procedure. A consumer who prevails in an action is entitled to an award of a reasonable attorney's fee. Although the Act is silent on the issue of damages, it appears that state law governs as to the measure of damages that may be awarded in actions brought under the Act's provisions.[34]

BANKRUPTCY

The U.S. Constitution (Article I, Section 8) grants Congress the power to establish uniform bankruptcy laws. The Bankruptcy Act (Title 11 U.S.C.) governs bankruptcy proceedings, which take place in federal bankruptcy courts before judges appointed by the U.S. Courts of Appeals. Bankruptcy laws are designed (1) to afford debtors whose liabilities exceed their assets an opportunity to make a fresh start; and (2) to provide a fair method of distributing the bankrupt debtor's assets among creditors.

Bankruptcy proceedings are usually identified by the chapter of the Bankruptcy Act under which they take place. In regular bankruptcy, called a Chapter 7 proceeding, the individual or corporate debtor files a petition itemizing all debts; however, certain businesses, for example, banks and insurance companies, have to proceed under other federal laws. The filing of the petition stays civil court actions against the debtor and the debtor's property. Under some circumstances, creditors can file an involuntary petition against the debtor to secure an adjudication of whether a person is bankrupt.

Creditors select a trustee who marshals the debtor's property, liquidates it, pays the expenses of the proceedings, and distributes the property among the creditors according to priorities set by law. An individual debtor has certain exemptions under state law; for example, in some states, a debtor's residence, life insurance, and personal property up to a certain value may be exempt. Alternatively, under certain state laws a debtor may choose to take advantage of similar federal exemptions. An honest debtor can secure a **discharge from debts** through operation of the bankruptcy law; however, certain debts, for example, alimony and child support, are not subject to discharge.

Other forms of bankruptcy are available through federal law. Under a Chapter 11 proceeding, often used by businesses, a reorganization plan is formulated under which the debtor pays a certain portion of debts while continuing in business. A Chapter 12 proceeding allows a debtor/family-farmer or debtor/family-fisherman to continue farming or fishing; and a Chapter 13 proceeding, also called a 'wage earner's plan', enables individuals with a regular income to develop a plan to repay all or part of their debts. Finally, Chapter 9 may be available for a city that tries to declare bankruptcy. In 2013, a federal judge stated that Detroit could enter into bankruptcy, making it the largest city to ever do that. Other municipalities that have declared bankruptcy in the last decade include Stockton, California; Jefferson County, Alabama; and Central Falls, Rhode Island.

The Bankruptcy Abuse Prevention and Consumer Protection Act of 2005

On April 20, 2005, President George W. Bush signed into law the **Bankruptcy Abuse Prevention and Consumer Protection Act of 2005**. Most provisions became effective October 17, 2005. The Act represented the culmination of congressional efforts that began in 1998; its final passage incorporated numerous compromises. The Act represents a comprehensive revision of bankruptcy laws. Its major thrust is to prevent perceived abuses by consumers. It calls for the debtor to document a good-faith effort to obtain and implement debt counseling before filing for bankruptcy. This burden is placed on the debtor and any legal counsel involved and, along with other administrative requirements, will increase the expenses for debtors' obtaining legal representation.

One of the major changes relates to an individual debtor's right to file and receive a discharge under Chapter 7. The Act requires a comparison of the debtor's income to the median income in the state where the debtor is domiciled. Currently, IRS guidelines will be used to determine what living expenses are reasonable, and these values, rather than the debtor's actual living expenses, will be used as a means for determining a debtor's net income. A debtor whose income exceeds the median and who has the ability to pay creditors at least a minimal amount per month is barred from filing under Chapter 7 and must be so informed by a "debt relief agency" or legal counsel assisting the debtor.

The "means test" is designed to reduce Chapter 7 filings and to force a larger percentage to reorganize their debts privately or to file under Chapter 13, which requires a repayment plan over a period of years instead of simply a discharging of the debtor. Now, filers under Chapter 13 can no longer receive a "super discharge," that is, one that previously allowed the debtor to be released from certain tax obligations.

Finally, the 2005 Act places limitations on certain exemptions available with bankruptcies under state laws, particularly the homestead exemption, which is available in some states and is designed to protect the value of homes, particularly in situations involving the death of a homeowner or a homeowner's spouse. Moreover, the Act also makes it more difficult for small businesses to reorganize under Chapter 11.

CONCLUSION

Formation of contracts is a daily occurrence. From a nod to the street vendor to purchase a hot dog to execution of a complex hundred-page document, contracts are the lifeblood of the American economy. Like personal liberties, contracts have constitutional protection from impairment by government. Further, because contracts create a binding legal relationship enforceable in a court of law, the need for enforcement is infrequent.

The law of contracts is part of our heritage of the English common law. It has been refined by judicial decisions, mostly from state courts. Understandably, the legal precedents diverged, and as they did, businesspersons, lawyers, legislators, and legal scholars crafted a restatement of contract principles, while states adopted uniform laws to provide clarity, stability, and uniformity in business transactions. Thus, the *Restatement of Contracts* and the Uniform Commercial Code became the outstanding accomplishments in contract law in the twentieth century.

Basic principles of contract law pervade such specialized areas as commercial paper, sales, and security transactions. And even where principles of real property law are controlling, elements of contract law are frequently present. These principles also are woven into the structure and business relationships of sole proprietorships, partnerships, limited liability companies, and that unique business entity, the corporation.

The close relationship that existed between the producer and consumer in earlier centuries has largely given way to a less personal relationship. This has transpired as the United States has progressed from an economy based largely on agriculture and small businesses to today's vast financial, industrial, and information economy. With this transition, the need developed for governmental regulation to assist consumers in the handling of their everyday business affairs. This role is being fulfilled by federal and state legislation and regulation—although the extent of government involvement in these matters remains a hotly contested political issue. Undoubtedly, as globalizations of economies continue, there will be discussions over the need for international economic regulations, as well.

SUMMARY OF KEY CONCEPTS

In this chapter, we have endeavored to impress the importance of the right to enter into contracts and the constitutional proscription against laws impairing contractual obligations. The American economy and social structure are based, to a considerable degree, on private property, as we discussed in the preceding chapter, and the right to contract, discussed in this chapter.

Contracts have their own legal nomenclature, which makes it important to understand how they are classified and the required elements of a contract. The student should grasp the meaning of "offer and acceptance," "consideration," "capacity to contract," and "legality of purpose." It is also necessary to understand the difference between a void and avoidable contract, how the statute of frauds requires certain contracts to be in writing, and how the parol evidence rule protects the sanctity of contracts by preventing oral modification of written agreements that are unambiguous.

As we have explained, many types of contracts can be assigned, but the assignor remains responsible for performance. The most common legal remedy for breach of a contract is a suit for damages; however, in some instances a contract may be rescinded, and for certain contracts, for example, a contract for the sale and purchase of real estate, the uniqueness of the subject of the contract may cause a court to order a party to specifically perform an obligation that has been undertaken.

The importance of commercial transactions in the American economy made it necessary for standard laws and procedures to regulate sales, commercial paper (checks, drafts, notes), secured transactions, and warranties so that commerce can flow freely. The Uniform Commercial Code (UCC), adopted in substance throughout the United States, has largely achieved that goal. It is important for the student to understand the distinction between non-negotiable and negotiable commercial paper and the requirements that must be present for a legal instrument to be negotiable.

Business is transacted largely through structured organizations. The simplest is the sole proprietorship. Somewhat more complex are the partnership and the limited partnership. But vastly important today is the corporation, which affords many advantages in management, perpetual existence, and ease of transferability of ownership, and affords investors the limited liability that attracts widespread ownership in the large publicly owned business in the United States.

Finally, in this chapter we have outlined some of the most significant laws that protect consumers and have provided a brief overview of how federal bankruptcy laws operate.

FOR FURTHER READING

Calamari, John D., and Joseph M. Perillo, *The Law of Contracts* (West 1998).

Helewitz, Jeffrey A., *Basic Contract Law for Paralegals* (5th ed., Aspen Publishers 2007).

Hillman, Robert A., *Principles of Contract Law* (West 2004).

Miller, Arthur S., *The Supreme Court and American Capitalism* (Free Press 1968).

Rohwer, Claude D., and Gordon D. Schaber, *Contracts in a Nutshell* (7th ed., West 2010).

Siegan, Bernard H., *Economic Liberties and the Constitution* (University of Chicago Press 1980).

Wright, Benjamin F., *The Contract Clause of the Constitution* (Harvard University Press 1938).

QUESTIONS FOR THOUGHT AND DISCUSSION

1. What are the essential elements of a contract?
2. In a casual conversation at a party Curtis offers to sell Donald his motorcycle for $600. Donald does not accept the offer; however, the following day he calls Curtis and says, "Get that motorcycle ready to go, I accept your offer." Is there a contract?
3. Trey owes Catherine $25. Catherine promises Trey that if he will pay her the $25 he owes plus an additional $5, she will give him a certain DVD in which he has expressed an interest. Trey pays Catherine the $30. Is there a consideration that will support a contract?
4. What is the purpose of the Statute of Frauds and to what contracts does it apply?
5. What specific areas of contract law are governed by the Uniform Commercial Code?
6. Discuss the advantages that consumers have gained from the spate of federal consumer acts passed during the 1970s.
7. If you were a state legislator assigned to a committee on consumer rights, what specific proposals would you offer?
8. What are the chief differences between a negotiable and a non-negotiable instrument?
9. What is the extent of a credit cardholder's liability when the cardholder loses the credit card?
10. What basic rights does a stockholder possess and how are they exercised?

11. Four individuals intend to lease a building and operate a restaurant. Two have substantial assets; two have experience in food management but minimal assets. What factors should they consider in determining whether to enter a partnership, form a corporation, or create a limited liability company?

12. Megan and Debra are general partners and Christine is a limited partner in a women's clothing shop. During the busy Christmas holiday season, at the request of the general partners, Christine came to the store and helped with sales for two weeks. A few months later a creditor of the partnership filed a suit for collection of an account naming all three as defendants. Christine's attorney asked the court to dismiss her suit, as she was a limited partner. What result is likely? Why?

13. Upon dissolution of a corporation how are the assets distributed?

14. Describe the requirements for an individual to file a voluntary bankruptcy petition under Chapter 11 under the Bankruptcy Abuse Prevention and Consumer Protection Act of 2005.

15. How is a trustee in bankruptcy selected? What are his or her functions?

KEY TERMS

abusive debt collection practices
accord and satisfaction
acts of God
adequacy of consideration
aggregation of capital
ambiguity
annual percentage rate of interest
anticipatory breach
APR
articles of incorporation
assignee
assignment
assignor
bait and switch advertising
Bankruptcy Abuse Prevention and
    Consumer Protection Act of
    2005
bankruptcy proceedings
bilateral contract
blue sky laws
breach of contract
capacity to contract
caveat emptor
certificate of incorporation
check
Check Clearing for the
    21st Century Act
closely held corporations
collateral
commercial paper
common stock

compensatory damages
consideration
continuity of management
corporate charter
corporation
covenant not to compete
credit cardholders
de jure corporation
delegatee
delegator
disaffirm
discharge from debts
domestic corporation
draft
drawee
drawer
Electronic Fund Transfer Act
executed contract
executory contract
express contract
express powers
fictitious name laws
financing statement
force majeure clauses
foreign corporation
formal contracts
full warranty
garnishee
garnishment
garnishor
general partner

holder in due course
illegal act
illusory
implied contract
implied powers
implied warranty
implied warranty of fitness of goods
implied warranty of merchantability
impossibility of performance
informal contracts
insider information
legal guardianship
lemon laws
limited liability
limited liability company
limited partner
limited partnership
limited warranty
liquidated damages
LLC
maker
mutual assent
mutual mistake
negotiable
negotiable instrument
nominal damages
non-delegable duties
non-negotiable
non-performance
offer
offeree

offeror
parol evidence rule
partnership
past consideration
payee
performance
perpetual existence
pierce the corporate veil
pre-existing duty
preferred stock
promisee
promisor
promissory estoppel

promissory note
public policy
publicly traded corporations
puffing
punitive damages
reasonably foreseeable
rescission
security
security agreements
sole proprietorship
specific performance
statute of frauds
suretyship

third-party creditor beneficiary
third-party donee beneficiary
transferability of ownership
ultra vires acts
unconscionability
unconscionable consumer
   contracts
Uniform Commercial Code
unilateral contract
unilateral mistake
usurious rate of interest
void contract
voidable contract

ENDNOTES

1. *Dartmouth Coll. v. Woodward*, 17 U.S. (4 Wheat.) 518, 4 L. Ed. 629 (1819).
2. 196 Va. 493, 84 S.E.2d 516 (1954).
3. *See, e.g., Ford Motor Co. v. Russell*, 519 N.W.2d 460 (Minn. 1994).
4. For a similar scenario, *see Lefkowitz v. Great Minneapolis Surplus Store, Inc.*, 86 N.W.2d 689 (Minn. 1957).
5. *Restatement (Second) of Contracts* §39(1).
6. *Restatement (Second) of Contracts* §61.
7. *See, e.g., Jewish Fedn. of Cent. N.J. v. Barondess*, 560 A.2d 1353 (N.J. 1989).
8. *Restatement (Second) of Contracts* §90(a).
9. *See Twin Forks Ranch, Inc. v. Brooks*, 907 P.2d 1013 (N.M. App. 1995).
10. *Christian v. Christian*, 365 N.E.2d 849, 855 (N.Y. 1977).
11. UCC §2-302. Where a contract is claimed to be or appears to be unconscionable, the parties are to be afforded an opportunity to present evidence as to its commercial setting, purpose, and effect to aid the court in making the determination.
12. Ian Austen, "The Comma That Cost One Million Dollars (Canadian)," *New York Times*, October 25, 2006; available at: http://www.nytimes.com/2006/10/25/business/worldbusiness/25comma.html?_r=0.
13. *United States v. Trans-Missouri Freight Assn.*, 166 U.S. 290, 17 S. Ct. 540, 41 L. Ed. 1007 (1897).
14. *See, e.g., C&A Constr. Co. v. Benning Constr. Co.*, 509 S.W.2d 302 (Ark. 1974).
15. 20 N.Y. 268 (1859).
16. *See Apex Mining Co. v. Chicago Copper Chem. Co.*, 340 F.2d 985 (8th Cir. 1985).
17. *Dartmouth Coll. v. Woodward*, 17 U.S. (4 Wheat.) 518, 636, 4 L. Ed. 629, 659 (1819).
18. *Paul v. Virginia*, 75 U.S. (8 Wall.) 168, 19 L. Ed. 357 (1868).
19. 15 U.S.C. §78(a).
20. 21 U.S.C. §§301-392.
21. 21 U.S.C. §453g.
22. 15 U.S.C. §§41, 45.
23. *See Toledo Pipe-Threading Mach. Co. v. Federal Trade Commn.*, 11 F.2d 337 (6th Cir. 1926).
24. 15 U.S.C. §§1601-1667.
25. 15 U.S.C. §§1671-1677.
26. 15 U.S.C. §1602(j)-(o); 15 U.S.C. §§1642-1644.
27. 15 U.S.C. §1642.
28. 15 U.S.C. §1643a.
29. 15 U.S.C. §§1681-1681t.
30. 15 U.S.C. §1666e-j.
31. 15 U.S.C. §1661i.
32. 15 U.S.C. §§1692-1692o.
33. 15 U.S.C. §2301 et seq.
34. *MacKenzie v. Chrysler Corp.*, 607 F.2d 1162 (5th Cir. 1979).

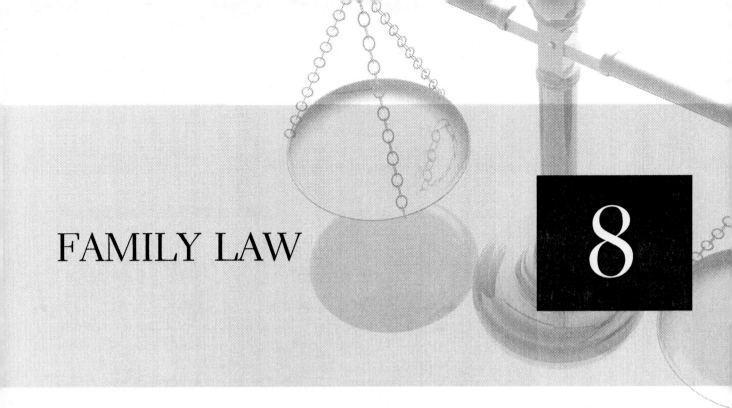

FAMILY LAW

LEARNING OBJECTIVES

This chapter should enable the student to understand:

- the historical background of marriage as an institution, legal consequences of the marriage contract and prenuptial agreements, and the contemporary issues of domestic partnerships and same-sex marriages
- annulment and divorce and the concept of no-fault divorce
- contractual and judicial resolution of issues of alimony and division of property between spouses
- changing attitudes about child custody and support and visitation rights of non-custodial parents, unmarried fathers, and grandparents
- the obligations of paternity and rights of children born out-of-wedlock

CHAPTER OUTLINE

LEARNING OBJECTIVES (CONT.)

- legal procedures for adoptions of children
- the basis of termination of parental rights
- the protection, through guardianship, of the personal and property rights of incapacitated persons
- basic constitutional rights to make reproductive decisions and continuing nuances in abortion rights
- the developing law concerning surrogate motherhood
- legal aspects regarding medical treatment and termination of life support systems.

INTRODUCTION

Family law is an area of the law that touches everyone. It is a dynamic field that is largely governed by state statutes. Many of these statutes have been based on precedent, but molded to a much different society from that which produced those precedents. Family law remains essentially within the domain of the states; however, the federal government has intervened to compel support of dependents, and to assist in health care and in the economic security of families.

Probably the most outstanding characteristic of the family, and hence the hallmark of family law, is change. Law generally follows societal change, and nowhere is this better illustrated than in family law. In earlier centuries, the family dictated one's education, occupation, choice of marriage partners, and social status. Yet, the role of the family has changed as an economy based on agriculture and family industry has given way to vast industrial complexes and is now being melded into a technological and informational society. With these developments comes social changes with an emphasis on privacy and gender equality in areas of life formerly controlled by the traditional family and greatly influenced by organized religion. Many argue that these changes have caused a decline in "family values," while others celebrate the new emphasis on individuality, personal growth, and "free choice." Irrespective of one's perspective, the reality is that the transition of the role of the family frequently has been reflected in divorce, irresponsibility in the support of dependents, and upheavals often resulting in social disorders. Considerable litigation has resulted as family law attempts to address these problems.

In this chapter, we examine the general state of family law. The reader is cautioned that statutes and court decisions usually are controlling in family law and they vary from state to state. Therefore, the principles we discuss should be regarded as illustrative rather than controlling. Moreover, the application of the law can vary considerably depending on the circumstances.

MARRIAGE

Marriage is the social institution that forms the basis of the family unit. In the western world, it has both secular and religious roots. In the United States, marriage is a religious rite for many, but for all, it is a civil contract formed under the laws of the state where it takes place, and it is governed by law. Thus, unlike contracts discussed in the preceding chapter, marriage results in a legal "status" of the parties. The state has a definite interest in regulating the institution of marriage and prescribes certain requirements for its formation and dissolution.

Historical Background of Marriage

Under the early Roman law, a man and woman who lived together and had consensual sexual relations were considered married. Later, Biblical concepts resulted in the Church's regarding marriage as sacramental and indissoluble, imposing age requirements, and forbidding marriage within certain degrees of kindred. As the English common law developed, marriage remained a matter of ecclesiastical law, which recognized informal marriages where a man and woman lived together in a committed relationship. These relationships came to be called **common law marriages**, but they were really informal marriages, not greatly influenced by the developing common law. In the latter half of the nineteenth century, the English Parliament passed the Matrimonial Causes Act, which called for **ceremonial marriages**.

The new American colonies did not insist on ceremonial marriages. But they did recognize what came to be known as common law marriages where a man and woman cohabited in a committed relationship. This institution served a vital function in the colonies and on the frontiers during the westward expansion of the country, as often parties were unable to reach either a civil or religious official to perform a ceremonial marriage. These non-ceremonial marriages became a part of the common law in the new states, and the term "common law marriage" aptly described them. Over time, judicial decisions developed various criteria as essential to the recognition of a common law marriage, one indispensable requisite being that the parties held themselves out to the community as being husband and wife.

Although the new states coming into the Union recognized common law marriage as practiced in the colonies and territories, they soon began to impose statutory requirements concerning age and capacity to marry. Laws prohibited marriage between persons within certain degrees of blood relationship and required a clergyperson or civil official to officiate at a marriage. Almost all states have now abolished common law marriages; however, they recognize the validity of such a marriage that occurred before their prohibitory laws became effective. The question of the validity of these unions can arise in connection with legitimacy of children, inheritance, contract rights, government benefits, and rights of action against a person who has injured or caused the wrongful death of a spouse. Historically, marriage in the United States has been defined as a union between a man and a woman; however, as we note later, in some states this has evolved to include the marriage of same-sex individuals.

Legal Requirements to Marry

Most states have laws stipulating that a marriage cannot be performed where the parties are within close degrees of blood kinship. In addition, one cannot be simultaneously married to two different people. In this regard, in *Reynolds v. United States,*[1] the Supreme Court specifically noted that religious beliefs could not be used as justification for violating a law that prohibited bigamy, which can be defined as marrying a person while still being legally married to a different person.

Otherwise, unmarried persons age eighteen or over who are mentally competent to understand the consequences of their acts are free to marry. With parental consent, most states permit persons age sixteen to marry. A few allow persons as young as fourteen to marry with parental consent. In many states, laws give judges the discretion to approve a marriage of underage parties if the parties are expectant parents or parents of a living child. For example, in Maryland parental consent is required for a person between sixteen and eighteen years of age. Persons under sixteen years of age need both the written consent of a custodial parent or guardian and the written approval of a judge. An individual under age fifteen may not marry. But, as in most states, if you are pregnant, or have a child, the parental consent requirement may be waived.[2]

State statutes prescribe not only the requirements to marry but also the procedures. The usual procedure is for a couple intending to be married to apply to the county clerk, magistrate, or judge for a license. Applicants are required to sign an affidavit that each is unmarried, that they are not within certain degrees of kinship, and that they understand the nature of the marital contract they are about to enter. Often, there is a waiting period before a license issues and the marriage is solemnized. This is to allow applicants in some states to be tested for sexually transmitted diseases and, in a few instances, for HIV. States impose a modest fee to obtain a marriage license and uniformly require that a civil official, priest, minister, or rabbi perform a marriage ceremony. In certain states, a notary public may officiate at a marriage. Marriage ceremonies vary from brief civil proceedings where the parties agree to be married and acknowledge the responsibilities of marriage to elaborate religious rites with extensive ceremonial trappings. Fees paid to those who officiate at marriages vary greatly according to custom and, more frequently, the generosity of the parties. Once the marriage ceremony has been completed, the officiating party endorses the license and returns it to the proper official, whereupon it becomes a public record.

Rights and Obligations of Marital Partners

Until the early nineteenth century, the law in most western countries followed the **unity concept of marriage** and deemed a married couple to legally be one person. Under the rationale of protecting the wife, a husband had legal control over his wife's property and laws restricted married women from entering into contracts or owning property. In 1920, the Nineteenth Amendment to the U.S. Constitution guaranteed women the right to vote, and in the early 1900s, states enacted various statutes known as **emancipation acts** to allow women to own and control their own property. Although these acts allowed women a measure of control over their own property, in most instances these rights were not widely granted to women until the mid-twentieth century.

Today, the law no longer looks upon a marriage in the unity concept of regarding the spouses legally as one person. Married women now have the right to freely enter contracts, the right to their own wages, the right to acquire and dispose of their own property, and the right to bring lawsuits in their own names. (In Chapter 11, we discuss more fully the evolution of the rights of women in the context of federal legislation.)

The contract of marriage differs from other contracts. It results in a **contractual status** that imposes mutual obligations beyond the traditional covenants of fidelity and care that parties orally assume in a marriage ceremony. The status of the relationship has changed. Historically, the husband was the provider with the legal obligation to support his wife and children. Today, spouses have a mutual obligation of support of one another and the offspring of the marriage. Since the 1960s, the emphasis has been on constitutional equality of the sexes. As a result, marriage has become an institution based more on gender equality.

Laws grant certain rights to married persons. For example, federal laws permit spouses to file joint federal income tax returns, allow benefits to surviving spouses in respect to federal estate and gift taxes, provide social security benefits to eligible surviving spouses, and impose certain requirements to enable a spouse to benefit from pension benefits. State laws usually allow one spouse to recover compensation for loss of **consortium**, which is the loss of the injured spouse's services and companionship when the other spouse is permanently injured (for example, in an auto accident) by another person's tort (see Chapter 5). Additionally, a spouse typically has certain entitlements under worker's compensation acts when the other spouse is killed in a work-related accident. State laws also provide certain benefits to spouses in respect to inheritance (see Chapter 6). Moreover, spouses have certain privileges not to testify against one another in court proceedings (see Chapter 9).

Domestic Partnerships and Civil Unions

Because married partners are able to receive special benefits from the government, certain groups have advocated for all those who live together in stable relationships to be granted rights concerning tax credits, health insurance, pensions, inheritance, and authority to make decisions concerning each other's health care. In 2000, Vermont became the first state to provide many of these benefits to same-sex couples by allowing for **civil unions**, which offered partners a legal status tantamount to marriage. Connecticut, New Jersey, and New Hampshire were the next states to permit civil unions, and others followed in subsequent years. Elsewhere, some cities have enacted ordinances to require that employers provide benefits such as health insurance and pension rights to persons in a **domestic partnership** (a term analogous to civil union).[3] A number of large national corporations and educational institutions have voluntarily conferred such benefits on their employees, as well.[4]

Nevertheless, these steps have failed to offer to some people the full connotations of actual marriage, and civil unions and domestic partnerships for same-sex couples have become less prevalent of late—largely because states that once offered these options have moved toward legalization of same-sex marriage. Among the first, the Connecticut Supreme Court ruled in 2008 that excluding same-sex couples from civil marriage violated the state's constitutional guarantee of equal protection of the laws.[5] That decision effectively brought an end to Connecticut's experiment with civil unions and provided for legalization of same-sex marriage. In March 2009, the Vermont legislature also voted to allow same-sex marriage, and existing civil unions in the state were converted to marriages.

As of 2014, a few states continued to offer domestic partner or civil union status to same-sex couples[6] and several states offered these options to different-sex, elderly couples;[7] the latter is connected to the notion that elderly widows and widowers are more likely to live together but opt not to marry in order to retain various social security benefits.

Same-Sex Marriage

For much of the United States' history, marriage was a covenant between a male and a female. Proponents of **same-sex marriage**, though, argue that the traditional limitation of marriage to heterosexual couples runs counter to the notion of equality before the law. In the 1990s, litigants began to challenge the constitutionality of state laws limiting marriage to heterosexual couples. Their first major victory came in Hawaii in 1993, when that state's supreme court ruled that the state must demonstrate a compelling interest in order to restrict marriage to a male and a female.[8]

Opponents of same-sex marriage, however, feared that if Hawaii were to license same-sex unions, other states would be required to do so, as well, under the Full Faith and Credit Clause of the U.S. Constitution.[9] Accordingly, over 30 states (including Hawaii) moved quickly to enact bans on same-sex marriage,[10] and Congress acted swiftly by adopting the Defense of Marriage Act (DOMA) of 1996, which sought to relieve states of the obligation to recognize same-sex marriages. It provided that:

> No State, territory, or possession of the United States, or Indian tribe, shall be required to give effect to any public act, record, or judicial proceeding of any other State, territory, possession, or tribe respecting a relationship between persons of the same sex that is treated as a marriage under the laws of such other State, territory, possession, or tribe, or a right or claim arising from such relationship.[11]

The next major development in this area occurred in December 1999 when the Supreme Court of Vermont ruled that its state constitution's "common benefits" clause required the state legislature to provide same-sex couples the same benefits conferred by law on married couples.[12] The court left it up to the state legislature as to whether to allow gay and lesbian couples to marry or whether to simply allow them the benefits of marriage through some form of domestic partnership, and the legislature opted, at the time, for civil unions.

Soon thereafter, Massachusetts moved a step further and legalized same-sex marriage—a process that commenced with a court ruling. In 2003, in *Goodridge v. Department of Public Health*, the Massachusetts Supreme Judicial Court held that "barring an individual from the protections, benefits, and obligations of civil marriage solely because that person would marry a person of the same sex violates the Massachusetts

Constitution."[13] This decision led to legislative action that legalized same-sex marriage in Massachusetts, making it the first state to do so. Several other states in the Northeast followed suit, and in 2009, Iowa became the first Midwestern state to permit same-sex marriage after its supreme court ruled a ban to be unconstitutional.

Elsewhere, California experienced a bitter and protracted battle over same-sex marriage that generated the first same-sex marriage case to reach the Supreme Court of the United States. In 2008, the California Supreme Court concluded "that the state interest in limiting the designation of marriage exclusively to opposite-sex couples ... cannot properly be considered a compelling state interest for equal protection purposes."[14] Consequently, California issued same-sex marriage licenses from June of 2008 through November of 2008. That practice was halted in November 2008, however, when California voters approved a ballot initiative,[15] Proposition 8, which amended the state constitution to limit marriage to heterosexual couples. This ban was later overturned in 2010 by a federal district court in *Perry v. Schwarzenegger*, but that decision was stayed. Subsequently, in February 2012, the U.S. Court of Appeals for the 9th Circuit also rejected California's Prop. 8 ban on gay marriage, affirming the district court ruling.[16] This appeared to pave the way for the return of same-sex marriage to California, but another appeal followed.

California officials actually refused to challenge the district and circuit court rulings, but the original proponents of the ballot initiative requested review by the Supreme Court of the United States, and certiorari was granted. In *Hollingsworth v. Perry*,[17] the Court stated that those looking to challenge these lower court rulings lacked standing to bring their claim to the Supreme Court, largely because the proponents of the original ballot initiative had not suffered any tangible injury. In effect, then, this decision left the lower court rulings intact, and thus allowed same-sex marriage in California to proceed; by deciding the case through the narrow lens of standing, though, the Supreme Court avoided making any broad proclamations about the legality of same-sex marriage bans in other parts of the country.

In another 2013 decision, *United States v. Windsor*,[18] the Supreme Court took the broader step of striking down the federal government's Defense of Marriage Act, a law that had made it impossible for same-sex partners to acquire certain federal benefits, such as tax credits. More specifically, the *Windsor* case concerned a woman who wished to receive an estate tax exemption typically provided to opposite-sex couples after the death of a spouse. The Court ruled in her favor, striking down the Defense of Marriage Act as violating principles of "due process;" in particular, the Court's decision referenced "a deprivation of the equal liberty of persons that is protected by the Fifth Amendment."[19] The practical effect of the ruling is that marriages recognized by a state also will be recognized by the federal government; accordingly, benefits such as IRS tax credits can be conferred upon those that have a valid same-sex marriage. However, the *Windsor* ruling is limited in that it does not require any state to allow same-sex marriages.[20]

Ultimately, the Supreme Court's decisions essentially have left this matter for the states and lower federal courts to untangle. By September 2014, 19 states and the District of Columbia had legalized same-sex marriage. The exact mechanism for legalization has varied across these states, and includes state supreme court decisions (Connecticut, Iowa, Massachusetts, New Jersey, New Mexico), federal court decisions (California, Oregon, Pennsylvania), popular vote (Maine, Maryland, Washington),[21] and acts of state legislatures (Delaware, Hawaii, Illinois, Minnesota, New Hampshire, Rhode Island, New York, Vermont).

In over a dozen other states, federal court decisions in 2014 struck down bans on same-sex marriage. The typical scenario in these states was for a federal district court to rule that such a ban violated the 14th Amendment's "equal protection clause" (as was the case, for example, in Utah, Michigan, Virginia, Idaho, Oklahoma, and Wisconsin); afterward, in all of these situations, a U.S. Court of Appeals granted review of the lower court ruling.

Throughout 2014, U.S. Courts of Appeals for the 4th, 7th, 9th, and 10th Circuits upheld lower court decisions in favor of allowing same-sex marriage. Later, in October 2014, the Supreme Court refused to review any of these U.S. Court of Appeals' decisions, effectively sanctioning those rulings. In practice, the high Court's denial of review brought the number of states that permit same-sex marriage to 25.

However, things became more complicated in November 2014 when the U.S. Court of Appeals for the Sixth Circuit became the first court of its kind to support a ban on same-sex marriage—a decision that directly affected the states of Michigan, Ohio, Kentucky and Tennessee. States in other circuits, including Kansas (which resides in the 10th Circuit), also attempted to use that 6th Circuit ruling to forge additional review of challenges to their bans. In the end, the presence of divergent circuit court opinions could spur the Supreme Court to hear a same-sex marriage case in the foreseeable future.

Such matters are further complicated when a Court of Appeals issues a stay while it examines a lower court decision. This occurred in March 2014, when the U.S. District Court for the Eastern District of Michigan overturned the state's ban on same-sex marriage. Marriage licenses then were granted to over 300 same-sex couples in the state, until the U.S. Court of Appeals for the 6th Circuit instituted a stay on the lower court ruling, pending review. Although the 6th Circuit eventually upheld Michigan's authority to ban same-sex marriage, U.S. Attorney General Eric Holder announced that the federal government would in fact honor those marriages performed in Michigan before the circuit court's stay was issued.

Lower courts also have been left to untangle ancillary matters related to this issue, such as what happens when a couple with a valid same-sex marriage from one state moves to another state that does not recognize same-sex marriage. This happened in Tennessee, when a federal district court judge allowed two women to be listed on a birth certificate after a same-sex couple from another state moved there.[22] In late 2014, the U.S. Court of Appeals for the 6th Circuit upheld Tennessee's right to refuse to recognize such a marriage. With 15 states still banning same-sex marriage in late 2014, and with many of these bans cemented by provisions in state constitutions, judicial decisions that force one state to recognize marriages from other locations could provide a viable pathway for change in this policy area.

Overall, many of the arguments against same-sex marriage are based on religious beliefs and affiliations. Most, but certainly not all, religions have opposed performance of rites that would give a blessing to a same-sex relationship. Across federal court cases, levels of judicial scrutiny have varied, with some courts using a rational basis test[23] and others, such as a district court in Virginia, using strict scrutiny.[24] Purported interests from government lawyers trying to support bans include promoting morality, preserving an appropriate environment for raising children, promoting procreation, maintaining a consistent definition of marriage, preserving a federalism interest, and maintaining tradition.[25] It remains to be seen whether any court will consider these to be valid interests, but the recent trend among federal district courts is to reject all of them as fitting neither the criteria of a compelling interest (under a strict scrutiny analysis) nor that of a legitimate interest (under the rational basis test).

Ultimately, recent lower court rulings reflect the fact that social attitudes in this area have changed markedly. Today, many people perceive the denial of marriage to same-sex couples as a form of **invidious discrimination**. And, as noted above, courts in several states have found it to be a violation of the principle of equal protection. In summary, it is clear that this issue is far from resolved. Debate will continue in legislative chambers and courtrooms across this country for some time to come. Most observers believe that, sooner or later, the Supreme Court of the United States will provide clarity by offering an opinion that directly uses the 14th Amendment to assess the constitutionality of state bans on same-sex marriage.

Prenuptial Agreements

The rising incidence of divorce, the fact that multiple marriages during one's lifetime are no longer uncommon, and the right of each spouse to separately accumulate property have caused an increase in the use of **prenuptial agreements**. A prenuptial agreement is a contract entered into by persons before they marry. The typical agreement stipulates the property rights of each spouse during marriage, upon death, and in the event of divorce. These agreements are more common where the parties' assets are disproportionate. Wealthy individuals often rely on such agreements to protect their substantial assets from transfer to a spouse. Older couples that are marrying for a second time, especially those who have children by their previous marriages and a desire to conserve their respective estates for their own children and grandchildren, may find a prenuptial agreement to be an attractive option.

If a spouse attacks the validity of a prenuptial agreement, courts often inquire as to whether the parties made a full disclosure of each other's financial resources before the agreement was entered into and whether the agreement meets basic standards of fairness. The issue of coercion sometimes arises, as well. For example, coercion may be found where just before a wedding ceremony, a wealthy male presents his bride with an agreement providing minimal rights. Courts tend to look more favorably on enforcement of a prenuptial agreement if, before the agreement was signed, each party made a full and fair disclosure of assets well in advance of the marriage ceremony, and each party reviewed the agreement with separate legal counsel.

Although not nearly as prevalent as prenuptial contracts, **post-nuptial agreements** are sometimes used where parties did not anticipate the need for a prenuptial agreement. Courts tend to scrutinize such an agreement to determine if it was fair when entered into and that it was not signed under the threat of a divorce. When a divorce follows, courts sometimes insist on determining if the agreement is fair and just as of the time of a divorce. As in the case of a prenuptial agreement, full disclosure of financial resources and independent legal counsel bolster the prospect that a court will look favorably upon enforcing of a post-nuptial agreement.

DIVORCE AND ANNULMENT

Divorce and **annulment** both have the same basic objective—**dissolution of a marriage** contract—but they differ in court processes and legal effects. A divorce presupposes a valid marriage and is a judicial decree dissolving the bonds of matrimony. An annulment, on the other hand, is a judicial recognition that a valid marriage did not take place. An annulment and a divorce each leave the parties free to contract a new marriage. However, a divorce does not necessarily relieve a party from obligations that have grown out of the marriage.

Annulment

An annulment is a judicial decree that no valid marriage existed. It is granted only on petition of a party who was unaware of an impediment to a valid marriage. These impediments might include a party's existing marriage, a party's mental incapacity, a party's physical incapacity to consummate the marriage, or the marriage's being the result of fraud or intoxication.

In earlier years, it was difficult to obtain a divorce, and a stigma was attached to being divorced. Thus, annulments were sought far more frequently than they are today. Although annulments are infrequent today in the civil courts, they are more common in the tribunals of the Roman Catholic Church, for if the church finds that a marriage is invalid from a canonical standpoint, under certain circumstances it will grant an annulment. While the annulment by the church has no legal effect, **canon law** allows a person whose marriage has been annulled to remarry within the church. Of course, before remarrying, a person whose marriage a religious tribunal has annulled must still obtain a decree of divorce from a civil court.

Legal Separation

When a marriage becomes an intolerable burden, some spouses voluntarily decide to live apart from one another. This does not alter the spouses' legal responsibilities to one another or to their children. In other instances, a husband and wife who agree to separate may opt for a more formal **legal separation** by entering into an agreement to live apart to await a resolution of problems that led to their separation or to await making a considered judgment of whether to dissolve their marriage. A formal separation agreement may simply provide for an agreement to live separately without interference from one another. But in many instances, the parties effectuate a settlement of their property rights and the custody of their children. Such an agreement is often a prelude to dissolving the marriage and usually contains a stipulation that should the marriage be dissolved, and subject to the approval of the court, the agreement is to become a part of any final judgment of divorce or dissolution. As in the case with prenuptial and post-nuptial agreements, separation agreements that settle support and custodial responsibilities and property rights can have long-lasting effects; thus, they should only be entered into advisedly, after careful review by each party's lawyer.

Separate Maintenance

Many states have statutory provisions regarding the award of what is sometimes known as **separate maintenance,** or allowing alimony without dissolution of marriage. A wife who is living apart from her husband and who is in need of support can file a petition for separate maintenance in some states. Separate maintenance proceedings were more common when states granted divorce based on fault rather than under modern no-fault dissolution-of-marriage laws. Sometimes this procedure is used as a way to provide a "cooling-off period" or is chosen because of religious scruples against divorce. The proceedings contemplate an award of alimony and support to a wife based on the economic circumstances of the husband and wife and may allow a parent, sometimes referred to as a custodial parent or one with shared responsibility, the right to the exclusive use and occupancy of the marital home. Such proceedings, however, do not ordinarily contemplate a resolution of the parties' interests in property acquired during the marriage. In some states, the court will award a reasonable attorney's fee to a party awarded separate maintenance who can demonstrate a need for such assistance.

Divorce

Before 1857, the English ecclesiastical court had jurisdiction over actions relating to marriage. These courts did not grant absolute divorces; rather, they could grant an annulment or a **divorce *a mensa et thoro*** (a divorce from bed and board). For a wife to obtain a divorce from bed and board, she had to demonstrate that her husband was at fault and that she was entitled to live separately and receive alimony from him. This is similar to the separate maintenance proceedings discussed in the preceding topic. In the United States, the idea of ecclesiastical courts was unacceptable to the new settlers, and jurisdiction over divorce and other domestic relations matters was vested in chancery courts.

Historically, a party seeking a divorce had to file a petition in the state that was considered the **matrimonial domicile** of the parties. As a result of a series of decisions from the U.S. Supreme Court, after 1942 it was no longer necessary that a divorce be granted in the state of the last matrimonial domicile. Rather, a petitioner can establish residence "in good faith" in the state where the petitioner seeks to obtain a divorce. Under the fault concept of divorce, this became important because the grounds for divorce varied greatly among the states. As an example, for many years, New York would grant divorce only on the ground of adultery. Thus, there was an incentive for a party seeking a divorce to apply for it in a state with liberal grounds for divorce and where residency could be established in a relatively short time. This brought many petitioners to establish residence and to seek a divorce in Florida, in Nevada, or in another state that had minimal residency requirements and a variety of grounds for divorce. A spouse who leaves the matrimonial domicile and obtains a divorce decree in another state, however, may still be subject to further proceedings concerning alimony, support, and custody rights in the state where the other spouse remained. This depends on various factors, one of which is whether the respondent spouse appears in the case in person or through counsel.

The Fault Concept

In the United States, courts granted a divorce only when a spouse alleged and proved one of the statutory grounds for divorce. These grounds varied among the states but usually included adultery, habitual intemperance, extreme cruelty, ungovernable temper, abandonment, impotency, non-support, and insanity. A few states allowed a divorce after a spouse disappeared for a period of seven years. The respondent could contest the grounds alleged and assert such defenses as condonation (my spouse condoned the actions now complained of) or recrimination (my spouse is just as guilty as I of the ground alleged for divorce), or the respondent spouse also could enter a countersuit for divorce.

If the court, after hearing the parties and their witnesses, determined that the petitioner or respondent had established grounds for divorce, it would enter a decree granting the divorce in favor of the party "not at fault." The **fault concept** had an important bearing on alimony that would be awarded and often on the issue of custody of the parties' children, as well as the visitation rights of the other party. Alimony and support money typically were awarded to the wife based upon her needs and the needs of the children, if any, and the husband's ability to pay. Historically, alimony was considered an obligation on the part of a husband which was to be paid periodically during the former wife's lifetime or until her remarriage. The obligated party (almost invariably the husband) was required to pay support money for children until each child attained majority or married.

Under the fault concept, the primary objective of each party was to prove the other party at fault, and this often led to incredible testimony. Sometimes, one spouse would be willing to "pay more" or "accept less" to avoid having to disclose the details of private matters in a public judicial forum. One spouse even might hire a detective to try to "get the goods" on the other spouse by proving some marital indiscretion. The emotional scars left by graphic court testimony often remained long after a contested divorce was final. By the 1960s, it became evident to most lawmakers that the time had come to change the laws concerning dissolution of marriage and, to some extent, the criteria to determine attendant responsibilities of the parties.

No-Fault Divorce

In the 1960s, the states began to move from eligibility for a divorce based on one spouse's being "at fault" to the concept of **no-fault dissolution of marriage.** By the 1980s, the transition to no-fault divorce was virtually complete. Today, some states retain grounds for divorce under the fault concept, but all states offer some basis of dissolving a marriage where the marriage is **irretrievably broken.**

The objective of the newer no-fault approach is to enable spouses to dissolve a marriage without becoming adversaries and to eliminate the accusations spouses formerly lodged against one another in attempting to prove the other to be at fault in the marriage. The no-fault approach effectively eliminates proof of a party's fault and the old defenses to divorce that we discussed in the preceding topic. And while some states continue to maintain some of the traditional grounds for divorce, the reality is that marriages usually are dissolved based on the no-fault concept of the marriage's being irretrievably broken. Should the respondent deny that the marriage is irretrievably broken, the court may refer the parties to counseling, postpone determination for a brief period, or simply take testimony to determine whether to grant the dissolution. Contests on the issue of a petitioner's ground for dissolution are now rare. If the petitioner convinces the court that the marriage is beyond reconciliation, that is usually sufficient. Contests in dissolution proceedings now focus on issues of alimony, property division, custody (shared parental responsibility) issues, and support of children. If a spouse has cause that the other spouse may react violently to a petition for dissolution, the court may be asked to issue a temporary restraining order that prohibits the apprehensive spouse from making contact with the other spouse.

All states require the petitioner to establish certain **residence requirements** to allow the court to take jurisdiction of the proceedings. The duration of such requirements varies from as little as ninety days to about two years. The petitioner must cause the respondent spouse to be served by legal process, as well as with a copy of the petition reciting the statutory ground for dissolution and demands for relief in other areas, such as alimony, support, custody arrangements, property division, and attorney's fees.

Today, parties in dissolution-of-marriage proceedings often resolve their problems concerning **alimony**, **child support**, and **visitation**, and memorialize their resolution of these points by written agreement—usually after consultation with their legal counsel. The parties can request the court to incorporate their agreement into the final judgment of dissolution of marriage. Such a request is normally granted if the court finds the agreement to be fair and reasonable.

As no-fault laws have progressed, the process of obtaining dissolution of marriage has become simpler. In 1983, a California appellate court pointed out that proceedings for dissolution of marriage are no longer actions by which one party seeks redress for wrongs committed by another and that the concept of a "cause of action" by one party against the other is wholly foreign to family proceedings under its Family Law Act.[26] This appears to be rather typical of the view courts now take of proceedings for dissolution of marriage. Indeed, where no children have been born of the marriage and the parties are each capable of self-support, many petitioners routinely appear in court without legal counsel. Ultimately, the court proceedings are essentially pro forma; dissolution will likely be granted based on proof of the petitioning spouse's durational residency requirement and minimal testimony by the petitioner that shows the irretrievable breakdown of the marriage.

Alimony

Alimony is the allowance to a spouse imposed by a court that grants a divorce. The concept of alimony stems from the English common law requirement that a husband must support his wife during her lifetime or until she remarries. A wife who was guilty of marital misconduct was not awarded alimony. In making awards of alimony, American courts generally required the husband to make weekly or monthly payments. Courts articulated many factors to be considered in determining the amount of alimony to be awarded. These included the ages and stations in life of the parties, their physical and mental health, the duration of the marriage, the wife's needs, and the husband's ability to pay. Often, the court's judgment was affected to some extent by which party was found to be at "fault" in the marriage. In some states, the legislature provided that no alimony could be awarded to a wife who was guilty of adultery.

In the United States, legislatures and courts characteristically viewed alimony much as did the common law, that is, as an obligation of the husband and an entitlement to a wife. This view was unacceptable to the U.S. Supreme Court, which in 1979 held that alimony statutes that provide for awards only to wives violated the Equal Protection Clause of the Fourteenth Amendment to the U.S. Constitution.[27] Thereafter, it was necessary for states to either amend their statutes to provide for awards to both the husband and the wife or, at least, that courts apply alimony statutes on a **sex-neutral basis**. By this time, the concept of alimony had undergone considerable change and courts tended to award permanent alimony primarily to spouses of long-term marriages or in those instances where disabling injuries prevented a spouse from achieving self-support. Usually, the scenario that would justify an award of permanent alimony would be where an older wife had fulfilled the traditional role of mother and homemaker and had not enjoyed the opportunity to pursue a career on her own—and thus was not capable of sustaining herself.

The Uniform Marriage and Divorce Act (UMDA) was approved by the National Conference of Commissioners on Uniform State Laws in 1970 and has been adopted in nine states. Even where the UMDA has not been adopted, courts refer to the criteria it offers for determining whether to award a party "maintenance," a term that the UMDA uses instead of alimony.[28] As amended in 1973, §308 of the UMDA provides for consideration of the following relevant factors when a court awards maintenance to a spouse:

(1) The financial resources of the party seeking maintenance, including marital property apportioned to him, his ability to meet his needs independently, and the extent to which a provision for support of a child living with the party includes a sum for the party as custodian;

(2) The time necessary to acquire sufficient education or training to enable the party seeking maintenance to find appropriate employment;

(3) The standard of living established during the marriage;

(4) The duration of the marriage;

(5) The age and physical and emotional condition of the spouse seeking maintenance; and

(6) The ability of the spouse from whom maintenance is sought to meet his needs while meeting those of the spouse seeking maintenance.

The above criteria seem to read like a mental checklist of the factors that judges traditionally consider, even absent statutory criteria.

The advent of no-fault divorce brought with it new perspectives on alimony awards. During the 1970s, the concept of **rehabilitative alimony** emerged through statutory enactments. Rehabilitative alimony is designed to provide short-term alimony and is awarded based on the time required for a divorced spouse to be educated or trained to become self-sufficient. The trial court fixes the amount of payments and a termination date for payments based on the proposed plan of rehabilitation for the recipient. The court also will consider a modification of the payments before the termination date if the recipient can show a justification. Trial judges are given broad discretion in awarding rehabilitative alimony, and absent an abuse of that discretion appellate courts are very reluctant to vacate or modify such awards. Traditionally, alimony terminated upon a former spouse's remarriage, but courts differ on whether remarriage should preclude instead of terminate an obligated spouse's liability for rehabilitative alimony. A strong argument can be made to have the payments continue until that rehabilitation has been accomplished.

Despite the tendency to award rehabilitative alimony, there are still instances where an award of **permanent alimony** serves an important role in dissolution-of-marriage proceedings. Consider, for example, dissolution of a long-term marriage. The male spouse is fifty-five years of age and possesses no marketable skills or talents and suffers from health problems. The parties have few marital assets, but the wife is gainfully employed at a good salary. Such a male spouse presents no actual and little potential capacity for self-support to enable him to live in the standard he enjoyed while married. A husband in those circumstances might present a court with a compelling case for an award of permanent alimony.

A spouse sometimes requests that the alimony be paid as a lump sum rather than in periodic installments, and the lump sum may consist of assets other than cash. Where a wife establishes entitlement to permanent alimony but the husband has limited resources and the wife requires the marital home as a place to raise the parties' minor children, courts sometimes award a husband's interest in the marital home place to the wife as lump sum alimony. In other instances, the wife may be given the right of occupancy of the home place until the youngest child attains majority, whereupon the home place might be sold and the proceeds distributed according to an order of the court.

Attorney's Fees

In many states, statutes allow courts to award **attorney's fees** to a spouse in a marital action "to level the playing field" if the requesting spouse can show an inability to retain counsel or where the other spouse has a greater ability to pay litigation expenses. Courts may sometimes award temporary attorney's fees to a spouse who requires such assistance to conduct litigation. Where the income flow of the parties is disproportionate, courts often award attorney's fees at final hearing incident to the equitable distribution of property.

Property Settlement Agreements

Parties in divorce litigation commonly enter into **property settlement agreements** to avoid the necessity for a judicial distribution of marital assets. Such agreements are generally executed only after counsel has had an opportunity to determine the nature and extent of the assets of the parties. This is usually accomplished through interrogatories and discovery depositions during the course of litigation.

Property settlement agreements can afford federal income tax advantages to a recipient, who is generally not taxed on the assets received, whereas alimony payments are taxable to the recipient and deductible to the party paying the alimony. But there also can be disadvantages. Alimony is subject to modification based on a substantial change in the needs of the recipient and the obligated party's ability to pay. In contrast, property settlement agreements are contractual and require far greater evidence of a party's unforeseeable change in circumstances before being subject to modification. Courts review these agreements, and if it appears that an agreement has been entered into advisedly, the court, upon request, can incorporate the agreement into the final judgment of dissolution of marriage.

Court-Imposed Distributions of Property

When the parties to a dissolution proceeding do not arrive at an amicable distribution of their marital assets, it becomes the trial court's responsibility to order a fair and equitable division of assets. The common law method was to allow each party to retain those assets titled in a party's name. This approach typically favored the husband in divorce litigation, and with the changing role of women in society it became essential for courts to look beyond legal titles in order to arrive at fair and just settlements of marital assets. Courts have developed different theories to cause a fair distribution of the marital assets.

One method of achieving a fair distribution of property in some states, while not disregarding the concept of title to assets, has been to award a spouse a **special equity** in property. Suppose the wife had received a substantial inheritance and used her separate funds to make the down payment on a home that became titled jointly in the husband and wife. A court might award the wife a special equity beyond her ordinary marital share equal to her special contribution to the marital residence. Courts have applied the special equity doctrine to all types of personal and real property. In other instances, courts have attempted to arrive at a fair distribution of property by awarding a party **lump sum alimony** to supplement that party's distributive share of the parties' assets. Nevertheless, more effective means of arriving at a fair distribution of marital property became essential.

One such method incorporated the notion of **community property**. Arizona, California, Idaho, Louisiana, Nevada, New Mexico, Texas, Washington, and Wisconsin are **community property states**. Statutes in these states treat all property as belonging equally to the husband and wife unless the property was acquired before the marriage, as a gift, or through inheritance. In these states, when a marriage is dissolved or annulled, the problem of making distribution of property is simpler because the marital assets belong equally to the husband and wife. Where community property is not susceptible to a division in kind, the court can order it sold and divide the proceeds equally between the husband and wife. Yet, even in community property states, courts sometimes must make adjustments in property distributions in order to arrive at a fair allocation of assets upon dissolution of marriage.

Today, most states (other than community property states) have moved toward distributing marital assets on a basis called **equitable distribution**. Equitable distribution does not mandate an equal distribution, although some courts have said that is a good starting point. Unlike the common law approach, the first step is for the court to determine which assets constitute marital property and which assets are separate properties. Many forms of real and personal property, for example, homes, vehicles, stocks and bonds, and pension rights, are subject to being divided and equitably distributed between spouses.

The Divorce Code of Pennsylvania sets forth factors that courts are to consider in their division of marital property. It also provides that the weight to be given to the factors in determining the equitable distribution of assets is within the discretion of the trial court.[29] These factors are:

(1) The length of the marriage.

(2) Any prior marriage of either party.

(3) The age, health, station, amount and sources of income, vocational skills, employability, estate, liabilities and needs of each of the parties.

(4) The contribution by one party to the education, training or increased earning power of the other party.

(5) The opportunity of each party for future acquisitions of capital assets and income.

(6) The sources of income of both parties, including, but not limited to, medical, retirement, insurance or other benefits.

(7) The contribution or dissipation of each party in the acquisition, preservation, depreciation or appreciation of the marital property, including the contribution of a party as homemaker.

(8) The value of the property set apart to each party.

(9) The standard of living of the parties established during the marriage.

(10) The economic circumstances of each party at the time the division of property is to become effective.

(10.1) The Federal, State and local tax ramifications associated with each asset to be divided, distributed or assigned, which ramifications need not be immediate and certain.

(10.2) The expense of sale, transfer or liquidation associated with a particular asset, which expense need not be immediate and certain.

(11) Whether the party will be serving as the custodian of any dependent minor children.

Some states' laws either prohibit or restrict the courts from treating public pension benefits as marital property. Federal law provides for civil service retirement benefits to be paid pursuant to a court decree of divorce, annulment, or legal separation.[30] But the Supreme Court's 1981 ruling that federal law precluded a state court from making a division of military pensions in proceedings involving military retirees proved to be an obstacle to equitable distribution.[31] The problem was short-lived, as the following year Congress enacted the Uniformed Services Former Spouses' Protection Act.[32] The Act allows a state court to order a division of military retired pay as part of a distribution of marital property in a divorce case. If the parties' marriage lasted for ten years or more concurrent with military service, a former spouse may receive court-ordered payments directly from the government's military finance center, though not in excess of 50 percent of the serviceperson's retired pay.

Elsewhere, the New York legislature has prescribed equitable distribution of **marital property** in divorce and annulment proceedings.[33] Marital property under New York law includes all property acquired by either or both spouses during marriage and before execution of a separation agreement or commencement of matrimonial action, regardless of the form in which title is held. The state's appellate division held that even a college degree obtained during the marriage is to be considered as marital property.[34]

Moreover, the New York courts are authorized to make orders concerning the use and occupancy of the marital home, regardless of the form of ownership. The court may make a distributive award where equitable distribution is impracticable, burdensome, or contrary to law, or to supplement distribution of marital property. Like most states, New York does not impose equitable distribution in respect to property that a spouse has acquired by will, inheritance, or gift.[35]

Because the dissolution of a marriage is absolute, courts attempt to make a distribution of property that will likewise be absolute. As the Supreme Court of Maine pointed out in 1995, courts should endeavor to divide marital property in such a manner as to avoid continued financial interaction between the parties.[36]

CHILD CUSTODY, SUPPORT, AND PATERNITY

The English common law principle of granting custody of minor children to a father yielded to an approach in the United States of courts' usually granting custody of young children, particularly **children of "tender years"** (considered to include preteen children), to the mother. This was based on the presumption that the mother was the primary caregiver. In some instances, courts would grant custody of older boys to their father. Under the "tender years" doctrine, it was very difficult for a father to obtain custody of young children unless he could prove the mother to be an unfit parent. In the early twentieth century, courts developed the **best interests of the child test** and attempted to award custody to the parent who could best serve the interests of the child. Again, in a time when most mothers of young children did not work outside the home, the mother was traditionally favored as being the parent who could serve the best interests of a child.

Changing Attitudes on Child Custody

With the increased number of mothers who now work outside the home, young children are often cared for by child care centers, and courts are prone to give more consideration to a father on issues of child custody. Fathers today occupy a somewhat different role in the family than in previous generations. Many fathers share household duties and have developed far more parenting skills than fathers in previous generations. Court opinions in custody matters often make declarations to the effect that custody must be determined on a gender-neutral basis, giving both parents equal consideration. A catalyst for this change was an opinion by the U.S. Supreme Court in 1971 (in a case unrelated to custody) holding that the Equal Protection Clause of the Fourteenth Amendment prevented courts from making judgments based on gender.[37,38] Yet, some courts still tend to find that circumstances dictate that the mother of younger children should be the caregiver of choice and so make custody awards accordingly.

In attempting to determine the best interests of the child, courts have articulated numerous criteria to be considered in making an award of custody. Reasons most commonly advanced by courts include:

- the parent more likely to allow the child frequent contact with the non-custodial parent
- the physical and mental health and moral fitness of the parents
- the emotional ties between the child and the parents
- the permanence of the existing or proposed custodial home
- the ability and disposition of parents to provide necessaries, including medical care.

Courts also may consider the expressed preference of older children, and such factors as the school and community affiliations and educational opportunities that will be served by the custodial parent. Historically, the religious preferences of the parents played a significant role in custody awards, but increasingly the religious practices of a parent are considered irrelevant as long as those practices do not pose a threat to a child's welfare. And while the issue of a party's misconduct has been largely removed by no-fault divorce laws with respect to most questions in dissolution-of-marriage cases, many courts still consider the moral conduct of the parties in deciding issues of child custody.[39] In former decades, an adulterous parent was routinely denied custody of children, but the trend today is for courts to determine whether such activities pose harm to a child and to make custody decisions accordingly.

In the past, gay and lesbian parents have experienced considerable difficulty in being awarded custody. Some states still have laws or court decisions stating that gay men and lesbians are not to be awarded custody of children; however, as society has come to more readily accept these lifestyles, several states now have statutes or court decisions declaring that sexual orientation is irrelevant in considering custody and visitation issues.

In cases with multiple children, the policy of the law typically has been to keep all children together rather than divide their custody between the parents. The rationale is that, absent compelling reasons to split the custody of children between the parents, children should not be deprived of growing up together with some common denominator of discipline and the advantages of sharing mutual experiences within the home and family unit.[40]

Traditionally, courts have awarded the custody of children to one parent and granted the **right of visitation** to the non-custodial parent. Court decrees frame this right as one allowing reasonable visitation, but where the parties cannot arrive at amicable visitation schedules, courts will define visitations with reference to times and places.

Shared Custody and Shared Parental Responsibility

During the 1980s, state legislatures began to provide a new concept for child custody called **shared parental responsibility**, which represented an expansion of a concept formerly referred to as **joint custody**. Shared parental responsibility recognizes that both parents continue to have responsibility for rearing a child. The objective in shared parental custody is for one parent to maintain the **primary physical residence** of the child but for both parents to retain full parental rights and responsibilities and to confer on major decisions affecting the welfare of the child. Thus, the concept of primary physical residence is divided from the responsibility for decisions regarding the child's education, discipline, and general upbringing. The court may allocate the parental rights and responsibilities for the care of the children to both parents and issue a shared parenting order that requires the parents to share all or some of the aspects of the physical and legal care of the children in accordance with the approved plan. Trial judges are vested with considerable discretion in determining whether to grant sole custody with rights of visitation or whether to grant joint custody. But, the recent trend of judicial decisions is to grant joint or shared custody, even in cases with children of "tender years."

Custody and Visitation Rights of Parents of Children Born Out-of-Wedlock

At common law, all courts recognized that the mother of a child born out-of-wedlock had sole custody of the child and the putative (or reputed) father had no rights unless he married the mother. But in 1972, the U.S. Supreme Court held that parents are constitutionally entitled to a hearing on their fitness before their children are removed from their custody.[41] In 1976, the Kentucky Supreme Court reasoned that if the biological father of children born out-of-wedlock has the constitutional right to a hearing before his right to custody is terminated, it follows that a biological father of a child born out-of-wedlock would have the right of visitation with his child.[42] The court went on to explain that a **putative father** has a right to reasonable access to his illegitimate child where he contributes to the child's support and there is no showing that such right would be detrimental to the child's best interests. Most courts have followed this view, often emphasizing that the visitation rights are to be determined in relation to the best interests of the child.

Modification of Custody Arrangements and Child Support Orders

Court decrees awarding child custody or shared parental rights are subject to modification; however, to promote stability in the parent-child relationship, courts hold that to obtain a **modification of custody** or shared parental rights the petitioner must show that there has been a substantial change in circumstance of either the parents or the child since the original custody decree. Likewise, a support order is subject to modification based on a substantial change in the needs of the child or in the ability of a parent to pay.

CASE IN POINT

IS JOINT CUSTODY APPROPRIATE FOR CHILDREN OF TENDER YEARS?
Church v. Church
North Carolina Court of Appeals
458 S.E.2d 732 (N.C. App. 1995)

The North Carolina Court of Appeals reviewed a trial court decision granting joint custody where the parents separated after some four years of marriage at a time when their son was about three years old and had been cared for primarily by the mother. The trial court awarded joint custody over the mother's objection, and she appealed. The appellate court cited the state statute providing that an order for custody of a minor should award custody to "such person . . . that will best promote the interest and welfare of the child." Despite the mother's contention that the father had testified that other parties also would care for the child in his absence, the appellate court noted that the evidence at trial sustained the trial court's findings that both parties were of excellent character, both were active in church activities, and both were fit and proper persons to have custody of their child; thus, the best interests of the child would be promoted by awarding joint custody. The appellate court affirmed the trial court's decision.

What About the Grandparents?

At common law, grandparents had no legal rights regarding their grandchildren. Today, those rights are governed by statutes. There are an estimated seventy million grandparents in the United States, and the increased longevity of the elderly afford them more opportunities to visit their grandchildren. Grandparents traditionally have played an important role through their relationships with grandchildren. Furthermore, given the proportion of marriages with minor children that have ended in dissolution in the past fifty years, the role of grandparents has become even more significant. To ensure that grandparents have rights to visit their grandchildren, all fifty states have enacted statutes allowing **grandparents' visitation** rights. In some instances, statutes allow visitation by others under varying circumstances that serve the best interests of the child.

Statutes that authorize judges to grant visitation rights to grandparents have met with different reactions from courts, usually based on their statutory criteria. Some courts have ruled that such statutes violate the **parents' right of privacy**; in other instances, courts have upheld such statutes. Overall, court decisions vary greatly depending on the language of the statute involved and the circumstances of the parties.

In 1994, the legislature in the State of Washington enacted Wash. Rev. Code §26.10.160(3), which permitted "[a]ny person to petition for visitation rights at any time and authorized trial judges to grant such rights whenever visitation may serve a child's best interest." In reviewing the statute, the Supreme Court of Washington held that a state may interfere with these parental rights only to prevent harm or potential harm to a child. The court then observed that the Washington statute did not require a threshold showing of harm and permitted any person to petition at any time, with the only requirement being that the visitation serves the best interest of the child. Thus, it held that the statute unconstitutionally infringed on the fundamental right of parents to rear their children.[43]

The U.S. Supreme Court granted review and on June 5, 2000, affirmed the judgment of the Washington Supreme Court.[44] Justice O'Connor wrote the plurality opinion of the Court, noting:

> A parent's estimation of the child's best interest is accorded no deference.... §26.10.160(3), as applied here, exceeded the bounds of the Due Process Clause.... There is a presumption that fit parents act in their children's best interests ... there is normally no reason for the State to inject itself into the private realm of the family to further question fit parents' ability to make the best decisions regarding their children.... Because the instant decision rests on §26.10.160(3)'s sweeping breadth ... there is no need to consider ... whether the Due Process Clause requires all nonparental visitation statutes to include a showing of harm or potential harm to the child as a condition precedent to granting visitation or to decide the precise scope of the parental due process right in the visitation context.[45]

Although such broad, sweeping statutes as enacted by the Washington legislature are doomed by the Supreme Court's decision, the Court's opinion does not seem to foreclose upholding grandparents' visitation rights on a case-by-case basis—perhaps under more narrowly drawn statutes that give special weight to parents' decisions regarding third-party visitation in the "best interests" of the children. In determining the best interests of the child, judges must exercise considerable discretion and consider a number of factors, including the moral fitness of the grandparents, the supervision they supply, and the grandparents' understanding that the rearing of grandchildren is the parents' responsibility. When statutes permit visitation where it serves the best interests of the child and courts craft a visitation order narrowly drawn to accomplish only a minimal intrusion on parental rights, courts tend to uphold grandparents' rights to visit. A question to ponder, though, is whether visitation statutes should make a distinction between children in intact families and children in the custody of one parent.

The Uniform Child Custody Jurisdiction Enforcement Act

As divorce has become more common and the population more mobile, the courts have been plagued with **interstate disputes concerning child custody**. Parents also have shifted children from one jurisdiction to another, thereby producing controversies over child custody and visitation rights. In 1968, this led the National Conference of Commissioners on Uniform State Laws to propose the Uniform Child Custody Jurisdiction Act. The Act received the approval of the American Bar Association and was adopted (sometimes with revisions) by legislatures in all fifty states. In 1997, the National Conference of Commissioners on Uniform State Laws revised and renamed the model statute the Uniform Child Custody Jurisdiction Enforcement Act (UCCJEA). The revised Act has been adopted in nearly all the states.

The basic purpose of the UCCJEA is to avoid jurisdictional competition and conflict with courts of other states. It is designed to promote cooperation toward the objective that a custody decree is rendered in the state that is in the best position to decide the case in the best interests of the child. More specifically, the Act seeks to ensure that litigation concerning custody takes place in the state where the child and the family have the closest connection and to limit custody determination to one state. This requires a court to decline to exercise jurisdiction when the child and the family have a closer connection with another state. Some of the practices the Act seeks to prevent are relitigation of custody disputes by a parent who loses custody in one jurisdiction and **child snatching** (the wrongful taking of a child by a parent, usually occurring incident to a custody dispute). To minimize the duration of the period of uncertainty and turmoil in a child's life, the UCCJEA directs courts to expeditiously handle jurisdictional issues.

The Parental Kidnapping Prevention Act

Some states made revisions in their adoption of the Uniform Child Custody Jurisdiction Enforcement Act that tended to weaken its application. So, despite the improvements in child custody proceedings that resulted from its adoption, Congress determined that further measures were necessary to deter **interstate abduction** of children by parents. In 1980, Congress enacted the Parental Kidnapping Prevention Act (PKPA).[46] The primary purposes of the Act are to prevent jurisdictional conflicts over child custody and to reduce any incentive for parental "child snatching" in custody matters. Because it is federal law, the PKPA takes precedence over any state law, including the UCCJA and UCCJEA.

The Support Requirement

The traditional view that the father is the parent charged with financial support of minor children has yielded to the modern view that support of children is the equal responsibility of the mother and father. Accordingly, a parent's responsibility for child support arises as a result of the child's birth; dissolution of marriage does not relieve a parent from that obligation. Of course, when dissolution occurs, the court may determine the **custodial parent** and non-custodial parent have disproportionate obligations for support of their children.

The obligation for support of an adopted child is the same as for a child born of the adoptive parents' marriage. An **illegitimate child** (sometimes referred to today as a **child-out-of-wedlock**) has the same right of support from the putative father as does a legitimate child. As we discuss in a later topic, courts must sometimes establish this responsibility through a judicial proceeding determining paternity. A parent's obligation to support a minor child can generally only be terminated by death of the parent or child, by the child's attaining majority or emancipation, by the child's marrying, or by his or her entry into the armed forces.

Determining the Amount of Child Support

In dissolution of marriage, the parties often seek agreement on the types and amounts of support for children. Sometimes these agreements are hammered out in a process of court-imposed or voluntary **mediation**. Any such agreement is subject to court approval. In the absence of the parents' agreeing on **child support requirements**, when making an award, a court considers each parent's assets, liabilities, and sources of income. In the past decade, many states have developed guidelines for support of children to cover the reasonable needs for housing, clothing, food, education, medical care, and other expenses related to child care and upbringing.

Usually, a court orders child support payments to be made on a periodic basis to the custodial or primary residential parent. Increasingly, the practice is to require the payments to be made through a central agency, such a court clerk, in order that accurate records are maintained. Court orders for child support are always subject to modification when the custodial parent experiences a substantial rise in costs of education, medical expenses, and housing. Another factor that often affects the amount of child support payments is inflation. Parents sometimes agree to adjust support payments based on the Department of Labor's Consumer Price Index. Where there is no agreement and there has been marked change in the inflation index, courts may sometimes alter support payments.

Enforcement of Child Support Orders

Failure of an obligated parent to pay child support to the custodial parent has become a major issue in the United States. This problem has been exacerbated by the drastic increase in out-of-wedlock births and the high rate of divorce, both of which have resulted in more single-parent families. Custodial parents often must resort to judicial proceedings by seeking to have a court find the defaulting parent in **contempt of court.** Other options include **garnishment** of an obligated parent's wages or even seeking criminal sanctions. These options are generally difficult for a custodial parent to pursue and normally necessitate the employment of a lawyer or assistance from a child support office. Of course, if the court punishes a parent for being in contempt or if a parent is prosecuted, it can result in that parent's inability to earn the money necessary to comply with support requirements.

Further, if a parent who is obligated to pay child support moves to another state, it presents an additional problem to the custodial parent who is trying to collect. To aid in the collection of support payments from out-of-state parties, most states have adopted the Uniform Reciprocal Enforcement of Support Act of 1950, commonly referred to as URESA, which became known as the Revised Uniform Reciprocal Enforcement of Support Act (RURESA) after revisions in 1968. The Act requires each state to enforce the support obligations imposed by other states. The Act itself creates no duties of family support; rather, it is concerned solely with the enforcement of existing duties when the person to whom a duty is owed is in one state and the person obligated to furnish support is in another. In an effort to streamline the procedures for **reciprocal enforcement of support obligations**, the Uniform Interstate Family Support Act (UIFSA) of 1992 superseded RURESA. UIFSA has now been adopted by all fifty states, albeit with modifications in some. Therefore, a child support modification case involving parties who live in different states is governed by the UIFSA. These acts generally have a positive effect on the ability of parents to compel assistance from those who might otherwise evade compliance with child support requirements.

Support of Dependents: The Federal Role

Congress has shown an increased interest in the federal government's taking an active role in compelling support of dependents. Federal law now provides a locator service at the disposal of the states to track down parents who default on their support obligations.[47] The revised Child Support Recovery Act (CSRA)[48] says that anyone who willfully fails to pay a support obligation with respect to a child who resides in another state is guilty of a federal offense if such obligation has remained unpaid for a period longer than one year, or is greater than $5,000. In 1999, a U.S. Court of Appeals said that "willfully" under CSRA can mean either having the money and refusing to use it for child support, or not having the money because one has failed to utilize the available means of obtaining it. The court concluded that Congress did not mean to let absentee parents evade their parental obligations by refusing to accept gainful employment or by failing to take other lawful steps to obtain necessary funds.[49]

Paternity

The presumption of legitimacy of a child is one of the strongest presumptions in law. A husband who contests **paternity** of a child born during his marriage must raise the issue promptly and not after dissolution of the marriage. In general, the following principles apply:

- A child born in wedlock is presumed legitimate. A husband who had access to his wife is presumed to be the father of her child.
- A child born during marriage is legitimate, even if conceived by the parties before marriage.
- A child born within the normal gestation period after the death of a husband is presumed to be the legitimate child of the deceased husband.

Under the common law, a putative father had no duty to support an illegitimate child. Today, in some states, statutes affix the responsibility of support on a male who acknowledges paternity. All states have laws that provide for judicial proceedings to determine paternity of an illegitimate child and to compel the father to contribute to the child's support. Any woman who is pregnant or who has delivered a child has standing to bring suit to determine paternity of her child. DNA analysis offers a reliable way to determine the biological parent, although older methods have included Human Leukocyte Antigen (HLA) tests. Putative fathers who contest their paternity often attack the reliability of these tests and raise as defenses impotency, sterility, and lack of access to the mother. In early years, a putative father might raise the issue of a female plaintiff's promiscuity; but today, attacking the mother's morals would likely fail as a defense.

Additionally, the Fourteenth Amendment to the U.S. Constitution forbids states to discriminate between legitimate and illegitimate children in granting the right to parental support.[50] Further, court decisions have held that the mother of an illegitimate child cannot contract away that child's right to support from the father. In some states, a government agency that provides support even has standing to bring a paternity suit in the mother's name to determine a putative father's liability for support. In recent decades, many legislatures also have revised their statutes of limitations to cause the time for an illegitimate child to bring suit to commence when a child attains majority.

ADOPTION

From a legal standpoint, adoption is the process of substituting the **adoptive parents** for the **biological parents**. Adoption has historic roots, particularly where a childless couple wanted to perpetuate their family. Yet, as a formal legal process, adoption was unknown under the English common law. In the United States, state statutes regulate adoption, and while these laws have certain commonalities, they vary considerably as to the eligibility of adoptive parents and rights of adoptees and as to the procedures for effecting adoption. Some states actually allow one adult to adopt another; however, the discussion that follows only refers to the adoption of children.

Types of Child Adoptions

There are three general categories of adoptions of children:

1. **Stepparent adoption.**   In some instances, an unmarried woman gives birth to a child and later marries a man who is not the father, and the new husband adopts the child. In other instances, a divorced parent who has custody of a child remarries, the non-custodial parent consents, and the custodial parent's new spouse adopts the child.
2. **Agency adoption.**   This is where a government agency or private adoption agency arranges for the adoption. Typically, the parents of the child have given their consent to adoption or their parental rights have been terminated by court action.
3. **Private placement adoption.**   Here, intermediaries, usually a physician and lawyer, arrange for birth parents to consent to adoption. However, not all states permit this category of adoptions.

Who May Adopt and Who May Be Adopted

In most situations, state statutes that provide for adoption of children are written in general terms stating that the adopting parents must be married, they must jointly agree to adopt, and the adoption must be in the best interests of the child. Before a child may be adopted, it is essential that the rights of the biological parents have terminated — either by their consent or by judicial decree. Often, statutes require a social services agency to interview the prospective adopting parents and to file a written report concerning their suitability as prospective parents and eligibility of the child to be adopted. These reports usually discuss the stability of the adopting parents' relationship, as well as their financial (and parental) ability to provide the potential adoptee with a suitable home environment. Normally, statutes impose a waiting period before adoption takes place, so that the adoptive parents and the child have an opportunity to bond.

Formalization of the Adoption

The legalities of adoption are formalized by a judicial hearing. At the hearing, the judge examines the documentation that releases the rights of the biological parents. Where such paperwork is in order, an adoption hearing is largely pro forma: the judge reviews any social report and listens to the parents acknowledge the responsibilities they are undertaking as well as the legal relationship that the adoptee will have with them and their biological children, if any. This process often involves a recitation of the adoptive parents' legal duty of support and the adoptee's right of inheritance.

If an adoption is contested, the hearing takes on a different complexion. Contests generally focus on the validity of the consent of the biological parent(s) or the issue of whether there has been a valid termination of the parental rights of such parent(s). The court carefully examines a consent to make certain that it conforms to the legal standards of the jurisdiction, that it was signed voluntarily, and that no fraud, duress, or undue influence was exerted in obtaining the consent. In some states, the necessity for obtaining the consent of the biological parents is waived if the evidence clearly shows the biological parent(s) to be unfit or to have abandoned or neglected the child. In other jurisdictions, the court looks to whether there has been a prior termination of the parental rights of the biological parent(s). If a birth mother or father is unknown, the court must make certain that the necessary legal procedures have been undertaken to ensure compliance with the standards of due process of law. In addition to the rights of a natural birth mother, the rights of an unwed father who demonstrates a full commitment as a responsible parent have been protected under the standards of due process of law.

Some Nontraditional Adoptions

In the past, social agencies have attempted to arrange adoptions based, in part, on the compatibility of the adoptive parents with the child to be adopted. They have considered a number of factors, including racial and religious compatibility of the adopting parents. However, there have been criticisms that the criteria established by adopting agencies have been too narrow. Indeed, some of these criteria are being challenged in court. For example, there has been an increase in the number of single parents and homosexual couples who have sought to adopt children. Ultimately, approval of adoptions is based on the adoption's being in the best interests of the child to be adopted. Therefore, court decisions do not always focus directly on the issue of homosexuality. A few states do not permit gay or lesbian couples to adopt children. Yet, in 1993, the New Jersey Supreme Court ruled that where a lesbian and the biological mother of a child had been in a committed relationship for approximately ten years, the lesbian could adopt her partner's child.[51] Today, many states will permit gay or lesbian individuals to petition to adopt a child.

TERMINATION OF PARENTAL RIGHTS

As previously noted, a child is not subject to adoption until the rights of the natural parents have been terminated. Parents may terminate their own parental rights, for example, by consent to adoption. A common instance is where the custodial parent remarries and the non-custodial parent consents to adoption of a child by the custodial parent's new spouse.

In some situations, one parent seeks to terminate the parental rights of the other, but these cases are the exception. The necessity to terminate parental rights most often begins with police action; however, police agencies generally refer cases of abused or neglected children to a state social agency. What constitutes abuse or neglect is defined by statute. Proceedings for **termination of parental rights** are usually initiated by a state agency. Such actions can be based on a parent's abuse of the child or a parent's neglect to provide for a child's welfare. When a social agency discovers such parental deficiencies, the child is often removed and placed in **foster care** while efforts are made to remedy the problems. A social agency may offer the family a case plan with the objective of reunification of the family once the social workers find the necessary improvements are accomplished.

A natural parent has a fundamental liberty interest in the care, custody, and management of children. Therefore, although the level of abuse or neglect necessary to justify termination of parental rights is not always capable of precise definition, when a state agency seeks to terminate parental rights, the state must establish termination of

CASE IN POINT

TERMINATION OF PARENTAL RIGHTS
In re Jennifer Ann Sprite & Michelle Marie Sprite, Minors
Michigan Court of Appeals
400 N.W.2d 320 (Mich. App. 1986)

The Juvenile Division of the Probate Court entered an order terminating the parental rights of the mother and father to their two young daughters. Only the mother appealed. She contended that termination of her parental rights was not in the best interests of the children. The Court of Appeals reviewed the evidence on which the Probate Court had based its findings and order. It revealed the two children were subjected to living in an unstable home with frequent and intense parental disputes, sexual abuse by the father, observation of sexual activity in the home, chronic deprivation of cleanliness, lack of food in the home, and a significant lack of medical attention for the children. The evidence also included evaluations by a psychiatrist who concluded that neither the father nor the mother was amenable to treatment and that regardless of how many parenting classes they attended or how much counseling they received, it was not going to make a great deal of difference in how they parented their children. The appellate court concluded that, based on the mother's intentional and negligent disregard of her children's needs, her demonstrated unwillingness to correct deficiencies in her parenting abilities, and her inability to protect her children, the Probate Court correctly terminated her parental rights. The Court of Appeals affirmed the judgment.

those rights by clear and convincing evidence of abuse, abandonment, or neglect. Decisions of the U.S. Supreme Court emphasizing the need to protect the due process rights of indigents have been persuasive in causing several jurisdictions to require appointment of counsel—at public expense—for indigent parents who face proceedings for termination of their parental rights.

GUARDIANSHIP

A **legal guardian** is a person, natural or corporate, appointed by a court to act on behalf of another (the **ward**) because of the latter's minority or incapacity. A guardian may act as guardian of the ward's person or property, or both. Sometimes, a guardian of the property is referred to as a **conservator**.

Parents are considered the natural guardians of their minor children. Accordingly, parents may make decisions concerning the welfare of the child and act on behalf of the child in regard to modest amounts of assets. However, if neither parent is living or if the assets of the child exceed state allowances, a guardian is required. Guardianship of a minor ends upon the minor's reaching the age of majority. Often, the appointment of a guardian of the property of a minor may be averted by giving property to a minor under a custodial or trust arrangement.

If an adult becomes mentally or physically incapable of handling his or her affairs and has not established the means for the management of his or her finances or the making of personal and medical decisions, then a guardianship may be required. In order to have a guardian of an adult appointed, the adult must be deemed incompetent or incapacitated by a court. This is accomplished by an interested person's petitioning the court for such a decree. In these cases, the court usually appoints a committee, often composed of three individuals, including a physician, to examine the individual.

Many states also require the appointment of an attorney to represent the allegedly incapacitated individual during the proceedings. After receiving reports and hearing testimony, the court makes a finding as to the individual's capacity. If the court finds that the person is incapacitated, it appoints a guardian, which may be a relative, a professional guardian, or a trust company. The guardian of a person who is a minor or an incapacitated person must oversee the welfare of the ward, including making medical and residential decisions, and typically must file an annual report concerning the ward's personal well-being. A guardian of a ward's property must manage and administer the ward's assets, file accountings and reports, and obtain court approval, if required by state law, to act on the ward's behalf to sell property owned by the ward. The guardian of an incapacitated ward also might be mandated to have the ward examined periodically to determine if any of the ward's rights should be restored. The court may even require the guardian to post a bond before taking charge of the ward's assets. The cost of the bond, court costs, and attorney's fees can make a guardianship quite expensive. Frequently, however, guardianship of an incapacitated person may be avoided through proper estate planning if the person, while still competent, executes a **durable power of attorney** and an **advance directive for medical decisions**.

REPRODUCTIVE DECISIONS

Reproductive rights have emerged over the years largely through decisions of the United States Supreme Court. These decisions concern the right to procreate, the right to use contraceptives, and the right to obtain an abortion.

Roe v. Wade: **The Supreme Court's Landmark Decision on Abortion**

Today, any discussion of a woman's right to choose whether to bear a child generally relates back to the Supreme Court's 1973 landmark decision in *Roe v. Wade*.[52] In writing for the majority of a divided Court, the late Justice Harry Blackmun opined that a woman's **right to privacy** under the U.S. Constitution is broad enough to encompass her decision of whether or not to terminate her pregnancy. The Court went on to hold that a fetus was not a "person" within the meaning of the Fourteenth Amendment to the U.S. Constitution, and therefore was not entitled to the constitutional protection guaranteed persons. More specifically, the Court's decision provided that during the first trimester of a woman's pregnancy, abortion was a matter between the woman and her physician—without state regulation. After the first trimester, procedures for abortion could be regulated when "necessarily related to maternal health," and in the final trimester, when the fetus has become "viable" (which means it could survive outside the mother's womb), the state could prohibit abortion except "when it is necessary, in appropriate medical judgment to preserve the life or health of the mother." In short, the state acquired an interest in the potential life of a fetus after viability. The Court's decision in *Roe v. Wade* remains controversial among both legislators and the general public—largely because the issue of abortion has deep philosophical, religious, ethical, medical, and political dimensions.

In 1992, in *Planned Parenthood v. Casey*, the Court revisited the issue of abortion, and although it retained the "core" holding of *Roe v. Wade* that a woman has a right to choose an abortion, the Court abandoned the trimester-by-trimester framework. Instead, it declared that abortion regulations that affect a woman **prior** to the viability of a fetus will be struck down if those regulations represent an "undue burden" on a woman's right to choose an abortion.[53] After viability, though, the state retains the right to prohibit abortion, except in situations where the mother's health is at issue.

Evolution of the Right of Privacy

Although *Roe v. Wade* provides the authority for a woman's right to control her reproductive functions, *Roe* was preceded by a number of decisions that developed the constitutional right of privacy. Some eight years earlier, in *Griswold v. Connecticut*, the Court struck down a Connecticut law that made the sale and possession of birth control devices a misdemeanor.[54] The late Justice William O. Douglas, writing for a divided Court, said that—although the Constitution itself did not reference a right to privacy—various other guarantees in the Constitution created a "penumbra," or "zone," of privacy. The 9th Amendment, which allows for the existence of un-enumerated (or unwritten) rights, played a large role in justifying the Court's creation of the right to privacy—as did the freedoms inherent in several other amendments (including the 1st, 3rd, 4th, and 5th). This notion of privacy, in turn, was used to justify the Court's decision to protect married couples who wished to use contraception. Significantly, the Court's 1965 ruling in *Griswold* began a trend for the Court to base decisions concerning sexual and reproduction matters on this newly found right of privacy. In 1972, the Court went a step further when it invalidated a Massachusetts law that prohibited unmarried persons

SIDEBAR

The U.S. Supreme Court's Abortion Decisions

Since its 1973 decision ruling (by a 7-2 margin) that a woman's constitutional right to privacy legalized abortion on a nationwide basis, the Supreme Court has issued numerous abortion-related decisions. The more significant rulings are summarized below:

1976: *Planned Parenthood v. Danforth.* By a 6-3 vote, the Court ruled that states cannot allow a husband to exercise veto power over his wife's decision to abort her pregnancy. By a 5-4 vote, the Court said that parents cannot be given absolute veto power over a minor's decision to have an abortion.

1979: *Colautti v. Franklin.* By a 6-3 vote, the Court said that states may protect a fetus that has reached viability, but the determination of viability is up to doctors, not courts or legislatures.

1983: *City of Akron v. Akron Center for Reproductive Health.* Among other things, the Court, by a 6-3 vote, ruled that state and local governments cannot require that abortions beyond the first trimester be performed in hospitals.

1986: *Thornburgh v. American College of Obstetricians & Gynecologists.* By a 5-4 vote, the Court struck down a Pennsylvania abortion regulation that would have required doctors to inform women seeking abortions about potential risks and available medical assistance for prenatal care and childbirth.

1989: *Webster v. Reproductive Health Services.* In a series of split votes, the Court upheld the right of the state of Missouri to restrict the use of public funds, personnel, and facilities in performing abortions and to require doctors to perform viability tests on fetuses at or beyond twenty weeks of gestation.

1992: *Planned Parenthood v. Casey.* The Court abandoned the trimester-by-trimester approach formulated in its 1973 decision in favor of a framework that provided the right to choose an abortion before the fetus was "viable" but restricted abortion post-viability. The Court also ruled that abortion regulations concerning the "pre-viability" phase will not be allowed if they impose an "undue burden" on a woman's constitutional right to obtain an abortion. An example of an "undue burden" was a Pennsylvania requirement that a woman notify her spouse before getting an abortion. However, the Court upheld a Pennsylvania regulation stating that a minor needed the consent of a parent before getting an abortion. It also upheld a regulation that mandated an "information session" and a 24-hour waiting period before a woman could procure an abortion. (Utah and South Dakota would later institute a 72-hour waiting period, and in 2014, Missouri's legislature passed a similar requirement, overriding the governor's veto in the process.)

2000: *Stenberg v. Carhart.* The Court struck down a Nebraska law banning "partial-birth abortion"[55] as unduly burdensome on a woman's "right to choose." In so doing, the Court reaffirmed its basic holding in *Roe v. Wade.*

2007: *Gonzales v. Carhart.* The Supreme Court upheld a federal ban on partial birth abortion, distinguishing the federal statute from the law invalidated in *Stenberg*—and thus not explicitly overruling the *Stenberg* decision.

2014: *McCullen v. Coakley:* The Supreme Court struck down a Massachusetts ban on protesting within 35 feet of an abortion clinic; the Court found the law to be an impermissible restriction on 1st Amendment free speech rights (see Chapter 3).

from buying and using contraceptives.[56] So, to many legal scholars, the 1973 decision on **abortion** in *Roe v. Wade* was simply an extension of the Supreme Court's determination to expand the right of privacy that it first declared in 1965.

The Future of the Abortion Issue

Although the Supreme Court's basic pronouncement in *Roe v. Wade* appears to be entrenched, the present Court remains divided on some of the ramifications of its 1973 decision. In a serious challenge in 1989, the Court split 5-4 in upholding the constitutionality of a Missouri statute that included a requirement that physicians conduct viability tests on the fetus at or beyond twenty weeks gestation. But, perhaps more troublesome to those who support a woman's right to choose to have an abortion was language in the preamble of the Missouri law stating, "[T]he life of each human being begins at conception."[57]

In 1992, the Court reaffirmed the essential holding of *Roe v. Wade* but upheld restrictions that Pennsylvania law imposed to require parental consent, waiting periods, and record-keeping and reporting provisions. The Court, however, did invalidate the requirement in the Pennsylvania law that required notification to a woman's spouse, as that was deemed an "undue burden."[58] Another example of an "undue burden" appeared in 2010, when a federal judge barred implementation of a Nebraska law that mandated mental health screenings for women who sought an abortion.[59] Similarly, in 2011, a federal court struck down provisions in a South Dakota law that required a physician to tell women about a supposed increased risk of suicide after abortion—although the same court upheld a provision that a woman be told that an abortion will "terminate the life of a whole, separate, unique, living human being."[60]

More recently, courts have struck down laws in Oklahoma[61] and North Carolina[62] that required a woman to view an ultrasound image of the fetus before having an abortion—although similar provisions in Louisiana, Texas, and Wisconsin are still valid. Additionally, in 2014, the U.S. Court of Appeals for the 5th Circuit said a Mississippi law requiring physicians who perform abortions to have admitting privileges at a local hospital was unconstitutional;[63] similar requirements in Wisconsin[64] and Alabama[65] have been struck down as well—although the 5th Circuit actually upheld such a provision in Texas.[66]

Additionally, Mississippi—which currently has one operational abortion clinic—also passed a requirement that only obstetricians could perform abortions. That was struck down for being a "substantial obstacle in the path of a woman's choice."[67] (California, by contrast, actually will allow physician's assistants, nurse practitioners, and even midwives to perform abortions.) Another recent trend has been for states to mandate elevated standards for abortion facilities to meet—in terms of criteria like square footage and required equipment. Such a law was passed in Texas in 2013—despite a filibuster from state senator Wendy Davis—and could result in the closing of more than half of the state's abortion clinics; judicial review is pending, and in October 2014, the Supreme Court of the United States barred the law from going into effect until the appeals process was completed.

The future of abortion cases may be tied in to efforts that some states—such as Nebraska—are taking to redefine the point at which viability occurs. Although viability is typically thought to occur between weeks 22 and 26 of a pregnancy, a 2010 Nebraska law set viability at 20 weeks, effectively prohibiting abortions that would occur after that point. Nebraska's legislation was connected to the supposition that a fetus could feel pain at that point. Similar '20-week bans' in Idaho[68] and Arizona[69] were struck down, as was a '12-week ban' in Arkansas[70] and a North Dakota law[71] that attempted to set viability at six weeks through a purported connection to "fetal heartbeat." In July 2014, Florida instituted a law that mandates "viability testing" before any abortion. Thus far, the Supreme Court has refused to hear a case on any of the above matters, and that helps to explain some of the inconsistent rulings across district and circuit courts. As with same-sex marriage, it remains to be seen whether the high Court will provide uniformity across the states when it comes to various attempts at restricting abortions.

Although it has been silent on many matters concerning abortion, in a 2000 case, *Stenberg v. Carhart*, the Supreme Court did address an ancillary aspect of the debate when it struck down a Nebraska law that banned a procedure commonly described as "partial-birth abortion."[72] Although the vote in the decision was 5-4, the Court made clear that the Constitution protects the fundamental right to choose abortion. In another 5-4 decision seven years later, the Court upheld a federal law banning partial-birth abortion, but in so doing restated *Roe*'s essential holding that, before fetal viability, the government may not prohibit a woman from exercising her right to terminate a pregnancy.[73] Although there are sharp disagreements on the Supreme Court regarding the abortion issue, the basic right announced in *Roe v. Wade* has been reiterated time and time again, and thus appears to be well established in constitutional law.

STENBERG v. CARHART
530 U.S. 914, 120 S. Ct. 2597, 147 L. Ed. 2d 743 (2000)

OPINION OF COURT

Justice Breyer delivered the opinion of the Court.

"We again consider the right to an abortion. We understand the controversial nature of the problem. Millions of Americans believe that life begins at conception and consequently that an abortion is akin to causing the death of an innocent child; they recoil at the thought of a law that would permit it. Other millions fear that a law that forbids abortion would condemn many American women to lives that lack dignity, depriving them of equal liberty and leading those with least resources to undergo illegal abortions with the attendant risks of death and suffering. Taking account of these virtually irreconcilable points of view, aware that constitutional law must govern a society whose different members sincerely hold directly opposing views, and considering the matter in light of the Constitution's guarantees of fundamental individual liberty, this Court, in the course of a generation, has determined and then predetermined that the Constitution offers basic protection to the woman's right to choose. . . ."

SURROGATE MOTHERHOOD

Surrogate motherhood is a modern development in **reproductive technology**. Until recently, adoption was the only option available to infertile couples who desired to have a child. However, with new reproductive technologies, couples unable to have children can enter a contract with a woman to bear a child for them. In the usual procedure, the woman employed to bear the child (surrogate mother) signs an agreement waiving any parental rights to the child to be born. The husband's sperm or an already fertilized egg is then implanted in the womb of the surrogate mother.

Will courts enforce a contract whereby a surrogate mother agrees to deliver the newborn child to the couple who employed her? In 1988, the New Jersey Supreme Court rendered the noteworthy decision on this point. The Sterns were unable to have children, so in 1985 Mr. Stern contracted with Mrs. Whitehead to bear a child for them. Mrs. Whitehead agreed to be impregnated by Mr. Stern's sperm and to bear a child that Mrs. Stern would legally adopt. Mrs. Whitehead was to receive $10,000 for her services. After the child (Baby M) was born, Mrs. Whitehead decided she wanted the child as her own, and a lengthy court battle on custody ensued. The case finally went to the state supreme court, which held that the surrogacy contract between Mr. Stern and Mrs. Whitehead conflicted with the New Jersey adoption laws, and was thus invalid and unenforceable. The court said that payment of money to a surrogate mother violated a state statute that prohibited payment or acceptance of money in connection with any placement of a child for adoption. Nevertheless, the court decided that the best interests of the child would be served by placing her in the custody of her biological father and his wife, with Mrs. Whitehead to enjoy rights of visitation.[74] Since this decision in 1988, several state legislatures have enacted laws barring enforcement of surrogacy contracts.

The scenario in the case reviewed by the New Jersey Supreme Court involved **traditional surrogacy**, where a woman is impregnated with the sperm of a married man with an understanding that the child to be born is to be legally the child of the married man and his wife. In contrast, **gestational surrogacy** involves artificially uniting the sperm of a married man with the egg of his wife and implanting the resulting **pre-embryo** in another woman's womb.

In 1993, the Supreme Court of California reviewed a gestational surrogacy case where a married couple, the Calverts, desired to have a child.[75] Mrs. Calvert was unable to become pregnant, although her ovaries remained capable of producing eggs. In 1990, the Calverts and Anna Johnson signed a contract providing that a pre-embryo created by Mr. Calvert's sperm and the egg of Mrs. Calvert would be implanted in Ms. Johnson, the surrogate. The agreement contemplated that the child to be born would be taken into the Calverts' home as their child. Ms. Johnson agreed she would relinquish "all parental rights" to the child in favor of the Calverts, and in return they would pay her $10,000 and provide a $200,000 life insurance policy on her life. After the **surrogate** became pregnant, relations between her and the couple deteriorated. The Calverts sued for a declaration that they were to become the legal parents of the unborn child. The surrogate then filed her own action seeking to be

CASE IN POINT

THE CASE OF THE FROZEN EMBRYOS
Davis v. Davis
Tennessee Supreme Court
842 S.W.2d 588 (Tenn. 1992)

Junior Davis and Mary Sue Davis married in 1980; however, the wife was unable to become pregnant. Several years later, the couple signed up for an in vitro fertilization program at a clinic in Knoxville. There was no agreement specifying what disposition should be made of any unused embryos that might result from the cryopreservation process, and no Tennessee statute governed such disposition. In 1989, the husband sought a divorce, and the wife sought custody of the frozen pre-embryos. The county court granted the divorce and awarded custody of the frozen pre-embryos to the wife. The husband appealed, and the Court of Appeals reversed, finding that the husband had a constitutionally protected right not to beget a child where no pregnancy had taken place. The Court of Appeals remanded the case to the county court with directions that the parties have joint control over the embryos and equal voice in their disposition.

The Tennessee Supreme Court granted review, believing the Court of Appeals directions to the lower court were insufficient. As the litigation progressed, Mrs. Davis remarried and no longer wanted the embryos for herself, but she desired the right to donate them. The court concluded that the embryos were neither persons nor property; rather, they were in a category that entitled them to special respect because of their potential for human life. The court found that Mr. Davis's constitutional right to avoid procreation overrode the former wife's right to keep the embryos or to donate them to others. The court directed that the clinic could proceed to dispose of them in a customary manner.

---

declared the mother. The cases were consolidated, the child was born, and a blood test excluded the surrogate as the genetic mother. The trial court ruled that the Calverts were the child's genetic, biological, and natural father and mother—and that the surrogate had no parental rights to the child, and that the contract was legal and enforceable against the surrogate's claims. Anna Johnson appealed from the trial court's judgment. The appellate court and the state supreme court affirmed, holding that gestational surrogacy contracts do not violate public policy, adoption statutes, parental rights termination statutes, or penal statutes making it a misdemeanor to pay for adoption.

In a 1998 California case, a husband and wife agreed to have a pre-embryo that was genetically unrelated to either of them implanted in a surrogate who would bear the child for them. After the fertilization, implantation, and pregnancy, the husband filed a petition for dissolution of marriage. He alleged that there were no children of the marriage. The wife responded, asserting that the parties were expecting a child by way of surrogate contract. The child was born six days later. The trial court declared that the parties were not the lawful parents of the child. The Court of Appeal reversed the judgment and held that both parties were the lawful parents of the child. The court said that even though neither party was biologically related to the child, they were still the child's lawful parents given their initiating role as the intended parents in the conception and birth of the child. Further, the court stated that the same statute that makes a husband the lawful father of a child born because of his consent to **artificial insemination** applied to both of the intended parents. The court reasoned that just as a husband is deemed to be the lawful father of a child unrelated to him when his wife gives birth after artificial insemination, a husband and wife should be deemed to be the lawful parents of a child after a surrogate bears a biologically unrelated child on their behalf.[76]

Medical advances have outstripped the law in this area of surrogacy, which has raised a number of moral and ethical problems leading to crucial legal issues. Some would argue that a comprehensive regulatory scheme for legislating surrogacy is needed and that Congress should pass uniform legislation to regulate surrogacy.[77]

DECISIONS REGARDING MEDICAL TREATMENT

One of the serious aspects of family life is the necessity to make decisions concerning medical treatments. Competent adults have the right to make decisions regarding their own medical treatment, and this includes the right to refuse treatment. A competent adult can also make **advance directives** addressing medical care through use of a **living will**, use of a durable power of attorney, and appointment of surrogates.

A spouse generally has the authority to make medical decisions for his or her spouse who is incompetent or unable to make decisions about medical treatments. Parents and guardians also have the right and obligation to make health care decisions for their children or their wards. Further, state statutes authorize physicians and hospitals to render needed medical treatments in an emergency when the parents or guardians are unavailable. There are, however, controversial issues concerning the requirement of parental consent for a minor female to obtain an abortion, and there are variations in requirements that pertain to the removal of life-sustaining support systems of terminally ill children.

Since the 1970s, considerably more attention has been given to matters surrounding health care, particularly those involving the discontinuance of life-sustaining measures. As a result, there is a movement in legislative bodies and courts to remove the issue of **extraordinary life-sustaining measures** from the courts and to permit the withdrawal or withholding of life-sustaining treatment for terminally ill patients at the direction of a surrogate based on competent medical advice.

Termination of Life Support Systems

In 1975, Karen Quinlan, age twenty-one, lay in a chronically vegetative state connected to a respirator and nourished by means of a nasogastric tube. After physicians advised her parents that she could not be restored to a sapient existence, her parents sought to have the respirator withdrawn. When the doctors refused, Karen's father sought approval from a local court to remove the life-sustaining equipment. That court refused, and an appeal was lodged in the New Jersey Supreme Court. In a landmark decision, the New Jersey Supreme Court found that use of a mechanical respirator was an "extraordinary" medical treatment and that Karen's constitutional right of privacy included her right to decline such treatment. The court recognized the right of Karen's father to assert her right of privacy.[78]

Today, courts typically accept a patient's right to order removal of **life support systems** based on the fundamental right of privacy discussed in the case involving Karen Quinlan. This is what occurred in 2005, when several appellate courts upheld the request of Michael Schiavo to remove a feeding tube that was keeping his wife, Terri, alive. Courts also have developed criteria to govern the removal of life support systems from children. In general, they have ruled that before courts may authorize the removal of life-sustaining equipment from a child or authorize the discontinuance of life-sustaining procedures for that child, competent medical evidence must disclose that the child's condition is terminal and irreversible, and that life is being sustained only through extraordinary life-prolonging measures. Courts usually allow parents or other surrogates to assert a minor's right of privacy and, through exercise of their **substituted judgment**, to approve of discontinuance of such extraordinary measures. Most courts have not required judicial approval unless there is a lack of concurrence among the family, physicians, and the hospital.[79]

All states now allow a competent adult to execute a durable power of attorney for health care, and most states have enacted statutes that provide a competent adult can sign a living will to stipulate the conditions under which life-sustaining treatment may be withheld or withdrawn. A durable power of attorney for health care becomes effective if the principal lacks capacity to make health care decisions. A living will becomes operative if the signer is incompetent and terminal, or lapses into a permanently unconscious state. Several real-world scenarios can help to illustrate these concepts.

As early as 1977, the Massachusetts Supreme Judicial Court permitted the guardian of an elderly, mentally challenged man to assert the right of his ward, who was suffering from leukemia, to refuse chemotherapy.[80] It seems clear, then, that a competent adult may reject extraordinary life-prolonging measures, but does that extend to the right to reject food and water? In 1986, the California Supreme Court ruled that a young woman who, although competent, was suffering from the effects of an advanced degenerative illness had the right to refuse food and water that was being administered through a nasogastric tube.[81]

By 1984, courts were issuing opinions concerning the rights of family members to approve the removal of extraordinary life-sustaining measures. In that year, the Supreme Court of Florida summarized the newer approach of the courts when it said:

> We hold that the right of a patient, who is in an irreversibly comatose and essentially vegetative state, to refuse extraordinary life-sustaining measures, may be exercised either by his or her close family members or by a guardian of the person of the patient appointed by the court. If there are close family members such as the patient's spouse, adult children, or parents, who are willing to exercise this right on behalf of the

patient, there is no requirement that a guardian be judicially appointed.... The decision to terminate artificial life support is a decision that normally should be made in the patient-doctor-family relationship. Doctors, in consultation with close family members, are in the best position to make these decisions.[82]

Legislatures and courts in states faced with the issue of whether or not artificial nutrition and hydration may be withdrawn or withheld have responded in various ways. Some state statutes permit the refusal or removal of some forms of life support but exclude those related to nutrition and hydration. Others allow the withdrawal or withholding of nutrition and hydration tubal feedings where the patient is terminally ill. Courts themselves have arrived at different conclusions concerning the withdrawal or withholding of nutrition and hydration. In 1989, the Supreme Court of the United States provided some guidance with its ruling in *Cruzan v. Director, Missouri Health Department*, which allowed a state to require "clear and convincing evidence" of a patient's wishes before medical officials terminated life support. As a result, many physicians and hospitals recommend that patients express their preferences in these matters through an advance care directive.

Although competent adults may refuse medical treatment on religious grounds, even if the refusal results in death, courts take a different view in respect to children. This sometimes poses problems where parents choose to rely on spiritual power to achieve healing or when they deny blood transfusions for children based on scripture. On this subject, the Supreme Court, in 1944, recognized that "parents may be free to become martyrs themselves. But it does not follow that they are free in identical circumstances to make martyrs of their children before they have reached the age of full legal discretion when they can make that choice for themselves."[83]

CONCLUSION

Family law touches each person's most intimate relationships. It embraces us from birth to death, with decisions and relationships in between. For many of us, family law regulates marriage—and unfortunately, in some instances, divorce, with its attendant problems of alimony, property division, and custody disputes. Even when we are not involved personally, laws and court decisions concerning the family shape the society in which we live. At times, attitudes toward family law seem paradoxical: we insist on privacy and personal autonomy in our interpersonal relationships, yet we demand that regulatory authorities require education and support of children and that they protect children and cohabitants from abuse.

As we speak, families are undergoing dramatic cultural changes, and laws must adjust to the factors bringing about such changes, while retaining the core concepts of family relationships. Our mobile, technologically-oriented society increasingly is characterized by diversity and pluralism and is less bound by traditional mores of family ties and the constraints of institutional religion. Today, the great unifying force in the United States is the law. Nowhere is this more evident than in family law.

SUMMARY OF KEY CONCEPTS

After studying this chapter, a student must surely realize how family law touches everyone and recognize the dynamic changes this area of the law has undergone since the last half of the twentieth century. Marriage has a firm secular and religious basis in the family unit. Although contractual, it results in a definite legal status of the parties. The legal obligations of the parties can be modified, to some extent, by prenuptial agreement. Today, the traditional concept of marriage as being an institution between an adult male and female is being challenged, with some states allowing same-sex individuals to enter civil unions—which, from a civil law standpoint, provide most of the attributes of marriage—and others states actually permitting the full benefits of same-sex marriage.

The process of dissolving a marriage also has undergone dramatic changes. In earlier years, laws severely restricted divorce; later, states allowed statutory grounds for divorce; and now, the no-fault concept allows dissolution of an irretrievably broken marriage. With the educational, economic, and social advances of women, concepts of alimony, child support, custody, and visitation rights also have seen considerable change. Except in long-term marriages, courts today tend to limit alimony to that necessary to rehabilitate a divorced spouse. The emphasis is now on a shared approach in resolving child custody, support, and visitation issues. Where divorcing parties cannot negotiate a fair and reasonable settlement of their property interests, courts today place less emphasis on permanent alimony and greater emphasis on ensuring an equitable distribution of marital and non-marital property. Shared parental responsibility is replacing the old concept of child custody and now is considered on a more gender-neutral basis. Finally, there is increased enforcement of child support obligations through interstate compacts and federal government assistance.

With the increasing divorced rate, adoption can solve many social problems in families. Many adoptions are by stepparents, although agencies and private placements play a significant role. One controversial issue is whether homosexual couples should be allowed to adopt children. In any adoption, where the consent of the biological parents of the child is not secured on a voluntary and knowing basis, the legal termination of parental rights must first be accomplished.

In some instances, it is necessary to secure the court appointment of a guardian for a minor or a minor's property, or guardianship for a person adjudged by a court to be physically or mentally incapable of handling his or her property.

After its evolving decisions on sexual privacy, in 1973 the Supreme Court issued its landmark abortion rights decision in *Roe v. Wade*. Today, its basic decision on a woman's reproductive rights appears entrenched; however, nuances continue to emerge, with seemingly irreconcilable views pitted against one another in discussion over a woman's liberty interest in deciding whether to continue a pregnancy.

Advances in medical technology also have brought additional new issues of family law to the forefront. Three prominent ones are (1) surrogate motherhood and its consequences to all parties involved; (2) an individual's right to make decisions concerning his or her medical treatment; and (3) the right of surrogates to substitute their judgment, where necessary, in making judgments whether to terminate life support systems of terminally ill patients.

FOR FURTHER READING

Dolgin, Janet, *Defining the Family: Law, Technology, and Reproduction in an Uneasy Age* (New York University Press 1997).

Glick, Henry, *The Right to Die: Policy Innovation and Its Consequences* (Columbia University Press 1992).

Luker, Kristin, *Abortion and the Politics of Motherhood* (University of California Press 1980).

Meisel, Alan, and Kathy L. Cerminara, *The Right to Die* (3d ed., Aspen Publishers 2004).

O'Brien, David M., *Privacy, Law and Public Policy* (Praeger 1979).

O'Connor, Karen, *No Neutral Ground? Abortion Politics in an Age of Absolutes* (Westview Press 1996).

Oliphant, Robert E., and Nancy Ver Steegh, *Family Law: Examples and Explanations* (Aspen Publishers 2004).

Reagan, Milton C., *Alone Together: Law and the Meanings of Marriage* (Oxford University Press 1999).

Strasser, Mark, *Legally Wed: Same-Sex Marriage and the Constitution* (Cornell University Press 1998).

Tribe, Laurence, *Abortion: The Clash of Absolutes* (Norton 1990).

QUESTIONS FOR THOUGHT AND DISCUSSION

1. Is there a justification for states to continue to recognize common law marriages? What about same-sex marriages? Explain.
2. What are the different legal consequences between a divorce and an annulment of a marriage?
3. What are the most common reasons that couples enter into prenuptial agreements?
4. What are the principal criteria courts look to in determining matters concerning custody of children? What criteria will courts not consider? What are the merits of courts' awarding shared parental responsibility for children as opposed to custody to one spouse with visitation rights to the other?
5. How did the Supreme Court's ruling in *Griswold v. Connecticut* in 1965 lay the groundwork for the Court's 1973 decision in *Roe v. Wade*?
6. Why would a court likely take a different view as to the rights of a surrogate mother in a case involving traditional surrogacy as opposed to one involving gestational surrogacy?
7. What is meant by the doctrine of "substituted judgment" in relation to the law governing the removal of life support systems and discontinuance of artificial nourishment for a comatose patient who has not indicated a preference in regard to these matters by advance directive or living will?
8. Should statutes governing adoption of children be specific in respect to requirements for adoptive parents and the suitability of a child for adoption? Why or why not?
9. What legal consequences affect adoptive parents as a result of a decree of adoption?
10. What is the rationale for a court to cause an equitable distribution of marital property? What property is ordinarily excluded from marital property?
11. Should the law provide for court-enforced rights of visitation of minor children by their grandparents? If so, what qualifications should be placed on such visitation rights?
12. Through what policy-making and legal processes have changes in same-sex marriage regulations been promulgated?

KEY TERMS

abortion
adoptive parents
advance directive for medical decisions
advance directives
agency adoption
alimony
annulment
artificial insemination
attorney's fees
best interests of the child test

biological parents
canon law
ceremonial marriages
child snatching
child support
child support requirements
child-out-of-wedlock
children of "tender years"
civil unions
common law marriages
community property

community property states
conservator
consortium
contempt of court
contractual status
custodial parent
dissolution of a marriage
divorce
divorce *a mensa et thoro*
domestic partnership
durable power of attorney

emancipation acts
equitable distribution
extraordinary life-sustaining
measures
fault concept
foster care
garnishment
gestational surrogacy
grandparents' visitation
illegitimate child
in vitro fertilization
interstate abduction
interstate disputes concerning child
custody
invidious discrimination
irretrievably broken
joint custody
legal guardian
legal separation
life support systems

living will
lump sum alimony
marital property
marriage
matrimonial domicile
mediation
modification of custody
no-fault dissolution of marriage
parents' right of privacy
paternity
permanent alimony
post-nuptial agreements
pre-embryo
prenuptial agreements
primary physical residence
private placement adoption
property settlement agreements
putative father
reciprocal enforcement of support
obligations

rehabilitative alimony
reproductive technology
residence requirements
right of visitation
right to privacy
same-sex marriages
separate maintenance
sex-neutral basis
shared parental responsibility
special equity
stepparent adoption
substituted judgment
surrogate
surrogate motherhood
termination of parental rights
traditional surrogacy
unity concept of marriage
ward

ENDNOTES

1. 98 U.S. 145, 25 L. Ed. 244; 8 Otto 145 (1878).
2. Md. Code Ann., Fam. Law §2-301.
3. Some cities that offer domestic partnerships include: Missoula, Montana; Phoenix, Arizona; Milwaukee, Wisconsin; Detroit, Michigan; Albuquerque, New Mexico.
4. A 2013 study suggested that 61% of Fortune 500 companies provide benefits to same-sex couples; see Blake Ellis, "Record Number of U.S. Companies Offering Same-Sex Benefits," CNN Money, December 9, 2013; available at: http://money.cnn.com/2013/12/09/pf/lgbt-corporate-equality/.
5. Kerrigan v. Commissioner of Pub. Health, 289 Conn. 135 (Conn. 2008).
6. As of September 2014, these states were Colorado and Nevada.
7. See, e.g., Cal. Fam. Code §297 (domestic partnership status includes individuals of the same sex or requires that at least one party be over age sixty-two); see also N.J. Stat. §26:8A-4 (domestic partnerships are limited to individuals who are of the same sex or who are both sixty-two years of age or older).
8. Baehr v. Lewin, 852 P.2d 44 (Haw. 1993).
9. U.S. Const. art. IV, §1.
10. Hawaii's ban was instituted in March 2000, before the Hawaii Supreme Court decreed that a same-sex marriage

license be issued; the state's voters, by a 61 percent to 39 percent margin, amended the state constitution to allow the state legislature to ban same-sex marriages. See: Haw. Const. art. 1, §23 ("The legislature shall have the power to reserve marriage to opposite-sex couples.").
11. 28 U.S.C. §1738C.
12. Baker v. State, 744 A.2d 864 (Vt. 2000).
13. 798 N.E.2d 941 (Mass. 2003).
14. In re Marriage Cases, 183 P.3d 384, 401 (Cal. 2008).
15. Ballot initiatives allow citizens to place a proposed law on the ballot during a general election if a predetermined amount of signatures are gathered on a petition bearing the text of the proposed law. At the election, if a majority vote "yes" in favor of the proposal becoming a law, it shall become a law. Similarly, citizens also can utilize a referendum, whereby they repeal an existing law through a similar procedure.
16. The 9th circuit case is Perry v. Brown (2012), while the district case is Perry v. Schwarzanegger, 704 F. Supp 2d. 921 (2010).
17. Hollingsworth v. Perry, 570 U.S. _____, 133 S. Ct. 2652, 186 L. Ed. 2d 768 (2013).
18. United States v. Windsor, 570 U.S. _____, 133 S. Ct. 2675,186 L.Ed.2d 808 (2013).

19. Id., slip op. at p.

20. The marriage in *Windsor* actually occurred in Canada, but it also was recognized by the state of New York; thus, the Supreme Court's decision allows for federal benefits when any state recognizes a marriage as valid, regardless of where the marriage itself took place.

21. Referendum votes in all three states followed the passage of laws that legalized same-sex marriage.

22. Joan Biskupic, "Two Moms, A Baby, and a Legal First for U.S. Gay Marriage," Reuters, April 9, 2014; available at: http://www.reuters.com/article/2014/04/09/us-usa-courts-samesexmarriage-idUSBREA380B420140409.

23. *See, e.g., Bishop, et al. v. United States of America, et al.* (2014), U.S. District Court for the Northern District of Oklahoma; opinion available at: http://www.oknd.uscourts.gov/docs/d50f87b8-eebd-49bf-a18a-cc6e8acda53e/04cv848.pdf.

24. *See Bostic v. Rainey,* 970 F. Supp. 2d 456, U.S. District Court for the Eastern District of Virginia; upheld by U.S. Court of Appeals for the 4th Circuit. Strict scrutiny also was used by the U.S. Court of Appeals for the 10th Circuit in upholding a Utah district court's decision to overturn that state's ban on same-sex marriage; *see Kitchen et al. v. Herbert and Swenson,* available at: https://www.ca10.uscourts.gov/opinions/13/13-4178.pdf.

25. *See, e.g.,* Id., and cases referenced in note 23.

26. *In re Marriage of Van Hook,* 195 Cal. Rptr. 541 (Cal. App. 1983).

27. *Orr v. Orr,* 440 U.S. 268, 99 S. Ct. 1102, 59 L. Ed. 2d 306 (1979).

28. Uniform Marriage and Divorce Act, U.L.A. §308 (1998).

29. 23 Pa. Cons. Stat. Ann. §3502.

30. 5 U.S.C. §8345(j).

31. *McCarty v. McCarty,* 453 U.S. 210, 101 S. Ct. 2728, 69 L. Ed. 2d 589 (1981).

32. 10 U.S.C. §1408.

33. N.Y. Dom. Rel. Law §236, pt. B.

34. *McGowan v. McGowan,* 535 N.Y.S.2d 990 (N.Y. App. Div. 1988). (Wife's teaching certificate, conferred as result of education program completed prior to marriage, was not marital property, but wife's master's degree, awarded based on completion of study undertaken during marriage, was marital property subject to equitable distribution.)

35. N.Y. Dom. Rel. Law §236, pt. B.

36. *Berry v. Berry,* 658 A.2d 1097 (Me. 1995).

37. The Supreme Court also noted that the race of a parent's boyfriend or girlfriend cannot play a role in custody decisions. *See Palmore v. Sidoti,* 466 U.S. 429, 80 L. Ed. 2d 421, 104 S. Ct. 1879 (1984).

38. *Reed v. Reed,* 404 U.S. 71, 92 S. Ct. 251, 30 L. Ed. 2d 225 (1971).

39. *See, e.g., In re Marriage of Dawson,* 214 N.W.2d 131 (Iowa 1974).

40. *See Doane v. Doane,* 330 So. 2d 753 (Fla. App. 1976).

41. *Stanley v. Illinois,* 405 U.S. 645, 92 S. Ct. 1208, 31 L. Ed. 2d 551 (1972).

42. *Phillips v. Horlander,* 535 S.W.2d 72 (Ky. 1976).

43. *In re Custody of Smith,* 969 P.2d 21 (Wash. 1998).

44. *Troxel v. Granville,* 530 U.S. 57, 120 S. Ct. 2054, 147 L. Ed. 2d 49 (2000).

45. 120 S. Ct. at 2061-2064.

46. 28 U.S.C. §1738A.

47. 42 U.S.C. §653.

48. 18 U.S.C. §228.

49. *United States v. Ballek,* 170 F.3d 871 (9th Cir. 1999).

50. *Gomez v. Perez,* 409 U.S. 535, 93 S. Ct. 872, 35 L. Ed. 2d 56 (1973).

51. *Matter of Adoption of Child by J.M.G.,* 632 A.2d 550 (N.J. 1993).

52. 310 U.S. 113, 93 S. Ct. 705, 35 L. Ed. 2d 147 (1973).

53. *Planned Parenthood v. Casey,* 505 U.S. 833, 112 S. Ct. 2791, 120 L. Ed. 2d 674 (1992).

54. *Griswold v. Connecticut,* 381 U.S. 479, 85 S. Ct. 1678, 14 L. Ed. 2d 510 (1965).

55. A "partial birth abortion" is a technique in which a fetus is removed intact from a woman's cervix. The term itself was coined by the National Right to Life Committee.

56. *Eisenstadt v. Baird,* 405 U.S. 438, 92 S. Ct. 1029, 31 L. Ed. 2d 349 (1972).

57. *Webster v. Reproductive Health Servs.,* 492 U.S. 490, 109 S. Ct. 3040, 106 L. Ed. 2d 429 (1989).

58. *Planned Parenthood v. Casey,* 505 U.S. 833, 112 S. Ct. 2791, 120 L. Ed. 2d 673 (1992).

59. *Planned Parenthood of the Heartland v. Heineman,* 724 F. Supp. 2d 1025 (2010). This decision was upheld by the United States 8th Circuit Court of Appeals in 2011.

60. *Planned Parenthood Minnesota v. Rounds,* 650 F. Supp. 2d 972 (2011).

61. The Oklahoma Supreme Court struck down a mandatory ultrasound law in December 2012, and the Supreme Court of the United States announced its refusal to hear an appeal in November 2013.

62. *Stuart v. Loomis* (2014), U.S. District Court for the Middle District of North Carolina; opinion available at: http://dig.abclocal.go.com/wtvd/docs/ultrasound_rluling_011714.pdf.

63. *Jackson Women's Health Organization v. Currier, et al.* (2014), U.S. Court of Appeals for the 5th Circuit; opinion available at: http://www.ca5.uscourts.gov/opinions%5Cpub%5C13/13-60599-CV0.pdf.

64. *Planned Parenthood of Wisconsin, Inc., et al. v. Van Hollen, et al.* (2013), U.S. District Court for the Western District of Wisconsin; opinion available at: http://www.aclu.org/files/assets/81__opinion__order.pdf; in 2014, the Supreme Court of the United States refused to hear an appeal.

65. *Planned Parenthood Southeast, Inc. v. Strange* (2014), U.S. District Court for the Middle District of Alabama; opinion available at: https://ecf.almd.uscourts.gov/cgi-bin/show_public_doc?2013cv0405-238.

66. *Planned Parenthood of Greater Texas Surgical Health Services, et al. v. Abbott, et al.* (2014), U.S. Court of Appeals for the 5th Circuit; opinion available at: http://www.ca5.uscourts.gov/opinions%5Cpub%5C13/13-51008-CV1.pdf.

67. *Jackson Women's Health Organization v. Currier, et al.* (2014), U.S. Court of Appeals for the 5th Circuit; opinion available at: http://www.ca5.uscourts.gov/opinions%5Cpub%5C13/13-60599-CV0.pdf; quote drawn from p. 8.

68. *McCormack v. Hiedeman*, 900 F. Supp.2d 1128 (2013).

69. *Isaacson, et al. v. Horne, et al.* 716 F.3d 1213 (2013). In January 2014, the Supreme Court of the United States refused to hear an appeal.

70. *Edwards v. Beck* (2014), U.S. District Court for the Eastern District of Arkansas; opinion available at: http://www.acluarkansas.org/contentitemdocuments/274.pdf.

71. *MKB Management Corp., et al. v. Birch Burdick*, 954 F. Supp.2d 900 (2013).

72. *Stenberg v. Carhart*, 530 U.S. 914, 120 S. Ct. 2597, 147 L. Ed. 2d 743 (2000).

73. *Gonzales v. Carhart*, 550 U.S. 124, 127 S. Ct. 1610, 167 L. Ed. 2d 480 (2007).

74. *See In re Baby M.*, 537 A.2d 1227 (N.J. 1988), *on remand*, 542 A.2d 52 (N.J. Super. 1988).

75. *Johnson v. Calvert*, 851 P.2d 776 (Cal. 1993).

76. *In re Marriage of Buzzanca*, 72 Cal. Rptr. 2d 280 (Cal. App. 1998).

77. Lisa L. Behm, "Legal, Moral, & International Perspectives on Surrogate Motherhood: The Call for a Uniform Regulatory Scheme in the United States," 2 *DePaul J. Health Care L.* 557 (Spring 1999).

78. *In re Quinlan*, 355 A.2d 647 (N.J. 1976).

79. *See In re Barry*, 445 So.2d 364 (Fla. App. 1984); *In re L.H.R.*, 321 S.E.2d 716 (Ga. 1984).

80. *See Superintendent of Belchertown State Sch. v. Saikewicz*, 370 N.E.2d 417 (Mass. 1977).

81. *Bouvia v. Superior Court*, 225 Cal. Rptr. 297 (Cal. App. 1986).

82. *John F. Kennedy Meml. Hosp. v. Bludworth*, 452 So.2d 921 926 (Fla. 1984).

83. *Prince v. Massachusetts*, 321 U.S. 158, 170, 64 S. Ct. 438, 444, 88 L. Ed. 645, 655 (1944).

THE LEGAL PROCESS

PART III

CIVIL PROCEDURE, EVIDENCE, AND THE APPELLATE PROCESS

9

LEARNING OBJECTIVES

This chapter should enable the student to understand:

- the jurisdiction of courts to hear civil disputes
- the parties involved in civil litigation
- court pleadings and service of process
- the social and economic role that class action suits play
- pretrial preparation and non-jury and jury trials of civil cases
- the mechanics and art of jury selection
- the evidentiary phases of a trial, arguments by counsel, jury deliberations, and verdicts
- classification of evidence, examination of expert and lay witnesses, exclusion of evidence, and privileges against testifying
- the role of appellate courts in error correction and law development
- how appellate courts function in hearing appeals of right and petitions for discretionary review
- the appellate decision-making process and dissemination of appellate court opinions and their importance to the law and lawyers

CHAPTER OUTLINE

INTRODUCTION

Civil lawsuits are brought in state and federal courts to redress injuries or to vindicate legal rights. Civil suits stem from a variety of causes, including personal injuries, conflicts over ownership of property, contractual disputes, and various business relationships. The civil jurisdiction of state courts is also invoked to determine whether a party is incompetent, to supervise guardianships of minors and incompetent persons, and to resolve issues in domestic relations cases, such as dissolution of marriage and custody of children.

Courts determine outcomes in civil suits based on relevant legal principles and precedents. The rules of civil procedure and evidence are the vehicles through which courts decide these cases in a fair and orderly manner.

Civil procedure embraces the processes by which claims and defenses are presented to and adjudicated by trial courts. It includes the pretrial, trial, and post-trial phases of civil litigation.

The procedures governing civil disputes, extremely complex and protracted at common law, have been greatly simplified and streamlined through the adoption of modern statutes and rules of court procedure. In the federal courts, civil procedure is governed by rules promulgated by the United States Supreme Court under authority delegated by Congress. Similarly, state legislatures have authorized state courts to establish rules of civil procedure, replacing what was known as **common law pleading** in civil cases.

The **rules of evidence** consist of principles applicable to the admission of evidence in judicial proceedings. These rules are largely of common law origin; however, they have been modified by statutory law and court decisions. In this chapter, we focus on civil procedure, the rules of evidence, and **appellate procedure** applicable to both civil and criminal disputes. Appellate procedure refers to the rules by which higher courts review lower court decisions. In Chapter 10, we amplify the rules of evidence and appellate procedure in relation to the adjudication of criminal cases.

CIVIL PROCEDURE

Those unable to resolve civil disputes informally have the right of access to the courts to attempt to obtain relief. One who files a **complaint** is known as the **plaintiff**; the party against whom the complaint is filed is known as the **defendant**. Of course, in some instances multiple plaintiffs may seek relief from more than one defendant. Plaintiffs and defendants are known as the **parties**, and their rights are determined in accordance with the principles of the substantive law, discussed in previous chapters. Civil procedure is the process that governs judicial resolution of civil disputes.

Jurisdiction: The First Step

One who seeks recourse through the judicial system must initially determine the appropriate court that has jurisdiction over the subject of the suit. **Jurisdiction** is the authority of a court to hear and determine a particular type of case, and it is conferred on courts either by constitution or by statute. Federal courts have jurisdiction over cases involving copyrights and patents, admiralty and maritime cases, bankruptcy proceedings, and other federal proceedings as well as over federal crimes. Congress has also vested federal courts with jurisdiction to determine cases between citizens of different states (**diversity jurisdiction**) where the party so elects and the amount in controversy exceeds $75,000.[1] Although federal procedural law is applied in diversity cases, the federal district courts apply the substantive law of the state where the court sits.[2] State courts hear most cases involving residents of the state and those affecting real property within the state.

In addition to filing suit in a court that has jurisdiction, the plaintiff must abide by the legal rules that relate to **venue**, the geographical place where a law action may be filed. Statutes generally designate the proper venue, commonly providing the place where a tort or breach of a contract occurs or where land in controversy is located. The rules become quite complex where multiple defendants are involved or when parties are from different states. Ultimately, the Supreme Court has suggested that an essential function of the courts is to respect the "due process" rights of the defendant by ensuring that a choice of venue does not "offend traditional notions of fair play and substantial justice."[3] In applying this principle, courts typically will assert one of two basic types of jurisdiction: general or specific.

General jurisdiction makes a party amenable to a lawsuit even for activity that has occurred outside the geographic scope of a particular court. More specifically, the Supreme Court has noted that a party with "continuous and systematic" ties to a location can be subject to general jurisdiction of its courts (see: *Perkins v. Benguet Mining*);[4] thus, general jurisdiction could expose a party to a lawsuit in its home state even for an incident that took place in another state. In a 2014 case, *Daimler AG v. Bauman*, however, the Court did place limits on the ability of U.S. courts to hold jurisdiction over corporations for the actions of subsidiaries in other countries.[5]

Specific jurisdiction applies when a party's activity is within a court's geographic reach and that activity leads to a lawsuit. Using this idea, the Supreme Court's landmark 1945 civil procedure decision in *International Shoe v. Washington*[6] stated that "sufficient minimum contacts" in a particular place are all that are needed to subject a party to jurisdiction of local courts. For example, driving a car in a state and causing an accident would create the "minimum contacts" needed for a local court to assert jurisdiction over a suit stemming from the accident, even if the defendant in such a suit were not a resident of that state.

Who Are Parties to Civil Suits?

Individuals, corporations, and government agencies may become parties to civil lawsuits as plaintiffs or defendants. For example, Harriet Hester, who was injured in an auto accident, can file a complaint against the driver and owner of a tanker truck that she claims caused the accident. The complaint might read, "Harriet Hester v. Damian Drivo and Economy Oil Company, a corporation." Individuals and entities also become parties in a representative capacity. For instance, Fidelity Trust Company, as personal representative of John Doe's estate or as trustee for John Doe, might file a complaint against Unexcelled Investments, Inc., a corporation. A minor's complaint through his guardian would likely be styled "Sharon Smith, as guardian of Jonathan Smith, a minor." Or, the citizen who disputes the tax assessment on her house may file a complaint styled, "Rhonda Roe, plaintiff v. James Jones, as tax assessor." In certain litigation, the party who files a complaint is known as a "petitioner" and the party against whom relief is sought is called the "respondent." Typically, a complaint for dissolution of a marriage may read, "Mary Jones, petitioner v. Paul Jones, respondent, or in some states it would be styled, "In re Dissolution of Marriage of Paul and Mary Jones."

Relief Sought by the Plaintiff

A civil suit is an attempt to obtain some form of relief through the courts. In addition to stating a **cause of action**, a lawsuit must specify the relief requested by the plaintiff. The most common form of relief sought by plaintiffs is **damages**. Damages represent monetary compensation for a party's injuries or economic losses. **General damages** are those the law implies to have accrued to the plaintiff due to a particular injury or loss. **Special damages** are those that have accrued or will accrue to the plaintiff although they did not necessarily flow from an injury or loss. To illustrate: a plaintiff who has been injured in an automobile accident suffers general damages, that is, pain and suffering. But the plaintiff may also have sustained such special damages as loss of wages and medical expenses. Finally, in some instances, where a plaintiff's rights have been violated, for example a technical trespass on the plaintiff's land, the court may award **nominal damages**, say $1.00, to recognize the plaintiff's rights have been violated but that no actual damages have accrued. Obviously, a plaintiff would not ordinarily seek to recover nominal damages.

Where a defendant's actions have been fraudulent, wanton, or outrageous, the plaintiff may be allowed to recover **punitive damages**. The object of punitive damages is to punish the defendant and to deter others from like conduct. Often, statutory law governs the award of punitive damages, perhaps through limitations, or "caps" on the amount that can be awarded.

In some instances, a plaintiff merely seeks **declaratory relief**, that is, the plaintiff requests the court to interpret the law in respect to a present factual situation where there is a genuine controversy between parties but applicability of the law is in doubt.

In other instances, a plaintiff will seek an **injunction** to prevent an injury from taking place or to terminate an ongoing injury. In unusual cases where a breach of contract cannot be remedied by recovering monetary damages, plaintiffs will ask the court to order **specific performance**, which means that the court will order the defendant to fulfill the contractual obligations that were breached. If, for example, a defendant breached a contract to sell a particular piece of artwork to the defendant, the plaintiff might not be content to accept monetary damages. For the billionaire who wishes to own an original Picasso, money is not the object. Such a plaintiff would likely seek to have the court force the defendant to deliver the painting. Generally, courts will not mandate specific performance when it would force a defendant to perform a service—such as finishing a roof on a house or playing a part in a movie—but will instead look to provide equivalent monetary damages.

The Initial Pleading

Recall that in Chapter 1 we discussed the historic differences between the common law and equity. At common law, the **initial pleading** (request to the court) in a civil case was called a declaration; in chancery court, it was referred to as a bill in equity. Today, in federal and most state courts, the plaintiff's complaint or the petitioner's petition is the initial pleading in a lawsuit. The purpose of the initial pleading is to demonstrate to the court that it has jurisdiction of the suit and to inform the defendant of the basis of the plaintiff's suit and the relief being sought. The plaintiff's complaint or petition must meet certain formal requirements. It must include a caption with the name of the court where the suit is filed and the names of the parties, a statement that alleges the jurisdiction of the court, the body of the complaint, which explains the basis of the suit, and a demand for a judgment. If the plaintiff is seeking to annul a contract between the parties, the demand for judgment may read, "Plaintiff seeks to rescind the contract described in this complaint." If the complaint seeks damages for injuries incurred in an auto accident, the demand for judgment might read, "Plaintiff demands judgment against the defendant for $10,000." In some cases, a plaintiff may add a demand for a jury trial.

Civil Process and How Accomplished

In order to notify the defendant that the plaintiff's complaint has been filed, the clerk of the court issues a formal document called a **summons**, which commands the defendant to answer the plaintiff's complaint. The summons directs the defendant to respond to the plaintiff's complaint within a set period, usually twenty days, from the date the complaint and summons are served. In federal court proceedings, the process may be served throughout the United States, but in state courts the process may be served only within the state. A marshal, sheriff, or process server usually accomplishes service of the complaint and summons.

When the summons and complaint are physically delivered to the defendant, the service is referred to as **personal service**. If the law authorizes these documents to be served on someone on the defendant's behalf, the service is known as **substituted service**. For example, many states allow a plaintiff to file suit against the driver and owner of an automobile involved in an accident in the state even though these defendants are nonresidents. The rationale of such laws is that when you drive your car in another state you designate the secretary of state or some other state official to receive a summons on your behalf. That official, in turn, sends the suit papers to the defendant.

Most states also have **long-arm statutes** that permit a plaintiff who is a resident of one state to sue a nonresident where the plaintiff has suffered a loss because of business the defendant has transacted in the plaintiff's state. The U.S. Supreme Court has established very definite requirements that must be met before long-arm service is permitted. In *Hanson v. Denckla* (1958), the Court explained that nonresidents may not constitutionally be subjected to the jurisdiction of another state unless the defendant by some act "purposefully avails" himself or herself of "the privilege of conducting activities" within the state, thus invoking the benefits of its laws.[7]

Beyond that, in some legal proceedings, the plaintiff can serve process on the defendant by publication of a notice to appear in the newspaper and by mailing a copy of the complaint to the defendant's last known address. This type of service is called **constructive service**, and the plaintiff is restricted as to the form of relief that can be obtained against a defendant.

If a defendant fails to respond to a summons in a timely fashion, the clerk of the court enters a **default**, and in due course the court may enter a **default judgment** against the defendant. In exceptional instances, a trial court may remove a default judgment and allow a defendant to proceed. While standards vary, in general, a party seeking to remove a default judgment must promptly seek relief and must demonstrate that failure to answer the plaintiff's complaint was due to excusable neglect and that the defendant has a meritorious defense.

The Defendant's Response to the Plaintiff's Complaint

The common law gave a defendant the option of filing a number of motions before responding to the substance of a plaintiff's complaint. Modern rules have greatly simplified these procedures in civil disputes.[8] Nevertheless, before filing an answer, a defendant may challenge the court's jurisdiction or the validity of the service of process or seek to dismiss the complaint on the ground that it does not state a legal cause of action, that is, a valid legal basis for the claim. The trial court disposes of such motions after hearing oral arguments or receiving written memoranda from the parties or their counsel. If the court determines that the plaintiff's complaint does not state a legal cause of action, the trial judge might allow the plaintiff to file an amended complaint to more precisely state the claim being asserted. If the plaintiff is unable to state a cause of action, the court will dismiss the case.

If the court denies the defendant's motions, or after the plaintiff alleges the basis of the complaint with more particularity, the defendant is required to file a written **answer** admitting or denying the plaintiff's allegations. The defendant's response may include specific defenses. The statute of limitations, which limits the time allowed for bringing different causes of action, and the statute of frauds, which requires certain contracts to be in writing, are examples of defenses asserted in civil cases.

A defendant may also file a **counterclaim**. For example, suppose the plaintiff sues the defendant claiming the defendant failed to pay the plaintiff the balance due for constructing the defendant's house. The defendant denies the plaintiff's claims and asserts a counterclaim alleging that the plaintiff contractor did not properly perform the contract and as a result the house has defects in construction. The counterclaim may accomplish one of three things. It may defeat the plaintiff's claim, mitigate the amount of the plaintiff's damages, or even result in the plaintiff's not receiving an award and the defendant's recovering damages from the plaintiff.

Pleadings in a civil lawsuit can become quite complex. In some instances, the defendant contends that a third party has an obligation to the defendant and brings a **cross-claim** against such party. In law, this is known as **third-party practice**. A cross-defendant, of course, has the same options to file motions and the same requirement to file an answer as the original defendant had.

Class Actions

A **class action** is a lawsuit brought against an alleged wrongdoer by a group of persons who have suffered a similar wrong or injury. Class actions are typically brought by parties who claim to represent a large group of unnamed persons who share a common interest in seeking relief. Class actions in federal and state courts have developed only since the mid-twentieth century. A class action may be maintained where joinder of the numerous plaintiffs is impracticable. Moreover, before the court permits a class action, the plaintiffs must establish that the questions of law or fact are common to a class of parties and that one or more parties suing on behalf of the class fairly represent the class. Likewise, representatives of the class of defendants being sued may maintain a defense. Once the trial court determines that a class action may be maintained, notice is given to all interested parties. The federal rules of civil procedure provide that any member of the class must be given the option to be excluded from the class action, and unless a party opts for exclusion, that party will be bound by the court's determination in the class action. Rules of procedure in state courts usually impose similar requirements.[9]

Class actions have become a major vehicle for social and economic reform. In recent years, class actions have been filed by persons claiming injuries resulting from exposure to cigarette smoke, asbestos, silicone breast implants, misrepresentations concerning insurance, and antitrust violations; prisoners also have instituted class actions to require states to improve prison facilities. Suits such as these frequently result in court-approved compromises. In some instances, the parties agree on the institution of certain reforms. In others, plaintiffs obtain monetary settlements and, after payment of attorney's fees and costs, the settlement proceeds are distributed to the class claimants. One of the more famous class action lawsuits involved residents of Hinkley, California, who brought suit against the Pacific Gas and Electric Company for allegedly polluting water sources with a contaminant that may have increased cancer rates in the town. The story of this case, which resulted in a $300 million settlement in 2000, was told in the movie *Erin Brockovich*.

Overall, it is critical that class action lawsuits comport with rules of civil procedure. In 2011, in *Wal-Mart v. Dukes*,[10] the Supreme Court dismissed a class action lawsuit on behalf of female employees claiming discrimination by their employer, Wal-Mart. The suit was rejected because the group did not present a common question of law or fact, thus invalidating the use of a class action lawsuit under Federal Rule of Civil Procedure 23(a). Similarly, in 2014, a federal district court judge in California ruled that Google would not face a class action lawsuit for alleged violations of email users' privacy rights; specifically, the judge stated that the various claims against Google were "too dissimilar" and thus could not be combined into one action.[11]

The Purpose, Scope, and Limitations on Discovery Proceedings

Discovery is the process whereby parties in a lawsuit can inquire into matters within the knowledge of the opposing party or that party's witnesses. Discovery rules allow inquiry into matters that may lead to relevant information concerning a claim or defense. The scope of inquiry is broad, but courts limit discovery of a party's "work product" (information prepared in anticipation of litigation) or information that is "privileged" (see later topic on Evidence in this chapter).

Discovery may be accomplished by a party's submitting written questions called **interrogatories** to another party and requiring answers to be given under oath. A more common method is by taking an oral **deposition** of a party or that party's witnesses. Such testimony is given under oath, often before a court reporter, and is subject to both direct and cross-examination. A party or witness can be compelled to produce documents for examination.

In recent years, many jurisdictions have amended their rules of procedure to allow depositions to be videotaped. One court required that a defendant being sued for injuries resulting from a karate maneuver afford the plaintiff the right to have that maneuver demonstrated and videotaped.[12]

Discovery proceedings often lead to **out-of-court settlements**. To illustrate, a defendant being sued for damages resulting from the plaintiff's injuries will usually take the plaintiff's deposition to determine the extent of those injuries and will depose the plaintiff's physicians to learn the plaintiff's diagnosis and prognosis. Often, the defendant will submit interrogatories requiring the plaintiff to itemize all claims for medical expenses, loss of income, and any other compensable items. After determining the plaintiff's injuries and economic losses, the defendant may initiate settlement negotiations.

The evidence developed by discovery processes may ordinarily be used at trial only to contradict or "impeach" the trial testimony of a party or witness. In some instances, however, if a person who has been deposed becomes unavailable for trial, courts may permit the deposition to be introduced as evidence.

Discovery proceedings are susceptible to abuse, and the trial judge may step in and exercise control over the extent of the proceedings. Where the discovery process becomes burdensome or seeks to obtain privileged materials, for example, trade secrets or an attorney's "work product," a judge can issue a **protective order** limiting the scope of discovery. One of the criticisms of the discovery process is that it has become very expensive and very time consuming.

Additional Pretrial Procedures

Parties may take depositions to perpetuate evidence in instances where it is unlikely the witness to be deposed will be available for trial. A party may also file a written request that the opposing party admit the genuineness of a document or other basic facts. The trial court can assess costs and attorney's fees against a party who improperly denies the genuineness of a document.

Where the mental or physical condition of a party is in controversy, the court may order a party to undergo a mental or physical examination. A report of the examination is made available to each party concerned.

Case Management and Pretrial Conferences

Trial judges often call for a **case management conference** to coordinate the progress of litigation and schedule and limit discovery. Once a case is ready for trial, the trial judge may call for a pretrial conference with counsel for the parties. A **pretrial conference** is designed to simplify the issues to be tried, obtain admissions of undisputed facts, obtain stipulation as to the genuineness of documentary evidence, agree on the witnesses to be presented and exhibits to be introduced at trial, and set the time for presentation of evidence by each side. Additionally, a trial judge might explore the possibilities of arriving at a settlement of the case. In some situations, this process of exploring a settlement may be overseen by a court-appointed mediator.

Will the Case Go to Trial?

Most civil suits are settled or otherwise disposed of before trial. One device available to parties in civil lawsuits is known as a Motion for Summary Final Judgment. No such device existed at common law. Rule 56 of the Federal Rules of Civil Procedure states:

> (a) For Claimant. A party seeking to recover upon a claim, counterclaim, or cross-claim or to obtain a declaratory judgment may, at any time after the expiration of 20 days from the commencement of the action or after service of a motion for summary judgment by the adverse party, move with or without supporting affidavits for a summary judgment in the party's favor upon all or any part thereof.
> (b) For Defending Party. A party against whom a claim, counterclaim, or cross-claim is asserted or a declaratory judgment is sought may, at any time, move with or without supporting affidavits for a summary judgment in the party's favor as to all or any part thereof.

By the latter half of the twentieth century, state courts began to include similar provisions in their rules of civil procedure. A party who moves for a **summary judgment** generally does so based on the discovery that has been completed and on affidavits submitted with the motion. The theory of the summary judgment procedure is that the right to a trial presupposes a genuine issue of material fact. Thus, the litigation should be terminated where there is no such issue as to material facts, or where, as a matter of law, the party against whom the motion is filed cannot legally recover or cannot legally defend against a claim. In determining whether to grant a summary judgment, the court resolves all doubts against the moving party. Summary judgments are particularly difficult to obtain in actions involving a person's negligence and are effectively precluded where a person's intent is material. Still, thousands of lawsuits are terminated at the summary judgment stage, thereby avoiding the time and expense of a trial.

Jury or Bench Trial?

In Chapter 1, we discussed traditional common law civil actions where parties were entitled to a jury trial and cases arising in equity where the chancellor made decisions without intervention of a jury. In general, courts today follow these practices in civil suits although the boundary between law and equity has become less distinct. The Seventh Amendment to the U.S. Constitution provides that for suits at common law the right to a **jury trial** is preserved where the value in controversy exceeds $20; however, this requirement applies only to the federal courts. In general, state constitutions preserve the right to a jury trial for common law civil actions, but this may be dependent on the dollar amount at stake in a particular controversy.

In many civil proceedings, there is no provision for a jury trial either because they are historically of equity origin or have been created as statutory proceedings unknown to the common law. Among the more common proceedings that were originally cases in equity are those involving domestic relations, suits to rescind contracts, suits to foreclose liens and mortgages, and those seeking an accounting or an injunction. Judges, not juries, hear statutory proceedings to change one's name and to adopt children, most proceedings concerning administration of estates and guardianships, and many disputes between lessors and lessees. A trial before a judge without a jury is known as a **bench trial**.

Jury Size

At common law, juries in both civil and criminal cases consisted of twelve persons. In *Colgrove v. Battin* (1973) (excerpted on page 337), the Supreme Court held that federal district court rules authorizing six-person juries in civil cases were permissible under the Seventh Amendment. The Court distinguished between the right to a jury trial in suits at common law and the incidents of the common law jury. States have generally followed this approach and most now permit six-person juries in civil cases.

Jury Selection

State and federal laws prescribe certain basic qualifications for jurors. Statutes commonly require that jurors be at least eighteen years of age and residents in the state or district from which they are to be selected. Convicted felons whose civil rights have not been restored are usually excluded from serving on juries. Beyond this, statutes frequently carve out exemptions for expectant mothers, mothers with young children, and persons over age seventy, as well as for physicians, dentists, attorneys, judges, teachers, elected officials, and police, fire, and emergency personnel. The trend has been for states to restrict exemptions from jury duty in order that the pool of prospective jurors reflects a cross-section of the community.

The goal is to select prospective jurors at random from lists of persons representative of the community. Local officials compile a list of persons qualified to serve as jurors, generally from the rolls of registered voters, driver's license lists, or some combination thereof. From this list, prospective jurors are randomly selected and summoned to court. Compensation paid to trial jurors ranges from meager to modest per diem travel and other expenses.[13]

The body of persons summoned to be jurors is referred to as the **venire**. After outlining the case to be tried and reciting the names of those expected to participate, the judge may excuse those whose physical disabilities or obvious conflicts of interest based on family relationships or business connections prevent them from serving. The judge swears in the remaining members of the venire to answer questions put to them by the court and counsel. Then six or twelve of these prospective jurors are called at random to take their seats in the jury box where the judge or counsel for each side may ask further questions of them in a process called the *voir dire*.

COLGROVE v. BATTIN
413 U.S. 149, 93 S. Ct. 2448, 37 L. Ed. 2d 522 (1973)

OPINION OF COURT

Mr. Justice Brennan delivered the Opinion of the Court.

. . . The pertinent words of the Seventh Amendment are: "In Suits at common law . . . the right of trial by jury shall be preserved. . . ." On its face, this language is not directed to jury characteristics, such as size, but rather defines the kind of cases for which jury trial is preserved, namely, "suits at common law." And while it is true that "[w]e have almost no direct evidence concerning the intention of the framers of the seventh amendment itself," the historical setting in which the Seventh Amendment was adopted highlighted a controversy that was generated, not by concern for preservation of jury characteristics at common law, but by fear that the civil jury itself would be abolished unless protected in express words. Almost a century and a half ago, this Court recognized that "[o]ne of the strongest objections originally taken against the constitution of the United States, was the want of an express provision securing the right of trial by jury in civil cases." . . . But the omission of a protective clause from the Constitution was not because an effort was not made to include one. On the contrary, a proposal was made to include a provision in the Constitution to guarantee the right of trial by jury in civil cases but the proposal failed because the States varied widely as to the cases in which civil jury trial was provided, and the proponents of a civil jury guarantee found too difficult the task of fashioning words appropriate to cover the different state practices. The strong pressures for a civil jury provision in the Bill of Rights encountered the same difficulty. Thus, it was agreed that, with no federal practice to draw on and since state practices varied so widely, any compromising language would necessarily have to be general. As a result, although the Seventh Amendment achieved the primary goal of jury trial adherents to incorporate an explicit constitutional protection of the right of trial by jury in civil cases, the right was limited in general words to "suits at common law." We can only conclude, therefore, that by referring to the "common law," the Framers of the Seventh Amendment were concerned with preserving the right of trial by jury in civil cases where it existed at common law, rather than the various incidents of trial by jury. In short, . . . constitutional history reveals no intention on the part of the Framers "to equate the constitutional and common law characteristics of the jury." . . .

The Voir Dire

Lawyers for the parties are permitted to challenge prospective jurors either for cause or peremptorily. A challenge is a request that a juror be excused from serving. Challenges are customarily asserted at a stage called the *voir dire* (French, meaning "to tell the truth"). The function of the *voir dire* is to enable the court and counsel to obtain the information necessary to ensure selection of a fair and impartial jury. To assist in obtaining background information, and thereby to expedite the *voir dire* process, trial courts often prepare a series of written questions to be answered by prospective jurors in advance of their appearance in court.

In some courts, the trial judge conducts the *voir dire* examination while in others the lawyers perform this function. In either event, the presiding judge exercises broad discretion to keep the questioning within proper bounds. A *voir dire* examination is generally conducted before the prospective jurors are initially selected; however, under certain circumstances some courts have allowed examination of individual jurors apart from the collective group.

Obviously, each trial lawyer wants jurors who may be sympathetic to the cause he or she advocates. Trial lawyers have their own peculiar theories on how to conduct a *voir dire* examination, but most would agree that a practical knowledge of psychology is helpful. In recent years, some have even retained social scientists for advice and assistance in the jury selection process. The process of excusing prospective jurors is accomplished by counsel's exercising challenges, either "for cause" or "peremptorily," that is, without assigning a reason.

In order to determine whether to exercise a challenge, an attorney conducting a *voir dire* examination attempts to determine the attitudes, background, and personalities of prospective jurors. Trial courts limit the questions that may be asked of prospective jurors, depending on the nature of the case. Some areas are considered very delicate and usually will not be permitted. For example, in 1985 the Supreme Court of Georgia upheld a trial judge's refusal to allow a defendant to ask prospective jurors questions concerning the kinds of books and magazine they read, whether they were members of any political organization, and the kinds of bumper stickers they had on their vehicles.[14]

Challenges for Cause

A **challenge for cause** may be directed to the venire on basis of the panel's having been improperly selected, for example, where a lawyer contends that the selection procedures exclude minority members. More commonly, challenges for cause are directed to a prospective juror individually concerning some fact that would disqualify that person from serving on the particular case. Among the more common reasons for disqualification of a prospective juror are having a close relationship with counsel or the parties to the litigation, or being involved in the case as a witness or in some other capacity. The court may excuse any prospective juror who acknowledges having formed an opinion on the merits of the case and who cannot disregard it. However, absent unusual circumstances concerning the parties involved in a case, a person would not be excused for cause because of religious or political affiliations.

Peremptory Challenges

Each side is allowed a limited number of **peremptory challenges** that may be exercised on *voir dire* to excuse prospective jurors without stating any reason. The number of peremptory challenges is usually provided by statute or court rules. In federal courts, each party in a civil suit is allowed three peremptory challenges.[15] States vary in the number of peremptory challenges they allow, with many following the federal practice.

Historically, lawyers were permitted to exercise peremptory challenges without advancing any reason; however, in the past two decades courts have reassessed this historic freedom. In 1986, the U.S. Supreme Court prohibited the exercise of **racially based peremptory challenges**, holding that such intentional discrimination based on race violates the Equal Protection Clause of the Fourteenth Amendment to the U.S. Constitution.[16] In 1994, the Court resolved conflict among lower federal courts and held that the Equal Protection Clause also prohibits **gender-based peremptory challenges**.[17] These decisions have required lawyers to be quite cautious in their exercise of peremptory challenges. Some commentators even believe that peremptory challenges are becoming a relic in trial practice.

Empanelling of the Jury

If a challenge is successful, the prospective juror is excused or "struck" and another prospective juror is seated and questioned until all challenges are exhausted. The jury is then selected. After selection is complete, the jury is sworn in as a body by the judge or the clerk of the court. The jury is advised not to discuss the case until instructed by the court to deliberate. If the court anticipates the trial will likely be protracted, the judge may have one or more alternate jurors selected to serve should any juror become ill or have to respond to an emergency. An alternate juror sits with the jury, but unless substituted for a regular juror, the alternate is excused just before the jury retires to deliberate.

Opening Statements by Counsel

At the beginning of a trial, each attorney is afforded the opportunity to make an **opening statement**. In a bench trial, that is, a case tried before a judge without a jury, the opening statement is usually quite brief, and frequently counsel waives it. On the other hand, an opening statement before a jury affords the attorneys an opportunity to "get acquainted" with the jury and outline the case to be presented, identify the participants, explain legal terms, and orient the jury as to how the case will proceed. Counsel must be careful to inform the jury that their statements are not evidence and that the case must be decided based on the evidence produced during the trial. Experienced trial lawyers emphasize that the opening statement should not be read or given in the form of a speech or lecture, but should "tell a story" informally in narrative form.

Direct and Cross-Examination

By the time a case goes to trial, the lawyers representing the parties are very conversant with the proof required to establish their case or defense. It is the plaintiff's task to effectively establish the case by a **preponderance** (greater weight) **of the evidence**. In most instances, counsel present events chronologically; however, logic and strategy often dictate another order of proof. The plaintiff's lawyer conducts a **direct examination** of each witness, after which the defendant's lawyer has the right of **cross-examination**. This can be followed by redirect and re-cross examinations.

The purpose of cross-examination is to weaken or disprove the testimony that the witness gave on direct examination. Skillful cross-examination is a hallmark of a successful trial lawyer. Although a juror is inclined to view the cross-examination as spontaneous, effective cross-examination is based on careful advance planning. Lawyers are aided greatly by the information that a witness has disclosed during the pretrial discovery phases. Unlike direct examination, the cross-examiner is permitted to ask leading questions, although the scope of inquiry is generally limited to matters brought out on the direct examination of the witness and any interest, bias, or motive of the witness. If a cross-examiner succeeds in showing that the witness's testimony is inconsistent with a prior statement, or that the witness has previously been convicted of a crime, or has a bad reputation in the community for telling the truth, it impeaches the credibility of the witness.

The defendant's lawyer must seek to disprove the plaintiff's contentions and in some instances must prove a specific defense. Consider a lawsuit where the plaintiff seeks damages for personal injuries sustained in an automobile collision. In some states, if the defendant proves the plaintiff's actions were a substantial contributing factor, the defendant can defeat the plaintiff's claim through the doctrine of contributory negligence; in other states, such proof can mitigate the award of damages to the plaintiff under the theory of comparative fault.

In most civil trials, the witnesses' testimony comprises most of the evidence, although documents and other exhibits, referred to as documentary evidence, are frequently introduced. Medical charts, x-rays, photographs, and mortality tables showing life expectancy are often introduced in personal injury and wrongful death actions. Increasingly, courts admit surveillance films or videotapes to confirm or contradict an injured party's claims. When a case involves contract rights, the parties will introduce written contracts, cancelled checks, memoranda, and business records. In a boundary dispute, counsel usually introduce deeds and land surveys.

Expert Witnesses

If scientific, technical, or other specialized knowledge will assist the court or jury in understanding the evidence presented or in determining an essential fact, a party may present expert testimony. An **expert witness** is one who by knowledge, skill, experience, training, or education is qualified to present testimony and offer opinion on a particular subject. Lawyers are given the opportunity to cross-examine witnesses offered as experts before the court rules as to whether the witness can testify as an expert. In many cases, lawyers for the parties stipulate as to the qualifications of a witness offered as an expert. Physicians normally are called to testify in personal injury and wrongful death cases. Engineers testify in cases involving patents and controversies over claims involving mechanical defects of products. In commercial litigation and antitrust cases, it is common to call accountants, economists, and statisticians. College professors are also frequent expert witnesses. While lay witnesses are restricted in voicing opinions, experts are permitted to give their opinions, often in response to hypothetical questions asked by lawyers.

CASE IN POINT

ADMISSIBILITY OF SCIENTIFIC EVIDENCE IN FEDERAL COURTS
Daubert v. Merrell Dow Pharmaceuticals, Inc.
United States Supreme Court
509 U.S. 579, 113 S. Ct. 2786, 125 L. Ed. 2d 469 (1993)

Jason Daubert and Eric Schuller brought suit against a major pharmaceutical company, alleging that their serious birth defects were caused by their mothers' prenatal ingestion of Bendectin, a prescription drug used to treat nausea. The federal district judge granted summary judgment for the defendant based on an expert's affidavit concluding that Bendectin had not been shown to cause birth defects. The judge rejected expert testimony introduced by the plaintiffs, determining that it did not meet the "general acceptance" test for the admission of expert testimony set forth in *Frye v. United States* (1923). The Court of Appeals affirmed. The Supreme Court reversed, holding that the Federal Rules of Evidence, not the *Frye* decision, provide the standard for admitting expert scientific testimony in federal court. Writing for the Court, Justice Blackmun concluded that " '[g]eneral acceptance' is not a necessary precondition to the admissibility of scientific evidence under the Federal Rules of Evidence, but the Rules of Evidence ... do assign to the trial judge the task of ensuring that an expert's testimony both rests on a reliable foundation and is relevant to the task at hand." Under this ruling, federal district judges must be the arbiters of what is legitimate and what is "junk" science.

Throughout most of the twentieth century, American courts approached questions relating to the validity of an expert's opinion by applying the "general acceptance" or *Frye* test.[18] If the principle expounded by the expert met with general acceptance in the scientific community, the testimony was admitted. However, in 1993 the U.S. Supreme Court, in *Daubert v. Merrell Dow Pharmaceuticals, Inc.*,[19] rejected the *Frye* test. The Court held that admissibility of scientific evidence is controlled by the Federal Rules of Evidence and must be based on several factors, including whether the evidence can be tested and whether it can be subjected to peer review. Because the Court's ruling is not one of constitutional dimension, state courts are not required to follow it. Many state courts continue to follow the *Frye* test; some have elected to follow *Daubert*; and a few have their own rules on admissibility of scientific evidence.

When the Plaintiff Rests

When the plaintiff's lawyer has completed presentation of the plaintiff's case, the lawyer "rests." At that point, the defense lawyer in a jury trial will often move for a **directed verdict** for the defense. This motion, sometimes called a motion for **involuntary dismissal** in a bench trial case, asks the trial judge to rule that the evidence presented by the plaintiff, taken most favorably to the plaintiff, is insufficient to support a verdict for the plaintiff. If the court rules with the defense, the action is terminated. If, as in most cases, the motion is denied, the defense is allowed to present its evidence and at the conclusion of the trial may again seek dismissal on the same ground.

The Case for the Defense and the Rebuttals

The defense lawyer proceeds to present the defendant's case much as outlined above for the plaintiff's lawyer, offering witnesses, perhaps including experts, and documentary evidence. If the defense has asserted a specific defense, then it must establish that defense by the preponderance (greater weight) of the evidence.

The plaintiff is allowed to introduce evidence in **rebuttal** to the evidence offered by the defendant. In turn, the defendant is usually allowed to rebut the plaintiff's rebuttal evidence. The presentation of rebuttal evidence is much less lengthy than the parties' main cases, and even might consist of the testimony of just one key witness.

The Court Instructs the Jury

At the close of all evidence in a jury trial, it is customary for the trial judge to confer with counsel outside the presence of the jury concerning the instructions on the law the judge will give to the jury. The trial court announces its intention to give certain standard instructions and offers to supplement them with specific instructions to be chosen from those submitted by counsel. A party is entitled to have the jury instructed on the law applicable to any legitimate issue that is supported by the evidence. **Jury instructions** are settled in advance of closing arguments by counsel so each can argue with assurance of how the judge will instruct the jury.

Closing Arguments

Because a judge is trained in evaluating evidence, counsel in bench trials frequently waive their right to make **closing arguments**; otherwise, their arguments are generally quite brief. But in jury trials, lawyers place great importance on their closing arguments. Closing arguments are designed to assist the jury in recalling and evaluating the evidence and in drawing inferences therefrom. Many lawyers begin by recapitulating the evidence in the light most favorable to their client. After that, the lawyer for each side entreats the jury to rule in favor of their client. Counsel may comment on the weight of the evidence and the credibility of the witnesses but may not state a personal belief about the merits of the case or refer to any matters—other than those of common, everyday knowledge—that have not been introduced in evidence. Improper comments by counsel may result in a **mistrial** if the judge determines that they have prejudiced the jury.

The Jury Deliberates and Returns Its Verdict

When directed to deliberate, the jurors are escorted to their quarters by a court bailiff. In some cases, the judge orders the jury sequestered, which means the jury must remain together until it reaches its verdict. **Sequestration of the jury**, however, is uncommon in civil cases. Once in the jury room, the jury's first order of business is to elect a foreperson. Then they are ready to commence their deliberations. Because jury deliberations are secret, we can only speculate about the reasoning processes of jurors. We do know, however, that juries usually take a preliminary vote shortly after electing a foreperson. On occasion, the jury will ask the court to reconvene to answer a question before concluding deliberations; the judge, after conferring with counsel, attempts to answer such questions succinctly so that their deliberations may be completed. If the jury is unable to reach a verdict, this is known as **hung jury**, and the court declares a mistrial.

Jury verdicts in civil cases may be either "general" or "special." An example of a **general verdict** is one where the jury finds that the defendant is liable to the plaintiff and assesses the plaintiff's damages as $10,000, or a verdict simply finding that the defendant is not liable to the plaintiff. A **special verdict** is one where the jury specifically answers questions posed by the court on the form of verdict submitted to the jury. For example, many states have comparative negligence laws. In such a state, in a suit to recover damages for personal injuries based on the defendant's negligence, the plaintiff's award is based on the percentage of fault the jury assigns against the defendant. A suit for damages arising out of an automobile accident is a typical example. The jury may find the defendant at fault but may answer a special verdict question that the plaintiff was also at fault to the extent of, say, 25 percent. If the jury determined the plaintiff should receive $20,000 in damages, those damages would be reduced by 25 percent and the court would award the plaintiff $15,000.

Upon return of the jury's verdict, the lawyers may exercise their right to poll the jury, that is, to ask each juror: "Is this your verdict?" Upon completion of this procedure, the trial judge usually discharges the jury. The losing party may then ask the trial judge for a new trial based on a claim of error in the trial proceedings. Such motions are rarely granted, but they can have an important bearing on issues that the losing party can raise on appeal. In addition, the court will generally award the prevailing party the court costs and, in some instances, attorney's fees.

Judgment Notwithstanding the Verdict

Under the common law, a judge in a civil trial could not set aside a jury verdict and enter judgment for the other party based on the judge's own assessment of the evidence. If the judge erred in failing to direct a verdict for the defense prior to submitting the case to the jury, the only remedy was to order a new trial. Under the Federal Rules of Civil Procedure and under most state rules, judges can, as a matter of law, enter a judgment contrary to the jury's verdict.[20] However, a judge may not do this if there is a substantial factual basis for the jury's verdict.[21]

THE RULES OF EVIDENCE

Rules of evidence govern the admissibility of factual information before a court. They are largely based on the common law and historically have been found in appellate court decisions. In the latter half of the twentieth century, it became common for legislative bodies and courts to codify the rules of evidence applicable to both civil and criminal cases. In this section, we discuss the general rules of evidence with emphasis on civil cases. In Chapter 10, we amplify those rules as they relate to criminal cases.

Judicial Notice

Certain matters that are beyond argument are accepted by a court without proof. Courts accept such facts, as well as laws, by taking **judicial notice**. Courts customarily take judicial notice of the calendar, names of certain public officials, the boundaries of a geographical area, and other undisputed facts well known in the jurisdiction where the court sits. Courts also take judicial notice of laws, rules of procedure, and the rules of evidence. Rule 201 of the Federal Rules of Evidence states that it is discretionary for a court to take judicial notice, whether requested or not, but that the court shall take judicial notice if requested by a party and supplied with the necessary information. In most states, statutes or rules of court include similar provisions.

Evidentiary Presumptions

An **evidentiary presumption** is an assumption of fact that the law makes from the existence of another fact or facts, although unproven by evidence. These are evidentiary devices designed to aid a party who has the burden of proof. Under this type of presumption, once evidence establishes a fact, the judge and jury may infer something else is true, provided there is a rational connection between the established fact and the presumed fact. In effect, this means that if a party proves certain facts, the judge or jury accepts the presumed fact as proven unless evidence rebuts the presumed fact. Most presumptions are rebuttable. For example, there is a **rebuttable presumption** that a child born during marriage is the child of the marital partners. There is a rebuttable presumption that a properly stamped, addressed, and mailed letter reached its intended recipient.[22] A party who rebuts the presumption has the burden of proving the presumption false.

Classifications of Evidence

There are several classifications of evidence. First, evidence may be real or testimonial. **Real evidence** consists of maps, blood samples, x-rays, photographs, fingerprints, knives, guns, and other tangible items. **Testimonial evidence** consists of sworn statements of witnesses. Watching a television drama might give the impression that a trial consists largely of real evidence, but the great majority of evidence presented in civil and criminal trials comes from the mouths of the witnesses, both lay and expert.

Next, evidence may be direct or indirect. **Direct evidence** is evidence that directly proves a fact in issue, and includes **eyewitness testimony**. In contrast, **indirect evidence** only tends to establish a fact in issue and usually consists of **circumstantial evidence**. In a civil trial, a witness who actually saw an automobile accident would be giving direct evidence. However, testimony by a witness who before the accident saw the defendant driving the vehicle that was later involved in the accident would be giving circumstantial evidence tending to indicate that the defendant was the driver. Testimony that reveals that the defendant's fingerprints were found on a window pane of that house shortly after it was broken into is also circumstantial evidence and depending on the circumstances, it may be inferred that the defendant entered the house through that window. The admissibility of circumstantial evidence is well established in American law. Contrary to popular belief, there is no real difference in the weight given circumstantial, as opposed to real, evidence.[23]

Requirements of Admissibility

Before a witness testifies in a judicial proceeding, the witness takes an oath to swear or affirm to tell the truth. The common law rule no longer bars a witness from testifying because the witness does not profess belief in a Supreme Being. Where a witness does not understand the English language, the court appoints an interpreter who must take an oath to properly interpret the questions asked and the witness's answers. Before evidence may be admitted in court, whether real or testimonial and whether direct or circumstantial, it must be relevant and must come from a competent witness.

Relevancy

To be admissible in court proceedings, evidence must also be relevant. **Relevant evidence** is that which tends to prove or disprove a material fact. Consequently, evidence that is relevant in one case may not necessarily be relevant in another. Trial judges have considerable discretion in determining whether evidence is relevant.

Certain relevant evidence may not be admissible in court proceedings. It may be needlessly cumulative. The following are examples where the probative value of relevant evidence is outweighed by the prejudice that would likely ensue for the party against whom the evidence is offered:

- A person's character is generally held to be inadmissible to prove that a person behaved in a certain way.
- An offer to compromise a disputed claim or statements made during settlement negotiations is inadmissible.
- The fact that the defendant carries liability insurance is generally inadmissible in a suit seeking to recover damages based on a defendant's alleged negligence.

Competency

To be admissible in court, evidence must also be **competent**. At common law, persons who had an interest in the case were not permitted to testify, and a person younger than age fourteen was presumed to be incapable of testifying. Statutes and court decisions have eliminated these disqualifications in the United States. A witness, regardless of age or interest, who has the ability to understand the nature and obligation of taking an oath to tell the truth is presumed to be competent. A party who asserts to the contrary must establish that the witness is not competent to testify. Even a person adjudged incompetent might be permitted to testify if the court finds that person is lucid at the time of testifying. In the case of a very young child, it is the judge's duty to determine if the child has sufficient maturity to understand, remember, and relate facts and that the child understands the obligation of taking an oath to tell the truth. In some instances, a child as young as five or six has been allowed to testify in cases of child abuse. Trial judges have broad discretion to make such a determination.

Privileges

A witness may be competent to testify and may be in a position to offer relevant evidence, yet in certain instances the court may not hear the evidence. Since early common law, courts have decided that it is in the interest of society that certain forms of communication remain confidential. Therefore, certain facts that may be relevant are not admissible in court proceedings because they are **privileged communications**. The most common privileges include the following:

- **Attorney-client privilege.** A communication between an attorney and client that is not intended to be disclosed to a third person is considered privileged, subject to certain exceptions. There is no privilege as to any communication by the client informing the attorney of the client's intent to commit a crime or to perpetrate a fraud.
- **Marital privilege.** Communications between spouses are intended to be confidential and privileged. The privilege emanates from the common law and is based on promoting and preserving domestic harmony and on the repugnance against convicting one person through the testimony of another who shares intimate secrets of domestic life. The temptation to perjure is another consideration. The privilege not only allows a spouse to refuse to disclose communications, but also allows one spouse to prevent the other spouse from disclosing them. Most courts hold that neither divorce nor death invalidates the privilege. But suppose a husband confessed to his wife that he had stolen building materials from a job where he was working. The wife would be prohibited from testifying to that conversation. On the other hand, the wife could testify that her husband arrived home with some building materials. Like other privileges, there are exceptions. The privilege does not apply when one spouse sues the other, when litigation arises out of child abuse, or when a spouse offers testimony on behalf of a spouse who is a defendant. States that have enacted laws providing for same-sex marriage usually incorporate the marital communications privilege and the benefits of the marital immunity from compelled testimony (see Chapter 8). A few jurisdictions have extended the privilege by making it applicable to confidential communications between a parent and minor child.
- **Clergy privilege.** Communications made by a person to a clergyperson seeking spiritual assistance are privileged. Generally, priests, ministers, and rabbis are prohibited from testifying about matters related to them in confidence by a penitent.
- **Additional privileges.** States frequently have added privileges such as those between an accountant and client, between a physician and patient, and between a psychotherapist and patient. Moreover, courts frequently allow a limited privilege not to disclose trade secrets.

Expert Witnesses

Today, **forensic experts** in nearly every field make a specialty of testifying in court. To qualify as an expert, a witness must present proper credentials and be received by the trial court as an expert. After one side offers a witness as an expert, opposing counsel may cross-examine the prospective witness about the witness's qualifications. Thus, a physician who is to give evidence as to the cause of death of someone is first asked to relate his or her educational background and experience in the specialized area of medical practice in question. The trial judge has considerable discretion in determining whether a witness is to be received as an expert.

Unlike lay witnesses, expert witnesses may respond to hypothetical questions and may express opinions within the realm of their expertise. Fingerprint identification, ballistics tests, handwriting exemplars, and medical tests have been prominent among areas where expert evidence is commonly received in criminal cases. More recently, evidence of speed detection devices and devices to test blood-alcohol content have become commonplace in civil and criminal trials.

An expert who has knowledge from personal observation may testify on that basis. For example, in some states, a psychiatrist who has examined the accused may offer an opinion as to the accused's sanity. If the expert is not acquainted with the person or subject from personal observation, the expert can base an opinion upon a **hypothetical question** that assumes the existence of facts the evidence tends to establish.

Testimony Generally Considered Unreliable

The majority of courts have held that hypnotically induced testimony is not sufficiently reliable to be admissible. In 1987, the Supreme Court held that excluding hypnotically induced testimony, when applied to prevent an accused from testifying as to his or her own posthypnotic recall, violated the constitutional right to testify on one's own behalf.[24] Accordingly, the position of the majority of courts to exclude all hypnotically induced testimony should not prevent an accused from testifying to the accused's own posthypnotic recall.

Courts also have been opposed to admitting evidence derived from a polygraph. A polygraph is a device that records the subject's physiological activities, such as blood pressure and heartbeat, as the subject is questioned by an examiner. The examiner poses certain questions and records the subject's responses. Historically, federal and state courts have declined to admit **polygraph evidence** on the ground that the reliability of polygraph testing has not been scientifically demonstrated to such a degree of certainty as to establish its reliability. However, some courts allow results of polygraph testing to be admitted in court on stipulation of counsel for both parties.

"Your Honor, I Object"

Anyone who has observed a trial, or even a television drama depicting one, is familiar with the advocates frequently addressing the court, "Your honor, I object. . . ." To this, the objecting lawyer may add, for example, "on the ground that the testimony is irrelevant." This is called a **general objection**. Or, the lawyer may make a **specific objection** by adding, for example, "because the testimony sought would be hearsay," "because the answer calls for an opinion of the witness which the witness is not qualified to give," or even one or more other grounds for specific objections. We consider some of the more common grounds for objections below.

Hearsay Evidence

Hearsay evidence refers to an oral or written statement by a person, other than the one testifying in court. The general rule is often stated as: A witness may not testify as to a statement made by another if that statement is offered as proof of the matter asserted. Thus, a witness who testifies, "I know the defendant was home on the night of March 13 because my sister told me so" would be giving hearsay testimony. The hearsay rule has many exceptions. Sometimes, a hearsay statement is admissible to prove something other than the truth of the statement itself. Further, a party's out-of-court statement is generally considered an exception to the hearsay rule if it is an admission, confession, or some other statement against that party's interest. The following are among the many exceptions to the hearsay rule.

- **Spontaneous or excited utterances.**   Where a statement is spontaneously made to describe or explain some event at or immediately following the event it is deemed sufficiently trustworthy to be an exception to the hearsay rule.
- **Dying declarations.**   A person's dying declaration is a statement made while the declarant believed that death was imminent. In 1961, the Maryland Supreme Court held such a statement might even be in response to a question asked by a bystander, thus not requiring the usual spontaneity.[25]
- **Reputation and records.**   Evidence of a person's reputation in the community and evidence of births, deaths, and other data contained in old family records are exceptions to the hearsay rule.
- **Business and public records.**   Business records kept in the ordinary course of business, hospital and medical records, and authenticated public records are exceptions to the hearsay rule.
- **Statements made for medical diagnosis.**   Because there is a slight chance that a person who is seeking treatment will relate incorrect facts to a physician, statements made to secure medical treatment are held to be an exception to the hearsay rule.

The Best Evidence Rule

Ordinarily, the best evidence of a transaction must be offered in court. The **best evidence rule** applies to writings and means that an original document must be offered unless the party who offers a copy can present a plausible explanation of why the original is not available. For example, the original contract being sued upon should be produced rather than photocopies. With modern photocopying processes, lawyers often stipulate that such copies of original documents be admitted in court.

Opinion Evidence

A lay witness is supposed to testify regarding facts within the witness's personal knowledge. In addition, lay witnesses are permitted to testify about such matters perceived through their physical senses and matters that are within the common knowledge of most people, such as speed of a vehicle, sizes, distances, or appearance of a person. They cannot give **opinion evidence** on matters beyond the common experience and understanding of laypersons. To illustrate: A driver can give an estimate of the speed of a vehicle observed traveling on the street. But a witness must be qualified as an expert to be permitted to testify as to the speed of a car based on observation of the car's skid marks on the pavement. Such an opinion must be based on facts perceived by the witness and not on hearsay statements.

APPELLATE PROCEDURE

Appellate courts perform dual functions in the civil and criminal process: **error correction** and **lawmaking**. Intermediate federal or state appellate courts review most civil and criminal appeals, although in the less populous states, the highest court of the state handles routine appeals. In these routine appeals, the primary function of appellate courts is to correct trial court errors. Appellate review is designed to ensure that substantive justice has been accomplished under constitutional standards of due process of law. Because of gaps in the statutory law and the inevitable need to interpret both statutory and constitutional provisions, appellate courts, in effect, must "make law." This lawmaking function is more characteristic of the highest courts than of intermediate appellate tribunals.

To the layperson, the jurisdictional requisites and procedures of appellate courts appear complex. Although these procedures vary in detail, they essentially follow the same basic path for both civil and criminal appeals. In some instances, a party who desires an appeal must first file a motion asking the trial court to order a new trial. This is often a pro forma measure, but it affords the trial judge an opportunity to review the defendant's claim of error and award a new trial if necessary. For some appellate courts, a motion for a new trial may be a prerequisite to challenging whether the evidence was sufficient to sustain the lower court's judgment.

Appellate courts possess both original and appellate jurisdiction. Most of the work of an appellate court concerns its appellate jurisdiction, that is, the power to review decisions of lower tribunals. We first discuss this phase of appellate procedure. At the conclusion of the chapter, we briefly mention the original jurisdiction of appellate courts.

Filing the Appeal

Once a party has determined the correct forum for an appeal or a petition for discretionary review, a series of steps follows. First, the **notice of appeal** or petition for review must be filed in the appropriate court within a specified period of time. The courts tend to strictly enforce the time requirement because it is this notice or petition that confers jurisdiction on the appellate court to act on the case.

Rule 4 of the Federal Rules of Appellate Procedure provides that an appeal in a civil case must be filed within thirty days after the entry of the judgment. In state courts, an aggrieved party usually has thirty days after entry of judgment to file an appeal. The filing of a notice of appeal must be accompanied by the payment of a required filing fee, although this fee can be waived in cases where an indigent party files a motion to proceed *in forma pauperis* ("in the manner of a pauper").

Filing Petitions for Discretionary Review

A party to a civil suit or a criminal defendant is generally limited to one appeal as a matter of right; however; additional review may be available on a discretionary basis with a higher court. In the U.S. Supreme Court and most state supreme courts, discretionary review occurs through the grant of a **writ of certiorari**. Rule 13 of the Rules of the United States Supreme Court states that a "petition for a writ of certiorari . . . shall be in time when it is filed . . . within 90 days after the entry of the judgment" of the lower court. State supreme courts have similar rules but usually allow less time to seek discretionary review.

"Cert petitions," as petitions of certiorari are commonly called, are granted at the discretion of the reviewing court. In deciding whether to exercise its discretion, the U.S. Supreme Court looks to whether there is a **substantial federal question** involved. If so, the Court is then interested in whether the petitioner has exhausted all other remedies available. In deciding whether to grant certiorari, the Court follows the **rule of four**, meaning that at least four of the nine justices must vote to place a case on the docket. The highest state courts usually follow a similar procedure, that is, they require that a certain number of justices agree to grant discretionary review.

Motions

During the early stages of the appellate process, counsel use **motions** to draw the court's immediate attention to procedural matters outside the routine of the appellate process. Counsel may request additional time to meet deadlines for filing briefs or move for expedited consideration of an appeal. By appropriate motions, counsel may request to sever or consolidate multiple appeals or to supplement the record the trial court has transmitted to the appellate court. Upon a showing of good cause, an appellate court may stay enforcement of a lower court judgment pending resolution of the appeal.

Filing of Briefs

Filing a notice of appeal or a petition for discretionary review sets in motion a series of procedural steps governed by the rules of appellate procedure of the federal or state appellate court. It is incumbent on the appellant or petitioner to have the clerk of the trial court forward to the appellate tribunal certified copies of pertinent records and transcripts of testimony relevant to the issues to be raised on appeal. Beyond this, procedures vary somewhat depending largely on whether the appeal is one of right or whether the defendant is seeking discretionary relief.

The party taking an appeal is called the **appellant**; the responding party is known as the **appellee**. In an appeal of right, the appellant files an **initial brief** summarizing the legal posture and the factual background of the case in the lower tribunal. Briefs are the principal instruments used to persuade the appellate court to reverse, affirm, or modify the decision being appealed. The extent of background information contained in the briefs depends on the points to be presented to the appellate court. Briefs are heavily laden with citations to constitutional provisions, statutes, and court decisions that the advocates regard as persuasive. The appellee is permitted to respond by filing an **answer brief**, and the appellant may then file a **reply brief**. The whole process resembles the order of a formal debate where the affirmative presents its case, followed by the negative and a rebuttal by the affirmative.

Where a petitioner seeks discretionary review, the appellate court must first decide whether to accept or deny the request to take jurisdiction. If the court determines to proceed on the petition, it will order all affected parties (respondents) to furnish the court a written response. As in an appeal of right, often the **petitioner** is permitted to file a reply to that response. Counsel must always furnish copies of briefs and other materials to their adversaries.

Oral Argument

After the appellate court has reviewed briefs, it may schedule **oral argument** where counsel for both parties appear. Typically, appellate courts conduct oral arguments in about half the cases they decide. During oral argument, counsel for both parties may summarize their positions orally and then respond to questions from the bench. Usually, each side is given fifteen to thirty minutes for an oral presentation. Increasingly, oral arguments are punctuated by questions from the bench. Indeed, today, many oral arguments take the form of a dialogue rather than that of a structured presentation.

The Judicial Conference

Unlike a trial court, where a single judge and jury decide the case, appellate decisions are made by panels of three or more judges without a jury. In intermediate appellate courts, these panels are generally selected by lot from the entire bench of judges who sit on that appellate court. Thus, appellate judges customarily confer on the disposition of appeals. The **judicial conference** is regarded as an essential part of the collegial process that distinguishes the appellate role from that of the trial court. If there has been oral argument, it is common for the panel of judges who heard the case to confer shortly thereafter. At that time, the panel frequently attempts to determine the disposition of the appeal but, in some instances, may find it necessary to further canvass the record or call upon counsel or the court's own staff lawyers for additional legal research. Where there has been no oral argument, the panel of judges assigned to the case usually confers after each judge has had the opportunity to review the briefs and pertinent records and the results of any research assignments given to the court's legal staff.

The Judgment of the Court

Essentially, an appellate court has three options in addressing a case before it. First, it may dismiss the appeal. This is uncommon in appeals of right, unless the appeal is untimely. Dismissal is more common in cases of discretionary review. Even after an appeal has been fully argued, the U.S. Supreme Court will sometimes dismiss a petition for certiorari as having been improvidently granted. When an appeal or cert petition is dismissed, the judgment of the lower tribunal remains undisturbed. The second option is to **affirm** the decision being reviewed, which preserves the judgment of the lower tribunal. The third option is to **reverse** the judgment of the lower tribunal. A reversal is usually accompanied by an order to **remand** the case to the lower tribunal for further proceedings consistent with the higher court's opinion. When a court of last resort remands a case to an intermediate appellate court, the latter must reconsider the case in light of the higher court's decision.

Appellate Court Opinions

After an appellate court has arrived at a decision, it remains for the court to issue an opinion announcing its decision. Some opinions simply announce the court's decision; others are quite lengthy in considering the arguments of counsel and articulating the reasons for the court's decision. An individual judge or justice generally prepares the court's opinion. If responsibility for preparation of an opinion has not been previously given to one judge, that responsibility is usually assigned at conference by the senior judge or the senior judge voting with the majority of the panel. A professional staff of law clerks and secretaries assists judges.

There are two basic types of appellate court opinions: per curiam and signed. A **per curiam opinion** represents the appellate court as a whole; it is not attributed to any individual judge or group of judges on the court. More commonly, appellate courts announce their decisions by an **opinion of the court** signed by one judge and joined by other judges comprising a majority. A judge who agrees with the court's decision but wishes to address or emphasize certain arguments not addressed or emphasized in the opinion of the court may write a separate **concurring opinion**. Sometimes, a judge writes an opinion **concurring in the judgment** only, meaning the judge supports the decision of the court but for reasons other than those articulated in the court's opinion. A judge who disagrees with the decision of the court may write a **dissenting opinion** explaining the judge's rationale for disagreeing with the majority opinion.

Publication of Appellate Decisions

Most decisions of appellate courts in America are published in books known as **reporters**. The publication of appellate decisions plays an important role in the development of the law, because judges and lawyers regularly consult the case reporters for guidance in pending cases.

Decisions of the United States Supreme Court are officially published in the *United States Reports* (abbreviated U.S.). Two private organizations also report these decisions in hard-cover volumes. The *Supreme Court Reporter* (abbreviated S. Ct.) is published by West, and *Lawyers' Edition*, now in its second series (abbreviated L. Ed. 2d), is published by the Michie Company. Although the three reporters have somewhat different editorial features, the opinions of the Supreme Court are reproduced identically in all three reporters.

References to judicial decisions found in the reporters are called **citations**. United States Supreme Court decisions are often cited to all three publications: for example, *Felker v. Turpin*, 518 U.S. 1051, 116 S. Ct. 2333, 135 L. Ed. 2d 827 (1996).

Since 1889, the decisions of the United States Courts of Appeals have been published in West's *Federal Reporter*, now in its third series (abbreviated F.3d). Decisions of federal district (trial) courts are published in West's *Federal Supplement*, now in its second series (abbreviated F. Supp. 2d). A citation to a case in *Federal Reporter* will read, for example, *Newman v. United States*, 817 F.2d 635 (10th Cir. 1987). This refers to a 1987 case reported in volume 817, page 635 of the *Federal Reporter*, second series, decided by the United States Court of Appeals for the Tenth Circuit. A citation to *United States v. Klopfenstine*, 673 F. Supp. 356 (W.D. Mo. 1987), refers to a 1987 federal district court decision from the western district of Missouri reported in volume 673, page 356 of the *Federal Supplement*.

Additional federal reporters publish the decisions from other federal courts (e.g., bankruptcy and military appeals), but the federal reporters referred to earlier are those most frequently used in specialized legal research.

The Regional Reporters

The decisions of the highest state courts (usually but not always called supreme courts) and the decisions of other state appellate courts (usually referred to as intermediate appellate courts) are found in seven regional reporters, West's *California Reporter*, and the *New York Supplement*. Regional reporters, with their abbreviations in parentheses, include decisions from the following states:

- *Atlantic Reporter* (A. and A.2d): Connecticut, Delaware, the District of Columbia, Maine, Maryland, New Hampshire, New Jersey, Pennsylvania, Rhode Island, and Vermont
- *North Eastern Reporter* (N.E. and N.E.2d): Illinois, Indiana, Massachusetts, New York (court of last resort only), and Ohio
- *North Western Reporter* (N.W. and N.W.2d): Iowa, Michigan, Minnesota, Nebraska, North Dakota, South Dakota, and Wisconsin
- *Pacific Reporter* (P., P.2d, and P.3d): Alaska, Arizona, California, Colorado, Hawaii, Idaho, Kansas, Montana, Nevada, New Mexico, Oklahoma, Oregon, Utah, Washington, and Wyoming
- *Southern Reporter* (So., So. 2d and So. 3d): Alabama, Florida, Louisiana, and Mississippi
- *South Eastern Reporter* (S.E. and S.E.2d): Georgia, North Carolina, South Carolina, Virginia, and West Virginia
- *South Western Reporter* (S.W., S.W.2d, and S.W.3d): Arkansas, Kentucky, Missouri, Tennessee, and Texas

The following examples of citation forms appear in some of the regional reporters:

- *State v. Hogan*, 480 So. 2d 288 (La. 1985). This refers to a 1985 decision of the Louisiana Supreme Court found in volume 480, page 288 of the *Southern Reporter*, second series.

■ *Molien v. Kaiser Foundation Hospitals,* 616 P.2d 813 (Cal. 1980). This refers to a 1980 decision of the Supreme Court of California found in volume 616, page 813 of the *Pacific Reporter,* second series.

■ *Tinsley v. Tinsley,* 512 S.W.2d 74 (Tex. Civ. App. 1974). This refers to a 1974 decision of the Texas Civil Court of Appeals found in volume 512, page 74 of the *South Western Reporter,* second series.

Syllabi, Headnotes, and Key Numbers

The National Reporter System and the regional reporters contain not only the official text of each reported decision but also a brief summary of the decision, called the "syllabus," and one or more topically indexed "headnotes." These headnotes briefly describe the principles of law expounded by the court and are indexed by a series of topic "key numbers." West assigns these key numbers to specific points of decisional law. For instance, decisions dealing with first-degree murder are classified under the topic "homicide" and are assigned a key number for each particular aspect of that crime. Thus, a homicide case dealing with the intent requirement in first-degree murder may be classified as: "Homicide 9—Intent and design to effect death." Using this key number system, a researcher can locate headnotes of various appellate decisions on this aspect of homicide and in turn, can uncover relevant decisional law.

Motions for Rehearing

Rules of appellate procedure uniformly permit the filing of a motion asking the appellate court to reconsider its decision in a given case. A **motion for rehearing** is designed to address some misstatement of material fact or to direct the court's attention to an overlooked or misapprehended proposition of law. In the U.S. Courts of Appeals, and in many state appellate courts, where cases are decided by panels of judges, a party may request that all judges of the court participate in an **en banc rehearing**. The likelihood that an appellate court will grant a motion for en banc rehearing is greater when there are conflicting opinions between or among panels within the court. Appellate courts view many motions for rehearing as little more than attempts by dissatisfied parties to have another chance to persuade the court of their position. Accordingly, motions for rehearing are seldom granted.

Original Jurisdiction of Appellate Courts

As noted at the beginning of this chapter, appellate courts also possess original jurisdiction. This power enables appellate courts to issue writs to either mandate or prohibit certain proceedings in lower tribunals and to cause persons holding someone in custody to show cause why that person should not be released. These **original writs** include **mandamus**, a writ commanding that a lower tribunal or government official take certain non-discretionary action; **prohibition**, a writ that orders a lower tribunal to cease exercising jurisdiction; and **habeas corpus**, a writ that requires the custodian of someone to either release the person or show cause why the court should not order the person released. Although habeas corpus is a civil writ, it is employed more frequently in a criminal law context. We discuss this writ further in Chapter 10.

CONCLUSION

Civil procedure enables courts to hear and resolve disputes in an orderly and fair manner. Further, the rules of evidence assure litigants that courts will uniformly apply known principles to determine proof in a non-prejudicial manner. Appellate procedures then furnish litigants a means of correcting errors and provide an accountability mechanism in the judicial system. Because these rules are published in advance in all jurisdictions, counsel trained in law can assist litigants to avoid litigation by evaluating their claims and defenses. Ultimately, when amicable settlements cannot be arranged, counsel can enter the judicial arena with a sense of predictability.

SUMMARY OF KEY CONCEPTS

A civil lawsuit is instituted by a plaintiff's filing a complaint in state or federal court. The threshold issue is determining the judicial forum that has jurisdiction. Suits involve a variety of claims, including matters relating to contracts, business, torts, property, and family—matters discussed in previous chapters. A plaintiff seeks damages or other relief, but in some instances the plaintiff(s) seek a declaration of their rights. In other instances, the plaintiff(s) bring "class actions" on behalf of numerous plaintiffs or against a number of defendants. Class actions often play a significant role in society. After a plaintiff files suit, and once the defendant(s) are served process according to law, the defendant(s) are afforded an opportunity to challenge the claims asserted.

Most lawsuits are settled or dismissed before trial. Settlements often occur after extensive pretrial preparation involving discovery of evidence. Other cases come on for trial either before a judge in a bench trial or before a jury with a judge presiding. Jury selection is an important stage of a trial, and counsel are allowed to challenge prospective jurors for causes that would disqualify a juror from sitting on a case. In addition, lawyers may exercise a limited number of peremptory challenges to remove a certain number of jurors without cause; however, such challenges cannot be based on gender or exercised in a racially discriminatory way. A lawyer also is permitted to make opening and closing statements to summarize his or her case; however, judges and juries must decide cases based on applying the law to the evidence presented.

Courts adjudicate disputes based on procedures and rules of evidence known in advance to litigants. We have endeavored to give the student an overview of judicial notice and various classes of evidence, the meaning of "relevancy" and "competency," and other basic rules of evidence. The rules of evidence are complex and have many exceptions, and there are privileges against testifying. The testimony of lay and expert witnesses, presented through direct and cross-examination, provide the bulk of evidence in a trial. Juries hear arguments of counsel, deliberate, and return verdicts, which result in courts' issuing judgments.

Appellate courts correct errors of lower tribunals and "make law" where necessary to "fill in gaps" in the law. They hear certain appeals as a matter of an aggrieved litigant's right and, in other instances, grant discretionary review. Counsel file briefs and, in many instances, orally argue their contentions. Unlike trial courts, which usually are presided over by one judge, an appellate court usually sits in panels of three judges, or in the case of the highest state courts and the U.S. Supreme Court, sit en banc. Appellate court decisions frequently include opinions on the law that are published in volumes widely used by lawyers.

FOR FURTHER READING

Barclay, Scott, *An Appealing Act: Why People Appeal in Civil Cases* (Northwestern University Press 1999).

Clermont, Kevin M., *Civil Procedure* (West Group 1999).

Elligett, Raymond T., and John M. Scheb, *Florida Appellate Practice and Advocacy* (5th ed., Stetson University College of Law 2008).

Glannon, Joseph W., *Civil Procedure: Examples and Explanations* (Little Brown and Co. 1996).

Hazard, Geoffrey C., Jr., *American Civil Procedure: An Introduction* (Yale University Press 1993).

Kane, Mary Kay, *Civil Procedure in a Nutshell* (West Publishing Co. 1996).

Litan, Robert E. (ed.), *Verdict: Assessing the Civil Jury System* (Brookings Institution 1993).

QUESTIONS FOR THOUGHT AND DISCUSSION

1. How is a complaint for damages instituted in a court of law?
2. What is meant by service of process? What are the various means by which service of process is accomplished?
3. What is a pretrial conference designed to accomplish?
4. What pretrial procedures are generally available to lawyers to learn facts within the knowledge of an opposing party or witnesses?
5. Should a trial judge be allowed to offer an opinion to the jury on the quality of evidence presented at trial?
6. What is meant by (a) a peremptory challenge; (b) a challenge for cause?
7. What restrictions has the U.S. Supreme Court placed on the use of peremptory challenges to jurors?
8. Name four major exceptions to the rule that hearsay testimony is not allowed in a trial.
9. What purposes are served by opening statements and closing arguments?
10. To what extent is a layperson permitted to offer an opinion in a civil trial?
11. What are the chief functions of an appellate court?
12. What are the key steps in the progress of an appeal?

KEY TERMS

affirm
answer
answer brief
appellant
appellate procedure
appellee
attorney-client privilege
bench trial
best evidence rule
business and public records
case management conference
cause of action

challenge for cause
circumstantial evidence
citations
civil procedure
class action
clergy privilege
closing arguments
common law pleading
competent
complaint
concurring in the judgment
concurring opinion

constructive service
counterclaim
cross-claim
cross-examination
damages
declaratory relief
default
default judgment
defendant
deposition
direct evidence
direct examination

directed verdict
discovery
dissenting opinion
diversity jurisdiction
dying declarations
en banc rehearing
error correction
evidentiary presumption
expert witness
eyewitness testimony
forensic experts
gender-based peremptory
  challenges
general damages
general objection
general verdict
habeas corpus
hearsay evidence
hung jury
hypothetical question
in forma pauperis
indirect evidence
initial brief
initial pleading
injunction
interrogatories
involuntary dismissal
judicial conference
judicial notice
jurisdiction

jury instructions
jury trial
lawmaking
long-arm statutes
mandamus
marital privilege
mistrial
motion for rehearing
motions
nominal damages
notice of appeal
opening statement
opinion evidence
opinion of the court
oral argument
original writs
out-of-court settlements
parties
per curiam opinion
peremptory challenges
personal service
petitioner
plaintiff
polygraph evidence
preponderance of the evidence
pretrial conference
privileged communications
prohibition
protective order
punitive damages

racially based peremptory
  challenges
real evidence
rebuttable presumption
rebuttal
relevant evidence
remand
reply brief
reporters
reputation
reverse
rule of four
rules of evidence
sequestration of the jury
special damages
special verdict
specific objection
specific performance
spontaneous or excited utterances
substantial federal question
substituted service
summary judgment
summons
testimonial evidence
third-party practice
venire
venue
voir dire
writ of certiorari

ENDNOTES

1. 28 U.S.C. §1332. In 1958 Congress set the amount for diversity jurisdiction at $10,000. Since then it has increased the amount presumably to take into consideration inflation and to diminish the burden that diversity jurisdiction imposes on federal courts.

2. *Erie R.R. Co. v. Tompkins*, 304 U.S. 64, 58 S. Ct. 817, 82 L. Ed. 1188 (1938).

3. *International Shoe v. Washington*, 326 U.S. 310, 66 S. Ct. 154; 90 L. Ed. 95 (1945).

4. *Perkins v. Benguet Mining Co., et al.*, 342 U.S. 437, 72 S. Ct. 413, 96 L.Ed. 485 (1958). Subsequent cases have helped to untangle the types of criteria that define "continuous and systematic" ties; *see, e.g., Hertz Corporation v. Friend*, 559 U.S. ___77, 130 S. Ct. 1181; 175 L. Ed. 2d 1029 (2010), which evaluated the "nerve center" of the company, as well as the "principal place of business." Chapter 4 contains additional information on the jurisdiction of U.S. courts over foreign companies.

5. *Daimler AG v. Bauman* 571 U.S. _____ (2014).

6. *International Shoe v. Washington*, 326 U.S. 310, 66 S. Ct. 154; 90 L. Ed. 95 (1945).

7. *Hanson v. Denckla*, 357 U.S. 235, 78 S. Ct. 1228, 2 L. Ed. 2d 1283 (1958). This matter was discussed in several subsequent cases, including: *World-Wide Volkswagen Corp. v Woodson*, 444 U.S. 286, 100 S. Ct. 559, 62 L. Ed. 2d 490 (1980), *Burger King v. Rudzewicz*, 471 U.S. 462, 105 S. Ct. 2174, 85 L. Ed. 2d 528 (1985), *Asahi Metal Industry Co. v. Superior Court*, 480 U.S. 102, 107 S. Ct. 1026, 94 L.Ed.2d 92 (1987).

8. Judges frequently take a more active role in the adjudication of disputes in small claims courts where, because the cost of retaining counsel may exceed the amount in controversy, parties usually appear without counsel.

9. Fed. R. Civ. P. 23.

10. *Wal-Mart Stores, Inc. v. Dukes,* 564 U.S. _____, 131 S. Ct. 2541, 180 L. Ed. 2d 374 (2011).

11. Jonathan Stempel, "Google Won't Face Email Privacy Class Action," *Reuters,* March 19, 2014; available at: http://mobile .reuters.com/article/idUSBREA2I13G20140319?irpc=932.

12. *Brown v. Bridges,* 327 So. 2d 874 (Fla. App. 1975).

13. While most states prohibit an employer from discharging an employee called for jury duty, Connecticut is one of a few states that require employers to continue to pay their employees while on jury duty. This requirement applies only to full-time employees and is limited to five days of jury service. Conn. Gen. Stat. Ann. §51-247.

14. *Alderman v. State,* 327 S.E.2d 168 (Ga. 1985).

15. 18 U.S.C. §1870.

16. *Batson v. Kentucky,* 476 U.S. 79, 106 S. Ct. 1712, 90 L. Ed. 2d 69 (1986).

17. *J.E.B. v. Alabama ex rel. T.B.,* 511 U.S. 127, 114 S. Ct. 1419, 128 L. Ed. 2d 89 (1994).

18. *Frye v. United States,* 293 F. 1013 (D.C. Cir. 1923).

19. 509 U.S. 579, 113 S. Ct. 2786, 125 L. Ed. 2d 469 (1993).

20. Mo. R. Civ. P. 72.01.

21. *See, e.g., Slocum v. New York Life Ins. Co.,* 228 U.S. 364, 33 S. Ct. 523, 57 L. Ed. 879 (1913).

22. *Konst v. Florida E. Coast Ry. Co.,* 71 F.3d 850 (11th Cir. 1996).

23. *Holland v. United States,* 348 U.S. 121, 75 S. Ct. 127, 99 L. Ed. 150 (1954).

24. *Rock v. Arkansas,* 483 U.S. 44, 107 S. Ct. 2704, 97 L. Ed. 2d 37 (1987).

25. *Connor v. State,* 171 A.2d 699 (Md. 1961).

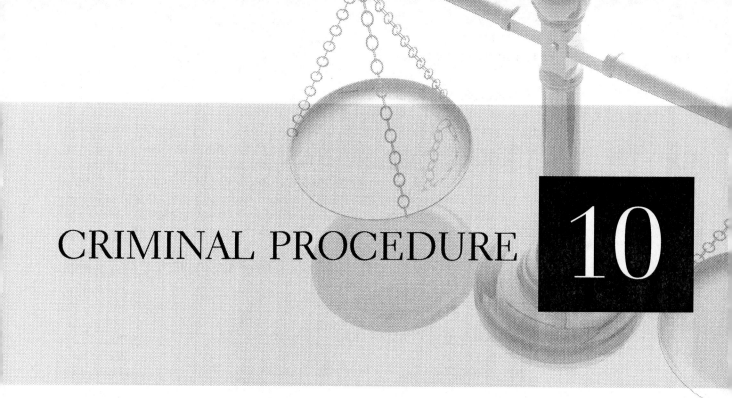

CRIMINAL PROCEDURE

10

LEARNING OBJECTIVES

This chapter should enable the student to understand:

▧ the Fourth Amendment rules governing searches and seizures

▧ the exclusionary rule designed to enforce the Fourth Amendment

▧ warrant and warrantless arrests and investigatory detentions

▧ the effect of *Miranda* rules on interrogation of suspects

▧ formal charging processes including the role of grand juries

▧ pretrial procedures, including arraignment and plea bargaining, and the roles of prosecutors, defense counsel, judges, and juries throughout the stages of a criminal trial

▧ sentencing options and processes in misdemeanor and felony convictions; sentencing procedures in capital cases

▧ the rights of victims in the criminal process; the rights of inmates

▧ appellate procedures and post-conviction remedies available in federal and state courts

▧ criminal procedure in military tribunals

359

INTRODUCTION

Criminal procedure consists of the processes by which crimes are investigated, prosecuted, and punished. It includes law enforcement activities such as search and seizure, arrest, interrogation, and identification of suspects. It also embraces the judicial processes that take place before, during, and after the trial of persons accused of crimes. The federal and state constitutions set the basic requirements for criminal procedure, but constitutional requisites are supplemented by federal and state statutes and by rules of criminal procedure promulgated by the courts. In recent decades, the courts have expanded the constitutional rights of criminal defendants, and many rules of criminal procedure reflect constitutional requisites as interpreted by the United States Supreme Court and the highest state courts.

SEARCH AND SEIZURE

A basic starting point in most criminal investigations is a police search or seizure. The Founders were acutely aware of the intrusive nature of such police activity. Thus, the Fourth Amendment to the United States Constitution prohibits unreasonable searches and seizures. A **search** occurs when government agents look for evidence in a manner that intrudes into a person's legally protected zone of privacy. A **seizure** takes place when agents take possession or control of property or persons. Although essential to the enforcement of the criminal law, search for and seizure of evidence often entails serious invasions of privacy and is subject to abuse. Therefore, the power of law enforcement agencies to conduct searches and seizures is limited by the federal and state constitutions, and even by a number of federal and state statutes. Most important among these legal limitations, though, is the Fourth Amendment to the United States Constitution, which prohibits unreasonable searches and seizures.

As a general rule, the Fourth Amendment requires law enforcement officers to obtain a **warrant** before conducting searches and seizures. Although some warrantless searches and seizures are permissible, they must all conform to a standard of reasonableness. Law enforcement officers are not permitted to conduct searches and seizures arbitrarily, or even based on their hunches about criminal activity. For a search to be reasonable under the Fourth Amendment, police generally must have **probable cause**, which simply means that a reasonable person has reasonable grounds to believe that a search will produce evidence of crime. In some instances, police may conduct limited searches (such as a "pat-down") based on the lesser standard of **reasonable suspicion**. Subject to certain exceptions, evidence obtained through unreasonable searches and seizures is not admissible in criminal prosecutions.

The Fourth Amendment, like all the protections of the Bill of Rights, was originally conceived as a limitation on the powers of the newly created national government. Under the original conception of the Bill of Rights, citizens seeking legal protection against actions of state and local governments had to look to their state constitutions and state courts for relief. But in 1949, the Supreme Court held that the freedom from unreasonable searches and seizures is "implicit in 'the concept of ordered liberty' and as such, enforceable against the States through the Due Process Clause [of the Fourteenth

Amendment]."[1] With that, the Fourth Amendment was "incorporated." Ultimately, the Fourth Amendment sets a minimal national standard; state courts are free to provide greater levels of protection under the search and seizure provisions of state constitutions. Several state courts have followed this latter approach.

When, Where, and to Whom Does the Fourth Amendment Apply?

The Fourth Amendment limits search and seizure activities by law enforcement agencies at all levels of government, whether federal, state, or local. Because the Constitution limits *government* action, the Fourth Amendment protects a person's rights against the police and other government agents, but not against searches and seizures conducted by private individuals—unless those individuals are acting under the direction of police. Moreover, the Amendment does not apply to searches and seizures conducted by United States agents outside the territory of the United States.

Travelers crossing the borders of the United States are routinely subjected to searches, even when they are not the targets of suspicion. Suspicionless **border searches** are justified by the assumption that persons crossing the national border are not entitled to the protections of the Fourth Amendment. The border search exception extends to searches conducted at established stations near the border or other functional equivalents of a border search, for example, the search of a ship when it first docks after entering the territorial waters of the United States.

In terms of its specific language, the Fourth Amendment protects "persons, houses, papers, and effects" from unreasonable search and seizure. The reference to "persons" places limitations on a law enforcement agent's ability to search an individual's actual body or clothing. As we shall discuss later, though, there are situations where law enforcement can engage in limited searches of an individual's outer clothing even without a warrant.

As to the Fourth Amendment's reference to "houses," it is worth noting that, historically, the English common law adopted the principle that "a man's home is his castle." And, although the Fourth Amendment refers specifically to "houses," its protections have been extended to stores, offices, and places of business, as well. However, the Supreme Court has noted that homeowners and overnight guests have a stronger claim to assert "standing" of a Fourth Amendment violation than do temporary visitors[2] to a dwelling.

Because it also mentions "papers" and "effects," the Fourth Amendment even applies to items of personal property, and not just to real estate. Even so, the Fourth Amendment does not apply to property that has been abandoned.[3] Therefore, police may search abandoned premises and seize abandoned property, and this notion has been interpreted to include police searches of trash that is left on the curb outside of a person's home[4] and even police efforts to procure DNA off utensils after they are used and left behind by a suspect.

Searches Based on Consent

Consent refers to situations where an individual voluntarily allows police to search themselves or their property. To date, the Supreme Court has refused to require law officers to inform suspects of their right to refuse to **consent to a search**.[5] More recently, the Court held that police are not required to inform motorists who are stopped for other reasons that they are "free to go" before asking them to consent to a search of their automobile.[6] For a person's consent to be valid, though, it must be truly voluntary and must involve more than mere acquiescence to the authority of the police. Accordingly, where police have claimed authority to search based on a nonexistent warrant, the Supreme Court held that their action was so coercive as to vitiate the defendant's consent.[7] Ultimately, individuals can assert their rights by simply invoking the phrase "I do not consent to a search."

College students may be interested to know that the Supreme Court has said that a landlord cannot consent to a search of a lessee's dwelling, and that a roommate can consent to a search of a "common area" in a shared dwelling, but cannot consent to a search of another person's private room.[8] Further, in *Georgia v. Randolph*, the Court noted that if two individuals who share a dwelling differ in their opinion on consent, the mere presence of one objector means the police may not search[9]—although concerns over domestic violence led Chief Justice Roberts to file a dissenting opinion. In 2014, the Supreme Court's decision in *Fernandez v. California* clarified the *Randolph* ruling by stating that if the original party that objected to the search had left the premises, then police could acquire consent for a search from another resident.[10]

The Scope of Privacy Protected by the Fourth Amendment

The term "seizure" refers to the taking into custody of physical evidence, property, or even a person. But what constitutes a "search" is not so clear. Originally, the protection of the Fourth Amendment was limited to physical intrusions on one's person or property, and courts looked at whether a trespass had taken place in deciding whether the Fourth Amendment was implicated. Thus, surveillance without physical contact with the suspect or the suspect's property was deemed to fall outside the protections of the Fourth Amendment. Accordingly, the Fourth Amendment was not applicable to **wiretapping** or **electronic eavesdropping**. But in *Katz v. United States* (1967), the Supreme Court abandoned the trespass doctrine, ruling that the Fourth Amendment protects people, not places.[11] In *Katz*, the Court held that a suspected bookie who was using a public telephone allegedly in conduct of a gambling business enjoyed a reasonable expectation of privacy, and that a police wiretap of the phone booth was a search within the meaning of the Fourth Amendment. This decision brought wiretapping and other forms of electronic eavesdropping within the limitations of the Fourth Amendment. Currently, any means of invading a person's **reasonable expectation of privacy** is considered a "search" for Fourth Amendment purposes. Thus, the critical question that courts must address in reviewing cases where police conduct surveillance or eavesdropping without probable cause or prior judicial authorization is whether such surveillance intruded on a suspect's reasonable expectation of privacy.

Along these lines, on January 23, 2012, the Supreme Court issued its opinion in *United States v. Jones*, a case where police had placed a GPS locator on an individual's car—without a warrant—and then proceeded to surveil that individual's movement for 28 days. The Court rejected evidence seized as a result of this search, and declared that police could not place a GPS locator on a car parked on private property and then electronically surveil the car's movements. Although the decision was a unanimous one, the justices split on the underlying rationale for the ruling, with five justices focusing on the physical intrusion of placing the GPS locator on the car (perhaps resurrecting the "trespass doctrine"), and four justices focusing on the overall violation of a "reasonable expectation of privacy" implied by lengthy electronic surveillance.[12]

On June 25, 2014, with its unanimous decision in *Riley v. California*, the Supreme Court took another step toward guarding privacy rights in the digital age. The Court specifically declared that police must acquire a warrant before searching the cell phone of a person who has been arrested. The majority opinion noted that cell phones contain a "broad array of private information" that is worthy of this protection. Even so, exceptions for police to conduct a warrantless cell phone search justified by exigent circumstances were preserved—including ones for public safety and imminent destruction of evidence.[13] Ultimately, new technology clearly raises unique 4th Amendment concerns—both in terms of police ability to conduct a search with enhanced tools and in terms of the places that individuals can store personal information. Chapter 11 expounds upon this discussion with an assessment of the National Security Agency's telephone and e-mail surveillance programs.

Diminished Expectations of Privacy

In certain situations, the Supreme Court has found individuals to possess "limited" or "diminished" expectations of privacy. In these scenarios, government officials have greater leeway to execute searches, even without a warrant—although this leeway may not be entirely unfettered.

One such situation includes searches of anyone lawfully incarcerated in a prison or jail, and it easy to understand why such a person has no reasonable expectation of privacy. As a result, jail and prison cells are routinely "swept" for weapons and other contraband, and inmates are routinely subjected to searches of their persons. A parolee is also said to have a diminished expectation of privacy, which permits searches of their person and property without a warrant.[14] The Supreme Court has even upheld **strip searches** of prison inmates because of the demands for institutional security, a decision that was subsequently made to apply to those arrested for minor offenses.[15] Nevertheless, in *Maryland v. King* (2013), the Supreme Court expanded the scope of police searches when it upheld DNA tests for those arrested on charges related to "serious offenses." The majority opinion noted that the nature of the intrusion—a 'cheek swab'—was low, while the government's "legitimate" interests in assessing the risk associated with an offender and in solving cold cases outweighed any infringement on individual privacy.[16]

Another area where the Court has found a "diminished expectation of privacy" is in electronic communication within a workplace setting. Specifically, in *City of Ontario v. Quon*,[17] the Court found no Fourth Amendment violation in searches of employee text messages at a police department in California. Two officers had raised a Fourth Amendment claim after the content of sexually explicit text messages (sent on phones provided by their department) led to internal disciplinary proceedings. Overall, case precedent has held that most "safety-sensitive" government jobs imply a diminished expectation of privacy. In fact, this principle has led the Supreme Court to uphold suspicionless drug testing of railway operators[18] and even U.S. customs officials.[19] (More on this below.)

Elsewhere, with increased concern over airplane hijacking and terrorism has come increased security at the nation's airports. Passengers attempting to board aircraft routinely pass through metal detectors; their carry-on baggage as well as checked luggage is routinely subjected to X-ray scans. Such searches are deemed reasonable, given their minimal intrusiveness, the gravity of the safety interests involved, and the reduced privacy expectations associated with airline travel.

Sobriety Checkpoints

One device increasingly used by law enforcement to combat the problem of intoxicated drivers is **sobriety checkpoints**, in which all drivers passing a certain point are stopped briefly and observed for signs of intoxication. To the extent that police officers at these checkpoints visually inspect the passenger compartments of stopped automobiles, these brief encounters involve searches, although in most instances these procedures entail only minor intrusion and inconvenience. Opponents of sobriety checkpoints argue that they amount to dragnet searches—the government searches many people in the hope of catching a few. Advocates of sobriety checkpoints argue that these measures save lives by reducing the number of drunk drivers on the streets. In 1990, the Supreme Court upheld the use of sobriety checkpoints to detect intoxicated drivers.[20] For the most part, state courts also have upheld sobriety checkpoints, but some have placed restrictions on how they are conducted. In November 2000, though, the Supreme Court did limit the use of checkpoints that are designed to detect "ordinary lawbreaking" (in that specific case, drug possession) as distinct from sobriety checkpoints.[21] And, the Court's 2013 decision in *Missouri v. McNeely* requires police to acquire a warrant for most compelled blood tests of drivers who are suspected of DUI—although exceptions to this warrant requirement can be made in certain exigent circumstances, such as in the case of an accident.[22]

The Warrant Requirement

The Fourth Amendment expresses a decided preference for searches and seizures to be conducted pursuant to a warrant. The warrant requirement is designed to ensure that the impartial judgment of a judge or magistrate is interposed between the citizen and the state. With the exception of warrants permitting administrative searches, search warrants must be based on probable cause. Probable cause exists when prudent and cautious police officers have trustworthy information leading them to believe that evidence of crime may be obtained through a particular search. The Supreme Court has said that courts should view the determination of probable cause as a commonsense, practical matter that must be decided in light of the **totality of**

circumstances in a given case.[23] Some state courts have declined to follow this approach and have opted to provide their citizens more protection under their state constitutions than allowed by the federal view.

Under normal circumstances, a police officer with probable cause to believe that evidence of a crime is located in a specific place must submit under oath an application for a search warrant to the appropriate judge or magistrate. An **affidavit** is a signed document attesting under oath to certain facts of which the **affiant** (the person submitting the affidavit) has knowledge. Usually, an affidavit by a law enforcement officer requesting issuance of a search warrant is presented to a judge or magistrate. The officer's affidavit in support of a search warrant must always contain a rather precise description of the place(s) or person(s) to be searched and the things to be seized, and must attest to specific facts that establish probable cause to justify a search. The information must be sufficiently fresh to ensure that the items to be seized are probably located on the premises to be searched.

A magistrate's finding of probable cause may be based on hearsay evidence. This rule permits police to obtain search warrants based on tips from anonymous or **confidential informants**. Confidential informants, or "CIs," are often persons who have been involved with the police and are seeking favorable consideration in respect to their own offenses. Because their motivation may be suspect, their reliability is checked carefully. For many years, the Supreme Court required magistrates to apply a rigorous test that made it very difficult for police to use **anonymous tips**. In 1983, however, the Supreme Court relaxed the test and permitted magistrates to consider the "totality of circumstances" when evaluating applications based on hearsay evidence.[24] Despite the relaxed standard approved by the U.S. Supreme Court, several state courts have opted to continue to require more rigorous standards in evaluating a CI's credibility and basis of knowledge before approving a search warrant based on information from a CI.

Exceptions to the Warrant Requirement

Courts have recognized that an absolute warrant requirement in all situations would be impractical. Consequently, they have upheld the reasonableness of **warrantless searches** under so-called **exigent circumstances**. Whenever possible, police officers should obtain warrants, because their failure to do so may jeopardize the fruits of a successful search. Nevertheless, the courts have articulated the following exceptions to the warrant requirement, all of which assume that police officers have probable cause to believe that a given search is likely to produce evidence of crime.

1. **Evidence in Plain View:**   A police officer may seize evidence in **plain view** provided that (1) the officer has a legal justification to be in a constitutionally protected area when the seizure occurs; (2) the evidence seized is in the plain view of the officer who comes across it; and (3) it is apparent that the object constitutes evidence of a crime.[25] This doctrine has been extended to include airplanes flying over an area in the hope of locating evidence that may be in "plain view" from the air. However, when "unusual technology," such as an

infrared heat sensor, is used to scan for evidence of marijuana heat lamps, then a search must be based on a warrant.[26]

2. **Emergency Searches:**   Police frequently must respond to emergencies involving reports of crime or injuries. Increasingly, law enforcement authorities are called upon to investigate, for example, bomb threats where explosive devices are possibly sequestered inside buildings. In these and other situations, police are called upon to conduct **emergency searches**. The law recognizes that police do not have the time to obtain search warrants in such instances. Of course, police must possess probable cause to make warrantless emergency searches of dwellings. Police who make warrantless entries and searches when they reasonably believe that a person within is in need of immediate aid do not violate protections against unreasonable search and seizure. Once inside, the police may justifiably seize evidence in plain view.[27]

3. **Preservation of Evidence:**   A frequently invoked justification for a warrantless search and seizure is the preservation of **evanescent evidence**—evidence that might be lost or destroyed. Where there is a reasonable belief that loss or destruction of evidence is imminent, a warrantless entry of premises may be justified, but a mere possibility of such is insufficient.[28] This principle has also been used to justify taking a blood sample from a driver suspected of being intoxicated at the time of an accident.[29]

4. **Roadside Searches of Motor Vehicles:**   The courts have long recognized the validity of the so-called **automobile exception**, assuming that the police officer has probable cause to believe the vehicle contains contraband or evidence of crime, on the premise that the mobile character of a motor vehicle creates a practical necessity for an immediate search.[30] A common justification for probable cause in these situations is an officer detecting the smell of drugs. Although the standard for a roadside search is probable cause, the Supreme Court has said that an officer merely needs to have a "reasonable suspicion" that a law is being violated (usually a traffic law) in order to pull over a car.[31]

5. **Canine Searches:**   In 2009, in *Illinois v. Caballes*, the Supreme Court noted that police do not require a warrant to walk a drug-sniffing dog around a car. Further, if a dog alerts to the presence of contraband, that would serve as probable cause for the officer to initiate a warrantless automobile search. The only clearly-defined limitation on this procedure is that police cannot prolong a traffic stop beyond a "reasonable" time frame in order to wait for a dog to arrive. Beyond that, in *Florida v. Harris*, the Supreme Court said that the litmus test of a dog's credibility is not its track record of "hits and misses" in the field, but rather, the quality of the dog's training.[32] Ultimately, this viewpoint presents a difficult burden for accused criminals. However, the rules shift when a dog search reaches the home, as the Supreme Court's decision in *Florida v. Jardines* said that police must obtain a warrant before bringing a drug-sniffing dog to a person's residence. In that case, police had walked a drug-sniffing canine on a

six-foot leash along Jardines' front porch. Justice Scalia's majority opinion noted that this warrantless activity represented a "trespass," and thus, was an unconstitutional search.[33] In the end, it appears as though the Supreme Court treats dog searches at the home differently than dog searches at roadside, with only the former requiring the procurement of a search warrant.

6. **Search Incident to a Lawful Arrest:** It has long been recognized that a **search incident to a lawful arrest**, to seize the fruits or evidence of crime, is allowed, but the Supreme Court has narrowed the permissible scope of searches incident to lawful arrests. The rule is that police may search the body of an arrestee and the area within that person's immediate control, that is, the area within the "grasp" or "lunge" of the arrestee. To conduct a more extensive search, police must obtain a search warrant.[34] And, as of June 2014, police also must acquire a warrant to search an arrestee's cell phone.[35]

7. **Hot Pursuit:** Officers in **hot pursuit** of a fleeing criminal already have probable cause to make an arrest. The Supreme Court has long recognized that police may pursue the suspect into a protected place, such as a home, without having to abandon pursuit until a warrant can be obtained.[36]

8. **Inventory Searches:** Most law enforcement agencies that impound automobiles for parking violations or abandonment, or pursuant to the arrest of a motorist, routinely conduct an inventory of the contents and remove any valuables for safekeeping. When conducted according to standard police procedures, an **inventory search** is generally regarded as an administrative search not subject to ordinary Fourth Amendment requirements. Inventory searches are justified by the needs to protect the owner's property and to protect the police from dangers that might be hidden inside closed automobiles. If a routine inventory search yields evidence of crime, it may be seized and admitted into evidence without violating the Fourth Amendment.[37]

Exceptions to the Probable Cause Requirement

Warrantless searches are often necessary and are generally deemed acceptable as long as there are exigent circumstances and police have probable cause. More controversial are situations in which the courts permit limited searches based on the lesser standard of "reasonable suspicion." In considering these special situations, one should keep in mind that the fundamental requirement of the Fourth Amendment is not probable cause, but reasonableness.

1. **Stop-and-Frisk:** The stop-and-frisk is a routine law enforcement technique whereby police officers may stop, question, check identification, and even 'patdown' exterior clothing of suspicious persons based on something "more than a hunch."[38] Concealed weapons and contraband that are discovered during the course of a legitimate frisk are admissible into evidence.[39]

2. **School Searches:** The Supreme Court has held that the Fourth Amendment protects children in the public schools from unreasonable searches and seizures, but that such searches are to be judged by a reasonableness standard and are not subject to the requirement of probable cause, much less the warrant requirement.[40] With the recent spate of school violence, there is considerable public support for giving school officials broad latitude in the area of search and seizure. However, in 2009, the Supreme Court placed some limits on the nature of school searches when it ruled that strip-searching a middle school girl who was suspected of possessing ibuprofen was in fact a violation of Fourth Amendment protections.[41]

3. **Drug Testing:** The national "war on drugs" has resulted in the widespread implementation of **drug testing** programs for public employees. As mentioned earlier, courts have routinely upheld regulations permitting urinalysis of public safety officers based on reasonable suspicion of drug abuse, and has even sustained a Customs Service policy requiring drug tests for persons seeking positions as customs inspectors. In 1995, the Supreme Court also held that a public school's policy of randomly drug testing athletes did not violate a student's right to be free from unreasonable searches, with the Court noting the diminished expectation of privacy associated with being a part of a sports team, particularly in a high school setting.[42] Outside of school settings, the Court has, on the other hand, invalidated a policy under which all political candidates were required to submit to drug testing as a condition of qualifying for the ballot.[43]

The Exclusionary Rule

The **exclusionary rule** prohibits the use of illegally obtained evidence in a criminal prosecution of the person whose rights were violated by the police in obtaining that evidence. In 1914, the U.S. Supreme Court first held that evidence obtained through an unlawful search and seizure could not be used to convict a person of a federal crime.[44] In *Mapp v. Ohio* (1961), the Court required the state courts to follow the exclusionary rule, largely on the rationale that there is no other effective means of enforcing the Fourth Amendment.[45] The *Mapp* decision certainly was one of the Warren Court's most important decisions in the criminal justice field and became emblematic of the Warren Court's efforts to enhance constitutional protections in this area.

During the 1960s and 1970s, however, the exclusionary rule came under attack from critics who argued that the social cost of allowing guilty persons to avoid prosecution outweighed the benefit of deterring police from violating the Fourth Amendment. In 1984, the Supreme Court revisited the issue and held that evidence obtained on the basis of a search warrant that is later held invalid may be admitted in evidence at trial if the police officer who conducted the search relied on the warrant in "good faith."[46] The **good-faith exception** to the exclusionary rule applies only in cases where police officers rely on warrants that are later held to be invalid; it does not apply to warrantless searches.

CASE IN POINT

THE STATE COURTS MUST FOLLOW THE FOURTH AMENDMENT EXCLUSIONARY RULE
Mapp v. Ohio
United States Supreme Court
367 U.S. 643, 81 S. Ct. 1684, 6 L. Ed. 2d 1081 (1961)

Cleveland, Ohio, police arrived at Dollree Mapp's home after receiving information that a bombing suspect was hiding there. They demanded access, but failing to produce a search warrant, they were denied. Police returned some four hours later and forced their way into the home. Mapp, who protested the entry, was forcibly detained while officers searched the home. Although police failed to locate the bombing suspect, they did find in a trunk in the basement some sexually explicit materials. Mapp was arrested, tried, and convicted under the Ohio statute proscribing possession of obscene materials. Dividing 7-2, the U.S. Supreme Court reversed her conviction, holding that the evidence had been improperly admitted against her since it had been obtained in violation of the Fourth Amendment warrant requirement. The Court overturned precedent and applied the exclusionary rule to the state courts for the first time. The Court said that this landmark decision "gives to the individual no more than that which the Constitution guarantees him, to the police officer no less than that to which honest law enforcement is entitled, and, to the courts, that judicial integrity so necessary in the true administration of justice."

ARREST AND INVESTIGATORY DETENTION

A formal arrest occurs when police take an individual into custody and charge that person with the commission of a crime. As a form of "seizure," an arrest is governed by the probable cause and warrant provisions of the Fourth Amendment. But the formal arrest is not the only type of encounter between police and citizens that implicates the Fourth Amendment. A seizure, for Fourth Amendment purposes, occurs when a police officer uses force or the threat of force to in some way restrain a person's liberty.

Arrest Warrants

An **arrest warrant** is routine in cases where an arrest is to be made based on an indictment by a grand jury. When a prosecutor files an information, a **capias** is issued by a court directing the arrest of the defendant. In such cases, suspects may not be aware that they are under investigation, and police officers have ample time to obtain an arrest warrant without fear that suspects will flee. However, most arrests are not made pursuant to secret investigations but rather are made by police officers who observe a criminal act, respond to a complaint filed by a crime victim, or have probable cause to arrest after completing an investigation. In these situations, it is often unnecessary for police to obtain an arrest warrant, but it is always essential that they have probable cause to make the arrest.

Warrantless Arrests

At common law, police had the right to make a **warrantless arrest** if they observed someone in the commission of a felony or they had probable cause to believe that a person had committed or was committing a felony. To make a warrantless arrest for a misdemeanor, an officer had to observe someone in the commission of the act. Otherwise, to make an arrest, a warrant was required. Many states enacted statutes adopting common law rules of arrest allowing police officers broad discretion to make warrantless arrests. As with warrantless searches and seizures, the Supreme Court has approved warrantless arrests: (1) where crimes are committed in plain view of police officers; or (2) officers possess probable cause to make an arrest, but exigent circumstances prohibit them from obtaining a warrant. Absent plain view or compelling exigencies, though, it is unclear whether police officers need to obtain an arrest warrant. As a matter of policy, it makes sense for them to obtain arrest warrants when possible. However, given the time it takes to obtain an arrest warrant and the fact that magistrates are not always available around the clock, it is not always feasible for police to obtain warrants prior to arrest.

Use of Force by Police Making Arrests

Because suspects frequently resist attempts to take them into custody, police officers must often use force in making arrests. Sometimes the use of force by police is challenged in civil suits for damages. Typically, in such cases, the courts have said that in making a lawful arrest, police officers may use such force as is necessary to effect the arrest and prevent the escape of the suspect.

Concern over police brutality took center stage in 1991, when the nation viewed, on television, a videotape of what appeared to be the unnecessarily brutal beating of motorist Rodney King by Los Angeles police officers. In response to public outrage, four police officers involved in the incident were prosecuted by state authorities for assault and battery and related crimes. On the motion of the defense, the trial was moved out of Los Angeles to a suburban community. A riot erupted in Los Angeles in April 1992 after the jury returned its verdict of "not guilty." In response to the widespread perception that a miscarriage of justice had occurred, the U.S. Department of Justice launched its own investigation of the case. In the summer of 1992, a federal grand jury indicted the four officers for violating Rodney King's Fourth Amendment rights. In April 1993, a trial jury returned verdicts of guilty against two of the officers; the other two were acquitted.

Investigatory Detention

A very common form of police encounter is the so-called stop-and-frisk or **investigatory detention**. Based on the Supreme Court's 1968 decision in *Terry v. Ohio*, police are permitted to stop pedestrians or automobiles temporarily as long as they have reasonable suspicion that criminal activity is afoot.[47] Police may then perform a limited pat-down search of the suspect's outer clothing to ascertain whether the suspect is armed. Under the doctrine of plain view, contraband discovered during a legitimate pat-down for weapons may be admissible into evidence. For example, if during the course of a lawful frisk, a police officer feels what the officer suspects is a knife concealed in the suspect's pocket, the officer may retrieve the object. If it turns out to be a metal smoking pipe wrapped inside a plastic bag containing "crack" cocaine, the crack would most likely be admissible as evidence of crime.[48]

Drug Courier Profiles

In recent years, police have developed **drug courier profiles** based on typical characteristics and behaviors of drug smugglers. The profiles include such factors as paying cash for airline tickets, taking short trips to drug-source cities, not checking luggage, appearing nervous, and so forth. Police often use these profiles to identify and detain suspected drug couriers, a controversial practice that has resulted in disparate court decisions. In 1989, the Supreme Court upheld an investigative stop of an air passenger for which a number of circumstances, including the use of the profile, furnished the police a reasonable suspicion of criminal activity. While the Court found that any one of the several factors relied on by the police may have been consistent with innocent travel, it observed that the evaluation of the validity of the stop requires a consideration of the totality of the circumstances.[49] Further, the Court explained that simply because the factors the police relied on may have been set forth in a "profile" did not detract from their evidentiary significance as seen by a trained agent.

Racial Profiling

A controversial aspect of law enforcement is the use of racial characteristics in determining which suspects to pull over or detain for questioning. In 2003, in response to reports that police in their state were targeting drivers of minority races for traffic stops, legislators in New Jersey actually made it a crime for police to use race as the seminal criterion in determining which individuals to stop. Other states have also taken steps to curtail the use of race as a primary factor in traffic stops.

However, some have suggested that Arizona's recent passage of a law designed to curtail illegal immigration may incorporate an aspect of racial profiling. The controversy began on April 23, 2010, when Arizona governor Jan Brewer signed a law called the Support Our Law Enforcement and Safe Neighborhoods Act, also known as Arizona Senate Bill 1070. Its most controversial provision asked state law enforcement to determine an individual's immigration status during any lawful detention when there was reasonable suspicion that the individual was in the United States illegally. Because the notion of reasonable suspicion in the context of this law seemed closely tied to race, a federal appeals court issued an injunction to bar implementation of this measure, but in *Arizona v. United States* (2012), the U.S. Supreme Court allowed the provision to stand , while noting that future challenges based on racial profiling would be allowed.[50]

INTERROGATION AND IDENTIFICATION OF SUSPECTS

Interrogation of suspects is an important and often necessary component of police practice. Historically, the practice of extracting confessions entailed serious abuses of the rights of suspects, although as far back as 1897 the Supreme Court held that a coerced confession violates the Self-Incrimination Clause of the Fifth Amendment.[51] The traditional test used by the courts was whether a challenged confession could reasonably be deemed to have been voluntary. But subjective voluntariness is extremely difficult to discern, even through direct observation, let alone through appellate hind-sight years later. Consequently, a number of early judicial decisions in this area were unclear and inconsistent.

The *Miranda* Decision

In its landmark decision in *Miranda v. Arizona* (1966), the Supreme Court held that before interrogating suspects who are in custody, police must warn them of their right to remain silent and their right to have counsel present during questioning.[52] Unless these warnings have been given, the Court said, no statement made by the suspect may be used in evidence.

The *Miranda* decision produced a firestorm of controversy, especially within the law enforcement community. Critics thought that the Court was "coddling the criminals" and "handcuffing the cops." Although the Court has recognized some exceptions to the *Miranda* requirements, it has been steadfast in maintaining the basic holding of the decision. This was clearly demonstrated in June 2000, when the Court struck down a federal statute aimed at reversing the *Miranda* decision. The statute, which had been passed in the late 1960s, made the admissibility of incriminating statements turn solely on whether they were made voluntarily.[53] The statute had been ignored for many years until 1999 when the United States Court of Appeals for the Fourth Circuit invoked it in a federal bank robbery case. The court concluded that, because the *Miranda* requirements were not themselves of constitutional origin, Congress could reverse these requirements by ordinary legislation.[54] In a 7-2 decision, the Supreme Court disagreed, holding that the *Miranda* decision announced a constitutional rule that could not be altered simply by enacting a countervailing statute.[55] Clearly, *Miranda* is the law of the land and will remain so for the foreseeable future.

In a 2010 case, *Berghuis v. Thompkins*,[56] the Court clarified the meaning of one's right to remain silent when it declared that an accused criminal must clearly invoke the right to remain silent in order for it to apply. By contrast, merely remaining silent for long periods of time while police asked questions would not be interpreted as an explicit invocation of the right, and would not force police to terminate an interrogation. The irony of having to speak to invoke one's right to remain silent was not lost on many Court observers. The same concept resurfaced more recently in *Salinas v. Texas*, where a suspect fell silent during an interrogation after police asked him whether shotgun shells at a crime scene would match a gun found in his home. That silence ultimately was used against him at trial and the Supreme Court once again declared that the individual had not clearly invoked his right to remain silent; thus, his conviction was upheld.[57]

In another 2010 case, *Maryland v. Shatzer*,[58] the Court provided some guidelines for handling those situations where a suspect does clearly invoke the right to remain silent; specifically, the majority opinion declared that if a suspect who is in custody asks for an attorney during (or even prior to) an interrogation, that interrogation must cease—but the Court added that, after a 14-day wait, the police can attempt to interrogate the suspect again, even without counsel present.

The Fruit of the Poisonous Tree Doctrine

Under the **fruit of the poisonous tree doctrine**, evidence that is derived from inadmissible evidence—such as that which is illegally seized or coerced—is likewise inadmissible.[59] Thus, for example, if police learn of the location of a weapon used in the commission of a crime by interrogating a suspect who is in custody, that weapon is considered **derivative evidence**. If the police failed to provide the *Miranda* warnings, not only the suspect's responses to their questions but also the weapon discovered as the fruit of the interrogation are tainted. On the other hand, if the physical evidence was located on the basis of independently and lawfully obtained information, it may be admissible under the **independent source doctrine**[60] (which is often referred to as the "inevitable discovery" doctrine). Thus, in our hypothetical case, if police also learned of the location of the weapon from an informant, the weapon might well be admissible in court, even though the suspect's statements are still inadmissible.

Police generally provide the *Miranda* warnings immediately upon arrest or as soon as is practicable, in order to preserve as evidence any statements that the suspect might make, as well as any other evidence that might be derived from these statements. However, in some situations the *Miranda* warnings are delayed because police are preoccupied with apprehending other individuals or taking actions to protect themselves or others on the scene. Accordingly, in 1984, the Supreme Court recognized a **public safety exception** to the *Miranda* exclusionary rule.[61] Police may ask suspects questions designed to locate weapons that might be used to harm the police or other persons before providing the *Miranda* warnings. If this interaction produces incriminating statements or physical evidence, the evidence need not be suppressed. Appellate courts also have carved an exception for any "spontaneous declaration" made by a suspect before police have a reasonable time to provide the Miranda warning; this exception would apply to statements made voluntarily by persons who are not in police custody.

Identification Procedures

Law enforcement agencies employ various means to identify suspects. The principal means is through eyewitness identification, often at "line-ups." The Supreme Court has noted that accused criminals are entitled to have counsel present at line-ups and that line-ups should not be "unnecessarily suggestive," as would be the case if, say, a 6-foot suspect were surrounding by 5-foot men in a line-up.[62] Beyond the use of line-ups,

CASE IN POINT

THE PUBLIC SAFETY EXCEPTION TO *MIRANDA*
New York v. Quarles
United States Supreme Court
467 U.S. 649, 104 S. Ct. 2626, 81 L. Ed. 2d 550 (1984)

Two New York City police officers were approached by a woman who claimed she had just been raped and that her assailant had gone into a nearby grocery store. The police were informed that the assailant was carrying a gun. The officers proceeded to the store and immediately spotted Benjamin Quarles, who matched the description given by the victim. Upon seeing the police, Quarles turned and ran. One of the police officers drew his service revolver and ordered Quarles to "freeze." Quarles complied with the officer's request. The officer frisked Quarles and discovered an empty shoulder holster. Before reading Quarles the *Miranda* warnings, the officer asked where the gun was.

Quarles nodded in the direction of some empty boxes and said, "The gun is over there." He was then placed under arrest and "Mirandized." Later, Quarles moved to have his statement suppressed from evidence since it was made prior to the *Miranda* warnings. He also moved for suppression of the gun under the fruit of the poisonous tree doctrine. The Supreme Court allowed both pieces of evidence to be used against Quarles, notwithstanding the delay in the *Miranda* warnings. Obviously, the Court felt that the officers were justified in locating a discarded weapon prior to Mirandizing Quarles. In so holding, the Court created the public safety exception to *Miranda*.

---

scientific methods have become increasingly important to police. Such methods include comparison of blood samples, matching of clothing fibers, comparison of head and body hair, identification of semen, and DNA tests. The Fifth Amendment privilege against compulsory self-incrimination does not apply to identification procedures,[63] although police may need to procure a warrant to compel a suspect to provide certain physical evidence. Further, the reliability and validity of particular procedures remains subject to due process–based challenges.

THE RIGHT TO COUNSEL

The Sixth Amendment to the U.S. Constitution provides: "In all criminal prosecutions, the accused shall enjoy the right . . . to have the Assistance of Counsel for his defense." The **right to counsel** is essential to preserving the fundamental fairness of all criminal procedures. The defense attorney not only represents the accused in pretrial court proceedings but also advises on strategy and often serves as the negotiator between the defendant and the prosecutor.

The Sixth Amendment has been consistently interpreted to allow defendants to employ counsel in all federal prosecutions. Similar provisions in the constitutions of the fifty states allow defendants to retain counsel in state criminal prosecutions. Irrespective of state constitutional protection, the accused is protected by the federal Constitution. In *Gideon v. Wainwright* (1963), the Supreme Court held that the Sixth Amendment right to counsel applies to prosecutions in the state courts by way of the Due Process Clause of the Fourteenth Amendment.[64]

Providing Counsel to Indigent Persons

Although criminal defendants have the right to employ attorneys to represent them, many defendants are too poor to afford private counsel. The Judiciary Act of 1790 required federal judges to assign counsel to indigent defendants in capital cases, at least where defendants requested representation. Some states emulated the act of Congress by providing for appointed counsel in capital cases, but most did not. In its 1963 *Gideon* decision, the Supreme Court decided that the Fourteenth Amendment requires states to provide counsel to indigent defendants in all felony cases, observing that "any person haled into court, who is too poor to hire a lawyer, cannot be assured a fair trial unless counsel is provided for him."[65] In 1972, the Supreme Court extended the *Gideon* decision to encompass defendants who face incarceration for misdemeanors.[66]

The representation provided to indigent defendants might take the form of a **public defender** or an attorney appointed ad hoc by the court. Many states have established successful public defender systems that operate much like prosecutors' offices. In other states, indigent defendants still depend largely on ad hoc appointment of counsel. Sometimes, the public defender's office has a conflict in which codefendants want to pursue inconsistent defenses. In such instances, an outside attorney should be appointed.

Federal and state laws generally leave the determination of indigency to the discretion of the courts. Courts tend to be liberal in this regard, refusing to equate indigency with destitution and are generally inclined to appoint counsel if the cost of hiring a lawyer would prevent the defendant from making bail. More than 75 percent of felony defendants are classified as indigent. Some state statutes provide for an assessment of an attorney's fee against a defendant who is represented by the public defender's office.

Self-Representation

The Supreme Court has held that there is a constitutional right to represent oneself in a criminal prosecution.[67] Moreover, the Court has said that the defendant's legal knowledge or skill has no bearing on the right to **self-representation**, but it has also stressed that the defendant who waives the right to counsel and proceeds *pro se* must do so knowingly and intelligently. A defendant who chooses self-representation is not required to evidence knowledge of the law, but a legion of decisions from state appellate courts hold that before approving a defendant's request, the trial court must conduct a thorough hearing to make sure he or she has intelligently exercised the right to choose self-representation. Moreover, the Supreme Court has ruled that "a defendant does not have a constitutional right to receive personal instruction from the trial judge on courtroom procedure."[68] Critics of the Court's approach in allowing laypersons to represent themselves in serious criminal cases argue that criminal law and procedure have become too complex and technical to permit the non-lawyer defendant to engage

OPINION OF COURT

GIDEON v. WAINWRIGHT
372 U.S. 335, 83 S. Ct. 792, 9 L. Ed. 2d 799 (1963)

Mr. Justice Black delivered the Opinion of the Court.

...[I]n our adversary system of criminal justice, any person haled into court, who is too poor to hire a lawyer, cannot be assured a fair trial unless counsel is provided for him. This seems to us to be an obvious truth. Governments, both state and federal, quite properly spend vast sums of money to establish machinery to try defendants accused of crime. Lawyers to prosecute are everywhere deemed essential to protect the public's interest in an orderly society. Similarly, there are few defendants charged with crime, few indeed, who fail to hire the best lawyers they can get to prepare and present their defenses. That government hires lawyers to prosecute and defendants who have the money hire lawyers to defend are the strongest indications of the widespread belief that lawyers in criminal courts are necessities, not luxuries. The right of one charged with crime to counsel may not be deemed fundamental and essential to fair trials in some countries, but it is in ours. From the very beginning, our state and national constitutions and laws have laid great emphasis on procedural and substantive safeguards designed to assure fair trials before impartial tribunals in which every defendant stands equal before the law. This noble ideal cannot be realized if the poor man charged with crime has to face his accusers without a lawyer to assist him....

in effective self-representation. This is why judges sometimes appoint standby counsel to assist defendants who choose self-representation.

THE PRETRIAL PROCESS

What happens during the pretrial process often determines the outcome of a criminal case, as the overwhelming majority of criminal cases never make it to trial. Some are dropped or dismissed for lack of sufficient evidence; others result in convictions pursuant to guilty pleas. Many guilty pleas result from negotiations between prosecutors and defense counsel, making trials unnecessary.

Disposition of Petty Offenses

Minor misdemeanors are often disposed through **summary justice**. In such cases, the accused usually is not placed under arrest but rather is simply issued a **summons** to appear in court to answer the charges. In many cases, such as those involving motor vehicle infractions, the individual who is charged is issued a **citation** and may simply elect to waive a court appearance and satisfy the charge by paying a predetermined fine.

If the individual appears in court to contest the charges, the entire matter is typically resolved in one proceeding. The accused enters a plea ("not guilty," "guilty," or "no contest"), evidence is taken, and the judge renders a verdict. If the defendant is found guilty, sentence is generally pronounced immediately. Although defendants clearly have a right to hire attorneys to represent them in minor misdemeanor cases, most people go it alone before the magistrate. If they lose, which is highly probable, they typically pay a fine, which tends to be substantially less expensive than hiring an attorney.

The Initial Court Appearance

In major misdemeanor and felony cases, the procedure is much more complex and protracted. Typically, individuals charged with felonies are placed under arrest prior to any appearance in court. However, all persons placed under arrest must promptly be taken before a judge or magistrate. Many jurisdictions require an **initial appearance** within twenty-four hours after arrest. The Supreme Court has ruled that suspects may be detained for as long as forty-eight hours before being taken before a judge or magistrate.[69]

The purpose of the initial appearance is to begin the formal charging process. Essentially, the judge or magistrate must perform three important functions at the initial appearance: (1) the charges must be read so that the accused will be formally notified of the charges; (2) the accused must be informed of relevant constitutional rights, including the right to remain silent and the right to counsel; and (3) a determination must be made of whether the accused should be released pending trial or remanded to custody to await the disposition of the case.

Pretrial Release and Pretrial Detention

The most important thing to a person who has been arrested and confined to jail is to secure release as soon as possible. **Pretrial release** is commonly referred to as granting **bail** and is usually granted by statutes or court rules. In determining whether a defendant is entitled to pretrial release, the court considers factors such as the accused's prior convictions (if any), character, employment history, and ties to family and the community, as well as the nature and scope of the current charges. Increasingly, courts are requiring that arrested persons be drug tested. While not used as evidence, the results of the drug test help inform the judge's decision whether to grant pretrial release and whether to impose conditions upon that release.

Excessive Bail

Recognizing the common law practice of allowing pretrial release on bail, the Eighth Amendment to the federal Constitution states that "excessive bail shall not be required." The Supreme Court has made it clear that the purpose of bail is to ensure the appearance of the accused in court, not to inflict punishment, as evidenced in its declaration that: "Bail set at a figure higher than an amount reasonably calculated to fulfill this purpose is 'excessive' under the Eighth Amendment."[70] However, the Supreme Court has never held that the Excessive Bail Clause of the Eighth Amendment is enforceable against the states via the Fourteenth Amendment, leaving the matter of **excessive bail** in state criminal cases to the state constitutions, state legislatures, and state courts.

Pretrial Detention

The constitutional prohibition against "excessive bail" is vague regarding the existence of a constitutional right to pretrial release. The Supreme Court has ruled that there is no right to bail under the Eighth Amendment.[71] The Federal Bail Reform Act of 1984[72] allows federal courts to hold arrestees in **pretrial detention** on the ground of dangerousness to the community, as well as the need to ensure future court appearances. And, in many states, a defendant who is charged with a crime punishable by death or life imprisonment is ineligible for pretrial release if there is substantial evidence of guilt.

The Formal Charging Process

Prosecutors have considerable influence in the determination of criminal cases. The prosecutor decides whether to proceed with a criminal case and whether to negotiate the charges with the defense. The prosecutor causes the court to issue subpoenas to compel the attendance of witnesses to testify, to bring in documents, and to provide non-testimonial physical evidence such as handwriting specimens and voice exemplars.

State and federal prosecutors have broad discretion in deciding whether to proceed with criminal charges initiated by a complainant or the police. The prosecutor may decide to drop a case for a variety of reasons, ranging from insufficient evidence to a judgment that the criminal sanction is inappropriate in a given situation. Alternatively, the prosecutor may decide to proceed on a lesser charge.

Prosecutorial discretion facilitates the widespread yet controversial practice of **plea bargaining**, which we discuss later. Although very broad, prosecutorial discretion is not unlimited. The Equal Protection Clause of the Fourteenth Amendment imposes limitations on **selective prosecution**. This means that prosecutors may not single out defendants for prosecution on the basis of race, religion, or other impermissible classifications.[73]

In a **preliminary hearing** (not to be confused with the initial appearance), a judge or magistrate examines the state's case to determine whether there is probable cause to bind the accused over to the grand jury or (in the absence of a grand jury requirement) hold the accused for trial. The Supreme Court has said that a preliminary hearing is constitutionally required in the absence of a grand jury review to determine the sufficiency of an **information**, where an arrest is made without a warrant.[74] However, preliminary hearings do not have to be full-blown adversarial proceedings. Typically, in a preliminary hearing, the defense has the privilege of cross-examining witnesses for the prosecution and is able to learn the details and strengths of the state's case. The preliminary hearing provides an inquiry into probable cause for arrest and detention and becomes a screening device for prosecutors, as well as an opportunity for defense counsel to discover the prosecutor's case.

The Grand Jury

In many jurisdictions, prosecutors must obtain an **indictment** or, true bill, from the **grand jury** in addition to, or instead of, the preliminary hearing. The Fifth Amendment to the United States Constitution states that "[n]o person shall be held to answer for a capital, or otherwise infamous crime, unless on a presentment or indictment of a grand jury." Grand jury indictments are routine in federal prosecutions, but the Supreme Court has held that states are not bound by the Fourteenth Amendment to abide by the grand jury requirement imposed on the federal courts by the Fifth Amendment. Nevertheless, about half the states have constitutional provisions or statutes requiring the use of grand juries in certain types of criminal cases. Other states use the grand jury primarily in an investigatory or supervisory capacity.

At common law, the grand jury comprised twenty-three persons, and at least twelve had to agree in order to hand down an indictment. Today, federal grand juries comprise sixteen to twenty-three persons, but the "twelve votes for indictment" rule applies in every case. States vary in regard to the size of grand juries, but in every state at least a majority of grand jurors must agree that there is probable cause for a trial in order to hand down an indictment against the accused. Today, grand juries seldom refuse to hand down indictments sought by prosecutors, causing some critics to question the utility of the institution as a safeguard for the rights of the accused. Perhaps it is this perception that has led a number of states to adopt the information/preliminary hearing mechanism in lieu of the grand jury. In most Midwestern and Western states, the grand jury is seldom used to charge persons with crimes.

The grand jury, like the magistrate presiding over the preliminary hearing, examines the evidence and testimony the prosecution has collected against the accused. Unlike the preliminary hearing, the grand jury proceeding is normally closed. The defendant is generally not represented by counsel or even present at the proceeding. Testimony is not always transcribed, and if it is, access to transcripts is either limited or nonexistent. While controversial, grand jury secrecy encourages uninhibited testimony by witnesses and prevents the circulation of derogatory statements about persons who are ultimately not indicted. After the prosecutor has presented testimony and physical evidence, the members of the grand jury vote whether to hand down an indictment. There is some variation among jurisdictions in the rules that determine grand jury indictments, but in no case can a grand jury return a "true bill" unless a majority of grand jurors votes to indict.

Grand Jury Powers

Grand juries possess the authority to compel the appearance of witnesses, to **subpoena** documents, to hold individuals in contempt, and to grant **immunity** from prosecution in exchange for testimony. Immunity is of two kinds. **Transactional immunity** bars any further prosecution of the witness in regard to the specific transaction to which the witness testified. **Use immunity** is more limited, barring only the use of the witness's testimony against him or her in a subsequent prosecution. Federal grand juries are authorized to grant use immunity. Many states follow the federal practice, but some permit grand juries to grant transactional immunity.

Evidence before the Grand Jury

Many of the rules of evidence that apply to the criminal trial do not apply to the grand jury. For example, hearsay evidence is admissible in proceedings before a grand jury, whereas at trial, except in certain instances, it is not admitted over the defendant's objection. Moreover, evidence excluded from trial on Fourth or Fifth Amendment grounds is also admissible before the grand jury. The theory is, of course, that the grand jury is an investigative body and that any infringement of the rights of the accused can be corrected in subsequent adversary court proceedings. Notwithstanding the fact that a grand jury may consider evidence that is inadmissible at trial, it may not violate a valid evidentiary privilege established by the Constitution, statutes, or the common law. (See discussion of evidentiary privileges in Chapter 9.)

Pretrial Motions

Pretrial motions are written requests to the court on behalf of the government or the defendant. Motions commonly filed in criminal cases include a **motion for continuance** (postponement), a **motion to dismiss** the indictment or information against the defendant, a **motion to suppress** a defendant's confession or admission, a motion to require the government to identify a confidential informant (CI), and a motion to determine the accused's competency to stand trial. In some instances, a motion to take a **deposition** is filed to preserve the testimony of a witness who may not be available for trial. More common in high profile cases is the **motion for change of venue** (seeking to move the trial to a different location).

In 2010, Jeffrey Skilling, former CEO of Enron, requested a change of venue at his trial for securities fraud. The Supreme Court ultimately rejected his claim that pre-trial publicity made it impossible for him to receive a fair trial in Houston. The Court noted, among other things, that Houston is the country's fourth-largest city, and publicity was more diffuse there than it would be in a smaller hamlet—and thus it was not probable that the entire jury pool had been prejudiced.[75]

Arraignment

The **arraignment** is the accused's first appearance before a court of law with the authority to conduct a criminal trial. At this stage of the process, the accused must enter a plea to the charges contained in the indictment or information. The accused may enter a **plea of not guilty**, in which case the plea is noted and a trial date is set. He or she may enter a **plea of guilty**, in which case no trial is necessary, guilt is pronounced, and sentencing follows, often after a presentence investigation has been completed. In some jurisdictions, the accused has the option of pleading *nolo contendere* (no contest). The **no contest plea**, although functionally equivalent to a guilty plea in a criminal trial, provides the accused the advantage that it generally cannot be construed as an admission of guilt in a related civil suit.

Because a plea of guilty or *nolo contendere* represents a waiver of constitutional rights, it is essential that the plea be made knowingly and voluntarily. A factual basis is necessary to ensure that the accused does not admit to an offense that does not fall within the bounds of the government's accusations. Judges employ various methods to determine voluntariness of a defendant's plea and to determine whether there is a factual basis for the offense. These methods usually include interrogation of the defendant by the judge, and sometimes by the prosecutor and defense counsel.

Plea Bargaining

In most jurisdictions, more than 90 percent of felony suspects arraigned plead guilty or no contest. Very often, the guilty plea is the result of a bargain struck between the defense and the prosecution. In a **plea bargain**, the accused agrees to plead guilty in exchange for a reduction in the number and/or severity of charges or a promise by the prosecutor not to seek the maximum penalty allowed by law. Plea negotiations are subject to the approval of the trial court. In most instances, the bargain is arrived at between experienced and knowledgeable counsel on both sides and is readily approved by the court. If the court is unwilling to approve the plea bargain, the defendant must choose between withdrawing the guilty plea (and thus going to trial), and accepting the plea bargain with such modifications as the judge may approve. Once the court has accepted a guilty plea pursuant to a plea bargain, the court cannot unilaterally alter it without permitting the defendant the opportunity to withdraw the plea.

In some jurisdictions, judges participate directly in plea-bargaining discussions. Yet, other courts disfavor the participation of a trial judge in such discussions on the basis that the power and position of the judge may improperly influence the defendant to enter a guilty plea. Plea bargaining has been sharply criticized by observers with different perspectives on the criminal process. Some critics fault plea bargaining for reducing the severity of criminal penalties. Others view plea bargaining as an unconstitutional effort to deprive defendants of their right to a fair trial. Plea bargaining has drawn criticism, but few critics stop to consider the tremendous costs and delays that would result if the numerous cases currently resolved through plea bargaining were to go to trial.

In addition to permitting a substantial conservation of prosecutorial and judicial resources, plea bargaining provides a means by which, through mutual concession, the parties may obtain a prompt resolution of criminal proceedings. The plea bargain, or negotiated sentence, avoids the delay and uncertainties of trial and appeal and permits swift and certain punishment of law violators with a sentence tailored to the circumstances of the case at hand. The Supreme Court has upheld the practice of plea bargaining, and has stated that a prosecutor's office should act in good faith during this process—that is, not making promises regarding sentencing recommendations and then reneging on those promises after a defendant pleads guilty, even when a different prosecutor takes over a case after an original prosecutor has agreed to a plea bargain.[76]

Pretrial Discovery

The courts have long recognized a prosecutorial duty to disclose **exculpatory information** (i.e., information that tends to vindicate the accused) to the defense. This is based on the fundamental concept of our system of justice that individuals accused of crimes must be treated fairly. In *Brady v. Maryland* (1963), the Supreme Court stated that "the suppression by the prosecution of evidence favorable to the accused upon request violates due process where the evidence is material either to guilt or punishment, irrespective of the good faith or bad faith of the prosecution."[77]

The Supreme Court also has held that, in addition to substantive exculpatory evidence, evidence tending to impeach the credibility of prosecution witnesses falls within *Brady*'s definition of evidence favorable to an accused. Therefore, under *Brady*, a defendant is entitled to disclosure of information that might be used to impeach government witnesses. Generally, the defense must request the disclosure of the exculpatory evidence. However, if the defense is unaware of the existence of the evidence, such a request is impossible. The Supreme Court has held that failure to request disclosure is not necessarily fatal to a later challenge based on *Brady v. Maryland*, but it may significantly affect the standard for determining materiality. In a similar vein, it has been held to be a denial of due process if a prosecutor knowingly allows perjured testimony to be used against the accused.[78]

Most states have now adopted liberal rules pertaining to **pretrial discovery**, rules designed to avoid unfairness to the defense. Using appropriate pretrial motions, the defense and prosecution can gain access to the evidence possessed by the opposing party. Much of this is accomplished by taking depositions of prospective witnesses. Discovery in a criminal case is somewhat more limited in federal than in state courts. Under the provisions of 18 U.S.C. §3500, a federal criminal defendant is not entitled to inspect a statement or report prepared by a government witness "until said witness has testified on direct examination in the trial of the case." After a witness testifies, the government, upon proper request of the defense, must then produce that portion of any statement or report that relates to the subject matter as to which the witness has testified. The federal statute is commonly referred to as the **Jencks Act** because its effect was first recognized by the Supreme Court in *Jencks v. United States* (1957).[79]

The Right to a Speedy Trial

The Sixth Amendment to the federal Constitution guarantees the defendant the **right to a speedy trial**. The Speedy Trial Clause of the Sixth Amendment is made applicable to the states through the Fourteenth Amendment.[80] In 1972, the Supreme Court refused to mandate a specific time limit between the filing of charges and the commencement of trial. Instead, it adopted a balancing test to determine whether a defendant was denied the right to a speedy trial. Under this test, courts must consider (1) the length of the delay; (2) the reasons for the delay; (3) the defendant's assertion of the right; and (4) prejudice to the defendant.[81]

In 1974, Congress enacted the Speedy Trial Act, which provides specific time limits for pretrial and trial procedures in the federal courts.[82] For example, an indictment must be filed within thirty days of arrest; arraignment must be held within ten days of indictment; and trial must commence within seventy days after indictment. Violations of the time limitations are remedied by dismissal of charges. However, there are a number of exceptions to the time limits, especially where defendants' motions cause delays. Most states have adopted legislation or court rules along the lines of the federal speedy trial statute.

Additionally, a defendant who can establish that the prosecutor intentionally delayed an indictment in order to gain a tactical advantage and that the defendant incurred actual prejudice as a result of the delay can assert a claim of denial of due process.

THE CRIMINAL TRIAL

A trial is the centerpiece of the criminal justice system. In criminal trials, the interests of the state and the individual are in sharp contrast. In general, the procedures in a criminal trial follow the sequence of those in a civil trial as outlined in Chapter 9. Historically, the standard of proof required to convict a defendant has been **proof beyond a reasonable doubt**, which is a more stringent standard than the preponderance of evidence standard that applies to civil trials. In 1970, the Supreme Court elevated the standard to constitutional status by ruling that the Due Process Clause of the Fourteenth Amendment requires the prosecution to establish all elements of a crime charged beyond a reasonable doubt.[83] Moreover, in a criminal trial a number of other significant constitutional guarantees come into play, and the rights of a criminal defendant must be scrupulously guarded.

The Prosecution's Case

Prosecutors are ever mindful that when a defendant pleads not guilty the government must establish the defendant's guilt beyond any reasonable doubt. In presenting the government's case, the prosecuting attorney usually calls as witnesses police officers, the victim, and any other available witnesses whose testimony can support the charge against the defendant. In addition to such testimonial evidence, the prosecution will present any available real evidence, that is, items such as X-rays, fingerprints, weapons, and so forth. The government's witnesses may also include experts. For example, in a homicide prosecution the prosecutor usually calls a physician; in a drug-trafficking case, a chemist; in a forgery prosecution, a handwriting expert. A technician who has conducted laboratory tests on DNA samples in homicide and sexual battery cases is often called to testify. The admissibility of scientific evidence is governed by standards set forth in the *Daubert* and *Frye* cases discussed in Chapter 9. The Supreme Court has also specifically noted that lie detector tests may not be admitted as evidence in criminal cases, even when the defense attempts to introduce them as evidence of innocence.[84]

Constitutional Rights of the Defendant

The Sixth Amendment to the U.S. Constitution is the basis of many trial rights for defendants. The Sixth Amendment is made applicable to state criminal trials by the Fourteenth Amendment.[85] The Sixth Amendment guarantees the defendant the right to confront witnesses for the prosecution. This means that the defendant has the right to be present at trial and to cross-examine each witness the prosecution presents. The **right of cross-examination** of an adversary's witness is absolute. The right of cross-examination is available to both the prosecutor and the defense counsel and is extremely valuable in the trial of criminal cases. The permissible scope of cross-examination, however, varies somewhat in different jurisdictions and is a matter largely within the discretion of the trial court. Courts typically agree that the right of cross-examination is limited to (1) questioning the witness about matters testified to on direct examination; and (2) asking any questions that may impeach the witness's credibility or demonstrate any bias, interest, or hostility on the part of the witness.

Although in most instances it is objectionable for a lawyer who is examining a witness to ask **leading questions** on direct examination, the rules of evidence permit a cross-examiner to ask leading questions. Frequently, a cross-examiner is successful in bringing out inconsistencies and contradictions and any bias or hostility of the witness. A witness may also be subject to **impeachment**, that is, having one's credibility attacked on cross-examination. A witness's credibility may be attacked by

- showing the witness's inability to have viewed or heard the matters the witness has testified to, or inability to recall the event testified to;
- demonstrating that the witness has made prior conflicting statements on an important point;
- showing the witness has been convicted of a crime;
- establishing that the witness bears a bad reputation for truth in the community; or
- showing bias, prejudice, or motive to misrepresent the facts, or that the witness has a definite interest in the result of the trial.

The defendant's right of confrontation guaranteeing a face-to-face meeting with witnesses appearing before the judge or jury is not absolute. It must occasionally give way to considerations of public policy and necessities of the case. The constitutional **right of confrontation** came into sharp focus in 1988 when the Supreme Court held that a defendant's Sixth Amendment right to confront witnesses was violated in a sexual abuse case in which the trial judge, pursuant to an Iowa law, allowed a screen to be erected between the defendant and the two thirteen-year-old girls that he was accused of assaulting. The two children were situated so they could not see the defendant during their testimony.[86] The Court left open the question of whether a procedure that shields a child sex abuse victim may be constitutionally acceptable if there is an individualized finding that the witness is in need of such protection.

Two years later in *Maryland v. Craig*, the Supreme Court revisited the problem. The Court ruled that if the trial court makes a specific finding of the necessity to protect a child witness from the trauma of testifying in the presence of the defendant in a child abuse case, it may use procedures such as one-way closed-circuit television.[87]

Recently, several states have refined their **child-shield statutes** affecting children who are victims of sexual abuse. These revised statutes have met with varying reactions from state appellate courts. To avoid the constitutional requirements of the Confrontation Clause, the prosecution must show, and the trial judge must make particularized findings that, a child victim of sexual abuse would suffer unreasonable and unnecessary mental or emotional harm if the child were to testify in the presence of the defendant.

Article 3, Section 2 of the U.S. Constitution provides that trial of all crimes, except in cases of impeachment, shall be by jury. Subsequently, the Sixth Amendment was adopted, guaranteeing that "[i]n all criminal prosecutions, the accused shall enjoy the right to a speedy and public trial, by an impartial jury." The constitutional mandate leaves unanswered questions concerning the qualifications of jurors, the method of their selection, and the requirements for a jury to convict a person accused of a crime.

An accused may waive the right to a **jury trial**. Indeed, many persons who plead not guilty to misdemeanor charges elect a **bench trial**. On the other hand, most defendants who plead not guilty to felony charges choose to be tried by jury. The Supreme Court has ruled that the constitutional right to a jury trial extends to the class of cases for which an accused was entitled to a jury trial when the Constitution was adopted. This did not include juvenile cases, hence there is no right to a jury trial for juveniles,[88] nor is the right to a jury trial applicable to military tribunals under the federal Constitution. As now interpreted, the Sixth Amendment guarantees an accused the right to a jury trial in criminal cases where a penalty of more than six months in jail can be imposed.[89] Offenses that carry a possible penalty of no more than six months' imprisonment are generally termed "petty offenses," and a jury trial is not required under the United States Constitution.[90] In some states, by constitutional provision or statute, a defendant may be entitled to a jury trial for an offense even if it is classified as a petty offense.

Composition of the Trial Jury

At common law, a jury consisted of twelve men. Rule 23(b) of the Federal Rules of Criminal Procedure requires a twelve-member jury in criminal cases in federal courts unless the defendant stipulates to fewer members in writing. All states require twelve-member juries in capital cases. Most require the same number for all felony prosecutions. Many, however, now use fewer than twelve jurors in misdemeanor cases. Six-person juries in both felony and misdemeanor cases are permissible, but states may not reduce the jury size below this level.[91]

In federal courts and in the great majority of state courts, a jury verdict in a criminal trial must be unanimous. A few states, however, accept less-than-unanimous verdicts. The Supreme Court has approved nonunanimous verdicts rendered by twelve-person juries, but it has ruled that a verdict by a six-person jury, even in a non-petty offense, must be unanimous.[92]

Jury Selection

As we discussed in Chapter 9, state and federal laws prescribe qualifications for jurors and set forth the processes by which citizens are summoned for jury duty. The body of persons summoned to be jurors is referred to as the **venire**. The jury is selected from the venire through a process known as *voir dire*. During *voir dire*, counsel will ask prospective jurors questions designed to detect biases. Counsel will challenge prospective jurors they believe to be biased against their side of the case. **Challenges for cause** require a ruling from the bench, while **peremptory challenges** do not require counsel to state a cause and are not subject to review by the court, except that peremptory challenges cannot be exercised on the basis of a prospective juror's race or gender. (For more discussion on this subject, see Chapter 9.)

The Supreme Court has said that **death qualification of a jury** (i.e., the exclusion of prospective jurors who will not under any circumstances vote for imposition of the death penalty) is designed to obtain a jury that can properly and impartially apply the law to the facts at both the guilt and sentencing phases of a capital trial. On this rationale, the Court upheld the removal, before the guilt phase in a capital trial, of prospective jurors whose opposition to the death penalty would impair or prevent performance of their duties at the sentencing phase.[93]

Free Press vs. Fair Trial

Because of First Amendment rights, the Supreme Court has held that trials may not be closed without findings sufficient to overcome the presumption of openness.[94] Nevertheless, First Amendment guarantees of freedom of the press often collide with a defendant's right to a fair trial before an impartial jury, particularly when heightened public interest results in mass media coverage of a trial, with potential prejudicial effects on witnesses and jurors. When this occurs, the trial court must protect the defendant's right to a fair trial by taking steps to prevent these influences from affecting the rights of a defendant. Failure to do so can result in a guilty verdict's being overturned by an appellate tribunal.

Cameras in the Courtroom

During the 1970s, many state courts began to allow radio, television, and still-camera coverage of court proceedings subject to limitations necessary to preserve the essential dignity of a trial (for example, equipment must be noiseless, and strong lights are not permitted). Also, judges may limit coverage by requiring pooling of media equipment. Nevertheless, Rule 53 of the Federal Rules of Criminal Procedure still prohibits the taking of photographs in the courtroom during the progress of judicial proceedings in federal courts. By 1993, cameras were allowed in the courtrooms in most state courts. And while there was some backlash regarding the televising of criminal trials following the O.J. Simpson case of 1995, many still feel that cameras in the courtroom have enhanced the public's awareness of the judicial processes.

Most state courts now permit television and photographic coverage of court proceedings. In many states, the consent of the presiding judge is required, and judges generally have considerable discretion in control of the coverage. Coverage of jurors is either prohibited or restricted, and most states prohibit coverage of cases involving juveniles and victims of sex crimes.

"Order in the Court"

Occasionally, a trial judge is confronted with a defendant or others in attendance at a trial whose disruptive behavior impedes the court from conducting a trial in a proper judicial atmosphere. This problem is more likely to be encountered in a so-called "political trial," where there may be support for the cause the defendant claims to represent. It is not too difficult for judges to exercise control over members of the public who attend court trials. The problem that confronts judges is when a defendant becomes unruly. In most instances, judges control disruption and defiance by defendants and others through exercise of the **power of contempt**. Yet, in recent years some courts have had to go further. In some cases, the defendant may be removed from the courtroom until he or she promises to conduct him- or herself properly. The defendant may even be bound and gagged, thereby keeping the defendant in the courtroom.

Opening Statements of Counsel

Once the jury is in place, the trial is ready to commence. In American jurisprudence, the judge ideally has been selected as an exemplar of justice. He or she serves as the "umpire" and makes rulings on the admissibility of evidence and conduct of the lawyers, rules on the qualifications of expert witnesses, and controls the extent of interrogation of witnesses. In addition, the trial judge controls various administrative matters that occur during trial. Counsel are permitted to make brief **opening statements** outlining to the court or jury their theories of the case and summarizing the evidence to be presented. Opening statements, though, may not be argumentative. Often, the defense counsel will defer an opening statement until the prosecution has presented its case. In a bench trial, counsel frequently waive making opening statements or limit their remarks to brief presentations.

The Defense Strategy in Moving for a Judgment of Acquittal

At the close of the prosecution's evidence, the defense counsel will frequently move the court to grant a **directed verdict** or, as it is called in federal courts and many state courts, a **judgment of acquittal**. At this point, the trial judge determines whether the evidence presented by the prosecution is legally sufficient to support a verdict of guilty. For the purpose of ruling on the motion, the trial judge must view the prosecution's evidence in the light most favorable to the government. Should the motion be granted, the defendant is discharged. If the motion is denied, defense counsel proceeds with the case on behalf of the defendant, and if additional evidence is offered, defense counsel may renew the motion at the close of all the evidence.

The Defense Case—Will the Defendant Take the Stand?

The defendant does not have to testify in a criminal case, and often defendants choose to rely simply on cross-examination of the government's witnesses in an effort to obtain an acquittal. Or, the defendant may present witnesses in support of an alibi, to contradict the prosecution's witnesses, or to establish an affirmative defense. Perhaps the major tactical decision a defendant and defense counsel must make at trial is whether the defendant will take the stand and testify in his or her own behalf. The Fifth Amendment privilege against self-incrimination, which applies to the states through the Fourteenth Amendment,[95] protects the defendant from being required to testify, absent a grant of immunity. Furthermore, it also forbids any direct or indirect comment by the prosecution on the accused's failure to testify. When an accused voluntarily chooses to testify in his or her own behalf, though, the prosecution may cross-examine the accused with the same latitude as with any other witness.

Jury Instructions

At the close of all the evidence in a jury trial, it is customary for the trial judge to confer with counsel outside the presence of the jury concerning the instructions on the law the judge will give to the jury. The prosecutor and defense counsel may be asked to present proposed instructions for the court to consider. More commonly, the trial judge announces that the court will give certain standard instructions and offers to supplement them with specific instructions to be chosen from those submitted by counsel. A defendant is entitled to have the jury instructed on the law applicable to any legitimate theory of defense that is supported by the evidence presented.

Closing Arguments

Each side in a criminal trial is allowed to make a **closing argument**. Usually, counsel waive the right to make a closing argument to the judge in a bench trial, but in a jury trial closing argument affords counsel an important opportunity to attempt to convince the jury of the merits of counsel's position. In their closing arguments, counsel may comment on the evidence and credibility of the witnesses but are not permitted to express their personal opinions on the defendant's guilt or innocence. Typically, at the conclusion of the closing arguments, the judge either reads the indictment or information or explains the charges against the defendant to the jury. This is followed by an admonition that the defendant is presumed innocent unless and until the government proves the defendant guilty beyond a reasonable doubt of each element of the crime. The judge defines the elements of any crime charged and explains any technical legal terms. Where the jury may convict the defendant of a lesser offense or an attempt, the judge must define the crime, any lesser included offenses, and attempts. For example, where the defendant is charged with first-degree murder, the judge must instruct the jury on such lesser offenses as second-degree murder and manslaughter.

    Jury instructions are given orally, and in some instances the jury is given a copy of the instructions. The clerk furnishes the jury forms of verdicts so they may find the defendant not guilty, guilty as charged, or guilty of some degree of the offense charged or of a lesser included offense. In federal criminal trials and in most state courts, the judge explains the requirement for a unanimous verdict. In some states, the judge is required to inform the jury of the penalties that can be imposed for the offense charged. Finally, the jury is directed to retire, select one of its members as **foreperson**, and deliberate on its verdict. Normally, a jury is allowed to take with it to the jury room all exhibits received in evidence.

The Jury Deliberates and Returns Its Verdict

When directed to deliberate, the jurors are escorted to their quarters by a court bailiff. In some cases, the judge orders the jury sequestered, which means the jury must remain together until it reaches its verdict. **Sequestration** often requires the bailiff to escort the jurors to a hotel and to be present with them during meals to ensure that no outside influences are brought to bear on their judgment. Once in the jury room, their first order of business is to elect a foreperson. Then they are ready to commence their deliberations.

When a jury has concluded its deliberations, it returns to the courtroom and delivers its written verdict. A defendant who is acquitted by a jury is immediately discharged. If a jury finds the defendant guilty, the defendant is normally taken into custody to await sentencing. In some instances, the defendant may be continued on bail, pending application for a new trial or an appeal. If a jury reports that it is a **deadlocked jury**, the trial judge can either declare a mistrial or urge the jury to make further attempts to arrive at a verdict.

If a mistrial is declared, the government usually will have the opportunity to re-try a defendant if it so chooses. A verdict of acquittal, though, is not subject to appeal from the government, in keeping with the Fifth Amendment prohibition against being "twice put in jeopardy." Further, if a mistrial is declared due to prosecutorial misconduct, a judge may rule that "jeopardy attaches" and preclude further prosecution. In 2012, the Court considered the case of an Arkansas man whose trial on homicide charges resulted in a hung jury. The jury's foreperson told the judge that jurors unanimously felt the defendant was not guilty of first-degree or second-degree murder, but that charges of voluntary manslaughter and involuntary manslaughter had resulted in a hung jury. The defendant argued that any re-trial should thus focus only on the latter two charges, in keeping with the notion of Double Jeopardy. On May 24, 2012, however, in *Blueford v. Arkansas*, the Supreme Court ruled that the prosecution could in fact retry the defendant on all counts, because no "final verdict" had been reached.[96]

SENTENCING

Although every jurisdiction requires that criminal sentences for adults be imposed in open court, in many instances juvenile offenders may be sentenced *in camera*. In misdemeanor cases, sentencing usually occurs immediately upon conviction. In felony cases, where penalties are greater, sentencing may be postponed to allow the court to conduct a **presentence investigation**.

In many states, as well as in the federal system, the court is required to order a presentence report where the offender to be sentenced is a first offender or under a certain age. In other state jurisdictions, the sentencing judge is accorded discretion in this area. The presentence report sets forth the defendant's history of delinquency or criminality, medical history, family background, economic status, education, employment history, and other relevant factors. Additionally, most jurisdictions allow courts to order physical and/or mental examinations of defendants.

In some states, statutes, court rules, or judicial interpretations mandate that courts release a presentence report to the defendant or defendant's counsel, usually allowing some exemptions for sensitive material. In other states, courts have ruled that this is a matter within the discretion of the sentencing judge. In some instances, courts will reveal factual material, such as police reports, but decline to disclose statements made in confidence to investigators. The Supreme Court requires release of presentence reports to defendants who may be sentenced to death.

The Sentencing Hearing

After the presentence report is completed, the court holds a **sentencing hearing**. At this hearing, the court considers the evidence received at trial, the presentence report, any evidence offered by either party in aggravation or mitigation of sentence, and any statement the defendant wishes to make. The **pronouncement of sentence** is the stage when the trial court imposes a penalty upon a defendant for the offense or offenses of which the defendant has been adjudged guilty. Sentences are pronounced in open court, usually by the judge who presided at the defendant's trial or entry of plea. In misdemeanor cases, sentencing often occurs immediately after entry of a plea or a finding of guilty by the judge or jury. In felony cases, the pronouncement is often delayed until the court has received a presentence investigation report or until the prosecutor and defense counsel have had an opportunity to prepare a presentation.

Sentencing is a "critical stage" of a criminal proceeding at which the defendant is entitled to be represented by counsel. Counsel must be supplied to indigent defendants.[97] The rules of evidence are relaxed during a sentencing proceeding. The procedure at the pronouncement stage is generally outlined in the criminal procedure rules of each jurisdiction. A verbatim account is made of the entire sentencing proceeding. Traditionally, a defendant has been afforded an opportunity to make a statement on his or her own behalf, a procedure often referred to as the right of **allocution**. Generally, special rules govern the sentencing of a defendant who is insane, and often sentencing must be deferred for a female defendant who is pregnant.

In many instances, where a defendant is convicted of a noncapital crime, courts are authorized to suspend the imposition of sentence and place the defendant on probation or under community control for some determinate period. Of course, if the defendant violates conditions set by the court, the original sentence may be imposed. A **suspended sentence** is most often used in cases of first offenses or nonviolent offenses. A defendant who is convicted of multiple crimes must be given separate sentences for each offense. These sentences may run consecutively or concurrently, usually at the discretion of the sentencing judge.

Indeterminate, Definite, Determinate, and Indefinite Sentencing

For much of the twentieth century, legislatures commonly allowed judges to sentence criminals to imprisonment for indeterminate periods in order to assist corrections officials in the process of rehabilitating offenders. Under this system, release from prison took the form of parole. Abuses of the system, combined with the decline of popular support for rehabilitation, have led most jurisdictions to abandon the concept of **indeterminate sentencing**. Despite this trend, a number of state laws retain indeterminate sentencing for youthful offenders.

At the opposite extreme from indeterminate sentencing is **definite sentencing**, an approach designed to eliminate discretion and ensure that offenders who commit the same crimes are punished equally. The definite sentence is set by the legislature with no leeway for judges or corrections officials to individualize punishment. Under **determinate sentencing**, a variation of the definite sentence, the judge sets a fixed term of years within statutory parameters, and the offender is required to serve that term without the possibility of early release. The most common approach is referred to as **indefinite sentencing**. Here there is judicial discretion to impose a sentence within a range of prescribed minimum and maximum penalties. What distinguishes indefinite from determinate sentencing is that indefinite sentencing allows for early release from prison on parole.

Mandatory Minimum Sentencing

Mandatory sentences result from legislative mandates that offenders who commit certain crimes must be sentenced to prison terms for minimum periods. Under **mandatory sentencing**, there is no option for judges to place offenders on probation. Most often, mandatory sentences are required for violent crimes, especially those involving the use of firearms. As a result of the "war on drugs" launched in the 1980s, federal law now mandates minimum prison terms for serious drug crimes. For example, a person charged with possession with the intent to distribute more than five kilograms of cocaine is subject to a mandatory minimum sentence of ten years in prison.[98] Federal courts have no authority to impose lesser sentences than those mandated by Congress unless prosecutors specifically request such departures. In many states, the legislature has enacted statutes requiring judges to impose mandatory sentences on defendants convicted of certain drug-trafficking offenses and offenses where a defendant used a firearm.

Penalty Enhancement Statutes

In an effort to incapacitate **habitual offenders**, the laws of many states require automatic increased penalties for persons convicted of repeated felonies. In 1980, the Supreme Court upheld a life sentence imposed under the Texas habitual offender statute mandating life terms for persons convicted of three felonies.[99] In a 1983 case, though, the Court rejected the life sentence of a South Dakota man who was deemed an habitual offender for seven non-violent crimes, the last of which involved writing a bad check for $100.[100]

A variation on the habitual offender law is known colloquially as **"three strikes and you're out."** In 1994, California voters overwhelmingly approved a ballot initiative under which persons convicted of a third violent or "serious" felony would be incarcerated for twenty-five years to life. Prosecutors immediately availed themselves of this new weapon, but in many instances the new law led to controversial results. However, in 1996, a California appellate court held that trial judges had the power to strike prior felony convictions, thus making a defendant ineligible for three-strikes sentencing.[101] This interpretation of the trial court's authority attenuated somewhat the harshness of the three-strikes policy.

The Violent Crime Control and Law Enforcement Act of 1994,[102] better known as the "Federal Crime Bill," provided for mandatory life sentences for persons convicted in federal court of a "serious violent felony" after having been previously convicted, in federal or state court, of two "serious violent felonies." Currently, the federal government and more than half the states have some form of habitual offender or "three strikes" statute.

Another approach to sentencing that has gained popularity in recent years is enhancing or extending penalties based on characteristics of the crime or the victim. For example, in 1993 the Supreme Court upheld a Wisconsin statute that increases the severity of punishment if a crime victim is chosen on the basis of race or other designated characteristics.[103]

Elsewhere, in an effort to strengthen law enforcement in the war on drugs, the 1994 Federal Crime Bill included several provisions for enhanced penalties. Drug trafficking in prisons and "drug free" zones, illegal drug use in federal prisons, or smuggling of drugs into federal prisons are now subject to enhanced penalties.

In 2000, however, the Supreme Court ruled that any fact that increases a defendant's punishment beyond the statutory maximum must be proven beyond a reasonable doubt before a jury, just as the prosecution is required to establish any element of the crime. The Court's decision greatly affected the practice of courts' imposing penalty enhancements at the federal and state levels.[104]

Sentencing Guidelines

In the face of considerable criticism of the exercise of judicial discretion, which often resulted in great disparities in sentences, Congress and a number of state legislatures adopted **sentencing guidelines**. Some states have adopted voluntary guidelines; others have mandated that sentencing conform to guidelines absent a compelling reason for departing from them. The federal guidelines came into being with the enactment of the Sentencing Reform Act of 1984, which applies to all crimes committed after November 1, 1987.[105] The Act created the United States Sentencing Commission and empowered it to promulgate sentencing guidelines. The resulting guidelines drastically reduced the discretion of federal judges by establishing a narrow sentencing range with the proviso that the sentencing court may depart from the guidelines if it "finds that there exists an aggravating or mitigating circumstance of a kind, or to a degree, not adequately taken into consideration . . . in formulating the guidelines that should result in a sentence different from that described." Of course, it is impermissible to depart from the guidelines on the basis of the defendant's race, sex, national origin, religion, or socioeconomic status. Other factors not ordinarily deemed relevant in determining whether to depart include the defendant's age, education, mental and physical condition, employment history, and family and community ties.

Congress intended the federal sentencing guidelines to be mandatory. But in 2005, the Supreme Court held that the guidelines violated a defendant's Sixth Amendment right to trial by jury because they authorized judges to increase sentences based on factual determinations not made by juries. The Court's decision effectively relegated the guidelines to a supplementary role. Although federal courts are no longer required to use the sentencing guidelines, many still tend to follow them as "advisory."[106]

States have experimented with sentencing guidelines with varying results. Minnesota, the first state to adopt presumptive sentencing guidelines in 1970, has a relatively simple system that has proven to be workable, although it has resulted in a higher incarceration rate. Washington's sentencing guidelines worked reasonably well until the state legislature began to mandate increased penalties overall as well as harsher minimum sentences for particular crimes. This has necessitated that the guidelines be revised. In Tennessee, the Commission that established sentencing guidelines was terminated, although the guidelines themselves remain in effect.

There is still considerable uncertainty about the efficacy of sentencing guidelines. There is evidence that they have reduced unwarranted sentencing disparities, but clearly they have not eliminated this problem altogether. There is also concern that sentencing guidelines have promoted higher incarceration rates and have thus contributed to the problem of prison overcrowding.

Granting and Revoking Probation

With the overcrowding of prisons, courts have come to rely increasingly on probation for first-time and non-violent offenders. Under federal law, a defendant who has been found guilty of an offense may be sentenced to a term of probation unless (1) the offense is a felony where the maximum term of imprisonment authorized is twenty-five years or more, life imprisonment, or death; or (2) the offense is one for which probation has been expressly precluded; or (3) the defendant is sentenced at the same time to a term of imprisonment for the same or a different offense. Probation terms for a felony must not be less than one nor more than five years, and for a misdemeanor not more than five years.[107] Certain conditions of probation are mandatory and others are discretionary with the federal judge who imposes probation.[108] In most states, the term of probation is limited to the maximum statutory term of confinement for the particular offense. In some instances, mandatory conditions are imposed by statute, but the trial court may impose additional conditions. Probation is often combined with a fine, restitution to the victim, or a short term of incarceration to give the probationer "a taste" of jail.

In every jurisdiction, the commission of a felony while on probation is grounds for revocation of probation. In many jurisdictions, certain misdemeanors qualify as grounds for revocation. Generally speaking, the violation of any substantive condition of probation is grounds for revocation. Typically, a probation officer is vested with broad discretion in determining when to seek revocation of probation. A probationer facing the loss of freedom is entitled to a fair hearing at which the probationer has the right to call favorable witnesses, to confront hostile witnesses, and to be represented by counsel. In 1974, the Supreme Court said that indigent probationers may have a constitutional right to have counsel appointed at revocation hearings, depending on the complexity of the issues involved, and that if counsel is not provided, the judge must state the reason.[109] In practice, counsel is usually provided. Additionally, there is a statutory right to appointment of counsel for those financially unable to obtain counsel in federal probation revocation proceedings.[110]

Prison Disciplinary Hearings and Revocation of Parole

Today, disciplinary measures in prisons often consist of removal of good-time credit toward early release. If officials pursue this policy, then due process of law demands that certain procedural requirements be observed before good-time credit is removed for disciplinary purposes. Specifically, there must be written notice of the disciplinary action, and the inmate has the right to an administrative hearing with a written record. The inmate must be accorded the right to produce evidence refuting the charges of misconduct and may even call witnesses on his or her behalf. These rights have not been extended to allow an inmate to have counsel present at **prison disciplinary hearings**, however.[111]

As in the case of internal prison disciplinary actions, the revocation of **parole** is affected by due process considerations. Essentially, before parole can be revoked, the parolee has the right to a hearing within a reasonable time after being retaken into custody. The Supreme Court has said, "[T]he process should be flexible enough to consider evidence including letters, affidavits, and other material that would not be admissible in an adversary criminal trial."[112] In addition, the Court has held that the right to counsel may apply to **parole revocation hearings**, depending on the complexity of the issues involved.[113] There is a statutory right to appointment of counsel for those financially unable to obtain counsel in federal parole revocation hearings.[114]

Sentencing in Capital Cases

In those cases where the prosecution is permitted by law to seek the death penalty, the sentencing procedure is considerably more complex. In *Furman v. Georgia* (1972), the Supreme Court imposed a moratorium on the death penalty, prompting state legislatures to rewrite their capital punishment statutes.[115] The post-*Furman* capital punishment laws require a **bifurcated trial** in cases where the prosecution seeks the death penalty. In the first stage, guilt is determined according to the usual procedures, rules of evidence, and standard of proof. If the jury finds the defendant guilty, the same jury considers the appropriateness of the death sentence in a separate proceeding where additional evidence is received in aggravation or mitigation of the punishment. In order to impose the death penalty, the jury must find at least one of several **aggravating factors** specified by law. The purpose of requiring aggravating factors before imposing the death penalty is to narrow the cases and persons eligible for capital punishment and make the imposition of the death penalty more predictable. In *Gregg v. Georgia* (1976), the Supreme Court upheld Georgia's revised death penalty statute by a 7-2 vote.[116] Apparently, the Court was satisfied that this scheme had sufficiently addressed the evils identified in *Furman*.

Thirty-two states now have death penalty statutes modeled along the lines of the law upheld in *Gregg*.[117] However, in recent cases, the Supreme Court has stated that the death penalty cannot be applied to the mentally retarded[118] or to those under the age of 18.[119] Further, in *Kennedy v. Louisiana*, the Court went so far as to prevent the execution of a child rapist, suggesting that a state's sentence of death should be reserved for those who take another's life.[120] Some states, though, have chosen to abolish the death penalty in all instances, with New York, New Mexico, Illinois, Connecticut, and Maryland doing so in the years since 2004. While elected officials in these states made the decisions to halt capital punishment, in July 2014, a federal judge in California stopped its application there. Specifically, Judge Cormac J. Carney decried "a system in which arbitrary factors, rather than legitimate ones like the nature of the crime or the date of the death sentence, determine whether an individual will actually be executed."[121] Appeals of the decision were forthcoming, and it remains to be seen whether higher courts actually would consider vacating the basic underpinnings of the *Gregg v. Georgia* decision.

Mitigating Factors and Victim Impact Evidence

During the sentencing phase of the capital trial, the defense usually introduces evidence of **mitigating factors**: the defendant's youth, alcoholism or drug dependency, the defendant's history of mental illness or instability, the absence of criminal record, the fact that there was some provocation by the defendant, and so forth. The jury can take anything into account by way of mitigation, assigning whatever weight it thinks appropriate. Sometimes, the defense will put the mother or other close relative of the defendant on the stand to plead for the defendant's life. Prosecutors counter emotional pleas on the defendant's behalf by presenting **victim impact evidence**. This evidence takes the form of testimony addressing the impact of the murder on the victim and the victim's family, including the physical, economic, and psychological effects of the crime. For example, the victim's surviving spouse might be called to testify to the toll the homicide has taken on the family. Needless to say, such testimony is often fraught with emotion and can have a powerful impact on the jury. Nevertheless, its constitutionality has been affirmed by the Supreme Court.[122] Federal and state decisions conflict as to the extent victim impact evidence can be presented. The issue usually turns on whether the evidence is inflammatory and unduly prejudicial. In the latest expression on the subject, the U.S. Supreme Court on November 10, 2008, denied a defendant's petition to review a California Supreme Court decision that allowed a twenty-minute montage consisting of still photos and video clips depicting the victim's entire life to be shown to a sentencing jury in a capital case.[123]

Recent Controversy in Capital Punishment: Lethal Injection

On April 29, 2014, the execution of an Oklahoma prisoner made headlines when it took forty-three minutes for him to die after the administration of a lethal injection (the normal length of time from injection to death is only a few minutes). Authorities said an improperly inserted IV line caused the delay, and the prisoner ended up dying of a heart attack. A similar incident occurred on July 23, 2014 in Arizona. There, an inmate took over two hours to die following administration of a lethal injection—a time frame that was long enough for his lawyers to actually file a request for a stay *during* the execution.

Recent controversy surrounding lethal injections is connected to the fact that drugs previously used in this process have become harder for states to acquire, perhaps because some are imported from European countries where objections to the death penalty are common. Consequently, states have been forced to utilize new combinations of drugs, with outcomes often an unknown. Some states, such as Oklahoma and

Tennessee, actually are refusing to reveal the drugs that comprise their lethal injection protocols. Tennessee also passed a law in May 2014 to mandate use of the electric chair if drugs for a lethal injection are not available; although seven other states allow a prisoner to choose the electric chair as the method of execution, Tennessee's decision to mandate its usage could result in appeals from death row inmates.

On May 22, 2014, the Supreme Court entered this debate by refusing to hear a claim from a Louisiana death row inmate who tried to force the revelation of a lethal injection's contents; the execution thus went forward. Later, in July 2014, after the U.S. Court of Appeals for the Ninth Circuit had halted an Arizona execution until the precise composition of a lethal injection protocol was released, the Supreme Court intervened and vacated the lower court's order.[124] These decisions were consistent with the Court's 2008 ruling in *Baze v. Rees*, which allowed the state of Kentucky to continue using lethal injections in spite of the possibility of adverse reactions if the drugs were improperly administered. The Court's opinion, however, did leave open the possibility that lethal injection could someday be ruled an example of "cruel and unusual punishment" if it could be determined that a better method of execution were feasible.[125] Ultimately, that matter could serve as the central issue for future capital punishment cases.

VICTIMS' RIGHTS IN THE CRIMINAL PROCESS

Although crime is by definition an injury against society as a whole, we must not forget that most serious crimes injure individual victims, often quite severely. The injury may transcend physical or economic injury to include emotional hardship. If during the 1960s the dominant concern of the criminal law was for the rights of the accused, since the 1990s, the trend has been to recognize the rights of crime victims. A number of states—including Arizona, California, Florida, Michigan, New Jersey, Rhode Island, Texas, and Washington—have adopted constitutional amendments specifically recognizing victims' rights. Other states have adopted statutes along these lines.[126] During the 1990s, a proposal to add a victims' rights amendment to the U.S. Constitution surfaced in Congress, but the amendment was not adopted. There are now more than 9,000 organizations (mostly private) dedicated to assisting crime victims. Clearly, there is substantial public support for efforts to recognize and enhance victims' rights.

The Uniform Victims of Crime Act

The Uniform Victims of Crime Act (UVCA) is an attempt to lend consistency to the patchwork of victims' rights laws that now exists at the state level. The UVCA was developed by the Uniform Law Commission, a voluntary association representing the legal profession. Like the Model Penal Code developed by the American Law Institute, the UVCA has no status as law unless and until it is adopted by a state legislature.

Under the UVCA, prosecutors or court personnel must notify victims of their rights under the Act, as well as the times of any court proceedings involving the person or persons who allegedly victimized them. A crime victim has a right to be present at any court proceeding that the defendant has a right to attend. If the defendant is convicted, the victim has the right to make an impact statement during the sentencing hearing and assert an opinion as to the proper sentence. Finally, the UVCA provides for victims to be compensated by the state, up to $25,000, for any physical or emotional injuries suffered as the result of the victimization. However, this amount may be denied or reduced if the victim receives compensation through insurance or restitution from the defendant.

Restitution

Restitution refers to "the return of a sum of money, an object, or the value of an object which the defendant wrongfully obtained in the course of committing the crime."[127] Although restitution was practiced under the early common law, it eventually was abandoned as a remedy in criminal cases in favor of fines payable to the Crown. In modern America, however, restitution is making a comeback in the criminal law. A number of states have enacted laws allowing trial courts to require restitution as a condition of probation, in lieu of sentencing offenders to prison.

Restitution is not practical in many criminal cases. Many offenders are not suited to probation and, even among those who are, there is no guarantee that they will be able to make payments to the victim. Recognizing this problem, a number of states have established victims' compensation commissions. For example, the Florida Crimes Compensation Act of 1977 makes victims and certain relatives eligible for compensation by a state commission where a crime results in injuries and is reported within seventy-two hours. Awards are limited to meeting the actual needs of victims.[128]

THE APPEALS PROCESS

Society's commitment to standards of fairness and procedural regularity is reflected in the opportunities that exist for defendants in criminal cases to seek higher judicial review of adverse court decisions. At common law, there was no right to appeal from a criminal conviction prior to the eighteenth century. On rare occasions, the Crown issued a "writ of error" to require a new trial, but there was no appeal in the modern sense. The government's right to appeal is limited, essentially allowing such appeals only in respect to adverse rulings on jurisdictional matters, suppression of evidence, and the validity of charging documents. Through judicial decisions and acts of Parliament, defendants eventually acquired the right to appeal their convictions to higher courts. The United States Constitution makes no mention of the right to appeal from a criminal conviction, although some might argue that the right to appeal is implicit in the Due Process Clauses of the Fifth and Fourteenth Amendments. In 1894, the United States Supreme Court held that the federal Constitution affords no right to appeal from a criminal conviction.[129] However, Congress and the state legislatures have provided for various types of appellate review. These remedies have increased greatly in recent decades, largely through judicial interpretation of statutory provisions.

Forms of Appellate Review

Forms of review in criminal cases include **trial *de novo*, appeal of right, discretionary review**, and **post-conviction relief**. Trial *de novo* occurs when a trial court of general jurisdiction reviews a conviction rendered by a court of limited jurisdiction. Appeal of right, the most common form of appeal, refers to an appellate court's review of a criminal conviction rendered by a trial court of general jurisdiction. A defendant whose conviction is affirmed on appeal may seek further review by a higher court by petitioning for discretionary review. Finally, a defendant confined to prison may seek additional review of a conviction or sentence by applying for a **writ of habeas corpus**, which allows a court of competent jurisdiction to review the legality of a prisoner's confinement. Literally, habeas corpus means "you have the body," and has been interpreted to mean "show the body," as if to refer to the act of bringing a prisoner into a public (i.e., court) for a hearing. Ultimately, each of the mechanisms referenced in this paragraph plays an important part in the determination of cases that move beyond the trial stage of the criminal process.

The mechanics of handling criminal appeals insofar as they relate to records, briefing, oral argument, and the court's decision-making processes are essentially as described in Chapter 9 in relation to appeals in civil cases.

What Defendants May Challenge on Appeal

In a direct appeal from a criminal conviction, a defendant may challenge any act of the trial court objected to by the defendant during the pretrial, trial, or post-trial phases of the defendant's case. Irrespective of whether an objection was made in the trial court, a defendant may challenge the trial court's jurisdiction and those trial court actions or rulings considered to be **fundamental errors**. Appellate courts take different approaches to how serious an error must be to be classified as fundamental. Courts are more liberal in reviewing errors first challenged at the appellate stage where the defendant has been convicted of a capital crime. The United States Supreme Court has said that when a person's life is at stake, fundamental errors not specifically challenged by the appellant should be corrected by the reviewing court.[130]

Although appellate review is designed to correct errors that occur during or before trial, not all errors necessitate reversal. This is referred to as the **doctrine of harmless error**. To obtain reversal of a judgment, the appellant must show that some prejudice resulted from the error and that the outcome of the trial or the sentence imposed would probably have been different in the absence of the error. Where an error involves provisions of the federal Constitution, appellate courts must find beyond a reasonable doubt that the error was harmless in order to affirm the trial court.[131]

The Right to Counsel on Appeal

The Supreme Court has said that states must provide counsel to indigent persons convicted of felonies who exercise their statutory right to appeal.[132] However, the Court has also held that a state's failure to provide counsel to an indigent defendant seeking discretionary review in the state and federal supreme courts does not violate due process or equal protection.[133]

Challenging State Court Convictions in Federal Court

The Supreme Court can review only a minute proportion of the cases in which persons convicted in state courts seek to challenge their convictions on federal constitutional grounds. The writ of habeas corpus is another means of obtaining federal judicial review of state court convictions. In recent decades, **federal habeas corpus review** of state criminal convictions has become a common form of appellate procedure. It also has greatly multiplied the opportunities for persons convicted of state offenses to obtain relief. Consequently, it has become the focus of considerable controversy.

The Federal Judiciary Act of 1789 recognized the power of federal courts to issue writs of habeas corpus only in respect to federal prisoners.[134] In 1867, federal law was amended to allow federal courts to entertain habeas petitions from state prisoners who allege that their incarceration violates provisions of the U.S. Constitution or federal statutes or treaties.[135]

Prior to the twentieth century, the federal habeas corpus jurisdiction was seldom used to review state criminal convictions. Federal law had long provided that federal habeas corpus relief was available only to state prisoners who had exhausted all available remedies in the state courts. But in 1963, the Supreme Court held that a state prisoner did not have to take a direct appeal to the state supreme court in order to seek federal habeas corpus review. Nor was the prisoner barred from raising constitutional issues in federal court merely because he had not raised them on direct appeal.[136] By the 1990s, the Supreme Court took a more conservative stance and in 1993 ruled that federal district courts may not overturn state criminal convictions unless the petitioner can show that he or she suffered "actual prejudice" from the errors cited in the petition.[137] Previously, the state carried the burden of proving beyond a reasonable doubt that any constitutional error committed during or prior to trial was "harmless," that is, not prejudicial to the defendant.

The Antiterrorism and Effective Death Penalty Act of 1996[138] curtailed second habeas corpus petitions by state prisoners who have already filed such petitions in federal court. Under the new statute, any second or subsequent habeas petition must meet a particularly high standard and must pass through a "gatekeeping" function exercised by the U.S. Courts of Appeals, which must grant a motion giving the inmate permission to file the petition in a district court; denial of this motion is not appealable to the Supreme Court. In 1996, an inmate awaiting execution in Georgia challenged the constitutionality of this provision, but in a unanimous decision the Supreme Court upheld the statute.[139]

Post-Conviction Relief in State Courts

The constitutional rights of criminal defendants were greatly expanded as a result of the Supreme Court's decisions of the 1960s, thereby effectively "nationalizing" criminal procedure. During those years, the states began to review the efficacy of the writ of habeas corpus as a basis for permitting challenges to judgments and sentences subsequent to conclusion of a direct appeal. As a result, most states adopted statutes or court rules that permit a post-appeal challenge to an illegal conviction or sentence. These procedures, known as **collateral attack** or post-conviction relief, provide a mechanism for a defendant who is incarcerated to obtain a review of judgments and sentences imposed in violation of the federal or state constitutions.

Ineffective counsel constitutes a common basis for post-conviction attacks on convictions and sentences. The issue of ineffective counsel is rarely raised on direct appeal as it is not a matter that would ordinarily be challenged in the trial court. In 1984, the Supreme Court articulated a uniform constitutional standard for determining the issue of ineffective counsel.[140] First, the defendant must show that counsel's performance was deficient, or below that standard that a reasonably competent lawyer would have provided. In essence, this requires showing that counsel made errors so serious that counsel was not functioning as the "counsel" guaranteed the defendant by the Sixth Amendment. Second, the defendant must show that the deficient performance prejudiced the defense. This requires showing that counsel's errors were so serious as to deprive the defendant of a fair trial, a trial whose result is reliable. In other words, the defendant must show that there was a reasonable probability that, but for the errors of counsel, the defendant would have received a different outcome.

CRIMINAL PROCEDURE IN MILITARY TRIBUNALS

The U.S. Constitution grants Congress the authority to regulate the armed forces.[141] Pursuant to this authority, Congress has enacted the **Uniform Code of Military Justice** (UCMJ).[142] The UCMJ gives courts-martial jurisdiction to try all offenses under the Code committed by military personnel in violation of the UCMJ.[143] (In Chapter 4 we mentioned some of the offenses unique to military service.) In *Solorio v. United States,* the Supreme Court noted that active military personnel can be subjected to court martial proceedings even for criminal activity that is unrelated to military service.[144] However, Reserve Officer Training Corps (ROTC) cadets at colleges and universities are not subject to the UCMJ unless placed on specific active duty orders, which normally occurs for summer training

Under an executive order issued by President George W. Bush on November 13, 2001, foreign nationals accused of acts of terrorism against the United States were to be tried by special military commissions. However, in *Hamdan v. Rumsfeld* (2006),[145] the Supreme Court ruled that the commissions created pursuant to the President's order were neither authorized by federal law nor required by military necessity, and ran afoul of the Geneva Conventions. In 2008, in *Boumediene v. Bush,*[146] the Supreme Court went a step further and noted that prisoners held at the U.S. military facility at Guantanamo Bay were entitled to the basic protections of habeas corpus regardless of the prisoners' national origin.

Preferral of Charges

Article 30 of the UCMJ authorizes any person subject to the UCMJ to prefer charges against a person subject to the UCMJ. In practice, it is the accused's immediate commander, after preliminary investigation, who files sworn charges against the accused. Whether such charges will be tried becomes a matter for the convening authority who exercises discretion as to whether to refer such charges for a court-martial.

Constitutional Rights of Service Personnel

Historically, members of the armed forces were viewed as sacrificing most of their individual rights upon entry into service. Courts did not recognize that the Bill of Rights to the United States Constitution was applicable to service members. But in *United States v. Jacoby* (1960),[147] the Court of Military Appeals held that the protections in the Bill of Rights, except those that are expressly—or by necessary implication—inapplicable, are available to members of the armed forces. Today, most of the protections of the Bill of Rights applicable to defendants in civilian courts are likewise applicable to servicepersons accused of offenses under the UCMJ.

Pretrial Proceedings

An accused must be brought to trial within 120 days after notice to the accused of preferral of charges, or the imposition of restraint, whichever is earlier. Absent delays occasioned by the defense, a violation of the right to a speedy trial is presumed if a service member is confined for more than ninety days before trial. Military and civilian defendants enjoy the right to a public trial, and those seeking to close a trial to the public must advance some "overriding interest," such as national security interests.

Pretrial Confinement

Although there is no right to bail in the military justice system, the UCMJ calls for pretrial confinement only as a last resort. In any event, the military services have a reputation for conducting prompt trials. A serviceperson is ordered into pretrial confinement only if the commander has probable cause to believe that the accused has committed an offense and that it is necessary to confine the accused to ensure that he or she will appear at trial, or that it is foreseeable that the accused will engage in serious misconduct, and that less severe forms of restraint would be inadequate. The commander's decision to order an accused into pretrial confinement must be reviewed promptly by a neutral and detached officer. The accused may appear with counsel and make a statement, if practicable. The reviewing officer must either approve continued pretrial confinement or order the prisoner to be immediately released.

Courts-Martial

Commanders of various military units convene court-martial proceedings and appoint military members who then sit similar to a civilian jury. These commanders are called the **convening authorities** and are assisted by military lawyers designated as staff judge advocates. Military trial procedures and rules of evidence are similar to the rules applied in federal district courts.

There are three classes of court-martial: summary, special, and general. The **summary court-martial** is composed of one military officer with jurisdiction to impose minor punishments over enlisted personnel. It is somewhat analogous to trial by a civilian magistrate, whereas special and general court-martial proceedings are formal military tribunals more analogous to civilian criminal courts of record.

A **special court-martial** must be composed of three or more members with or without a military judge, or a military judge alone, if requested by the accused. It can impose more serious punishments on both officers and enlisted personnel. A general court-martial tries the most serious offenses and must consist of five or more members and a military judge (or a military judge alone, if requested by the accused).

A **general court-martial** may try any offense made punishable by the UCMJ and may impose any punishment authorized by law against officers and enlisted personnel, including death for a capital offense. Trial by a military judge alone is not permitted in capital cases. Before charges are sent to a general court-martial, an investigation (called an Article 32 investigation) somewhat akin to that undertaken by the civilian grand jury is conducted by a military officer who makes a nonbinding recommendation concerning the disposition of the charges.

A **military judge** presides at special and general courts-martial. A trial counsel serves as prosecutor, and a defendant is furnished legal counsel by the government unless the accused chooses to employ private defense counsel. If less than two-thirds of the members vote for a finding of guilty—or, when the death penalty is mandatory, fewer than all the members vote for a finding of guilty—a finding of not guilty results as to the particular charge. The extent of punishment that may be imposed varies according to the offense and the authority of the type of court-martial convened. Punishment may include confinement, reduction in pay grade, and/or discharge under less-than-honorable conditions.

Appeals from Decisions of Courts-Martial

Decisions of courts-martial are reviewed by **military courts of review** in each branch of the armed forces. In specified instances, appeals are heard by the United States **Court of Appeals for the Armed Forces**. This court is staffed by civilian judges who are appointed to fifteen-year terms by the President with the consent of the Senate. The Supreme Court of the United States could also hear appeals emanating from military proceedings.

CONCLUSION

The Framers of the Bill of Rights imposed constraints on law enforcement not because they were opposed to law and order, but because they were deeply distrustful of power. They feared what well-meaning but overzealous officials might do if not constrained by the rule of law. Consequently, they gave us a Bill of Rights, which makes it more difficult for government to investigate, prosecute, and punish crime. During the 1960s, the Supreme Court, under Chief Justice Warren, interpreted these protections more broadly than courts traditionally had viewed them. In the 1980s, the pendulum swung back in the other direction, as more conservative justices were appointed to the Court. Since then, a more moderate (yet still conservative) Court has refrained from making major changes in constitutional interpretation affecting the criminal justice system. Of course, the great challenge to the Supreme Court, indeed to all courts, is to strike the proper balance between society's need for crime control and our equally strong desire for individual privacy and freedom.

SUMMARY OF KEY CONCEPTS

The U.S. Constitution protects the rights of an individual accused of crime, from the earliest stages of investigation to the finality of appellate review of a conviction. Central to procedural requirements are three Amendments to the Constitution. The Fourth Amendment protects against unreasonable searches and seizures. Its safeguards have been fleshed out by the Supreme Court in respect to the preference for warrants and the requirements of probable cause in most instances. The Fifth Amendment and the Court's familiar 1966 *Miranda* requirements protect the right against self-incrimination. The "exclusionary rule," imposed against the states by the Court's 1961 *Mapp* decision, operates to restrain law enforcement from violating these rights. Finally, the Sixth Amendment guarantees a defendant the right to a speedy and public jury trial in all but cases involving minor offenses, as well as the right to legal counsel. Constitutional constraints also reach investigatory detentions, the investigatory process, and the methods used by police in securing eyewitness and scientific means of identifying suspects.

In all felony and major misdemeanor cases, the accusatorial processes of the law occur through grand juries' returning indictments at the federal, and often, at the state level; however, states have the right to develop their own means of initiating prosecution and many have done so through prosecutors' filing of sworn accusatorial documents known as informations. An accused in many instances is available for pretrial release through a variety of methods, the most common being the posting of a bail bond.

Once the federal or state government has instituted charges against a defendant, the defendant can opt to plead guilty or not guilty. A number of pretrial procedures are available to allow a defendant to learn of the strength of the prosecution's case before deciding whether to stand for trial. A defendant may be represented by counsel at all important pretrial and trial stages of a criminal prosecution, and since the Supreme Court's seminal decision in *Gideon v. Wainwright* in 1963, indigent defendants have the right to be represented by public defendants or court-appointed counsel.

In this chapter, we discussed the effects of pleas of guilty, not guilty, and *nolo contendere*, the process of plea bargaining, and the availability of pretrial discovery processes. Yet, we also emphasized that a trial is the centerpiece of the criminal justice system. We have endeavored to take the student through the steps of a criminal trial, with emphasis on the requirement for proof beyond a reasonable doubt, and to explain the processes from the selection of a jury to the return of the jury's verdict. These processes include the role of counsel in making opening statements, examining and cross-examining witnesses, and making closing arguments to the jury. We mentioned the role of the court in instructing the jury on the law and the jury's functions in deliberating and returning a verdict.

Beyond those of accused criminals, the rights of inmates also have received constitutional protection; however, because victims are not the first-line players in a criminal prosecution, in the past their rights have not been accorded the attention many think victims deserve. Increasingly, legislative bodies and courts are responding to the demands of citizens to ensure that the rights of victims of crime are considered by the criminal justice system.

Legislative bodies set the statutory parameters of punishment for criminal offenses; historically, though, judges have exercised discretion in imposing a sentence within those boundaries. The trend has been to restrict judicial discretion in order to minimize disparities in punishment. The present approach relies heavily on sentencing guidelines that require courts to consider numerous factors when crafting a sentence within stated parameters. In jurisdictions where capital punishment is imposed, judges and juries must follow strict guidelines and consider aggravating and mitigating factors to ensure that death sentences comport with strict judicially-imposed safeguards.

We also have discussed the appeals process in criminal cases. The government's right to appeal is limited, essentially allowing such appeals only in respect to adverse rulings on jurisdictional matters, suppression of evidence, and the validity of charging documents. A defendant, on the other hand, has the right to appeals from a final order of conviction and sentence and to seek post-conviction remedies available in federal and state courts.

Finally, we have provided a brief outline of criminal procedure in the military justice system. Under the Uniform Code of Military Justice, Congress has provided that courts-martial have jurisdiction to try all offenses committed by military personnel in violation of the UCMJ. Courts-martial follow somewhat different procedures from civilian criminal courts, but servicepersons accused of crimes have many of the same rights as civilian defendants, including the right to counsel, freedom from compulsory self-incrimination, and the right to appeal. Certain basic protections, then, extend across the spectrum of criminal proceedings in the United States of America.

FOR FURTHER READING

Amar, Akhil Reed, *The Constitution and Criminal Procedure: First Principles* (Yale University Press 1997).

Baker, Liva, *Miranda: Crime, Law and Politics* (Atheneum Press 1983).

Dershowitz, Alan M., *The Best Defense* (Random House 1982).

Heumann, Milton, *Plea Bargaining: The Experiences of Prosecutors, Judges and Defense Attorneys* (University of Chicago Press 1978).

Jacob, Herbert, *Law and Politics in the United States* (Little, Brown 1986).

Lewis, Anthony, *Gideon's Trumpet* (Vintage Books 1964).

Scheb, John M., and John M. Scheb II, *Criminal Procedure* (5th ed., Wadsworth/Cengage 2009).

Stith, Kate, and Jose A. Carbranes, *Fear of Judging; Sentencing Guidelines in the Federal Court* (University of Chicago Press 1998).

Wishman, Seymour, *Anatomy of a Jury: The System on Trial* (Times Books 1986).

QUESTIONS FOR THOUGHT AND DISCUSSION

1. In what instances and to what extent may a law enforcement officer conduct a search based on less than probable cause to believe the search will produce evidence of a crime?

2. What is the rationale for the exclusionary rule? Should the "good-faith exception" be extended to a situation where a police officer makes a warrantless arrest?

3. What constitutes an arrest? Is the use of arrest procedures for minor traffic offenses unnecessary? Is it better policy for a state to adopt procedures such as decriminalizing minor traffic offenses or to simply give an officer discretion in handling these matters?

4. What scientific and non-scientific methods are used by the police to identify suspects?

5. What alternatives can you suggest to the traditional bail bond system to ensure the appearance of a defendant in court?

6. Explain the role of plea bargaining in the criminal justice system. Should a judge participate directly in the process of plea bargaining? Why or why not?

7. Would the American system of criminal justice be more credible if the *voir dire* was conducted exclusively by the trial judge and only challenges for cause were permitted?

8. In some jurisdictions, trial judges now give basic instructions to the jury at the commencement of a trial. Evaluate this approach.

9. Describe and evaluate the most common forms of contemporary punishment.

10. What must a prosecution demonstrate during the penalty phase of a bifurcated trial in order to secure a capital sentence?

11. Do you favor the use of sentencing guidelines or would giving the trial judge discretion to impose a penalty within statutory parameters be more effective?

12. What are the most common grounds urged by criminal defendants in direct appeals of right?

13. On what grounds may an incarcerated defendant seek post-conviction relief?

14. How does the military justice system differ from the civilian justice system? What rights do servicepersons accused of offenses against the UCMJ have when they are prosecuted before courts-martial?

KEY TERMS

affiant
affidavit
aggravating factors
allocution
anonymous tips
appeal of right
arraignment
arrest warrant
automobile exception
bail
bench trial
bifurcated trial
border searches
capias
challenges for cause
child-shield statutes
citation
closing argument
collateral attack
confidential informants
consent to a search
convening authorities
Court of Appeals for the Armed
     Forces
criminal procedure
deadlocked jury
death qualification of a jury
definite sentencing
deposition
derivative evidence
determinate sentencing
directed verdict
discretionary review
doctrine of harmless error
drug courier profiles

drug testing
electronic eavesdropping
emergency searches
evanescent evidence
excessive bail
exclusionary rule
exculpatory information
exigent circumstances
federal habeas corpus review
foreperson
fruit of the poisonous tree doctrine
fundamental errors
general court-martial
good-faith exception
grand jury
habitual offenders
hot pursuit
immunity
impeachment
indefinite sentencing
independent source doctrine
indeterminate sentencing
indictment
information
initial appearance
inventory search
investigatory detention
Jencks Act
judgment of acquittal
jury instructions
jury trial
leading questions
mandatory sentencing
military courts of review
military judge

mitigating factors
motion for change of venue
motion for continuance
motion to dismiss
motion to suppress
no contest plea
opening statements
parole
parole revocation hearings
peremptory challenges
plain view
plea bargain
plea bargaining
plea of guilty
plea of not guilty
post-conviction relief
power of contempt
preliminary hearing
presentence investigation
pretrial detention
pretrial discovery
pretrial motions
pretrial release
prison disciplinary hearings
probable cause
pronouncement of sentence
proof beyond a reasonable doubt
prosecutorial discretion
public defender
public safety exception
reasonable expectation of privacy
reasonable suspicion
restitution
right of confrontation
right of cross-examination

right to a speedy trial
right to counsel
search
search incident to a lawful arrest
seizure
selective prosecution
self-representation
sentencing guidelines
sentencing hearing
sequestration
sobriety checkpoints

special court-martial
stop-and-frisk
strip searches
subpoena
summary court-martial
summary justice
summons
suspended sentence
"three strikes and you're out"
totality of circumstances
transactional immunity

trial *de novo*
Uniform Code of Military Justice
use immunity
venire
victim impact evidence
voir dire
warrant
warrantless arrest
warrantless searches
wiretapping
writ of habeas corpus

ENDNOTES

1. *Wolf v. Colorado*, 338 U.S. 25, 27-28, 69 S. Ct. 1359, 1361, 93 L. Ed. 1782, 1785 (1949).
2. *See Minnesota v. Carter*, 525 U.S. 83, 119 S. Ct. 469, 142 L. Ed. 2d 373 (1998); and *Minnesota v. Olsen*, 495 U.S. 91, 110 S. Ct. 1684, 109 L. Ed. 2d 85 (1990).
3. *Abel v. United States*, 362 U.S. 217, 80 S. Ct. 683, 4 L. Ed. 2d 668 (1960).
4. *California v. Greenwood*, 1981 486 U.S. 35, 108 S. Ct. 1625, 100 L. Ed. 2d 30 (1988).
5. *Schneckloth v. Bustamonte*, 412 U.S. 218, 93 S. Ct. 2041, 36 L. Ed. 2d 854 (1973).
6. *Ohio v. Robinette*, 519 U.S. 33, 117 S. Ct. 417, 136 L. Ed. 2d 347 (1996).
7. *Bumper v. North Carolina*, 391 U.S. 543, 88 S. Ct. 1788, 20 L. Ed. 2d 797 (1968).
8. *U.S. v Matlock*, 415 U.S. 164, 94 S. Ct. 988, 39 L. Ed. 2d 242 (1974).
9. *Georgia v. Randolph*, 547 U.S. 103, 126 S. Ct. 1515, 164 L. Ed. 2d 208 (2006).
10. *Fernandez v. California*, 573 U.S. _____, 134 S. Ct. 1126, 188 L.Ed2d 25 (2014).
11. 389 U.S. 347, 88 S. Ct. 507, 19 L. Ed. 2d 576 (1967).
12. *United States v. Jones* 132 S.Ct. 945 (2012).
13. *Riley v. California*, 573 U.S. _____, 134 S. Ct. 2473, 1899 L. Ed. 2d 430 (2014); this case was combined with the case of *U.S. v. Wurie*.
14. *Samson v. California*, 547 U.S. 843, 126 S.Ct. 2193, 165 L. Ed. 2d 258 (2006).
15. *Bell v. Wolfish*, 441 U.S. 520, 99 S. Ct. 1861, 60 L. Ed. 2d 447 (1979). *See also Florence v. Board of Chosen Freeholders*, 566 U.S. ____, 132 S. Ct. 1510, 182 L. Ed. 2d 566 (2012); this case extended such strip searches to those arrested for minor offenses.
16. *Maryland v. King*, 569 U.S. _____, 133 S. Ct. 1958, 186 L. Ed. 2d 1 (2013).

17. *City of Ontario v. Quon*, 560 U.S. 746, 130 S. Ct. 2619, 177 L. Ed. 2d 216 (2010).
18. *Skinner v. Railway Labor Executives Association*, 489 U.S. 602, 109 S. Ct. 1402, 103 L. Ed. 2d 639 (1989).
19. *National Treasury Employees Union v. Von Raab*, 489 U.S. 656, 109 S. Ct. 1384, 103 L. Ed. 2d 685 (1989).
20. *Michigan Dept. of State Police v. Sitz*, 496 U.S. 444, 110 S. Ct. 2481, 110 L. Ed. 2d 112 (1990).
21. *Indianapolis v. Edmonds*, 531 U.S. 32, 121 S. Ct. 447, 148 L. Ed. 2d 333 (2000).
22. *Missouri v. McNeely*, 569 U.S. _____, 133 S. Ct. 1552, 185 L. Ed. 2d 696 (2013).
23. *Illinois v. Gates*, 462 U.S. 213, 103 S. Ct. 2317, 76 L. Ed. 2d 527 (1983).
24. *Id.* However, some states continue to request that the credibility of anonymous informants be assessed more vigorously, on an individual case-by-case basis. These states (AK, MA, NY, TN, VM, and WA) are said to utilize the Aguilar-Spinelli standard, which is derived from two Supreme Court cases that pre-dated *Illinois v. Gates. See Aguilar v. Texas*, 378 U.S. 108, 84 S. Ct. 1509, 12 L. Ed. 2d 723 (1964); and *Spinelli v. United States*, 393 U.S. 410, 89 S. Ct. 584, 21 L. Ed. 2d 637 (1969).
25. *Coolidge v. New Hampshire*, 403 U.S. 443, 91 S. Ct. 2022, 29 L. Ed. 2d 564 (1971).
26. *California v. Ciraolo*, 476 U.S. 207, 106 S. Ct. 1809, 90 L. Ed. 2d 210 (1986); *Kyllo v. U.S.*, 533 U.S. 27, 121 S. Ct. 2038, 150 L. Ed. 2d 94 (2001).
27. For discussion of the "emergency aid" exception, *see Michigan v. Fisher*, 558 U.S. 45, 130 S. Ct. 546, 175 L. Ed. 2d 410 (2009) and *Brigham City v. Stuart*, 547 U.S. 398, 126 S. Ct. 1943, 164 L. Ed. 2d 650 (2006).
28. *Kentucky v. King*, 563 U.S. _____, 131 S. Ct. 1849, 179 L. Ed. 2d 865 (2011).

29. *Schmerber v. California*, 384 U.S. 757, 86 S. Ct. 1826, 16 L. Ed. 2d 908 (1966).

30. *Carroll v. United States*, 267 U.S. 132, 45 S. Ct. 280, 69 L. Ed. 543 (1925).

31. *Delaware v. Prouse*, 440 U.S. 648, 99 S. Ct. 1391, 59 L. Ed. 2d 660 (1979).

32. *Florida v. Harris*, 568 U.S. _____, 133 S. Ct. 1050, 185 L. Ed. 2d 61 (2013).

33. *Florida v. Jardines*, 569 U.S. _____, 133 S. Ct. 1409, 185 L. Ed. 2d 495 (2013).

34. *Chimel v. California*, 395 U.S. 752, 89 S. Ct. 2034, 23 L. Ed. 2d 685 (1969). This decision was buttressed when the Supreme Court placed limits on searches of an arrestee's vehicle in *Arizona v. Gant*, 556 U.S. 332, 129 S. Ct. 1710, 173 L. Ed. 2d 485 (2009).

35. *Riley v. California*, 573 U.S. _____, 134 S. Ct. 2473 (2014).

36. *Warden v. Hayden*, 387 U.S. 294, 87 S. Ct. 1642, 18 L. Ed. 2d 782 (1967).

37. *South Dakota v. Opperman*, 428 U.S. 364, 96 S. Ct. 3092, 49 L. Ed. 2d 1000 (1976).

38. *Terry v. Ohio*, 392 U.S. 1, 88 S. Ct. 1868, 20 L. Ed. 2d 889 (1968). The officer's ability to ask for identification is justified by the following case: *Hiibel v. Sixth Judicial District Court of Nevada*, 542 U.S. 177, 124 S. Ct. 2451, 159 L. Ed. 2d 292 (2004).

39. *Minnesota v. Dickerson*, 508 U.S. 366, 113 S. Ct. 2130, 124 L. Ed. 2d 334 (1993).

40. *New Jersey v. T.L.O.*, 469 U.S. 325, 105 S. Ct. 733, 83 L. Ed. 2d 720 (1985).

41. *Safford Unified School District v. Redding*, 557 U.S. 364, 129 S. Ct. 2633, 174 L. Ed. 2d 354 (2009).

42. *Vernonia Sch. Dist. v. Acton*, 515 U.S. 646, 115 S. Ct. 2386, 132 L. Ed. 2d 564 (1995). This principle was extended from sports teams to all extracurricular activities in *Board of Education v. Earls*, 536 U.S. 822, 122 S. Ct. 2559, 153 L. Ed. 2d 735 (2002).

43. *National Treasury Employees Union v. Von Raab*, 489 U.S. 656, 109 S. Ct. 1384, 103 L. Ed. 2d 685 (1989).

44. *Weeks v. United States*, 232 U.S. 383, 34 S. Ct. 341, 58 L. Ed. 652 (1914).

45. 367 U.S. 643, 81 S. Ct. 1684, 6 L. Ed. 2d 1081 (1961).

46. *United States v. Leon*, 468 U.S. 897, 104 S. Ct. 3405, 82 L. Ed. 2d 677 (1984); *Massachusetts v. Sheppard*, 468 U.S. 981, 104 S. Ct. 3424, 82 L. Ed. 2d 737 (1984).

47. *Terry v. Ohio*, 392 U.S. 1, 88 S. Ct. 1868, 20 L. Ed. 2d 889 (1968).

48. See *Minnesota v. Dickerson*, 508 U.S. 366, 113 S. Ct. 2130, 124 L. Ed. 2d 334 (1993). The Court stated that an officer must have probable cause to suggest that what is touched during a pat-down amounts to contraband.

49. *United States v. Sokolow*, 490 U.S. 1, 109 S. Ct. 1581, 104 L. Ed. 2d 1 (1989).

50. *Arizona v. United States*, 567 U.S. ___, 132 S. Ct. 2492, 183 L. Ed. 2d 351 (2012).

51. *Bram v. United States*, 168 U.S. 532, 18 S. Ct. 183, 42 L. Ed. 568 (1897).

52. *Miranda v. Arizona*, 384 U.S. 436, 86 S. Ct. 1602, 16 L. Ed. 2d 694 (1966).

53. 18 U.S.C. §3501.

54. *Dickerson v. United States*, 166 F.3d 667 (4th Cir. 1999).

55. *United States v. Dickerson*, 530 U.S. 428, 120 S. Ct. 2326, 147 L. Ed. 2d 405 (2000).

56. *Berghuis, Warden v. Thompkins*, 560 U.S. 370, 130 S. Ct. 2250, 176 L. Ed. 2d 1098 (2010).

57. *Salinas v. Texas*, 570 U.S. _____, 133 S. Ct. 2174, 186 L. Ed. 2d 376 (2013).

58. *Maryland v. Shatzer*, 559 U.S. 98, 130 S. Ct. 1213, 175 L. Ed. 2d 1045 (2010).

59. *Wong Sun v. United States*, 371 U.S. 471, 83 S. Ct. 407, 9 L. Ed. 2d 441 (1963).

60. *Segurra v. United States*, 468 U.S. 796, 104 S. Ct. 3380, 82 L. Ed. 2d 599 (1984).

61. *New York v. Quarles*, 467 U.S. 649, 104 S. Ct. 2626, 81 L. Ed. 2d 550 (1984).

62. *Foster v. California*, 394 U.S. 440, 89 S. Ct. 1127, 22 L. Ed. 2d 402.

63. *Schmerber v. California*, 384 U.S. 757, 86 S. Ct. 1826, 16 L. Ed. 2d 908 (1966).

64. *Gideon v. Wainwright*, 372 U.S. 335, 83 S. Ct. 792, 9 L. Ed. 2d 799 (1963).

65. *Gideon v. Wainwright*, 372 U.S. 335, 344, 83 S. Ct. 792, 796, 9 L. Ed. 2d 799, 805 (1963).

66. *Argersinger v. Hamlin*, 407 U.S. 25, 92 S. Ct. 2006, 32 L. Ed. 2d 530 (1972).

67. *Faretta v. California*, 422 U.S. 806, 95 S. Ct. 2525, 45 L. Ed. 2d 562 (1975).

68. *McKaskle v. Wiggins*, 465 U.S. 168, 183-184, 104 S. Ct. 944, 954, 79 L. Ed. 2d 122, 136-137 (1984).

69. *County of Riverside v. McLaughlin*, 500 U.S. 44, 111 S. Ct. 1661, 114 L. Ed. 2d 49 (1991).

70. *Stack v. Boyle*, 342 U.S. 1, 5, 72 S. Ct. 1, 3, 96 L. Ed. 3, 6 (1951).

71. *United States v. Salerno*, 481 U.S. 739, 107 S. Ct. 2095, 95 L. Ed. 2d 697 (1987).

72. 18 U.S.C. §3141 et seq.

73. *Oyler v. Boles*, 368 U.S. 448, 82 S. Ct. 501, 7 L. Ed. 2d 446 (1962).

74. *Gerstein v. Pugh*, 420 U.S. 103, 95 S. Ct. 854, 43 L. Ed. 2d 54 (1975).

75. *Skilling v. United States*, 561 U.S. _____, 130 S. Ct. 2896, 177 L. Ed. 2d 619 (2010).

76. *Santobello v. New York*, 404 U.S. 257, 260, 92 S. Ct. 495, 498, 30 L. Ed. 2d 427, 432 (1971).

77. *Brady v. Maryland*, 373 U.S. 83, 87, 83 S. Ct. 1194, 1996, 10 L. Ed. 2d 215, 218 (1963).

78. *Stickler v. Greene*, 527 U.S. 263, 119 S. Ct. 1936, 144 L. Ed. 2d 286 (1999).

79. 353 U.S. 657, 77 S. Ct. 1007, 1 L. Ed. 2d 1103 (1957).

80. *Klopfer v. North Carolina*, 386 U.S. 213, 87 S. Ct. 988, 18 L. Ed. 2d 1 (1967).

81. *Barker v. Wingo*, 407 U.S. 514, 92 S. Ct. 2182, 33 L. Ed. 2d 101 (1972).

82. 18 U.S.C. §3161.

83. *In re Winship*, 397 U.S. 358, 90 S. Ct. 1068, 25 L. Ed. 2d 368 (1970).

84. *United States v. Scheffer*, 523 U.S. 303, 118 S. Ct. 1261, 140 L. Ed. 2d 413 (1998).

85. *Pointer v. Texas*, 380 U.S. 400, 85 S. Ct. 1065, 13 L. Ed. 2d 923 (1965).

86. *Coy v. Iowa*, 487 U.S. 1012, 108 S. Ct. 2798, 101 L. Ed. 2d 857 (1988).

87. 497 U.S. 836, 110 S. Ct. 3157, 111 L. Ed. 2d 666 (1990).

88. *In Re Gault* was a Supreme Court case that did grant basic due process rights, such as fair notice, fair hearing, right to confront witnesses, and right to counsel, to accused juveniles. 387 U.S. 1, 87 S. Ct. 1428, 18 L. Ed. 2d 527 (1967).

89. *Codispoti v. Pennsylvania*, 418 U.S. 506, 94 S. Ct. 2687, 41 L. Ed. 2d 912 (1974).

90. *Baldwin v. New York*, 399 U.S. 66, 90 S. Ct. 1886, 26 L. Ed. 2d 437 (1970).

91. In *Williams v. Florida*, 399 U.S. 78, 90 S. Ct. 1893, 26 L. Ed. 2d 446 (1970), the Supreme Court upheld the use of six-person juries in the trial of felony offenses in Florida. Subsequently, in *Ballew v. Georgia*, 435 U.S. 223, 98 S. Ct. 1029, 55 L. Ed. 2d 234 (1978), the Court held that a jury of only five persons was not acceptable under the Sixth Amendment.

92. See *Johnson v. Louisiana*, 406 U.S. 356, 92 S. Ct. 1620, 32 L. Ed. 2d 152 (1972); *Burch v. Louisiana*, 441 U.S. 130, 99 S. Ct. 1623, 60 L. Ed. 2d 96 (1979).

93. *Lockhart v. McCree*, 476 U.S. 162, 106 S. Ct. 1758, 90 L. Ed. 2d 137 (1986).

94. *Richmond Newspapers, Inc. v. Virginia*, 448 U.S. 555, 100 S. Ct. 2814, 65 L. Ed. 2d 973 (1980).

95. *Malloy v. Hogan*, 378 U.S. 1, 84 S. Ct. 1489, 12 L. Ed. 2d 653 (1964).

96. *Blueford v. Arkansas*, 560 U.S. ___, 132 S. Ct. 2044, 182 L. Ed. 2d 937 (2012).

97. *Mempa v. Rhay*, 389 U.S. 128, 88 S. Ct. 254, 19 L. Ed. 2d 336 (1967).

98. See 21 U.S.C. §841(b)(1)(A).

99. *Rummel v. Estelle*, 445 U.S. 263, 100 S. Ct. 1133, 63 L. Ed. 2d 382 (1980).

100. *Solem v. Helm*, 463 U.S. 277, 103 S. Ct. 3001, 77 L. Ed. 2d 637 (1983).

101. *People v. Romero*, 53 Cal. Rptr. 2d 789 (Cal. App. 1996).

102. Pub. L. No. 103-322, 108 Stat. 1796.

103. *Wisconsin v. Mitchell*, 508 U.S. 476, 113 S. Ct. 2194, 124 L. Ed. 2d 436 (1993).

104. *Apprendi v. New Jersey*, 530 U.S. 466, 120 S. Ct. 2348, 147 L. Ed. 2d 435 (2000).

105. *Codified at* 18 U.S.C. §§3551-3586, 28 U.S.C. §§991-998.

106. *United States v. Booker*, 543 U.S. 220, 125 S. Ct. 738, 160 L. Ed. 2d 621 (2005).

107. 18 U.S.C. §3561.

108. 18 U.S.C. §3563.

109. *Gagnon v. Scarpelli*, 411 U.S. 778, 93 S. Ct. 1756, 36 L. Ed. 2d 656 (1973).

110. 18 U.S.C. §3006A.

111. *Baxter v. Palmigiano*, 425 U.S. 308, 96 S. Ct. 1551, 47 L. Ed. 2d 810 (1976).

112. *Morrissey v. Brewer*, 408 U.S. 471, 92 S. Ct. 2593, 33 L. Ed. 2d 484 (1972).

113. *Gagnon v. Scarpelli*, 411 U.S. 778, 93 S. Ct. 1756, 36 L. Ed. 2d 656 (1973).

114. 18 U.S.C. §3006A; *Baldwin v. Benson*, 584 F.2d 953 (10th Cir. 1978).

115. 408 U.S. 238, 92 S. Ct. 2726, 33 L. Ed. 2d 346 (1972).

116. 428 U.S. 153, 96 S. Ct. 2909, 49 L. Ed. 2d 859 (1976).

117. In three states (Connecticut, Maryland, New Mexico), capital punishment has been abolished but inmates previously sentenced to death remain eligible for execution.

118. *Atkins v. Virginia*, 536 U.S. 304, 122 S. Ct. 2242, 153 L. Ed. 2d 335 (2002).

119. *Roper v. Simmons*, 543 U.S. 551, 125 S. Ct. 1183, 161 L. Ed. 2d 1 (2005).

120. *Kennedy v. Louisiana*, 554 U.S. 407, 128 S. Ct. 2641; 171 L. Ed. 2d 525 (2008).

121. Jones v. Chappell, U.S. District Court Central District of California, July 16, 2014.

122. *Payne v. Tennessee*, 501 U.S. 808, 111 S. Ct. 2597, 115 L. Ed. 2d 720 (1991).

123. *Kelly v. California*, 555 U.S. 1020, 129 S. Ct. 564, 172 L. Ed. 2d 445 (2008).

124. *Ryan, et al. v. Wood*, 573 U.S.; order released July 22, 2014; available at: http://www.supremecourt.gov/orders/court orders/072214zr1_m6io.pdf.

125. *Baze v. Rees*, 553 U.S. 35, 128 S. Ct. 1520, 170 L. Ed. 2d 420.

126. See, e.g., Cal. Penal Code §679.

127. *State v. Stalheim*, 552 P.2d 829, 832 (Or. 1976).

128. Fla. Stat. Ann. §§960.001-960.297.

129. *McKane v. Durston*, 153 U.S. 684, 14 S. Ct. 913, 38 L. Ed. 867 (1894).

130. *Fisher v. United States*, 328 U.S. 463, 66 S. Ct. 1318, 90 L. Ed. 1382 (1946).

131. *Chapman v. California*, 386 U.S. 18, 87 S. Ct. 824, 17 L. Ed. 2d 705 (1967).

132. *Douglas v. California*, 372 U.S. 353, 83 S. Ct. 814, 9 L. Ed. 2d 811 (1963).
133. *Ross v. Moffitt*, 417 U.S. 600, 94 S. Ct. 2437, 41 L. Ed. 2d 341 (1974).
134. 1 Stat. 82 (1789).
135. Habeas Corpus Act of 1867, 14 Stat. 385, 386 (1867).
136. *Fay v. Noia*, 372 U.S. 391, 83 S. Ct. 822, 9 L. Ed. 2d 837 (1963).
137. *Brecht v. Abrahamson*, 507 U.S. 619, 113 S. Ct. 1710, 123 L. Ed. 2d 353 (1993).
138. Pub. L. No. 104-132, 110 Stat. 1214.
139. *Felker v. Turpin*, 518 U.S. 1047, 117 S. Ct. 25, 135 L. Ed. 2d 1119 (1996).
140. *Strickland v. Washington*, 466 U.S. 668, 104 S. Ct. 2052, 80 L. Ed. 2d 674 (1984).
141. U.S. Const. art. I, §8.
142. 10 U.S.C. §§801-940.
143. *Solorio v. United States*, 483 U.S. 435, 107 S. Ct. 2924, 97 L. Ed. 2d 364 (1987).
144. *Solorio v. United States*, 483 U.S. 435, 107 S. Ct. 2924, 97 L. Ed. 2d 364 (1987).
145. 548 U.S. 557, 126 S. Ct. 2749, 165 L. Ed. 2d 723 (2006).
146. *Boumediene v. Bush*, 553 U.S. 723, 128 S. Ct. 2229, 171 L. Ed. 2d 41 (2008).
147. 11 C.M.A. 428, 430, 29 C.M.R. 244, 246 (1960).

LEGISLATIVE AND ADMINISTRATIVE DEVELOPMENTS IN THE LAW

PART IV

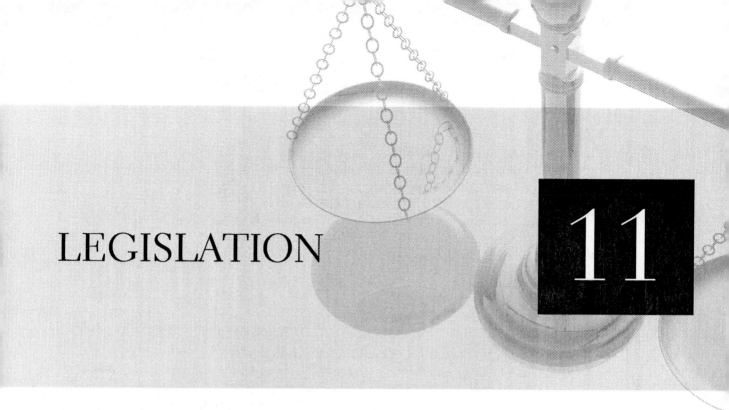

LEGISLATION

11

LEARNING OBJECTIVES

This chapter should enable the student to understand:

- how the federal and state constitutions empower Congress and state legislatures, respectively, to enact laws
- why Congress enacted antitrust legislation and how antitrust law evolved through legislation, judicial decisions, and administrative actions
- how federal law and administrative regulation have brought stability to the nation's banking system
- how the federal government regulates the securities markets
- how federal legislation has allowed organized labor to bargain collectively with management
- how social security, Medicare, Medicaid, and unemployment insurance have become key elements in the maintenance of social welfare

CHAPTER OUTLINE

LEARNING OBJECTIVES (CONT.)

▓ how Congress and the courts have supported the struggle to end various forms of invidious discrimination through enactment and interpretation of civil rights laws
▓ how the federal government has attempted to protect the natural environment through the enactment of legislation and through administrative regulations

INTRODUCTION

During the last century, the role of government at all levels changed dramatically. The industrial revolution of the nineteenth century and the technological revolution of the twentieth century gave rise to new demands on government and on the legal system. Many of these demands have resulted in the adoption by Congress and the state legislatures of new statutes regulating specific areas of economic activity and providing social benefits. As a result, the fabric of American law has been altered dramatically. In this chapter, we examine some of the more prominent areas of modern legislation, including antitrust law, banking and securities law, social insurance and welfare legislation, civil rights statutes, environmental law, and national security. Due to constraints of space, our treatment will focus entirely on federal legislation. The student should be aware, though, that in addition to having their own legislative approaches, many states have adopted their own counterparts to these federal statutes.

CONSTITUTIONAL AUTHORITY TO LEGISLATE

Although state legislatures have plenary legislative authority, the United States Congress is limited in its exercise of legislative power to its enumerated and implied powers (see Chapter 3). Of course, over the two centuries since the Constitution was adopted, Congress has stretched its enumerated and implied powers to legislate in many areas of social life and economic activity unimagined by the Framers. To a great extent, the confrontation between President Franklin Delano Roosevelt (FDR) and the Supreme Court over the constitutionality of the New Deal (FDR's policy response to the Great Depression) was a fundamental difference of opinion about the legislative power of Congress. Ultimately, this battle was won by FDR and Congress.

In the modern era, Congress has relied to a very great extent on its power to regulate interstate commerce as enumerated in Article I, Section 8. The Commerce Clause has come to be regarded as a kind of substitute **police power**, the power to legislate comprehensively to further the public welfare. Because almost everything relates in some way (however remotely) to interstate commerce, Congress has effectively acquired the power to legislate in furtherance of the public welfare. From the late 1930s until very recently, the Supreme Court permitted Congress to legislate under the Commerce Clause without restraint. In 1995 and, then again, in 2000 the Court began to impose limits on Congress's legislative power under the Commerce Clause. In *United States v. Lopez* (1995)[1] and *United States v. Morrison* (2000),[2] the Court made it clear that the Commerce Clause does not confer upon Congress plenary legislative power. Still, Congress's legislative power is quite broad. That notion was reinforced with the Court's 2005 decision in *Gonzales v. Raich,*[3] which effectively sanctioned Congress' authority, under the Commerce Clause, to regulate "medical marijuana" within the state of California. Although there was no evidence that this marijuana was leaving the state of California, the Court implied that the drugs could have a "substantial effect" on

OPINION
OF
COURT

UNITED STATES v. MORRISON
529 U.S. 598, 120 S. Ct. 1740, 146 L. Ed. 2d 658 (2000)

Chief Justice Rehnquist delivered the opinion of the Court.

. . . As we discussed at length in [*United States v.*] *Lopez* [1995], our interpretation of the Commerce Clause has changed as our Nation has developed. . . . We need not repeat that detailed review of the Commerce Clause's history here; it suffices to say that . . . since *NLRB v. Jones & Laughlin Steel Corp.* (1937), Congress has had considerably greater latitude in regulating conduct and transactions under the Commerce Clause than our previous case law permitted. . . .

Lopez emphasized, however, that even under our modern, expansive interpretation of the Commerce Clause, Congress' regulatory authority is not without effective bounds. "[E]ven [our] modern-era precedents which have expanded congressional power under the Commerce Clause confirm that this power is subject to outer limits. In *Jones & Laughlin Steel,* the Court warned that the scope of the interstate commerce power 'must be considered in the light of our dual system of government and may not be extended so as to embrace effects upon interstate commerce so indirect and remote that to embrace them, in view of our complex society, would effectually obliterate the distinction between what is national and what is local and create a completely centralized government.'" . . .

As we observed in *Lopez,* modern Commerce Clause jurisprudence has "identified three broad categories of activity that Congress may regulate under its commerce power." . . . "First, Congress may regulate the use of the channels of interstate commerce." . . . "Second, Congress is empowered to regulate and protect the instrumentalities of interstate commerce, or persons or things in interstate commerce, even though the threat may come only from intrastate activities." "Finally, Congress' commerce authority includes the power to regulate those activities having a substantial relation to interstate commerce, . . . *i.e.,* those activities that substantially affect interstate commerce." . . .

marijuana prices across state lines. Thus, Congress had the power to regulate marijuana usage that appeared to be confined to one state. In the end, even that which Congress cannot mandate directly through its constitutionally provided powers, it can actually bring about through the use of its spending power, perhaps by imposing conditions on state officials regarding the receipt of federal funds.[4]

Delegation to the Executive Branch

Legislation usually is written in general terms. It is difficult for a legislative body to specify rules with great particularity. Therefore, Congress typically relies on agencies within the executive branch of government to make specific rules to supplement statutes. For example, the Clean Air Act, one of the most important federal statutes in the environmental field, is supplemented by more than 300 regulations adopted by the Environmental Protection Agency. Thus, throughout this chapter, we will often refer to rules imposed by regulatory agencies pursuant to delegations of power from Congress. (Delegation of legislative power to the executive branch and administrative rulemaking are discussed extensively in Chapter 12.)

ANTITRUST LAW

One of the undesirable by-products of the tremendous economic expansion of the late nineteenth century was the emergence of monopolies or near-monopolies in a number of major industries, most notably oil refining, mining, and manufacturing. These monopolies, or "trusts," came about as corporations were consolidated by exchanging stock for "trust certificates." The monopolies were able to dictate prices in the marketplace, as there was little competition to exert downward pressures on prices. When a competitor arose, the monopoly could force it out of business by selling goods at a loss. Once the competitor was vanquished, prices would return to artificially high levels. The victims of the trusts were not only the would-be competitors, but also the consumers who had to pay artificially high prices for goods.

The common law had prohibited contracts that had the effect of restraining trade, but in practice, American courts did little to stem the emergence of the monopolies. The doctrine of *laissez-faire*, which was widely adopted in the business community, held that government should refrain from interfering in the workings of the economy. But increasingly, the public demanded that the government intervene to prevent and dismantle monopolies. In 1890, Congress enacted the Sherman Antitrust Act, the cornerstone of American **antitrust law**.[5] The Act was adopted with almost unanimous support in both houses of Congress. The Sherman Act contained two sections. Section 1 prohibited contracts, combinations, or conspiracies in restraint of trade; Section 2 prohibited individuals from monopolizing or attempting to monopolize particular areas of interstate commerce. Violations of either section were punishable by fines of up to $5,000 and/or incarceration for up to a year.[6] Of course, today, penalties are much more stringent.

In 1910, in its first great antitrust decision, the Supreme Court upheld a federal district court order dissolving the Standard Oil Company into thirty-three separate companies.[7] Still, many believed that federal antitrust law needed to be strengthened. Congress responded by adopting the Clayton Act of 1914.[8] The Clayton Act prohibited price discrimination—charging similarly situated buyers different prices for the same goods or services. It also proscribed sales contracts that contained provisions that buyers no longer deal with the seller's competitors. Finally, the Clayton Act outlawed interlocking directorates, the practice of having the same members serve on boards of directors of competing companies. However, these practices were not prohibited per se but only to the extent that they worked to "substantially lessen competition" or "tend[ed] to create a monopoly." This language permitted the courts broad discretion in applying the prohibitions of the statute.[9] The Robinson-Patman Act of 1936 amended the Clayton Act to deal specifically with price discrimination.[10] It prohibited any firm engaged in interstate commerce from selling the same commodity at different prices to different purchasers when the effect would be to lessen competition or to create a monopoly.

In 1914, Congress also enacted the Federal Trade Commission Act, which prohibited "unfair methods of competition . . . and unfair or deceptive acts or practices in or affecting commerce."[11] The Act established a new federal regulatory agency, the Federal Trade Commission (FTC), to enforce federal antitrust laws. Congress gave the FTC rulemaking authority, which means that it can implement the general provisions of federal antitrust law by making and enforcing specific rules for business and industry. (The FTC's rules are located in Title 16 of the Code of Federal Regulations.) FTC rules, as well as federal court decisions, help to clarify the rather vague terms of federal antitrust law—terms such as "unfair competition," "restraint of trade," "collusion," and "intent to monopolize."

Enforcement of Antitrust Laws

Antitrust law is enforced three ways:

1. The FTC can issue cease and desist orders. These orders are issued only after the FTC has conducted an investigation and afforded the party or parties being investigated the opportunity to contest the matter in an administrative hearing (see Chapter 12).[12]
2. The Antitrust Division of the Department of Justice can file civil suits in federal court. States and private parties also can bring federal civil actions. In addition to recovering compensatory damages, plaintiffs in federal antitrust suits can collect treble (triple) punitive damages.
3. United States Attorneys can initiate criminal prosecutions. Antitrust violations are felonies carrying fines of up to $10 million for corporations, and fines of up to $350,000 and prison sentences of up to three years for individuals.

Landmark Antitrust Cases

The Bell Telephone Company, founded by the inventor of the telephone, Alexander Graham Bell, evolved into the American Telephone and Telegraph Co. (AT&T) in

1899. The settlement of a federal antitrust case in 1913 established AT&T as a government-sanctioned monopoly. For many decades thereafter, AT&T exercised a virtual monopoly over telephone service in the United States, although its rates were regulated by government. In 1974, the federal government brought another antitrust suit against AT&T, which at the time was the largest company in the world. After many years of litigation, in 1982, AT&T agreed to a settlement that resulted in the breakup of the Bell System into the so-called "Baby Bells" and greatly energized the telecommunications industry.[13] Today, there are numerous providers of local, long-distance, and cellular telephone services. Most commentators agree that consumers benefited from the breakup of the AT&T monopoly.

In the early 1990s, the FTC investigated allegations of unfair trade practices by the software giant Microsoft but ultimately decided against pursuing an antitrust action. In 1994, the Department of Justice compelled Microsoft to sign a consent decree prohibiting certain restrictive licensing practices pertaining to its Windows operating system and other programs. After competitors continued to fault Microsoft's practices, the federal government and twenty states sued Microsoft in 1998, alleging a number of illegal practices designed to suppress competition. After a long trial, a federal judge found that Microsoft was indeed a monopoly within the meaning of the antitrust laws, that it used its monopoly power to coerce customers, and that it had harmed consumers by stifling competition and innovation.[14] The court delayed issuing a judgment,

CASE IN POINT

CAN MANUFACTURERS SET MINIMUM RETAIL PRICES FOR THEIR PRODUCTS?
Leegin Creative Leather Products, Inc. v. PSKS

United States Supreme Court
551 U.S. 877, 127 S. Ct. 2705, 168 L. Ed. 2d 623 (2007)

Leegin Creative Leather Products required its retailers to agree to charge minimum prices for its products, claiming that this would encourage competition among its retailers with regard to promotion of products and customer service. Leegin dropped PSKS, a retailer, after learning that it had sold Leegin products below the minimum price. PSKS sued in federal court, arguing that Leegin was engaging in price fixing in violation of the Sherman Antitrust Act. In *Dr. Miles Medical Co. v. John D. Park & Sons Co.* (1911), the Supreme Court had ruled that manufacturers were prohibited from requiring retailers to sell their goods at or above specified prices, regardless of the circumstances. Following this precedent, the trial court found for PSKS and the U.S. Court of Appeals for the Fifth Circuit

affirmed. In a dramatic departure from precedent, the Supreme Court reversed the Fifth Circuit and overturned its long-standing decision in *Dr. Miles*. The Court abandoned the position that minimum price agreements between manufacturers and retailers are *per se* unlawful under the Sherman Act and adopted instead a "rule of reason." Writing for a sharply divided Court, Justice Anthony Kennedy observed that vertical agreements establishing minimum resale prices can have either procompetitive or anticompetitive effects, depending upon the circumstances in which they are formed. And although the empirical evidence on the topic is limited, it does not suggest efficient uses of the agreements are infrequent or hypothetical.

however, allowing the government and Microsoft to attempt to settle the case. After settlement talks broke down, the court issued a judgment finding Microsoft liable under Section 2 of the Sherman Act. The court ordered that Microsoft be broken into two separate companies—one to produce and sell the Windows operating system and the other to handle Microsoft's applications software.[15] Microsoft appealed and won a partial reversal, due in part to improper conduct by the trial judge.[16] This ruling reinvigorated settlement talks and in 2001 Microsoft agreed to a settlement under which it would be required to share its application programming interfaces with other companies so that their programs would work with the Windows operating system. The settlement was approved by a federal appeals court in 2004.[17]

BANKING AND SECURITIES

The national government first experimented with a central bank when Congress chartered the Bank of the United States in 1791. In 1816, five years after the charter expired, Congress established a second Bank of the United States, once again with a twenty-year charter. In *McCulloch v. Maryland* (1819),[18] the Supreme Court upheld Congress's authority to establish the bank despite the fact that the Constitution did not expressly authorize this action (see Chapter 3). The Court said that establishment of a national bank was necessary and proper in light of Congress's enumerated powers to coin money, regulate the value thereof, borrow, tax and spend, and regulate interstate commerce. This decision created a constitutional foundation for the Federal Reserve System, the Federal Deposit Insurance Corporation, and the elaborate federal regulation of the banking industry that would come about in the twentieth century.

The Federal Reserve Act of 1913

The Federal Reserve System, which acts as this nation's central bank, was established by Congress in 1913. The System, which is commonly known as the "Fed," consists of twelve Federal Reserve Banks located in major cities throughout the country. In addition to supervising and regulating the banking industry, the Fed determines **monetary policy** by adjusting the interest rates that it charges its member banks, which in turn lend money to large commercial banks. By controlling interest rates, the Fed attempts to smooth out the business cycle, stimulating the economy when it approaches recession and putting on the brakes when it overheats.

A seven-member Board of Governors oversees the Federal Reserve System. Members of the Board are nominated by the President subject to confirmation by the Senate. Each serves one fourteen-year term, although a member who completes the unexpired portion of a term may be reappointed. From the seven Board members, one is appointed by the President to serve as Chairperson, again with the consent of the Senate. The Chairperson serves a four-year term and may be reappointed throughout his or her term as Board member. The Chair of the Federal Reserve Board is one of the most powerful individuals in the country. When the Chair speaks, financial markets listen and usually respond.

Securities Legislation

The stock market crash of 1929 and the Great Depression that followed greatly undermined public confidence in the nation's capital markets. To reestablish faith in public offerings of securities and to protect investors, Congress enacted the Securities Act of 1933[19] and the Securities Exchange Act of 1934.[20]

The 1933 Act is designed to ensure that investors receive truthful information concerning securities. It requires securities to be registered before being offered for sale through the mails, on securities exchanges, or through any other facility of interstate commerce. It allows certain exemptions for securities offered and sold exclusively to residents of the issuer's state; however, states usually have their own laws, often called "Blue-sky laws," that frequently parallel federal laws and regulations. The 1933 Act defines "securities" to include notes, stocks, bonds, investment contracts, and so forth, but does not define an "investment contract." The U.S. Supreme Court has interpreted that term very broadly, stating that an investment contract means "a contract, transaction or scheme whereby a person invests his money in a common enterprise and is led to expect profits solely from the efforts of the promoter or a third party, it being immaterial whether the shares in the enterprise are evidenced by formal certificates. . . ."[21]

The 1934 Act established the Securities and Exchange Commission (SEC) to enforce this new legislation and set standards for fair dealing and trading in securities. The SEC is headed by five Commissioners who are appointed to five-year terms by the President with the consent of the Senate. The SEC enforces statutory requirements and promulgates regulations consistent with those requirements. For example, the SEC's Rule 10(b) stipulates that "insiders" who have material information about a company must refrain from dealing in the company's securities until such information is available to the general public. To enforce the securities laws, the SEC can file civil suits, invoke its own administrative processes, or refer matters to the Justice Department for criminal prosecution.

The Federal Deposit Insurance Corporation

The Great Depression also produced a crisis of confidence in America's financial institutions. Depositors rushed to withdraw their funds from banks. More than 9,000 banks closed between October 1929 and March 1933. In June 1933, Congress, at the urging of President Roosevelt, established the Federal Deposit Insurance Corporation (FDIC) to restore confidence and stability to the nation's banking system. Since the establishment of the FDIC, depositors have not suffered the loss of their insured deposits as result of a bank failure. Today, the FDIC insures deposits in nearly all of this nation's banks and savings and loan associations. It also regulates state-chartered banks that are not members of the Federal Reserve System. The FDIC ensures that such banks are complying with federal consumer protection and equal credit laws, such as the Truth in Lending Act and the Community Reinvestment Act.

The Truth in Lending Act

The federal Truth in Lending Act (TILA) was adopted in 1968 as part of the broader Consumer Credit Protection Act.[22] The purpose of TILA is to protect borrowers by requiring lenders to disclose all the terms of loans, including the annual percentage rate (APR) of interest, the term of the loan, and the total cost to the borrower. TILA applies to closed-ended credit (e.g., a car loan) as well as open-ended credit (e.g., a credit card issued by a bank). The Federal Reserve Board has promulgated Regulation Z to implement the general provisions of TILA. This regulation "gives consumers the right to cancel certain credit transactions that involve a lien on a consumer's principal dwelling, regulates certain credit card practices, and provides a means for fair and timely resolution of credit billing disputes."[23]

The Community Reinvestment Act

The Community Reinvestment Act (CRA)[24] was enacted by Congress in 1977 to encourage banks to make loans to residents and businesses in low-income neighborhoods. The Act was intended to eliminate a practice known as "redlining," in which banks allegedly drew red lines around areas to which they refused to extend credit. The Act also was intended to revitalize inner cities by making credit available to entrepreneurs who would redevelop blighted areas. The Act is enforced by the Federal Reserve and the FDIC, as well as the Office of Thrift Supervision (OTS) and the Office of the Comptroller of the Currency (OCC). CRA requires that banks be evaluated periodically to determine if they have met the credit needs of their communities. Banks are given CRA ratings based on the extent to which they have made loans to low-income communities.

The Economic Stabilization Act of 2008

In fall of 2008, the nation's financial markets spiraled downward when it was revealed that a number of major financial institutions, including banks, brokerage firms, and insurance companies, were on the verge of collapse due to a proliferation of bad mortgage debt. For years, the government had encouraged home ownership through low interest rates and easy credit. The nation's financial institutions accumulated more than a trillion dollars in bad debts as thousands of borrowers defaulted on ill-advised mortgages. Some critics faulted inadequate regulation of the financial industry while others blamed government policies (such as the Community Reinvestment Act) that encouraged very risky home loans. Facing a financial crisis that threatened to drive the economy into a severe recession, the federal government decided to intervene to rescue the financial industry. The Emergency Economic Stabilization Act of 2008,[25] known popularly as the financial bailout bill, authorized the Secretary of the Treasury to spend up to $700 billion to acquire bad debts from, and/or purchase preferred stock in, financial institutions. The law also temporarily increased FDIC insurance on bank deposits from $100,000 to $250,000 per account. The bailout represented the most significant government intervention into the nation's financial markets since the Great Depression.

LABOR LAW

Since the late nineteenth century, labor rights activists had been trying to form unions to strengthen the bargaining position of workers in mines, mills, and factories. These efforts were steadfastly resisted by management, which regarded labor unions as a form of creeping socialism. The courts tended to side with management when strikes or boycotts threatened to disrupt production. For example, in 1911 the Supreme Court upheld an injunction against a union that had called for a boycott of the employer.[26] The Great Depression and the ensuing New Deal would forever change the legal status of organized labor.

The Wagner Act

One of the great accomplishments of the New Deal of the 1930s was the adoption of the National Labor Relations Act of 1935, better known as the Wagner Act.[27] The new law recognized the right of industrial workers to unionize and bargain collectively with management over wages, hours, and working conditions. The Act also created the National Labor Relations Board (NLRB) to investigate charges of unfair labor practices. The Wagner Act was challenged in federal court by the Jones and Laughlin Steel Corporation, which refused to abide by an enforcement order obtained against it by the NLRB. Jones and Laughlin argued that the Wagner Act transcended Congress's power to regulate commerce, and there was good reason to think the Supreme Court would agree. In 1918, the Court had struck down a federal law aimed at restricting the use of child labor in manufacturing, holding that manufacturing precedes commerce but is not a part of it.[28] Moreover, the Supreme Court was locked in battle with President Roosevelt over the constitutionality of the New Deal and had already struck down several key pieces of New Deal legislation. But in a stunning reversal, the Supreme Court upheld the statute, splitting 5-4.[29] Writing for the Court, Chief Justice Hughes concluded that

> [e]mployees have as clear a right to organize and select their representatives for lawful purposes as the [company] has to organize its business and select its own officers and agents. Discrimination and coercion to prevent the free exercise of the right of employees to self-organization and representation is a proper subject for condemnation by competent legislative authority.[30]

The four dissenters in the case thought that Congress had clearly transcended its power to regulate interstate commerce. They argued that if Congress could regulate labor relations under the Commerce Clause, then nothing was beyond the scope of Congress's legislative power. Additionally, they believed that the Wagner Act interfered with employers' freedom to enter into contracts with individuals regarding the terms and conditions of labor. While this view had earlier prevailed in the Supreme Court,[31] by 1937 the Court was prepared to relinquish this position in favor of a more modern interpretation of the law.

The Taft-Hartley Act

As the result of the passage of the Wagner Act and its validation by the Supreme Court, labor unions and **collective bargaining** became staples of the American economy. In 1947, Congress passed a second statute of immense importance in this field. A more conservative piece of legislation, the Taft-Hartley Act imposed limits on organized labor.[32] Specifically, the Act prohibited "closed shops," a policy under which one's job is contingent on belonging to the union. The Act also prohibited secondary boycotts, where striking workers take action against third-party suppliers or buyers that deal with the company being struck. Finally, Taft-Hartley allowed the President to impose an eighty-day "cooling off period" when a strike created a national emergency. Proponents of Taft-Hartley saw it as a necessary correction to the excesses permitted by the Wagner Act. On the other hand, organized labor has always considered the Taft-Hartley Act as one of two major impediments to unionization in this country, the other being the **right to work laws** enacted by twenty-two states. These laws forbid labor unions and companies from establishing union security agreements under which all workers who benefit from union representation are required to share the cost of maintaining the union, even if they decide to remain non-members.

The Landrum-Griffin Act

In 1959, Congress enacted the Labor Management Reporting and Disclosure Act, better known as the Landrum-Griffin Act.[33] Among other things, this legislation imposed financial disclosure requirements on unions and their officers, regulated union elections, and created a bill of rights for union members. This legislation was motivated by concerns over corruption in organized labor as well as ties to organized crime. Members of Congress were particularly concerned about corruption within the Teamster's Union, a reservation that has not altogether vanished six decades later.

SOCIAL WELFARE LEGISLATION

Modern democratic governments have assumed the responsibility for the welfare of their populations. In this country, the assumption of this responsibility by the federal government began during the New Deal. Since then, Congress has enacted a wide array of **social welfare legislation**.

Social Security

Without question, the most important piece of legislation to emerge from the New Deal was the Social Security Act of 1935.[34] Never intended as a "welfare program,"

social security was designed as social insurance. Essentially, it works like this: employers withhold a portion of their employees' wages, match these amounts, and transfer these sums to the government. Self-employed individuals pay into the system at a higher rate. The government places social security receipts in a trust fund from which benefits are paid to retirees and surviving spouses and dependents, as well as to workers who have become disabled. The amount of retirement benefits one receives is a function of how much one has paid into the system.

Social security was conceived at a time when relatively few Americans invested money for retirement. The program was designed to ensure that Americans would not have to spend their retirement years in poverty. The Supreme Court upheld the new social security program against a constitutional challenge in 1937.[35] Since then, what was conceived as a grand experiment has become an almost sacred institution in this country. Politicians are loath to discuss the issue, let alone consider serious reform of the system, which is facing potential insolvency due to the impending retirement of the Baby Boom generation.

The Social Security Amendments of 1954 created a federal disability insurance program. This program has considerably reduced the economic insecurity of American workers, and it also has generated considerable business for lawyers. Some lawyers specialize in assisting citizens with disability claims filed with the Social Security Administration. To receive benefits under the Social Security Disability program, a person must have a physical or mental health problem that is severe enough to prevent them from working in an income-producing job for at least one year. One of the more interesting legal issues in this field is what constitutes a physical or mental disability. During President Clinton's first term, the Social Security Administration recognized alcoholism and drug abuse as disabilities, a policy that generated sizable political controversy. Critics claimed that the federal government was subsidizing alcohol and drug abuse. Currently, as a result of the Contract With America Advancement Act of 1996,[36] people are not eligible for disability benefits if drug or alcohol abuse is a "material factor" in their disability.

Medicare and Medicaid

Established as part of the Social Security Amendments of 1965, **Medicare** is the federal government's health insurance program for senior citizens; individuals with Amyotrophic Lateral Sclerosis (ALS) are also eligible.[37] Before they become eligible for Medicare, workers pay a tax in addition to their social security contributions to help support the system. When they go on Medicare, seniors pay a monthly premium, which is deducted from their social security benefits. However, the bulk of Medicare costs are borne by the federal government's general fund. The Medicare program has two primary components: Hospital Insurance (Part A), which helps pay for inpatient hospital services, skilled nursing facility services, home health services, and hospice care; and Medical Insurance (Part B), which covers doctor services, outpatient hospital services, medical equipment and supplies, and other health services and supplies. Beneficiaries are subject to "deductibles" when they obtain services. Moreover, coverage is limited, so today, many people have supplemental insurance obtained from a private insurer.

In 2000, Congress considered a series of bills to make the Medicare system more efficient and provide coverage for prescription drugs, a major concern among the elderly. More than a decade later, discussions over how to reform the Medicare program in order to make it more financially sustainable were continuing in Congress, with Democrats and Republicans finding it difficult to agree on a suitable long-term plan.

Medicaid is a federal program that offers grants to the states to provide medical care for their indigent populations.[38] Together, Medicare and Medicaid provide benefits to more than 75 million people in this country. Both Medicare and Medicaid are administered by the Health Care Financing Administration (HCFA), located within the U.S. Department of Health and Human Services. Under the Clinton Administration, HCFA allowed states greater flexibility in the administration of Medicaid. Like health services generally, Medicaid in many states has adopted a system of **managed care**, where recipients of services are required to be members of health maintenance organizations (HMOs) operated by insurance companies. The Supreme Court's decision in *National Federation of Independent Business v. Sebelius*[39] upheld the rights of states to define their own standards for Medicaid eligibility even in the face of federal expansion of the program.

One of the areas of legal activity surrounding Medicare and Medicaid in recent years has been the government's effort to prosecute health care providers who file fraudulent claims for reimbursement. The Government Accountability Office has estimated that 10 percent of Medicare funds are spent in paying fraudulent claims. Violators include physicians, hospitals, nursing homes, clinical laboratories, and various other providers of medical services to the elderly. Medicare and Medicaid fraud includes the filing of false or inflated claims, misrepresentation of a diagnosis order to perform unnecessary medical services, and waiving patient deductibles and co-payments. The following list shows some prominent examples of health care fraud:

- In 1997, the Department of Justice launched an investigation of Columbia/HCA, the nation's largest health care provider. Two former Columbia/HCA executives were found guilty of criminal fraud in 1999. In May 2000, Columbia agreed to pay $745 million to settle civil claims filed against it by the Justice Department.
- In March 2000, the Alabama Attorney General's Office reached a settlement with Providence Hospital of Mobile resulting from the state's investigation of allegations of improper Medicaid billing practices. The half-million-dollar settlement covered actual damages incurred by the state, administrative fines, and reimbursement for the cost of the investigation. Similar investigations by state and federal authorities have become commonplace in recent years.
- According to a report from the Office of the Inspector General, in 2011, the government paid out approximately $23 million in Medicare and Medicaid benefits to dead people. This can occur when criminals make use of a deceased person's identity or when doctors engage in improper billing practices to acquire payments.[40]

In May 2014, a total of 90 individuals around the United States—including 16 doctors—were arrested as a part of the federal government's widespread attempt to crack down on fraud, including reimbursements for products and services that were never rendered, billing for medically unnecessary procedures, and improper kickbacks for referrals of business. This investigation revealed fraud estimated at $260 million. The inquiry was led by the government's Medicare Fraud Strike Force, which was formed by the Justice Department and the Department of Health and Human Services in 2009.

Health Care Legislation

Most Americans get their health insurance through group plans provided by their employers. Enacted by Congress in 1996, the Health Insurance Portability and Accountability Act (HIPAA)[41] protects employees' access to health insurance by limiting the extent to which they can be excluded from coverage due to preexisting medical conditions. It also prohibits discrimination against participants in group plans based on their health status, medical history, disability, genetic information, or insurability. HIPAA authorizes the Department of Health and Human Services (HHS) to promulgate regulations in support of its statutory objectives. Based on this authority, HHS has promulgated national standards to protect the privacy of personal health information. These rules are enforced by the Office for Civil Rights within HHS.[42] That office also has enforcement responsibilities under the Civil Rights Act of 1964, the Rehabilitation Act of 1973, the Age Discrimination Act of 1975, and the Americans with Disabilities Act of 1990. Collectively, these laws, along with the Obama administration's Patient Protection and Affordable Care Act of 2010, prohibit discrimination based on race, gender, age, and disability in the provision of health care services.

In 2010, at the urging of President Barack Obama, Congress enacted the Patient Protection and Affordable Care Act,[43] which was designed to expand health care coverage to the uninsured and generally lower the cost of health care in this country. The Act contained numerous regulations of the insurance industry as well as significant changes to Medicare and Medicaid. At the heart of the statute was a provision mandating that all Americans obtain health coverage, either through their employers, the private market, or a government program. Immediately upon passage of the law, states and individuals filed suit in federal court seeking to have aspects of the law declared unconstitutional. In 2011, the Supreme Court granted certiorari to address specifically the validity of the mandate. On June 28, 2012, the Court handed down its decision in *National Federation of Independent Business v. Sebelius.*[44] By a vote of five to four, the Court upheld the mandate at the heart of the Affordable Care Act. Most of the discussion of the constitutionality of the mandate had turned on the scope of congressional power under the Commerce Clause of Article I, Section 8 of the Constitution. But Chief Justice John Roberts, writing for the Court, held that the mandate could reasonably be viewed as an exercise of Congress' broad taxing powers. This approach avoided the difficult problem of reconciling the mandate with what the Court had previously said with respect to the Commerce Clause in cases like *United States v. Lopez* and *United States v. Morrison* (see page 415). The Court's decision did not end the national debate over the Affordable Care Act, as congressional Republicans vowed to seek repeal of this legislation.

Other components of the Affordable Care Act provide for the following: allowing individuals under the age of 26 to be covered under a parent's health care plan;

eliminating the concept of "pre-existing conditions" (which had been used by many insurance companies to deny coverage); requiring insurance companies to provide that certain 'preventative services' are covered at no additional charge to the consumer; and mandating that businesses with more than 50 full-time employees[45] provide health insurance options.[46] Increased payroll and capital gains taxes (and even a "tanning services tax") were also a part of the legislation, as were tax credits and subsidies for low-income earners and small businesses that provide health care options for employees. Critics have suggested that the Affordable Care Act has caused individuals who were happy with their existing plans to either lose access to that coverage or to see increases in premiums.

Additional litigation may be forthcoming in regard to interpretation of the law's language. In this regard, some have contended that the Affordable Care Act authorizes the application of tax credits and subsidies to plans purchased on both state and federal health care "exchanges." Others suggest, though, that the law only authorizes tax credits and subsidies on the state exchanges—and not the federal exchanges. In July 2014, two federal circuit courts reached conflicted conclusions on this matter. The U.S. Court of Appeals for the D.C. Circuit found that the lack of a clear statutory guideline made the use of tax credits and subsidies on the federal exchange improper.[47] However, the U.S. Court of Appeals for the 4th Circuit stated that the IRS could reasonably interpret the Affordable Care Act to provide such discounts.[48] In September 2014, the D.C. Circuit agreed to reconsider its decision *en banc*, a motion rendered largely irrelevant two months later when the Supreme Court agreed to hear this matter.

Unemployment Compensation

Another important program established by the Social Security Act of 1935 was a federal program to provide temporary benefits to workers who become unemployed through no fault of their own. The program was designed to give an unemployed worker time to find a new job without suffering major financial distress. Although **unemployment compensation** programs are actually administered by state agencies (a la Medicaid), the program is funded through a combination of federal and state taxes that are levied on employers. States also determine eligibility requirements and levels of benefits, although the minimum benefits are set by federal law. The federal courts also have imposed constitutional constraints on state unemployment programs. States may not deny unemployment benefits to workers who are fired for refusing to work in a manner that violates their religious beliefs, even if they adopted those beliefs after taking their jobs.[49] Nor may states deny compensation to women fired solely because they became pregnant or chose to terminate their pregnancy.[50]

Welfare

In the decades following the Second World War, the world's advanced democracies established **welfare programs** to assist the poor. For many years, the basic component of welfare in this country was Aid to Families with Dependent Children (AFDC), a program that had its genesis in the Social Security Act of 1935. AFDC provided cash benefits to families with children deprived of parental support. Like Medicaid and unemployment compensation, AFDC was set up on the model of **cooperative federalism**—most of the money came from the federal government while the states actually administered the program and set eligibility requirements and benefits within parameters established by federal law.

As in the case of unemployment compensation, the federal courts have imposed constraints on state operation of welfare programs. Although the courts have never held that there is a constitutional right to welfare, benefits cannot be terminated without due process of law.[51] And, states may not discriminate against new residents in providing access to benefits.[52]

Welfare has never been particularly popular, as taxpayers have always been suspicious of those who remain on welfare over the long term. In the 1980s and 1990s, conservative social critics decried the existence of a large underclass that had become permanently dependent on government for its subsistence. Critics also voiced concern about the effect of welfare entitlements on family life, in that men might abandon their parental responsibilities knowing that their children and the mothers of their children could subsist on welfare. These concerns led to demands for **welfare reform**, which was accomplished with bipartisan support in 1996.

Under the Responsibility and Work Opportunity Reconciliation Act of 1996,[53] AFDC was renamed Temporary Assistance to Needy Families (TANF). Under TANF, welfare is no longer an open-ended personal entitlement—five years is the maximum that a recipient can be paid from federal funds. During this period, recipients must demonstrate that they are making reasonable efforts to secure employment and must avail themselves of job training programs. Of course, states are free to supplement federal assistance with their own programs, which they control entirely. The implementation of welfare reform caused the nation's welfare rolls to be reduced dramatically. Further, the economic boom of the late 1990s, characterized by historically low unemployment, facilitated the implementation of reform. Time will tell whether these reforms will survive periods of recession characterized by high unemployment.

CIVIL RIGHTS LEGISLATION

The term **civil rights legislation** refers to the set of laws designed to ensure that everyone is treated fairly by society. These laws take many forms, including federal and state constitutional provisions, federal and state statutes, local ordinances, and regulations adopted by federal, state, and local government agencies. Perhaps most significant of all are the rulings of federal and state courts interpreting all of the foregoing. Civil rights policy is extremely complex, involving conflicts over race, gender, religion, ethnicity, disability, age, and sexual orientation in areas such as education, employment, housing, criminal justice, government contracts, and voting.

The essential purpose of civil rights laws is to prevent and/or provide remedies for unlawful forms of discrimination. The term **discrimination** refers to the denial of equal treatment to a person based on membership in some recognizable group. Thus, discrimination may be based on race, gender, ethnicity, religion, age, sexual orientation, socioeconomic status, or any number of other factors. To say that a particular action, decision, or policy is discriminatory does not necessarily mean that it is unlawful. Some forms of discrimination are entirely permissible; others are almost never so. For example, a licensing law that prohibits untrained individuals from practicing medicine discriminates against those who have not completed medical school. Yet there is little question as to the validity of the licensure requirement. On the other hand, a law that prohibited members of a particular religious sect from holding public office would unquestionably be declared invalid. The difference is that there is a rational basis for the licensure requirement, while the political restriction based on religion lacks any compelling foundation.

Most contemporary questions of civil rights are not nearly so clear-cut. Lawmakers and courts struggle with difficult civil rights questions in a highly-charged political environment. Valid arguments can be made on both sides of many of these issues. Consider, for instance, the issue of whether gay men and lesbians should be permitted to serve in the military. From December 1993 to September 2011, the military's official policy on sexual orientation was called "Don't Ask, Don't Tell," which essentially prohibited openly gay individuals from serving. Some in the military believed that permitting gay men and lesbians to serve in the military was bad for morale, discipline, and, ultimately, the ability of the military to function. Others, both within and outside the military, disagreed with this assessment. Gay rights activists insisted that gay men and lesbians had as much of a right, indeed a duty, to serve their country as anyone else. They compared the ban on openly gay individuals in the military to the racial segregation that characterized the armed forces prior to and during World War II. Public opinion was divided on the issue, with many people looking for a "middle ground," which effectively became: "Don't Ask, Don't Tell." That policy, however, was repealed on September 20, 2011, which allowed gay members of the military to freely discuss their sexual orientation. This example illustrates that, when it comes to questions of civil rights, compromise can be difficult to achieve.

Laws Prohibiting Racial Discrimination

The development of civil rights law in the United States is linked historically with the evolving status of African-Americans. The fundamental fact that defined the status of African-Americans at the time of the Constitutional Convention in 1787 was that they had been brought forcibly to this country to work as slaves. As slaves, they enjoyed no rights, for they were regarded as less than fully human. Summing up the legal status of blacks prior to the Civil War, the Supreme Court in 1857 observed that African-Americans "were not intended to be included under the word 'citizens' in the Constitution."[54]

While the Civil War and subsequent amendments to the Constitution formally abolished slavery and guaranteed the right to vote and equal protection of the law regardless of race, these rights were not readily forthcoming. African-Americans found themselves in a society in which both the power of government officials and the actions of private individuals made life incredibly unequal. Before African-Americans could begin to enjoy full participation in American society, they had to overcome a vast array of institutions, practices, and policies that were geared against them. They faced both public and private discrimination at the local, state, and national levels. This discrimination took on a multitude of forms. It would take well over a century until the battle could even be fully joined, let alone won.

The Civil War Amendments to the Constitution

Slavery was formally abolished by the ratification of the Thirteenth Amendment to the Constitution in 1865. Three years later, the Fourteenth Amendment was ratified. It effectively overturned the *Dred Scott* decision by announcing that "[a]ll persons born or naturalized in the United States, and subject to the jurisdiction thereof, are citizens of the United States and of the State wherein they reside." Second, in a clause that would play a major role in many civil rights cases in the following century, the Fourteenth Amendment provided: "[N]or shall any State deprive any person of life, liberty, or property, without due process of law; nor deny to any person within its jurisdiction the equal protection of the laws." The Fifteenth Amendment, ratified in 1870, forbade the United States, or any state, to deny the right to vote "on account of race, color, or previous condition of servitude." Known collectively as the Civil War Amendments, the Thirteenth, Fourteenth, and Fifteenth Amendments provided a constitutional basis for the protection of civil rights. In addition to outlawing slavery, guaranteeing the right to vote, and prohibiting states from denying persons due process and **equal protection of the law**, the Civil War Amendments granted Congress the power to adopt "appropriate legislation" to foster civil rights.

Early Civil Rights Legislation

In the decade following the Civil War, Congress utilized its new authority under the Civil War Amendments by enacting a number of important civil rights laws. Two of these laws, the Civil Rights Act of 1870 and the Civil Rights Act of 1871, remain extremely important today. The 1870 statute made it a federal crime to conspire to "injure, oppress, threaten or intimidate any citizen in the free exercise of any right or privilege secured to him by the Constitution or laws of the United States."[55] The 1871 law permitted individuals to bring civil actions in federal court against those violating their civil rights under color of state law. Civil suits under this statute are commonly referred to as "Section 1983 actions" because the Act is now codified at Title 42 of the U.S. Code at Section 1983. In addition to recovering compensatory damages, plaintiffs can recover treble punitive damages under Section 1983.

One of the Reconstruction Era civil rights laws, the Civil Rights Act of 1875, attempted to eradicate racial discrimination in **places of public accommodation**, including hotels, taverns, restaurants, theaters, and "public conveyances." This was an ambitious act, which, if enforced, would have represented a direct confrontation to existing practices in many states. Not surprisingly, it was challenged in federal court. In 1883, the Supreme Court struck down the key provisions of the law, ruling that the Fourteenth Amendment limited congressional action to the prohibition of official, state-sponsored discrimination, as distinct from discrimination practiced by privately owned places of public accommodation.[56] This reading of the Constitution recognized an implicit right for private individuals to discriminate against other citizens. Moreover, this decision severely limited the meaning of the Equal Protection Clause of the

Fourteenth Amendment. It would be eighty years before Congress would again attempt to pass legislation outlawing such discrimination. Meanwhile, individuals were free to discriminate. The white-dominated political culture of the South, and to some degree the rest of the country, fully supported such discrimination.

The Civil Rights Act of 1964

The Civil Rights Act of 1964 was a far-reaching, even visionary piece of legislation, and it remains the foundation of national policy on the rights of minorities. The Act's most important and controversial section, Title II, prohibited racial discrimination in places of public accommodation that affected interstate commerce, including restaurants, stadiums, theaters, as well as motels or hotels with more than five rooms. In adopting Title II, Congress relied on its broad constitutional power to regulate interstate commerce (Article I, Section 8) as well as its enforcement powers under the Fourteenth Amendment. In upholding Title II, the Supreme Court gave its blessing to a broad extension of federal power to regulate virtually any business in the country.[57] As a result, African-Americans found restaurants, motels, and hotels throughout the South available for the first time. In addition, stores removed the "Colored" and "White" designations from their drinking fountains and restrooms. Without question, the public accommodations section of the Civil Rights Act of 1964 had an immediate impact on people's lives, especially in the South.

SIDEBAR

"Civil Rights Laws Passed During Reconstruction"

During the Reconstruction Era, Congress enacted four major civil rights acts. Most provisions of these statutes remain important components of contemporary federal civil rights law.

The Civil Rights Act of 1866. Provided that citizens of all races have the same rights to make and enforce contracts, to sue and give evidence in the courts, and to own, purchase, sell, rent, and inherit real and personal property. The statute was designed to invalidate the "Black Codes" enacted in the South during the Civil War. The modern counterparts can be found at 42 U.S.C. §§1981, 1982; 18 U.S.C. §242.

The Civil Rights Act of 1870. Made it a federal crime to conspire to "injure, oppress, threaten, or intimidate any citizen in the free exercise of any right or privilege secured to him by the Constitution or laws of the United States." The statute also criminalized any act under color of state law that subjects persons to deprivations of constitutional rights. The modern counterparts are codified at 42 U.S.C. §1985 and 18 U.S.C. §241.

The Civil Rights Act of 1871. Made individuals acting "under color of state law" personally liable for acts violating the constitutional rights of others. The Act of 1871 also permitted civil suits against those conspiring to violate the civil rights of others. Civil suits under this statute are commonly referred to as "Section 1983 actions" because the Act is now codified at 42 U.S.C. §1983.

The Civil Rights Act of 1875. Forbade denial of equal rights and privileges by places of public accommodation. The statute was declared invalid by the Supreme Court as applied to privately owned public accommodations in *The Civil Rights Cases* (1883). (Access to public accommodations was ultimately achieved under Title II of the Civil Rights Act of 1964.)

The 1964 Civil Rights Act did more than ensure equal access to restaurants and hotels. Title VII prohibited **employment discrimination** on the basis of race, color, or national origin (later amended to include sex discrimination as well). Title VII made it unlawful for employers to intentionally discriminate in hiring, firing, or setting levels of compensation by adopting employment practices that are not racially neutral. It also prohibited employment practices that have a **disparate impact** on minorities unless such practices are a business necessity.[58] Various sorts of pre-employment tests and requirements have been challenged on the basis of disparate impact. To prevail, a plaintiff must be able to demonstrate that the challenged practice has an adverse impact on a protected class to which the plaintiff belongs. If the plaintiff makes this showing, the burden shifts to the employer to show that the challenged practice constitutes a business necessity. If that burden is carried, the plaintiff must prove that a less discriminatory business practice would be equally useful in achieving the employer's objective.

Another important component of the Civil Rights Act was the requirement that federal funding be withheld from any government or organization that practiced discrimination under the Act. Practically speaking, this gave tremendous power to federal officials. Virtually every public school and university system, as well as almost all private colleges, depend on federal funding, even if it is the federally insured student loans upon which students rely. These institutions would later find themselves under careful scrutiny in areas they would not have anticipated at the time of the Act's passage. This is an important extension of congressional power to government agencies, which promulgate rules in order to carry out the intent of the law. These rules reach far beyond the government itself to all those who rely on federal funding. Indeed, when in 1984 the Supreme Court attempted to restrict enforcement of civil rights requirements against private colleges that received federal funds,[59] Congress responded by adopting the Civil

CASE IN POINT

CONGRESS OUTLAWS RACIAL DISCRIMINATION IN PLACES OF PUBLIC ACCOMMODATION
Heart of Atlanta Motel v. United States

United States Supreme Court
379 U.S. 241, 85 S. Ct. 348, 13 L. Ed. 2d 258 (1964)

In order to perpetuate their policy of refusing to accommodate black customers, owners of the Heart of Atlanta Motel, located on Courtland Street in downtown Atlanta, brought suit attacking the constitutionality of Title II of the 1964 Civil Rights Act. Even though approximately 75 percent of the guests at the motel were from other states, the owners claimed that Title II could not constitutionally be applied to their establishment. In a unanimous decision, the Supreme Court ruled that the racially restrictive practices of the Heart of Atlanta Motel could impede commerce among the states and could therefore be appropriately regulated by Congress. The Court noted that in enacting Title II, "Congress was also dealing with what it considered to be a moral problem. But that fact does not detract from the overwhelming evidence of the disruptive effect that racial discrimination has had on commercial intercourse."

Rights Restoration Act of 1988. This Act stipulated that educational institutions that receive any amount of federal funding must refrain from discrimination in all of their activities and programs.

Affirmative Action

It is unlikely that Congress intended to allow for any "reverse" or "corrective" discrimination under the 1964 Civil Rights Act. However, during the late 1960s and early 1970s, the Act came to be interpreted in such a way as to allow for preferential treatment of members of racial minorities in order to bring minorities into the economic mainstream. President Lyndon Johnson actually issued an executive order that called for "affirmative action" in federal government hiring.[60] In some cases, African-Americans and members of certain other minority groups were also accepted into colleges and professional programs on the basis of lower grades and lower standardized test scores than applied to non-minorities. Similar preferences were established in employment both in the public and private sectors. Proponents argued that such policies were necessary to make up for past discrimination and to enhance the diversity of the educational experience and the workplace. Opponents characterized **affirmative action** as "reverse discrimination," which they believed violated the principle of equal opportunity. They sought relief in the courts under the Equal Protection Clause of the Fourteenth Amendment and, where applicable, the Civil Rights Act of 1964.

SIDEBAR

Federal Law on Employment Discrimination
Excerpt from 42 U.S.C. §2000e-2: "Unlawful Employment Practices"

(a) Employer practices. **It shall be an unlawful employment practice for an employer—(1) to fail or refuse to hire or to discharge any individual, or otherwise to discriminate against any individual with respect to his compensation, terms, conditions, or privileges of employment, because of such individual's race, color, religion, sex, or national origin; or (2) to limit, segregate, or classify his employees or applicants for employment in any way which would deprive or tend to deprive any individual of employment opportunities or otherwise adversely affect his status as an employee, because of such individual's race, color, religion, sex, or national origin.**

(b) Employment agency practices. **It shall be an unlawful employment practice for an employment agency to fail or refuse to refer for employment, or otherwise to discriminate against, any individual because of his race, color, religion, sex, or national origin, or to classify or refer for employment any individual on the basis of his race, color, religion, sex, or national origin.**

(c) Labor organization practices. **It shall be an unlawful employment practice for a labor organization—(1) to exclude or to expel from its membership, or otherwise to discriminate against, any individual because of his race, color, religion, sex, or national origin; (2) to limit, segregate, or classify its membership or applicants for membership, or to classify or fail or refuse to refer for employment any individual, in any way which would deprive or tend to deprive any individual of employment opportunities, or would limit such employment opportunities or otherwise adversely affect his status as an employee or as an applicant for employment, because of such individual's race, color, religion, sex, or national origin; or (3) to cause or attempt to cause an employer to discriminate against an individual in violation of this section.**

Initially, the Supreme Court steered a middle course through the affirmative action controversy. In a landmark 1978 case, a white man named Alan Bakke filed suit after he was denied admission to UC-Davis Medical School. UC-Davis reserved sixteen spaces in its yearly 100 person incoming class for minorities. In *Regents of UC-Davis v. Bakke*, the Supreme Court upheld the concept of affirmative action in principle, but barred the use of rigid quotas for admitting minorities to programs of public higher education.[61] One year later, in the area of employment, the Court upheld affirmative action programs that were voluntarily established by private companies.[62] However, as the Court became more conservative throughout the 1980s, it indicated in a number of decisions that it would not tolerate affirmative action programs unless they were tailored to remedy specific instances of discrimination. For example, it upheld an affirmative action program established for promotions within Alabama's Department of Public Safety; the Court's plurality opinion in that case was based on a finding of long-standing discrimination.[63] Conversely, in 1989, the Court struck down a Richmond, Virginia, policy that set aside a certain proportion of city public works contracts for "minority business enterprises." The Court based its decision in that case largely on the fact that African-Americans constituted a majority of the city population and held a majority of seats on the city council. Moreover, there was no evidence that black-owned construction companies seeking public works contracts were being discriminated against by the city of Richmond.[64] In a key decision in 1994, the Court said that it would subject all race-based affirmative action programs established by government agencies to the highest level of judicial scrutiny, strict scrutiny.[65] The late 1990s witnessed a roll-back of affirmative action programs across the country, either as the result of lawsuits or merely in response to the threat of litigation.[66]

Affirmative action in education returned to the Supreme Court's docket in 2003. In *Grutter v. Bollinger,*[67] the Court—using strict scrutiny—examined the University of Michigan Law School's plan of enrolling a "critical mass" of diverse candidates each year. In upholding this plan under strict scrutiny, the Court found that diversity in the classroom was in fact a valid compelling interest, and because diversity was not exclusively connected with race (with the university using race as "one of many factors" considered), the school's program also was seen as narrowly tailored. However, in a companion case, *Gratz v. Bollinger*, decided on the same day, the Court struck down a University of Michigan undergraduate admissions policy that awarded extra SAT points to all minority applicants simply on the basis of their being minorities.[68]

Voters in the state of Michigan responded by passing a ballot initiative that barred any consideration of race in the college admissions process—even if race were merely "one of many factors." In 2014, in *Schuette v. Coalition to Defend Affirmative Action*, the Supreme Court upheld the constitutionality of this ballot initiative.[69] This decision could have far-reaching implications, as seven other states already have similar bans in place (Washington, Florida, Nebraska, Oklahoma, New Hampshire, Arizona, and California). In effect, states now can decide for themselves whether race should play any role in the college admissions process, and ballot initiatives addressing this topic are likely to become more common in forthcoming elections.

The *Schuette* decision, however, did not speak directly to the matter of whether considering race as "one of many factors" is itself compatible with the 14th Amendment, but a subsequent case may address this matter. In 2012, the Supreme Court agreed to hear an affirmative action case stemming from policies in place at the University of Texas. It ultimately remanded that case back to the U.S. Court of Appeals for the Fifth Circuit without offering a definitive ruling, but the Supreme Court did observe that the lower court had failed to utilize strict scrutiny when it upheld the university's admissions policies. The Fifth Circuit re-heard oral arguments on this matter in November 2013, and after it issues a revised ruling, the Supreme Court could conceivably hear the matter again.

Based on the precedents established in *Grutter* and *Gratz,* moving forward, it seems as though the Supreme Court is only willing to justify educational affirmative action programs that are based on the compelling interest of increasing diversity in the classroom—and not on the compelling interest of remedying past discrimination. Further, in order to survive the narrow-tailoring aspect of strict scrutiny, it seems as though the Court requires a showing that race is one of many factors that is used to essentially "break ties" among similarly qualified candidates. The specific application of these principles, though, remains an evolving area of law.

The Fair Housing Act

Historically, one of the biggest obstacles facing African-American families wishing to move out of inner city ghettoes was that they faced discrimination in obtaining housing. In 1948, the Supreme Court held that **restrictive covenants** under which homeowners agreed not to sell or rent their homes to minorities could not be judicially enforceable under the Fourteenth Amendment.[70] Twenty years later, Congress enacted major legislation to address the problem of discrimination in housing. Under Title VIII of the Civil Rights Act of 1968 (also known as the Fair Housing Act), anyone selling or renting a house or apartment through a licensed agent became subject to penalty by refusing to sell or rent the unit on the basis of race, color, national origin, or religion. The Act was later amended to include **housing discrimination** based on gender, disability, or familial status.[71]

The Voting Rights Act

After Reconstruction ended, southern states systematically excluded African-Americans from the electoral process. As was the case with desegregation of the public schools, the process of opening political participation began in the courts. In 1944, the Supreme Court had struck down the infamous white primary (a primary election limited to white voters).[72] Subsequently, the Civil Rights Act of 1964 limited the use of literacy tests that had been employed by local officials to keep blacks from voting. In that same year, the states ratified the Twenty-Fourth Amendment, which outlawed the use of the poll tax in federal elections.[73]

In 1965, Congress saw the need to act further to ensure African-Americans access to the ballot box. The Voting Rights Act[74] completely outlawed the use of literacy tests as a condition for voting in seven southern states where African-American voting had lagged far behind that of whites. In addition, the Act had a triggering mechanism by which federal registrars would be sent to any county in these states in which fewer than 50 percent of those of voting age population were registered to vote in the 1964 Presidential election.

The effect of the Voting Rights Act was significant. Black registration and voting increased dramatically. By the mid 1970s, African-Americans were voting in numbers that approached that of whites, and several thousand African-Americans had been elected to state and local office. Blacks became such a force in the politics of the southern states that very few politicians could afford to risk alienating them.

After the completion of the federal census every ten years, state legislatures must redraw their own members' districts as well as the congressional districts in their state. Under the Supreme Court's famous reapportionment decisions of the 1960s, these districts must be drawn so as to be nearly equal in population.[75] These decisions limited **gerrymandering**, which is the intentional drawing of district borders to reach a desired political end. By the early 1990s, the Department of Justice was using its authority under the Voting Rights Act to "pre-clear" changes in state election systems to force states to maximize the number of minority-majority districts (those in which minority voters are in the numerical majority).[76] For example, in order to create a congressional district with a safe African-American majority, the legislature of North Carolina extended boundary lines of a particular district for hundreds of miles along an interstate highway to connect different concentrations of black voters. In 1996, the Supreme Court said that this sort of racial gerrymandering was unconstitutional unless the state could articulate a compelling interest.[77] In effect, the Court invalidated the Justice Department's policy of forcing states to maximize minority-majority districts. In January 2000, the Supreme Court further restricted the Justice Department's **preclearance** authority under the Voting Rights Act.[78] Nevertheless, the overall impact of the Voting Rights Act had been to enfranchise and empower African-Americans and other minorities. In 2006, Congress extended the Voting Rights Act for another twenty-five years.

In 2013, though, the Supreme Court's decision in *Shelby County v. Holder* essentially struck down the portion of the Voting Rights Act that required states to "pre-clear" changes in their voting procedures. In eliminating this requirement, Chief Justice Roberts, writing for the majority, stated, "History did not end in 1965."[79] One tangible outcome of this decision has been the proliferation of "Voter ID laws," which require an individual to show a government-issued photo ID before voting. Some have suggested that such laws will make it harder for poor people to vote, while others have noted that photo IDs are often available for free in many locations and also are required for numerous purposes in society, including something as basic as filling a prescription. Careful analysis of voter turnout in subsequent elections will help society to evaluate these competing positions.

Laws Addressing Gender Discrimination

At the time of the founding of the American republic, women were not accorded anything resembling legal equality. Even with the addition of the Bill of Rights and the Civil War Amendments, the U.S. Constitution contained no explicit recognition of women's rights. In fact, the right to vote was not guaranteed until 1920, with ratification of the Nineteenth Amendment. Given the lack of women participants in the Constitutional Convention, and, until quite recently, the dearth of women holding political office of any kind, there can be no doubt that, in the eyes of many Founders, women were intended to hold second-class citizenship at best. However, it would be simplistic to categorize this sort of systematic discrimination as merely an extension of the racism that defined the treatment of African-Americans.

The inferior citizenship status granted women in this country was certainly not unique to the United States. Indeed, under the common law, women were regarded as little more than personal property. This was widely accepted because of deeply ingrained cultural norms. Western culture was decidedly patriarchal in nature. Men had long assumed a superior status within the whole structure of family and religion. Whereas the institution of slavery represented the exploitation of a whole people by another, the institutions regarding the role of women were tightly woven into a cultural fabric so pervasive that it was beyond any hope of consideration by the Founders. One would be hard-pressed to find any race, tribe, or group of people whose cultural identity was defined by submission to others. However, most women in the United States, as well as elsewhere, were essentially forced to accept their social status outside the political and economic mainstream.

Cultures evolve, though, and many individuals simply will never accept second-class treatment, regardless of the circumstances. As women confronted their status in American politics and the broader society, they faced a dual set of challenges not unlike those faced by African-Americans. First, women were kept by law from full participation in society. Second, many individuals would discriminate for their own reasons. The former demanded the elimination of laws; the latter demanded new laws outlawing discrimination.

Again, however, the situation was somewhat more complex than was the case for racial minorities. While some would claim that one race was "different" from another, and would use this difference as the basis for passing discriminatory legislation, many more would do so for women. The motivations for such a claim might be grounded in a belief that biological differences made such laws necessary. Or, they might purely represent customs that unfairly recognized men as the only legitimate owners of property. Through the 1800s and into the 20th century, in fact, some states actually barred women from certain professions, particularly if they were married or pregnant; states also provided few financial rights for women upon the dissolution of a marriage.

The beginnings of the women's struggle for political equality were rooted in the fight for the vote. Supporters of the vote for women were known as Suffragists. Under the leadership of figures like Elizabeth Cady Stanton and Susan B. Anthony, they utilized grassroots movements, such as the Seneca Falls Convention of 1848, to lobby politicians for constitutional change. Ultimately, the Nineteenth Amendment, which gave women the right to vote, was passed by Congress in 1919 and ratified by the states in 1920. However, the right to vote did not bring about many substantial changes in public policy, or in acceptance of women as public officeholders.

Overall, the modern women's movement began to take form in the 1960s. Led by interest groups like Betty Friedan's National Organization for Women, the movement employed many of the tactics that had been utilized successfully by African-Americans in the civil rights movement, including marches, protests, demonstrations, and boycotts.

The Equal Pay Act and Title VII

Congress first responded to growing demands for legal equality between the sexes by passing the Equal Pay Act of 1963, which prohibits unequal pay for equal or "substantially equal" work performed by men and women. In 1972, Congress amended Title VII of the Civil Rights Act of 1964 to add gender to the list of prohibited forms of employment discrimination. In 1981, the Supreme Court ruled that Title VII goes beyond the Equal Pay Act to proscribe discrimination not only in pay between jobs that are equal but also between jobs that are different.[80]

Traditionally, the socially prescribed role of woman as wife and mother, combined with a protectionist attitude on the part of men, served to keep women out of the work force in significant numbers, although women were mobilized to fill jobs vacated by men during the two world wars. Today, most adult women are employed, at least part time. Indeed, roughly half of all women with children under the age of one are employed outside the home.

Despite recent gains, women on average earn only about 75 cents for every dollar earned by men. This discrepancy is partially due to the fact that women are much more likely than men to be employed in relatively low-paying service, clerical, sales, and manufacturing jobs. They are still less likely than men to be doctors, engineers, accountants, and lawyers, although the gender gap in the professions is narrowing. Finally, women have yet to gain access to the top-paying positions in corporations. Some have even complained of a "glass ceiling," an invisible barrier that keeps women out of top managerial positions.

Although women are not a minority, in that they make up roughly 53 percent of the population, women have had to struggle as hard as minority groups to gain acceptance in the workplace. Early on, the issue was whether women should be permitted to work at all. Later the issue became which jobs, if any, were unsuitable for women. Then, the issue became "equal pay for equal work." In the 1980s, women's groups attempted to define the issue as equal pay for work of "comparable worth." Women's groups argued that women should receive the same pay as men, even if their jobs were different, as long as the jobs entailed similar levels of education and experience. Critics of comparable worth argued that there was no way to implement this idea without a massive program of government regulation or numerous lawsuits, either of which would be costly and disruptive to business. Today, some of the highest-priority issues for working women are access to affordable day care and family leave. Although these are primarily economic issues, they are related to women's search for social equality.

In 2009, Congress furthered that search for equality by passing the Lily Ledbetter Fair Pay Act, which ostensibly altered the scope of the Supreme Court's decision in *Ledbetter v. Goodyear* (see Case in Point on next page); this law broadened the time frame for filing lawsuits brought pursuant to the Equal Pay Act, allowing plaintiffs to raise a claim within 180 days after each paycheck, as opposed to 180 days after the start of discriminatory action.

CASE IN POINT

AN "UNTIMELY" SEX DISCRIMINATION CLAIM BARRED
BY A STRICT READING OF TITLE VII
Ledbetter v. Goodyear
United States Supreme Court
550 U.S. 618, 127 S. Ct. 2162, 167 L. Ed. 2d 982 (2007)

Lily Ledbetter filed a complaint with the Equal Employment Opportunity Commission (EEOC) alleging sex discrimination by Goodyear Tire and Rubber Co. in violation of Title VII of the Civil Rights Act of 1964. Title VII prohibits discrimination "against any individual with respect to his compensation ... because of such individual's... sex." Under Title VII, failure to submit a claim to the EEOC within 180 days "after the alleged unlawful employment practice occurred" results in the claimant's being barred from filing suit in federal court. In her EEOC claim, Ledbetter claimed that her work performance had been unfairly evaluated due to her sex and that by the time she quit working for Goodyear, she was making significantly less than male colleagues who were doing the same work. After investigating the claim, the EEOC authorized Ledbetter to sue Goodyear in federal district court. At trial, Goodyear alleged that Ledbetter's evaluations had been nondiscriminatory. Nevertheless, the jury found for the plaintiff and awarded back pay and damages. On appeal,

Goodyear argued that Ledbetter's pay discrimination claim was untimely with respect to any allegedly discriminatory actions that took place more than 180 days before she filed her EEOC claim. The U.S. Court of Appeals for the Eleventh Circuit agreed with Goodyear and reversed the trial court's judgment. In a 5-4 ruling, the Supreme Court upheld the Court of Appeals. Speaking for the Court, Justice Samuel Alito concluded that Ledbetter's "arguments for giving special treatment to pay claims find no support in the statute and are inconsistent with our precedents." Adopting a strict construction of Title VII, Alito observed, "We apply the statute as written, and this means that any unlawful employment practice, including those involving compensation, must be presented to the EEOC within the period prescribed by statute." In dissent, Justice Ruth B. Ginsburg objected to a "cramped interpretation of Title VII, incompatible with the statute's broad remedial purpose." Ginsburg called on Congress "to correct this Court's parsimonious reading of Title VII."

Title IX

Another significant enactment in the area of **gender discrimination** is Title IX of the Higher Education Amendments of 1972,[81] which authorized the withholding of federal funds from educational institutions that engage in sex discrimination. The most obvious result of this statute has been the movement toward **gender equity** in collegiate athletics, through which young women across the country have been afforded opportunities to participate in athletic, competition that was once the sole province of men.

Specifically, Title IX requires universities to provide extracurricular opportunities for women in proportionality to the overall female student population. Thus, a school with a 50 percent female population should have approximately 50 percent of its overall extracurricular opportunities reserved for females. Title IX also requires that women's teams receive comparable facilities and benefits to those received by men's teams. A school can avoid exact proportionality standards if it can demonstrate an ongoing trend of increasing opportunities for females, or if the school can demonstrate a lack of interest among female students in participating in certain extracurricular activities. Ultimately, as a result of Title IX, many young women who might not otherwise have received a college education have been able to go to college with an athletic scholarship.

Under President Reagan and the elder President Bush, though, enforcement of Title IX was less than rigorous. Some have suggested that this was out of fear that aggressive enforcement may have led to men's programs being cut in order to facilitate compliance with the letter of Title IX's proportionality requirements. Regardless of the exact reason, the Office for Civil Rights in the Department of Education, which is primarily responsible for Title IX enforcement, was not adequately funded to aggressively pursue Title IX complaints. Consequently, in the 1990s, many women with Title IX complaints bypassed the OCR and filed suit directly, often with great success. For example, in 1993, Howard University women's basketball coach Sanya Tyler sued Howard for sex discrimination under Title IX because she was paid substantially less than the men's head basketball coach. Tyler's case broke new ground in that it resulted in the first monetary award given by a jury in a Title IX case. Tyler was awarded $2.4 million in damages, although the amount was later reduced to $250,000.

Affirmative Action on Behalf of Women

Desiring to facilitate the integration of women into the social and economic mainstream, federal, state, and even some local agencies have adopted a variety of affirmative action programs to benefit women. Employers that do business with government, as well as educational institutions that receive public funds, have been encouraged to adopt their own affirmative action programs. Like the policies that grant preferred status to black applicants, affirmative action programs that benefit women have been controversial and even have been challenged in court.

In 1987, the Supreme Court handed down a landmark decision on affirmative action for women. It upheld a program under which a woman had been promoted to the position of road dispatcher in the Santa Clara (California) Transportation Agency, even though a man had scored higher on a standardized test designed to measure aptitude for the job. The man who had been passed over for the job brought a lawsuit, claiming reverse discrimination, as Alan Bakke had done some years earlier. The Supreme Court rejected the plaintiff's claim, stressing that the affirmative action program was a reasonable means of correcting the sexual imbalance in the Transportation Agency's personnel, who were overwhelmingly male.[82]

An interesting hypothetical question to ponder is this: Would affirmative action programs that benefit women be eliminated if women did achieve economic parity with men? Although many supporters of affirmative action have characterized it as a temporary corrective measure, experience indicates that once a right or benefit is established in law, it is difficult to disestablish.

In a somewhat different form of affirmative action, some cities and states have gone so far as to require all-male social and civic clubs to admit women. The courts have generally approved such measures, even though they are sometimes challenged as violating the concept of freedom of association, which is protected by the First Amendment. In a notable 1984 decision, a unanimous Supreme Court found that the state of Minnesota's interest in eradicating sex discrimination was sufficiently compelling to justify a decision of its human rights commission requiring local chapters of the Jaycees to admit women.[83] Later decisions of the Court extended this ruling to embrace chapters of the Rotary Club, as well as private athletic clubs that served liquor and food to their members.

A 1996 Supreme Court decision also mandated that Virginia Military Institute (VMI) open its doors to female students.[84] The Court applied the test of intermediate scrutiny to this gender discrimination case, and noted that VMI lacked a narrowly tailored, significant state interest for justifying its exclusion of women. The Court also noted that VMI might have been able to avoid admitting women if it had provided an "ample alternative," but went on to say that a VMI "sister program" was not in fact an "ample alternative" because it lacked the rigorous training and alumni network of the main VMI program. As a result of the decision, female students are currently enrolled at VMI.

We should point out that the Supreme Court has also protected the rights of men to attend certain specialized "all-female" programs, as it did in *Mississippi University for Women v. Hogan*, where a man who wished to attend an all-female nursing school was afforded the right to do so.[85]

Sexual Harassment

In the 1980s, the issue of **sexual harassment** appeared on the public agenda as a civil rights issue. The sexual harassment issue has been particularly noticeable on college campuses, where it has entered the debate over issues related to dating, dormitory visitation, and student-teacher relationships.

The issue of sexual harassment was aired in a particularly dramatic fashion when law professor Anita Hill appeared before the Senate Committee on the Judiciary in October 1991 to make allegations of misconduct against Clarence Thomas, who had been nominated by President Bush to serve on the Supreme Court. Hill alleged that Thomas, when he was chairman of the Equal Employment Opportunity Commission, made sexual advances toward her, told off-color jokes in her presence, and generally harassed her in a sexual manner. Thomas categorically denied the charges. Because there was little supporting evidence, the Senate ultimately approved Thomas's nomination to the Supreme Court. Many women believed that the all-male Senate Judiciary Committee had been insensitive to Professor Hill and to the whole issue of sexual harassment. The Clarence Thomas–Anita Hill episode was apparently one factor that led women in record numbers to run for public office in 1992.

The Supreme Court itself has played a prominent role in addressing the problem of sexual harassment. For example, in 1986, the Court ruled that sexual harassment in the workplace constituted unlawful gender discrimination in violation of federal civil rights laws.[86] Later, in 1993, the Court adopted a legal standard that made it easier for victims of sexual harassment to sue in federal court.[87] The decision, which was joined by all nine justices (including Clarence Thomas), came in a case brought by Teresa Harris, who worked for a truck leasing company in Nashville. Harris complained that her boss subjected her to repeated comments and suggestions of a sexual nature. The federal judge who heard the case in Nashville described the boss's behavior as vulgar and offensive, but ruled that it was not likely to have had a serious adverse psychological effect on the employee. He dismissed the case before it could go to a jury trial. The U.S. Court of Appeals for the Sixth Circuit upheld the district court's ruling. In reversing the lower courts, the Supreme Court, speaking through Justice Sandra Day O'Connor, said that it was not necessary for a plaintiff in a sexual harassment case to show "severe psychological injury." It is enough that the work environment would be perceived by a reasonable person as being "hostile or abusive." The Court's decision reinstated Teresa Harris's complaint, thus allowing the case to go before a jury in the district court. More importantly, the decision increased the likelihood that women (and men) who believe that they are victims of sexual harassment in the workplace will file and win federal lawsuits. Thus, the Supreme Court effectively put employers on notice that their conduct would be subject to judicial scrutiny. To avoid litigation, employers should have appropriate policies and training programs in place and must take immediate action whenever complaints are filed.

Discrimination Against Persons with Disabilities

Although there are few laws that overtly discriminate against them, persons with disabilities have always faced physical barriers as well as societal prejudice. For the most part, it has been Congress, not the courts, which has taken the lead in recognizing the rights of handicapped persons. With the passage of Title V of the Rehabilitation Act of 1973,[88] the Education for all Handicapped Children Act of 1975,[89] and, especially, the Americans with Disabilities Act (ADA) of 1990,[90] Congress has established a comprehensive regime of federal law protecting persons with disabilities. The ADA prohibits **discrimination against persons with disabilities** in all programs and services provided by state and local governments, private industries, and commercial establishments. Private employers that have fifteen or more employees are prohibited from discriminating on the basis of disability in their employment practices. The Department of Justice (DOJ) enforces the ADA through civil litigation. The DOJ has established a toll-free hotline, making it easy for citizens to file complaints. If DOJ prevails in litigation, the court can order compensatory damages and back pay for the complainant. It also can impose penalties of up to $50,000 for the first violation and $100,000 for any subsequent violation of the statute. The ADA authorizes various federal agencies to promulgate regulations in furtherance of the ADA's policy goals. For example, the Equal Employment Opportunity Commission has adopted extensive regulations implementing the ADA's provisions relative to employment discrimination.[91]

In essence, the ADA requires **reasonable accommodation** of persons with disabilities. An individual is considered "disabled" if that individual has a physical or mental impairment that substantially limits one or more major life activities or has a record of such an impairment.

Discrimination Based on Sexual Orientation

How far should the law go in protecting people against discrimination based on their sexual identity or orientation? Advocates of gay rights have called for the enactment of legislation that would protect people against such discrimination in the workplace.

There is no such protection currently available under federal civil rights laws, although **gay rights** groups have been calling for Congress to establish such protections. Given the controversial nature of the issue, it may be some time before a political consensus emerges that supports federal legislation in this area. However, it is important to note that in 1998, President Bill Clinton issued Executive Order 13087, which prohibited employment discrimination on the basis of sexual orientation by federal agencies. It is also important to note a number of states and cities have enacted laws prohibiting discrimination based on sexual orientation in employment, housing, and the enjoyment of public accommodations. And, recent developments with respect to same-sex marriage and civil unions have increased public support for gay rights generally (although same-sex marriage has been rejected by voters in several state ballot propositions). Clearly, this issue will be on the public agenda for some time to come, and it is reasonable to expect continued legislative and judicial activity at the state and federal levels of government.

Age Discrimination

Discrimination against the young is usually not legally problematic because persons below the age of legal majority are presumed not to enjoy the full rights of citizenship. Most questions of age discrimination involve elderly Americans who claim that they have been discriminated against. Federal courts typically employ the rational basis test to determine the constitutionality of government policies that discriminate on the basis of age. Most age discrimination cases are not constitutional cases, however. Rather, they are based on provisions of statutes enacted by Congress and the state legislatures. In 1967, Congress passed the Age Discrimination in Employment Act, which bars companies that deal in interstate commerce or do business with the government from discriminating against their employees on the basis of age.[92] In 1988, Congress passed a measure that prohibits all organizations that receive federal funds from engaging in **age discrimination**.[93] Today, there is substantial litigation in the state and federal courts dealing with age discrimination by employers. These cases frequently grow out of attempts by companies to save money by dismissing people who are approaching retirement age. As our society ages, with people living and working longer, conflicts involving age discrimination will undoubtedly grow more numerous and more intense.

Family and Medical Leave

Congress enacted the Family and Medical Leave Act of 1993 (FMLA)[94] to balance the demands of the workplace with the medical needs of families. FMLA applies to private employers with fifty or more employees, but federal, state, and local public agencies are covered regardless of the number of employees. A covered employer must grant an eligible employee up to a total of twelve workweeks of unpaid leave during any twelve-month period due to a serious health condition, the birth of a child, or the need to care for a spouse, a child, or parent with a serious health condition. The statute makes it unlawful for an employer to interfere with or to restrain an employee from exercising his or her rights under the law or to discharge or discriminate against an employee for the exercise of those rights. The U.S. Department of Labor is authorized to investigate and resolve complaints of violations and is granted the power to subpoena necessary records in connection with investigations. An eligible employee may bring a civil action against an employer for violations. FMLA does not affect any federal or state law prohibiting discrimination, nor does it supersede any state or local law or collective bargaining agreement that provides greater family or medical leave rights.

ENVIRONMENTAL LEGISLATION

One of the more important social developments of the 1960s was the emergence of the environmental movement. Within a few years, concern for the environment moved beyond the realm of a few scientists and activists and into the societal mainstream. Reflecting this new social awareness, Congress enacted a series of landmark environmental laws beginning in the late 1960s. In adopting these statutes, Congress relied on its power to regulate interstate commerce. A question to ponder is whether a strict reading of the Commerce Clause would support Congress's authority in this area. Of course, states can act in this field and many have done so, either at the behest of Congress or on their initiative. Consequently, there is now a substantial body of federal and state **environmental law**.

The National Environmental Policy Act

Enacted in 1969, the National Environmental Policy Act (better known as NEPA) requires federal agencies to consider the environmental impacts of their proposed actions.[95] Because of this mandate, the **environmental impact statement** (EIS) has become a staple of American public administration. Title II of NEPA created the Council on Environmental Quality (CEQ), which oversees federal agency implementation of the Act. NEPA requires the CEQ to report to the President annually on the conditions and trends in environmental quality.

The Clean Air Act

The Clean Air Act of 1970 set federal standards designed to enhance the quality of the air by deterring air polluters.[96] In 1977, Congress passed a series of amendments establishing stricter standards for air quality. As amended, the Act provides criminal sanctions for violation of any provisions for which civil penalties apply, and for any person who knowingly makes any false representation in a document filed under the Act. Enforcement may be delegated to the states pursuant to the State Implementation Plan (SIP), but the states are not required to enact minimum criminal provisions to receive EPA approval of their implementation plans. Nevertheless, states are increasingly toughening criminal penalties in this area.

SIDEBAR

The Clean Air Act and "Cooperative Federalism"
Excerpt from 42 U.S.C. §7402: "Cooperative Activities"

The Clean Air Act is one of many federal laws that is implemented not only by the national government but also through cooperative arrangements involving federal, state, and local government agencies. The following excerpt from the Clean Air Act clearly manifests Congress's intent that the Act be implemented based on a "cooperative federalism" model.

Sec. 7402. Cooperative activities

(a) Interstate cooperation; uniform State laws; State compacts

The Administrator [of the Environmental Protection Agency] shall encourage cooperative activities by the States and local governments for the prevention and control of air pollution; encourage the enactment of improved and, so far as practicable in the light of varying conditions and needs, uniform State and local laws relating to the prevention and control of air pollution; and encourage the making of agreements and compacts between States for the prevention and control of air pollution.

(b) Federal cooperation

The Administrator shall cooperate with and encourage cooperative activities by all Federal departments and agencies having functions relating to the prevention and control of air pollution, so as to assure the utilization in the Federal air pollution control program of all appropriate and available facilities and resources within the Federal Government.

(c) Consent of Congress to compacts

The consent of the Congress is hereby given to two or more States to negotiate and enter into agreements or compacts, not in conflict with any law or treaty of the United States, for (1) cooperative effort and mutual assistance for the prevention and control of air pollution and the enforcement of their respective laws relating thereto, and (2) the establishment of such agencies, joint or otherwise, as they may deem desirable for making effective such agreements or compacts. No such agreement or compact shall be binding or obligatory upon any State a party thereto unless and until it has been approved by Congress. . . .

The Clean Water Act

Better known as the Clean Water Act, the Federal Water Pollution Control Act of 1972 is designed to control water pollution by regulating industrial and other discharges.[97] Although the Clean Water Act is enforced primarily through civil means, criminal sanctions have been imposed for willful or negligent violations of certain provisions concerning permits and the making of false statements. Amendments in 1987 eliminated the "willful" requirement and imposed more stringent penalties for negligent violations and even more severe penalties for knowing violations of the Act's criminal provisions.[98]

A majority of the states have programs approved by the EPA. While states vary somewhat in their approaches, many provide penalties similar to those in the federal Act for either willful or negligent violations of water pollution provisions.

The Endangered Species Act

One of the best-known federal environmental statutes is the Endangered Species Act of 1973.[99] This Act is designed to conserve ecosystems by preserving wildlife, fish, and plants. And while enforcement is largely accomplished through civil penalties, criminal liability can be imposed against any person who knowingly violates regulations issued under the Act. The Act also permits federal courts to issue injunctions against projects that threaten **endangered species**. The Endangered Species Act is a powerful weapon in the arsenal of the environment movement, because enforcement of the Act does not depend solely on government agencies charged with protecting the environment. Assuming they meet the requirements of standing, citizens can bring suit under the Endangered Species Act to prevent or halt projects that threaten animals on the endangered species list. Hospitals, highways, dams, subdivisions, and office parks have been delayed, relocated, or stopped altogether as the result of civil actions brought by environmentalists under the Endangered Species Act. One of the most famous (or infamous, depending on one's point of view) case involving the Endangered Species Act was *TVA v. Hill* (1978) (see Case in Point below).

Hazardous Waste Legislation

One of the most serious environmental threats facing this country is the accumulation of hazardous waste. Congress has responded to this threat by enacting a series of statutes. Enacted in 1976, the Resource Conservation and Recovery Act (RCRA)[100] sought to encourage the states—through grants, technical assistance, and advice—to establish standards and provide for civil and criminal enforcement of state **hazardous waste regulations**. The EPA sets minimum standards requiring the states to enact

CASE IN POINT

TVA, THE SNAIL DARTER, AND THE ENDANGERED SPECIES ACT
TVA v. Hill
United States Supreme Court
437 U.S. 153, 98 S. Ct. 2279, 57 L. Ed. 2d 117 (1978)

In 1973, an ichthyologist at the University of Tennessee discovered an isolated species of perch in the waters of the Little Tennessee River. Named the "snail darter," this little fish was designated as "endangered" by the Secretary of the Interior under the Endangered Species Act. Another federal agency, the Tennessee Valley Authority, was nearing completion of the Tellico Dam, which, when operational, would destroy the habitat of the snail darter. A group of conservationists obtained a federal court injunction to prevent the dam from becoming operational. The case became a national political issue—a confrontation between environmentalism and economic development. In 1978, the Supreme Court upheld the injunction, saying that "Congress has spoken in the plainest of words, making it abundantly clear that the balance has been struck in favor of affording endangered species the highest of priorities...." Ultimately, the snail darter was discovered in another nearby river and Congress enacted legislation specifically authorizing completion of the Tellico Dam. Today, the Dam is operational, much of the Little Tennessee River has become Tellico Lake, and the snail darter remains in existence, although it is still endangered. The Supreme Court's decision in *TVA v. Hill* remains an important moral victory for environmentalists.

criminal penalties against any person who knowingly stores or transports any hazardous waste to an unpermitted facility, who treats such waste without a permit, or who makes false representations to secure a permit. All states have enacted statutes pursuant to the criteria specified in RCRA.

Toxic Substances Control Act

The Toxic Substances Control Act of 1976 authorizes the EPA to require testing and to prohibit the manufacture, distribution, or use of certain chemical substances that present an unreasonable risk of injury to health or the environment, and to regulate their disposal.[101] Although the Act depends primarily on civil penalties, a person who knowingly or willfully fails to maintain records or submit reports as required violates the criminal provisions of the Act.

The Superfund Law

In 1980, Congress enacted the Comprehensive Environmental Response, Compensation, and Liability Act (CERCLA), commonly known as the Superfund Law.[102] Its purpose is to finance cleanup and provide for civil suits by citizens. As revised in 1986, the Act requires notice to federal and state agencies of any "release" of a "reportable quantity" of a listed hazardous substance. "Release" is broadly defined, and "reportable quantity" is relative to each of the several hundred "hazardous substances." CERCLA also provides for the EPA to promulgate regulations for the collection and disposal of solid wastes. The Act imposes criminal sanctions against those who fail to report as required, or who destroy or falsify records.

NATIONAL SECURITY LEGISLATION

In the aftermath of World War II, Harry Truman signed the National Security Act of 1947 into law—with the objective of reconfiguring the United States' foreign intelligence and national defense infrastructure.[103] The law merged the War Department and Navy Department into the Department of Defense, which was to be overseen by a Secretary of Defense. Additionally, the National Security Act created the Central Intelligence Agency (C.I.A.), which was designed to gather intelligence and direct covert action abroad.

This law also established the National Security Council, a group that included the President, Vice President, Secretary of State, Secretary of Defense, Director of the C.I.A., and other key members of the President's cabinet. Different presidents have utilized the National Security Council in different ways, with some using it regularly to help formulate key foreign policy decisions (such as Eisenhower), and others using it sparingly (such as John Kennedy and Lyndon Johnson).

The Central Intelligence Agency Act

In 1949, the Central Intelligence Agency Act[104] expanded the scope of the C.I.A.'s authority by allowing it to use federal money in a confidential fashion and by exempting it from disclosing information about its personnel. Further, the law enabled the C.I.A. to bring individuals from other countries to the United States without utilizing normal immigration channels—ostensibly to allow potential defectors to transition into clandestine operations.

The Supreme Court upheld the constitutionality of this act in a 1974 case, *United States v. Richardson*.[105] The respondent was a taxpaying citizen who had challenged the act as being incompatible with Article 1, Section 9 of the Constitution, which requires disclosure of how public funds are used. The Court ultimately found that Richardson lacked standing to contest the law because he had not suffered a tangible injury from its passage.

In 2014, the C.I.A. became embroiled in controversy amidst revelations that it had spied on computers used by staff members of U.S. senators serving on the Senate Intelligence Committee. During testimony in front of a Senate panel investigating the incident, C.I.A. director John Brennan issued a formal apology to the affected parties. Even so, Colorado Senator Mark Udall, a member of the committee, demanded that Brennan tender his resignation.

The Foreign Intelligence Surveillance Act

In addition to the C.I.A., the U.S. government uses the National Security Agency (N.S.A.) to engage in worldwide, secretive collection of intelligence. The N.S.A. has its origins in the U.S. Army's old "Cipher Bureau" (also known as Military Intelligence Branch, Section 8—or M.I.-8), which was used to gather information during World War I. Its name evolved into Signal Security Agency during World War II, and it acquired its current moniker during a reorganization initiated by President Harry Truman in 1952.

The Foreign Intelligence Surveillance Act (F.I.S.A) was passed in 1978 to craft some parameters for the N.S.A.'s authority—boundaries that some say have been vitiated recently. F.I.S.A. specifically limits the N.S.A to physical or electronic collection of "foreign intelligence information" and further specifies that the information be drawn from communications between "foreign powers and agents of foreign powers."[106] The law also created F.I.S.A. courts, which would meet secretly to evaluate warrant requests for such surveillance; warrants were supposed to be based on the legal standard of probable cause. Beyond that, the law also made it illegal to gather intelligence under the guise of an official purpose where none exists.

Other legislation has impacted the scope of F.I.S.A. For example, the PATRIOT Act's Section 207 made extensions or renewals of F.I.S.A. warrants easier to acquire and its Section 215 indicated that the government can compel businesses to turn over records of customers' activity, perhaps cell phone records. In 2008, F.I.S.A. was amended to provide a seven-day warrantless search "grace period" for government officials (although a corresponding warrant request is supposed to be filed with a F.I.S.A. court during that time frame); the previous "grace period" had been 48 hours. The F.I.S.A. Amendments Act of 2008 also limited civil liability for businesses that turn individuals' telecommunications records over to the government, and the law even sanctioned the government's ability to destroy records of searches.[107]

In 2013, whistleblower Edward Snowden revealed that the N.S.A. had been using its authority to spy on the private communications of millions of people living in America and abroad, including some world leaders. More specifically, the N.S.A. appeared to be collecting "meta-data" from phone calls and e-mails; this involved cataloging the phone numbers called by individuals, as well as the email addresses to which messages were sent. Snowden also revealed that when he worked for an N.S.A. contractor, he had the ability to look into the actual content of private communications. Additional reports even suggested that F.I.S.A. courts had rejected only 0.03% of warrant requests over a thirty-three year time span.[108]

In 2014, President Obama stated that limits will be placed on how long the N.S.A. stores the information it gathers, and lawsuits have been filed against the agency in federal district courts around the country. However, there is no sign that the Supreme Court is prepared to hear a case that addresses the N.S.A.'s information collection methods. Even if it did, the Court could adhere to its precedent from *Smith v. Maryland,* where it upheld a police department's warrantless use of a "pen register,"[109] a device that tracks the numbers that are called by a telephone. That case could provide an interesting starting point for evaluating the constitutionality of the N.S.A.'s surveillance tactics.

THE USA PATRIOT ACT

In the aftermath of the terrorist attacks of September 11, 2001, Congress passed the USA PATRIOT Act,[110] which serves as an acronym for the law's more lengthy name: Uniting and Strengthening America by Providing Appropriate Tools Required to Intercept and Obstruct Terrorism. Additionally, the Homeland Security Act of 2002 created a bureaucratic infrastructure to support many of the objectives of the PATRIOT Act by combining several existing departments and agencies under the broader umbrella of U.S. Department of Homeland Security. The PATRIOT Act itself has ten sections that help to clarify its overall objectives:

Title I: Enhancing Domestic Security Against Terrorism

Title II: Enhanced Surveillance Procedures

Title III: International Money Laundering Abatement and Anti-Terrorist Financing Act of 2001

Title IV: Protecting the Border

Title V: Removing Obstacles to Investigating Terrorism

Title VI: Providing for Victims of Terrorism, Public Safety Officers, and Their Families

Title VII: Increased Information Sharing for Critical Infrastructure Protection

Title VIII: Strengthening the Criminal Laws Against Terrorism

Title IX: Improved Intelligence

Title X: Miscellaneous

In general terms, Title I provided increased funding for counter-terrorist activity, and also criticized any discrimination against Arabs or Muslims. Title II contained some of the more controversial aspects of the PATRIOT Act. For example, it allowed for delayed notification of search warrants—such that searches actually could be conducted before an affected party was aware of them, a practice that observers pejoratively refer to as a "sneak and peek" search.[111] Section 215 in Title II also enabled the FBI to access different types of documents that might reveal a terror suspects' pattern of activity—a provision interpreted by some to sanction even the searches of library material. Additionally, Title II expanded the number of F.I.S.A. court judges and contained trade sanctions against North Korea and Afghanistan.

Title V permitted the Attorney General to offer reward money related to efforts at stopping terrorist activity, and it also allowed DNA samples of suspected terrorists to be entered into a national database. Title V generated controversy because it permitted use of "National Security Letters," which could compel businesses to provide the government with records of an individual's activity—even without use of a search warrant; this component was struck down by a federal court but revised versions were signed into law by both the Bush and Obama administrations.[112] Title VI addressed compensation for families of public safety officers who are injured or killed in the line of duty; specifically, it increased the amount of money available for the U.S. Victims of Crime Fund and mandated that payments be made within thirty days of injury or death.

Title VIII extended statutes of limitation for certain terrorist offenses, increased penalties for many crimes (including attempts or conspiracies to commit terrorist activities), and even created new infractions, such as the possession of biological weapons and the harboring of terrorist suspects. It also allowed for civil forfeiture of assets connected to terrorist activity. However, Title VIII has drawn the ire of some for defining terrorism as activity "to influence government policy by intimidation or coercion"—language that could be construed very broadly.[113]

On March 9, 2006, President Bush signed additional legislation, the USA PATRIOT Improvement and Reauthorization Act of 2005.[114] This law made almost all of the provisions of the original PATRIOT Act permanent, a step necessitated by the fact that most of them were set to expire on December 31, 2005. On May 26, 2011, President Obama also signed a similar piece of legislation, called the PATRIOT Sunsets Extension Act of 2011;[115] this extended components related to the following: 1. "Roving wiretaps"—which can follow a suspect even if they make use of different phones; 2. Business record searches—such as those related to electronic communications or perhaps the aforementioned "library searches"; 3. Investigations of "lone wolves," who are terrorist suspects that bear no connection to formal organizations. Ultimately, future revisions may be required as courts untangle the constitutionality of the PATRIOT Act's numerous directives.

The National Defense Authorization Act and Guantanamo Bay

The National Defense Authorization Act is a law that creates the budget of the Department of Defense for an upcoming fiscal year; a version of this law is passed annually. The 2014 law contained a provision (Section 1035) that required the President to notify Congress 30 days before transferring any detainees held in the U.S. military facility at Guantanamo Bay.[116] That directive became a source of controversy when the Obama administrations swapped five Guantanamo Bay detainees to the Taliban in exchange for U.S. Army soldier Bowe Bergdahl, who had been held captive in Afghanistan for approximately five years.

In this case, the president failed to provide appropriate notification to Congress—and his administration attempted to justify this action by pointing to a "signing statement" that accompanied the 2014 N.D.A.A. This statement suggested that the 30-day notification requirement violated the president's authority to serve as "Commander in Chief" and thus was contrary to the constitutional principle of "separation of power." Nevertheless, signing statements are merely advisory declarations from the President and do not carry any legal weight. In fact, President Obama had previously criticized President Bush's use of signing statements. (The 2007 N.D.A.A. included a signing statement from Bush that implied that executive branch power should be expanded.)

Another version of the National Defense Authorization Act that led to controversy was its 2011 rendition, whose Section 1021 has been interpreted by some as allowing the government to detain . . . allowing the government to indefinitely detain individuals—including American citizens—who are suspected of terrorist activity, even without a formal hearing. (This power was originally proposed in a 2001 law called the Authorization for Use of Military Force[117]—which the Obama administration has used to justify drone strikes on American citizens abroad.) Ultimately, the application of such authority could violate criminal procedure protections embedded in the 5th and 6th Amendments. In the end, forging a balance between such protections and the ultimate goal of protecting public safety lies as the forefront of any legislation designed to preserve national security.

CONCLUSION

This chapter has provided a thumbnail sketch of some of the more important pieces of legislation enacted by Congress throughout our nation's history. As evidenced herein, although Congress does not possess plenary legislative power, it has ample authority to legislate in those areas that the states cannot or will not enter. Historically, Congress has taken the lead in dealing with social and economic problems through legislation. Today, however, the states have become very active in addressing these issues. Consequently, legislation in this country is a complex and often confusing tapestry of state and federal statutes, the interplay of which must be interpreted by courts. Of course, this is one of the reasons why American law is so dynamic and exciting.

SUMMARY OF KEY CONCEPTS

Since the late 1800s, the federal government has achieved far-reaching social and economic reforms. This occurred through Congress's exercise of its delegated and implied powers and through the Supreme Court's broad interpretation of the Constitution's "Commerce Clause." Antitrust, banking, securities, and labor legislation has brought a large measure of economic stability to the nation's financial, business, and labor forces. These policies aided the United States in becoming the world's financial and industrial giant. On occasions, the states, through exercise of their inherent police powers, have served as testing grounds for development of legislation; in other instances, they have supplemented federal legislative policies. For example, the Social Security Act and much of the social welfare legislation emerged in the 1930s as a part of the New Deal during the presidency of Franklin D. Roosevelt.

After the Civil War, Congress began to enact laws to end discrimination based on race; however, the real impetus in the struggle to end racial, gender, age, and disability discrimination awaited the social and cultural changes of the 1960s, which preceded the enactment of modern civil rights laws. Legislation that was passed in the latter half of the twentieth century continues to remain vital today. For example, enactment of the Civil Rights Act of 1964 represented a significant victory in the struggle for racial equality. Since then, major legislative, administrative, and judicial accomplishments have furthered the movement to end discrimination based on race, gender, age, and disability. Guaranteeing all adults the right to vote

and the right to fairness in housing also has posed major legislative challenges. Beyond that, with the advent of large numbers of women entering the work force, legislation has achieved modest gains in the equality of pay and prohibition of sexual harassment. Obviously, challenges remain. The struggle to end discrimination continues in contemporary America, as evidenced by the legislation being continually offered to support social and cultural changes now occurring in society.

In other contexts, as the nation has moved into an age of technological advancement, the watchwords of society are to conserve, protect, and preserve. Along these lines, major federal legislative enactments are still being tested in an effort to achieve a workable balance between protection of the environment and private property interests. Ultimately, the design and enforcement of environmental legislation is a major challenge today and will remain so in the years to come.

Similar themes also resonate in regard to society's ability to craft an appropriate balance between protecting national security and preserving individual liberties. As the nation tries to respond to the threats posed by terrorist organizations around the world—many of which are unaffiliated with formal government entities—new legislation has attempted to provide officials with the tools necessary for combatting evolving dangers. Ensuring that such newfound authority does not infringe upon essential constitutional protections remains an important matter for future generations.

FOR FURTHER READING

Baer, Judith, *Women in American Law: The Struggle toward Equality from the New Deal to the Present* (2d ed., Holmes and Meier 1996).

Bork, Robert H., *The Antitrust Paradox* (The Free Press 1993).

Dalton, James A., and Stanford L. Levin (eds.), *The Antitrust Dilemma* (Lexington Books 1974).

Davidson, Chandler, and Bernard Grofman (eds.), *Quiet Revolution in the South: The Impact of the Voting Rights Act, 1965-1990* (Princeton University Press 1994).

Findley, Roger W., and Daniel A. Farber, *Environmental Law in a Nutshell* (7th ed., Thomson West 2008).

Frickey, Philip P., Elizabeth Garrett, and William N. Eskridge, *Legislation and Statutory Interpretation* (2d ed., Foundation Press 2006).

Goren, William D., Understand the Americans with Disabilities Act (2d ed., American Bar Association 2007).

Kubasek, Nancy K., and Gary Silverman, *Environmental Law* (6th ed., Prentice-Hall 2007).

McKinnon, Catherine, *Sexual Harassment of Working Women* (Yale University Press 1979).

Mezey, Susan Gluck, *In Pursuit of Equality: Women, Public Policy and the Federal Courts* (St. Martin's Press 1992).

Santos, Miguel A., *Limits and Scope of Environmental Law* (Charles C. Thomas 1996).

Terry, Evan, *Americans with Disabilities Act Facilities Compliance: A Practical Guide* (John Wiley & Sons 1992).

Vietzen, Laurel A., *Practical Environmental Law* (Aspen Publishers 2008).

QUESTIONS FOR THOUGHT AND DISCUSSION

1. What three methods does the federal government employ to enforce the antitrust laws?

2. The authors state that "the most important piece of legislation to emerge from the New Deal was the Social Security Act of 1935." Identify three major functions that social security programs serve at the present time.

3. How does the Federal Reserve Board of Governors act to regulate the monetary policies of the nation?

4. What major changes in labor-management relations were accomplished by passage of the Wagner Act in 1935, and how did enactment of the Taft-Hartley Act in 1947 affect unionization practices?

5. What is meant by "cooperative federalism," and how has it been employed in respect to administration of Medicaid and unemployment compensation benefits?

6. How has Congress implemented the guarantees of the Thirteenth, Fourteenth, and Fifteenth Amendments to the U.S. Constitution?

7. What has been the impact of the Voting Rights Act enacted in 1965 with respect to city and county governments?

8. Explain the difference between the concepts of "equal pay for equal work" and equal pay for work of "comparable worth."

9. What standard of proof do federal courts require before a plaintiff can recover damages in a sexual harassment suit?

10. What, if any, new federal legislation is needed for protection of the environment?

11. How has Congress responded to the ongoing threat of terrorism in the wake of the terrorist attacks of September 11, 2001?

KEY TERMS

affirmative action
age discrimination
antitrust law
civil rights legislation
collective bargaining
cooperative federalism
discrimination
discrimination against persons with disabilities
disparate impact
employment discrimination
endangered species
environmental impact statement

environmental law
equal protection of the law
gay rights
gender discrimination
gender equity
gerrymandering
hazardous waste regulations
housing discrimination
managed care
Medicaid
Medicare
monetary policy
places of public accommodation

police power
preclearance
reasonable accommodation
restrictive covenants
right to work laws
sexual harassment
social security
social welfare legislation
unemployment compensation
welfare programs
welfare reform

ENDNOTES

1. 514 U.S. 549, 115 S. Ct. 1624, 131 L. Ed. 2d 626 (1995).
2. 529 U.S. 598, 120 S. Ct. 1740, 146 L. Ed. 2d 658 (2000).
3. *Gonzales v. Raich*, 545 U.S. 1, 125 S. Ct. 2195, 162 L. Ed. 2d 1 (2005).3.
4. *Printz v. United States*, where Congress' mandate that local law enforcement conduct background checks for gun purchases was deemed unconstitutional, seems to provide some limits on the directives that the federal government can provide to state actors. 521 U.S. 898, 117 S. Ct. 2365, 138 L. Ed. 2d 914 (1997).
5. 15 U.S.C. §1 et seq.
6. 26 Stat. 209, chap. 647, U.S. Comp. Stat. 1901, at 3200.
7. *Standard Oil Co. of N.J. v. United States*, 221 U.S. 1, 31 S. Ct. 502, 55 L. Ed. 619 (1910).
8. 15 U.S.C. §12 et seq.
9. *See, e.g., United States v. United States Steel Corp.*, 251 U.S. 417, 40 S. Ct. 293, 64 L. Ed. 343 (1920).
10. 15 U.S.C. §13 et seq.
11. 15 U.S.C. §§41-58.
12. The FTC's orders are archived at http://www.ftc.gov/os/case list/index.shtm.
13. *United States v. American Tel. & Tel. Co.*, 552 F. Supp. 131 (D.D.C. 1982), *affd in Maryland v. United States*, 460 U.S. 1001, 103 S. Ct. 1240, 75 L. Ed. 2d 472 (1983).
14. *United States v. Microsoft Corp.*, 87 F. Supp. 2d 30 (D.D.C. 2000).
15. *United States v. Microsoft Corp.*, 97 F. Supp. 2d 59, 64-65 (D.D.C. 2000).
16. *United States v. Microsoft Corp.*, 253 F.3d 34 (D.C. Cir. 2001).
17. *Massachusetts v. Microsoft Corp.*, 373 F.3d 1199 (D.C. Cir. 2004).
18. 17 U.S. (4 Wheat.) 316, 4 L. Ed. 579 (1819).
19. *See* 15 U.S.C. §77a et seq.
20. *See* 15 U.S.C. §78a et seq.
21. *SEC v. W.J. Howey Co.*, 328 U.S. 293, 298, 66 S. Ct. 1100, 1103, 90 L. Ed. 1244, 1250 (1946).
22. Pub. L. No. 90-321, 82 Stat. 146, *codified at* 15 U.S.C. §1601 et seq.
23. 12 C.F.R. §226.1(b).
24. Pub. L. No. 95-128, 91 Stat. 1147, 12 U.S.C. §2901 et seq.
25. Pub. L. No. 110-343, div. A (enacted Oct. 3, 2008).
26. *Gompers v. Buck's Stove & Range Co.*, 221 U.S. 418, 31 S. Ct. 492, 55 L. Ed. 797 (1911).
27. Pub. L. No. 74-198, *codified at* 29 U.S.C. §151 et seq.
28. *Hammer v. Dagenhart*, 247 U.S. 251, 38 S. Ct. 529, 62 L. Ed. 1101 (1918).
29. *N.L.R.B. v. Jones & Laughlin Steel Corp.*, 301 U.S. 1, 57 S. Ct. 615, 81 L. Ed. 893 (1937).
30. 301 U.S. at 33, 57 S. Ct. at 622, 81 L. Ed. at 909 (1937).
31. *See, e.g., Lochner v. New York*, 198 U.S. 45, 25 S. Ct. 539, 45 L. Ed. 937 (1905).
32. Labor Management Relations Act of 1947, 61 Stat. 136, *codified at* 29 U.S.C. §141 et seq.
33. *Codified at* 29 U.S.C. §401 et seq.
34. Act of Aug. 14, 1935, 49 Stat. 620.
35. *Chas. C. Steward Mach. Co. v. Davis*, 301 U.S. 548, 57 S. Ct. 883, 81 L. Ed. 1279 (1937).
36. Pub. L. No. 104-121.
37. *See* 42 U.S.C. §§1395-1395ccc.
38. *See* 42 U.S.C. §§1396-1396v.
39. *National Federation of Independent Business v. Sebelius*, 567 U.S. _____, 132 S. Ct. 2566; 183 L. Ed. 2d 450 (2012).
40. Blake Ellis, "Medicare Paid $23 Million to Dead People," *CNN*, November 1, 2013; available at: http://money.cnn.com/2013/11/01/pf/medicare-deceased/.
41. *Codified at* 29 U.S.C. §1181 et seq.
42. *See* http://www.hhs.gov/ocr/hipaa/.
43. Pub. L. 111-148, 124 Stat. 119.
44. *National Federation of Independent Business v. Sebelius*, 567 U.S. _____, 132 S. Ct. 2566; 183 L. Ed. 2d 450 (2012).
45. Full-time employees are those that work 30 hours or more per week; an employer could also fall within the scope of these requirements merely by having a substantial number of "full-time equivalents"; a formula in the law can be used to calculate this figure—essentially to prevent a business from having an incentive to exclusively employ individuals who work 29 hours per week.
46. Implementation of this provision has been delayed until 2015.
47. *Halbig v. Burwell*, U.S. Court of Appeals for the D.C. Circuit, July 22, 2014; full opinion available at: http://www.cadc.uscourts.gov/internet/opinions.nsf/10125254D91F8BAC85257D1D004E6176/$file/14-5018-1503850.pdf.
48. *King v. Burwell*, U.S. Court of Appeals for the 4th Circuit, July 22, 2014; full opinion available at: http://www.ca4.uscourts.gov/Opinions/Published/141158.P.pdf.
49. *Hobbie v. Unemployment Appeals Commn.*, 480 U.S. 136, 107 S. Ct. 1046, 94 L. Ed. 2d 190 (1987).
50. *Wimberly v. Labor & Industrial Relations Commn.*, 479 U.S. 511, 107 S. Ct. 821, 93 L. Ed. 2d 909 (1987).
51. *Goldberg v. Kelly*, 397 U.S. 254, 90 S. Ct. 1011, 25 L. Ed. 2d 287 (1970).
52. *Saenz v. Roe*, 526 U.S. 489, 119 S. Ct. 1518, 143 L. Ed. 2d 689 (1999).
53. Pub. L. No. 104-193.
54. *Dred Scott v. Sandford*, 19 Howard 393 (1857).
55. *Codified at* 42 U.S.C. §1985.

56. *The Civil Rights Cases*, 109 U.S. 3, 3 S. Ct. 18, 27 L. Ed. 835 (1883).

57. *Heart of Atlanta Motel v. United States*, 379 U.S. 421, 85 S. Ct. 348, 13 L. Ed. 2d 258 (1964); *Katzenbach v. McClung*, 379 U.S. 294, 85 S. Ct. 377, 13 L. Ed. 2d 290 (1964).

58. *Griggs v. Duke Power Co.*, 401 U.S. 424, 91 S. Ct. 849, 28 L. Ed. 2d 158 (1971). In the Civil Rights Act of 1991, Congress codified the Court's holding in *Griggs*. *See* 42 U.S.C. §2000e-2.

59. *Grove City Coll. v. Bell*, 465 U.S. 555, 104 S. Ct. 1211, 79 L. Ed. 2d 516 (1984).

60. Executive Order 11246.

61. *University of Cal. Bd. of Regents v. Bakke*, 438 U.S. 265, 98 S. Ct. 2733, 57 L. Ed. 2d 750 (1978).

62. *United Steelworkers of Am. v. Weber*, 443 U.S. 193, 99 S. Ct. 2721, 61 L. Ed. 2d 480 (1979).

63. 480 U.S. 149, 107 S. Ct. 1053, 1064, 94 L.Ed.2d 203 (1987).

64. *City of Richmond v. J.A. Croson Co.*, 488 U.S. 469, 109 S. Ct. 706, 102 L. Ed. 2d 854 (1989).

65. *Adarand Constructors, Inc. v. Pena*, 512 U.S. 1288, 115 S. Ct. 41, 129 L. Ed. 2d 936 (1994).

66. *See, e.g., Hopwood v. Texas*, 78 F.3d 932 (5th Cir. 1996).

67. *Grutter v. Bollinger*, 539 U.S. 306, 123 S. Ct. 2325, 156 L. Ed. 2d 304 (2003).

68. *Gratz v. Bollinger*, 539 U.S. 244, 123 S. Ct. 2411, 156 L. Ed. 2d 257 (2003).

69. *Schuette v. Coalition to Defend Affirmative Action*, 572 U.S. _____, 134 S. Ct. 1623, 188 L. Ed. 2d 613 (2014).

70. *Shelley v. Kraemer*, 334 U.S. 1, 68 S. Ct. 836, 92 L. Ed. 1161 (1948).

71. 45 U.S.C. §§3604-3606.

72. *Smith v. Allwright*, 321 U.S. 649, 64 S. Ct. 757, 88 L. Ed. 987 (1944).

73. In 1966, the Supreme Court struck down the poll tax in state elections as a violation of the Fourteenth Amendment Equal Protection Clause. *See Harper v. Virginia State Bd. of Elections*, 383 U.S. 663, 86 S. Ct. 1079, 16 L. Ed. 2d 169 (1966).

74. *See* 42 U.S.C. §1971 et seq.

75. *Reynolds v. Sims*, 377 U.S. 533, 84 S. Ct. 1362, 12 L. Ed. 2d 506 (1964); *Wesberry v. Sanders*, 376 U.S. 1, 84 S. Ct. 526, 11 L. Ed. 2d 481 (1964).

76. Section 5 of the Voting Rights Act of 1965 requires designated states and their political subdivisions to obtain "pre-clearance," either from the Attorney General or from the District Court for the District of Columbia, before implementing changes in their election systems. *See* 42 U.S.C. §1973c.

77. *Shaw v. Hunt*, 517 U.S. 899, 116 S. Ct. 1894, 135 L. Ed. 2d 207 (1996).

78. *Reno v. Bossier Parish Sch. Bd.*, 528 U.S. 320, 120 S. Ct. 866, 145 L. Ed. 2d 845 (2000).

79. *Shelby County v. Holder*, 570 U.S. _____, 133 S. Ct. 2612, 186 L. Ed. 2d 651 (2013). The decision struck down Section 4(b), which contained the formula for determining which states would be subject to pre-clearance requirements; in effect, this voided Section 5, which mandated the pre-clearance.

80. *County of Washington v. Gunther*, 452 U.S. 161, 101 S. Ct. 2242, 68 L. Ed. 2d 751 (1981).

81. Pub. L. 92-318.

82. *Johnson v. Transportation Agency of Santa Clara County*, 480 U.S. 616, 107 S. Ct. 1442, 94 L. Ed. 2d 615 (1987).

83. *Roberts v. United States Jaycees*, 468 U.S. 609, 104 S. Ct. 3244, 82 L. Ed. 2d 462 (1984).

84. *United States v. Virginia*, 518 U.S. 515, 116 S. Ct. 2264, 135 L. Ed. 2d 735 (1996).

85. *Mississippi University for Women v. Hogan*, 458 U.S. 718, 102 S. Ct. 3331, 73 L. Ed. 2d 1090 (1982).

86. *Meritor Sav. Bank, FBD v. Vinson*, 477 U.S. 57, 106 S. Ct. 2399, 91 L. Ed. 2d 49 (1986).

87. *Harris v. Forklift Sys., Inc.*, 510 U.S. 17, 114 S. Ct. 367, 126 L. Ed. 2d 295 (1993).

88. *Now codified at* 29 U.S.C. §701 et seq.

89. *Now codified at* 20 U.S.C. §1400 et seq.

90. 104 Stat. 337, 42 U.S.C. §12101 et seq.

91. 29 C.F.R. pt. 1630.

92. *Now codified at* 29 U.S.C. §621 et seq.

93. *Now codified at* 42 U.S.C. §6101 et seq.

94. 29 U.S.C. §2601 et seq.

95. 42 U.S.C. §§4321-4345.

96. 42 U.S.C. §§7401-7642.

97. 33 U.S.C. §§1251-1270.

98. 33 U.S.C. §1319(c).

99. 16 U.S.C. §§1531-1544.

100. 42 U.S.C. §§6901-6992.

101. 15 U.S.C. §§2601-2671.

102. 42 U.S.C. §§9601-9675.

103. 50 U.S.C. §401 et seq.

104. 50 U.S.C. §403a.

105. 418 U.S. 166, 94 S. Ct. 2940, 41 L. Ed. 2d 678 (1974).

106. 50 U.S.C. §1801 et seq.

107. Pub. L. 110-261.

108. Evan Perez, "Secret Court's Oversight Gets Scrutiny," *Wall Street Journal*, June 9, 2013; available at: http://online.wsj.com/news/articles/SB10001424127887324904004578535670310514616?mg=reno64-wsj&url=http%3A%2F%2Fonline.wsj.com%2Farticle%2 FSB10001424127887324904004578535670310514616.html.

109. *Smith v. Maryland*, 442 U.S. 735, 99 S. Ct. 2577; 61 L. Ed. 2d 220 (1979).

110. Pub. L. 107-56.

111. This provision was struck down in 2007 by a U.S. District Court in Oregon.

112. The Bush version was passed and then also struck down by a federal court; the Obama version was signed into law in 2011.
113. Pub. L. 107-56.
114. Pub. L. 109-177.
115. Pub. L. 112-14
116. H.R. 3304.
117. Pub. L. 107-40; *see* Chapter 12 for information on this law's connection to recent drone strikes.

ADMINISTRATIVE LAW AND PROCEDURE

12

LEARNING OBJECTIVES

This chapter should enable the student to understand:

- the means by which Congress and state legislatures have delegated power to administrative and regulatory agencies to carry out legislative programs
- the executive, legislative, and judicial restraints on administrative rulemaking
- the exercise of agency investigatory authority
- the available means for enforcement of agency decisions
- the role of administrative agencies, in adjudicating disputes
- standing and exhaustion of administrative remedies as prerequisites to judicial review of agency decisions
- open meeting requirements, access to governmental information, and "sunshine laws"
- the legal protections afforded to public employees

CHAPTER OUTLINE

INTRODUCTION

Bureaucracy is the hallmark of modern government. As government has taken on more and more responsibility for solving social and economic problems, it has found it necessary to create agencies to administer programs and to promulgate and enforce regulations. These agencies are located within the executive branches of federal, state, and local governments. While we often refer to the sum total of these agencies as the "bureaucracy," a basic distinction can be made between **administrative agencies** and **regulatory agencies**.[1]

Administrative agencies carry out government programs such as highway construction, education, or the delivery of social services. At the federal level, the Social Security Administration is a good example. Its function is not to regulate but rather to administer this country's social insurance program for the elderly, widowed, and disabled. At the state and local levels, one finds agencies devoted to highway construction, education, public housing, social welfare, public health, and various other functions.

Regulatory agencies promulgate and enforce rules pursuant to authority delegated by legislatures. For example, at the federal level, the Nuclear Regulatory Commission (NRC), the Federal Aviation Administration (FAA), and the Securities and Exchange Commission (SEC) are just a few of the many agencies created by Congress to regulate particular industries. States also have regulatory agencies that deal with everything from alcoholic beverages to the licensing of physicians. At the state level, agencies have long regulated professional and occupational licensing, adjudicated the need to issue bank charters, alcoholic beverage licenses, and insurance company licenses, and regulated public utilities. In recent years, the determinations of eligibility for certificates of need for health care facilities and environmental and natural resource permits have assumed an increasing role in state administrative proceedings.

Administrative law is the branch of the law that governs the activities of administrative and regulatory agencies. It is designed to apply the rule of law to the bureaucracy to reduce arbitrariness, enhance the quality of decision making, and promote democratic values. Administrative law involves such questions as:

- Does an agency have the authority to regulate a certain product or industry? For example, in 1996, the federal Food and Drug Administration (FDA) undertook the regulation of tobacco as a drug. Cigarette makers went to court, arguing that Congress had never given the FDA such authority. The Supreme Court agreed with the tobacco industry.[2] (See Case in Point on page 464.) Currently, the Food and Drug Administration is attempting to enact rules that regulate electronic cigarettes (or e-cigs), which deliver nicotine in the form of smokeless vapor. These regulations could include setting age restrictions, eliminating sales in vending machines, and requiring health warnings on packages. How might courts evaluate these attempts?
- What access do citizens have to information held by government agencies? In 1966, Congress enacted the Freedom of Information Act to give citizens such access, but the Act contains a number of exemptions and continues to be the source of considerable litigation.

▨ What procedures must agencies follow when they deny program benefits to individuals or impose sanctions on industries they regulate? Clearly, agencies must afford parties **due process of law**, as required by the federal and state constitutions, but, as we shall see, the exact nature of due process depends greatly on the context.

▨ When can private citizens bring suits to challenge agency actions? The answer is, when they have **standing**, but there are a variety of legal rules governing standing in the federal and state courts.

As government in the modern era has become more pervasive, administrative law has become more important. Virtually everyone in this country has had or will have contact with an administrative or regulatory agency. The encounter may be as simple as registering to vote, paying property taxes, or obtaining a fishing license. But it may be much more complex and serious, such as when a business owner is penalized for violating safety conditions in the workplace, when an undocumented immigrant is deported by Immigration and Customs Enforcement (ICE), or when a taxpayer is subjected to a field audit by the Internal Revenue Service (IRS). In such situations, administrative law becomes very relevant.

DELEGATION OF LEGISLATIVE AUTHORITY

Under our constitutional system, legislatures have the primary authority to make law. However, the expansive role now played by government at all levels makes the legislative function much more difficult. The complexity of problems demanding government attention and the practical difficulties of regulation obviously limit the ability of legislatures to legislate comprehensively, much less effectively. Moreover, the slow pace of the legislative process makes it all but impossible for legislatures to respond promptly to changing conditions. Thus, Congress and state legislatures have come to rely increasingly on experts for the development, as well as the implementation, of regulations. These experts are found in a host of government departments, commissions, agencies, boards, and bureaus that make up the modern administrative state.

Through a series of broad **delegations of power**, legislatures have transferred to the bureaucracy much of the responsibility for making and enforcing the rules and regulations deemed necessary for a technological society. Frequently, the **enabling legislation** creating these agencies provides little more than vague generalities to guide agency **rulemaking**. For example, in 1970, Congress gave the Occupational Safety and Health Administration (OSHA) the power to make rules that are "reasonably necessary or appropriate to provide safe and healthful employment and places of employment." As a result, the rules promulgated by OSHA as "necessary" or "appropriate" take on all the force of law. A business that is found to be in violation of these rules is subject to civil penalties. For example, after a trainer at Sea World was killed by a whale, OSHA fined Sea World and placed restrictions on the ability of trainers to be in the water with a whale without a barrier. Sea World appealed this administrative ruling, but the U.S. Court of Appeals for the D.C. Circuit upheld OSHA's actions.[3]

SIDEBAR

Three Essential Publications for the Serious Student or Practitioner of Administrative Law

■ The *United States Government Manual* provides basic information on all federal government agencies, including their histories, functions, programs, officials, and so forth. It is updated annually.

■ The *Federal Register* contains all executive orders, notice of agency hearings, proposed and adopted rules, and amendments to proposed or adopted rules. It is published daily.

■ The *Code of Federal Regulations* (CFR) is the codification of all final rules of all federal agencies. It is updated annually.

Broad delegations of legislative power are generally seen as necessary so that agencies can develop the programs required to deal with targeted problems. Others would say that broad delegations are inevitable because Congress and the state legislatures simply do not have the expertise to write detailed policies into legislation.

To a great extent, broad delegations of power may be desirable or even inevitable, but they do raise serious constitutional questions. Delegation is difficult to square with the principle of **separation of powers** implicit in the very structure of the United States Constitution. Specifically, Article I vests "all legislative power" in Congress. Thus, when Congress delegates legislative power to the executive branch, it can be viewed as violating the implicit constitutional principles of representative government and separation of powers, as well as the express language of Article I. Chief Justice William Howard Taft recognized the constitutional problem raised by legislative delegation: "[I]n carrying out that Constitutional division into three branches it is a breach of the national fundamental law if Congress gives up its legislative power and transfers it to the President, or to the judicial branch, or if by law attempts to vest itself of either executive or judicial power."[4]

Chief Justice Taft's essential point was that if the Constitution imposes meaningful limitations on government, then Congress must be very careful in transferring its own power to the other branches. In 1935, as part of an epic struggle with President Franklin Roosevelt over the New Deal, the Supreme Court struck down a major government program on the ground that Congress had delegated too much authority to the bureaucracy. In 1933, on the recommendation of President Roosevelt, Congress adopted the National Industrial Recovery Act. This statute created the National Recovery Administration (NRA), which became the centerpiece of the New Deal. NRA was empowered to create "Codes of Fair Competition" in major industries. In *Schechter Poultry Corp. v. United States* (1935), the Supreme Court held that Congress had granted "virtually unfettered" discretion to the bureaucracy to enact "laws for the government of trade and industry throughout the country."[5] Thus, the Court dealt a body blow to the New Deal and intensified a political conflict already under way, a battle that eventually was won by the President.

A Constitutional Revolution?

Because he was elected to four terms of office, President Roosevelt was able to fill eight vacancies on the Supreme Court, effectively remaking the Court to reflect his political views. As a result, the Court's orientation changed dramatically. Beginning in the 1940s, the Court manifested much more tolerance of delegation of legislative power. In effect, the Court acknowledged the legitimacy of the modern administrative state. As Cass Sunstein has noted, President Roosevelt's remaking the Court "altered the constitutional system in ways so fundamental as to suggest that a constitutional amendment had taken place."[6] Gary Lawson has made the point more forcefully: "The post-New Deal administrative state is unconstitutional, and its validation by the legal system amounts to nothing less than a bloodless constitutional revolution."[7]

Despite numerous opportunities, not since the *Schechter* decision has the Court struck down an act of Congress on delegation grounds. In the early 1980s, certain members of the Court indicated a desire to scrutinize legislative delegations more carefully. For example, in 1981 the Court sustained an OSHA "cotton dust" regulation against a challenge from the textile industry.[8] Joined by Chief Justice Warren Burger, Justice William Rehnquist asserted that in enacting the OSH Act of 1970, Congress "simply abdicated its responsibility for the making of a fundamental and most difficult policy choice."[9] But, a majority of the Court could never be mustered to rally around Rehnquist's position.

In 1989, in *Mistretta v. United States*,[10] eight members of the Court rejected the argument that Congress had impermissibly delegated its power to prescribe ranges of criminal sentences that federal judges were required to impose on persons convicted of crimes. The Court also rejected the argument that Congress had violated the separation of powers principle by placing the sentencing commission within the judicial branch and authorizing it to establish legally binding sentencing guidelines. In a lone dissent, Justice Antonin Scalia asserted that the separation of powers principle had been violated, concluding that the new sentencing commission amounted to a "junior varsity Congress with extensive lawmaking power."[11] (See the excerpts from the *Mistretta* decision in the Opinion of the Court on page 462.)

The argument over delegation of legislative power is not confined to the federal level. State courts have wrestled with this problem over the years. Like the U.S. Supreme Court, though, most state courts have come down on the side of permitting broad delegations of legislative authority to the bureaucracy. The nondelegation doctrine remains viable, however, at least in theory. It remains available as a tool to invalidate a particularly egregious instance of legislative abdication of responsibility.

Legislative Control of the Bureaucracy

Congress and the state legislatures have employed a variety of mechanisms to retain control over agency decisions. These include attaching riders to agency appropriations bills, conducting oversight hearings, reducing agency budgets, and amending statutes. Of course, if the legislature is extremely dissatisfied with the performance of a particular agency, it may rewrite the statute that created the agency in the first instance.

MISTRETTA v. UNITED STATES
488 U.S. 361, 109 S. Ct. 647, 102 L. Ed. 2d 714 (1989)

Justice Blackmun delivered the opinion of the Court.

... The Constitution provides that "[a]ll legislative Powers herein granted shall be vested in a Congress of the United States," ... and we long have insisted that "the integrity and maintenance of the system of government ordained by the Constitution" mandate that Congress generally cannot delegate its legislative power to another Branch.... We also have recognized, however, that the separation-of-powers principle, and the nondelegation doctrine in particular, do not prevent Congress from obtaining the assistance of its coordinate Branches.... So long as Congress "shall lay down by legislative act an intelligible principle to which the person or body authorized to [exercise the delegated authority] is directed to conform, such legislative action is not a forbidden delegation of legislative power." ... Applying this "intelligible principle" test to congressional delegations, our jurisprudence has been driven by a practical understanding that in our increasingly complex society, replete with ever changing and more technical problems, Congress simply cannot do its job absent an ability to delegate power under broad general directives. ... "The Constitution has never been regarded as denying to the Congress the necessary resources of flexibility and practicality, which will enable it to perform its function." ... Accordingly, this Court has deemed it "constitutionally sufficient if Congress clearly delineates the general policy, the public agency which is to apply it, and the boundaries of this delegated authority." ...

By amending the appropriate statute, the legislature may enlarge or contract the agency's **jurisdiction**, as well as the nature and scope of its **rulemaking authority**.

The Legislative Veto

A **legislative veto** is a device whereby the legislature as a whole, one house thereof, or even one legislative committee can override an agency decision that is made pursuant to delegated authority. Prior to 1986, a legislative veto provision typically was written into the original act delegating legislative power to an executive agency. However, in *Immigration & Naturalization Service v. Chadha* (1986), the Supreme Court held that the legislative veto is unconstitutional.[12] The essence of the Court's opinion was that all legislative vetoes are invalid because the President is not given the opportunity to veto the legislative veto of the agency's action. Obviously, the Court in *Chadha* assumed that a legislative veto is a legislative act that must conform to the requirements of Article I, an assumption that the dissenting justices and numerous commentators have found unpersuasive.

The *Chadha* decision not only invalidated the veto provision actually before the Court but also rendered some 230 similar statutory provisions presumptively unconstitutional, making it the most sweeping exercise of judicial review in the history of the Supreme Court. As noted previously, Congress retains a number of mechanisms whereby it can control agency action of which it disapproves. Furthermore, the Court's decision applied only to legislative vetoes enacted by Congress; it said nothing of similar provisions at the state level.

Many, but certainly not all, of the state legislative veto provisions have been struck down by state courts following the reasoning of the *Chadha* decision. The Idaho Supreme Court actually has approved the legislative veto, viewing it as a reasonable condition on the delegation of legislative power to executive agencies.[13] Some commentators on the *Chadha* decision itself have taken this position. That notwithstanding, *Chadha* remains the law of the land, and there is little likelihood that the Court will reconsider its position in the foreseeable future.

Through enactment of the Contract with America Act of 1996, Congress has created a new procedure that is functionally similar to the legislative veto. Under a section entitled "Congressional Review of Agency Decisionmaking," an agency must submit a report to Congress on every new proposed rule.[14] Through simple majority vote of either house, the rule is stayed for sixty days, giving Congress ample time to prevent the adoption of the rule through the process of joint resolution. Unlike the legislative veto, the joint resolution must be presented to the President before it can become law. Thus, even though the new procedure restores some measure of control to the Congress, Congress cannot act autonomously to veto administrative action of which it disapproves.

RULEMAKING

When Congress and the state legislatures delegate regulatory authority to agencies, they are not authorizing agencies to make policy ad hoc. Rather, they are permitting agencies to engage in the process of rulemaking. Rulemaking is like legislation — it produces rules of general applicability. Kenneth Culp Davis, a leading authority on administrative law, observed in the late 1960s that "the chief hope for confining discretionary power does not lie in statutory enactments but in much more extensive administrative rulemaking."[15] The federal government may have heeded his words, for the 1970s initiated the "era of rulemaking" as federal agencies became much more active in this regard. Indeed, the trend toward increased rulemaking by federal agencies continues to the present time, despite efforts by Presidents Reagan and Bush in the 1980s and early 1990s to stem the regulatory tide. In 1997 alone, federal agencies produced nearly three thousand new regulations. Keeping pace with the changing regulatory environment is a daunting task for business, but it is a "growth industry" for lawyers.

At the federal level, the rulemaking process is governed by the Administrative Procedure Act (APA) of 1946, as amended.[16] Most states have similar statutes. Either they have adopted the Model State Administrative Procedure Act of 1961 or its 1981 update, or they have crafted their own legislation.

The federal APA is codified in Title 5 of the U.S. Code. Section 553 of the Act (see Sidebar below) requires agencies to publish a **notice of proposed rulemaking** (NPRM)

CASE IN POINT

CAN THE FDA REGULATE TOBACCO AS A DRUG?
Food & Drug Administration v. Brown & Williamson Tobacco Corp.
United States Supreme Court
529 U.S. 120, 120 S. Ct. 1291, 146 L. Ed. 2d 121 (2000)

Under the federal Food, Drug and Cosmetic Act, the Food and Drug Administration has the authority to regulate "drugs" and "devices." In 1996, the FDA adopted regulations governing the promotion and labeling of tobacco products. The regulations were concerned specifically with making these products less accessible to children and adolescents. The FDA based its regulatory authority on the grounds that nicotine is a "drug" and tobacco products are "devices" that deliver nicotine to the body. Brown and Williamson, a manufacturer of tobacco products, filed suit challenging the FDA's authority in this area.

The federal district court upheld the FDA's authority, but the Court of Appeals reversed, holding that Congress had not granted the FDA jurisdiction over tobacco products. Splitting 5-4, the Supreme Court also ruled against the FDA. Notwithstanding its customary deference to agency interpretations of statutes, the Court concluded that Congress clearly had not intended to give the FDA the authority to regulate tobacco products. Of course, as a matter of statutory interpretation, the Court's decision can be overturned by ordinary legislation clearly authorizing the FDA to regulate tobacco.

---

in the *Federal Register*. Such notice must include "a statement of the time, place, and nature of public rulemaking proceedings; reference to the legal authority under which the rule is proposed; and either the terms or substance of the proposed rule or a description of the subjects and issues involved...."[17] The law requires that before the rule can go into effect, interested parties must be afforded an opportunity to comment orally or in writing. Agencies are required to take comments into account before adopting a final rule. Once adopted, the final rule must be published in the *Federal Register* at least thirty days prior to its effective date. Even then, the law requires the agency to provide interested parties the right to petition for the issuance, amendment, or repeal of a rule. After a rule is finalized, it is incorporated into the *Code of Federal Regulations*.

The Administrative Procedure Act sets forth minimal requirements for agency rulemaking. Congress will often require that particular agencies go well beyond these simple, relatively informal procedures. For example, the Toxic Substances Control Act requires the Environmental Protection Agency (EPA) to follow more elaborate procedures when regulating hazardous materials.[18] Another example is the extensive process the Food and Drug Administration is required to follow before approving new drugs and medical devices.[19]

Rulemaking also is affected by a number of general statutes. For example, the National Environmental Policy Act (NEPA) requires agencies to provide an environmental impact statement before undertaking or approving any major action affecting the environment. The Paperwork Reduction Act of 1995 requires agencies to assess the impact of proposed rules on the need for data collection and archiving. Similarly, the Unfunded Mandates Act of 1995 requires agencies to assess the fiscal impact of proposed rules on state and local governments.

The Regulatory Flexibility Act, which was enacted during the Carter Administration and strengthened in 1996, was adopted to ease the regulatory burden on small business. Large companies can generally withstand economic costs associated with complying with government regulations. Small businesses, though, are at a disadvantage in this respect. Specifically, small businesses often encounter great difficulty in trying to comprehend and comply with government regulations. Accordingly, federal law now requires that before agencies adopt rules that significantly impact small business, they consider how rules can be made and enforced in such a way so as to minimize the regulatory burden on small business.[20]

SIDEBAR

The Administrative Procedure Act Section on Rule Making (5 U.S.C. §553)

§553. Rule making

(a) This section applies, according to the provisions thereof, except to the extent that there is involved—

(1) a military or foreign affairs function of the United States; or

(2) a matter relating to agency management or personnel or to public property, loans, grants, benefits, or contracts.

(b) General notice of proposed rulemaking shall be published in the Federal Register, unless persons subject thereto are named and either personally served or otherwise have actual notice thereof in accordance with law. The notice shall include—

(1) a statement of the time, place, and nature of public rule making proceedings;

(2) reference to the legal authority under which the rule is proposed; and

(3) either the terms or substance of the proposed rule or a description of the subjects and issues involved.

Except when notice or hearing is required by statute, this subsection does not apply—

(A) to interpretative rules, general statements of policy, or rules of agency organization, procedure, or practice; or

(B) when the agency for good cause finds (and incorporates the finding and a brief statement of reasons therefor in the rules issued) that notice and public procedure thereon are impracticable, unnecessary, or contrary to the public interest.

(c) After notice required by this section, the agency shall give interested persons an opportunity to participate in the rule making through submission of written data, views, or arguments with or without opportunity for oral presentation. After consideration of the relevant matter presented, the agency shall incorporate in the rules adopted a concise general statement of their basis and purpose. When rules are required by statute to be made on the record after opportunity for an agency hearing, sections 556 and 557 of this title apply instead of this subsection.

(d) The required publication or service of a substantive rule shall be made not less than 30 days before its effective date, except—

(1) a substantive rule which grants or recognizes an exemption or relieves a restriction;

(2) interpretative rules and statements of policy; or

(3) as otherwise provided by the agency for good cause found and published with the rule.

(e) Each agency shall give an interested person the right to petition for the issuance, amendment, or repeal of a rule.

Executive Control of Rulemaking

Excessive government regulation of business became a political issue in the 1970s. In 1978, President Carter issued an executive order requiring federal agencies to conduct a "regulatory analysis" before adopting new rules in order to ensure that economic costs were taken into account.[21] President Reagan greatly expanded on this mandate by requiring agencies to conduct **cost-benefit analyses** and by adopting only those rules that maximized net benefits to society.[22] Agencies that fail to satisfy White House **preclearance** of proposed rules are prevented from publishing NPRMs in the *Federal Register.*

White House preclearance of proposed rules is effectuated by the Office of Management and Budget (OMB), which is part of the Executive Office of the President. Presidents can control rulemaking to an extent because agencies depend on the White House, more specifically the OMB, to submit their annual budget requests to Congress.

Adequacy of Rulemaking Procedures

In the absence of more specific congressional guidance, the Supreme Court has tended to rely on the Administrative Procedure Act as an adequate framework for agency rulemaking procedures. For example, in 1978 the Court considered the adequacy of procedures used by the Atomic Energy Commission (now the Nuclear Regulatory Commission) for the licensure of nuclear power plants.[23] Of particular concern was the agency's procedure in promulgating a rule governing spent nuclear fuel. The procedure in question included the scheduling of hearings prior to adoption of the rule, as required by the APA. These hearings were somewhat informal, however, and did not include full **adjudicatory procedures**, such as discovery and cross-examination. The Court of Appeals for the District of Columbia Circuit held that the existing procedure was inadequate under the Due Process Clause of the Fifth Amendment. The Supreme Court reversed without a dissenting vote. In his opinion for the Court, Justice Rehnquist sharply criticized the court of appeals decision, complaining that "this sort of unwarranted judicial examination of perceived procedural shortcomings of a rulemaking proceeding can do nothing but seriously interfere with that process prescribed by Congress. . . ."[24]

Although courts usually uphold agency interpretations of rulemaking authority, that was not the case with the Supreme Court's 2006 decision in *Gonzales v. Oregon.*[25] This case stemmed from Oregon voters' 1994 decision to legalize assisted suicide via a ballot proposition. In 2001, the U.S. Attorney General, John Ashcroft, responded by using his perceived authority under the Controlled Substances Act to issue a rule. The rule banned physicians from using regulated drugs for the act of assisted suicide. (While Ashcroft's rule led to the court case, the case name ultimately came to include the name of Ashcroft's successor, Alberto Gonzales.) In its decision, the Supreme Court found that the Attorney General lacked the authority, under the Controlled Substances Act, to pass a rule that prohibited doctors from using drugs for assisted suicide (when state law permitted the procedure). The Court did note that agency interpretations typically would receive "substantial deference," but found that such deference was not absolute.[26]

AGENCY INVESTIGATIONS

Agencies have the authority to conduct investigations within the purview of their regulatory authority. For example, the EPA investigates alleged violations of the Clean Air Act, Clean Water Act, and other federal environmental laws. In their investigations, agencies have powers to subpoena records and compel individuals to testify, as long as compelled testimony is not used as evidence in a criminal prosecution.[27] Agencies cannot enforce their own subpoenas, however, so they may file enforcement petitions in federal district courts.[28] Courts often hold hearings on these petitions, but usually uphold agency subpoenas.

Search and Seizure

One of the most important investigative tools agencies possess is that of search and seizure. Despite the Fourth Amendment's prohibition against unreasonable searches and seizures, agencies have routinely conducted administrative inspections of the industries they regulate. In general, the courts have been more permissive toward **administrative searches** directed at business and industry than toward police searches directed at private individuals. In 1959, the Supreme Court found no violation of the Fourth Amendment when administrative searches were conducted without notice and without search warrants.[29] In the 1960s, the Court became stricter, holding that, as a general rule, warrants must be obtained to justify administrative searches.[30] The Court made an exception, though, for "closely regulated industries," stating that administrative searches in these settings do not require a warrant or consent; examples of closely regulate industries include food service businesses, such as catering companies,[31] junkyards,[32] pawn shops,[33] and mines[34] (see below).

An example of the stricter judicial approach to administrative searches can be seen in *Marshall v. Barlow's, Inc.* (1978).[35] There, the Supreme Court struck down a provision of the Occupational Safety and Health Act of 1970 that allowed OSHA to conduct warrantless searches of the workplace. (The specific case dealt with an electrical and plumbing business). However, the Court was careful to point out that to obtain **administrative search warrants**, OSHA inspectors did not have to meet the same strict standards of probable cause that govern the issuance of warrants in criminal investigations.

In the 1980s, a more conservative Supreme Court backed away from the strict scrutiny of regulatory searches manifested by the Court in the 1960s and 70s. For example, in 1981, the Court refused to invalidate a provision of the Federal Mine Safety and Health Act of 1977 that allowed the Department of Labor to conduct **warrantless inspections** of mines.[36] The Court attempted to distinguish the case from *Barlow's*, but it seems clear that a majority of the justices preferred the more permissive approach that prevailed prior to the 1960s.

In 1987, in upholding a warrantless inspection of a junkyard, the Court laid out a contemporary framework for evaluating **warrantless administrative searches**.[37] The Court said that such inspections should be upheld as long as three conditions are met:

1. There must be a substantial government interest that informs the regulatory scheme pursuant to which the inspection is made;

2. the warrantless inspection must be necessary to further the regulatory scheme; and

3. the inspection program must provide a constitutionally adequate substitute for a warrant.

This approach gives government agencies considerable latitude in conducting warrantless inspections of regulated industries and, accordingly, has been highly criticized. Of course, state courts can adopt stricter rules for administrative searches under their own state constitutional provisions relative to search and seizure.

Deportation and Administrative Detention

Immigration and Customs Enforcement (ICE) has the responsibility for carrying out the nation's immigration laws.[38] Historically, ICE (formerly INS) has possessed broad discretion. ICE conducts immigration inspections of travelers entering the United States, regulates permanent and temporary immigration (including legal permanent residence status), and maintains control of the nation's borders. ICE also identifies and removes people who do not have lawful immigration status, a process known as deportation. Under the Illegal Immigration Reform and Immigrant Responsibility Act of 1996, ICE could detain illegal aliens indefinitely without bond, regardless of whether they were likely to appear for deportation proceedings and posed no danger to the community.[39] In such cases, administrative detention of less than six months often is not subject to judicial review.[40] This approach is justified on the basis that illegal aliens are not entitled

---

CASE IN POINT

WARRANTLESS AERIAL INSPECTION OF A CHEMICAL PLAT
Dow Chemical Co. v. United States
United States Supreme Court
476 U.S. 227, 106 S. Ct. 1819, 90 L. Ed. 2d 226 (1986)

Acting without a warrant, Environmental Protection Agency officials employed a commercial aerial photographer to take pictures of a chemical plant from an altitude of twelve hundred feet. When the plant's owners learned of the photographic flyover, they filed suit in federal court, claiming that the EPA had violated their Fourth Amendment rights. Splitting 5-4, the Supreme Court sided with the EPA, holding that the flyover was not a "search" within the meaning of the Fourth Amendment. The Court observed:

"It may well be, as the Government concedes, that surveillance of private property by using highly sophisticated surveillance equipment not generally available to the public, such as satellite technology, might be constitutionally proscribed absent a warrant. But the photographs here are not so revealing of intimate details as to raise constitutional concerns. Although they undoubtedly give EPA more detailed information than naked-eye views, they remain limited to an outline of the facility's buildings and equipment. The mere fact that human vision is enhanced somewhat, at least to the degree here, does not give rise to constitutional problems."

to the protections of the Constitution, a theory that not everyone accepts.[41] In 2014, though, President Obama used executive action to protect illegal immigrants that have lived in the United States more than five years from being deported.

AGENCY ENFORCEMENT POWERS

Agencies have a variety of sanctions available. Of course, agencies cannot impose sanctions without statutory authority. Agencies that issue licenses, such as the Federal Communications Commission and the Nuclear Regulatory Commission, have the authority to revoke such licenses where licensees engage in repeated violations of regulations. Agencies also have the power to impose their own administrative fines. Certain agencies, such as the Securities and Exchange Commission and the National Labor Relations Board, even have the power to issue **cease and desist orders**.

Civil Suits

A number of federal agencies have the authority to file civil suits against violators. For example, the Civil Rights Act of 1964 authorizes the Department of Justice to file suit to vindicate citizens' civil rights:

> Whenever the Attorney General has reasonable cause to believe that any person or group of persons is engaged in a pattern or practice of resistance to the full enjoyment of any of the rights secured by this subchapter, and that the pattern or practice is of such a nature and is intended to deny the full exercise of the rights herein described, the Attorney General may bring a civil action in the appropriate district court of the United States by filing with it a complaint . . . setting forth facts pertaining to such pattern or practice, and . . . requesting such preventive relief, including an application for a permanent or temporary injunction, restraining order or other order against the person or persons responsible for such pattern or practice, as he deems necessary to insure the full enjoyment of the rights herein describe.[42]

It was under this provision that the Justice Department filed a highly publicized suit in 1993 against Flagstar Corporation, the operator of Denny's Restaurants. The suit alleged racial discrimination against black patrons. In a settlement, Flagstar paid $45 million in damages and established a program to prevent future discrimination at its restaurants.[43]

Often, the civil rights suits filed by the Justice Department are referred to it by other federal agencies. For example, the Office for Civil Rights (OCR) in the U.S. Department of Education is responsible for enforcing a number of civil rights laws that apply to public education, including Title VI of the Civil Rights Act of 1964, Title IX of the Education Amendments of 1972, Section 504 of the Rehabilitation Act of 1973, and Title II of the Americans with Disabilities Act of 1990. The OCR investigates complaints filed by parties who believe they are the victims of unlawful discrimination, but it has no power to bring lawsuits on its own. The OCR prefers to settle discrimination complaints through negotiation with school officials, but in some situations it refers cases to the Justice Department, which then decides whether to file suit against the school district.

One agency that can bring civil suits directly against violators is the Securities and Exchange Commission (SEC). The SEC routinely files suit in federal district court against parties who are accused of securities fraud under federal law and the Commission's own regulations.[44] The SEC is empowered to seek injunctions, the "disgorgement" of ill-gotten gains, and civil penalties.

Citizen-Initiated Lawsuits

In some instances, citizens can go to court directly rather than wait for a government agency to act on a violation of public policy. For example, Section 505(a) of the Clean Water Act authorizes private citizens to commence a civil action for injunctive relief and/or the imposition of civil penalties in federal district court against any person "alleged to be in violation" of the conditions of a National Pollutant Discharge Elimination System (NPDES) permit. However, Section 505(a) does not allow citizen suits for "wholly past violations."[45]

An increasingly popular form of citizen-initiated litigation is the **qui tam action**. *Qui tam* is short for the Latin phrase *qui tam pro domino rege quam pro sic ipso in hoc parte sequitur,* which means "who sues for the king sues for himself as well." According to *Black's Law Dictionary*, a *qui tam* suit is "an action brought by an informer, under a statute which establishes a penalty for the commission or omission of a certain act, and provides that the same shall be recoverable in a civil action, part of the penalty to go to any person who will bring such action and the remainder to the state or some other institution." The federal False Claims Act allows private citizens to file suit on behalf of the U.S. Government charging fraud by government contractors and others who receive federal funds.[46] If the plaintiff prevails, the government can recover triple its damages in addition to civil penalties ranging from $5,000 to $10,000 per violation. The citizen (referred to as the "relator") shares in the monetary damages collected up to a maximum of 30 percent. The False Claims Act was enacted by Congress during the Civil War in order to ferret out fraud in military procurement. Today, the law provides an incentive to whistleblowers to reveal evidence of fraud in programs like Medicare and Medicaid. In recent years, there have been a number of million-dollar settlements.[47] Currently, about five hundred *qui tam* actions are filed in federal courts each year, and the number is growing rapidly.

Beyond suits filed by actual citizens, states themselves can bring legal action against federal agencies. In 2007, a unique case ensued when 12 states, joined by the cities of New York and Baltimore and the District of Columbia, filed suit against the EPA after the agency refused to regulate greenhouse gases (like carbon dioxide) that were emitted from motor vehicles. An EPA administrator essentially claimed that the Clean Air Act did not require it to regulate such activity, and the agency was even joined, as respondents, by several different states. In issuing its ruling for *Massachusetts v. EPA*, the Supreme Court first stated that the petitioners did in fact have standing to sue the EPA, and then the Court noted that the EPA's reasons for not regulating vehicle greenhouse gas emissions were inadequate, since this authority fell within its purview.[48] Subsequently, in 2009, the EPA—now under the control of President Obama's administration—would end up establishing rules for regulating automobile emissions.

In 2014, the Supreme Court recognized EPA authority to regulate "greenhouse gases" in industrial contexts as well—but the Court did place some limits upon the scope of this power. More specifically, in *Utility Air v. EPA*, the Supreme Court addressed EPA authority under the Clean Air Act. Pursuant to that law, the EPA requires that so-called "stationary polluters" (e.g., power plants, steel mills, and refineries) must procure permits before expanding existing facilities or creating new ones. The EPA typically grants these permits if it is clear that appropriate technology is implemented in order to reduce pollution. In the *Utility Air* decision, the Court stated the EPA could not mandate that companies acquire such permits *solely* because of "potential greenhouse emissions." However, if a company had to acquire a permit regarding *other* pollutants, then the EPA also could necessitate using the "best available control technology" for greenhouse gas emissions. (This decision did not affect the holding from *Massachusetts v. EPA*, and thus, the EPA can still regulate all greenhouse emissions from automobiles.)[49]

Overall, numerous media outlets have characterized this decision as something of a "mixed bag" for the EPA. In this regard, Justice Scalia's opinion actually observed: "It bears mention that the EPA is getting almost everything it wanted in this case." Scalia specifically suggested that the EPA could still regulate 83% of greenhouse-gas emissions, but he added that the regulation the court struck down would have raised that to 86%. Although this might not seem like a substantial difference, Scalia articulated an important underlying principle by saying, "To permit the extra 3%, however, we would have to recognize a power in EPA and other government agencies to revise clear statutory terms . . . [contradicting] the principle that Congress, not the president, makes the law." In the end, that sentiment could prove to be the key rationale that emanates from this decision.

Criminal Prosecutions

Federal agencies do not have the authority to initiate criminal prosecutions. But when they obtain evidence of criminal wrongdoing, they can refer the matter to the Department of Justice. If the Attorney General believes the matter warrants prosecution, the case is presented to a federal grand jury for indictment (see Chapter 10).

Liens, Levies, and Garnishments

Without question, the federal agency most feared by average Americans is the Internal Revenue Service (IRS). It is also among the most vital, in that it collects 95 percent of the federal government's revenues through personal and corporate income taxes, excise, gift, and estate taxes, as well as social security employment taxes. The IRS is empowered to conduct audits of taxpayers' returns, impose liens and levies on assets in order to recover unpaid taxes, and even garnish wages. However, in 1988, 1996, and 1998, Congress enacted legislation to protect taxpayers from the abuse of IRS powers. A taxpayer's principal residence is now protected from **levy** to satisfy tax liabilities of less than $5,000. The taxpayer must be provided with a levy statement at least thirty days before property is seized, during which time the taxpayer may request a hearing to challenge the levy. With respect to garnishments, the law now requires a twenty-one-day hold on bank accounts garnished by the IRS, which provides more time to challenge an improper **garnishment**. Finally, taxpayers who are the victims of reckless or intentional disregard of proper tax collection procedures may sue the IRS in federal district court for damages up to $1 million.[50]

Forfeitures

Federal law provides for the **forfeiture** of real estate and other property used in illegal drug trafficking and other criminal activities.[51] Cars, boats, and airplanes are commonly seized under the forfeiture laws. In 1984, federal law enforcement agencies began a program called "Equitable Sharing," under which federal agencies recruit state and local police to assist them in seizing property under federal statutes. Local or state police seize property and turn it over to the federal government. If the forfeiture is upheld, the state or local police agency that made the seizure shares equally in the proceeds when the forfeited assets are sold at auction.

In 1993, the Supreme Court held that a property forfeiture stemming from a drug crime is subject to limitation under the Eighth Amendment.[52] Writing for the Court, Justice Blackmun concluded that "forfeiture . . . constitutes 'payment to a sovereign as punishment for some offense,' and, as such, is subject to the limitations of the Eighth Amendment's Excessive Fines Clause."[53]

Until recently, real estate, including a residence or business, could be seized on the basis of an ex parte seizure warrant, and the property owner ousted from the property pending trial—without notice or an opportunity to be heard. The Supreme Court has held that such practices are unconstitutional when they apply to seizures of real estate.[54] Due process requires notice and the opportunity to be heard before real estate can be seized, the Court held, and in most situations this should mean that the property owner not be disturbed in the right of possession of the property pending trial. But the Supreme Court expressly limited the holding to real property—residential or commercial. It did not affect pretrial detention of cars, bank accounts, cash, and other personal property.

AGENCY ADJUDICATION

Agencies often must settle disputes with parties they regulate or the beneficiaries of their programs. In this respect, agencies act as **quasi-judicial bodies**. Unlike judicial proceedings, however, the rules of evidence for administrative hearings are quite liberal, with hearsay evidence generally admitted and only irrelevant, immaterial, or repetitive evidence excluded.

The Administrative Procedure Act (APA)

Federal agency adjudicatory procedures are governed by the Administrative Procedure Act (APA). Most states have their own counterpart to the APA. The APA requires the most basic elements of due process, that is, notice and hearing. Regarding notice, it provides that "[p]ersons entitled to notice of an agency hearing shall be timely informed of (1) the time, place, and nature of the hearing; (2) the legal authority and jurisdiction under which the hearing is to be held; and (3) the matters of fact and law asserted."[55] As to the hearing, the agency is required to "give all interested parties opportunity for ... the submission and consideration of facts, arguments, offers of settlement, or proposals of adjustment when time, the nature of the proceeding, and the public interest permit. ..."[56]

The APA's requirement of a public administrative hearing applies where a statute requires that adjudication is to be determined on the record after opportunity for an agency hearing.[57] Where a statute fails to use the words "on the record" or fails to otherwise indicate that the APA applies, there is some conflict in judicial decisions as to the applicability of hearing requirements of the APA. But the APA is not the only source of procedural requirements. Depending on the agency and issue involved, other statutory requirements may come into play. The agency's enabling legislation, that is, the act of Congress that established and empowered the agency, may dictate certain additional procedural requirements. So, too, may the substantive statute being enforced. Contracts between agencies and private contractors also may specify additional procedural requirements respecting the termination of contracts. And, some agencies develop their own internal rules of procedure that go beyond the APA and other statutory requirements. As a result, it is difficult to generalize about the procedural aspects of agency adjudication. They vary considerably along a continuum from **informal adjudication** that observes only the minimal requirements of the APA to **formal adjudication** that resembles a civil trial (see Chapter 9).

The Presiding Officer

Less formal agency adjudications are overseen by "administrative judges" or "hearing examiners." More formal proceedings are conducted by **administrative law judges** (ALJs).[58] Although ALJs are technically employees of the agencies they serve, they are supposed to function as impartial arbiters of disputes. It is essential that disputes be adjudicated by impartial decision-makers.[59] Accordingly, federal law contains a number of measures designed to enhance the independence of ALJs from their agencies.[60]

Due Process Requirements

Beyond the statutory requirements regarding agency adjudication, the U.S. Constitution looms as the ultimate source of procedural protection. The Supreme Court has applied the Due Process Clauses of the Fifth and Fourteenth Amendments when it has found statutory procedures inadequate to ensure fairness or to protect the fundamental rights of individuals. During the 1970s, the Supreme Court seemed more willing to apply constitutional due process requirements in cases where agency decisions affected the economic interests of specific individuals. For example, in *Goldberg v. Kelly* (1970), the Supreme Court held that the Fourteenth Amendment Due Process Clause required a state agency to provide an evidentiary hearing before terminating a person's welfare benefits after the agency determined that the individual was no longer eligible for such benefits.[61] Additionally, in *Goss v. Lopez* (1975), the Court held that the ten-day suspension of a student from a public school constituted deprivation of property within the meaning of the Due Process Clause.[62] Thus, the school was required to provide basic procedural safeguards. Other Supreme Court decisions in the 1970s extended due process protections to a wide variety of claimants, including public employees, automobile drivers, prisoners, and debtors.

In administrative due process cases, the Court must make two determinations. First, it must decide whether the Due Process Clause is applicable. Administrative decisions are constrained by the Due Process Clause only if they in some meaningful way deprive an individual of "life, liberty or property." Of course, today, those interests are broadly defined. Second, assuming the Due Process Clause does apply, the Court must determine what "process" is due in order to ensure fundamental fairness. Here, the Court has been reluctant to adopt a one-size-fits-all approach to administrative due

CASE IN POINT

DUE PROCESS AND TERMINATION OF SOCIAL SECURITY DISABILITY BENEFITS
Mathews v. Eldridge

United States Supreme Court
424 U.S. 319, 96 S. Ct. 893, 47 L. Ed. 2d 18 (1976)

George Eldridge, who had been disabled due to "chronic anxiety and back strain," was informed by the Social Security Administration that, according to medical reports, his disability no longer existed and that benefit payments would be terminated. Although agency procedures required ample notification and an evidentiary hearing prior to final termination, the payments could be stopped initially without a hearing. Provision was also made for retroactive payments to any recipient whose disability was later determined not to have ended. Eldridge, who was concerned with the initial decision to terminate payments, relied on *Goldberg v. Kelly* in arguing that the Due Process Clause required an evidentiary hearing before any termination of benefits.

Writing for the Court, Justice Lewis Powell conceded the existence of a property interest in Social Security ben-

efits and thus the applicability of the Due Process Clause. But Powell said that "due process is flexible and calls for such procedural protections as the particular situation demands." In other words, the degree of procedural safeguards required by the Constitution depends on how much one stands to lose. In this case, the Court distinguished social security from welfare benefits and held that the "potential deprivation ... is generally likely to be less" when social security payments are denied than when welfare benefits are terminated. In this way, the Court significantly narrowed the potential application of *Goldberg v. Kelly* without formally overruling it. In *Mathews*, the Court was willing to regard the existing agency procedures as adequate safeguards.

process. In *Mathews v. Eldridge* (see Case in Point on page 474), the Court said that "due process is flexible and calls for such procedural protections as the particular situation demands."[63] Beyond the general requirements of fair notice and fair hearing, it is difficult to say precisely what due process requires in a specific administrative context. But, one guiding principle is that the greater the magnitude of the individual's life, liberty, or property interest, the greater the requirement for procedural protections. For instance, in *Jones v. Flowers* (2006),[64] the Supreme Court held that notice of a tax foreclosure sale sent by certified by mail to the homeowner who occupied the residence, but returned unclaimed, failed to meet due process standards. The Court indicated that publication of a notice in the newspaper was not sufficient and suggested that notice could have been resent by regular mail or that a notice could have been posted on the front door.

Historically, procedural due process has been applied only to government action. However, in *Thomas M. Cooley Law School v. American Bar Assn.* (2006),[65] a federal appeals court said "that quasi-public professional organizations and accrediting agencies such as the ABA have a common law duty to employ fair procedures when making decisions affecting their members."[66] The court went on to hold that it would conduct its review based on standards drawn from the federal APA.

JUDICIAL REVIEW OF AGENCY ACTIONS

One of the functions of the federal courts is to ensure that the federal bureaucracy conforms to the rule of law. In certain instances, parties can go directly to federal district court to challenge agency actions. In most cases, however, parties must first exhaust available remedies internal to the agency. Having done so and failing to get relief, they can then file an appeal with the appropriate circuit court. For obvious reasons, the U.S. Court of Appeals for the District of Columbia Circuit has an extensive caseload of these administrative cases. There is an elaborate body of law, both statutory and decisional, governing **judicial review of agency actions**. At the outset, it is important to understand the distinction between decisions on threshold issues, which govern access to judicial review, and decisions on the merits.

Access to Judicial Review

Before a federal court can reach the merits of an administrative law case, a number of threshold issues must be addressed. These threshold issues govern access to judicial review. By limiting access to judicial review, courts maintain manageable caseloads and, moreover, maintain comity with the executive branch. The most fundamental threshold issue is jurisdiction. The court must have jurisdiction over the parties, the subject matter, and the geographical area before it can grant review. Because the jurisdiction of the lower federal courts is wholly dependent on Congress, the legislature can preclude judicial review altogether or under certain circumstances. This is known as **statutory preclusion of judicial review**. For example, in 1994, the Supreme Court ruled that the Federal Mine Safety and Health Amendments Act of 1977 precludes a federal court from exercising subject matter jurisdiction over a pre-enforcement challenge to the Act.[67] Similarly, in 1988, the Court held that the National Security Act of 1947 precludes judicial review of the CIA Director's decisions to terminate employees regardless of cause.[68]

Standing and Exhaustion of Remedies

The Administrative Procedure Act provides, "A person suffering legal wrong because of agency action, or adversely affected or aggrieved by agency action within the meaning of a relevant statute, is entitled to judicial review thereof."[69] State statutes usually provide parallel recourse for persons adversely affected by final administrative state agency action. Federal and state courts generally require that persons seeking judicial review have "standing" and must first exhaust their administrative remedies. To have standing to challenge an agency action, one must be adversely affected by that action in a way that is direct, substantial, and immediate. Parties who are direct targets of agency actions, such as beneficiaries who are denied benefits and licensees whose licenses are suspended or revoked, have virtually automatic standing to challenge adverse agency decisions in court, once they have exhausted all of their administrative remedies. Even so, simply being a taxpayer does not confer standing on an individual or group to challenge government actions. Many states, however, have enacted statutes to confer standing on taxpayers to challenge state and local public expenditures. At the state level, the issue of standing becomes particularly important to property owners who seek to challenge land-use zoning decisions that indirectly affect their property.

When a statute provides for administrative review within an agency, such review must be pursued before seeking review by the courts. Agencies are given every opportunity to correct their own errors before courts become involved. This **exhaustion of remedies** doctrine prevents judicial review that is premature or unnecessary. In 2006, in *Woodford v. Ngo*,[70] Justice Alito, writing for a six-Justice majority of the Supreme Court, pointed to the strictures of the doctrine when he noted, "Proper exhaustion [of remedies] demands compliance with an agency's deadlines and other critical procedural rules because no adjudicative system can function effectively without imposing some orderly structure on the course of its proceedings."[71]

Individuals and groups that are not direct parties to agency proceedings have more difficulty in establishing standing to challenge agency actions. Certainly, the status of being a disgruntled taxpayer is not enough to give one standing to challenge an agency action of which one disapproves, no matter how strong a legal challenge one can mount.[72] Similarly, an interest group does not have standing to challenge an agency action merely because its members oppose what the agency has done.[73] If an interest group is unable to show "individualized harm" to itself or its members, it does not have standing. On the other hand, standing is not confined to those who show economic harm. If a group can show that agency action adversely affects its quality of life, it may be successful in overcoming this threshold issue.[74]

Review on the Merits

A plaintiff who seeks judicial relief from an administrative agency decision faces an uphill legal battle in challenging agency actions. Federal courts typically review agency actions with a fairly strong presumption of validity. In other words, the burden of proof rests with the party challenging the agency to show that the agency's action was contrary to statute or the agency's own policies. In matters of statutory interpretation, the agency's construction of a statute is presumed to be valid unless it is contradicted by unambiguous legislative intent.[75] However, when constitutional issues involving fundamental rights such as freedom of speech or the right to privacy are concerned, the burden shifts to the agency to show that its action is constitutional. Nevertheless, the Supreme Court is reluctant to invalidate agency actions on constitutional grounds.[76] With regard to factual determinations, federal courts generally do not overturn agency conclusions unless they are clearly erroneous or at least not based on **substantial evidence**. Likewise, state courts usually uphold factual determinations by administrative agencies when the record is supported by substantial evidence.

It is fair to say that the federal courts show substantial deference to the actions of administrative agencies. A certain degree of deference is necessary to maintain the

CASE IN POINT

DEFERENCE TO ADMINISTRATIVE AGENCIES: THE ELIAN GONZALES CASE
Gonzales v. Reno
United States Court of Appeals for the Eleventh Circuit
211 F.3d 1338 (11th Cir. 2000)

In late 1999 and early 2000, the Immigration and Naturalization Service (INS) became the focus of national and international attention for its handling of the unusual case of Elian Gonzales, a six-year-old Cuban boy who was rescued at sea after his mother and nine other people drowned when their boat capsized. The INS gave temporary custody of the boy to relatives in Miami. When the boy's natural father came from Cuba to claim Elian, the Miami relatives refused to relinquish custody. After negotiations between the INS and the Miami relatives broke down, the INS used force to remove the boy from the home of the Miami relatives and reunite him with his father. While they had custody of Elian, the Miami relatives initiated a federal lawsuit to force the INS to grant Elian a political asylum hearing. The INS took the position that legally, only Elian's father could speak for him in this regard. The federal district court in Miami dismissed the case. The Miami relatives appealed to the U.S. Court of Appeals for the Eleventh Circuit in Atlanta. On June 1, 2000, the Eleventh Circuit ruled that the INS had acted within its legal authority in refusing to hold a political asylum hearing. The Miami relatives vowed

to appeal. The following is a brief excerpt from the Eleventh Circuit's opinion:

EDMONDSON, Circuit Judge:

. . . When the INS was confronted with Plaintiff's purported asylum applications, the immigration law of the United States provided the INS with no clear answer. The INS accordingly developed a policy to deal with the extraordinary circumstances of asylum applications filed on behalf of a six-year-old child, by the child himself and a non-parental relative, against the express wishes of the child's parents (or sole parent). The INS then applied this new policy to Plaintiff's purported asylum applications and rejected them as nullities.

Because the preexisting law compelled no particular policy, the INS was entitled to make a policy decision. The policy decision that the INS made was within the outside border of reasonable choices. And the INS did not abuse its discretion or act arbitrarily in applying the policy and rejecting Plaintiff's purported asylum applications. The Court neither approves nor disapproves the INS's decision to reject the asylum applications filed on Plaintiff's behalf, but the INS decision did not contradict [the law].

viability of the administrative state. As the *Brown & Williamson* case demonstrates, however, this deference is not unlimited. In extreme cases, the courts will say that agencies have operated outside the law.

PUBLIC ACCESS TO AGENCY INFORMATION

In the information age, information is power. In a democratic society, it is therefore essential that citizens have access to information held by government agencies. Of course, there must be exceptions to this principle in order to protect personal privacy, ensure national security, and foster effective law enforcement. At the federal level, the linchpin of this debate is the Freedom of Information Act (FOIA).[77] Adopted in 1966, FOIA establishes a presumption that records in the possession of agencies and executive departments of the U.S. government are accessible to the people. The statute sets standards for determining which records must be disclosed and which records can be withheld. The law provides administrative and judicial remedies for those denied access to records. Above all, the statute requires federal agencies to provide the fullest possible **disclosure of information** to the public. Together with the Privacy Act, the FOIA restricts the **improper disclosure of personal information** and provides for civil remedies where an individual's rights have been violated.

The Freedom of Information Act applies to documents held by agencies in the executive branch of the federal government, including the Cabinet-level departments, military departments, government corporations, independent regulatory agencies, law enforcement agencies, and other establishments in the executive branch. FOIA does not apply to elected officials of the federal government, including the President, Vice President, senators, and representatives. It does not apply to the federal courts. Nor does it apply to private companies or persons who receive federal contracts or grants. FOIA also does not apply to state or local governments, but note that all states and some localities have passed "open records" laws that, like the FOIA and Privacy Act, permit individuals access to records.

FOIA provides that a party making a request must ask for existing records rather than information. The law requires that each request must reasonably describe the records being sought. A request must be specific enough to permit the agency to locate the record in a reasonable period of time. Once an FOIA request is filed, an agency is required to determine within ten days (excluding Saturdays, Sundays, and legal holidays) whether to comply. The actual disclosure of documents is required to follow promptly thereafter. FOIA permits an agency to extend the time limits up to ten days in unusual circumstances. If a request is denied, the agency must provide reasons for the denial. FOIA contains a number of exemptions designed to protect against the disclosure of information that would jeopardize national security, privacy of individuals, proprietary interests of business, and the functioning of the government. For example, classified documents are exempt, as are records relating to internal personnel matters, internal government communications, and confidential business information. In denying a request, the agency must also indicate whether there is a mechanism internal to the agency to appeal a denial. Of course, the ultimate review lies with the federal courts.

Often, it is a federal court that must decide whether an agency has properly invoked one of the exemptions in denying an FOIA request.

All states have laws allowing the public access to public records. For example, the Delaware act provides, "All public records shall be open to inspection and copying by any citizen of the State." In *Lee v. Miner*,[78] Matthew Lee, a journalist and consumer advocate residing in New York, sought to obtain certain public records but was denied access because he was not a citizen of Delaware. The U.S. Court of Appeals for the Third Circuit held that the Privileges and Immunities Clause of the federal constitution prevented the State of Delaware from denying Lee's request for the reason that he was not a citizen of Delaware.

A recent case concerning FOIA involved a request by *The New York Times* to acquire an internal Obama administration document that justified using drone strikes to kill American citizens who were suspected of terrorist activity. (The administration has stated that such action will only be taken abroad.) The document in question was specifically connected to the 2011 killing of an American citizen in Yemen. In April 2014, the U.S. Court of Appeals for the 2nd Circuit mandated the release of this document,[79] and members of the executive branch complied in June 2014. The 41-page document ultimately revealed that the administration was relying on a law called the Authorization to Use Military Force as justification for the use of drone strikes against individuals who are deemed threats to national security; further, the individual killed in the 2011 drone strike was said to have ties to the terrorist organization Al-Qaeda. The government did, however, redact sections of the report that addressed implications for the 4th Amendment.

GOVERNMENT IN THE SUNSHINE

In the contemporary era, government secrecy is considered anathema to democracy. The Government in the Sunshine Act requires federal agencies headed by a collegial body composed of two or more members to hold their meetings in public.[80] There are numerous exceptions to this requirement, however. The Sunshine Act does not require agencies, for example, to hold public meetings that would reveal matters that must be kept secret for reasons of national security or those that relate solely to the internal agency personnel rules and practices. The Act also exempts the disclosure of ongoing law enforcement investigations, personal information that would be an unwarranted invasion of personal privacy, as well as disclosures that would lead to speculation in currencies, securities, or commodities.

While the federal Sunshine Act is in fact fairly narrow in its requirements of **open meetings**, state **sunshine laws** are often much broader. Florida has one of the strictest sunshine laws, and violations are punishable by fine.[81] Florida appellate courts have said the law must be broadly construed to effectuate its remedial and protective purpose. That purpose, one court opined, is to prevent crystallization of secret governmental decisions at nonpublic meetings to the point just short of ceremonial acceptance.[82] The Florida Sunshine Law stipulates that all meetings of any board or commission of any state, county, political subdivision, or municipality at which official acts are to be taken, are to be public meetings open to the public at all times, except as otherwise provided in the state constitution. Minutes of all such meetings must be recorded and made available for public inspection. The law does permit agencies to meet in private to discuss pending litigation, but a record must be made of such discussions, and it must be made available after the litigation has been concluded. The law has been held to apply only to a meeting of two or more public officials at which decision making, as opposed to fact-finding or information gathering, will occur. At the point where decisions are being made, such discussions must be conducted in public meetings after notice to the public. In an early opinion construing the law, a Florida appellate court held that a junior college president was neither a "board" or "commission" nor an alter ego of the college board of trustees. Accordingly, the court held that he was outside the ambit of the Sunshine Law and was not required to open his meetings with representatives of career employees of the college.[83]

THE LAW OF PUBLIC EMPLOYMENT

Public officers hold positions created by federal and state constitutions or statutes. To be eligible to be elected or appointed to a public office, one must possess the qualifications prescribed by law. When a period of residency in a given state or locality is a prerequisite, such requirement is generally upheld by courts if it is of a reasonable duration. Likewise, prohibiting one who has been convicted of a felony involving moral turpitude from holding a public office is usually acceptable to courts. A public officer also is required to take an oath to uphold the U.S. Constitution before assuming official duties as a member of Congress, as a member of a state legislature, or as a federal or state executive or judicial officer. States require the oath to include the obligation to uphold the constitution of the state. The U.S. Constitution also stipulates that no religious test may be required to hold office.[84]

The Civil Service

Historically, public employees at all levels of government served at the pleasure of chief executives. Under the so-called **spoils system**, mayors, governors, and presidents had virtually total discretion in hiring and firing government employees. However, beginning in 1883, the federal government enacted civil service laws and regulations to establish a merit system of employment, promotion, and discharge of public employees. The creation of this system was spurred by public outcry in the aftermath of President Garfield's 1881 assassination by Charles Guiteau, a man who felt that he was entitled to a government job because he had campaigned for Garfield.

Today, numerous federal statutes regulate federal civil service. The Office of Personnel Management is responsible for the general administration of the federal **civil service** system. The Merit Systems Protection Board is charged with adjudicating employment issues involving federal civil service employees. States and their political subdivisions, and in many instances municipalities, have emulated the federal system. Even so, civil service laws at the local level often apply to limited classes of employees, for example, police, firefighters, and other public safety officers.

In 1978, Congress enacted the Civil Service Reform Act, which provides a statutory basis for collective bargaining by federal government employees through their unions. Federal employees, however, have long been forbidden from striking against the federal government.[85] Many states now allow public employees to bargain collectively but uniformly restrict them from striking. Nevertheless, in recent years, some strikes have taken place.

Public officers and employees also are uniformly prohibited from furthering their own interest through public employment. For example, federal employees are barred from lobbying and are limited in their participation in proceedings affecting the federal government.[86] Many states have similar laws.

Discrimination and Harassment

Title VII of the Civil Rights Act of 1964, as amended, prohibits employment discrimination on the basis of race, religion, or sex. These prohibitions apply to federal, state, and local agencies as well as to the private sector.[87] Actionable issues include racial and gender discrimination in hiring and promotions, including the controversial question of affirmative action, as well as racial and sexual harassment. (For more discussion of civil rights issues in the workplace, see Chapter 11.)

Constitutional Issues

Public employees cannot be dismissed merely for exercising their constitutional rights. In *Pickering v. Board of Education* (1968), a public school teacher was dismissed for sending a letter to a newspaper criticizing the board of education. On review of her dismissal, the Supreme Court held that a public employee cannot be discharged for

CASE IN POINT

DO AIR TRAFFIC CONTROLLERS HAVE THE RIGHT TO STRIKE?
Professional Air Traffic Controllers Organization v. Federal Labor Relations Authority
United States Court of Appeals for the District of Columbia Circuit
685 F.2d 547 (D.C. Cir. 1982)

The Professional Air Traffic Controllers Organization (PATCO) was the recognized exclusive bargaining representative for air traffic controllers employed by the Federal Aviation Administration. Following a breakdown in negotiations for a new contract, PATCO announced a strike deadline, and on August 3, 1981, more than 70 percent of the nation's federally employed air traffic controllers walked off the job. The FAA revoked PATCO's status as bargaining representative and obtained a restraining order against the strike. This was followed by civil and criminal contempt citations when the restraining order was not heeded. The Federal Labor Relations Authority (FLRA) upheld the FAA's actions and eventually the case came before the U.S. Court of Appeals for the District of Columbia Circuit. In 1985, that court upheld the FLRA's actions in revoking PATCO's status as union representative for the Air Traffic Controllers.

comments in exercise of First Amendment rights.[88] In 1987, the Court reaffirmed this holding in the context of a case where a clerical worker in a Texas constable's office was fired after making an intemperate political remark.[89] When Ardith McPherson heard that John Hinckley had tried unsuccessfully to kill President Reagan, she said, "If they go for him again, I hope they get him." The Supreme Court held that her dismissal violated the First Amendment.

However, in a 2006 case, *Garcetti v. Ceballos*,[90] the Court placed some limitations on the First Amendment rights of public employees. Ceballos, a deputy district attorney in the Los Angeles County District Attorney's office, said that he had not received a promotion because of comments that he made about a search warrant's validity; thus, he claimed a violation of his right to free speech. The Supreme Court rejected his argument, noting that when public officials make comments related to their jobs, they are not entitled to First Amendment protections, and therefore, can be disciplined for what they say. Even so, the *Garcetti* case did not disturb the ability of public employees to speak, as citizens, about matters unconnected to their jobs. As a result, the precedents mentioned in the previous paragraph are still valid.

Another of the more controversial constitutional questions involving public employees today is drug testing. Many local, state, and federal agencies, especially in the field of law enforcement, require their employees to submit to periodic or random drug testing as a condition of employment or promotion. The Supreme Court has recognized that drug testing by public agencies is a form of search and is therefore subject to challenge under the Fourth Amendment. But at the same time, the Court has upheld drug testing of Customs Inspectors, who are directly involved in drug interdiction.[91] In 1997, though, the Court struck down a Georgia law requiring all candidates for state office to submit to drug tests.[92] Between the two decisions lies a gray area that is now the subject of considerable litigation in state and federal courts.

Malfeasance, Misfeasance, and Nonfeasance

An employee may be discharged for **malfeasance** involving commission of illegal acts under "color of office." An employee also may be dismissed for **misfeasance**, that is, performing legal acts in an improper or illegal manner, or for **nonfeasance**, which is neglect of duties. Issues are currently arising as to whether a public employee can be discharged for failing to take a polygraph test or for refusing to take a drug test. There are conflicting court decisions on these matters, but the courts tend to uphold such requirements for law enforcement personnel.

CONCLUSION

Administrative law embraces the legal rules that govern administrative and regulatory agencies at all levels of government. Agencies bring expertise to focus on special areas of governmental concern. Indeed, they have become indispensable to the functioning of modern government. In general, agencies are reasonably diligent and efficient in performing the essential functions of rulemaking and adjudication.

However, despite its efficiency and expertise, "the bureaucracy" often suffers the wrath of the citizenry because of its insulation from direct political control. One of the great challenges of modern democratic government, it follows, is to make the bureaucracy function with regard to the traditional rule of law and constitutional protections, while at the same time preserving the discretion and flexibility necessary to address the constantly changing demands of society. Ultimately, this is the purpose of administrative law.

SUMMARY OF KEY CONCEPTS

Because of their pervasive influence in the social and economic life of American citizens, administrative agencies have been termed by some commentators as "America's Fourth Branch of Government." Others simply refer to the federal and state administrative framework as the "bureaucracy." But an overview of the American legal system is incomplete without considering the role of administrative law, which governs such administrative agencies as the Social Security Administration and such regulatory agencies as the Securities and Exchange Commission and the Food and Drug Administration.

In this last chapter, we have endeavored to depict for the student how, under the American constitutional system—even though Congress and the state legislatures make the law—the nation's vast social and economic problems demand that an increasingly large degree of authority be delegated to experts in various fields. Many criticize such delegation, but who would opt to have elected officials control the Nuclear Regulatory Commission? At the federal level, through legislative and executive control of budgeting and oversight over rulemaking, Congress and the President maintain a degree of authority over administrative agencies. The Supreme Court and the lower federal courts also exercise substantial control over federal agencies through judicial review.

In carrying out their functions, administrative agencies conduct investigations within the scope of their regulatory authority as they grant and revoke licenses and permits and issue orders. Where necessary, agencies impose administrative fines and bring civil suits to enforce compliance with their directives. Under certain conditions, citizens can initiate enforcement. When an agency seeks to impose a criminal penalty, though, it must refer the matter to other governmental authorities.

Agencies adjudicate disputes through informal and formal proceedings. Interested parties must be afforded due process of law, but administrative due process is a flexible concept that depends on the magnitude of issues being resolved. In most instances, aggrieved parties who have standing and who have exhausted their administrative remedies may seek judicial review of final agency actions. Delegation of authority to administrative agencies also has given rise to many constitutional issues as to whether delegation is warranted and whether agency rules, directives, and orders result from actions that have afforded interested parties due process of law.

To effectively participate in a democratic society, a citizen must have access to information concerning the government. To further this end, at the federal level, Congress adopted the Freedom of Information Act as well as the Government in the Sunshine Act, which requires federal agencies to hold their meetings in public. Many states have companion laws.

Ultimately, most federal and many state career employees fall beneath the scope of civil service laws, which provide a merit system of employment, promotion, and discharge. The Civil Rights Act of 1964 and other legislation and regulations prohibit sexual harassment and protect these public employees from discrimination because of race, religion, gender, and disability.

Although this chapter has illustrated the processes of administrative law primarily from a federal standpoint, state and local administrative agencies function in a manner that is parallel to many of the principles and the processes we have discussed. State and local agencies tend to focus on licensing, permitting, franchising, land-use zoning, and ratemaking. Additionally, due process of law in state and local administrative proceedings and judicial review in state courts closely parallel those issues at the federal level. In the end, decisions from all of these legal entities can have a dramatic impact in shaping the American legal system.

FOR FURTHER READING

Cooper, Philip, *Public Law and Public Administration* (4th ed., F.E. Peacock Publishers 2000).

Davis, Kenneth Culp, *Discretionary Justice* (Louisiana State University Press 1969).

Kerwin, Cornelius M., *Rulemaking: How Government Agencies Write Law and Make Public Policy* (3d ed., CQ Press 2003).

Rohr, John, *To Run a Constitution: The Legitimacy of the Administrative State* (University of Kansas Press 1986).

Scheb, John M., and John M. Scheb II, *Law and the Administrative Process* (Wadsworth 2004).

Shapiro, Martin, *Who Guards the Guardians? Judicial Control of Administration* (University of Georgia Press 1988).

Sunstein, Cass R., *After the Rights Revolution: Reconceiving the Regulatory State* (Harvard University Press 1990).

Warren, Kenneth F., *Administrative Law in the American Political System* (West 1982).

Wilson, James Q., *Bureaucracy: What Government Agencies Do and Why They Do It* (Basic Books 1991).

QUESTIONS FOR THOUGHT AND DISCUSSION

1. Evaluate the following statement made by former Supreme Court Justice Robert Jackson: "Administrative agencies have become a veritable fourth branch of government, which has deranged our three-branch legal theories as much as the concept of a fourth dimension unsettles our three-dimensional thinking."

2. Why has Congress found it necessary to delegate so much of the responsibility for public policymaking to regulatory agencies?

3. Why did the Supreme Court hold that the Food and Drug Administration lacked the authority to regulate the marketing of tobacco products?

4. What was the Supreme Court's rationale for declaring the legislative veto unconstitutional? How does Congress maintain a measure of control over administrative action of which it disapproves?

5. Explain the premise of, procedures under, and exceptions to the Freedom of Information Act.

6. What are the essential elements of administrative due process?

7. What are the general principles governing judicial review of agency actions? Be sure to discuss both access to judicial review and review on the merits.

8. Is government in the sunshine always consistent with good policymaking?

9. Under what circumstances can public employees lawfully be dismissed?

10. What is the ultimate goal of administrative law?

KEY TERMS

adjudicatory procedures
administrative agencies
administrative detention
administrative law
administrative law judges
administrative search warrants
administrative searches
cease and desist orders
civil service

cost-benefit analyses
delegations of power
deportation
disclosure of information
due process of law
enabling legislation
exhaustion of remedies
forfeiture
formal adjudication

garnishment
improper disclosure of personal information
informal adjudication
judicial review of agency actions
jurisdiction
legislative veto
levy
malfeasance

misfeasance
nonfeasance
notice of proposed rulemaking
open meetings
preclearance
quasi-judicial bodies
qui tam action

regulatory agencies
rulemaking
rulemaking authority
separation of powers
spoils system
standing

statutory preclusion of judicial
 review
substantial evidence
sunshine laws
warrantless administrative searches
warrantless inspections

ENDNOTES

1. Another important distinction is that between "independent agencies" and those that are located within the major departments of the executive branch. For example, at the federal level, the Food and Drug Administration is located within the Department of Health and Human Services, whereas the Consumer Products Safety Commission is an independent agency. Similarly, the Occupational Safety and Health Administration is located within the Department of Labor. The Environmental Protection Agency, by contrast, is an independent regulatory agency.

2. *Food & Drug Admin. v. Brown & Williamson Tobacco Corp.*, 529 U.S. 120, 120 S. Ct. 1291, 146 L. Ed. 2d 121 (2000).

3. *Sea World v. Perez*, U.S. Court of Appeals for the D.C. Circuit, April 11, 2014; opinion available at: http://www.cadc .uscourts.gov/internet/opinions.nsf/5AF8A4C12F19AE21852 57CB700516292/$file/12-1375-1487925.pdf.

4. *J.W. Hampton & Co. v. United States*, 276 U.S. 394, 406, 48 S. Ct. 348, 351, 72 L. Ed. 624, 629 (1928).

5. *A.L.A. Schechter Poultry Corp. v. United States*, 295 U.S. 495, 55 S. Ct. 837, 79 L. Ed. 1570 (1935).

6. Cass Sunstein, "Constitutionalism after the New Deal," 101 *Harv. L. Rev.* 421, 447-448 (1987).

7. Gary Lawson, "The Rise and Rise of the Administrative State," 107 *Harv. L. Rev.* 1231, 1237 (1994).

8. *American Textile Mfrs. Institute v. Donovan*, 452 U.S. 490, 101 S. Ct. 2478, 69 L. Ed. 2d 185 (1981).

9. 452 U.S. at 547, 101 S. Ct. at 2509, 60 L. Ed. 2d at 225 (1981).

10. 488 U.S. 361, 109 S. Ct. 647, 102 L. Ed. 2d 714 (1989).

11. 488 U.S. at 427, 109 S. Ct. at 683, 102 L. Ed. 2d at 765.

12. *INS. v. Chadha*, 462 U.S. 919, 103 S. Ct. 2764, 77 L. Ed. 2d 317 (1983).

13. *Mead v. Arnell*, 791 P.2d 410 (Idaho 1990).

14. *See* 5 U.S.C. §801 et seq.

15. Kenneth Culp Davis, *Discretionary Justice: A Preliminary Inquiry* 27 (1969).

16. *See* 5 U.S.C. §553.

17. 5 U.S.C. §533b.

18. 15 U.S.C. §2601.

19. *See* 21 U.S.C. §355.

20. *See* 5 U.S.C. §600 et seq.

21. Exec. Order No. 12044.

22. Exec. Order No. 12291.

23. *Vermont Yankee Nuclear Power Corp. v. Natural Res. Defense Council, Inc.*, 435 U.S. 519, 98 S. Ct. 1197, 55 L. Ed. 2d 460 (1978).

24. 435 U.S. at 548, 98 S. Ct. at 1214, 55 L. Ed. 2d at 482.

25. *Gonzales v. Oregon*, 546 U.S. 243, 126 S. Ct. 904, 163 L. Ed. 2d 748 (2006).

26. In discussing this deference, the opinion in *Gonzales v. Oregon* referred to two previous cases: *Chevron U.S.A. v. Natural Resource Defense Council*, 467 U.S. 837, 104 S. Ct. 2778, 81 L. Ed. 2d 694 (1984); and *Auer v. Robbins*, 519 U.S. 452, 117 S. Ct. 905, 137 L. Ed. 2d 79 (1997).

27. *Murphy v. Waterfront Commn.*, 378 U.S. 52, 84 S. Ct. 1594, 12 L. Ed. 2d 678 (1964).

28. *Interstate Commerce Commn. v. Brimson*, 154 U.S. 447, 14 S. Ct. 1125, 38 L. Ed. 1047 (1894).

29. *Frank v. Maryland*, 359 U.S. 360, 79 S. Ct. 804, 3 L. Ed. 2d 877 (1959).

30. *See, e.g., Camara v. Municipal Court*, 387 U.S. 523, 87 S. Ct. 1727, 18 L. Ed. 2d 930 (1967), *overruling Frank v. Maryland*, 359 U.S. 360, 79 S. Ct. 804, 3 L. Ed. 2d 877 (1959).

31. *Colonnade Catering Corp. v. United States*, 397 U.S. 72, 90 S. Ct. 774, 25 L. Ed. 2d 60 (1970).

32. *New York v. Burger*, 482 U.S. 691, 107 S. Ct. 2636, 96 L. Ed. 2d 601 (1987).

33. *United States v. Biswell*, 406 U.S. 311, 315-17, 92 S. Ct. 1593, 32 L. Ed. 2d 87 (1972).

34. *Donovan v. Dewey*, 452 U.S. 594, 101 S. Ct. 2534, 69 L. Ed. 2d 262 (1981).

35. 436 U.S. 307, 98 S. Ct. 1816, 56 L. Ed. 2d 305 (1978).

36. *Donovan v. Dewey*, 452 U.S. 594, 101 S. Ct. 2534, 69 L. Ed. 2d 262 (1981).

37. *New York v. Burger*, 482 U.S. 691, 107 S. Ct. 2636, 96 L. Ed. 2d 601 (1987).

38. *See* 8 U.S.C. §1181 et seq.

39. 8 U.S.C. §1226a.

40. 8 U.S.C. §1226e.

41. The counterargument is that illegal immigrants, as persons within the jurisdiction of the United States, should be provided due process of law; *see Zadvydas v. Davis*, 533 U.S. 678, 121 S. Ct. 2491, 150 L. Ed. 2d 653 (2001).

42. 42 U.S.C. §2000a-5.

43. *Ridgeway v. Flagstar Corp.*, 1994 WL 665414 (N.D. Cal. 1994).

44. *See* Section 17(a) of the Securities Act of 1933, Section 10(b) of the Securities Exchange Act of 1934, and SEC Rule 10b-5.

45. *Gwaltney v. Chesapeake Bay Found.*, 484 U.S. 49, 108 S. Ct. 376, 98 L. Ed. 2d 306 (1987).

46. 31 U.S.C. §§3729-3733.

47. For a list of False Claims Act settlements from 2000-2014, *see* the following document from Crowell & Moring LLP: http://www.crowell.com/files/false-claims-act-fca-settlements-crowell-moring.pdf.

48. *Massachusetts v. EPA*, 549 U.S. 497, 127 S. Ct. 1438, 167, L. Ed. 2d 248 (2007).

49. *Utility Air v. EPA*, 570 U.S. _____ (2014).

50. *See* Internal Revenue Code, 26 U.S.C. §§1-1563.

51. *See, e.g.*, 21 U.S.C. §881.

52. *Austin v. United States*, 509 U.S. 602, 113 S. Ct. 2801, 125 L. Ed. 2d 488 (1993).

53. 509 U.S. at 622, 113 S. Ct. at 2812, 125 L. Ed. 2d at 505.

54. *United States v. James Daniel Good Real Prop.*, 510 U.S. 43, 114 S. Ct. 492, 128 L. Ed. 2d 490 (1992).

55. 5 U.S.C. §554b.

56. 5 U.S.C. §554c.

57. 5 U.S.C. §554(a).

58. For more information on administrative judges and ALJs, *see* Verkuil, "Reflections Upon the Federal Administrative Judiciary," 39 *UCLA L. Rev.* 1341 (1992).

59. *See* M. Redish & L. Marshall, "Adjudicatory Independence and the Values of Procedural Due Process," 95 *Yale L.J.* 455 (1986).

60. *See* 5 U.S.C. §§551-559, 701-706, 3105, 3344, 5372, 7521.

61. 397 U.S. 254, 90 S. Ct. 1011, 25 L. Ed. 2d 287 (1970).

62. 419 U.S. 565, 95 S. Ct. 729, 42 L. Ed. 2d 725 (1975).

63. *Mathews v. Eldridge*, 424 U.S. 319, 334, 96 S. Ct. 893, 902, 47 L. Ed. 2d 18, 33 (1976).

64. 547 U.S 220, 126 S. Ct. 708, 164 L. Ed. 2d 415 (2006).

65. 459 F.3d 705 (6th Cir. 2006).

66. 459 F.3d at 711.

67. *Thunder Basin Coal Co. v. Reich*, 510 U.S. 200, 114 S. Ct. 771, 127 L. Ed. 2d 79 (1994).

68. *Webster v. Doe*, 486 U.S. 592, 108 S. Ct. 2047, 100 L. Ed. 2d 632 (1988).

69. 5 U.S.C. §702.

70. 548 U.S. 81, 126 S. Ct. 2378, 165 L. Ed. 2d 368 (2006).

71. 548 U.S. at 91, 126 S. Ct. at 2386, 165 L. Ed. 2d at 378.

72. *Frothingham v. Mellon*, cited as *Massachusetts v. Mellon*, 262 U.S. 447, 43 S. Ct. 497, 87 L. Ed. 1078 (1923), the two cases having been consolidated.

73. *Sierra Club v. Morton*, 405 U.S. 727, 92 S. Ct. 1361, 31 L. Ed. 2d 636 (1972).

74. *See, e.g., United States v. Students Challenging Regulatory Agency Procedures*, 412 U.S. 669, 93 S. Ct. 2405, 37 L. Ed. 2d 254 (1973).

75. *Chevron U.S.A. v. Natural Res. Defense Council*, 467 U.S. 837, 104 S. Ct. 2778, 81 L. Ed. 2d 694 (1984).

76. *See, for example, Bob Jones University v. United States*, 461 U.S. 574, 103 S. Ct. 2017, 76 L. Ed. 2d 157 (1983), where the Court upheld a decision of the Internal Revenue Service to deny tax-exempt status to a private religious college that practiced racial discrimination.

77. 5 U.S.C. §552.

78. 458 F.3d 194 (3d Cir. 2006).

79. The document can be viewed at: http://www.washington post.com/r/2010-2019/WashingtonPost/2014/06/23/National-Security/Graphics/memodrones.pdf. The case is from the U.S. Court of Appeals for the 2nd Circuit: *New York Times v. United States Department of Justice*, decided April 21, 2014; citation: 2014 U.S. App. LEXIS 7387.

80. 5 U.S.C. §552b(b).

81. Fla. Stat. ch. 286.

82. *News-Press Publg. Co. v. Carlson*, 410 So. 2d 546 (Fla. App. 1982).

83. *Bennett v. Warden*, 333 So. 2d 97 (Fla. App. 1976).

84. U.S. Const. art. VI, §3.

85. 5 U.S.C. §7311.

86. 18 U.S.C. §207.

87. 42 U.S.C. §2000e.

88. 391 U.S. 563, 88 S. Ct. 1731, 20 L. Ed. 2d 811 (1968).

89. *Rankin v. McPherson*, 483 U.S. 378, 107 S. Ct. 2891, 97 L. Ed. 2d 315 (1987).

90. *Garcetti v. Ceballos*, 547 U.S. 210, 126 S. Ct. 1951, 164 L. Ed. 2d 689 (2006).

91. *National Treasury Employees Union v. Von Raab*, 489 U.S. 656, 109 S. Ct. 1384, 103 L. Ed. 2d 685 (1989).

92. *Chandler v. Miller*, 520 U.S. 305, 117 S. Ct. 1295, 137 L. Ed. 2d 513 (1997).

THE CONSTITUTION OF THE UNITED STATES OF AMERICA

APPENDIX

A

We the People of the United States, in Order to form a more perfect Union, establish Justice, insure domestic Tranquility, provide for the common defence, promote the general Welfare, and secure the Blessings of Liberty to ourselves and our Posterity, do ordain and establish this Constitution for the United States of America.

ARTICLE I

Section 1

All legislative Powers herein granted shall be vested in a Congress of the United States, which shall consist of a Senate and House of Representatives.

Section 2

(1) The House of Representatives shall be composed of Members chosen every second Year by the People of the several States, and the Electors in each State shall have the Qualifications requisite for Electors of the most numerous Branch of the State Legislature.

(2) No Person shall be a Representative who shall not have attained to the age of twenty-five Years, and been seven Years a Citizen of the United States, and who shall not, when elected, be an Inhabitant of that State in which he shall be chosen.

(3) Representatives and direct Taxes shall be apportioned among the several States which may be included within this Union, according to their respective Numbers, which shall be determined by adding to the whole Number of free Persons, including those bound to Service for a Term of Years, and excluding Indians not taxed, three fifths of all other Persons. The actual Enumeration shall be made within three Years after the

first Meeting of the Congress of the United States, and within every subsequent Term of ten Years, in such Manner as they shall by Law direct. The Number of Representatives shall not exceed one for every thirty Thousand, but each State shall have at Least one Representative; and until such enumeration shall be made, the State of New Hampshire shall be entitled to chuse three, Massachusetts eight, Rhode Island and Providence Plantations one, Connecticut five, New York six, New Jersey four, Pennsylvania eight, Delaware one, Maryland six, Virginia ten, North Carolina five, South Carolina five, and Georgia three.

(4) When vacancies happen in the Representation from any State, the Executive Authority thereof shall issue Writs of Election to fill such Vacancies.

(5) The House of Representatives shall chuse their Speaker and other Officers; and shall have the sole Power of Impeachment.

Section 3

(1) The Senate of the United States shall be composed of two Senators from each State, chosen by the Legislature thereof, for six Years; and each Senator shall have one Vote.

(2) Immediately after they shall be assembled in Consequence of the first Election, they shall be divided as equally as may be into three Classes. The Seats of the Senators of the first Class shall be vacated at the Expiration of the second Year, of the second Class at the Expiration of the fourth Year, and of the third Class at the Expiration of the sixth Year, so that one third may be chosen every second Year; and if Vacancies happen by Resignation, or otherwise, during the Recess of the Legislature of any State, the Executive thereof may make temporary Appointments until the next Meeting of the Legislature, which shall then fill such Vacancies.

(3) No Person shall be a Senator who shall not have attained, to the Age of thirty Years, and been nine Years a Citizen of the United States, and who shall not, when elected, be an Inhabitant of that State for which he shall be chosen.

(4) The Vice President of the United States shall be President of the Senate, but shall have no Vote, unless they be equally divided.

(5) The Senate shall chuse their other Officers, and also a President pro tempore, in the Absence of the Vice President, or when he shall exercise the Office of the President of the United States.

(6) The Senate shall have the sole Power to try all Impeachments. When sitting for that Purpose, they shall be on Oath or Affirmation. When the President of the United States is tried, the Chief Justice shall preside: And no Person shall be convicted without the Concurrence of two thirds of the Members present.

(7) Judgment in Cases of Impeachment shall not extend further than to removal from Office, and disqualification to hold and enjoy any Office of honor, Trust or Profit under the United States: but the Party convicted shall nevertheless be liable and subject to Indictment, Trial, Judgment and Punishment, according to Law.

Section 4

(1) The Times, Places and Manner of holding Elections for Senators and Representatives, shall be prescribed in each State by the Legislature thereof; but the Congress may at any time by Law make or alter such Regulations, except as to the Places of chusing Senators.

(2) The Congress shall assemble at least once in every Year, and such Meeting shall be on the first Monday in December, unless they shall by Law appoint a different Day.

Section 5

(1) Each House shall be the Judge of the Elections, Returns and Qualifications of its own Members, and a Majority of each shall constitute a Quorum to do Business; but a smaller Number may adjourn from day to day, and may be authorized to compel the Attendance of absent Members, in such Manner, and under such Penalties as each House may provide.

(2) Each House may determine the Rules of its Proceedings, punish its Members for disorderly Behaviour, and, with the Concurrence of two thirds, expel a Member.

(3) Each House shall keep a Journal of its Proceedings, and from time to time publish the same, excepting such Parts as may in their Judgment require Secrecy; and the Yeas and Nays of the Members of either House on any question shall, at the Desire of one fifth of those Present, be entered on the Journal.

(4) Neither House, during the Session of Congress, shall, without the Consent of the other, adjourn for more than three days, nor to any other Place than that in which the two Houses shall be sitting.

Section 6

(1) The Senators and Representatives shall receive a Compensation for their Services, to be ascertained by Law, and paid out of the Treasury of the United States. They shall in all Cases, except Treason, Felony and Breach of the Peace, be privileged from Arrest during their Attendance at the Session of their respective Houses, and in going to and returning from the same; and for any Speech or Debate in either House, they shall not be questioned in any other Place.

(2) No Senator or Representative shall, during the Time for which he was elected, be appointed to any civil Office under the Authority of the United States, which shall have been created, or the Emoluments whereof shall have been increased during such time; and no Person holding any Office under the United States, shall be a Member of either House during his Continuance in Office.

Section 7

(1) All Bills for raising Revenue shall originate in the House of Representatives; but the Senate may propose or concur with Amendments as on other Bills.

(2) Every Bill which shall have passed the House of Representatives and the Senate, shall, before it become a Law, be presented to the President of the United States; If he approve he shall sign it, but if not he shall return it, with his Objections to that House in which it shall have originated, who shall enter the Objections at large on their Journal, and proceed to reconsider it. If after such Reconsideration two thirds of that House shall agree to pass the Bill, it shall be sent, together with the Objections, to the other House, by which it shall likewise be reconsidered, and if approved by two thirds of that House, it shall become a Law. But in all such Cases the Votes of both Houses shall be determined by Yeas and Nays, and the Names of the Persons voting for and against the Bill shall be entered on the Journal of each House respectively. If any Bill shall not be returned by

the President within ten Days (Sunday excepted) after it shall have been presented to him, the Same shall be a Law, in like Manner as if he had signed it, unless the Congress by their Adjournment prevent its Return, in which Case it shall not be a Law.

(3) Every Order, Resolution, or Vote to which the Concurrence of the Senate and House of Representatives may be necessary (except on a question of Adjournment) shall be presented to the President of the United States; and before the Same shall take Effect, shall be approved by him, or being disapproved by him, shall be repassed by two thirds of the Senate and House of Representatives, according to the Rules and Limitations prescribed in the Case of a Bill.

Section 8

(1) The Congress shall have Power To lay and collect Taxes, Duties, Imposts and Excises, to pay the Debts and provide for the common Defence and general Welfare of the United States; but all Duties, Imposts and Excises shall be uniform throughout the United States;

(2) To borrow Money on the credit of the United States;

(3) To regulate Commerce with foreign Nations, and among the several States, and with the Indian Tribes;

(4) To establish an uniform Rule of Naturalization, and uniform Laws on the subject of Bankruptcies throughout the United States;

(5) To coin Money, regulate the Value thereof, and of foreign Coin, and to fix the Standard of Weights and Measures;

(6) To provide for the Punishment of counterfeiting the Securities and current Coin of the United States;

(7) To establish Post Offices and post Roads;

(8) To promote the Progress of Science and useful Arts, by securing for limited Times to Authors and Inventors the exclusive Right to their respective Writings and Discoveries;

(9) To constitute Tribunals inferior to the supreme Court;

(10) To define and punish Piracies and Felonies committed on the high Seas, and Offenses against the Law of Nations;

(11) To declare War, grant Letters of Marque and Reprisal, and make Rules concerning Captures on Land and Water;

(12) To raise and support Armies, but no Appropriation of Money to that Use shall be for a longer Term than two Years;

(13) To provide and maintain a Navy;

(14) To make Rules for the Government and Regulation of the land and naval Forces;

(15) To provide for calling forth the Militia to execute the Laws of the Union, suppress Insurrections and repel Invasions;

(16) To provide for organizing, arming, and disciplining, the Militia, and for governing such Part of them as may be employed in the Service of the United States, reserving to the States respectively, the Appointment of the Officers, and the Authority of training the Militia according to the discipline prescribed by Congress;

(17) To exercise exclusive Legislation in all Cases whatsoever, over such District (not exceeding ten Miles square) as may, by Cession of particular States, and the Acceptance of Congress, become the Seat of the Government of the United States, and to exercise like Authority over all Places purchased by the Consent of the Legislature of the State in which the Same shall be, for the Erection of Forts, Magazines, Arsenals, dock-Yards, and other needful Buildings;—And

(18) To make all Laws which shall be necessary and proper for carrying into Execution the foregoing Powers, and all other Powers vested by this Constitution in the Government of the United States, or in any Department or Officer thereof.

Section 9

(1) The Migration or Importation of such Persons as any of the States now existing shall think proper to admit, shall not be prohibited by the Congress prior to the Year one thousand eight hundred and eight, but a Tax or Duty may be imposed on such Importation, not exceeding ten dollars for each Person.

(2) The Privilege of the Writ of Habeas Corpus shall not be suspended unless when in Cases of Rebellion or Invasion the public Safety may require it.

(3) No Bill of Attainder or ex post facto Law shall be passed.

(4) No Capitation, or other direct, Tax shall be laid, unless in Proportion to the Census or Enumeration herein before directed to be taken.

(5) No Tax or Duty shall be laid on Articles exported from any State.

(6) No Preference shall be given by any Regulation of Commerce or Revenue to the Ports of one State over those of another; nor shall Vessels bound to, or from, one State, be obliged to enter, clear or pay Duties in another.

(7) No Money shall be drawn from the Treasury, but in Consequence of Appropriations made by Law; and a regular Statement and Account of the Receipts and Expenditures of all public Money shall be published from time to time.

(8) No Title of Nobility shall be granted by the United States: And no Person holding any Office of Profit or Trust under them, shall, without the Consent of the Congress, accept of any present, Emolument, Office, or Title, of any kind whatever, from any King, Prince or foreign State.

Section 10

(1) No State shall enter into any Treaty, Alliance, or Confederation; grant Letters of Marque and Reprisal; coin Money; emit Bills of Credit; make any Thing but gold and silver Coin a Tender in Payment of Debts; pass any Bill of Attainder, ex post facto Law, or Law impairing the Obligation of Contracts, or grant any Title of Nobility.

(2) No State shall, without the Consent of Congress, lay any Imposts or Duties on Imports or Exports, except what may be absolutely necessary for executing its inspection Laws: and the net Produce of all Duties and Imposts, laid by any State on Imports or Exports, shall be for the Use of the Treasury of the United States; and all such Laws shall be subject to the Revision and Control of the Congress.

(3) No State shall, without the Consent of Congress, lay any Duty of Tonnage, keep Troops, or Ships of War in time of Peace, enter into any Agreement or Compact with

another State, or with a foreign Power, or engage in War, unless actually invaded, or in such imminent Danger as will not admit of Delay.

ARTICLE II

Section 1

(1) The executive Power shall be vested in a President of the United States of America. He shall hold his Office during the Term of four Years, and, together with the Vice President, chosen for the same Term, be elected, as follows:

(2) Each State shall appoint, in such Manner as the Legislature thereof may direct, a Number of Electors, equal to the whole Number of Senators and Representatives to which the State may be entitled in the Congress: but no Senator or Representative, or Person holding an Office of Trust or Profit under the United States, shall be appointed an Elector.

The Electors shall meet in their respective States, and vote by Ballot for two Persons, of whom one at least shall not be an Inhabitant of the same State with themselves. And they shall make a List of all the Persons voted for, and of the Number of Votes for each; which List they shall sign and certify, and transmit sealed to the Seat of the Government of the United States, directed to the President of the Senate. The President of the Senate shall, in the presence of the Senate and House of Representatives, open all the Certificates, and the Votes shall then be counted. The Person having the greatest Number of Votes shall be the President, if such Number be a Majority of the whole Number of Electors appointed; and if there be more than one who have such Majority, and have an equal Number of Votes, then the House of Representatives shall immediately chuse by Ballot one of them for President; and if no Person have a Majority, then from the five highest on the List the said House shall in like Manner chuse the President. But in chusing the President, the Votes shall be taken by States, the Representation from each State having one Vote; a quorum for this Purpose shall consist of a Member or Members from two thirds of the States, and a Majority of all the States shall be necessary to a Choice. In every Case, after the Choice of the President, the Person having the greatest Number of Votes of the Electors shall be the Vice President. But if there should remain two or more who have equal Votes, the Senate shall chuse from them by Ballot the Vice President.

(3) The Congress may determine the Time of chusing the Electors, and the Day on which they shall give their Votes; which Day shall be the same throughout the United States.

(4) No Person except a natural born Citizen, or a Citizen of the United States, at the time of the Adoption of this Constitution, shall be eligible to the Office of President; neither shall any Person be eligible to that Office who shall not have attained to the Age of thirty five Years, and been fourteen Years a Resident within the United States.

(5) In Case of the Removal of the President from Office, or of his Death, Resignation, or Inability to discharge the Powers and Duties of the said Office, the Same shall devolve on the Vice President, and the Congress may by Law provide for the Case of

Removal, Death, Resignation or Inability, both of the President and Vice President, declaring what Officer shall then act as President, and such Officer shall act accordingly, until the Disability be removed, or a President shall be elected.

(6) The President shall, at stated Times, receive for his Services, a Compensation, which shall neither be increased nor diminished during the Period for which he shall have been elected, and he shall not receive within that Period any other Emolument from the United States, or any of them.

(7) Before he enter on the Execution of his Office, he shall take the following Oath or Affirmation: — "I do solemnly swear (or affirm) that I will faithfully execute the Office of President of the United States, and will to the best of my Ability, preserve, protect and defend the Constitution of the United States."

Section 2

(1) The President shall be Commander in Chief of the Army and Navy of the United States, and of the Militia of the several States, when called into the actual Service of the United States; he may require the Opinion, in writing, of the principal Officer in each of the executive Departments, upon any Subject relating to the Duties of their respective Offices, and he shall have Power to grant Reprieves and Pardons for Offenses against the United States, except in Cases of Impeachment.

(2) He shall have Power, by and with the Advice and Consent of the Senate, to make Treaties, provided two thirds of the Senators present concur; and he shall nominate, and by and with the Advice and Consent of the Senate, shall appoint Ambassadors, other public Ministers and Consuls, Judges of the supreme Court, and all other Officers of the United States, whose Appointments are not herein otherwise provided for, and which shall be established by Law: but the Congress may by Law vest the Appointment of such inferior Officers, as they think proper, in the President alone, in the Courts of Law, or in the Heads of Departments.

(3) The President shall have Power to fill up all Vacancies that may happen during the Recess of the Senate, by granting Commissions which shall expire at the End of their next Session.

Section 3

He shall from time to time give to the Congress Information of the State of the Union, and recommend to their Consideration such Measures as he shall judge necessary and expedient; he may, on extraordinary Occasions, convene both Houses, or either of them, and in Case of Disagreement between them, with Respect to the Time of Adjournment, he may adjourn them to such Time as he shall think proper; he shall receive Ambassadors and other public Ministers; he shall take Care that the Laws be faithfully executed, and shall Commission all the Officers of the United States.

Section 4

The President, Vice President and all Civil Officers of the United States, shall be removed from Office on Impeachment for, and Conviction of, Treason, Bribery, or other high Crimes and Misdemeanors.

ARTICLE III

Section 1
The judicial Power of the United States, shall be vested in one supreme Court, and in such inferior Courts as the Congress may from time to time ordain and establish. The Judges, both of the supreme and inferior Courts, shall hold their Offices during good Behaviour, and shall, at stated Times, receive for their Services, a Compensation, which shall not be diminished during their Continuance in Office.

Section 2
(1) The judicial Power shall extend to all Cases, in Law and Equity, arising under this Constitution, the Laws of the United States, and Treaties made, or which shall be made, under their Authority;—to all Cases affecting Ambassadors, other public Ministers and Consuls;—to all Cases of admiralty and maritime Jurisdiction;—to Controversies to which the United States shall be a party;—to Controversies between two or more States;—between a State and Citizens of another State;—between Citizens of different States;—between Citizens of the same State claiming Lands under Grants of different States, and between a State, or the Citizens thereof, and foreign States, Citizens or Subjects.

(2) In all Cases affecting Ambassadors, other public Ministers and Consuls, and those in which a State shall be Party, the supreme Court shall have original Jurisdiction. In all the other Cases before mentioned, the supreme Court shall have appellate Jurisdiction, both as to Law and Fact, with such Exceptions, and under such Regulations as the Congress shall make.

(3) The Trial of all Crimes, except in Cases of Impeachment, shall be by Jury; and such Trial shall be held in the State where the said Crimes shall have been committed; but when not committed within any State, the Trial shall be at such Place or Places as the Congress may by Law have directed.

Section 3
(1) Treason against the United States, shall consist only in levying War against them, or in adhering to their Enemies, giving them Aid and Comfort. No Person shall be convicted of Treason unless on the Testimony of two Witnesses to the same overt Act, or on Confession in open Court.

(2) The Congress shall have Power to declare the Punishment of Treason, but no Attainder of Treason shall work Corruption of Blood, or Forfeiture except during the Life of the Person attainted.

ARTICLE IV

Section 1
Full Faith and Credit shall be given in each State to the public Acts, Records, and judicial Proceedings of every other State. And the Congress may by general Laws

prescribe the Manner in which such Acts, Records and Proceedings shall be proved, and the Effect thereof.

Section 2

(1) The Citizens of each State shall be entitled to all privileges and Immunities of Citizens in the several States.

(2) A Person charged in any State with Treason, Felony, or other Crime, who shall flee from Justice, and be found in another State, shall on Demand of the executive Authority of the State from which he fled, be delivered up, to be removed to the State having Jurisdiction of the Crime.

(3) No Person held to Service of Labour in one State, under the Laws thereof, escaping into another, shall, in Consequence of any Law or Regulation therein, be discharged from such Service or Labour, but shall be delivered up on Claim of the Party to whom such Service or Labour may be due.

Section 3

(1) New States may be admitted by the Congress into this Union; but no new State shall be formed or erected within the Jurisdiction of any other State; nor any State be formed by the Junction of two or more States, or Parts of States, without the Consent of the Legislatures of the States concerned as well as of the Congress.

(2) The Congress shall have power to dispose of and make all needful Rules and Regulations respecting the Territory or other Property belonging to the United States; and nothing in this Constitution shall be so construed as to Prejudice any Claims of the United States, or of any particular State.

Section 4

The United States shall guarantee to every State in this Union a Republican Form of Government, and shall protect each of them against Invasion; and on Application of the Legislature, or of the Executive (when the Legislature cannot be convened) against domestic Violence.

ARTICLE V

The Congress, whenever two thirds of both Houses shall deem it necessary, shall propose Amendments to this Constitution, or, on the Application of the Legislatures of two thirds of the several States, shall call a Convention for proposing Amendments, which, in either Case, shall be valid to all Intents and Purposes, as Part of this Constitution, when ratified by the Legislatures of three fourths of the several States, or by Conventions in three fourths thereof, as the one or the other Mode of Ratification may be proposed by the Congress; Provided that no Amendment which may be made prior to the Year One thousand eight hundred and eight shall in any Manner affect the first and fourth Clauses in the Ninth Section of the first Article; and that no State, without its Consent, shall be deprived of its equal Suffrage in the Senate.

ARTICLE VI

(1) All Debts contracted and Engagements entered into, before the Adoption of this Constitution, shall be as valid against the United States under this Constitution, as under the Confederation.

(2) This Constitution, and the Laws of the United States which shall be made in Pursuance thereof; and all Treaties made, or which shall be made, under the Authority of the United States, shall be the supreme Law of the Land; and the Judges in every State shall be bound thereby, any Thing in the Constitution or Laws of any State to the Contrary notwithstanding.

(3) The Senators and Representatives before mentioned, and the Members of the several State Legislatures, and all executive and judicial Officers, both of the United States and of the several States, shall be bound by Oath or Affirmation, to support this Constitution; but no religious Test shall ever be required as a Qualification to any Office or public Trust under the United States.

ARTICLE VII

The Ratification of the Conventions of nine States, shall be sufficient for the Establishment of this Constitution between the States so ratifying the Same.

ARTICLES IN ADDITION TO, AND AMENDMENT OF, THE CONSTITUTION OF THE UNITED STATES OF AMERICA, PROPOSED BY CONGRESS, AND RATIFIED BY THE SEVERAL STATES, PURSUANT TO THE FIFTH ARTICLE OF THE ORIGINAL CONSTITUTION

AMENDMENT I (1791)

Congress shall make no law respecting an establishment of religion, or prohibiting the free exercise thereof; or abridging the freedom of speech, or of the press; or the right of the people peaceably to assemble, and to petition the Government for a redress of grievances.

AMENDMENT II (1791)

A well regulated Militia, being necessary to the security of a free state, the right of the people to keep and bear Arms, shall not be infringed.

AMENDMENT III (1791)

No Soldier shall, in time of peace be quartered in any house, without the consent of the Owner, nor in time of war, but in a manner to be prescribed by law.

AMENDMENT IV (1791)

The right of the people to be secure in their persons, houses, papers, and effects, against unreasonable searches and seizures, shall not be violated, and no Warrants shall issue, but upon probable cause, supported by Oath or affirmation, and particularly describing the place to be searched, and the persons or things to be seized.

AMENDMENT V (1791)

No person shall be held to answer for a capital, or otherwise infamous crime, unless on a presentment or indictment of a Grand Jury, except in cases arising in the land or naval forces, or in the Militia, when in actual service in time of War or public danger; nor shall any person be subject for the same offence to be twice put in jeopardy of life or limb; nor shall be compelled in any criminal case to be a witness against himself, nor be deprived of life, liberty, or property, without due process of law; nor shall private property be taken for public use, without just compensation.

AMENDMENT VI (1791)

In all criminal prosecutions, the accused shall enjoy the right to a speedy and public trial, by an impartial jury of the State and district wherein the crime shall have been committed, which district shall have been previously ascertained by law, and to be informed of the nature and cause of the accusation; to be confronted with the witnesses against him; to have compulsory process for obtaining witnesses in his favor, and to have the Assistance of Counsel for his defence.

AMENDMENT VII (1791)

In Suits at common law, where the value in controversy shall exceed twenty dollars, the right of trial by jury shall be preserved, and no fact tried by a jury, shall be otherwise re-examined in any Court of the United States, than according to the rules of the common law.

AMENDMENT VIII (1791)

Excessive bail shall not be required, nor excessive fines imposed, nor cruel and unusual punishments inflicted.

AMENDMENT IX (1791)

The enumeration in the Constitution, of certain rights, shall not be construed to deny or disparage others retained by the people.

AMENDMENT X (1791)

The powers not delegated to the United States by the Constitution, nor prohibited by it to the States, are reserved to the States respectively, or to the people.

AMENDMENT XI (1798)

The Judicial power of the United States shall not be construed to extend to any suit in law or equity, commenced or prosecuted against one of the United States by Citizens of another State, or by Citizens or Subjects of any Foreign State.

AMENDMENT XII (1804)

The Electors shall meet in their respective states and vote by ballot for President and Vice-President, one of whom, at least, shall not be an inhabitant of the same state with themselves; they shall name in their ballots the person voted for as President, and in distinct ballots the person voted for as Vice-President, and they shall make distinct lists of all persons voted for as President, and of all persons voted for as Vice-President, and of the number of votes for each, which lists they shall sign and certify, and transmit sealed to the seat of the government of the United States, directed to the President of the Senate;—The President of the Senate shall, in the presence of the Senate and House of Representatives, open all the certificates and the votes shall then be counted;—The person having the greatest number of votes for President, shall be the President, if such number be a majority of the whole number of Electors appointed; and if no person have such majority, then from the persons having the highest numbers not exceeding three on the list of those voted for as President, the House of Representatives shall choose immediately, by ballot, the President. But in choosing the President, the votes shall be taken by states, the representation from each state having one vote; a quorum for this purpose shall consist of a member or members from two-thirds of the states, and a majority of all the states shall be necessary to a choice. And if the House of Representatives shall not choose a President whenever the right of choice shall devolve upon them, before the fourth day of March next following, then the Vice-President shall act as President, as in the case of the death or other constitutional disability of the President—The person having the greatest number of votes as Vice-President, shall be the Vice-President, if such number be a majority of the whole number of Electors appointed, and if no person have a majority, then from the two highest numbers on the list, the Senate shall choose the Vice-President; A quorum for the purpose shall consist of two-thirds of the whole number of Senators, and a majority of the whole number shall be necessary to a choice. But no person constitutionally ineligible to the office of President shall be eligible to that of Vice-President of the United States.

AMENDMENT XIII (1865)

Section 1
Neither slavery nor involuntary servitude, except as a punishment for crime whereof the party shall have been duly convicted, shall exist within the United States, or any place subject to their jurisdiction.

Section 2
Congress shall have power to enforce this article by appropriate legislation.

AMENDMENT XIV (1868)

Section 1
All persons born or naturalized in the United States and subject to the jurisdiction thereof, are citizens of the United States and of the State wherein they reside. No State shall make or enforce any law which shall abridge the privileges or immunities of citizens of the United States; nor shall any State deprive any person of life, liberty, or property, without due process of law; nor deny to any person within its jurisdiction the equal protection of the laws.

Section 2
Representatives shall be apportioned among the several States according to their respective numbers, counting the whole number of persons in each State, excluding Indians not taxed. But when the right to vote at any election for the choice of electors for President and Vice-President of the United States, Representatives in Congress, the Executive and Judicial officers of a State, or the members of the Legislature thereof, is denied to any of the male inhabitants of such State, being twenty-one years of age, and citizens of the United States, or in any way abridged, except for participation in rebellion, or other crime, the basis of representation therein shall be reduced in the proportion which the number of such male citizens shall bear to the whole number of male citizens twenty-one years of age in such State.

Section 3
No person shall be a Senator or Representative in Congress, or elector of President and Vice-President, or hold any office, civil or military, under the United States, or under any State, who, having previously taken an oath, as a member of Congress, or as an officer of the United States, or as a member of any State legislature, or as an executive or judicial officer of any State, to support the Constitution of the United States, shall have engaged in insurrection or rebellion against the same, or given aid or comfort to the enemies thereof. But Congress may by a vote of two-thirds of each House, remove such disability.

Section 4

The validity of the public debt of the United States, authorized by law, including debts incurred for payment of pensions and bounties for services in suppressing insurrection or rebellion, shall not be questioned. But neither the United States nor any State shall assume or pay any debt or obligation incurred in aid of insurrection or rebellion against the United States, or any claim for the loss or emancipation of any slave; but all such debts, obligations and claims shall be held illegal and void.

Section 5

The Congress shall have power to enforce, by appropriate legislation, the provisions of this article.

AMENDMENT XV (1870)

Section 1

The right of citizens of the United States to vote shall not be denied or abridged by the United States or by any State on account of race, color, or previous condition of servitude.

Section 2

The Congress shall have power to enforce this article by appropriate legislation.

AMENDMENT XVI (1913)

The Congress shall have power to lay and collect taxes on incomes, from whatever source derived, without apportionment among the several States, and without regard to any census or enumeration.

AMENDMENT XVII (1913)

The Senate of the United States shall be composed of two Senators from each State, elected by the people thereof, for six years; and each Senator shall have one vote. The electors in each State shall have the qualifications requisite for electors of the most numerous branch of the State legislatures.

When vacancies happen in the representation of any State in the Senate, the executive authority of such State shall issue writs of election to fill such vacancies: Provided, That the legislature of any State may empower the executive thereof to make temporary appointments until the people fill the vacancies by election as the legislature may direct.

This amendment shall not be so construed as to affect the election or term of any Senator chosen before it becomes valid as part of the Constitution.

AMENDMENT XVIII (1919)

Section 1
After one year from the ratification of this article the manufacture, sale, or transportation of intoxicating liquors within, the importation thereof into, or the exportation thereof from the United States and all territory subject to the jurisdiction thereof for beverage purposes is hereby prohibited.

Section 2
The Congress and the several States shall have concurrent power to enforce this article by appropriate legislation.

Section 3
This article shall be inoperative unless it shall have been ratified as an amendment to the Constitution by the legislatures of the several States, as provided in the Constitution, within seven years from the date of the submission hereof to the States by the Congress.

AMENDMENT XIX (1920)

The right of citizens of the United States to vote shall not be denied or abridged by the United States or by any State on account of sex.

Congress shall have power to enforce this article by appropriate legislation.

AMENDMENT XX (1933)

Section 1
The terms of the President and Vice President shall end at noon on the 20th day of January, and the terms of Senators and Representatives at noon on the 3d day of January, of the years in which such terms would have ended if this article had not been ratified; and the terms of their successors shall then begin.

Section 2
The Congress shall assemble at least once in every year, and such meeting shall begin at noon on the 3d day of January, unless they shall by law appoint a different day.

Section 3

If, at the time fixed for the beginning of the term of the President, the President elect shall have died, the Vice President elect shall become President. If a President shall not have been chosen before the time fixed for the beginning of his term, or if the President elect shall have failed to qualify, then the Vice President elect shall act as President until a President shall have qualified; and the Congress may by law provide for the case wherein neither a President elect nor a Vice President elect shall have qualified, declaring who shall then act as President, or the manner in which one who is to act shall be selected, and such person shall act accordingly until a President or Vice President shall have qualified.

Section 4

The Congress may by law provide for the case of the death of any of the persons from whom the House of Representatives may choose a President whenever the right of choice shall have devolved upon them, and for the case of the death of any of the persons from whom the Senate may choose a Vice President whenever the right of choice shall have devolved upon them.

Section 5

Sections 1 and 2 shall take effect on the 15th day of October following the ratification of this article.

Section 6

This article shall be inoperative unless it shall have been ratified as an amendment to the Constitution by the legislatures of three-fourths of the several States within seven years from the date of its submission.

AMENDMENT XXI (1933)

Section 1

The eighteenth article of amendment to the Constitution of the United States is hereby repealed.

Section 2

The transportation or importation into any State, Territory or possession of the United States for delivery or use therein of intoxicating liquors, in violation of the laws thereof, is hereby prohibited.

Section 3

This article shall be inoperative unless it shall have been ratified as an amendment to the Constitution by conventions in the several States, as provided in the Constitution, within seven years from the date of the submission hereof to the States by the Congress.

AMENDMENT XXII (1951)

Section 1

No person shall be elected to the office of the President more than twice, and no person who has held the office of President, or acted as President, for more than two years of a term to which some other person was elected President shall be elected to the office of the President more than once. But this Article shall not apply to any person holding the office of President when this Article was proposed by the Congress, and shall not prevent any person who may be holding the office of President, or acting as President, during the term within which this Article becomes operative from holding the office of President or acting as President during the remainder of such term.

Section 2

This Article shall be inoperative unless it shall have been ratified as an amendment to the Constitution by the legislatures of three-fourths of the several States within seven years from the date of its submission to the States by the Congress.

AMENDMENT XXIII (1961)

Section 1

The District constituting the seat of Government of the United States shall appoint in such manner as the Congress may direct:

A number of electors of President and Vice President equal to the whole number of Senators and Representatives in Congress to which the District would be entitled if it were a State, but in no event more than the least populous State; they shall be in addition to those appointed by the States, but they shall be considered, for the purposes of the election of President and Vice President, to be electors appointed by a State; and they shall meet in the District and perform such duties as provided by the twelfth article of amendment.

Section 2

The Congress shall have power to enforce this article by appropriate legislation.

AMENDMENT XXIV (1964)

Section 1

The right of citizens of the United States to vote in any primary or other election for President or Vice President, for electors for President or Vice President, or for Senator or Representative in Congress, shall not be denied or abridged by the United States or any State by reason of failure to pay any poll tax or other tax.

Section 2
The Congress shall have power to enforce this article by appropriate legislation.

AMENDMENT XXV (1967)

Section 1
In case of the removal of the President from office or of his death or resignation, the Vice President shall become President.

Section 2
Whenever there is a vacancy in the office of the Vice President, the President shall nominate a Vice President who shall take office upon confirmation by a majority vote of both Houses of Congress.

Section 3
Whenever the President transmits to the President pro tempore of the Senate and the Speaker of the House of Representatives his written declaration that he is unable to discharge the powers and duties of his office, and until he transmits to them a written declaration to the contrary, such powers and duties shall be discharged by the Vice President as Acting President.

Section 4
Whenever the Vice President and a majority of either the principal officers of the executive departments or of such other body as Congress may by law provide, transmit to the President pro tempore of the Senate and the Speaker of the House of Representatives their written declaration that the President is unable to discharge the powers and duties of his office, the Vice President shall immediately assume the powers and duties of the office as Acting President. Thereafter, when the President transmits to the President pro tempore of the Senate and the Speaker of the House of Representatives his written declaration that no inability exists, he shall resume the powers and duties of his office unless the Vice President and a majority of either the principal officers of the executive department or of such other body as Congress may by law provide, transmit within four days to the President pro tempore of the Senate and the Speaker of the House of Representatives their written declaration that the President is unable to discharge the powers and duties of his office. Thereupon Congress shall decide the issue, assembling within forty-eight hours for that purpose if not in session. If the Congress, within twenty-one days after receipt of the latter written declaration, or, if Congress is not in session, within twenty-one days after Congress is required to assemble, determines by two-thirds vote of both Houses that the President is unable to discharge the powers and duties of his office, the Vice President shall continue to discharge the same as Acting President; otherwise, the President shall resume the powers and duties of his office.

AMENDMENT XXVI (1971)

Section 1
The right of citizens of the United States, who are eighteen years of age or older, to vote shall not be denied or abridged by the United States or by any State on account of age.

Section 2
The Congress shall have power to enforce this article by appropriate legislation.

AMENDMENT XXVII (1992)

No law, varying the compensation for the services of the Senators and Representatives, shall take effect, until an election of Representatives shall have intervened.

GLOSSARY OF LEGAL TERMS

abandoned property   Property over which an owner or possessor has relinquished control with no intent to regain control.

abortion   The intentional termination of a pregnancy through medical intervention.

abusive debt collection practices   Actions or threats used by debt collectors to harass a debtor.

accession   An addition or increase in property.

accessory   A person who aids in the commission of a crime.

accord and satisfaction   Payment by one party and acceptance of it by another in full satisfaction of a disputed claim.

Acts of God   Unforeseen occurrences not caused by a human being or a human agency.

actual possession   Possession of property with the possessor's having immediate control over it.

actus reus   A "wrongful act" that, combined with other necessary elements of crime, constitutes criminal liability.

ad valorem **taxes**   Taxes based on the assessed value of the property taxed.

adequacy of consideration   A consideration that is reasonably proportional under the circumstances.

adjudicatory procedures   Procedures leading to adjudication in administrative or judicial proceedings.

adjusted gross estate   Value of an estate after subtracting all deductions allowed by law or regulations.

administrative agencies   Departments of federal, state, and local governments exercising regulatory authority over designated areas of services or control.

administrative law   The body of law dealing with the structure, authority, policies, and procedures of administrative and regulatory agencies.

administrative law judges   Officers appointed to hear and determine controversies before administrative agencies of governments.

administrative search warrants   Court orders authorizing searches to determine if there are violations of regulatory laws and ordinances.

administrative searches   Searches of premises by a government official to determine compliance with health and safety regulations.

adoptive parents   Parents who have adopted a child, as distinct from "birth parents."

advance directive for medical decisions   A written document signed by a person stating his or her desires concerning health care, often appointing a surrogate to exercise judgment as to the extent of medical procedures to be taken should the person signing the directive be incompetent or unable to give directions.

adversarial system   A system of justice involving conflicting parties where the role of the judge is to remain neutral.

adverse possession   Possession of real property without consent of the owner that can result in acquiring title after a period of prescribed years upon compliance with requirements of statutes.

affiant   A person who makes an affidavit.

affidavit   A written document attesting to specific facts of which the affiant has knowledge, and sworn to or affirmed by the affiant.

affirm   To uphold, ratify, or approve.

affirmative action   A program under which women and/or persons of particular minority groups are granted special consideration in employment, government contracts, and/or admission to programs of higher education.

affirmative defenses   Defenses to a criminal charge where the defendant bears the burden of proof. Examples include automatism, intoxication, coercion, and duress.

after-born children   Children born after a testator executes a last will and testament.

age discrimination   Giving unequal considerations to persons because of their age. This type of discrimination is especially applicable to employment situations.

agency adoption   An adoption arranged by an adoption agency, typically for a fee.

aggravated assault   An assault committed with a dangerous weapon or with intent to commit a felony.

aggravated battery   A battery committed by use of an instrument designed to inflict great bodily harm on the victim.

aggravating factors   Factors attending the commission of a crime that make the crime or its consequences worse.

aggregation of capital   Accumulation of capital assets, usually cash, from different sources. In corporations this usually occurs as a result of the sale of securities to investors.

aiding and abetting   Assisting in or otherwise facilitating the commission of a crime.

alibi   Defense to a criminal charge that places the defendant at some place other than the scene of the crime at the time the crime occurred.

alimony   Regular payments of money to a former spouse as required by a court that grants a divorce.

allocution   Oral statement made by a defendant prior to sentencing.

alternative dispute resolution   A method of resolving disputes without judicial adjudication. The usual means employed are arbitration and mediation.

ambiguity   Unclear meaning of terms or words.

ancillary administration   An auxiliary administration of a decedent's estate in a state other than the state of the decedent's domicile.

annual percentage rate of interest (APR)   The rate of interest actually paid by a borrower when the lender's fees and "points" are considered; the true rate of interest received from money invested when the compounding factor is included.

annulment   Judicial dissolution of marriage on the ground that a valid marriage did not take place.

anonymous tip   Information from an unknown source concerning alleged criminal activity.

answer   The defendant's response to the allegations of the plaintiff's complaint or petition.

answer brief   The appellee's written response to the appellant's law brief filed in an appellate court.

antitrust law   The body of law defining antitrust violations and providing remedies for such violations.

antitrust violations   Violations of laws designed to protect the public from price-fixing, price discrimination, and monopolistic practices in trade and commerce.

appeals of right   Appeals brought to higher courts as a matter of right under federal or state law.

appellant   A person who takes an appeal to a higher court.

appellate courts   Judicial tribunals that review decisions from lower tribunals.

appellate jurisdiction   The legal authority of a court of law to hear an appeal from or otherwise review a decision by a lower court.

appellate procedure The rules of procedure followed by appellate courts in deciding appeals.

appellee The party against whom a case is appealed to a higher court.

arbitration Procedure whereby controversies are resolved by a referee or a panel of referees who make a decision on the merits of a controversy after presentations by the disputants.

arraignment An appearance before a court of law for the purpose of pleading to a criminal charge.

arrest warrant A document issued by a magistrate or judge directing that a named person be taken into custody for allegedly having committed an offense.

arson The crime of intentionally burning someone else's house or building, now commonly extended to other property as well.

Articles of Confederation The constitution under which the United States was governed between 1781 and 1789.

articles of incorporation Document signed by organizers of a corporation setting forth the name, purpose, authorized capital stock, and other requirements of the corporation.

artificial insemination Medical procedure in which semen is injected into a woman's vagina in order to achieve pregnancy.

***Ashwander* rules** Rules of judicial self-restraint articulated by Justice Louis D. Brandeis in a concurring opinion in *Ashwander v. TVA* (1936).

assault The attempt or threat to inflict bodily injury upon another person.

assignee One to whom a legal right is transferred.

assignment Transfer of legal rights.

assignor One who assigns legal rights.

assisted suicide An offense (in some jurisdictions) of aiding or assisting a person to take his or her life.

assume the mortgage Agreement to pay the balance due on a note secured by a mortgage.

assumption of risk A person's voluntary exposure to known or obvious risks.

attempt An intent to commit a crime coupled with an act taken toward committing the offense.

attorney-client privilege The right of a person (client) not to testify about matters discussed in confidence with an attorney in the course of the attorney's representation of the client.

Attorney General The highest legal officer of a state or of the United States.

attorney's fees (1) Sums charged by a lawyer for representation of a client. (2) Sums awarded by a court to reimburse a litigant for fees the litigant is obligated to pay an attorney. Attorney's fees are generally awarded only when authorized by a statute or a contract.

attractive nuisance A condition or machine on premises that poses a danger or special peril to children because of its attractiveness to them.

authority of law Force of law backed by the coercive power of the state.

automatism The condition under which a person performs a set of actions during a state of unconsciousness. For example: sleepwalking.

automobile exception Exception to the Fourth Amendment warrant requirement allowing the warrantless search of a vehicle by police who have probable cause to search but because of exigent circumstances are unable to secure a warrant.

bail The conditional release from custody of a person charged with a crime pending adjudication of the case.

bailee Person or entity entrusted with someone's property.

bailment Entrustment of property to someone to perform some service or repair on the property. Example: One takes a car to a mechanic to have it repaired.

bailor One who entrusts property to another for a specified purpose.

bait and switch advertising Attempting to sell a customer a higher-priced item after having advertised a similar item for a lower price.

bankruptcy Legal process by which honest debtors obtain relief under laws designed to protect them from their creditors.

battered child syndrome A set of symptoms typically manifested by a child who has suffered continued physical or mental abuse, often from a parent or person having custody of the child.

battered woman syndrome A set of symptoms typically manifested by a woman who has suffered continued physical or mental abuse, usually from a male with whom she lives.

battery The unlawful use of force against another person that entails some injury or offensive touching.

bench trial A trial held before a judge without a jury present.

beneficiaries Persons designated to receive property from another person's insurance policy, will, or trust.

best evidence rule The requirement that the original document or best facsimile must be produced in court to prove the content of a writing.

best interests of the child test The doctrine under which custody of a child is awarded to the parent who is better able to foster the child's best interests.

bid rigging An illegal manipulation in submitting bids to obtain a contract, usually from a public body.

bifurcated trial A capital trial with separate phases for determining guilt and punishment.

bilateral contract A contract between parties based on an exchange of promises.

bill of attainder A legislative act imposing punishment without trial upon persons deemed guilty of treason or felonies. (Prohibited by the U.S. Constitution.)

Bill of Rights The first ten amendments to the U.S. Constitution, ratified in 1791, concerned primarily with individual rights and liberties.

biological parents The male and female who are biologically responsible for conceiving a child.

Blackstone's Commentaries A codification of principles of the English Common Law published in 1769 by Sir William Blackstone, an author and professor.

***Blockburger* test** A test applied by courts to determine if the charges against a defendant would constitute a violation of the constitutional prohibition against double jeopardy, that is, being tried twice for the same offense. The *Blockburger* test holds that it is not double jeopardy for a defendant to be tried for two offenses if each offense includes an element that the other offense does not.

blue sky laws Common name for statutory laws designed to protect investors from securities frauds.

board of adjustment A local board authorized to grant exceptions and variances from land use zoning ordinances and regulations.

board of equalization A local board authorized to revise the assessed values of properties subject to *ad valorem* taxation.

bona fide purchaser One who makes a purchase in good faith, that is, without the attempt to defraud or deceive.

boot camps Institutions that provide systematic discipline in a military-like environment designed to rehabilitate an offender; employed as a sentencing alternative.

border searches Searches of persons entering the borders of the United States.

breach of contract The violation of a provision in a legally enforceable agreement that gives the damaged party the right to recourse in a court of law.

breach of duty Failure to act or refrain from acting as required by law.

bribery The crime of offering, giving, requesting, soliciting, or receiving something of value to influence a decision of a public official.

building codes Governmental regulations specifying the requirements for the construction of buildings.

Bureau of Alcohol, Tobacco and Firearms Federal agency located within the Department of the Treasury empowered to enforce federal statutes dealing with intoxicating beverages, tobacco products, guns, and explosives.

burglary At common law, the crime of breaking and entering a house at night with the intent to commit a felony therein. Under modern statutes, burglary frequently consists of breaking and entering a structure or conveyance at any time with the intent to commit any offense therein.

business and public records Records kept in the ordinary course of business and records required to be kept by governments.

"but for" test A test to determine causation in negligence actions. The test asks, "Would an injury have occurred 'but for' the defendant's actions?"

canon law The laws of a church.

capacity to contract   Legal ability to enter into a binding agreement.

capias   A general term for various court orders requiring that some named person be taken into custody.

capital crimes   Crimes punishable by death.

carjacking   Taking a motor vehicle from someone by force and violence or by intimidation.

case management conference   A meeting between a judge and counsel to review the status of a case before the court and to plan necessary steps to conclude the case.

castle doctrine   "A man's home is his castle." At common law, the right to use whatever force is necessary to protect one's dwelling and its inhabitants from an unlawful entry or attack.

causation   An act that produces an event or an effect.

cause of action   A right to bring suit based on someone's breach of a legal duty.

caveat emptor   "Let the buyer beware." Common law maxim requiring the consumer to judge the quality of a product before making a purchase.

cease and desist orders   An order issued by an administrative agency requiring a person to stop certain designated activities.

ceremonial marriages   A marriage celebrated in conformity with requirements of the law.

certificate of incorporation   A legal charter to conduct business as a corporation issued by a government, usually the state.

challenges for cause   Objections to prospective jurors on some specified ground (e.g., a close relationship to a party to the case).

charitable immunity   Doctrine of law that relieves a charitable organization from liability for its acts. (Doctrine of declining importance in the United States.)

check   A written document by a depositor directing the bank to pay a certain sum to the order of a named payee.

checks and balances   Refers to constitutional powers granted each branch of government to prevent one branch from dominating the others.

child-out-of-wedlock   A child born of parents who were not married at the time the child was born and who did not subsequently marry one another.

child shield statutes   Laws that allow a screen to be placed between a child victim of sexual abuse and a defendant while the child testifies in court.

child snatching   A parent's removal of his or her child from jurisdiction of the court in order to obtain custody either by self-help or from a court in another jurisdiction.

child support   Financial obligation of a parent to support a minor child.

child support requirements   Amount required to be paid (by agreement or court order) for support of minor children.

child visitation rights   Rights of a divorced non-custodial parent to visit his or her child. Visitation rights may be established by agreement of the parents or by court order.

children of tender years   Young children; sometimes pre-teen children are referred to as children of tender years.

chose in action   A right not reduced to possession but recoverable by a lawsuit. Example: A right to receive wages is a chose in action.

circumstantial evidence   Indirect evidence from which the existence of certain facts may be inferred.

citation   (1) A summons to appear in court, often used in traffic violations. (2) A reference to a statute or court decision, often designating a publication where the law or decision appears.

civil contempt   Intentional disobedience of a court order.

civil disobedience   Purposeful, peaceful lawbreaking to dramatize one's opposition to the law.

civil law   (1) The law relating to rights and obligations of parties. (2) The body of law, based essentially on Roman Law, that prevails in most non-English-speaking nations.

civil procedure   The rules of procedure followed by courts in adjudicating civil cases.

civil rights legislation   Statutes protecting persons against various forms of unlawful discrimination.

civil service   The system under which government employees are selected and retained based on merit rather than political patronage.

civil suit   Any court action other than a criminal prosecution.

civil union A legally sanctioned same-sex relationship carrying all of the rights and duties of marriage.

class action A lawsuit brought by one or more parties on behalf of themselves and others similarly situated.

clear and present danger doctrine The doctrine that the First Amendment protects expression up to the point that it poses a clear and present danger of bringing about some substantive evil that government has a right to prevent.

clergy privilege The exemption of a clergyperson and a penitent from disclosing communications made in confidence by the penitent.

closely held corporation A corporation whose stock is held by a small group of stockholders who often actively conduct the corporate business.

closing arguments Arguments presented at trial by counsel at the conclusion of the presentation of evidence.

Code of Justinian Code of laws compiled by the Roman Emperor Justinian c. 535 A.D.

codicil An amendment to a last will and testament.

codification Collection of laws usually indexed by subject matter.

coercive federalism Refers to efforts by the federal government to use its spending power to induce the states to adopt policies they would not otherwise adopt, such as raising the legal drinking age to twenty-one.

collateral Cash or other asset pledged as security for repayment of a debt.

collateral attack The attempt to defeat the outcome of a judicial proceeding by challenging it in a different proceeding or court.

collateral source rule A rule that allows a jury, when considering an award of damages to an injured plaintiff, to consider the sums the plaintiff will receive from sources other than the defendant. For example, workers compensation or other insurance.

collective bargaining Negotiations between representatives (usually union leaders) on behalf of employees and representatives on behalf of an employer. Bargaining usually focuses on wages and working conditions.

collegial courts A judicial tribunal consisting of more than one judge, for example, federal and state appellate courts.

commercial paper Short-term unsecured debt instruments.

common law marriages Marriages recognized at common law simply on the basis of cohabitation.

common law pleading English common law system of filing various written documents in litigation to arrive at the issues to be resolved by the court.

common stock Class of corporate security whose holders have the right to vote to elect directors.

community-oriented policing Style of policing in which officers attempt to form constructive and respectful relationships with the communities they serve.

community property Property acquired by a husband and wife during their marriage, other than property acquired by gift or inheritance, in a state that has community property laws.

community property states States (primarily in the western United States) that have community property laws.

community service A sentence requiring that the criminal perform some specific service to the community for some specified period of time.

comparative negligence Doctrine of tort law that allows a plaintiff to recover damages from a defendant in a negligence action even though the plaintiff is negligent to some degree but that reduces the plaintiff's award based on the amount of the plaintiff's negligence.

compensatory damages Amount awarded a plaintiff to compensate for injury or losses suffered.

competent Legally qualified.

complaint An initial document filed in court to inform the defendant of the nature and extent of the plaintiff's claim against the defendant.

compounding a crime The acceptance of money or something else of value in exchange for an agreement not to prosecute a person for committing a crime.

compulsory process The requirement that witnesses appear and testify in court or before a legislative committee. See also subpoena.

compulsory self-incrimination   The requirement that an individual give testimony leading to his or her own criminal conviction. Forbidden by the U.S. Constitution, Amendment V.

computer crimes   Crimes perpetrated through the use of computer technology.

concurrent jurisdiction   Jurisdiction that is shared by different courts of law.

concurrent powers   Powers exercised jointly by the state and federal governments.

concurring in the judgment   An opinion by a judge or justice agreeing with the judgment of an appellate court without agreeing with the court's reasoning process.

concurring opinion   An opinion by a judge or justice agreeing with the decision of the court. A concurring opinion may or may not agree with the rationale adopted by the court in reaching its decision (see opinion of the court).

condominium   Building whose owners have title to individual units in a multi-unit structure and who have title in common with other owners to the amenities and other common elements of the property.

condominium association   Organization of condominium owners that governs the maintenance and uses of the amenities and other common elements of the property. (1) A form of ownership in common with other owners; (2) as presently defined.

confidential informant (CI)   An informant known to the police but whose identity is held in confidence.

confusion   Mixing of goods belonging to different owners.

Congress   The national legislature of the United States established by Article I of the U.S. Constitution.

consent   Voluntarily yielding to the will or desire of another person.

consent to a search   The act of a person's voluntarily permitting police to conduct a search of person or property.

consideration   A benefit or detriment bargained for by parties who form a contract.

consortium   The right of companionship and services that each spouse has in relation to the other spouse.

conspiracy   The crime of two or more persons agreeing or planning to commit a crime. The crime of conspiracy is distinct from the crime contemplated by the conspirators (the "target crime").

constitution   A nation's fundamental law.

constructive notice   Knowledge of facts imputed to someone who by proper diligence should have become aware of the facts.

constructive possession   The ability to effectively control something, even if it is not actually in one's possession.

constructive service   A form of service of court process other than by personal delivery to the intended recipient. Constructive service is sometimes accomplished by a notice published in a newspaper with a copy sent to the last known address of the intended recipient.

contempt   An action that embarrasses, hinders, obstructs, or is calculated to lessen the dignity of a judicial or legislative body.

contempt of court   Any action that embarrasses, hinders, obstructs, or is calculated to lessen the dignity of a court of law.

contingent fee   A fee to be paid to an attorney only in the event the attorney prevails in court on behalf of the client.

continuity of management   Pattern of uninterrupted management.

contractual status   In family law, the recognition that marriage not only involves a contractual relationship but also, because of the state's interest in the institution of marriage, results in a contractual status.

contributory negligence   A common law rule that provides that where a plaintiff's own negligence contributed to an injury, the plaintiff is barred from recovering damages against a defendant.

conversion   The unlawful assumption of the rights of ownership to someone else's property.

cooperative   A form of ownership where a person buys shares of stock in a corporation in order to occupy a unit in an apartment or business building.

cooperative federalism   A modern approach to American federalism in which powers and functions are shared among national, state, and local authorities.

corporal punishment   Punishment that inflicts pain or injury on a person's body.

corporate charter   A certificate of incorporation issued by federal or state government authorizing an organization to conduct business as a corporation.

corporation   "... [a]n artificial being, invisible, intangible, and existing only in contemplation of law..." *Dartmouth College v. Woodward* (1819); an entity with legal powers chartered under law and designed to exist indefinitely where ownership is vested in stockholders.

corpus delicti "The body of the crime." The material thing upon which a crime has been committed (for example, a burned-out building in a case of arson).

cost-benefit analysis   Systematic assessment of the costs and benefits that will result from a given transaction.

counterclaim   A request by the defendant for relief against the plaintiff.

court-martial   A military court.

Court of Federal Claims   Specialized federal trial court established to adjudicate tort claims brought against agencies of the United States government.

Court of International Trade   A federal court that hears cases involving the federal government and importers of goods.

court of last resort   The highest court in a judicial system, the last resort for deciding appeals.

court of limited jurisdiction   A trial court with narrow authority to hear and decide cases, typically misdemeanors and/or small claims.

Court of Veterans' Appeals   A federal court that hears appeals from denials of veterans benefits.

covenant not to compete   A contract not to act in competition.

covenants   Agreements; promises.

credit card fraud   The offense of using a credit card to obtain goods or services by a person who knows that the card has been stolen, forged, or canceled.

credit cardholders   One who possesses a credit card that allows the cardholder to obtain credit in accordance with the terms of a contract between the cardholder and the issuing institution.

crime   An offense against society punishable under the criminal law.

criminal contempt   See contempt.

criminal intent   A necessary element of a crime—the evil design associated with the criminal act.

criminal law   The law defining crimes and punishments.

criminal procedure   The rules of law governing the procedures by which crimes are investigated, prosecuted, adjudicated, and punished.

criminal prosecution   The process by which a person is charged with a criminal offense.

cross-claim   A claim asserted in a lawsuit by one party against a co-party.

cross-examination   The process of interrogating a witness who has testified on direct examination by asking the witness questions concerning testimony given. Cross-examination is designed to bring out any bias or inconsistencies in the witness's testimony.

cruel and unusual punishments   Punishment that shocks the moral conscience of the community, for example, torturing or physically beating a prisoner.

custodial parent   A parent that has legal custody of a minor child.

custody   The right and obligation to shelter and care for a minor child.

damages   Monetary compensation awarded by a court to a person who has suffered injuries or losses to person or property as a result of someone else's conduct.

dangerous instrumentality   An instrument that has inherently dangerous characteristics.

de jure **corporation**   A body corporate organized and existing under law.

deadlocked jury   A jury where the jurors cannot agree on a verdict.

deadly force   The degree of force that may result in the death of the person against whom the force is applied.

death penalty   Capital punishment; a sentence to death for the commission of a crime.

death qualification of a jury   The process by which a jury is selected whose members do not entertain scruples against imposing a death sentence.

decisional law   Law declared by appellate courts in their written decisions and opinions.

Declaration of Independence   Formal document of July 4, 1776, establishing the United States of America as an independent nation.

declaratory relief   A court decision establishing rights of parties.

deed of trust   A deed by which a borrower conveys legal title to real estate to a trustee who holds title as security for a lender.

defamation   A tort involving the injury to one's reputation by the malicious or reckless dissemination of a falsehood.

default   Failure to do some act required by contract or by law.

default judgment   A judgment entered by a court due to a defendant's failure to respond to legal process or to appear in court to contest the plaintiff's claim.

defendant   A person charged with a crime or against whom a civil action has been initiated.

defense of a third person   Aiding or assisting a person being attacked.

deficiency judgment   A judgment entered by a court for sums remaining due a creditor or mortgagee after the creditor repossesses and sells goods or after a mortgagee forecloses and causes the mortgaged property to be sold.

definite sentence   Criminal penalty set by law with no discretion for the judge or correctional officials to individualize punishment.

definite sentencing   Legislatively determined sentencing with no discretion given to judges or corrections officials to individualize punishment.

delagatee   One to whom a power, authority, or responsibility has been transferred.

delegation   Act of transferring a power, authority, or responsibility to a person or agency.

delegations of power   Transfer of legal right to act.

delagator   One who transfers a power, authority, or responsibility.

Department of Justice   The department of the federal government that is headed by the Attorney General and staffed by United States Attorneys.

deportation   The legal process by which an alien is expelled from a host country.

deposition   The recorded sworn testimony of a witness; not given in open court.

derivative evidence   Evidence that is derived from or obtained only as a result of other evidence.

determinate sentencing   The process of sentencing whereby the judge sets a fixed term of years within statutory parameters and the offender must serve that term without possibility of early release.

deterrence   Prevention of criminal activity by punishing criminals so that others will not engage in such activity.

devisees   Beneficiaries of real property under a last will and testament.

diplomatic immunity   A privilege to be free from arrest and prosecution granted under international law to diplomats, their staffs, and household members.

direct evidence   Evidence that applies directly to proof of a fact or proposition. For example, a witness who testifies to having seen an act done or heard a statement made is giving direct evidence.

direct examination   Interrogation by an attorney of a party or a witness called to testify.

directed verdict   A verdict rendered by a jury upon direction of the presiding judge.

disaffirm   Repudiate; disavow. For example, a minor can ordinarily disaffirm a contract.

discharge from debts   The object of a debtor who files a bankruptcy proceeding. In such a proceeding, an honest debtor who complies with all requirements of the law receives a discharge, that is, a release, from most debts.

disclosure of information   To reveal or make known certain facts.

discovery   A process whereby counsel seek to obtain information from parties in a lawsuit through interrogatories and depositions.

discretionary activities   Actions taken that are not prescribed by law.

discretionary review   Form of appellate court review of lower court decisions that is not mandatory but occurs at the discretion of the appellate court. See also certiorari.

discrimination   Treatment of persons unequally based on their race, religion, sex, or national origin.

discrimination against persons with disabilities   Treatment of persons unequally based on their disabilities.

disinherited   Deprived of receiving an inheritance from a decedent.

disorderly conduct   Illegal behavior that disturbs the public peace or order.

disparate impact   A facially neutral law or policy that has a differential impact on members of different races or genders.

dissenting opinion   A written opinion by a judge or justice setting forth reasons for disagreeing with a particular decision of the court.

dissolution of marriage   Legal termination of a marriage through divorce or annulment.

distributive articles   Articles I, II, and III of the U.S. Constitution, delineating the powers and functions of the legislative, executive, and judicial branches, respectively, of the national government.

diversity of citizenship jurisdiction   The authority of federal courts to hear lawsuits in which the parties are citizens of different states and the amount in controversy exceeds $75,000.

divine law   Law ascribed to a Supreme Being.

divorce   Termination of a marriage by a court judgment.

divorce *a mensa et thoro*   A divorce from bed and board; a divorce judgment that does not legally terminate a marriage.

doctrine of harmless error   Legal principle that holds that an appellate court should not reverse a decision of a lower tribunal because of an error that does not affect the substantial rights of the parties.

doctrine of incorporation   (1) The practice of allowing one document to be made part of another by specific reference. (2) In constitutional law, the doctrine that the Fourteenth Amendment incorporates the provisions of the Bill of the Rights and thus makes them applicable to the states.

doctrine of original intent   Doctrine that holds that a court should interpret a constitution based on the intent of those who drafted it.

domestic corporation   A corporation doing business in the state of its incorporation.

domestic partnership   An agreement between two persons of the same sex to live and cohabit together.

domicile   Place of a person's permanent residence.

dominion and control   Ability to exercise the right to property and authority to direct its disposition.

donee   One who receives a gift.

donor   One who makes a gift.

double jeopardy   The condition of being tried twice for the same criminal offense.

draft   A written order drawn on one party by another and requesting that payment be made to a third party.

dram shop acts   Statutes prohibiting sales of alcoholic beverages to minors or intoxicated persons.

drawee   Party on whom a draft is drawn.

drawer   Party who draws an order on another party (drawee) requesting the drawee to make payment to a third party.

drug courier profile   A controversial law enforcement practice of identifying possible drug smugglers by relying on a set of characteristics and patterns of behavior believed to typify persons who smuggle drugs.

drug testing   The practice of subjecting employees to urine tests to determine whether they are using illegal substances.

dual federalism   A concept of federalism in which the national and state governments exercise authority within separate, self-contained areas of public policy and public administration.

DUBAL   Driving with an unlawful blood alcohol level.

due-on-sale clause   A provision in a mortgage that stipulates that the entire unpaid balance due on the mortgaged indebtedness will become due upon transfer of the property that is collateral for the mortgage debt.

due process of law   Procedural and substantive rights of citizens against government actions that threaten the denial of life, liberty, or property.

durable power of attorney   A written document in which a person (the principal) designates another person to act as an agent for specified purposes, especially for making health care decisions. The "durable" characteristic means the power of attorney remains effective even if the principal becomes incapacitated.

duress The use of illegal confinement or threats of harm to coerce someone to do something he or she would not do otherwise.

duty An obligation that a person has by law or contract.

dying declaration Statement made by a person who believes that his or her death is imminent. A dying declaration is generally considered an exception to the hearsay rule of evidence.

easement A right of use over the property of another. This term frequently refers to a right-of-way across privately owned land.

easement of necessity Right to use a part of someone else's land as a right-of-way for purposes of ingress to and egress from otherwise landlocked property.

elective share A share of a deceased spouse's estate that a surviving spouse is entitled to claim in some states.

Electoral College The body of electors chosen by the voters of each state and the District of Columbia for the purpose of formally electing the President and Vice President of the United States. The number of electors (538) is equivalent to the total number of representatives and senators to which each state is entitled, plus three electors from the District of Columbia.

electronic eavesdropping Covert listening to or recording of a person's conversations by electronic means.

emancipation acts (1) Laws that allow persons considered legally incapable of entering into legal transactions to enter contracts and other legal transactions. In past decades applied to married women. (2) Laws that remove the disability of a minor to enter contracts once the minor marries. (3) Laws that allow courts to permit mature minors to enter legal transactions.

embezzlement The crime of using a position of trust or authority to transfer or convert the money or property of another to oneself.

emergency searches Warrantless searches performed during an emergency, such as a fire or potential explosion.

eminent domain The power of government, or of individuals and corporations authorized to perform public functions, to take private property for public use.

The Fifth Amendment requires that private property cannot be taken for public use without just compensation.

employment discrimination Denying employment or treating employees unequally based on their disabilities, race, religion, sex, or national origin.

en banc rehearing A rehearing in an appellate court in which all or a majority of the judges participate.

enabling legislation As applied to public law, a statute authorizing the creation of a government program or agency and defining the functions and powers thereof.

endangered species An animal species that has been officially designated as endangered by the Secretary of Interior under the Endangered Species Act.

English common law A system of legal rules and principles recognized and developed by English judges prior to the colonization of America and accepted as a basic aspect of the American legal system.

entrapment The act of government agents in inducing someone to commit a crime that the person otherwise would not be disposed to commit.

enumerated powers Powers specified in the text of the federal and state constitutions.

environmental crimes Statutes that impose punishment for violations of laws enacted to protect the environment and natural resources.

environmental impact statement A document required by law outlining the effects that a proposed land development will likely have on the surrounding environment.

environmental law The body of law protecting the natural environment from pollution and despoliation.

environmental regulations Regulations adopted by administrative agencies designed to implement statutory protections of the environment.

equal protection of the laws Constitutional requirement that the government not engage in prohibited forms of discrimination against persons under its jurisdiction.

equitable distribution A distribution of property that is fair, just, and reasonable.

equity Historically, a system of rules, remedies, customs, and principles developed in England to supplement the harsh common law by emphasizing the concept of fairness. In addition, because the common law served only to recompense after injury, equity was devised to prevent injuries that could not be repaired or recompensed after the fact. While American judges continue to distinguish between law and equity, these systems of rights and remedies are, for the most part, administered by the same courts.

error correction   See error correction function.

error correction function   The function of appellate courts in correcting errors committed by lower tribunals in their interpretation and application of law, evidence, and procedure.

escape   Unlawfully fleeing to avoid arrest or confinement.

estates during the life of another   An interest in real property that can be enjoyed only during the lifetime of a named person.

estates in real property   Interests in lands and property attached thereto.

evanescent evidence   Evidence that tends to disappear or to be destroyed. Often police seek to justify a warrantless search on the ground that destruction of the evidence is imminent.

evidentiary presumption   Establishment of one fact allows inference of another fact or circumstance.

ex post facto law   A retroactive law that criminalizes actions that were innocent at the time they were taken or increases punishment for a criminal act after it was committed.

excessive bail   Where a court requires a defendant to post an unreasonably large amount or imposes unreasonable conditions as a prerequisite for a defendant to be released before trial. The Eighth Amendment to the U.S. Constitution prohibits courts from requiring "excessive bail."

excessive fines   Fines that are deemed to be greater than is appropriate for the punishment of a particular crime.

exculpatory information   That which exonerates or tends to exonerate a person from fault or guilt.

excusable homicide   A death caused by accident or misfortune.

executed contract   A contract that has been completely performed.

executive order   An order by a president or governor directing some particular action to be taken.

executive power   The power to enforce the law and administer the government.

executive privilege   The right of the President to withhold certain information from Congress or a court of law.

executory contract   An agreement not yet performed by the parties.

exhaustion of remedies   The requirement that a party seeking review by a court first exhaust all legal options for resolution of the issue by nonjudicial authorities or lower courts.

exigent circumstances   Situations that demand unusual or immediate action.

expert witness   A witness with specialized knowledge or training called to testify in his or her field of expertise.

express contract   A contract where the terms have been expressed orally or in writing by the parties.

express powers   Powers explicitly granted by some instrument, whether a constitution, statute, or contract.

expressive conduct   Conduct undertaken to express a message.

extortion   The crime of obtaining money or property by threats of force or the inducement of fear.

extradition   The surrender of a person by one jurisdiction to another for the purpose of criminal prosecution.

extraordinary life-sustaining measures   Medical measures to prolong life beyond ordinary feeding and care. A good example is a mechanical respirator.

eyewitness testimony   Testimony given by a person based on personal observation of an event.

fair hearing   A hearing in a court of law that conforms to standards of procedural justice.

fair notice   The requirement stemming from due process that government provide adequate notice to a person before it deprives that person of life, liberty, or property.

false imprisonment   The crime of holding someone against their will without legal justification.

false pretenses   The crime of obtaining money or property through misrepresentation.

fault concept   (1) In family law, the requirement that one spouse must prove the other spouse to be at fault before a court grants a divorce. (2) In tort law, the basis of imposing liability because of a person's failure to act as a reasonably prudent individual would act under given circumstances.

Federal Bureau of Investigation (FBI)   The primary federal agency charged with investigating violations of federal criminal laws.

federal bureaucracy   The collective term for the myriad departments, agencies, and bureaus of the federal government.

federal estate tax   A tax imposed by the U.S. government on the estates of decedents.

federal habeas corpus review   Review of a state criminal trial by a federal district court on a writ of habeas corpus after the defendant has been convicted, has been incarcerated, and has exhausted appellate remedies in the state courts.

federal magistrate judges   Judges appointed to preside over pretrial proceedings, try misdemeanor case, and with consent of parties handle civil trials in federal courts.

federal question jurisdiction   The authority of federal courts to decide issues of national law.

federalism   The constitutional distribution of government power and responsibility between the national government and the states.

fee simple estate   The highest interest in real property that the law recognizes.

fee tail estates   An estate in real property conveyed to a person (grantee) and to the heirs of the grantee's body.

felony   A serious crime for which a person may be incarcerated for more than one year.

felony murder   A homicide committed during the course of committing another felony other than murder (e.g., armed robbery). The felonious act substitutes for malice aforethought ordinarily required in murder.

fictitious name laws   A law that requires persons who operate a business under a name other than their own to register that fact with a government office.

fighting words   Utterances that are inherently likely to provoke a violent response from the audience.

financing statement   A document filed with an appropriate government office that notifies the public that specified property is subject to existing loans.

fines   Sums of money exacted from criminal defendants as punishment for wrongdoing.

firefighter's rule   English common law doctrine applied in many states. Treats a police officer or firefighter as a licensee, thereby limiting a landowner's liability to such persons who enter premises as part of their duties.

first-degree murder   The highest degree of unlawful homicide, usually defined as "an unlawful act committed with the premeditated intent to take the life of a human being."

flight to avoid prosecution   Unlawful travel to escape prosecution for a crime.

force majeure **clauses**   A contract provision excusing performance when a superior force makes performance impossible. See Acts of God.

foreign corporation   A corporation doing business or maintaining an office in a state other than its state of incorporation.

forensic evidence   Evidence usually in the form of testimony offered by a forensic expert. See forensic experts.

forensic experts   Persons qualified in the application of scientific knowledge to legal principles, usually applied to those who participate in discourse or who testify in court.

foreperson   The person selected by fellow jurors to chair deliberations and report the jury's verdict.

foreseeable   An event that a reasonable person would ordinarily anticipate from one's act or failure to act.

forfeiture   Sacrifice of ownership or some right (usually property) as a penalty.

forgery   The crime of making a false written instrument or materially altering a written instrument (e.g., a check, promissory note, or college transcript) with the intent to defraud.

formal adjudication   Official determination (usually by an administrative tribunal).

formal contracts   A contract that complies with specific requirements of law. Examples: a check or draft.

foster care   Placing a child in the care of person(s) who perform the duties of a parent, usually under supervision of a social welfare agency.

Fourteenth Amendment   Amendment to the U.S. Constitution, ratified in 1868, prohibiting states from depriving persons in their jurisdictions of due process and equal protection.

fraud   Intentional deception or distortion in order to gain something of value.

fraud, duress, or undue influence   Intentional deception or false representations, unlawful coercion, or pressure to override a person's free will. (Terms frequently used in contests concerning execution of a last will and testament.)

freedom of association   Implicitly protected by the First Amendment, the right of people to associate freely without unwarranted interference by government.

freedom of expression   A summary term embracing freedom of speech and freedom of the press as well as symbolic speech and expressive conduct.

fruit of the poisonous tree doctrine   A doctrine based on judicial interpretation of the Fourth Amendment that holds that evidence that is derived from illegally seized evidence cannot be used by the prosecution.

full warranty   A written consumer product warranty that complies with the Magnuson-Moss Warranty Act.

fundamental error   An error in a judicial proceeding that adversely affects the substantial rights of the accused.

gambling   Operating or playing a game for money in the expectation of gaining more than the amount played.

garnishee   A party (usually a bank or employer) who is required to withhold payment due or to become due to someone and pay it over to the garnishor.

garnishment   Court action requiring a party (garnishee) who is indebted to a person to withhold payment and pay a sum over to a creditor (garnishor) who instituted garnishment proceedings.

garnishor   A party who institutes a garnishment proceeding.

gay rights   Summary term referring to the idea that persons should be permitted to engage in private homosexual conduct and be free from discrimination based on their sexual orientation.

gender-based peremptory challenge   A challenge to a prospective juror's competency to serve based solely on the prospective juror's gender.

gender discrimination   Treating a person in an unequal manner based on the person's sex.

gender equity   Idea that women should receive equal benefits conferred by government.

general damages   Damages that have accrued to the plaintiff due to a particular injury or loss.

general intent   The state of mind to do something prohibited by law without necessarily intending to accomplish the harm that results from the illegal act.

general objection   An objection raised against a witness's testimony or introduction of evidence when the objecting party does not recite a specific ground for the objection.

general partner   A member of a partnership who shares with other partners the management and the profits and losses of the business.

general verdict   Ordinary form of jury verdict in civil case that finds for the plaintiff or defendant in general terms; in criminal case, finds the defendant not guilty or guilty of specified crime(s).

gerrymandering   The intentional manipulation of legislative districts for political purposes.

gestational surrogacy   A method of surrogate parenthood where the sperm of a married man is artificially united with the egg of his wife and the resulting pre-embryo is implanted in another woman's womb.

good-faith exception   An exception to the exclusionary rule that bars use of evidence obtained by a search warrant found to be invalid. The exception allows use of the evidence if the police relied in good faith on the search warrant, even though the warrant is subsequently held to be invalid.

good-time credit   Credit toward early release from prison based on good behavior during confinement (often referred to as "gain time").

grand jury   A group of twelve to twenty-three citizens convened to hear evidence in criminal cases to determine whether indictment is warranted.

grandfathered in   Allowed to continue. Example: If a land use zoning ordinance changes the classification of zoning, an existing use that is permitted to continue is said to be "grandfathered in."

grandparents' visitation   The right of grandparents to visit their grandchildren.

grantee   One to whom a grant is made. Usually refers to a person or entity that acquires title to real estate.

grantor   One who makes a grant. Usually refers to a person or entity that deeds property to another person or entity.

grantor or settlor   Person who executes a document creating a trust.

gratuitous bailments   Entrustment of property for benefit of bailor to a person (bailee) who receives no compensation and has a limited responsibility.

gross negligence   Carelessness of an outrageous character.

gun control legislation   Laws restricting the manufacture, design, importation, sale, or possession of firearms.

habeas corpus   "You have the body." A judicial order issued to an official holding someone in custody, requiring the official to bring the prisoner to court for the purpose of allowing the court to determine whether that person is being held legally.

habitual offender   One who has been repeatedly convicted of crimes.

hazardous waste regulations   Government regulations affecting the shipment, storage, and disposal of toxic and radioactive waste products.

hearsay evidence   Statements made by someone other than a witness offered in evidence at a trial or hearing to prove the truth of the matter asserted.

heirs   Persons entitled to succeed to the property of a decedent who dies intestate.

hot pursuit   (1) The right of police to cross jurisdictional lines to apprehend a suspect or criminal. (2) The Fourth Amendment doctrine allowing warrantless searches and arrests where police pursue a fleeing suspect into a protected area.

house arrest   A sentencing alternative to incarceration where the offender is allowed to leave home only for employment and approved community service activities.

housing discrimination   Treatment of applicants for housing or tenants on terms unequally applied based on race, religion, sex, or national origin.

hung jury   A trial jury unable to reach a verdict.

hypothetical question   A question based on an assumed set of facts. Hypothetical questions may be asked of expert witnesses in criminal trials.

illegal act   Any act that violates a provision of law.

illegitimate child   A child born out-of-wedlock.

illusory   Deceptive; based on a false impression. Courts will not enforce an illusory contract where a party has made a vague, insubstantial, or deceptive promise.

imminent lawless action   Unlawful conduct that is about to take place and that is inevitable unless there is intervention by the authorities.

immunity   Exemption from civil suit or prosecution. See also use immunity; transactional immunity.

impeachment   (1) A legislative act bringing a charge against a public official that, if proven in a legislative trial, will cause his or her removal from public office. (2) Impugning the credibility of a witness by introducing contradictory evidence or proving his or her bad character.

implied consent   An agreement or acquiescence manifested by a person's actions or inaction.

implied contract   An agreement formed based on actions or inactions of the parties.

implied powers   Powers not specifically enumerated but implied by an instrument such as a constitution, statute, or contract.

implied warranty   A warranty that is implied based on the nature of the transaction, the relationship of the parties, and the circumstances and customs.

implied warranty of fitness of goods   A warranty under the Uniform Commercial Code that goods are suitable for the buyer's intended use.

implied warranty of merchantability   A warranty imposed on merchants that goods sold are such as to allow the buyer to assume they are as defined in the Uniform Commercial Code.

impossibility of performance   Where circumstances beyond the control of a contracting party make it impossible to perform under a contract.

impoundment   (1) Action by a president in refusing to allow expenditures approved by Congress. (2) In criminal law, the seizure and holding of a vehicle or other property by the police.

improper disclosure of personal information   Revealing a person's private information without that person's consent and when not required by law.

in camera   "In a chamber." In private. Refers to a judicial proceeding or conference from which the public is excluded.

in forma pauperis   "In the manner of a pauper." Waiver of filing costs and other fees associated with judicial proceedings to allow an indigent person to proceed.

in vitro fertilization   A technique whereby human ova are placed in a laboratory dish with human sperm, and after fertilization the embryo is transferred into the uterus of a woman who is to serve as surrogate mother of the developing fetus.

incapacitation   Making it impossible for someone to do something.

incarceration   Imprisonment.

inchoate offense   An offense preparatory to committing another crime. Inchoate offenses include attempt, conspiracy, and solicitation.

indefinite sentencing   Form of criminal sentencing whereby a judge imposes a term of incarceration within statutory parameters, and corrections officials determine actual time served through parole or other means.

independent agencies   Federal agencies located outside the major Cabinet-level departments.

independent contractor   A party to a contract who agrees to perform specified work under his or her own methods and supervision.

independent counsel   A special prosecutor appointed to investigate and, if warranted, prosecute official misconduct.

independent source doctrine   The doctrine that permits evidence to be admitted at trial as long as it was obtained independently from illegally obtained evidence.

indeterminate sentencing   Form of criminal sentencing where criminals are sentenced to prison for indeterminate periods until corrections officials determine that rehabilitation has been accomplished.

indictment   A formal document handed down by a grand jury accusing one or more persons of the commission of a crime or crimes.

indirect evidence   Inferences and presumptions that tend to establish a fact or issue.

infancy   The condition of being below the age of legal majority.

inflammatory remarks   Remarks by counsel during a trial designed to excite the passions of the jury.

informal adjudication   A form of administrative adjudication that observes only minimal procedural requirements.

informal contracts   Contract for which the law does not prescribe a set form.

information   A document filed by a prosecutor under oath charging one or more persons with commission of a crime.

informed consent   A doctrine of consent applicable in professional malpractice cases, especially those involving surgery. Example: An informed consent to surgery is based on the physician's explaining the risks before a patient consents to a procedure.

inheritance tax   A tax imposed by many states on the receipt of property from a decedent.

initial appearance   After arrest, the first appearance of the accused before a judge or magistrate.

initial brief   Appellant's brief filed in support of issues raised in appellate court.

initial pleading   Petition or complaint filed to initiate a proceeding in a judicial tribunal.

injunction   A court order prohibiting someone from doing some specified act or commanding someone to undo some wrong or injury.

Inns of Court   English institutions founded in the fourteenth century where judges and experienced barristers served as teachers and mentors to those aspiring to become barristers.

insanity   A degree of mental illness that negates the legal capacity or responsibility of the affected person.

insider information   Information concerning financial matters and prospective actions of a corporation available only to persons within the corporation.

insider trading   Transactions in securities by a person who operates "inside" a corporation and by using material nonpublic information trades to his or her advantage without first disclosing that information to the public.

intangible personal property   Property with no tangible value, such as bonds, promissory notes, and stock certificates.

intentional acts   Acts committed purposely.

intentional infliction of emotional distress   Outrageous conduct that causes a person mental and emotional suffering. Recognized as a tort in many jurisdictions.

intentional tort committed under color or authority of law   An act committed under color of state authority that deprives a person of a federal constitutional right.

intentions of the Framers   The intentions of the Framers of the United States Constitution with respect to the meaning of its provisions.

intermediate appellate courts   Appellate courts positioned below the supreme or highest appellate court. Their primary function is to decide routine appeals not deserving review by the Supreme Court.

interrogatories   Written questions put to a witness.

interspousal immunity   A common law doctrine that prevented spouses from suing one another for commission of a tort.

interstate abduction   In family law, a non-custodial parent's removal of his or her child to another state usually to attempt to escape the exercise of jurisdiction by the courts of the child's residence.

interstate disputes concerning child custody   Conflicting claims of jurisdiction between courts in different states concerning control and supervision of children.

intervening act   An act (either human or natural) that occurs after an original tortious act. An intervening act can excuse the original tortfeasor from liability unless the tortfeasor should have anticipated the occurrence of the intervening act.

inter vivos **trust**   A trust established during the lifetime of the grantor or settlor.

intestate succession   The descent of property of a decedent who dies intestate. See also heirs; inheritance tax.

intoxication   A state of drunkenness resulting from the use of alcoholic beverages or drugs.

invasion of privacy   A tort involving the unreasonable or unwarranted intrusion on the privacy of an individual.

inventory search   An exception to the warrant requirement that allows police who legally impound a vehicle to conduct a routine inventory of the contents of the vehicle.

investigatory detention   Brief detention of suspects by a police officer who has reasonable suspicion that criminal activity is afoot. See also stop-and-frisk.

invitee   One who is expressly or impliedly invited. Generally refers to entry on another's land or into another's premises.

involuntary dismissal   Dismissal of a law action based on legal grounds.

irretrievably broken   Unable to be repaired (a term of art pertaining to divorce).

irrevocable trust   A trust that cannot be revoked.

Jencks **Act**   The common name for a federal statute that permits a defendant to review a witness's prior written or recorded statement after the witness has testified on direct examination.

joint and several liability   Liability that usually applies where two or more wrongdoers cause an injury or where two or more makers sign a promissory note. A judgment obtained against parties who are jointly and severally liable can be enforced against any one of parties.

joint custody   Shared responsibility of divorced parents concerning control and supervision of children.

joint ownership with right of survivorship　A method of ownership where upon death of one joint owner that owner's interest passes to the surviving owner, irrespective of the deceased owner's last will and testament.

joint tenancy　A form of holding title to property where two or more persons share in the ownership.

joint tenants with right of survivorship　A form of property ownership whereby upon death of one party, that party's interest in the property becomes the property of the surviving joint tenant(s).

judgment of acquittal　(1) In a nonjury trial, a judge's order exonerating a defendant based on a finding that the defendant is not guilty. (2) In a case heard by a jury finding a defendant guilty, a judge's order exonerating a defendant on the ground that the evidence was not legally sufficient to support the jury's finding of guilt.

judicial accountability　The idea that judges should answer to the public for their decisions, primarily through the ballot box.

judicial activism　Defined variously, but the underlying philosophy is that judges should exercise power vigorously.

judicial conference　A meeting of judges to deliberate on disposition of a case.

judicial decision　A decision by a court of law.

judicial disciplinary commissions　Agencies established by state legislatures to investigate complaints of judicial misconduct.

judicial independence　The idea that judges should be free from public pressure in making decisions based on the rule of law.

judicial notice　The act of a court recognizing, without proof, the existence of certain facts that are commonly known. Such facts are often brought to the court's attention through the use of a calendar or almanac.

judicial review　Generally, the review of any issue by a court of law. In American constitutional law, judicial review refers to the authority of a court to invalidate acts of government on constitutional grounds.

judicial review of agency actions　Process by which courts of law review actions or decisions of administrative and regulatory agencies.

judicial self-restraint　The idea that judges should exercise the power of judicial review cautiously and should defer to the decisions of the elective branches of government.

jurisdiction　The geographical area within which, the subject matter with respect to which, and the persons over whom a court can properly exercise its power.

jury instructions　A judge's explanation of the law applicable to a case being heard by a jury.

jury trial　A judicial proceeding to determine a defendant's guilt or innocence conducted before a body of persons sworn to render a verdict based on the law and the evidence presented.

just compensation　The constitutional requirement that a party whose property is taken by government under the power of eminent domain be justly compensated for the loss, normally at fair market value.

justifiable homicide　Killing another in self-defense or defense of others when there is serious danger of death or great bodily harm to self or others, or when authorized by law.

justifiable use of force　The necessary and reasonable use of force by a person in self-defense, defense of another, or defense of property.

kidnapping　The forcible abduction and carrying away of a person against that person's will.

knock and announce　The provision under federal and most state laws that requires a law enforcement officer to first knock and announce his or her presence and purpose before entering a person's home to serve a search or arrest warrant.

land tenure　System developed under the feudal system where an occupier or tenant held lands subordinate to a superior, usually a lord.

land use planning　Developing criteria for present and future uses of lands. Land use zoning is a principal tool in land use planning.

land use zoning　See zoning.

landlord-tenant law　The branch of the civil law that deals with relationships between owners and tenants.

larceny　At common law, the unlawful taking of property with the intent of permanently depriving the owner of same.

law enforcement agencies Government agencies empowered to arrest and detain persons who violate the criminal law.

lawmaking See lawmaking function.

lawmaking function One of the principal functions of an appellate court, often referred to as the law development function, in which the appellate court makes law by interpreting or reinterpreting a constitutional or statutory provision.

leading question A question that suggests an answer. Leading questions are permitted at a civil or criminal trial on cross-examination of witnesses and in other limited instances.

leasehold The legal interest in property that a tenant acquires by lease (usually written) from the owner.

legal codes Compilations of statutory laws usually indexed according to subject matter.

legal guardianship Court proceeding resulting in appointment of a guardian to exercise control over a ward, the ward's property, or both.

legal separation (1) An agreement whereby married parties agree to live separate and apart from one another. (2) A court order providing for spouses to live separate and apart from one another, often making provisions for support of a spouse and children, but not dissolving the parties' marriage.

legatees Those who receive personal property under a decedent's last will and testament.

legislative veto A statutory provision under which a legislative body is permitted to overrule a decision of an executive agency.

legislators Members of a legislature.

legislature An elected lawmaking body such as the Congress of the United States or a state assembly.

lemon laws Statutes that provide a means for a consumer who buys goods that are defective (frequently a motor vehicle) to obtain necessary repairs or replacement of the goods.

lessee A party who leases real or personal property from a lessor (owner).

lessor A party (sometimes called a landlord) who leases real or personal property to a lessee (tenant).

levy (1) Imposition of a tax or assessment by a government agency. (2) Procedure whereby a court official takes possession of property and causes it to be sold to satisfy a judgment lien.

lex talionis The ancient law of retaliation, commonly referred to as "an eye for an eye."

libel The tort of defamation through published material. See defamation.

libertarian view of law The idea that law should protect people from one another but not protect the individual from his or her own vices or unfortunate choices.

licensee A party who holds a license.

licenses Permits to act for specified purposes.

lien A claim of a right or interest in or charge against another's property.

life estates An interest in property (usually real estate) that allows the life tenant to use and control the property during his or her lifetime.

life support systems Artificial means of sustaining life (usually refers to extraordinary means of medical treatment such mechanical respirators).

life tenant A holder of a life estate in property.

limited liability A characteristic of certain forms of investment where the investor's liability is limited to his or her investment. Example: Liability of a corporate stockholder is generally limited to his or her investment.

limited partner A partner in a limited partnership whose liability for debts of the partnership is generally limited to the partner's investment.

limited partnership A partnership with at least one general partner and one or more limited partners organized under statutory law; a form of partnership that distinguishes between general and limited partners.

limited warranty (1) A warranty that expressly includes certain limitations of the warrantor's liability. (2) A written consumer product warranty that does not conform to the requirements for a full warranty specified by the Magnuson-Moss Warranty Act.

liquidated damages A fixed amount of damages that parties agree to in the event of a breach of contract.

living trust A trust created by a grantor during his or her lifetime. Also known as an inter vivos trust.

living will　A document enforceable in court stating a person's wishes regarding the use of extraordinary medical treatment in the event that person is injured and is unable to communicate.

loitering　Standing around idly, "hanging around."

long-arm statute　A state law authorizing service of process on a nonresident defendant as a basis for the court's jurisdiction. To be constitutionally applied, the defendant served must have had minimal contacts within the state where the court is to acquire jurisdiction.

lost property　Property that the owner has involuntarily parted with and about which the owner is without knowledge as to how or where to find it.

lump sum alimony　Payment of alimony at one time rather than a continuing basis. See alimony.

Magna Carta　The "Great Charter" signed by King John in 1215 guaranteeing the legal rights of English subjects. Generally considered the foundation of Anglo-American constitutionalism.

maker　One who executes a document; a term commonly applied to a person who signs a promissory note.

mala in se　"Evil in itself." Refers to crimes such as murder that are universally condemned.

mala prohibita　"Prohibited evil." Refers to crimes that are wrong primarily because the law declares them to be wrong.

malfeasance　Misconduct that adversely affects the performance of official duties.

malicious mischief　The crime of willful destruction of the personal property of another.

managed care　Medical services generally furnished through a health maintenance organization (HMO).

mandamus　"We command." A judicial order or writ commanding a public official or an organization to perform a specified non-discretionary duty.

mandatory sentencing　Sentencing practice in which trial courts are constrained by law to impose prison terms of certain minimum duration.

manslaughter　The crime of unlawful killing of another person without malice.

marital privilege　The privilege of married persons not to be compelled to testify against one another.

marital property　Property acquired by spouses, other than by gift or inheritance, during their marriage.

marriage　A special contractual relationship formed according to law between a man and a woman that results in the regulation of the social and economic status of the parties by law.

matrimonial domicile　Place where a husband and wife live during their marriage.

mayhem　At common law, the crime of injuring someone so as to render that person less able to fight.

mediation　An informal, non-adversarial process whereby a neutral third person facilitates resolution of a dispute between parties by exploring issues and settlement alternatives.

Medicaid　Federal program that provides grants to states to furnish medical care to indigent persons.

Medicare　Federal health insurance program primarily for senior citizens.

Megan's Law　Law requiring convicted sex offenders released from prison to register with local law enforcement authorities.

mens rea　Guilty mind, criminal intent.

misdemeanor　A minor offense usually punishable by fine or imprisonment for less than one year.

misfeasance　Improper performance of a lawful act.

misrepresentation　An untrue statement of fact made to deceive or mislead.

Missouri Plan　Plan for merit-based selection and retention of state judges; originated in Missouri in 1940.

mistake of fact　Unconscious ignorance of a fact or belief in the existence of something that does not exist.

mistake of law　An erroneous opinion of legal principles applied to a set of facts.

mistrial　A trial that is terminated due to misconduct, procedural error, or a "hung jury" (one that is unable to reach a verdict).

mitigating factors　Circumstances or factors that tend to lessen culpability.

M'Naghten **Rule**   Under this rule, for a defendant to be found not guilty by reason of insanity, it must be clearly proved that, at the time of committing the act, the defendant was suffering such a defect of reason, from disease of the mind, as not to know the nature and quality of the act he was doing; or, if he did know it, that he did not know what he was doing was wrong.

Model Penal Code (MPC)   Published by the American Law Institute (ALI), the MPC consists of general provisions concerning criminal liability, sentences, defenses, and definitions of specific crimes. The MPC is not law; rather, it is designed to serve as a model code of criminal law for all states.

modification of custody   A court judgment revising previous court-ordered arrangements for control and supervision of minor children.

monetary policy   Area of public policy affecting the supply of money in the economy.

money laundering   The offense of disguising illegal income to make it appear legitimate.

mortgage   Written contract creating a lien against specifically described real property to secure payment of a note or other undertaking. In some states, a conditional conveyance of real property to secure a debt.

mortgagee   One who takes or holds a mortgage (usually a lender).

mortgagor   One who executes a mortgage (usually a borrower) to secure payment of an obligation.

motion for change of venue   A formal request to a court to designate a different location for conduct of legal proceedings.

motion for continuance   A formal request to a court to postpone a hearing or trial.

motion for rehearing   A formal request made to a court of law to convene another hearing in a case in which the court has already ruled.

motion to dismiss   (1) A formal request to a court to dismiss a plaintiff's complaint, often on the ground the complaint fails to state a legal basis for relief sought by the plaintiff. (2) A formal request to a trial court to dismiss the criminal charges against the defendant.

motion to suppress   A request asking a court to rule that a confession or admission, pretrial identification, or fruits of a search or seizure were unlawfully obtained and cannot be used against a defendant in court.

motions   Formal applications to courts to obtain an order or grant some relief to the movant.

motive   A person's conscious reason for acting.

murder   The unlawful killing of a person by another with malice aforethought or premeditation, or through depraved indifference to human life.

mutual assent   An understanding between parties manifested by an offer and an acceptance.

mutual benefit bailments   A type of bailment where the owner of the property and the person receiving the property each receive a benefit. Example: a lease of a motor vehicle.

mutual mistake   Where each of the parties to a contract was mistaken as to a fact material to the formation of the contract.

Napoleonic Code   The codification of the civil and criminal laws of France promulgated under Napoleon Bonaparte in 1804.

natural law   Principles of human conduct believed to be ordained by God or nature, existing prior to and superseding human law.

natural rights   Rights believed to be inherent in human beings, the existence of which is not dependent on their recognition by government. In classical liberalism, natural rights are "life, liberty and property." As recognized by the Declaration of Independence, they are "life, liberty and the pursuit of happiness."

necessity   A condition that compels or requires a certain course of action.

negative defenses   Any criminal defenses not required to be specifically pled.

negligence   The failure to exercise ordinary care or caution.

negligence per se   An act or omission in violation of a duty imposed by statute or ordinance for the protection of persons or property.

negligent acts or omissions   Acts or omissions committed by a person who fails to act as a reasonably prudent individual would act under the circumstances.

negligent hiring A tort consisting of employing a person whom the employer knew or should have known would pose a threat to the security of others.

negligent infliction of emotional distress A tort in some states where a person in a zone of physical risk suffers demonstrable physical consequences from fright or shock as a result of outrageous acts against another person.

negotiable Transferable by endorsement and delivery.

negotiable instrument Commercial paper signed by the maker or drawer containing an unconditional promise or order to pay a sum certain in money, made payable on demand or at a fixed time to the order of someone or to the bearer.

negotiation (1) As respects commercial paper, a transfer in a manner that the transferee becomes a holder in due course. (2) Method of settling a dispute between parties without a formal trial.

no contest plea A plea to a criminal charge that, although it is not an admission of guilt, generally has the same effect as a plea of guilty.

no-fault automobile insurance laws Statutes in some states that require automobile owners to carry insurance that reimburses the insured irrespective of who is at fault in a vehicular accident. Statutes sometimes allow an action against a party at fault in instances of major injuries or death.

no-fault dissolution of marriage A court judgment dissolving a marriage without the necessity of one spouse's proving the other spouse to be at fault in the marriage.

nominal damages A token amount awarded to a plaintiff who proves the defendant liable but fails to prove actual damages.

non-custodial parent A parent that does not have legal custody of one or more of that parent's children.

non-delegable duties Duties that cannot legally be transferred to others.

nonfeasance Failure to perform a duty.

non-negotiable Refers to contracts that do not comply with the requirements for negotiability under the Uniform Commercial Code. One who acquires a non-negotiable instrument or contract takes it subject to all defenses between the original parties.

non-performance Failure to perform as required by a contract.

notice of appeal Document filed notifying an appellate court of an appeal from a judgment of a lower court.

notice of proposed rulemaking Notification to interested parties of an agency's intention to promulgate a rule.

nuisance An unlawful or unreasonable use of a person's property that results in an injury to another or to the public.

obscenity Explicit sexual material that is patently offensive, appeals to a prurient or unnatural interest in sex, and lacks serious scientific, artistic, or literary content.

obstruction of justice The crime of impeding or preventing law enforcement or the administration of justice.

offer Statement or conduct by a person constituting a proposal to enter a contract.

offeree One to whom an offer has been made.

offeror One who makes an offer.

open meetings Meetings open to the general public.

open public trial A trial that is held in public and is open to spectators.

opening statement A prosecutor's or defense lawyer's initial statement to the judge or jury in a trial.

opinion A written statement accompanying a judicial decision, authored by one or more judges, supporting or dissenting from that decision.

opinion of the court The opinion expressing the views of the majority of judges participating in a judicial decision.

oral argument Verbal presentation made to an appellate court in an attempt to persuade the court to affirm, reverse, or modify a lower court decision.

ordinance An enactment of a local governing body such as a city council or commission.

organized crime Syndicates involved in racketeering and other criminal activities.

original jurisdiction The authority of a court of law to hear a case in the first instance.

original writs   Writs issued by a court in an original, as opposed to an appellate, proceeding. Original writs include mandamus, prohibition, quo warranto, and habeas corpus.

out-of-court settlements   Compromises arrived at between parties that result in dismissal of cases before formal trials occur.

oversight   Refers to the responsibility of a legislative body to monitor the activities of government agencies it created.

paralegal   A legal assistant trained to perform certain legal functions under supervision of a lawyer.

parents' right of privacy   Right of parents to deny visitation rights to grandparents and others.

parol evidence rule   A rule of law providing that when a contract is complete, oral agreements made prior to or at the time of execution of the contract cannot be admitted in evidence to vary or contradict the terms of the contract absent fraud, mistake, or illegality.

parole   Conditional release from jail or prison of a person who has served part of his or her sentence.

parole board   An administrative board that determines if a prisoner should be released on parole and, if so, under what conditions.

parole revocation hearing   An administrative hearing held for the purpose of determining whether an offender's parole should be revoked.

parties   Persons involved in court actions; persons who enter contracts.

partition suit   A legal proceeding to apportion undivided interests of owners of real property. Example: a court can divide land owned as tenants in common, or if division is not practicable, it can order the land sold and the proceeds divided according to the parties' interests.

partnership   An association of two or more persons who carry on a business for profit as co-owners and share in the profits and losses.

past consideration   Something done or given in the past that cannot serve as a consideration in the present for a contract.

patents, copyrights, and trademarks   Species of intangible property rights, often referred to today as intellectual property.

paternity   Biological fatherhood.

payee   Party to whom a negotiable instrument is payable.

penitentiary   A prison.

per curiam opinion   An opinion rendered "by the court" as distinct from one attributed to one or more judges.

peremptory challenge   An objection to the selection of a prospective juror in which the attorney making the challenge is not required to state the reason for the objection.

performance   Fulfillment of a promise under a contract.

perjury   The crime of making a material false statement under oath.

perjury by contradictory statements   Commission of the offense of perjury by a witness who makes conflicting statements under oath.

permanent alimony   Requirement to pay alimony on a permanent basis.

perpetual existence   Indefinite lifetime, a characteristic of a corporation.

personal property   All species of property other than land and things attached to the land.

personal representative   One who administers an estate, sometimes known as an executor or executrix of a testate estate or an administrator or administratrix of an intestate estate.

personal service   Service of legal process by delivery to the named person.

petitioner   A person who brings a petition before a court of law.

pierce the corporate veil   To disregard the identity of a corporation as an entity separate from its shareholders and hold the stockholders liable.

places of public accommodation   Businesses that open their doors to the general public.

plain view   Readily visible to the naked eye.

plaintiff   The party initiating legal action; the complaining party.

plea bargaining   Negotiations leading to an agreement between a defendant and a prosecutor whereby the defendant agrees to plead guilty in exchange for some concession (such as a reduction in the number of charges brought).

plea of guilty   A formal answer to a criminal charge in which the accused acknowledges guilt and waives the right to trial.

plea of not guilty   A formal answer to a criminal charge in which the accused denies guilt and thus exercises the right to a trial.

police power   The power of government to legislate to protect public health, safety, welfare, and morality.

polygraph evidence   Results of lie detector tests (generally inadmissible into evidence).

positive law   The written law enforced by government.

post-conviction relief   Term applied to various mechanisms a defendant may use to challenge a conviction after other routes of appeal have been exhausted.

post-nuptial agreements   Contracts entered into by a husband and wife settling their property rights upon death of one party or in the event of divorce.

power of contempt   The authority of a court of law to punish someone who insults the court or flouts its authority.

power to investigate   Refers to the power of a legislative body to conduct hearings and subpoena witnesses in order to investigate an issue or area in which it has legislative authority.

precedent   A judicial decision cited as authority controlling or influencing the outcome of a similar case.

preclearance   Requirement under the Voting Rights Act that changes in state voting and election laws must be approved by the Attorney General before they can take effect.

preconception tort   A new tort based on a physician's failure to advise a prospective mother of the likelihood of conceiving a defective child.

pre-embryo   A fertilized ovum or zygote.

pre-existing duty   A duty, the performance of which does not constitute a valid consideration for a contract.

preferred stock   Shares of corporate stock that receive preference in payment of fixed dividends and priority in receiving assets upon dissolution of the corporation.

preliminary hearing   A hearing held to determine whether there is sufficient evidence to hold an accused for trial.

preliminary injunction   An injunction issued pending a trial on the merits of the case.

prenuptial agreements   Contracts entered into by a man and woman before their marriage settling their property rights upon death of one party or in the event of divorce.

preponderance of evidence   Evidence that has greater weight than countervailing evidence.

prescription   Refers to acquiring an easement by long, continued, uninterrupted use, that is, by prescription.

presentence investigation   An investigation held before sentencing a convicted criminal to aid the court in determining the appropriate punishment.

presumption of constitutionality   The doctrine of constitutional law holding that laws are presumed to be constitutional, with the burden of proof resting on the plaintiff to demonstrate otherwise.

pretrial conference   A meeting of attorneys and the trial judge in advance of a jury trial to define issues, stipulate as to evidentiary exhibits, estimate the time required for trial, and discuss other details concerning the trial.

pretrial detention   The holding of a defendant in custody prior to trial.

pretrial discovery   The process by which counsel for parties gain access to the evidence possessed by the opposing party prior to trial.

pretrial motions   Request for certain rulings or orders before the commencement of a trial.

pretrial release   The release of a defendant pending trial.

price fixing   Sellers' unlawfully entering into agreements as to the price of products or services.

primary physical residence   In family law, the place where a child remains with a parent who has custodial responsibility for the child.

principal   (1) A perpetrator of or aider and abettor in the commission of a crime (as distinguished from an accessory). (2) The amount of a debt excluding interest.

prior restraint   An official act preventing publication of a particular work.

prison disciplinary hearings   Informal administrative hearing required before removal of "good time" credits earned by a prisoner.

prisoners' rights   Refers to the set of rights that prisoners retain or attempt to assert through litigation.

private placement adoption   An adoption arranged by private intermediaries, usually by a doctor and lawyer.

privilege   A right extended to persons by virtue of law, for example, the right accorded a spouse in not being required to testify against the other spouse.

privileged communications   Confidential communications that persons are not required to disclose in court proceedings.

probable cause   A reasonable ground for belief in certain alleged facts.

probate court   A court that exercises jurisdiction over the probate of wills and administration of estates of decedents.

probation   Conditional release of a convicted criminal in lieu of incarceration.

procedural criminal law   The branch of the criminal law that deals with the processes by which crimes are investigated, prosecuted, and punished.

procedural due process   Set of procedures designed to ensure fairness in a judicial or administrative proceeding.

procedural legitimacy   Popular acceptance of an institution based on the perception that it operates by valid procedures.

products liability   The legal responsibility of a manufacturer, seller, or distributor of products that cause injuries to consumers.

professional responsibility   Requirement that members of the legal profession adhere to a code of professional ethics.

prohibition   A provision of law forbidding a particular form of conduct.

prohibition, writ of   A judicial order issued by a superior court directing a lower tribunal to cease acting in excess of its lawful jurisdiction.

promisee   Party to whom a contractual promise has been made.

promisor   Party who makes a contractual promise.

promissory estoppel   A doctrine of contract law under which a promise, even though made without consideration, may be legally enforceable if the promise induces action on the part of the promisee.

promissory note   A written promise to pay a certain sum to or to the order of another.

pronouncement of sentence   Formal announcement of a criminal punishment by a trial judge.

proof beyond a reasonable doubt   The standard of proof in a criminal trial or a juvenile delinquency hearing.

proper forum   The correct court or other institution in which to press a particular claim.

property rights   Refers to the bundle of rights that exist relative to private ownership and control of property.

property settlement agreement   A contract entered into by married persons providing for disposition of their assets and liabilities. In most instances the agreement becomes effective upon approval of the court, upon dissolution of the parties' marriage.

proportionality   The degree to which a particular punishment matches the seriousness of crime or matches the penalty other offenders have received for the same crime.

proprietary or operational activities   Non-governmental activities of municipal government that may subject a municipality to tort liability.

prosecutor   A public official empowered to initiate criminal charges and conduct prosecutions.

prosecutorial discretion   The leeway afforded prosecutors in deciding whether or not to bring charges and to engage in plea bargaining.

prostitution   The act of selling sexual favors.

protective order   A court order protecting a person from whom discovery is sought prior to trial from annoyance, oppression, or undue expense in complying with demands of a party seeking discovery.

proximate cause   The cause that is nearest a given effect in a causal relationship.

public defender   An attorney responsible for defending indigent persons charged with crimes.

public figures   Persons who are in the public eye.

public officials   Persons who hold public office by virtue of election or appointment.

public policy   Guidelines (usually unwritten) by which courts make determinations whether certain acts are beneficial or harmful to society.

public safety exception   Exception to the requirement that police officers promptly inform suspects taken into custody of their rights to remain silent and have an attorney present during questioning. Under the public safety exception, police may ask suspects questions motivated by a desire to protect public safety without jeopardizing the admissibility of suspects' answers to those questions or subsequent statements.

publicly traded corporations   Corporations whose securities are traded in the public markets, for example, on a national stock exchange.

puffing   Exaggerated, but not fraudulent, claims by a seller or sales person.

punitive damages   A sum of money awarded to the plaintiff in a civil case as a means of punishing the defendant for wrongful conduct.

purchase money mortgage   A document executed by a buyer creating a lien in favor of a seller of real property for the unpaid balance of the purchase price.

putative father   A man who is regarded to be the father of a child although paternity has not been established.

quasi-judicial bodies   Public boards of administrative officers who make factual determinations as a basis for their rulings.

qui tam action   Civil suit brought by a private party on behalf of the government against a party that has allegedly defrauded the government.

quitclaim deed   A legal conveyance by a grantor to a grantee of an interest, if any, the grantor has in land described in the deed.

racially based peremptory challenges   Peremptory challenges to prospective jurors that are based solely on racial animus or racial stereotypes.

rape   Common law crime involving sexual intercourse by a male with a female, other than his wife, by force and against the will of the female. See also sexual battery.

rape shield laws   Laws that protect the identity of rape victims or prevent disclosure of victims' sexual history.

rape trauma syndrome   A recurring pattern of physical and emotional symptoms experienced by rape victims.

rational basis test   The most basic test of the validity of a statute, in which the court determines whether the challenged law is rationally related to a legitimate government objective.

real evidence   Refers to maps, blood samples, x-rays, photographs, stolen goods, fingerprints, knives, guns, and other tangible items introduced into evidence.

real property   Land and buildings permanently attached thereto.

reapportionment   The redrawing of legislative district lines so as to remedy malapportionment.

reasonable accommodation   Requirement under the Americans with Disabilities Act that employers take reasonable steps to accommodate employees with disabilities.

reasonable expectation of privacy   A person's reasonable expectation that his or her activities in a certain place are private; society's expectations with regard to whether activities in certain places are private.

reasonable force   The maximum degree of force that is necessary to accomplish a lawful purpose.

reasonable person   The hypothetical person referred to by courts as the objective standard for judging a person's actions.

reasonable suspicion   A person's suspicion based on objective standards that criminal activity is afoot.

reasonableness standard   Objective standard that courts employ in determining whether a person's conduct is negligent.

reasonably foreseeable   An act or event that a reasonable person would anticipate to occur as a result of a prior act or event.

rebuttable presumption   A legal presumption that may be refuted by evidence.

rebuttal   Refutation by an attorney of the opposing attorney's argument.

recidivism   Repetitive criminal activity.

reciprocal enforcement of support obligations   Statutory method whereby the states cooperate in enforcing legal obligations of support of dependents. Involves proceedings in an initiating state and responding state.

regulation   A legally binding rule or order prescribed by a controlling authority. The term is generally used with respect to the rules promulgated by administrative and regulatory agencies.

regulatory agencies   Agencies empowered by statutes to promulgate and enforce regulations within particular substantive areas.

regulatory taking   Governmental regulations that result in a substantial diminishment in the value of an owner's property.

rehabilitation   Restoring someone or something to its former status; a justification for punishment emphasizing reform rather than retribution.

rehabilitative alimony   A court-ordered sum paid by one spouse to the other to enable the recipient to become financially self-sufficient. Rehabilitative alimony is usually paid for a definite number of months or years.

relevant evidence   Evidence tending to prove or disprove an alleged fact.

remainderman   Person designated to receive an estate in real property upon expiration of the prior estate. Example: If H conveys a life estate to W with the remainder to C, C is a remainderman who succeeds to title upon W's death.

remand   To send back, as from a higher court to a lower court for the latter to take specified action in a case or to follow proceedings designated by the higher court.

reply brief   A brief submitted in response to an appellee's answer brief.

reporters   Books that are a part of the National Reporter Series that contain judicial decisions and accompanying opinions, for example, the Supreme Court Reporter Series includes Supreme Court decisions; other regional reporters contain decisions of federal and state decisions.

representative government   Form of government in which officials responsible for making policy are elected by the people in periodic free elections.

reproductive technology   Modern medical devices that assist in achieving pregnancy.

reputation evidence   Evidence admitted under a rule of evidence that provides that when a person's character is in issue, proof of good character may be made by showing a person's reputation in the community.

res ipsa loquitur   "The thing speaks for itself." In tort law, where an injury occurs to a plaintiff who is without fault, by an instrumentality or event in control of the defendant where the injury would not occur in absence of the defendant's negligence. The event raises an inference of a defendant's negligence. For example, where a plaintiff is injured when struck by rocks falling from a vehicle.

rescission   Cancellation. An equitable remedy that annuls a contract.

residence requirements   Legal requirements that parties have resided in a jurisdiction for a minimum period of time before voting, running for office, marrying, or receiving certain benefits to which residents are entitled.

resisting arrest   The crime of obstructing or opposing a police officer making an arrest.

restitution   The act of compensating someone for losses suffered.

restraining orders   Court orders prohibiting named persons from taking specified actions.

restrictive covenants   Agreements among property holders restricting the use of property or prohibiting the rental or sale of it to certain parties.

retaliatory eviction   Action by a lessor to terminate a tenant's occupancy because the tenant has angered the lessor, usually by reporting a housing violation to public authorities.

retribution   Something demanded in payment for a debt; in criminal law, the demand that a criminal pay his or her debt to society.

reverse   To set aside a decision on appeal.

revocable trust   A trust that the grantor reserves the right to revoke.

RICO   Acronym for Title IX (Racketeer Influenced and Corrupt Organizations) of the Organized Crime Control Act of 1970.

right of confrontation   The right to face one's accusers in a criminal case.

right of cross-examination   Right of an attorney to ask questions of a witness who has testified on behalf of the opposing party.

right of privacy   Right to be let alone, that is, free from governmental interference.

right of redemption   A mortgagor's right to pay all sums due the mortgagee before a foreclosure sale and thus redeem the mortgagor's right to the property that has been foreclosed.

right of visitation   The court-ordered right of a non-custodial parent to visit with his or her child.

right to a speedy trial   Right guaranteed by the Sixth Amendment to U.S. Constitution; however, statutes and court rules frequently specify the time periods within which a trial must be held.

right to counsel   Right to be represented by an attorney in a court, including the right of an indigent criminal defendant to have court-appointed counsel when subject to incarceration if convicted.

right to die   The right of persons who are terminally ill to refuse further medical treatment and be allowed to die.

right to keep and bear arms   Right to possess certain weapons, protected against federal infringement by the Second Amendment to the U.S. Constitution.

right to vote   The right of an individual to cast a vote in an election.

right to work laws   State statutes that provide a person cannot be required to join a union in order to obtain or hold a job.

rights of prisoners   Rights to adequate food, clothing, shelter, medical care, and sanitation as well as access to the courts; limited rights of expression and to exercise religious practices that do not disrupt prison routine.

rights of the accused   All of the rights belonging to persons accused of crimes, such as the right to counsel, the right to a fair trial, the right to due process, and so forth.

riot   A public disturbance involving acts of violence, usually by three or more persons.

robbery   The crime of taking money or property from a person against that person's will by means of force.

Roman Law   Laws that prevailed among the Romans first codified in the Twelve Tables; basis of the modern civil law in most European countries.

rule of four   U.S. Supreme Court rule whereby the Court grants certiorari only on the agreement of at least four justices.

rule of law   The idea that law, not the discretion of officials, should govern public affairs.

rulemaking   Formal process by which regulatory agencies make rules that carry the force of law.

rulemaking authority   Authority of federal and state regulatory agencies to promulgate rules of general applicability over matters within the agency's jurisdiction.

rules of evidence   Rules that govern the introduction of evidence in courts.

rules of practice   Rules regulating the practice of law before courts and administrative agencies.

rules of procedure   Rules promulgated by courts of law under constitutional or statutory authority governing procedures for trials and other judicial proceedings.

same-sex marriages   Marriages between persons of the same sex.

search   Intrusion by law officers or other government officials that affects an individual's legally protected zone of privacy.

search incident to a lawful arrest   Search of a person placed under arrest and the area within the arrestee's grasp and control.

second-degree murder   Typically refers to a killing perpetrated by any act imminently dangerous to another and evincing a depraved mind with no regard for human life, although without any premeditated design to effect the death of any particular individual.

Secret Service   A federal law enforcement function located within the Treasury Department that protects the President and the President's family and enforces federal laws against forgery of government checks and bonds, and investigates credit card and computer fraud.

security   An investment in a stock or bond issued by a corporation.

security agreement   A written contract between a debtor and a creditor granting the creditor a security interest in collateral.

security deposit   A sum deposited by a tenant either with a lessor or in escrow to guarantee performance of the tenant's obligations under a lease.

security interest An interest in collateral that a creditor acquires to ensure repayment of a debt.

seizure Action of police in taking possession or control of property or persons.

selective prosecution Singling out defendants for prosecution on the basis of race, religion, or other impermissible classifications.

self-defense The protection of one's person against an attack.

sentencing guidelines Legislative guidelines mandating that sentencing conform to guidelines absent a compelling reason for departing from them.

sentencing hearing A hearing held by a trial court prior to the pronouncement of sentence.

separate maintenance An allowance that a court orders paid to a wife who is living apart from her husband in order to provide for the wife and the parties' children.

separation of church and state The First Amendment states, "Congress shall make no law respecting an establishment of religion, or prohibiting the free exercise thereof." The Supreme Court has sometimes used a "wall of separation" metaphor, attributed to Thomas Jefferson, to describe the relationship between church and state.

separation of powers Constitutional assignment of legislative, executive, and judicial powers to different branches of government.

sequestration The seclusion of a jury from outside influences under supervision of a law officer acting under direction of a court.

sequestration of the jury Isolation of jurors (usually in a high-profile criminal case) from contact with the general public until a trial jury has reached a verdict.

session laws Laws enacted at a given session of a legislature.

sex-neutral basis Without regard to the sex of a party.

sexual harassment Offensive interaction of a sexual nature in the workplace.

shared custody The joint responsibility of divorced parents for the supervision and control of their children.

shared parental responsibility A court-ordered relationship in which both parents retain their parental rights and responsibilities with respect to their child and are to confer with each other on major decisions affecting the child's health, education, and welfare.

sheriff The chief law enforcement officer of the county.

slander The tort of defaming someone's character through verbal statements.

sobriety checkpoints Roadblocks set up for the purpose of administering field sobriety tests to motorists who appear to be intoxicated.

social host One who furnishes alcoholic beverages to guests.

social security A federal government program instituted by Congress in 1935 where employers withhold a portion of their employees' wages, match these amounts, and transfer these sums to the government. Self-employed individuals also pay into the system. From these funds, the government pays benefits to disabled persons, retirees, surviving spouses, and dependents.

social welfare legislation Laws enacted by federal and state governments to assist socially and economically disadvantaged people.

sodomy Oral or anal sex between persons, or sex between a person and an animal, the latter commonly referred to as bestiality. In 2003, the Supreme Court declared unconstitutional a Texas Law prohibiting sodomy.

sole proprietorship A business owned and operated by one individual.

solicitation The crime of offering someone money or other thing of value in order to persuade that person to commit a crime; an active effort on the part of an attorney or other professional to obtain business.

sovereign immunity A common law doctrine under which the sovereign may be sued only with its consent.

sovereignty The authority of an independent nation or state to govern within its territorial limits.

special damages Compensation awarded by a court to reimburse a plaintiff for out-of-pocket losses sustained as a result of a defendant's actions. In a typical tort action, special damages included compensation for medical expenses and loss of wages.

special equity Court-ordered interest in an asset awarded to a spouse based on his or her superior contribution to a particular marital asset.

special exceptions   Approvals by zoning boards that permit uses within a particular district conditioned upon compliance with special requirements.

special prosecutor   A prosecutor appointed specifically to investigate a particular episode and, if criminal activity is found, to prosecute those involved.

special verdict   A jury verdict with the jury answering specific questions as to its findings on issues posed by the court.

specific intent   The mental purpose to accomplish a certain prohibited act.

specific objection   Counsel's objection to a question posed to a witness by opposing counsel where a specific reason is given for the objection, for example, that the question calls for hearsay evidence.

specific performance   A court-imposed requirement that a party perform obligations incurred under a contract.

spoils system   A political term based on the old adage that "to the victor go the spoils." In practice, the award of contracts and jobs to supporters of a winning candidate.

spontaneous or excited utterances   Exceptions to the hearsay rule of evidence. The former is a spontaneous statement describing or explaining an event made while the declarant is perceiving the event or immediately thereafter. The latter is a statement made relating to a startling event made while the declarant was under stress caused by the event.

stalking   Following or placing a person under surveillance and threatening that person with bodily harm, sexual assault, confinement, or restraint or placing that person in reasonable fear of bodily harm, sexual assault, confinement, or restraint.

standing   The right to initiate a legal action or challenge based on the fact that one has suffered or is likely to suffer a real and substantial injury.

stare decisis   "To stand by decided matters." The principle that past decisions should stand as precedents for future decisions. This principle, which stands for the proposition that precedents are binding on later decisions, is said to be followed less rigorously in constitutional law than in other branches of the law.

state-sponsored discrimination   Discrimination that is endorsed, permitted, or backed by government.

state supreme court   The highest state court; however, in New York the supreme court refers to a court with trial and appellate divisions and the highest state court is the Court of Appeals.

state's attorney   A state prosecutor.

statute   A generally applicable law enacted by a legislature.

statute of frauds   A statutory law patterned after an English statute that requires certain contracts to be in writing.

statute of limitations   (1) A law proscribing prosecutions for specific crimes after specified periods of time. (2) A statutory law setting time limits for filing court actions involving contract and tort claims.

statutory construction   The official interpretation of a statute rendered by a court of law.

statutory preclusion of judicial review   Because the jurisdiction of the lower federal courts is dependent on federal legislation, legislative act enacted by Congress to preclude judicial review altogether or under certain circumstances.

stepparent adoption   Adoption of a child by the spouse of the child's natural parent, usually with consent of the child's natural parents.

stop-and-frisk   An encounter between a police officer and a suspect during which the latter is temporarily detained and subjected to a "pat-down" search for weapons.

strict judicial scrutiny   Judicial review of government action or policy in which the ordinary presumption of constitutionality is reversed.

strict liability   Doctrine of law whereby liability is imposed upon a party irrespective of that party's fault.

strict liability offenses   Offenses that do not require proof of the defendant's intent.

strict necessity, doctrine of   The doctrine that a court should consider a constitutional question only when strictly necessary to resolve the case at bar.

strict neutrality   Refers to the doctrine that government must be strictly neutral on matters of religion.

strict scrutiny   The most demanding level of judicial review in cases involving alleged infringements of civil rights or liberties.

strip search   A search of a suspect's or prisoner's private parts.

structuring   Engaging in multiple smaller transactions to avoid currency reporting requirements.

subornation of perjury   The crime of procuring someone to lie under oath.

subpoena   "Under penalty." A judicial order requiring a person to appear in court or before a legislative committee in connection with a designated proceeding.

subpoena duces tecum   A judicial order requiring a person to produce documents sought by a court or legislative committee.

substantial capacity test   The doctrine that a person is not responsible for criminal conduct if at the time of such conduct, as a result of mental disease or defect, the person lacks substantial capacity either to appreciate the wrongfulness of his or her conduct or to conform his or her conduct to the requirements of the law.

substantial evidence   Evidence that reasonable minds accept as sufficient to support a rational conclusion.

substantial federal question   A significant legal question pertaining to the U.S. Constitution, a federal statute, treaty, regulation, or judicial interpretation of any of the foregoing.

substantive criminal law   That branch of the criminal law that defines criminal offenses and defenses, and specifies criminal punishments.

substantive due process   Doctrine that Due Process Clauses of the Fifth and Fourteenth Amendments to the United States Constitution require legislation to be fair and reasonable in content as well as application.

substantive legitimacy   The belief that the government or legal system is enacting rules and policies that are fair, reasonable, and just.

substituted judgment   Decisions by a relative or surrogate in respect to health care matters for an incapacitated individual. Judgment presumably is exercised on the basis of the decision-maker's view as to the decision the incapacitated individual would ordinarily make.

substituted service   Any form of service of process other than by personal service, such as service by mail or by publication in a newspaper.

summary judgment   A decision rendered by a trial court without extended argument where there is no genuine issue of material fact and the moving party is entitled to a judgment as a matter of law.

summary justice   Trial held by a court of limited jurisdiction without benefit of a jury.

summons   A court order requiring a person to appear in court to answer a criminal charge.

sunshine laws   Federal and state laws requiring certain government meetings to be conducted in public.

suretyship   A written contract whereby one party agrees to become liable for the debt or default of another party.

surrogate   One who acts in the place of another.

surrogate motherhood   A woman who relinquishes her parental rights as the biological mother of a child she has delivered as a result of having been artificially inseminated.

survival statutes   Statutes that provide that tort actions survive the plaintiff and defendant.

suspect classification doctrine   The doctrine that laws classifying people according to race, ethnicity, and religion are inherently suspect and subjected to strict judicial scrutiny.

suspended sentence   Trial court's decision to place a defendant on probation or under community control instead of imposing an announced sentence on the condition that the original sentence may be imposed if the defendant violates the conditions of the suspended sentence.

tangible personal property   Property that has physical form and substance and value in itself.

target crime   A crime that is the object of a conspiracy. Example: In a conspiracy to traffic in illegal drugs, the offense of trafficking in illegal drugs is the target crime.

Tax Court   A federal court established by Congress in 1924 to resolve disputes between taxpayers and the Internal Revenue Service.

tax fraud   False or deceptive conduct performed with the intent of violating revenue laws, especially the Internal Revenue Code.

tenancy by the entirety   A form of ownership of property by a husband and wife. Upon the death of either party, the survivor becomes the owner of the property.

tenants in common   A form of ownership of property whereby each tenant in common owns an undivided interest in the property.

termination of parental rights   A court judgment declaring an end to a natural parent's rights over his or her child.

testamentary capacity   The legal capability to execute a last will and testament.

testamentary trust   A trust created under a last will and testament.

testator   A person (male) who executes a last will and testament.

testatrix   A person (female) who executes a last will and testament.

testimonial evidence   Evidence received by a court from witnesses who have testified under oath.

testimony   Evidence given by a witness who has sworn to tell the truth.

the living Constitution   The idea that the meaning of the Constitution changes to adapt to changing social and economic conditions.

third-party creditor beneficiary   A person designated to receive payment of an obligation as a result of a contract between other persons. Example: A party to whom money is owed is named as a beneficiary of a life insurance policy.

third-party donee beneficiary   A person designated to receive something of value as a result of a contract between other persons. Example: A person gratuitously named as a beneficiary under a life insurance policy is a typical donee beneficiary.

third-party practice   Where a defendant in a civil suit makes a third party an additional defendant in the litigation. The basis to join a third party is the defendant's allegation that such party is or may be liable to the defendant for all or part of the plaintiff's claim against the defendant.

three-strikes-and-you're-out law   Popular term for a statute that provides for mandatory life imprisonment for a convicted felon who is convicted of a third violent or serious felony after having been previously convicted of two or more serious felonies.

time, place, and manner regulations   Government limitations on the time, place, and manner of expressive activities.

tort   A wrong or injury other than a breach of contract for which the remedy is a civil suit for damages.

tort claims   Claims asserted for alleged torts.

tortfeasor   One who commits a tort.

totality of circumstances   The entire collection of relevant facts in a particular case.

toxic torts   Acts involving human or property exposure through absorption, contact, ingestion, inhalation, implantation, or injection of toxins.

traditional surrogacy   Impregnation of a woman with the sperm of a married man with an understanding that the child to be born is to be legally the child of the married man and his wife.

transactional immunity   A grant of immunity applying to offenses that a witness's testimony relates to.

transcript   A written record of a trial or hearing.

transferability of ownership   Ability to readily transfer ownership interests in a corporation by simply endorsing stock certificates.

treason   The crime of attempting by overt acts to overthrow the government or of betraying the government to a foreign power.

treaty   A legally binding agreement between two or more countries. In the United States, treaties are negotiated by the President but must be ratified by the Senate.

trespass to land   An unlawful entry onto another person's real property.

trespasser   One who unlawfully interferes with another person's property.

trial   A judicial proceeding held for the purpose of making factual and legal determinations.

trial by jury   A trial in which the verdict is determined not by the court but by a jury of the defendant's peers.

trial courts   Courts whose primary function is the conduct of civil and/or criminal trials.

trial *de novo*   "A new trial." Refers also to trial court review of convictions for minor offenses by courts of limited jurisdiction by conducting a new trial instead of merely reviewing the record of the initial trial.

trust   A legal relationship created when a party known as the grantor or settlor transfers legal title to assets to a second party known as the trustee for the benefit of a third party known as a beneficiary.

trustee   One who holds legal title to assets transferred by a grantor or settlor to be held and administered for the benefit of a third-party beneficiary.

ultra vires **acts**   Refers to acts committed by a corporation beyond the scope of its legal authority.

unconscionable conduct   Conduct that is unfair and oppressive but not necessarily fraudulent.

unconscionable consumer contracts   Contracts that result in oppression against consumers who have no real choice as to the terms imposed.

unemployment compensation   A federal program administered by state agencies and funded through taxes on employers that provides temporary payments to unemployed workers.

unified bar   A statewide bar association that regulates the legal profession, usually under the oversight of the state's highest court, and that requires lawyers to be dues-paying members of the association.

unified credit   A credit against federal estate taxes; in effect an exemption from the tax. The credit was $675,000 in 2001, increasing to $3,500,000 in 2009.

Uniform Code of Military Justice (UCMJ)   A federal statute enacted by Congress in 1950 that consolidated and modified prior laws regulating the conduct of military personnel; established a revised code of military justice to apply uniformly in all the military services; and established a civilian court of appeals. The Act authorizes the President to promulgate a Manual for Courts-Martial binding on all persons subject to the UCMJ.

uniform codes   A collection of laws designed to be uniformly adopted by the various states. The Uniform Commercial Code (UCC) is a classic example of a uniform code of laws.

unilateral contract   A contract formed by a promise being made in exchange for performance of an act.

unilateral mistake   Mistake by only one party to a contract concerning a material aspect of the contract.

unitary system   A political system in which all power is vested in one central government.

United States Attorneys   Attorneys appointed by the President with consent of the U.S. Senate to prosecute federal crimes in a specific geographical area of the United States.

United States Court of Appeals for the Armed Forces   A civilian court established by Congress consisting of five civilian judges appointed by the President for fifteen-year terms. Serves as a court of review for specified cases and may grant petitions for review beyond the normal channels of military review in courts-martial cases.

United States Courts of Appeals   The intermediate appellate courts of appeals in the federal system that sit in geographical areas of the United States and in which panels of appellate judges hear appeals in civil and criminal cases primarily from the U.S. District Courts.

United States District Courts   The principal trial courts in the federal system that sit in ninety-four districts where usually one judge hears proceedings and trials in civil and criminal cases.

United States Sentencing Commission   A federal body that proposes guideline sentences for defendants convicted of federal crimes.

United States Supreme Court   The highest court in the United States, consisting of nine justices and having jurisdiction to review, by appeal or writ of certiorari, the decisions of lower federal courts and many decisions of the highest courts of each state.

unity concept of marriage   Common law doctrine whereby courts treated a husband and wife as one person for legal purposes. Courts have now generally discarded the unity concept.

unlawful assembly   A meeting of a group of individuals who intend to commit an unlawful act or to commit a lawful act in an unlawful manner.

unreasonable searches and seizures   Searches that violate the Fourth Amendment to the Constitution.

U.S. Code   Official code of the laws of the United States.

use immunity   A grant of immunity that forbids prosecutors from using immunized testimony as evidence in criminal prosecutions.

usurious rate of interest   A rate of interest charged to a borrower that exceeds the maximum rate allowed by law.

uttering a forged instrument   The crime of passing a false or worthless instrument, such as a check, with the intent to defraud or injure the recipient.

vandalism   The willful destruction of the property of another person.

variances   Deviations granted by a Board of Adjustment where enforcement of zoning regulations would impose an undue hardship on the property owner.

vehicular homicide   Homicide resulting from the unlawful and negligent operation of a motor vehicle.

venire   The group of citizens from whom a jury is chosen in a given case.

venue   The location of a trial or hearing.

veto   The power of a chief executive to block adoption of a law by refusing to sign the legislation.

vicarious liability   Liability of one party in place of another.

vice of vagueness   The constitutional infirmity of a law that is so vague that a person of ordinary intelligence cannot determine what it permits, requires, or prohibits.

victim   A person who is the object of a crime or tort.

victim impact evidence   Evidence relating to the physical, economic, and psychological impact that a crime has on the victim or victim's family.

violations of civil rights   Violations of federal and state statutes, local ordinances, and regulations designed to ensure that society treats everyone equally.

void contract   An agreement that cannot be enforced by law.

voidable contract   An agreement that a party can set aside. Example: A minor can usually set aside (avoid) a contract.

void-for-vagueness doctrine   See vice of vagueness.

voir dire   "To speak the truth." The process by which prospective jurors are questioned by counsel and/or the court before being selected to serve on a jury.

ward   A minor or incapacitated individual placed under guardianship by a court.

warrant   A judicial writ or order directed to a law enforcement officer authorizing the doing of a specified act, such as arrest or search.

warrant requirement   The Fourth Amendment's "preference" that searches be based on warrants issued by judges or magistrates.

warrantless administrative searches   Reasonable searches of premises by government officials to determine compliance with health and safety regulations.

warrantless arrest   An arrest made by police who do not possess an arrest warrant.

warrantless inspection   See warrantless administrative searches.

warrantless searches   Searches conducted by police or other officials acting without search warrants.

warranty deed   A deed from a grantor conveying an interest in real property to the grantee with various covenants, including the grantor's warranty to defend the title to the property conveyed.

welfare programs   Government-sponsored programs such as those that furnish financial assistance for dependent children, medical assistance for the poor, and unemployment compensation for persons out of work.

welfare reform   Congressional action revising the criteria for entitlements in welfare programs.

white-collar crimes   Various criminal offenses committed by persons in the upper socioeconomic strata of society, often in the course of the occupation or profession of such persons.

will   An expression (in most instances written) that makes known the intent of the signer (testator or testatrix) as to the disposition of his or her property. Also referred to as a last will and testament.

wiretapping   The use of highly sensitive electronic devices to intercept electronic communications.

worker's compensation acts   Statutes that require payments of monetary benefits to workers injured within the scope of their employment and to dependents of workers killed within the scope of their employment.

writ   An order issued by a court of law requiring or prohibiting the performance of some specific act.

writ of certiorari   Order from a higher court directing a lower court to send up the record of a case for appellate review.

writ of habeas corpus   See habeas corpus.

writ of mandamus   See mandamus.

writ of prohibition   See prohibition, writ of.

wrongful act or omission   An act or omission that infringes on the rights of another person.

wrongful birth action   A tort action by parents for the birth of an impaired or deformed child because a physician's negligent treatment or advice deprived them of the opportunity to avoid or terminate the wife's pregnancy.

wrongful death acts   Statutory laws that allow a tort action against a person responsible for the wrongful death of an individual. The class of persons eligible to bring suit and the elements of damages recoverable vary among the states.

wrongful life action   A tort action brought on behalf of a child born with birth defects whose birth would not have occurred but for negligent medical advice or treatment.

INDEX

abortion, 5, 51, 52, 79, 80, 81, 98, 109, 155, 156, 310-313
absent without leave (AWOL), 47
abusive offenses, 133
accession, in property law, 215-220
accessories to crimes, 128-129
accused, rights of the, 104
acts of God, in contract law, 259
actus reus, 127
Adams, John, 21
adjudication, by administrative agencies, 472-475
adjudication, formal, 473
adjudication, informal, 473
adjustable rate mortgages, 227
administration of justice, offenses against, 150
administrative agencies, 29, 53-54, 458, 476-477
administrative detention, 468-469
administrative law, 54, 457-483
administrative law judge (ALJ), 473
Administrative Procedure Act, 463-466, 473, 476
administrative search warrant, 467
administrative searches, 467-468
administrator of estate, 238
admissibility, requirements of, 345-346
adoption, 306-307
adultery, 120, 165
advance directive for medical decisions, 309
adversarial system, 15, 65-66
Aereo Inc., 216-217
affiant, 365
affidavit, 365
affirmance, by appellate court, 352
affirmative action, 25, 110-111, 433-435, 440-441
affirmative defenses, 152-159, 182
"affluenza" defense, 162
African-Americans, discrimination against, 429-438
after-born children, 237
age discrimination, 426, 443
Age Discrimination Act of 1975, 426
Age Discrimination in Employment Act, 426

agency enforcement powers, 469-472
agency investigations, 467-468
aggravating factors, in death penalty cases, 394
Aid to Families with Dependent Children (AFDC), 427-428
aiding and abetting, 128
aiding the enemy, 151
air traffic controllers, 481
alcohol-related offenses, 146-147
Alcohol, Tobacco, Firearms and Explosives, Bureau of (ATF), 56-57
alcoholic beverages, prohibition of, 143, 197-198
alibi, 151-152, 387
alimony, 291, 293-295, 296
Alito, Samuel, 42, 85, 96, 99, 439, 476
allocution, right of, 390
alternative dispute resolution (ADR), 61, 67-68
American Bar Association (ABA), 64
American Law Institute (ALI), 26, 123, 153, 178, 248, 396
American Revolution, 17, 18, 38, 92, 122
American Telephone and Telegraph Co. (AT&T), 272, 417, 418
American Taxpayer Relief Act, 230
Americans with Disabilities Act (ADA), 27, 426
Amish, 124
ancient legal systems, 10-11
ancillary administration of estate, 239
annual percentage rate (APR), 272
annulment, 290-291
answer to complaint, 331-332
Anthony, Susan B., 437
Antitrust Division, U.S. Department of Justice, 417
antitrust law, 417-419
antitrust violations, 143
appeal, notice of, 349
appeals of right, 43, 350, 351, 398
appeals process, 397-400
appellant, 350
appellate courts, 27, 38, 40, 48, 52, 123
appellee, 350
Aquinas, Thomas, 4

arbitration, 37, 67
Arizona v. United States, 371-372
arms, right to keep and bear, 101-102, 107, 149
arraignment, 380-381
arrest, 369-370
arrest warrant, 369
arson, 132, 134, 141, 142, 165
Articles of Confederation, 18, 36, 90
Ashcroft, John, 466
Ashcroft v. ACLU, 125
Ashwander rules, 80
Ashwander v. Tennessee Valley Authority, 79
assault and battery, tort of, 184
assault, aggravated, 133
assaultive offenses, 133
assembly, freedom of, 22, 95
association, freedom of, 101
Association for Molecular Biology v. Myriad Genetics, 216
assumption of risk, 182-183
attempt, offense of, 129-130
Attorney General, U.S., 35, 59, 136, 160
attorney's fees, 223, 235, 293, 295, 309, 333, 334, 343
attorneys general, state, 35, 59, 160, 269
authority of law, as defense to tort claim, 189
Authorization to Use Military Force, 479
automatism, defense of, 152-154
automobile exception, 366

Bachelor of Laws degree (LL.B.), 60
bail, 23, 104-105, 375, 377-378
bailee, 219
bailments, 219
bailments, gratuitous, 219
bailor, 219
bait and switch advertising, 272
banking and securities, 419-422
bankruptcy, 37, 83, 274-275
Bankruptcy Abuse Prevention and Consumer Protection Act of 2005, 275
bankruptcy courts, 40, 41
bankruptcy proceedings, 274
bar, admission to the, 60-61